Lawyers and Ethics

Professional Responsibility and Discipline

Gavin MacKenzie
of the Ontario Bar

Canadian Cataloguing in Publication Date

MacKenzie, Gavin, 1952-
Lawyers and ethics: professional responsibility and discipline

3rd ed.
Includes index
ISBN 0-459-24032-3

1. Legal ethics. 2. Lawyers—Discipline. I. Title.

KE339.M33 2001 173'.3 C2001-903339-7

One Corporate Plaza, 2075 Kennedy Road, Toronto, Ontario M1T 3V4
Customer Service:
Toronto 1-416-609-3800
Elsewhere in Canada/U.S. 1-800-387-5162
Fax 1-416-298-5094

To Rosemary, Charlotte, Travis, and Brooke

About the Author

Gavin MacKenzie is a partner in the Toronto office of Heenan Blaikie, where his practice includes professional liability and discipline work, commercial litigation, class actions, and advocacy before courts and tribunals.

Since his call to the bar in 1977, Mr. MacKenzie has frequently represented lawyers, other professionals, and regulatory bodies in disciplinary proceedings. From 1990 to 1993 he served as the Law Society of Upper Canada's Senior Counsel with responsibility for professional discipline. He has frequently been retained by lawyers and law firms to provide opinions and expert evidence on issues of professional responsibility.

Mr. MacKenzie was elected as a bencher of the Law Society of Upper Canada in 1995 and was re-elected in 1999. He has served as chair of the Society's professional regulation committee (which is responsible for professional conduct and discipline policy), and proceedings authorization committee (which is responsible for authorizing the initiation of discipline proceedings against lawyers). He has also served as chair of the Society's special committee on defence counsel's duties in relation to physical evidence, and co-chair of the Society's strategic planning committee. From 1998 to 2000 he served as co-chair of the task force on the reform of the Law Society's *Rules of Professional Conduct*, a process that culminated in the adoption of new *Rules of Professional Conduct* that came into force on November 1, 2000.

In addition to *Lawyers and Ethics: Professional Responsibility and Discipline* Mr. MacKenzie is the author of articles published in the *Canadian Bar Review*, the *Law Society of Upper Canada Gazette*, the *Advocates' Society Journal*, *Reid's Administrative Law*, the *Canadian Journal of Law & Jurisprudence*, and the *Alberta Law Review*. He writes *The Profession* column for the *Law Times* and is a frequent speaker at continuing education programs. He has taught civil litigation, administrative law and the Charter of Rights, and professional responsibility in the Ontario bar admission course.

Mr. MacKenzie is a former director of the Advocates' Society and of LINK – the Lawyer's Assistance Programme, and a former council member of the Canadian Bar Association – Ontario and the Toronto Medico-Legal Society. He has been honoured by induction as a Fellow of the American College of Trial Lawyers.

Mr. MacKenzie lives near Unionville, Ontario with his wife Rosemary and their three children, Charlotte, Travis, and Brooke.

Acknowledgments

I am grateful to Dean Marilyn Pilkington of Osgoode Hall Law School, who read the manuscript and made many valuable suggestions.

I am also grateful to Allan Rock, who somehow found time to read the manuscript and wrote a thoughtful foreword during a period of his life when he had many other pressing responsibilities.

My friend and sometime colleague, Stephen Traviss, generously made available his extensive library of materials on professional responsibility. Anna Burnowicz, Charlene Weston and Josephine Cunningham typed the manuscript and made countless revisions without once losing the good humour that has made them such a pleasure to work with.

My most important debt of gratitude is owed to my wife Rosemary. In the two and a half years of evenings, weekends and so-called holidays during which I researched and wrote this book she has proven that, contrary to popular belief, it is she who is the patient one.

Foreword

Among the challenges facing the legal profession in the current age, none is more urgent than the need to preserve and foster its ethical values at a time when the business aspects of practice demand so much of our attention. Faced with increased competition, the relentless pressure of cost, the disappearance of many traditional sources of work and the growing complexity of the law, lawyers in practice must struggle on a daily basis to balance their roles as professionals and as proprietors.

The profession has attempted to meet this challenge in various ways. Professional responsibility is now taught in both law school curricula and in bar admission courses. Leaders of the profession have spoken out against the rising trend toward commercialism, and law societies everywhere are encouraging a critical re-assessment of our approaches and standards. These measures have succeeded only partially.

Until now, those engaged in efforts to maintain ethical standards have been without a reliable reference work capable of relating rules of professional conduct to the daily demands of practice. With his work on Lawyers and Ethics, Gavin MacKenzie has met that need. By furnishing a text that combines a restatement of ethical norms with a realistic understanding of the modern law office, Mr. MacKenzie has made a lasting contribution to legal literature and to the cause of professionalism.

The book's value derives in great part from the rounded perspective that Mr. MacKenzie brings to the task. For many years a busy litigation lawyer with both civil and criminal retainers, he has extensive first-hand knowledge of the demands of the practice environment. Mr. MacKenzie's caseload included, as a significant component, the defence of lawyers and other professionals facing allegations of misconduct. For a time, he served as counsel to the Discipline Committee of the College of Physicians and Surgeons. He also carried briefs for individuals seeking admission and re-admission to professions in circumstances in which their fitness was in issue. He therefore had occasion to test and examine, in a wide variety of contexts, the very essence of what it means to be a professional.

In recent years, Mr. MacKenzie has served as Senior Counsel, Discipline, for the Law Society of Upper Canada, a role in which he has earned a widespread reputation not only for his skills as an advocate, but also for his fairness in the process and the soundness of his judgment in issues relating to professional conduct.

Mr. MacKenzie's varied and balanced experience ensures that this book is not merely an academic or theoretical analysis: on every page, there is evidence of his keen awareness of the highly complex task that the modern lawyer faces. The rules of professional conduct are brought to life in examples often drawn from the author's own experience, and the principles underlying the rules are illustrated dynamically. By these means, the rules are rendered more meaningful than ever before to those of us who must, in practice, harmonize those obligations that we owe at once to clients, colleagues, the court and our governing body, and which all too often seem to pull us in different directions.

The appealing blend of principle and practice is perhaps best exemplified in Mr. MacKenzie's insightful treatment of the subject of conflicts, a difficult, elusive area requiring an especially rigorous effort in order to reconcile competing considerations and values.

Nor is the work intended just for courtroom lawyers, despite the emphasis on litigation in Mr. MacKenzie's own professional experience. The book takes on, in a straightforward manner, the way in which the rules of conduct find application in a variety of other practice settings, whether in the boardroom, in the service of government, among corporate counsel or in a general practice.

Canadian lawyers have waited a very long time for a text that treats these subjects fully and with authority. In Mr. MacKenzie's work, we now have a thorough and scholarly resource, the enduring value of which is that it relates every principle to a practical setting and every rule to the realities of practice. The profession, and ultimately the public, are in Mr. MacKenzie's debt.

Allan M. Rock Q.C.

Table of Contents

About the Author v
Acknowledgments vii
Foreword ix
Consolidated Table of Cases TC-1

Introduction to the 1995 Supplements i
Introduction 1

PART I — IN COURT

CHAPTER 1 LAWYERS AND ETHICS 1-1

1.1 The Public Perception of Lawyers 1-1
1.2 Legal Education and Training 1-4
1.3 Lawyers and Commercialism 1-6.1
1.4 The Importance of Lawyers' Ethics 1-8
1.5 Improving Lawyers' Ethics 1-9

CHAPTER 2 THE ADVERSARY SYSTEM 2-1

2.1 Introduction 2-1
2.2 The Sporting Theory of Justice 2-2
2.3 Forensic Excesses and the Prisoner Dilemma 2-3
2.4 Discovery Abuse 2-4
2.5 Legal Ethics and the Public's Ethics 2-6
2.6 Rules of Professional Conduct 2-9
2.7 Justifications of the Adversary System 2-10
2.8 Criminal Prosecutions 2-11
2.9 Civil Litigation 2-12
2.10 Should We Abolish the Adversary System? 2-15
2.11 The Adversary System Today 2-16
2.12 Public Law Commissions of Inquiry and Administrative Tribunal Hearings 2-18
2.13 Family Law 2-19
2.14 Expert Witnesses 2-19
2.15 Conclusion 2-20

CHAPTER 3 CONFIDENTIALITY 3-1

3.1 Introduction 3-1
3.2 The Confidentiality Rule 3-3
3.2.1 Inadvertent Disclosure of Confidential Information 3-9
3.3 Confidentiality and the Corporate Client 3-11
3.4 The Future Crime or Harm Exception 3-12

3.5 Lawyer Self-Interest Exceptions 3-15
3.6 Balancing Confidentiality and Other Interests 3-17

CHAPTER 4 ADVOCACY 4-1

4.1 The Ethics of Advocacy 4-1
4.2 The Retainer and the Right to Decline Employment 4-2
4.3 Children and Clients Under a Disability 4-6
4.4 Advising Clients Concerning Possible Litigation 4-8
4.5 Medical-Legal Reports 4-9
4.6 Discovery 4-10
4.7 Other Lawyers 4-13
4.8 The Duty to Settle 4-14
4.9 The Law's Delay 4-17
4.10 Withdrawal as Counsel 4-19
4.11 Duty to Follow Instructions 4-23
4.11.1 Communicating with Represented Parties and With Witnesses Prior to Trial 4-24
4.12 Preparing Witnesses 4-26.2
4.13 Leading Evidence: The Perjury Problem 4-31
4.14 Cross-Examination 4-37
4.15 Communicating With Witnesses Giving Evidence 4-40
4.16 Argument 4-42
4.17 Costs 4-44
4.18 Counsel's Liability in Negligence 4-45
4.19 Lawyers as Witnesses 4-49
4.20 *Ex Parte* Proceedings 4-50
4.21 Agreements Guaranteeing Recovery (Mary Carter Agreements) 4-51
4.22 Control of Advocacy 4-53
(a) Cost Sanctions Against Lawyers 4-53
(b) Contempt of Court 4-56
(c) Law Society Disciplinary Sanctions 4-58
4.23 Lawyers and Judges 4-59
4.24 Lawyers and Jurors 4-62

CHAPTER 5 CONFLICTS OF INTEREST IN LITIGATION 5-1

5.1 Introduction 5-1
5.2 Appearances of Impropriety 5-1
5.3 Acting For Adverse Parties in Same Litigation 5-4
5.4 Acting Against Current Clients in Unrelated Litigation 5-5
5.5 Acting For Co-Parties in Same Litigation 5-8
5.6 Acting Against Former Clients 5-13
5.7 Acting Against Former Co-Clients and Co-Parties 5-20
5.8 Issue and Procedural Conflicts Between Clients 5-20.1
5.9 Lawyer-Client Conflicts of Interest 5-20.1
5.10 Imputed Disqualification 5-20.5
5.11 Payment of Fees by Non-Clients 5-37

5.12 Class Actions 5-37
5.13 Derivative Proceedings 5-39
5.14 Indemnity Insurance Litigation 5-40

CHAPTER 6 PROSECUTING 6-1

6.1 Doing Justice 6-1
6.2 Who is the Client? 6-5
6.3 The Charging Decision 6-5
6.4 Disclosure 6-10
6.5 Plea Bargaining 6-12
6.6 Impermissible Tactics 6-14
6.7 The Magisterial Prosecutor 6-17

CHAPTER 7 CRIMINAL DEFENCE 7-1

7.1 The Ethics of the Criminal Defence Lawyer 7-1
7.2 Confidentiality and Truth 7-6
7.3 The Duty Not to Destroy or Conceal Physical Evidence 7-8
7.4 Cross-Examining the Truthful Witness 7-9
7.5 The Perjurious Client 7-11
7.6 Conflicts of Interest 7-15
7.7 Plea Bargaining 7-20
7.8 Withdrawal as Counsel 7-23

CHAPTER 8 CIVILITY 8-1

PART II — ACCESS TO JUSTICE

CHAPTER 9 HOW MUCH JUSTICE CAN YOU AFFORD? 9-1

CHAPTER 10 ADVERTISING 10-1

CHAPTER 11 SOLICITATION 11-1

CHAPTER 12 CONTINGENCY FEES 12-1

CHAPTER 13 THE MEDIA 13-1

PART III — OUT OF COURT

CHAPTER 14 COUNSELLING 14-1

CHAPTER 15 NEGOTIATION 15-1

TABLE OF CONTENTS

CHAPTER 16 MEDIATION 16-1

CHAPTER 17 REAL ESTATE 17-1

17.1 Ethics in Real Estate Practice 17-1
17.2 The Ontario Rules 17-1
7.3 Unauthorized Use of Client Funds in Speculative Real Estate Ventures and the Ontario Spot Audit Programme 17-3
17.4 Conflicts of Interest in Real Estate Practice 17-4
17.5 Undertakings 17-7

CHAPTER 18 ESTATES 18-1

18.1 Testamentary Capacity and Undue Influence 18-1
18.2 Wills Benefitting Lawyers 18-3
18.3 Other Conflicts of Interest 18-5
18.4 Confidentiality 18-8
18.5 Competence and Quality of Service 18-9

CHAPTER 19 TAX 19-1

CHAPTER 20 THE CORPORATE COUNSEL 20-1

20.1 House Counsel 20-1
20.2 Moonlighting 20-4
20.3 Responsibility to Law Society 20-5
20.4 Non-Legal Advice 20-6
20.5 Who is the Client? 20-7
20.6 Whistleblowing 20-10

CHAPTER 21 GOVERNMENT LAWYERS 21-1

21.1 Introduction 21-1
21.2 Who is the Client? 21-1
21.3 Limitations on Forensic Strategies 21-3
21.4 Whistleblowing 21-4
21.5 Conflicts of Interest 21-6

CHAPTER 22 CONFLICTS OF INTEREST 22-1

22.1 Introduction 22-1
22.2 Other Client Conflicts of Interest 22-3
22.3 Lawyer-Client Conflicts of Interest 22-8
22.4 Conflicts of Interest Involving Non-Clients 22-13

22.5 Errors and Omissions Claims 22-15

PART IV — THE REGULATION OF THE PROFESSION

CHAPTER 23 ADMISSION TO THE BAR 23-1

23.1 Introduction 23-1
23.2 Purposes of the Good Character Requirement 23-2
23.3 History and Application of the Good Character Requirement 23-4
23.4 Alternatives to the Good Character Requirement 23-16

CHAPTER 24 REGULATING LAWYER COMPETENCE AND QUALITY OF SERVICE 24-1

24.1 Rules of Professional Conduct 24-1
24.2 Discipline Proceedings 24-3
24.3 Continuing Legal Education 24-4
24.4 Insurance Loss Prevention Programmes 24-4
24.5 Practice Review Programmes 24-4
24.6 Solicitors' Negligence Litigation 24-5
24.7 Judicial Intervention 24-7
24.8 Conclusion 24-8

CHAPTER 25 RULES OF PROFESSIONAL CONDUCT 25-1

25.1 Introduction 25-1
25.2 History, Nature, and Application of Rules of Professional Conduct 25-2
25.3 Client Property 25-10
25.4 Borrowing From Clients 25-12
25.5 Fees 25-13
(a) Fairness of Fees 25-13
(b) Fee Splitting and Referral Fees 25-16
25.6 Lawyers and the Administration of Justice 25-17
25.7 Responsibility to the Profession 25-18
25.8 Retired Judges Returning to Practice 25-21
25.9 Practice by Unauthorized Persons and Delegation to Non-Lawyers 25-22
25.10 Outside Interests and the Practice of Law 25-25
25.11 Interprovincial Law Firms 25-27
25.12 Duties of Articling Principals and Students 25-27
25.13 Sexual Harassment 25-28
25.14 Representation of Clients Under a Disability 25-29
25.15 Discrimination 25-30

CHAPTER 26 DISCIPLINE PROCEEDINGS 26-1

26.1 Purposes of Discipline Proceedings 26-1
26.2 Are Discipline Proceedings Civil or Criminal? 26-2

26.3 Impartiality of Adjudicators and the Independence of Law Society's Counsel 26-6
26.4 Investigation of Complaints 26-7
26.5 Parallel Criminal and Civil Proceedings 26-12
26.6 Disclosure Pending Hearing 26-17
26.7 Professional Misconduct 26-19
26.8 Conduct Unbecoming a Barrister and Solicitor 26-25
26.9 Public Hearings 26-26.3
26.10 Effect of Delay 26-26.5
26.11 Disqualification for Bias 26-28
26.12 Duty to Act Judicially 26-34
26.13 Adjournments and Interim Suspensions 26-36.1
26.14 Hearing Panel's Use of Own Expertise 26-37
26.15 Use of Transcripts of Previous Testimony—Section 13 of the *Charter* 26-38
26.16 Standard of Proof 26-40
26.17 Penalty 26-42
26.18 Decision and Reasons 26-54
26.18.1 Costs 26-56
26.19 Judicial Review and Appeal 26-56
26.20 Special Cases: Crown Attorneys, Judges, Legislators 26-58
26.21 Incapacity Proceedings 26-60
26.22 Readmission 26-60

CHAPTER 27 THE INDEPENDENCE OF THE BAR 27-1

27.1 Introduction 27-1
27.2 The Independence of the Bar from the State 27-2
27.3 Rules of Professional Conduct 27-6
27.4 Independence from Clients 27-6
27.5 Independence from the Courts 27-8
27.6 The American Experience: Discipline by the Courts 27-13
27.7 Conclusion 27-15

APPENDIX CODE OF PROFESSIONAL CONDUCT (CANADIAN BAR ASSOCIATION) A-1

INDEX I-1

Consolidated Table of Cases

[All references are to part numbers.]

Abraham v. Jutsun, [1963] 2 All E.R. 402 (C.A.). . . . . 4.22(a), 27.5

Abse v. Smith, [1986] Q.B. 536, [1986] 1 All E.R. 350 (C.A.) 4.23

Adcock v. Algoma Steel Corp., [1970] 3 O.R. 560 (H.C.) 4.9

Adair v. Health Disciplines Board (Ontario) (*sub nom.* Adair v. Ontario (Health Disciplines Board) 15 O.R. (3d) 705, 68 O.A.C. 202 (Div. Ct.). 26.18

Adams v. Law Society of Alberta, [2000] A.J. 1031 (Alta. C.A.) 26.8, 26.17

Advocate, An [1964] M.L.J. 1. . . . . 25.10

Aerojet Properties Inc. v. New York, 138 A.D. 2d 39, 530 N.Y.S. 2d 624 (N.Y. App., 1988) 5.4

Ainsworth Electric Co. v. Alcatel Canada Wire Inc. (1998), 40 O.R. (3d) 123 (Master). 5.6

Airst v. Airst (1998), 37 O.R. (3d) 654, 21 C.P.C. (4th) 146 (Gen. Div.) 3.2.1

Alberta Treasury Branches v. Invictus Financial Corp. (1985), 38 Alta. L.R. (2d) 36, 56 C.B.R. (N.S.) 239, 63 A.R. 4 (Q.B.). 25.3

Aldrich v. Struk, 1 B.C.L.R. (2d) 71, [1986] 3 W.W.R. 341, 12 C.P.C. (2d) 6, 12 C.P.R. (3d) 118, 26 D.L.R. (4th) 352 (S.C.). 5.6

Alfred Crampton Amusement Machines Ltd. v. Commissioners of Custom and Excise (No. 2), [1972] 2 All E.R. 353 (C.A.) 20.1, 20.4

Algonquin Mercantile Corporation v. Cockwell (1996), 2 C.P.C. (4th) 231, 3 O.T.C. 97 (Gen. Div.) 5.6

Allen v. Manitoba (Judicial Council), [1990] 5 W.W.R. 236, 46 Admin. L.R. 247, 65 Man. R. (2d) 307, 70 D.L.R. (4th) 164 (Q.B.), reversed (1990), 46 Admin. L.R. 252, [1991] 2 W.W.R. 337, 70 Man. R. (2d) 234, 78 D.L.R. (4th) 576 (C.A.) 26.11

Allinson v. General Medical Council, [1844] 1 Q.B. 750. . . . . 4.23

Amacher v. Erickson (1963), 42 W.W.R. 348, 40 D.L.R. (2d) 251 (B.C. S.C.). 12

American Farm Bureau Federation v. Canadian Import Tribunal. See National Corn Growers Assn. v. Canada (Canadian Import Tribunal)

Amourgis v. Law Society (Upper Canada) (1984), 48 O.R. (2d) 91, 5 O.A.C. 286, 12 D.L.R. (4th) 759 (Div. Ct.). 26.13

Analytica, Inc. v. NPD Research, Inc., 708 F. 2d 1263 (7th Cir., 1983) 5.6

Andrews v. Law Society (British Columbia), [1989] 1 S.C.R. 143, [1989] 2 W.W.R. 289, 34 B.C.L.R. (2d) 273, 25 C.C.E.L. 255, 10 C.H.R.R. D/5719, 36 C.R.R. 193, 56 D.L.R. (4th) 1, 91 N.R. 255 . . . . 23.1

Anns v. Merton London Borough Council, [1978] A.C. 728, [1977] 2 All E.R. 492 (H.L.). 24.6, 25.3

Applebaum, Re, report adopted by Convocation, July 15, 1982 . . . . 26.17

Application of A.T., Re, 286 Md. 507, 408 A. 2d 1023 (1979) 23.3

Application of Allan S. for Admission to the Bar of Maryland, Re, 387 A. 2d 271 (1978) 23.3

Application of G.L.S. for Admission to the Bar of Maryland, Re, 439 A. 2d 1107 (1982) 23.3

Aptowitzer v. Ontario (1995), 23 O.R. (3d) 315 (Gen. Div.) 5.6, 5.10

Arlington Crane Service Ltd. v. Ontario (Minister of Labour) (1988), 67 O.R. (2d) 225, 89 C.L.L.C. 14,019, 56 D.L.R. (4th) 209 (H.C.) 26.2

Arnold v. Teno, [1978] 2 S.C.R. 287, 3 C.C.L.T. 272, 83 D.L.R. (3d) 609, 19 N.R. 1 12

Arthur v. Meaford (Town) (1915), 34 O.L.R. 231, 24 D.L.R. 878 (H.C.) 4.7, 8

Arthur J.S. Hall & Co. v. Simons, [2000] H.L. J. 43 .... 4.18, 27.5

Artinian v. College of Physicians & Surgeons (Ontario) (1990), 73 O.R. (2d) 704, 40 O.A.C. 51 (Div. Ct.) 26.4

Ashburton (Lord) v. Pape, [1913] 2 Ch. 469, [1911-13] All E.R. Rep. 708 (C.A.) 3.2.1

Ashburton Oil Ltd. v. Sharp (1992), 67 B.C.L.R. (2d) 64 (S.C.) 5.10

Ashby, Re, [1934] O.R. 421, 62 C.C.C. 132, [1934] 3 D.L.R. 565 (C.A.) 26.11

Asian Video Movies Wholesaler Inc. v. Mathardoo (1991), 36 C.P.R. (3d) 29, 46 F.T.R. 19 .... 5.10

Assoc. des officiers de direction du service de police de Québec (Ville) v. Québec (Commission de police) (1995), 119 D.L.R. (4th) 484, [1994] R.J.Q. 1505 (C.A.) 26.11

Atamanchuk v. DeBruin (1992), 14 C.P.C. (3d) 259, 106 Sask. R. 288 (Q.B.) 4.6

Atlantic Shipping Ltd. v. Payne (1992), 122 N.B.R. (2d) 211, 306 A.P.R. 211 (Q.B.) 5.10

Attorney Grievance Commission of Maryland v. Goldberg, 292 Md. 650, 441 A. 2d 338 (1982) 26.17

Ayre v. Barristers' Society (Nova Scotia) (June 8, 1998), Doc. C.A. 139683 (N.S. C.A.) 26.19

B.C.T.W. v. Manitoba (Man. Human Rights Commission). See McGavin Toastmaster Ltd. v. Powlowski

B.X. Developments Ltd. v. R., [1976] 4 W.W.R. 364, 31 C.C.C. (2d) 14, 70 D.L.R. (3d) 366 (B.C. C.A.) 3.2

Bagambiire, re, June 1, 1997 .... 26.18.1

Baker v. Law Society of Upper Canada (1997), (*sub nom.* Law Society of Upper Canada v. Baker) 143 D.L.R. (4th) 551, 97 O.A.C. 244 (Div. Ct.), leave to appeal refused (April 10, 1997), Doc. CA M19885 (Ont. C.A.) 26.6

Baker v. R., N.S. C.A., 1988 (unreported) 7.7

Bakht v. College of Physicians & Surgeons (New Brunswick) (1989), 95 N.B.R. (2d) 81, 241 A.P.R. 81, 59 D.L.R. (4th) 156 (C.A.) 26.22

Balaban, Re, report adopted by Convocation, May 24, 1984 .... 4.6, 4.22(c), 8, 26.17

Balaban (No. 2), report adopted by Convocation, September 25, 1986........... 4.22(c), 8

Balla v. Gambro Inc., 560 N.E. 2d 1043 (Ill. App. Ct., 1990) 20.1

Bank of B.C. v. M. [1981] 2 W.W.R. 351, 24 B.C.L.R. 49, 120 D.L.R. (3d) 177 (C.A.) 17.5

Bank of Montreal v. Arvee Cedar Mills Ltd. (No. 2), [1979] 1 W.W.R. 219, 9 C.P.C. 249 (*sub nom.* Bank of Montreal v. Arvee Cedar Mills Ltd.), 93 D.L.R. (3d) 58 (B.C. S.C.) 4.8

Bank of Montreal v. Wilson (1867), 2 Ch. 117 .... 4.7

Bank of Nova Scotia v. Imperial Developments (Canada) Ltd., [1988] 2 W.W.R. 141, 67 C.B.R. (N.S.) 58, 49 Man. R. (2d) 53, 46 D.L.R. (4th) 190 (C.A.) 25.3

Banks v. Goodfellow (1870), L.R.S. Q.B. 549 .... 18.1

Banks v. Hall, [1941] 2 W.W.R. 534, [1941] 4 D.L.R. 217 (Sask. C.A.) 26.12

Banque provinciale du Canada v. Adjutor Lévesque Roofing Ltd. (1968), 68 D.L.R. (2d) 340 (N.B. C.A.) 5.6

Baron v. F., [1945] 4 D.L.R. 525 (B.C. Law Society Visitorial Trib.) 26.7, 26.16

Barrister, Re (1953), 33 M.P.R. 146, 108 C.C.C. 92, [1954] 1 D.L.R. 814 (N.B. C.A.) 26.16

Barry v. Alberta (Securities Commission) (1986), 67 A.R. 222, 24 C.R.R. 9, 25 D.L.R. (4th) 730 (C.A.), affirmed [1989] 1 S.C.R. 301, 35 Admin. L.R. 1, (*sub nom.* Brosseau v. Alberta (Securities Commission)) 65 Alta. L.R. (2d) 97, [1989] 3 W.W.R. 456, 93 N.R. 1, 96 A.R. 241, 57 D.L.R. (4th) 458 .... 26.11

Barry v. Law Society (New Brunswick) (1989), 100 N.B.R. (2d) 245, 252 A.P.R. 245 (Q.B.) 5.6

Barsoum v. Pape (1988), 34 Admin. L.R. 100, [1988] N.W.T.R. 368 (S.C.) 26.3, 26.11

Bassett v. College of Physicians & Surgeons (Saskatchewan) (1987), 63 Sask. R. 45 (Appeal Trib. under the Medical Profession Act), affirmed (1988), 70 Sask. R. 283 (C.A.) 26.15

Batchelor v. Pattison and Mackersy (1876), 3 R. 914 (Sct. Ct. of Sess.) 4.11, 27.4

Bater v. Bater, [1950] 2 All E.R. 458, [1951] p. 35 (C.A.) 26.16

Bates v. Arizona State Bar, 433 U.S. 350, 97 S. Ct. 2691 (1977) 10, 11

Batorski v. Moody (1983), 42 O.R. (2d) 647, [1983] Admin. L.R. 60, 150 D.L.R. (3d) 114 (Div. Ct.) 26.11

Baum, re, reasons of Convocation, September 28, 1995 .... 26.17

Baumann v. Bonderove (1986), 45 Alta. L.R. (2d) 168 (C.A.) 26.15

Baumgartner v. Baumgartner, 2 B.C.L.R. (3d) 126, [1995] 5 W.W.R. 289, 122 D.L.R. (4th) 542, 55 B.C.A.C. 277, 90 W.A.C. 277 (C.A.) 5.10

Bazant, Re. See Bilson v. University of Saskatchewan

Beckon, Re. See Becon v. Ontario (Deputy Chief Coroner)
Beckon v. Ontario (Deputy Chief Coroner) (1992), (*sub nom.* Re Beckon) 9 O.R. (3d) 256, 57 O.A.C. 21, 93 D.L.R. (4th) 161 (C.A.) 26.16

Belhumeur c. Barreau du Québec (*sub nom.* Belhumeur v. Discipline Committee of Que. Bar Assn.) (1983), 34 C.R. (3d) 279 (C.S. Qué), affirmed (*sub nom.* Belhumeur v. Comité de discipline du Barreau du Québec) 16 Q.A.C. 1, (*sub nom.* Belhumeur c. Savard) [1988] R.J.Q. 1526, 54 D.L.R. (4th) 105, 35 C.R.R. 193 (C.A.) 26.2

Béliveau c. Comité de discipline (Barreau du Québec), [1992] R.J.Q. 1822, 50 Q.A.C. 67 .... 26.2

Bell v. Commercial Insurance Co., 280 F. 2d 514 (3rd Cir., 1990) 5.14

Bell v. Smith, [1968] S.C.R. 664, 68 D.L.R. (2d) 751 .... 3.2

Beltz v. Law Society (British Columbia) (1986), 7 B.C.L.R. (2d) 353, [1987] 1 W.W.R. 427, 27 C.R.R. 152, 31 D.L.R. (4th) 685 (S.C.) 27.2

Benaiah, re, order of Convocation, September 22, 1993 .... 26.17

Bennett v. British Columbia (Securities Commission) (1992), 69 B.C.L.R. (2d) 171, [1992] 5 W.W.R. 481, 94 D.L.R. (4th) 339, 18 B.C.A.C. 191, 31 W.A.C. 191 (C.A.), leave to appeal to Supreme Court of Canada dismissed, [1992] 6 W.W.R. lvii (note), 70 B.C.L.R. (2d) xxxii (note), 143 N.R. 396 (note), 20 B.C.A.C. 80 (note), 35 W.A.C. 80 (note), 97 D.L.R. (4th) vii (note) (S.C.C.) 26.11

Bergel & Edson v. Wolf (2000), 50 O.R. (3d) 777 (S.C.) 12

Berger v. United States, 295 U.S. 78, 55 S. Ct. 629 (1935) 6.1

Bernstein v. College of Physicians & Surgeons (Ontario) (1977), 15 O.R. (2d) 447, 1 L.M.Q. 56, 76 D.L.R. (3d) 38 (Div. Ct.) 26.16

Betts v. Allstate Insurance Co., 1954 Cal. App. 3d 688, 201 Cal. Rptr. 528 (1984)... 5.14

BeVill, Bresler & Schulman Asset Management Corp., Re, 805 F. 2d 210 (1986).... 20.5

Bhandari v. Advocates Committeee, [1956] 1 W.L.R. 1442, [1956] 3 All E.R. 742 (P.C.) 26.16

Biderman, Re, report adopted by Convocation, March 28, 1991 .... 26.17

Bilson v. University of Saskatchewan, [1984] 4 W.W.R. 238, 33 Sask. R. 1 (*sub nom.* Re Bazant; Bilson v. University of Sask.) (C.A.) 4.19

Bishop v. College of Physicians & Surgeons (British Columbia), 65 B.C.L.R. 315, [1985] 6 W.W.R. 234, 17 C.R.R. 59, 22 D.L.R. (4th) 185 (S.C.), affirmed 1 B.C.L.R. (2d) 36, [1986] 3 W.W.R. 377, 23 C.R.R. 267, 26 D.L.R. (4th) 15 (C.A.) 26.4

Bisyk (No. 2), Re (1980), 32 O.R. (2d) 281 (H.C.), affirmed (1981), 32 O.R. (2d) 281n (C.A.) .... 4.17, 4.22(a)

Black, re, adopted by Convocation, November 25, 1993 .... 26.17

Black v. Law Society (Alberta), [1989] 1 S.C.R. 591, 37 Admin. L.R. 161, 66 Alta. L.R. (2d) 97, [1989] 4 W.W.R. 1, 96 A.R. 352, 38 C.R.R. 193, 93 N.R. 266, 58 D.L.R. (4th) 317 .... 23.1, 25.11

Blackledge v. Allison, 431 U.S. 63, 97 S. Ct. 1621 (1977)........................6.5

Blackledge v. Perry, 417 U.S. 21 (1974)..6.5

Blumenfeld v. Borenstein, 247 Ga. 406, 276 S.E. (2d) 607 (S. Ct. Ga., 1981).......5.9

Board of Education v. Nyquist, 590 F. 2d 1241 (2nd Cir., 1979)...................5.4

Bodily v. Intermountain Health Care Corp., 649 F. Supp. 468 (Utah, 1986).........5.4

Bolkiah v. KPMG (1998), [1999] 2 W.L.R. 215, [1999] 1 All E.R. 517, 45 B.L.R. (2d) 201 (U.K. H.L.)....................................5.4, 5.6, 5.10

Bolton v. Law Society, [1993] 1 W.L.R. 512 (C.A.).......... Intro, 26.1, 26.17, 26.19

Booth v. Huxter (1994), 16 O.R. (3d) 530 (Div. Ct.).............................5.5

Booth v. Mary Carter Paint Co., 202 So. 2d 8 (Fla. 1967)........................4.21

Bordenkircher v. Hayes, 434 U.S. 357, 98 S. Ct. 663 (1978)......................6.5

Boucher v. R., [1955] S.C.R. 16, 20 C.R. 1, 110 C.C.C. 263............. 4.16, 6.1, 6.6

Boudreau v. Benaiah (1998), 154 D.L.R. (4th) 650, 37 O.R. (3d) 686 (Gen. Div.)..4.18

Boughner, Re, report adopted by Convocation, April 21, 1994.................26.17

Bovbel v. Canada (Minister of Employment & Immigration) (1994), 18 Admin. L.R. (2d) 169, 167 N.R. 10, 113 D.L.R. (4th) 415 (Fed. C.A.)................26.18

Bow Valley Energy Inc. v. San Diego Gas and Electric Co. (1995), 36 Alta. L.R. (3d) 269, 43 C.P.C. (3d) 384, [1996] 4 W.W.R. 115, 179 A.R. 75 (Q.B.), affirmed (1996), 38 Alta. L.R. (3d) 116, 181 A.R. 261, 116 W.A.C. 261, 48 C.P.C. (3d) 99 (C.A.)..5.6

Box, re, order of Convocation, November 24, 1994..........................26.17

Bradbury, Re, report adopted by Convocation, May 27, 1983..................26.17

Bradwell v. Illinois, 83 U.S. (16 Wall) 130 (1872).............................23.3

Brady v. Maryland, 373 U.S. 83 (1962)..6.4

Brampton Engineering Inc. v. Alros Products Ltd. (1986), 8 C.P.C. (2d) 48 (Ont. Master)..4.6

Brand v. College of Physicians & Surgeons (Saskatchewan), [1989] 5 W.W.R. 516, 77 Sask. R. 252 (Q.B.), affirmed [1990] 3 W.W.R. 272 (Sask. C.A.)......26.10

Brar v. Brar, [1990] 3 W.W.R. 495, 24 R.F.L. (3d) 459, 84 Sask. R. 261 (Q.B.)......5.6

Breault, Re, report adopted by Convocation, September 21, 1984...............26.17

Brethour v. Law Society (British Columbia) (1950), 1 W.W.R. 34, [1951] 2 D.L.R. 138 (B.C. C.A.)...................................26.12, 26.16, 26.19

Brett v. Board of Directors of Physiotherapy (Ontario) (1991), 77 D.L.R. (4th) 144, 48 O.A.C. 24 (Div. Ct.)..26.18

Brett v. Board of Directors of Physiotherapy (Ontario) (1992), 9 O.R. (3d) 613, 56 O.A.C. 29, (*sub nom.* Brett v. Ontario (Board of Directors of Physiotherapy) 92 D.L.R. (4th) 693 (Div. Ct.)............................26.11

Bridges v. California, 314 U.S. 252, 62 S. Ct. 190 (1941).......................4.23

Briginshaw v. Briginshaw, 60 C.L.R. 336, [1938] A.L.R. 334..................26.16

Brinkley v. Hassig, 83 F. 2d 351 (1936) 26.11

British Columbia (Attorney General) v. Jabour. See Law Society (British Columbia) v. Canada (Attorney General)

British Columbia (Securities Commission) v. Branch (1992), 63 B.C.L.R. (2d) 331, [1992] 3 W.W.R. 165, 88 D.L.R. (4th) 381 (C.A.), leave to appeal to S.C.C. granted [1992] 6 W.W.R. lvii (note), 70 B.C.L.R. (2d) xxxii (note), 142 N.R. 160 (note) (S.C.C.) 26.15

Broda v. Law Society (Alberta) (1993), 7 Alta. L.R. (3d) 305, 138 A.R. 68 (Q.B.) 26.4

Brookman v. State Bar, 46 Cal. 3d 1004 (1988) 26.22

Brooks, re, reasons of Convocation, November 14, 1996 . . . . 26.17

Brosseau v. Alberta (Securities Commission). See Barry v. Alberta (Securities Commission)

Brounsall, Ex parte (1778), 2 Cowp. 829, 98 E.R. 1385 . . . . 26.1

Brown, re, adopted by Convocation, March 27, 1997 . . . . 26.17

Brown & Williamson Tobacco Corp. v. Daniel International Corp., 563 F. 2d 671 (1977) 5.3

Browne v. Dunn (1893), 6 R. 67 (H.L.) 4.14

Brown v. General Dental Council (1990), 123 N.R. 315 (P.C.) 26.19

Brumer v. Gunn, [1983] 1 W.W.R. 424, 18 Man. R. (2d) 155 (Q.B.) 14

Buchanan v. Buchanan, 99 Cal. App. 3d 587, 160 Cal. Rptr. 577 (1979) 5.14

Buffalo, Re, 390 U.S. 544, 88 S. Ct. 1222 (1968) 26.12

Burger v. Kemp, 107 S. Ct. 3114 (1987) 7.6

Burk, Re, report adopted by Convocation, May 24, 1984 . . . . 26.17

Burke v. Burke, 425 N.W. 2d 550 (Mich. App., 1988) 4.17

Burnham v. Metropolitan Toronto Chief of Police, (*sub nom.* Burnham v. Metropolitan Toronto Police), [1987] 2 S.C.R. 572, 29 Admin. L.R. 94, 37 C.C.C. (3d) 115, (*sub nom.* Burnham v. Ackroyd (Chief of Police) 32 C.R.R. 250, (*sub nom.* Burnham v. Toronto Police Force) 81 N.R. 207, 24 O.A.C. 367, (*sub nom.* Burnham v. Ackroyd) 45 D.L.R. (4th) 309 . . . . 26.2

Burns v. Chiropractic Assn. (Alberta), (1981), 16 Alta. L.R. (2d) 120, 31 A.R. 176, 125 D.L.R. (3d) 475 (C.A.) 26.14

Burns v. Stewart, 290 Minn. 289, 188 N.W. 2d 760 (1971) 12

Butler v. United States, 414 A. 2d 844 (D.C. App., 1980) 7.5

C., Re, report of admission committee, December 19, 1991 . . . . 23.3

C. (J.M.N.) v. Winnipeg Child and Family Services (May 26, 1997), AH 97-30-03267 (Man. C.A.) 3.2.1

Cairns v. Cairns, 26 Alta. L.R. 69, [1931] 3 W.W.R. 335, [1931] 4 D.L.R. 819 (C.A.) 4.19

Calgas Investments Ltd. v. 784688 Ontario Ltd. (1991), 4 O.R. (3d) 459, 1 C.P.C. (3d) 64, 81 D.L.R. (4th) 518 (Gen. Div.), additional reasons at (1991), 1 C.P.C. (3d) 64n (Ont. Gen. Div.), leave to appeal to Div. Ct. refused (1991), 4 O.R. (3d) 459n (Gen. Div.) 5.10

California v. Meredith, 29 Cal. 3d 682 (1981) 7.3

Camera v. Fogg, 658 F. 2d 80 (2nd Cir., 1981) 7.6

Camgoz v. College of Physicians & Surgeons (Saskatchewan) (1989), (*sub nom.* Re Camgoz) 74 Sask. R. 73 (C.A.) 26.16

Canada v. McKinlay Transport Ltd. See R. v. McKinlay Transport Ltd.

Canada v. Pharmaceutical Society (Nova Scotia), [1992] 2 S.C.R. 606, 114 N.S.R. (2d) 91, 15 C.R. (4th) 1, (*sub nom.* R. v. Nova Scotia Pharmaceutical Society) 43 C.P.R. (3d) 1, 10 C.R.R. (2d) 34, (*sub nom.* R. v. Nova Scotia Pharmaceutical Society (No. 2)) 139 N.R. 241, 313 A.P.R. 91, 10 C.C.C. (3d) 289, 93 D.L.R. (4th) 36 . . . . . 23.3

Canada (Attorney General) v. Law Society (British Columbia) (*sub nom.* Jabour v. Law Society (British Columbia)), [1982] 2 S.C.R. 307, 37 B.C.L.R. 145, [1982] 5 W.W.R. 289, 66 C.P.R. (2d) 1, 66 B.L.R. 234, 43 N.R. 451, 137 D.L.R. (3d) 1 . . . . . 26.7, 27.2

Canada (Attorney General) v. P.S.A.C., [1991] S.C.R. 614, 48 Admin. L.R. 161, 91 C.L.L.C. 14,017, (*sub nom.* Canada (Procureur général v. A.F.P.C.) 123 N.R. 161, 80 D.L.R. (4th) 520 . . . . . 26.19

Canada (Attorney General) v. Veinotte (1987), 81 N.S.R. (2d) 356, 203 A.P.R. 356 (T.D.), affirmed (June 7, 1989), Doc. No. S.C.A. 02014 (N.S. C.A.) 4.8

Canada (Procureur général) v. A.F.P.C. See Canada (Attorney General) v. P.S.A.C.

Canada (Solicitor General) v. Ontario (Royal Commission of Inquiry into Confidentiality of Health Records) (*sub nom.* Re Inquiry into Confidentiality of Health Records in Ontario) (1979), 24 O.R. (2d) 545, 13 C.P.C. 239, 47 C.C.C. (2d) 465, 98 D.L.R. (3d) 704 (C.A.), reversed on other grounds [1981] 2 S.C.R. 494, 23 C.R. (3d) 338, 23 C.P.C. 99, 38 N.R. 588, 128 D.L.R. (3d) 193 . . . . . 26.9

Canada Southern Railway v. Kingsmill, Jennings (1978), 8 C.P.C. 117, 4 B.L.R. 257 (Ont. H.C.) 5.6

Canadian Newspapers Co. v. Law Society (Upper Canada) (1986), 10 O.A.C. 361 (Div. Ct.) 26.9

Canadian Pacific Railway v. Aikins, MacAulay & Thorvaldson, 157 D.L.R. (4th) 473, 123 Man. R. (2d) 281, 159 W.A.C. 281, [1998] 6 W.W.R. 351, 23 C.P.C. (4th) 55 (C.A.) 5.10

Canadian Southern Petroleum v. Amoco Canada Petroleum Ltd., [1997] 5 W.W.R. 395, 193 A.R. 273, 135 W.A.C. 273, 144 D.L.R. (4th) 30, 48 Alta. L.R. (3d) 382, 7 C.P.C. (4th) 26 (C.A.), leave to appeal to S.C.C. refused (1997), 216 N.R. 159 (note) (S.C.C.) 5.6, 5.10

Canbook Distribution Corp. v. Borins (1999), 7 C.B.R. (4th) 121 (Ont. Gen. Div. [Commercial List]) 3.2

Cannon, Re, Sask., March 26, 1992 (unreported) 26.17

Cannon v. U.S. Acoustic Corp., 532 F. 2d 1118 (7th Cir., 1976) 5.13

Cappe, Re, report adopted by Convocation, June 20, 1991 .... 26.22

Carruthers v. College of Nurses of Ontario (1996), 31 O.R. (3d) 377, 96 O.A.C. 41, 141 D.L.R. (4th) 325 (Div. Ct.) 26.2

Carson v. Law Society (Saskatchewan), [1975] 6 W.W.R. 544, 61 D.L.R. (3d) 652 (Sask. C.A.) 5.6

Cartledge (Litigation Guardian of) v. Brown (1998), 41 O.R. (3d) 376, 27 C.P.C. (4th) 292 (Gen. Div.) 5.10

Carvell, Re (1977), 21 N.B.R. (2d) 642, 37 A.P.R. 642 (Prob. Ct.) 18.1

Casey v. Law Society (Newfoundland) (1986), 58 Nfld. & P.E.I.R. 349, 174 A.P.R. 349 (Nfld. T.D.) 23.1

Caskie, Re, report adopted by Convocation, June 24, 1983 .... 26.8, 26.17

Cavallin v. King (1984), 51 B.C.L.R. 149 (S.C.) 22.3

Central & Eastern Trust Co. v. Rafuse, (*sub nom.* Central Trust Co. v. Rafuse), [1986] 2 S.C.R. 147, 75 N.S.R. (2d) 109, 42 R.P.R. 161, 34 B.L.R. 187, 37 C.C.L.T. 117, 186 A.P.R. 109, 69 N.R. 321, 31 D.L.R. (4th) 481, (*sub nom.* Central Trust Co. c. Cordon) [1986] R.R.A. 527 (headnote only), varied [1988] 1 S.C.R. 1206, 44 C.C.L.T. xxxiv 24.6, 25.3

Champlain Lending Corp. v. Orillia (City), Ont. Gen. Div., July 1992 (unreported) 5.10

Channan v. Professional Examination Board in Law (1980), 12 Alta. L.R. (2d) 301, 110 D.L.R. (3d) 671 (Q.B.) 23.1

Chapman v. 3M Canada Inc. (1995), 25 O.R. (3d) 658, 43 C.P.C. (3d) 142 (Gen. Div.) 5.5

Charboneau v. College of Physicians & Surgeons (Ontario) (1985), 52 O.R. (2d) 552, 20 C.R.R. 68, 22 D.L.R. (4th) 303 (H.C.) 26.4

Chassure Brown's Inc. v. Québec. See Ford v. Quebec (Attorney General)

Chaukalos Woodburn McKenzie Maranda Ltd. v. Smith, Lyons, Torrance, Stevenson & Mayer (1994), 97 B.C.L.R. (2d) 122, [1995] 1 W.W.R. 3 (S.C.) 5.10

Chief Industries v. Equisource Corp., Ont. Gen. Div., July 1, 1992 (unreported) 5.10

Chin v. Wong (1991), 53 B.C.L.R. (2d) 288 (S.C.) 5.10

Chippewas of Kettle & Stony Point v. Canada (Attorney General) (1993), 17 C.P.C. (3d) 5 (Ont. Gen. Div.), affirmed (*sub nom.* Chippewas of Kettle & Stony Point v. Canada (Ministry of Indian Affairs)) (1993), [1994] 2 C.N.L.R. 33 (Ont. Div. Ct.) 5.10

Chodos, re, adopted by Convocation, December 8, 1995 .... 26.8, 26.17

Chodos (No. 1), Re, report adopted by Convocation, November 22, 1986 .... 3.2, 5.9, 26.17

Chodos (No. 2), Re, report adopted by Convocation, April 16, 1989 .... 26.17

Christo v. Bevan (1982), 36 O.R. (2d) 797, 27 C.P.C. 209, 28 R.F.L. (2d) 197 (H.C.) 5.6

Chrysler Credit Canada Ltd. v. 734925 Ontario Ltd. (1991), 5 O.R. (3d) 65 (Gen. Div.) 4.7

Chua, Re (1995), 11 B.C.L.R. (3d) 393, [1996] 1 W.W.R. 121 (S.C.) 5.6

Ciglen, Re, report adopted by Convocation, October 16, 1970 .... 26.8, 26.17

Ciglen, Re, report adopted by Convocation, September 18, 1980 .... 26.17

Cincinnati Bar Assn. v. Fettner, 8 Ohio St. 3d 17, 455 N.S. 2d 1288 (1983) 25.13

Cinema 5, Ltd. v. Cinerma, Inc., 528 F. 2d 1384 (1976) 5.4

Cini v. Micallef (1987), 60 O.R. (2d) 584, 20 C.P.C. (2d) 229 (H.C.) .... 4.22(a), 27.5

Cirillo, Re, report adopted by Convocation, October 22, 1992 .... 26.22

Clarence Construction Ltd. v. Lavallee (1980), 111 D.L.R. (3d) 582 (B.C. S.C.), affirmed [1982] 2 W.W.R. 760, 132 D.L.R. (3d) 153 (B.C. C.A.) 17.4

Clark Boyce v. Mouat, [1993] 4 All E.R. 268 (P.C.) 22.1, 22.2

Clarkson v. R. See R. v. Clarkson

Clarkson Co. v. Chilcott (1984), 48 O.R. (2d) 545, 53 C.B.R. (N.S.) 251, 6 O.A.C. 291, 13 D.L.R. (4th) 481, 13 C.R.R. 41 (C.A.) 3.2

Coates v. Ontario (Registrar of Motor Vehicle Dealers & Salesmen) (1988), 65 O.R. (2d) 526, 34 Admin. L.R. 70, 28 O.A.C. 307, 52 D.L.R. (4th) 272 (Div. Ct.) 26.16

Coccimiglio, Re, report adopted by Convocation, June 20, 1991 .... 25.13

Coccimiglio, Re, report adopted by Convocation, September 26, 1991 .... 26.17

Cochrane, Re, report adopted by Convocation, November 28, 1988 .... 18.3

Coffee, Re, report adopted by Convocation, September 23, 1982 .... 26.17

Colborne Capital Corp. v. 542775 Alberta Ltd. (1995), 20 Alta. L.R. (3d) 127, [1993] 7 W.W.R. 671 (Q.B.) 5.10

College of Nurses (Ontario) v. Quiogue (1993), 13 O.R. (3d) 325, 63 O.A.C. 241, 104 D.L.R. (4th) 44 (Div. Ct.) 26.19

College of Physicians & Surgeons (Manitoba) v. Morgentaler (1986), 42 Man. R. (2d) 28, 28 D.L.R. (4th) 283 (C.A.) 26.13

College of Physicians & Surgeons (Ontario) v. Casullo (1976), [1977] 2 S.C.R. 2, 9 N.R. 239, 67 D.L.R. (3d) 351 .... 26.11

College of Physicians & Surgeons (Ontario) v. K. (1985), 59 O.R. (2d) 1, 19 O.A.C. 51 (*sub nom.* College of Physicians & Surgeons (Ont.) v. Keil), 36 D.L.R. (4th) 707 (C.A.) 26.12

College of Physicians & Surgeons (Ontario) v. Petrie (1989), 68 O.R. (2d) 100, 37 Admin. L.R. 119, 32 O.A.C. 248 (Div. Ct.) 26.12

Collison v. Hurst, [1946] O.W.N. 668, [1946] 4 D.L.R. 27 (C.A.) 4.10

Columbia Realty Associates Ltd., Re, 71 Bankr. 804 (Bankr. N.D. Ill., 1987) 5.6

Comden v. Superior Court, 20 Cal. 3d 906, 576 P. 2d 791, cert. denied 439 U.S. 981, 99 S. Ct. 568 (1978) 4.19

Commission on Professional Ethics and Conduct of Iowa State Bar Assn. v. Floy, 334 N.W. 2d 739 (Iowa, 1983) 25.13

Committee for Justice & Liberty v. Canada (National Energy Board), [1978] 1 S.C.R. 369, 9 N.R. 115, 68 D.L.R. (3d) 716 .... 26.11

Commonwealth v. Alderman, 292 Pa. Super 263, 437 A. 2d 36 (1981) 7.5

Commonwealth v. D'Amato, 514 Pa. 471, 526 A. 2d 300 (1987) 6.6

Commonwealth v. Kozec, 399 Mass. 514, 505 N.E. 2d 519 (1987) 6.6

Commonwealth v. Kozec, 505 N.G. 2d 519 at 522 (Mass. Sup. Jud. Ct., 1987) 6.6

Commonwealth v. Steinhach, 514 A.2d 114 (Penn., 1986) 7.3

Commonwealth Investors Syndicate Ltd. v. Laxton (1990), 50 B.C.L.R. (2d) 186, [1991] W.W.R. 315, 74 D.L.R. (4th) 260 (C.A.), leave to appeal to S.C.C. refused 54 B.C.L.R. (2d) xxxiv (note), [1991] 4 W.W.R. lxiv (note), 79 D.L.R. (4th) vii (note), 135 N.R. 77 (note) (S.C.C.) 12

Commonwealth Investors Syndicate Ltd. v. Laxton (1994), 117 D.L.R. (4th) 382 (B.C.C.A.) 12

Connor v. Law Society (British Columbia), [1980] 4 W.W.R. 638 (B.C. S.C.) 26.11

Consiglio (No. 2), Re, [1973] 3 O.R. 329, 36 D.L.R. (3d) 661 (C.A.) .... 4.22(a)

Consumers Glass Co. v. Foundation Co. of Can./Cie foundation du Can. (1985), 51 O.R. (3d) 385, 1 C.P.C. (2d) 208, 30 B.L.R. 87, 33 C.C.L.T. 104, 13 C.L.R. 149, 9 O.A.C. 193, 20 D.L.R. (4th) 126 (C.A.) 25.3

Continental Insurance Co. v. Dalton Cartage Ltd. [1982] 1 S.C.R. 164, 25 C.P.C. 72, [1982] I.L.R. 1-1487, 131 D.L.R. (3d) 559, 40 N.R. 135 (*sub nom.* Dalton Carton Ltd. v. Continental Ins. Co.) 26.16

Cooke, Re (1889), 5 T.L.R. 407 (C.A.) 26.7

Cooper, Re, report adopted by Convocation, May 23, 1991 .... 26.17

Copperview Haven Ltd. v. Waverley Park Estates Ltd., [1981] 4 W.W.R. 673 (B.C. S.C.), additional reasons at [1984] 4 W.W.R. 673 at 675, [1984] 4 W.W.R. 673 at 676 (B.C. S.C.), varied [1984] 4 W.W.R. 673, 55 B.C.L.R. 230 (C.A.) 22.3

Cornacchia and Law Society of Upper Canada, Re, Div. Ct., September 26, 1985 (unreported) 26.5, 26.8

Coulombe (Litigation Guardian of) v. Beard (*sub nom.* Coulombe v. Beard) (1993), 16 O.R. (3d) 627, 22 C.P.C. (3d) 101 (Gen. Div.) 3.2, 3.2.1

Coulumbe v. Horner Ont. S.C., 1988 (unreported) 4.8

Courtright v. Canadian Pacific Ltd. (1983), 45 O.R. (2d) 52, 26 B.C.L.R. 17, 4 C.C.E.L. 152, 5 D.L.R. (4th) 488 (H.C.), affirmed (1985), 50 O.R. (2d) 560, 18 D.L.R. (4th) 639 (C.A.) 20.1

Cousineau v. Vancouver (City), [1926] 2 W.W.R. 433, 37 B.C.R. 266, [1926] 3 D.L.R. 265 (C.A.) 4.16

Cox v. College of Optometrists (Ontario) (1988), 65 O.R. (2d) 461, 28 O.A.C. 337, 33 Admin. L.R. 287, 52 D.L.R. (4th) 298 (Div. Ct.), leave to appeal to C.A. refused (1988), 33 Admin. L.R. xliv (Ont. C.A.) 26.19

Crawford W. Long Memorial Hospital of Emory University v. Yerby, 373 S.E. 2d 749 (S. Ct. Ga., 1988) 5.6

Crompton v. Williams, [1938] O.R. 543, [1938] 4 D.L.R. 237 (S.C.).............. 18.2

Cross, Re, report adopted by Convocation, April 23, 1982...................... 26.17

Cunliffe v. Law Society (British Columbia), [1984] 4 W.W.R. 451, 40 C.R. (3d) 67, 13 C.C.C. (3d) 560, 11 D.L.R. (4th) 280 (B.C. C.A.) 26.20

Currie & Co. v. Law Society, [1976] 3 All E.R. 832, [1977] Q.B. 990............. 27.5

Cwinn, Re, report adopted by Convocation, September 12, 1979 .... 26.17

Cwinn v. Law Society (Upper Canada) (1980), 28 O.R. (2d) 61, 33 N.R. 358, 108 D.L.R. (3d) 381 (Div. Ct.), leave to appeal denied and appeal quashed (1980), 28 O.R. (2d) 61n, 33 N.R. 358n, 108 D.L.R. (3d) 381 (S.C.C.) 23.2, 25.10, 26.8, 26.12

Dabbs v. SunLife Assurance Co. of Canada (1997), 35 O.R. (3d) 708 (Gen. Div.), leave to appeal dismissed (1998), 36 O.R. (3d) 770 (Gen. Div.)......... ,5.12

Dale v. Toronto Railway Co. (1915), 34 O.L.R. 104 (C.A.).............. 4.16, 4.22(b)

Dalfen's Ltd. v. Bay Roberts Shopping Centre Ltd. (1989), 78 Nfld. & P.E.I.R. 128, 244 A.P.R. 128 (Nfld. T.D.)... 5.6

Dalke, Re (1981), 21 C.R. (3d) 380, (*sub nom.* R. v. Dalke) 59 C.C.C. (2d) 477 (B.C. S.C.).. 4.22(b)

Danson v. Ontario (Attorney General) (1987), 60 O.R. (2d) 676, 19 C.P.C. (2d) 249, 41 C.R.R. 48, 41 D.L.R. (4th) 129, 22 O.A.C. 38 (C.A.), affirmed [1990] 2 S.C.R. 1086, 74 O.R. (2d) 763 (note), 43 C.P.C. (2d) 165, 50 C.R.R. 59, 112 N.R. 362, 41 O.A.C. 250, (*sub nom.* R. v. Danson) 73 D.L.R. (4th) 686 .... 4.17

Davey v. Woolley, Hames, Dale & Dingwall (1982), 35 O.R. (2d) 599, 133 D.L.R. (3d) 647 (C.A.), leave to appeal to S.C.C. refused (1982), 37 O.R. (2d) 499n (S.C.C.) 5.10, 22.2, 22.3

Davies, re, order of Convocation, June 23, 1994 .... 26.17

Davies, Ward & Beck v. Baker & McKenzie (1998), 111 O.A.C. 352, 164 D.L.R. (4th) 423, 40 O.R. (3d) 257, 18 C.C.P.B. 225, 26 C.P.C. (4th) 51 (C.A.) 5.10

Davy-Chiesman v. Davy-Chiesman, [1984] 1 All E.R. 321 (C.A.)................ 27.5

Deans v. Armstrong (1983), 46 B.C.L.R. 273, 149 D.L.R. (3d) 295 (S.C.) 12

Deck v. Rody (1977), 2 C.P.C. 348 (Sask. Q.B.) 12

Deep v. College of Physicians & Surgeons (Ontario) (1974), 5 O.R. (2d) 435, 50 D.L.R. (3d) 515 (Div. Ct.) 26.11

Del Core v. Ontario College of Pharmacists (1985), 51 O.R. (2d) 1, 15 Admin. L.R. 227, 10 O.A.C. 57, 19 D.L.R. (4th) 68 (C.A.), leave to appeal to S.C.C. refused (1986), 57 O.R. (2d) 296 (note), 17 O.A.C. 79 (note), 70 N.R. 82 (note) (S.C.C.)... 26.5, 26.14, 26.18

Delgado, Re, 306 S.E. 2d 591 (1983), cert. denied 464 U.S. 1057 (1984) 4.23

Demarco v. Ungaro (1979), 21 O.R. (2d) 673, 8 C.C.L.T. 207, 95 D.L.R. (3d) 385 (H.C.) 4.2, 4.18, 27.5

Demerara Bauxite Co. v. Hubbard, [1923] A.C. 673 (P.C.) 22.3

Demeter v. British Pacific Life Insurance Co., 43 O.R. (2d) 33, 37 C.P.C. 277, 2 C.C.L.I. 246, [1983] I.L.R. 1-1689, 150 D.L.R. (3d) 249 (H.C.), affirmed 48 O.R. (2d) 266, 8 C.C.L.I. 286, 7 O.A.C. 143, [1985] I.L.R. 1-1862, 13 D.L.R. (4th) 318 (C.A.) 26.5

Deptuck v. Law Society (Saskatchewan) (1984), [1985] 2 W.W.R. 433, 9 Admin. L.R. 275, 35 Sask. R. 296, 15 D.L.R. (4th) 636 (C.A.) 26.22

Dersch v. Canada (Attorney General). See R. v. Dersch

Descôteaux v. Mierzwinski, [1982] 1 S.C.R. 860, 28 C.R. (3d) 289, 70 C.C.C. (2d) 385, 1 C.R.R. 318, 141 D.L.R. (3d) 590 .... 3.2

Desmoulin v. Blair (1994), (*sub nom.* Desmoulin (Committee of) v. Blair) 21 O.R. (3d) 217, 76 O.A.C. 1, 120 D.L.R. (4th) 700 (C.A.) 12

Desmoulin (Committee of) v. Blair. See Desmoulin v. Blair

Després c. Assn des Arpenteurs-géomètres du Nouveau-Brunswick (*sub nom.* Després v. L'Association des arpenteurs-géomètres du Nouveau-Brunswick) (1992), 130 N.B.R. (2d) 210, 328 A.P.R. 210, 8 Admin. L.R. (2d) 136 (C.A.) 26.18

DiCarlo v. United States, 6 F. 2d 364 (2nd Cir., 1925) 6.1

Dingle, Re, report adopted by Convocation, September 21, 1984 .... 26.17

Disciplinary Board v. Amundson, 297 N.W. 2d 433 (N.D., 1980) 26.17

Disciplinary Proceedings Against Webster, 452 N.W. 2d 374 (S. Ct. Wis., 1990) 5.9

Dobud v. Herbertz (1985), 50 C.P.C. 283 (Ont. Dist. Ct.) 4.17

Donald v. Law Society (British Columbia), [1984] 2 W.W.R. 46, 48 B.C.L.R. 210, 7 C.R.R. 305n, 2 D.L.R. (4th) 385 (C.A.), additional reasons at [1985] 2 W.W.R. 671 (B.C. C.A.), leave to appeal to S.C.C. refused (1984), 7 C.R.R. 305, 55 N.R. 237 (S.C.C.) 26.15

Donaldson, Re, report adopted by Convocation, June 26, 1992 .... 26.17

Donnelly v. De Christoforo, 416 U.S. 637 (1974) 6.1

Dorion v. Roberge [1991] 1 S.C.R. 374, (*sub nom.* Roberge v. Bolduc) 78 D.L.R. (4th) 666, (*sub nom.* Dorion c. Roberge) 124 N.R. 1, [1991] R.R.A. 314 (headnote only), [1991] R.D.I. 239, 39 Q.A.C. 81 .... 24.6

Down, Re, [1999] B.C.J. 1809 (S.C.) 5.10

Drabinsky v. KPMG (1998), 41 O.R. (3d) 565, 45 B.L.R. (2d) 196 (Gen. Div.), leave to appeal allowed (November 4, 1998), Doc. Toronto 664/98 (Ont. Div. Ct.), affirmed (1999), 10 C.B.R. (4th) 130 (Ont. Div. Ct.) 5.4, 5.6, 5.10

Duarte v. Perreault (1991), 83 Alta. L.R. (2d) 92, 1 C.P.C. (3d) 227 (Master) 26.15

Dubinsky, Re, report adopted by Convocation, September 21, 1984 .... 4.22(c), 26.17

Dudzic v. Law Society (Upper Canada) (1989), 71 O.R. (2d) 272, 36 O.A.C. 314, 64 D.L.R. (4th) 527 (Div. Ct.) 26.19

Dudzik, Re, report adopted by Convocation, October 27, 1989 .... 18.2

Dulmage v. Ontario (Police Complaints Commissioner) (1994), 21 O.R. (3d) 356, 75 O.A.C. 305, 120 D.L.R. (4th) 590, 30 Admin. L.R. (2d) 203 (Div. Ct.) 26.11

Dumais v. Zarnett (1996), 30 O.R. (3d) 431, 6 O.T.C. 264 (Gen. Div.) 4.6, 25.9

Duncan, Re (1957), [1958] S.C.R. 41, 11 D.L.R. (2d) 616 .... 4.22(b)

Duncan v. Law Society of Alberta Investigating Committee (1991), 49 Admin. L.R. 142, 79 Alta. L.R. (2d) 228, (*sub nom.* Duncan v. Law Society (Alberta)) 115 A.R. 161, 80 D.L.R. (4th) 702 (C.A.), leave to appeal to S.C.C. refused (1991), 7 Admin. L.R. (2d) 219 (note), 82 Alta. L.R. (2d) lxv (note), 127 A.R. 393 (note), 20 W.A.C. 393 (note), 137 N.R. 160 (note), 85 D.L.R. (4th) viii (note) (S.C.C.) 26.10, 26.11

Dunkley v. R., [1995] 1 All E.R. 279 (P.C.) 7.8

Dupuis v. R. (1967), 3 C.R.N.S. 75 (Que. C.A.) 6.6

Duriancik v. Ontario (Attorney General) (1994), 114 D.L.R. (4th) 504 (Ont. Div. Ct.) 26.10

Dwyer v. Spry (1981), 27 B.C.L.R. 253 (S.C.) 22.2

E.A. Manning Ltd. v. Ontario (Securities Commission) (1994), 3 C.C.L.S. 221, 17 O.S.C.B. 2339, 18 O.R. (3d) 97, (*sub nom.* Manning (E.A.) Ltd. v. Ontario (Securities Commission)) 72 O.A.C. 34 (Div. Ct.) 26.11

E.F. Hutton & Co. v. Brown, 305 F. Supp 371 (S.D. Tex., 1969) 5.6

Eastholme Realty Ltd. v. Grundy, [1954] O.W.N. 583 (C.A.) 4.19, 5.6

Eaton, Re, [1924] 3 W.W.R. 562, [1924] 4 D.L.R. 873 (Alta. C.A.) 26.22

Ebert Howe & Associates v. Optometric Assn. (British Columbia), 66 B.C.L.R. 72, [1985] 6 W.W.R. 394, 21 D.L.R. (4th) 421 (C.A.) 10

Eckstein v. Law Society (Manitoba), [1981] 1 W.W.R. 566, 6 Man. R. (2d) 161, 116 D.L.R. (3d) 60 (Q.B.), reversed on other grounds [1981] 3 W.W.R. 171, 7 Man. R. 415, 121 D.L.R. (3d) 677 (C.A.) 14

Edwards v. Edwards, [1958] P. 235, [1958] 2 All E.R. 179 .... 27.5

Edwards v. Law Society of Upper Canada (1988), 37 O.R. (3d) 279, 156 D.L.R. (4th) 348 (Gen. Div.) 26.4

Edmondson v. State Bar, 29 Cal. 3d 339, 625 P. 2d 812 (1981) 26.16

Edwards Books & Art Ltd. v. R. See R. v. Videoflicks Ltd.

Elyria & Steel Co. v. Mohegan Tube Co., 7 F.2d 827 (2d Cir. 1925) 2.14

Emerson v. Law Society (Upper Canada) (1983), 44 O.R. (2d) 729, 41 C.P.C. 7, 5 D.L.R. (4th) 294 (H.C.) 26.7, 26.14, 26.18

Enerchem Shipmanagement Inc. v. "Coastal Canada" (The), [1988] F.C. 421, 83 N.R. 256 (C.A.) 25.2

Enns v. Panju, [1978] 5 W.W.R. 244, 5 R.P.R. 248 (B.C. S.C.) 25.2

Essa (Township) v. Guergis (1993), 12 O.R. (3d) 97 (Gen. Div.) 4.19

Essa (Township) v. Guergis (1993), 15 O.R. (3d) 573, (*sub nom.* Heck v. Royal Bank) 22 C.P.C. (3d) 63, 52 C.P.R. (3d) 372 (Div. Ct.) 4.19, 5.6, 5.10

Estates Theatres, Inc. v. Columbia Pictures Industries, Inc., 345 F. Supp. 93 (S.D.N.Y., 1972) 5.8

Evans v. Savarin Ltd. (1980), 27 O.R. (2d) 705, 109 D.L.R. (3d) 510 (H.C.) .... 4.22(a)

Everingham v. Ontario (1992), 8 O.R. (3d) 121, 5 C.P.C. (3d) 118, 54 O.A.C. 224, 88 D.L.R. (4th) 755 (Div. Ct.) 4.12, 21.3

F., Re, [1945] 3 W.W.R. 31, (*sub nom.* Re Legal Professions Act & Benchers Society of B.C.) [1945] 4 D.L.R. 702 (B.C. Law Society Visitorial Trib.) 26.12

Faber-Castell Canada Ltd. v. Woods, Ont. Gen. Div., Matlow J., March 14, 1994 (unreported) 4.22

Fabian v. Bud Mervyn Construction Ltd. (1981), 35 O.R. (2d) 132, 23 C.P.C. 40, 127 D.L.R. (3d) 119 (Div. Ct.) 4.8

Fan v. Law Society (British Columbia) (1977), 4 B.C.L.R. 16, 77 D.L.R. (3d) 97 (C.A.) 25.2, 26.18

Faraci, Re, report adopted by Convocation, May 24, 1984 .... 26.17

Farkas, Re, report adopted by Convocation, March 24, 1983 .... 26.17

Farm-Rite Equipment Ltd. (Receiver of) v. Robinson Alamo Sales Ltd., [1989] 5 W.W.R. 673, 78 Sask. R. 161, 9 P.P.S.A.C. 204 (C.A.) 5.6

Farrelly v. Corrigan, [1899] A.C. 563 (P.C.) 18.2

Fasken Campbell Godfrey v. Seven-up Canada Inc. (1997), 142 D.L.R. (4th) 456 (Ont. Gen. Div.) 24.6

Fawell v. Atkins (1981), 28 B.C.L.R. 32 (S.C.) 4.12

Feherguard Products Ltd. v. Rocky's of B.C. Leisure Ltd., [1993] 3 F.C. 619, 54 C.P.R. (3d) 545 (C.A.) 5.10

Fejes, re, adopted by Convocation, June 23, 1994 .... 26.17

Feldman v. Law Society (Upper Canada) (November 1, 1988), Doc. No. 639/85 (Ont. Div. Ct.) 26.11

Feldman v. Law Society of Upper Canada (December 3, 1987), Doc. 639/85 (Ont. Div. Ct.) 26.2

Fenton v. College of Physicians & Surgeons (Ontario) (1974), 6 O.R. (2d) 193, 52 D.L.R. (3d) 321 (Div. Ct.) 26.18

Ferguson v. Georgia, 365 U.S. 570 (1961) 7.5

Ferris v. Rusnak (1983), 50 A.R. 297, 9 D.L.R. (4th) 183 (Q.B.), supplementary reasons at (1984), 54 A.R. 319 (Q.B.) 22.2

Fickett v. Superior Court, 27 Ariz. App. 793, 558 P. 2d 988 (1976) 22.4

Filmlab Systems International Ltd. v. Pennington, [1994] 4 All E.R. 673 .... 4.22

Fisher v. Fisher (1986), 76 N.S.R. (2d) 326, 14 C.P.C. (2d) 263, 189 A.P.R. 326 (C.A.) 5.10

Fitzpatrick, Re, 54 O.L.R. 3, [1924] 1 D.L.R. 981 (Ont. S.C.) 26.7

Flak, re, order of Convocation, September 28, 1995 .... 26.17

Fleischer, Re, 102 N.J. 440, 508 A. 2d 1115 (1986) 26.17

Fletcher & Son v. Jubb, Booth & Helliwell, [1920] 1 K.B. 275 (C.A.) 4.14

Florida Bar v. Levin, 570 So. 2d 917 (Fla., 1990) 26.8

Florida Bar v. Newhouse, 498 So. 2d 935 (1986) 4.16

Flynn Developments Ltd. v. Central Trust Co. (1985), 51 O.R. (2d) 57 (H.C.)....... 5.6

Fogel, Re, 422 A. 2d 966 (D.C., 1980) 26.17

Ford v. Quebec (Attorney General), [1988] 2 S.C.R. 712, (*sub nom.* Chassure Brown's Inc. v. Québec (P.G.)) 19 Q.A.C. 69, 90 N.R. 84, 10 C.H.R.R. D/ 5559, 54 D.L.R. (4th) 577 10

Ford Motor Company of Canada, Limited v. Osler, Hoskin & Harcourt (1996), 27 O.R. (3d) 181, 24 B.L.R. (2d) 217, 43 C.P.C. (3d) 156, 131 D.L.R. (4th) 419 (Gen. Div. [Commercial List]). 5.6, 5.10

Fox v. General Medical Council, [1960] 1 W.L.R. 1017, [1960] 3 All E.R. 225 (P.C.) 4.14

Fraser, re, order of Convocation, November 26, 1992 .... 26.17

Freedman, Re, report adopted by Convocation, September 22, 1983 .... 26.17

French, Re (1982), 39 O.R. (2d) 666 (Div. Ct.) 26.3, 26.7, 26.11

French v. Law Society (Upper Canada) (1975), 9 O.R. (2d) 473, 61 D.L.R. (3d) 28 (C.A.) 26.4

French v. Law Society (Upper Canada) (No. 2) (1975), 8 O.R. (2d) 193, 57 D.L.R. (3d) 481 (C.A.), application for leave to appeal to S.C.C. dismissed without written reasons (1975), 8 O.R. (2d) 193n, 57 D.L.R. (3d) 481n (S.C.C.) 26.3, 26.11

Friedman, Re, 76 Ill. 2d 392, 392 N.E. 2d 1333 (Ill. S.C., 1979) 26.17

Fuller v. Oregon, 417 U.S. 40, 94 S. Ct. 2116 (1974) 9

G. (D.L.) v. Wood (1995), 125 D.L.R. (4th) 712 (N.S. C.A.)..................... 5.10

GM&A Advertising Ltd. v. Chubb Insurance Company of Canada................ 5.10

Gage v. Reid (1917), 38 O.L.R. 514, 34 D.L.R. 46 (C.A.)....................... 4.16

Gainers Inc. v. Pocklington (1995), 29 Alta. L.R. (3d) 323, [1995] 7 W.W.R. 413, 165 A.R. 274, 89 W.A.C. 274, 125 D.L.R. (4th) 50 (C.A.)................. 5.10

Garlow v. State Bar of California, 30 Cal. 3d 912, 640 P. 2d 1106 (1982).......... 26.1

Garofoli v. Kohm (1989), 77 C.B.R. (N.S.) 84 (Man. Q.B.)....................... 22.2

Garofoli v. Raimondi. See Garofoli v. Kohm

Garrant v. Moskal, [1985] 6 W.W.R. 31, 47 R.F.L. (2d) 1, 40 Sask. R. 155 (*sub nom.* Garrant v. Moskal; Garrant v. Cawood; Garrant v. Garrant) (C.A.) 4.18

Gault, Re, 387 U.S. 1, 87 S. Ct. 1428 (1967) 4.3

Geller v. Brisseau, 36 N.S.R. (2d) 689, 29 N.B.R. (2d) 517, [1979] 6 W.W.R. 416, 20 A.R. 317, 64 A.P.R. 689, 25 Nfld. & P.E.I.R. 221, 31 N.R. 125, 66 A.P.R. 517 (B.C. C.A.) 27.5

General Medical Council v. Spackman, [1943] A.C. 627, [1943] 2 All E.R. 337 (H.L.) 26.5

Gentile v. State Bar of Nevada, 111 S. Ct. 2720 (1991) 13

German v. Law Society (Alta.), [1974] 5 W.W.R. 217, 45 D.L.R. (3d) 535 (Alta. C.A.) 26.7

Giacomelli v. O'Reilly (1979), 23 O.R. (2d) 469, 9 C.P.C. 65, 96 D.L.R. (3d) 126 (Master) 4.16

Giannarelli v. Wraith (1988), 62 A.L.J.R. 611 (H.C.) 4.18

Giddens v. State Bar, 28 Cal. 3d 730, 621 P. 2d 851 (1981) 26.12

Gideon v. Wainwright, 372 U.S. 335 (1963) 7.1, 9

Gillen v. College of Physicians & Surgeons (Ontario) (1989), 68 O.R. (2d) 278 (Div. Ct.) 26.2

Girardet v. Crease & Co. (1987), 11 B.C.L.R. (2d) 361 at 362 (S.C.) 24.6

Girones, Re, report adopted by Convocation, January 19, 1973 .... 26.17

Gladstone, Re, [1972] 2 O.R. 127, 7 R.F.L. 176, 25 D.L.R. (3d) 43 (C.A.) 4.10

Glasser v. United States, 315 U.S. 60, 62 S. Ct. 457 (1942) 7.6

Glassman v. College of Physicians & Surgeons (Ontario), [1966] 2 O.R. 81, 55 D.L.R. (2d) 674 (C.A.) 26.16

Glebe Sugar Refining Co. Ltd. v. Greenock Port & Harbour Trustees, [1921] 2 A.C. 66 (H.L.) 4.16

Glueck v. Jonathan Logan, Inc., 653 F. 2d 746 (1981) 5.4

Gnat, Re, report of discipline hearing panel, January 9, 1990 .... 27.1

Goddart v. Nationwide Building Society, [1987] Q.B. 670 (C.A.) 3.2.1

Goldberg v. Goldberg (1982), 31 R.F.L. (2d) 453, 141 D.L.R. (3d) 133 (Ont. Div. Ct.) 5.6

Goldman, Re, report adopted by Convocation, May 14, 1981 .... 26.8, 26.17

Goldman, Re, report adopted by Convocation, May 5, 1987 .... 26.22

Goldstein v. Friedmann (1997), 32 O.R. (3d) 212 (Gen. Div.) 5.6, 5.9

Golomb v. College of Physicians & Surgeons (Ontario) (1976), 12 O.R. (2d) 73, 68 D.L.R. (3d) 25 (Div. Ct.) 26.11, 26.12, 26.16, 26.18

Goodell, Re, 39 Wis. 232 (S.C., 1875) 23.3

Goodman v. R., [1939] S.C.R. 446, 72 C.C.C. 305, [1939] 4 D.L.R. 361 12

Goodman & Carr v. Minister of National Revenue, [1968] 2 O.R. 814, 70 D.L.R. (2d) 670, [1968] C.T.C. 484, 68 D.T.C. 5288 (H.C.), additional reasons at [1968] 2 O.R. 819, 70 D.L.R. (2d) 675, 68 D.T.C. 5310 (H.C.) 3.2

Gower, Re, report adopted by Convocation, April 23, 1992 .... 26.17

Graham v. Conroy (1983), 29 Sask. R. 13 (Q.B.) 12

Gray, re, order of Convocation, October 22, 1992 .... 26.17

Green, Carter v. Law Society (Northwest Territories) (1980), [1981] 1 W.W.R. 662, 28 A.R. 143 (*sub nom.* Green v. Law Society of N.W.T.), 114 D.L.R. (3d) 762 (N.W.T. S.C.) 25.9

Greenberg v. United States, 280 F. 2d 472 (1st Cir., 1960) 6.6

Greening, Re, report adopted by Convocation, May 17, 1974 .... 26.17

Gregg v. Georgia, 428 U.S. 153 (1976) 6.3

Gridley v. United States, 44 F. 2d 716 (6th Cir., 1930), cert. denied 283 U.S. 827 (U.S. S. Ct., 1931) 6.6

Grier v. Alta. Optometric Assn., 53 Alta. L.R. (2d) 289, [1987] 5 W.W.R. 539, 42 D.L.R. (4th) 327, 79 A.R. 36 (C.A.) 10

Grievance Committee v. Rottner, 203 A. 2d 82 (1964) 5.4

Griffin v. College of Dental Surgeons (B.C.) (1989), 40 B.C.L.R. (2d) 188, [1990] 1 W.W.R. 503, 64 D.L.R. (4th) 652 (C.A.) 10

Griffiths, Re, 413 U.S. 717, 93 S. Ct. 2851 (1973) 7.1

Grochowski v. Assn. of Architects (Alberta) (1996), 184 A.R. 233, 38 Admin. L.R. (2d) 132, 122 W.A.C. 233 (C.A.) 26.18.1

Grossman v. Toronto General Hospital (1983), 41 O.R. (2d) 457, 35 C.P.C. 11, 146 D.L.R. (3d) 280 (H.C.) 2.4, 4.6

Guay v. Société Franco-Manitobaine (1985), 37 Man. R. (2d) 16 (Q.B.) 3.2

Guiness Peat Properties Ltd. v. Fitzroy Robinson Partnership, [1987] 2 All E.R. 716 (C.A.) 3.2.1

Gunn v. Washek, 405 Pa. 521, 176 A. 2d 635 (1961) 11

Hall v. Ball (1923), 54 O.L.R. 147 (H.C.) 26.19

Hamulka v. Golfman, [1985] 5 W.W.R. 597, 35 Man. R. (2d) 189, 20 D.L.R. (4th) 540 (C.A.) 26.15

Handelman, Re, report adopted by Convocation, January 23, 1992 .... 26.8

Hands v. Law Society (Upper Canada) (1888), 16 O.R. 625 (Q.B.), reversed (1888), 17 O.R. 300 (Div. Ct.), reversed (1890), 17 O.A.R. 41 (C.A.) 27.1

Hanes v. Wawanesa Mutual Insurance Co., [1963] S.C.R. 154, [1963] 1 C.C.C. 321, 36 D.L.R. (2d) 718 .... 26.16

Hargrave, Re, report adopted by Convocation, March 21, 1980 .... 26.17

Harris, Re (1914), 6 W.W.R. 628, 7 Alta. L.R. 272, 14 D.L.R. 103 (C.A.) 26.22

Harris v. Law Society (Alberta), [1936] S.C.R. 88, [1936] 1 D.L.R. 401 .... 26.19

Harvard Investments Ltd. v. Winnipeg (City), [1994] 6 W.W.R. 127, 25 C.P.C. (3d) 185, 93 Man R. (2d) 269 (Q.B.) 4.19

Harvey v. Law Society (Newfoundland) (1992), 2 Admin. L.R. (2d) 306, 93 Nfld. & P.E.I.R. 339, 292 A.P.R. 339, 88 D.L.R. (4th) 487 (Nfld. T.D.) 26.2, 26.10

Hauck v. Dixon (1975), 10 O.R. (2d) 605, 64 D.L.R. (3d) 201 (H.C.) 24.6

Haunholter v. Law Society (Alberta) (1988), 88 A.R. 313 (C.A.) 26.19, 26.22

Hawitt v. Campbell, 46 B.C.L.R. 260, [1983] 5 W.W.R. 760, 37 C.P.C. 52, 148 D.L.R. (3d) 341 (C.A.) 4.8

Hawkins, Re 532 So. 2d 669 (Fla. 1988) 26.22

Hearing on Immunity for Ethics Complainants, Re, 96 N.J. 669, 477 A. 2d 339 (1984) 26.4

Heck v. Royal Bank (1993), 12 O.R. (3d) 111 (Gen. Div.) 4.19

Hedley Byrne & Co. v. Heller & Partners, [1963] 2 All E.R. 575, [1964] A.C. 465, [1963] 1 Lloyd's Rep. 485 (H.L.) 22.4, 24.6, 25.3

Hein, Re, 104 N.J. 297, 516 A. 2d 1105 (1986) 26.17

Hendin (No. 1), Re, report adopted by Convocation, July 15, 1982 .... 26.17

Herbster v. North American Co., 501 N.E. 2d 343, appeal dismissed 508 N.E. 728, cert. denied 108 S. Ct. 150 (1987) 20.1

Herman v. Klig, [1938] O.W.N. 270 (H.C.) 4.20

Hermanns v. Ingle (1996), 80 O.T.C. 23 (Gen. Div.) 5.10

Heslin, re, order of Convocation, September 26, 1996 .... 26.17

Hess v. Mandzuk (1984), 44 C.P.C. 179, 34 R.P.R. 90 (Ont. H.C.) 4.20

Hill v. Berkshire Farm Center and Service for Youth, 521 N.Y.S. 2d 358 (N.Y.S. Ct., 1987) 5.5

Hill v. Church of Scientology. See Hill v. Church of Scientology of Toronto

Hill v. Church of Scientology of Toronto, [1995] 2 S.C.R. 1130, (*sub nom.* Hill v. Church of Scientology) 30 C.R.R. (2d) 189, 25 C.C.L.T. (2d) 89, 184 N.R. 1, 126 D.L.R. (4th) 129, 24 O.R. (3d) 865n, 84 O.A.C. 1 13

Himmel, Re, 125 Ill. 2d 531 (1988) 25.7

Hippard, Re, 49 Cal. 3d 1084, 782 P. 2d 440 (1989) 26.22

Hirt v. College of Physicians & Surgeons (British Columbia) (1986), 63 B.C.L.R. 185 (S.C.), affirmed (1986), 10 B.C.L.R. (2d) 314, 34 D.L.R. (4th) 331 (C.A.) 26.11

Hoem v. Law Society (British Columbia) (1985), 63 B.C.L.R. 36, [1985] 5 W.W.R. 1, 20 C.C.C. (3d) 239, 20 D.L.R. (4th) 433 (C.A.) 26.20

Hiss, Re, 368 Mass. 447, 333 N.E. 2d 429 (1975) 26.22

Holden & Co. v. Crown Prosecution Service, [1990] 1 All E.R. 368 (C.A.) 27.5

Holizki v. Reeves (1997), 154 Sask. R. 179, 10 C.P.C. (4th) 63 (Q.B.) 5.6

Holloway v. Arkansas, 98 S. Ct. 1173 (1978) 7.6

Holmes v. National Benzole Co. (1965), 109 S.J. 971 (Q.B.) 27.5

Holowaty v. Holowaty, [1949] 1 W.W.R. 1064 (Sask. K.B.) 4.13

Holt v. Jesse (1876), 3 Ch. D. 177 .... 4.8

Horman, Re, report adopted by Convocation, February 24, 1994 .... 26.17

Hosein v. College of Physicians & Surgeons (Ontario) (1974), 5 O.R. (2d) 204, 50 D.L.R. (3d) 14 (H.C.) 26.14

Howard v. The Queen (1989), 48 C.C.C. (3d) 38 (S.C.C.) 4.14

Howard, Re 512 N.W. 2d 300 (Iowa 1994) 26.22

Howe v. Institute of Chartered Accountants (Ontario) (1994), 21 O.R. (3d) 315, 31 Admin. L.R. (2d) 119, 121 D.L.R. (4th) 149, 77 O.A.C. 145 (Div. Ct.), affirmed (1995), 25 O.R. (3d) 96, 31 Admin. L.R. (2d) 133 (C.A.) 26.2, 26.5, 26.6

Hryciuk v. Ontario (Lieutenant Governor) (1994), 18 O.R. (3d) 645 (Div. Ct.) 26.16

Huerto v. College of Physicians & Surgeons (Saskatchewan), [1994] 9 W.W.R. 457, 117 D.L.R. (4th) 129, 26 Admin. L.R. (2d) 169, 124 Sask. R. 33 (Q.B.) 26.11

Hutton v. Law Society (Newfoundland) (1992), 96 D.L.R. (4th) 670 (Nfld. T.D.) 23.3

I.B.M. Corp. v. Levin, 579 F. 2d 271 (3rd Cir., 1978) 5.4

Iannetta, re, reasons of Convocation, September 28, 1995 .... 26.17

Imrie v. Institute of Chartered Accountants (Ontario), [1972] 3 O.R. 275, 28 D.L.R. (3d) 53 (H.C.) 26.4, 26.7, 27.5

Inquiry into Confidentiality of Health Records in Ontario. See Canada (Solicitor General) v. Ontario (Royal Commission of Inquiry into Confidentiality of Health Records)

International Capital Corp. v. Schafer, (*sub nom.* Schafer v. International Capital Corp.) [1997] 8 W.W.R. 412 (C.A.) 5.6

Irwin Toy Ltd. v. Quebec (A.G.), [1989] 1 S.C.R. 927, 24 Q.A.C. 2, 25 C.P.R. (3d) 417, 94 N.R. 167, 39 C.R.R. 193, 58 D.L.R. (4th) 577 10

Ishmael v. Millington, 50 Cal. Rptr. 592 (1966) 5.3

J. & M. Chartrand Realty Ltd. v. Martin (1981), 22 C.P.C. 186 (Ont. H.C.) 4.21

J. & P. Goldfluss Ltd. v. 306569 Ontario Ltd. (1977), 4 C.P.C. 296 (Ont. H.C.) 4.20

J.C. and S.C., Re (1980), 31 O.R. (2d) 53 (Prov. Ct.) 4.3

Jabour v. Law Society (British Columbia). See Canada (Attorney General) v. Law Society (British Columbia)

Jacks v. Bell (1828), 3 C. & P. 316 15

Jackson v. United States, 297 F. 2d 195 (D.C. Cir., 1961) 7.1

Jain v. College of Physicians & Surgeons (British Columbia) (1974), 52 D.L.R. (3d) 616 (B.C. S.C.) 26.13

James v. Law Society (British Columbia), [1982] 2 W.W.R. 647, 132 D.L.R. (3d) 181 (B.C. S.C.) 26.13

Jarson, re, order of Convocation, September 23, 1993 .... 26.17

John v. Rees, [1970] Ch. 345 4

Johnson v. Emerson & Sparrow (1871), L.R. 6 Ex. 329 .... 7.1

Johnson v. Law Society (Alberta) (1985), 66 A.R. 345 (Q.B.) 26.10

Johnston, Re, [1946] 3 W.W.R. 424 (Alta. Dist. Ct.) 18.1

Johnston v. Law Society (Prince Edward Island) (1982), 37 Nfld. & P.E.I.R. 142, 104 A.P.R. 142 (P.E.I. S.C.), reversed (1985), 53 Nfld. & P.E.I.R. 181, 156 A.P.R. 181 (P.E.I. C.A.) 26.4

Johnston v. Law Society (Prince Edward Island) (1991), 1 Admin. L.R. (2d) 265, 91 Nfld. & P.E.I.R. 126, 286 A.P.R. 126, 80 D.L.R. (4th) 725 (P.E.I. C.A.), leave to appeal to S.C.C. refused (1991), 93 Nfld. & P.E.I.R. 270 (note), 292 A.P.R. 270 (note), 137 N.R. 79 (note), 85 D.L.R. (4th) viii (note) (S.C.C.) 26.11

Johnstone v. Law Society (British Columbia), [1987] 5 W.W.R. 637, 15 B.C.L.R. (2d) 1, 40 D.L.R. (4th) 550 (C.A.) 26.15

Jones, Re, 506 F. 2d 527 (8th Cir., 1974) 26.12

Jones, Re, report of admissions committee of Law Society of Upper Canada, August 31, 1993 .... 26.22

Jones v. Barnes, 463 U.S. 745 (1983) 4.11

Jones v. Smith. See Smith v. Jones Barnes, 463 U.S. 745 (1983) 4.11

Justices of Antigua, Re (1830), 1 Knapp 267 .... 27.5

Kalina v. Directors of Chiropractic (Ontario) (1981), 35 O.R. (2d) 626 (Div. Ct.), leave to appeal to Ont. C.A. refused (1982), 35 O.R. (2d) 626 (C.A.) 26.11

Karfilis, Re, report adopted by Convocation, September 24, 1987 .... 18.4

Karpenko v. Paroian, Courey, Cohen & Houston (1980), 30 O.R. (2d) 776, 117 D.L.R. (3d) 383 (H.C.) 4.8, 4.18, 4.19

Kelley, Re, 801 P. 2d 1126 (1990) 26.8

Kempner v. Oppenheimer & Co., 662 F. Supp. 1271 (S.D.N.Y., 1987) 5.6

Kent v. Waldock, [2000] 7 W.W.R. 10 (B.C. C.A.) .... 4.22(a)

Kenyeres (Litigation Guardian of) v. Cullimore (1992), 13 C.P.C. (3d) 385 (Ont. Gen. Div.) 12

Khaliq-Kareemi, Re (*sub nom.* Khaliq-Kareemi v. Nova Scotia (Health Services & Insurance Commission) (1988), 84 N.S.R. (2d) 425, 213 A.P.R. 425 (T.D.), reversed (1989), 89 N.S.R. (2d) 388, 35 Admin. L.R. 131, 227 A.P.R. 388, 57 D.L.R. (4th) 505 (C.A.), leave to appeal to S.C.C. refused (1989), 93 N.S.R. (2d) 269 (note), 242 A.P.R. 269 (note), 105 N.R. 158 (note) (S.C.C.) 26.2, 26.16

Khan v. College of Physicians & Surgeons (Ontario) (1992), 9 O.R. (3d) 641, 76 C.C.C. (3d) 10, 57 O.A.C. 115, 94 D.L.R. (4th) 193 (C.A.) 26.18

Kimmerly v. Law Society of Yukon (1987), 3 Y.R. 54 (S.C.) 26.20

King, Re, report adopted by Convocation, January 25, 1991 .... 22.3

Kinnaird, re, reasons of Convocation, April 9, 1997 .... 26.17

Kirsch v. Duryea, 578 P. 2d 935 (1978) 4.18

Klein v. Law Society (Upper Canada) (1985), 50 O.R. (2d) 118, 13 C.R.R. 120, 8 O.A.C. 161, 16 D.L.R. (4th) 489 (Div. Ct.) 10, 25.2, 26.7, 27.2

Knight v. Indian Head School Division No. 19, [1990] 1 S.C.R. 653, 43 Admin. L.R. 157, [1990] 3 W.W.R. 289, 30 C.C.E.L. 237, 106 N.R. 17, 83 Sask. R. 81, 90 C.L.L.C. 14,010, 69 D.L.R. (4th) 489 .... 26.11

Knippel v. Institute of Chartered Accountants of Saskatchewan (Discipline Committee), Sask. Q.B. April 10, 1991, (unreported) 26.14

Knutson v. Registered Nurses' Assn. (Saskatchewan) (1990), 46 Admin. L.R. 234, [1991] 2 W.W.R. 327, 4 C.R.R. (2d) 168, 90 Sask. R. 120, 75 D.L.R. (4th) 723 (C.A.) 26.15

Konigsberg v. State Bar of California, 353 U.S. 252 (1957) 23.3

Kopyto, Re, report adopted by Convocation, November 8, 1989 .... 26.17

Kopyto v. Law Society of Upper Canada (1993), 18 Admin. L.R. (2d) 54, 107 D.L.R. (4th) 259, 67 O.A.C. 297, 19 C.R.R. (2d) 351 (Div. Ct.) 26.2

Korman, Re, report adopted by Convocation, April 21, 1994 .... 26.17

Korponey v. Canada (Attorney General), [1982] 1 S.C.R. 41, 26 C.R. (3d) 343, 65 C.C.C. (2d) 65, 132 D.L.R. (3d) 354, 44 N.R. 103 (*sub nom.* R. v. Korponey) 7.6

Korz v. St. Pierre (1987), 61 O.R. (2d) 609, 23 O.A.C. 226, 43 D.L.R. (4th) 528 (C.A.), leave to appeal to S.C.C. refused (1988), 62 O.R. (2d) ix (note), 30 O.A.C. 239 (note), 89 N.R. 322 (note) (S.C.C.) 22.3

Kramer, re, order of Convocation, September 26, 1997 .... 26.17

Kramer v. Scientific Control Corp., 534 F. 2d 1085 (3rd Cir., 1976), cert. denied 429 U.S. 830, 97 S. Ct. 90 (1976) 5.12

Krieger v. Law Society (Alberta), [2000] A.J. 1129 (C.A.) 26.20

Kuntz v. Assn. of Optometrists (Saskatchewan) (1992), 8 Admin. L.R. (2d) 312, [1993] 3 W.W.R. 651, (*sub nom.* Kuntz v. Saskatchewan Assn. of Optometrists) 107 Sask. R. 81 (Q.B.) 26.4

Kupferstein v. Gottlieb, Hoffman & Kumer (1989), 40 C.P.C. (2d) 111 (Ont. Master) 3.2

Kyuquot Logging Ltd. v. B.C. Forest Products Ltd. (1986), 5 B.C.L.R. (2d) 1, [1986] 5 W.W.R. 481, 15 C.P.C. (2d) 52, 12 C.P.R. (3d) 347, 30 D.L.R. (4th) 68 (C.A.) 26.15

Laan, re, reasons of Convocation, March 24, 1994 .... 26.17

Laba v. Dental Assn. (Manitoba) (1988), 54 Man. R. (2d) 17 (Q.B.) 26.7

Laba v. Dental Assn. (Manitoba) (1989), 61 Man. R. (2d) 24 (Q.B.), reversed in part (1990), 63 Man. R. (2d) 289, 70 D.L.R. (4th) 154 (Man. C.A.) 26.22

Laidlaw Environmental Services (Sarnia) Ltd. v. Ontario (Minister of Environment and Energy) (1997), 32 O.R. (3d) 795 (Gen. Div.) 5.2, 5.5, 7.6

Lamontagne v. Law Society (Saskatchewan), [1991] 4 W.W.R. 481, 89 Sask. R. 219, 81 D.L.R. (4th) 64 (C.A.), leave to appeal to S.C.C. refused (1991), [1992] 1 W.W.R. lxv (note), 137 N.R. 384 (note), 100 Sask. R. 240 (note), 18 W.A.C. 240 (note) (S.C.C.) 26.19

Landmark Communications v. Virginia, 435 U.S. 829, 98 S. Ct. 1535 (1978) 4.23

Landru v. Landru, [1989] 3 W.W.R. 705, 42 C.P.C. (2d) 186, 19 R.F.L. (3d) 113, 58 D.L.R. (4th) 85, 73 Sask. R. 196 (C.A.) 5.6

Lane v. Chowning, 610 F. 2d 1385 (1979) 20.5

Lanford v. General Medical Council (1989), [1990] 1 A.C. 13, [1989] 2 All E.R. 921 (P.C.) 26.16

Lang v. Ramsay (1992), 11 O.R. (3d) 190, (*sub nom.* Ramsay v. Toronto (City) Commissioners of Police) 96 D.L.R. (4th) 594 (Div. Ct.), additional reasons at 96 D.L.R. (4th) 594 at 606 (Ont. Div. Ct.) 26.11

Lapedus, re, order of Convocation, February 26, 1987 .... 27.17

LaPierre v. Young (1980), 30 O.R. (2d) 319, 117 D.L.R. (3d) 643 (H.C.)............. 22.2

Larson v. Land Surveyors Assn. (Sask.) (1988), 65 Sask. R. 292 (Q.B.)............... 26.7

Lasch v. Annapolis (County) (1992), 118 N.S.R. (2d) 418, 327 A.P.R. 418 (Co. Ct.) 5.10

Launch! Research & Development Inc. v. Essex Distributing Co. (1977), 4 C.P.C. 261 (Ont. H.C.) 4.20, 4.23

Law Society (Alberta) v. Randhawa, [1996] 7 W.W.R. 664, 39 Alta. L.R. (3d) 226, 185 A.R. 220, 48 C.P.C. (3d) 21 (Q.B.) 26.6

Law Society (British Columbia) v. Canada (Attorney General), [1982] 2 S.C.R. 307, 37 B.C.L.R. 145, 5 W.W.R. 289, 66 C.P.R. (2d) 1 (*sub nom.* British Columbia (A.G.) v. Jabour), 19 B.L.R. 234, 43 N.R. 451, 137 D.L.R. (3d) 1 10

Law Society (British Columbia) v. MacKrow (1968), 64 W.W.R. 550, (*sub nom.* R. v. Law Society of B.C.) 68 D.L.R. (2d) 179 (B.C. C.A.) 26.8

Law Society (Manitoba) v. Crump (1982), 14 Man. R. (2d) 405 (C.A.)............... 26.12

Law Society (Manitoba) v. Frohlinger, [1997] 7 W.W.R. 747, 47 Admin. (2d) 1, 118 Man. R. (2d) 89, 149 W.A.C. 89, 148 D.L.R. (4th) 710 (C.A.).............................. 26.19

Law Society (Manitoba) v. Giesbrecht (1983), [1984] 1 W.W.R. 430, 39 C.P.C. 26, 30 R.P.R. 77, 2 D.L.R. (4th) 354, 24 Man. R. (2d) 228 (C.A.)............................. 5.10

Law Society (Manitoba) v. Savino, [1983] 6 W.W.R. 538, 6 C.R.R. 336, 23 Man. R. (2d) 293, 1 D.L.R. (4th) 285 (C.A.) 10, 26.7

Law Society (Saskatchewan) v. Robertson Stromberg (*sub nom.* Robertson Stromberg, Re) (1994), [1995] 1 W.W.R. 112, 119 D.L.R. (4th) 551, 124 Sask. R. 259 (Q.B.), affirmed, [1995] 3 W.W.R. 601, (*sub nom.* Robertson Stromberg, Re) 122 D.L.R. (4th) 433, 128 Sask. R. 107, 85 W.A.C. 107 (C.A.).. 26.4

Law Society of Upper Canada v. Baker. See Baker v. Law Society of Upper Canada

Law Students Civil Rights Research Council v. Wadmond, 401 U.S. 154 (1971)..... 23.4

Leask v. Cronin, 66 B.C.L.R. 187, [1985] 3 W.W.R. 152, 18 C.C.C. (3d) 315 (S.C.) 4.10

Legal Professions Act & Benchers Society of B.C., Re. See F., Re

Lennan, Re, 102 N.J. 518, 509 A. 2d 1979 (1986)... 26.17

Leshner v. Ontario (Deputy Attorney General) (1992), 10 O.R. (3d) 732, 8 Admin. L.R. (2d) 132, 57 O.A.C. 238, 96 D.L.R. (4th) 41 (Div. Ct.) 26.11

Lewin c. Barreau (Québec), [1988] R.J.Q. 619, 24 Q.A.C. 106 .... 23.3

Lewis v. Ogden (1984), 53 A.L.R. 53 (H.C.) .... 4.22(b)

Li v. College of Pharmacists (1994), 116 D.L.R. (4th) 606, 95 B.C.L.R. (2d) 153, 49 B.C.A.C. 115, 80 W.A.C. 115 (C.A.) 8

Liani v. The Queen (1980), 13 M.P.L.R. 161 (Ont. Div. Ct.) 6.1, 6.6

Liebowitz, Re, 101 N.J. 632 (1985) 25.13

Lischka v. Ontario (Criminal Injuries Compensation Board) (1982), 37 O.R. (2d) 134 (Div. Ct.) 26.12

Lister v. College of Physicians & Surgeons (Ontario) (February 12, 1987), Doc. No. 1188/85 (Ont. Div. Ct.) 26.10

Lloyd, Re, 12 W.W.R. 445, [1954] 3 D.L.R. 834 (Man. C.A.) 18.3

Lockhart v. MacDonald (1980), 42 N.S.R. (2d) 29, 77 A.P.R. 29, 118 D.L.R. (3d) 397 (C.A.), varied on other grounds (1980), 44 N.S.R. (2d) 261, 31 C.P.C. 81, 83 A.P.R. 261, 118 D.L.R. (3d) 397 at 420 (*sub nom.* MacDonald v. Lockhart) (C.A.), leave to appeal to S.C.C. denied (1980), 118 D.L.R. (3d) 397n, 35 N.R. 265n (S.C.C.) 14

Loftus v. Harris (1914), 30 O.L.R. 479, 19 D.L.R. 670 (C.A.) 18.2

London Loan & Savings Co. v. Brickenden, [1933] S.C.R. 257, [1933] 3 D.L.R. 161, affirmed [1934] 2 W.W.R. 545, [1934] 3 D.L.R. 465 (P.C.) 22.2

London Trust & Savings Corp. v. Corbett (1994), 24 C.P.C. (3d) 226 (Ont. Gen. Div.) 3.2

Louisiana State Bar Assn. v. Chatelain, 513 So. 2d 1178 (1987) 26.4

Lowery v. Cardwell, 575 F. 2d 727 (9th Cir., 1978) 7.5

Luchka v. Zens (1989), 37 B.C.L.R. (2d) 127, 36 C.P.C. (2d) 271 (C.A.) 4.10

Lukas v. Lawson (1993), 13 O.R. (3d) 447, 19 C.P.C. (3d) 238 (Master) 3.2

Lynch v. Checker Cabs Ltd. (June 30, 1999), Doc. Calgary 9701-16341 (Alta. Q.B.) .... 4.17, 4.22(a)

MTS International Services Inc. v. Warnat Corp. (1980), 31 O.R. (2d) 221, 18 C.P.C. 212, 118 D.L.R. (3d) 561 (H.C.) 5.6

MacDonald v. Lockhart. See Lockhart v. MacDonald

MacDonald (No. 1), Re, report adopted by Convocation, February 20, 1981 .... 24.2

MacDonald Estate v. Martin, [1989] 3 W.W.R. 653, 58 D.L.R. (4th) 67, 57 Man. R. (2d) 161 (C.A.), reversed (1990), (*sub nom.* Martin v. Gray), [1990] 3 S.C.R. 1235, [1991] 1 W.W.R. 705, 48 C.P.C. (2d) 113, 70 Man. R. (2d) 241, 121 N.R. 1, 77 D.L.R. (4th) 249 .... Intro, 5.2, 5.6, 5.10, 25.2

Macfarlane v. MacLaughlin, [1975] 1 W.W.R. 764, 50 D.L.R. (3d) 140 (B.C. S.C.) 12

MacGregor, Re, report adopted by Convocation, April 22, 1993 .... 26.17

MacGregor, re, reasons of Convocation, April 23, 1993 . . . 26.17

MacMillan Bloedel Ltd. v. Freeman & Co. (1992), 78 B.C.L.R. (2d) 325 (S.C.) . . . 4.11.1

MacPhee v. Barristers' Society (New Brunswick) (1983), 50 N.B.R. (2d) 61, 131 A.P.R. 61, 1 D.L.R. (4th) 156 (Q.B.) . . . 26.10

Maddox v. State, 613 S.W. 2d 275 (1981) . . . 7.5

Mady v. Royal College of Dental Surgeons (Ontario) (1974), 5 O.R. (2d) 414, 50 D.L.R. (3d) 494 (Div. Ct.) . . . 26.11, 26.13

Maillet v. Haliburton (1983), 55 N.S.R. (2d) 311, 32 C.P.C. 33, 114 A.P.R. 311 (T.D.) . . . 4.8

Maine v. Horton, 561 A. 2d 488 (1989) . . . 26.4

Major v. Higgins (1932), 53 Que. K.B. 277 (C.A.) . . . 25.2

Malartic Hygrade Gold Mines (Canada) Ltd. v. Ontario (Securities Commission) (1986), 54 O.R. (2d) 544, 19 Admin. L.R. 21, 24 C.R.R. 1, 15 O.A.C. 124, 9 O.S. C.B. 2286, 27 D.L.R. (4th) 112 (Div. Ct.), leave to appeal to Ont. C.A. refused (1986), 19 Admin. L.R. xiiv (note) (Ont. C.A.) . . . 26.11

Mallal, re, order of Convocation, March 25, 1993 . . . 26.17

Maloney, Re, report adopted by Convocation, March 28, 1991 . . . 26.17

Manitoba (A.G.) v. Groupe Quebecor Inc., [1987] 5 W.W.R. 270, 59 C.R. (3d) 1, 37 C.C.C. (3d) 421, 31 C.R.R. 313, 45 D.L.R. (4th) 80, 47 Man. R. (2d) 187 (C.A.) . . . 13

Mans v. State Farm Mutual Insurance Company (1996), 32 O.R. (3d) 786 (Gen. Div.) . . . 4.10, 4.22(a)

Manville Canada Inc. v. Ladner Downs, [1992] 2 W.W.R. 323, 63 B.C.L.R. (2d) 102, 88 D.L.R. (4th) 208 (S.C.), affirmed (1993), 76 B.C.L.R. (2d) 273, [1993] 5 W.W.R. 36, 100 D.L.R. (4th) 321, 25 B.C.A.C. 121, 43 W.A.C. 121 (C.A.) . . . 5.6, 5.10

Mara (Guardian ad litem of) v. Blake, 134 D.L.R. (4th) 716, [1996] 10 W.W.R. 277, (*sub nom. Mara v. Blake*) 74 B.C.A.C. 296, 121 W.A.C. 296, 23 B.C.L.R. (3d) 225 (C.A.) . . . 5.5, 5.14

Markandey v. Board of Ophthalmic Dispensers (Ontario) (March 14, 1994), Doc. Toronto RE 2661/93 (Ont. Gen. Div.) . . . 26.2, 26.6

Markovina, Re (1991), 57 B.C.L.R. (2d) 73, [1991] 6 W.W.R. 47 (S.C.) . . . 5.10

Marks, Re, 72 A. 2d 399, 424 N.Y.S. 2d 229 (1980) . . . 26.17

Markus v. Barristers' Society (Nova Scotia) (1989), 90 N.S.R. (2d) 156, 230 A.P.R. 156 (C.A.) . . . 26.19

Maroist v. Barreau du Québec, [1987] R.J.Q. 2322 (C.A.) . . . 10

Martin v. Goldfarb (1997), 31 B.L.R. (2d) 265 (Ont. Gen. Div.), reversed in part (August 26, 1998), Doc. CA C27477 (Ont. C.A.) . . . 24.6

Martin v. Gray. See MacDonald Estate v. Martin

Martin v. Law Society (British Columbia), [1950] 3 D.L.R. 173 (B.C. C.A.), affirming [1949] 1 D.L.R. 105 (*sub nom.* Re Martin) . . . 23.3

Martin v. Martin (1987), 19 C.P.C. (2d) 97, 61 Sask. R. 74 (Q.B.)........................4.17

Martin v. Rose, 717 F. 2d 295 (1983)..7.7

Mastercraft Construction Corp. v. Baker (1978), 19 O.R. (2d) 652, 3 R.P.R. 65, 86 D.L.R. (3d) 121 (H.C.), affirmed (1979), 26 O.R. (2d) 389, 104 D.L.R. (3d) 767 (C.A.)..22.2

Matthews v. Board of Directors of Physiotherapy (Ontario) (1990), 44 Admin. L.R. 147, 40 O.A.C. 60 (Div. Ct.).. 26.18

Matter of Anis, 599 A. 2d 1265, 126 N.J. 448 (1992).. 11

Matthews v. Board of Directors of Physiotherapy (1986), 54 O.R. (2d) 375, 18 Admin. L.R. 303, 15 O.A.C. 37, 26 D.L.R. (4th) 626 (Ont. Div. Ct.), affirmed (1987), 61 O.R. (2d) 475 (*sub nom.* Re Matthews and Board of Directors of Physiotherapy), 24 O.A.C. 319, 43 D.L.R. (4th) 478 (C.A.)...26.2, 26.4, 26.7

Maurice v. Priel, [1989] 1 S.C.R. 1023, [1989] 3 W.W.R. 673, 36 Admin. L.R. 169, 96 N.R. 178, 77 Sask. R. 22, 58 D.L.R. (4th) 736 .... 26.20

Maxwell v. Law Society (New Brunswick) (1990), 103 N.B.R. (2d) 342, 259 A.P.R. 342, 65 D.L.R. (4th) 754 (Q.B.)..26.4

May, Re, report adopted by Convocation, January 24, 1985............4.22(c), 26.8, 26.17

May Department Stores v. Williamson, 549 F. 2d 1147 (1977)...........................21.3

McCafferty v. Law Society of Alberta, [1941] S.C.R. 430.............................. 26.19

McCauley v. McVey, [1980] 1 S.C.R. 165, 9 R.P.R. 35, 27 N.R. 604, 98 D.L.R. (3d) 577...22.1, 22.2

McCoan v. General Medical Council, [1964] 3 All E.R. 143 (P.C.) 26.19

McDonald, Re, report adopted by Convocation, November 21, 1985 .... 22.3, 26.17

McDonald, Re, report adopted by Convocation, November 26, 1985 .... 18.2, 18.3

McDonald, re, order of Convocation, January 26, 1995 .... 26.17

McDonald v. Law Society (Alberta) (1993), 15 Alta. L.R. (3d) 298, 147 A.R. 135, [1994] 3 W.W.R. 697, 19 C.R.R. (2d) 186 (Q.B.) 26.15

McGavin Toastmaster Ltd. v. Powlowski, [1973] 5 W.W.R. 388, 37 D.L.R. (3d) 100 (*sub nom.* B.C. T.W. v. Manitoba (Man. Human Rights Comm.)) (Man. C.A.) 26.11

McGough, Re, 115 Wash. 2d 1, 793 P. 2d 430 (1990)......................................26.1

McGrath v. Goldman (1975), [1976] 1 W.W.R. 743, 64 D.L.R. (3d) 305 (B.C. S.C.) 22.2

McKay, re, order of Convocation, September 28, 1995 .... 26.17

McKee v. College of Psychologists (British Columbia) (1994), 95 B.C.L.R. (2d) 66, [1994] 9 W.W.R. 374, 116 D.L.R. (4th) 555, (*sub nom.* McKee v. College of Psychologists (British Columbia) (No. 2)) 47 B.C.C.A. 189, 76 W.A.C. 189 (C.A.).............. 26.17

McKee v. College of Psychologists (British Columbia (No. 2)). See McKee v. College of Psychologists (British Columbia)

McKeown, Re, report adopted by Convocation, March 25, 1983 .... 26.17

McLellan v. Milne, [1937] O.R. 742, [1937] 3 D.L.R. 659 (H.C.) 22.3

McLennan, Re, 93 Ill. 2d 215, 443 N.E. 2d 533 (1982) 26.17

McMaster v. Byrne, [1952] 1 All E.R. 1362, [1952] 3 D.L.R. 337 (P.C.), reversing [1951] O.W.N. 1, [1951] 1 D.L.R. 593 .... 22.3

McQuarrie v. Foote, [1983] 2 W.W.R. 283, 41 B.C.L.R. 123, 143 D.L.R. (3d) 354 (C.A.), reversing [1982] 1 W.W.R. 359, 31 B.C.L.R. 323, 25 C.P.C. 111, 129 D.L.R. (3d) 437 (S.C.) 12

Meadwell Enterprises Ltd. v. Clay & Co., 44 B.C.L.R. 188, [1983] 3 W.W.R. 742, 27 R.P.R. 257 (S.C.) 8

Meek v. Fleming, [1961] 2 Q.B. 366, [1961] 3 All E.R. 148 (C.A.) 4.12, 4.13

Mehr v. Law Society (Upper Canada), [1954] O.R. 337 (H.C.), affirmed [1954] O.R. 692, [1954] 3 D.L.R. 796 (C.A.), reversed [1955] S.C.R. 344, [1955] 2 D.L.R. 289 ..26.12, 27.5

Membery v. Hill. See Essa (Township) v. Guergis

Mercator Enterprises Ltd. v. Harris (1978), 29 N.S.R. (2d) 703, 6 C.P.C. 297, 45 A.P.R. 703 (T.D.) 5.6

Merchant v. Law Society (Saskatchewan), [1973] 2 W.W.R. 109, 32 D.L.R. (3d) 178 (Sask. C.A.) 10

Merck & Co. v. Interpharm Inc., [1992] 3 F.C. 774, 44 C.P.R. (3d) 440, 57 F.T.R.306 .... 5.10

Merker v. Leader Terrazzo Tile Mosaic Ltd. (1983), 43 O.R. (2d) 632, 37 C.P.C. 1, 2 D.L.R. (4th) 417 (H.C.) 4.20

Merrill Lynch, Royal Securities Ltd./Ltée. v. Granove, [1985] 5 W.W.R. 589, 35 Man. R. (2d) 194 (C.A.) 26.15

Messinger v. Bramalea Ltd. (1989), 35 C.P.C. (2d) 260 (Ont. H.C.) 5.6

Meyerhofer v. Empire Fire and Marine Insurance Co., 497 F. 2d 1190 (1974) 20.6

Michel v. Lafrentz (1992), 85 Alta. L.R. (2d) 1, 4 C.P.C. (3d) 155, 120 A.R. 355, 8 W.A.C. 355 (C.A.) 5.10

Milgaard v. Kujawa, [1995] 2 W.W.R. lxiv (note), 32 C.P.C. (3d) 101 (note), 119 D.L.R. (4th) vi (note) (S.C.C.) 6.4

Millennium (Diagnostic) Corp. v. Canadian Blood Bank Corp. (1998), 168 Nfld. & P.E.I.R. 168, 517 A.P.R. 168, 25 C.P.C. (4th) 162 (Nfld. T.D.) 5.10

Miller v. Saskatchewan Psychiatric Nurses' Assn. (1992), 103 Sask. R. 61 (Q.B.) 26.16

Millican v. Tiffin Holdings Ltd. (1964), 50 W.W.R. 673, 49 D.L.R. (2d) 216 (Alta. T.D.), reversed (1965), 53 W.W.R. 505, 53 D.L.R. (2d) 674 (Alta. C.A.), reversed [1967] S.C.R. 183, 59 W.W.R. 31, 60 D.L.R. (2d) 469 .... 24.6

Milligan v. Gemini Mercury Sales Ltd. (1977), 1 B.L.R. 63 (Ont. H.C.) 22.3

Millroy, Re, report adopted by Convocation, February 19, 1989 . . . . . 26.17

Milne, Re, report adopted by Convocation, September 23, 1990 . . . . . 26.8

Milne v. Joint Chiropractic Professional Review Committee (Saskatchewan), [1992] 3 W.W.R. 354, 97 Sask. R. 299, 12 W.A.C. 299, 90 D.L.R. (4th) 634 (C.A.) 26.11

Milrod, Re, report adopted by Convocation, January 30, 1986 . . . . . 26.1, 26.17

Milstein v. College of Pharmacy (Ontario) (1978), (*sub nom.* Re Milstein and Ontario College of Pharmacy) 20 O.R. (2d) 283, 87 D.L.R. (3d) 392 (C.A.) 26.11, 26.18

Mireau v. Saskatchewan, [1995] 4 W.W.R. 389, (*sub nom.* Mireau v. Canada) 128 Sask. R. 142, 85 W.A.C. 142 (C.A.) 4.22

Misra v. College of Physicians & Surgeons (Saskatchewan), [1988] 5 W.W.R. 333, 36 Admin. L.R. 298, 70 Sask. R. 116, 52 D.L.R. (4th) 477 (C.A.), leave to appeal to S.C.C. granted (1989), 79 Sask. R. 80 (note), 102 N.R. 156 (note) (S.C.C.), appeal to S.C.C. discontinued January 27, 1992 . . . . . 26.5, 26.10, 26.11

Mitchell v. Institute of Chartered Accountants (Manitoba), [1994] 10 W.W.R. 768, 97 Man. R. (2d) 66, 79 W.A.C. 66 (C.A.) 26.18

Moffat v. Wetstein (1996), 135 D.L.R. (4th) 298, 5 C.P.C. (4th) 128, 4 O.T.C. 364, 29 O.R. (3d) 371 (Gen. Div.), leave to appeal refused (1997), 144 D.L.R. (4th) 188, 29 O.T.C. 65 (Gen. Div.) 5.3, 5.4, 5.5, 5.6

Monaghan, Re, 122 Vt. 199, 167 A. 2d 81 (1961) 23.3

Montreal Trust Co. of Canada v. Basinview Village Ltd. (1995), 126 D.L.R. (4th) 61, 39 C.P.C. (3d) 200, 142 N.S.R. (2d) 337, 407 A.P.R. 337 (C.A.) 5.10

Morgan v. Land Surveyors Assn. (Ontario) (1980), 28 O.R. (2d) 19, 108 D.L.R. (3d) 643 (Div. Ct.) 26.13

Morrell v. State, 575 P. 2d 1200 (Alaska, 1978) 7.3

Morris v. Jackson (1984), 34 R.P.R. 269 (Ont. H.C.) 22.2

Morton v. Asper, 21 C.P.C. (2d) 95, [1988] 1 W.W.R. 47, 49 Man. R. (2d) 167 (Q.B.), affirmed [1988] 2 W.W.R. 317, 45 D.L.R. (4th) 374, 51 Man. R. (2d) 207 (C.A.) 5.10

Morton v. Registered Nurses Assn. (N.S.) (1989), 92 N.S.R. (2d) 154, 237 A.P.R. 154 (T.D.) 26.7

Moseley, Re (1924), 57 N.S.R. 209 (T.D.) 26.22

Moskalyk-Walker v. College of Pharmacy (Ontario) (1975), 8 O.R. (2d) 609, 58 D.L.R. (3d) 665 (Div. Ct.) 26.11

Moss v. Chin (1994), 99 B.C.L.R. (2d) 332, [1995] 3 W.W.R. 233, 120 D.L.R. (4th) 406, 6 E.T.R. (2d) 49 (S.C.) 2.5

Mourad v. Automobile Club Insurance Assn., 465 N.W. 2d 395 (1991) 20.1

Moynihan, Re, 113 Wash. 2d 219, 778 P. 2d 521 (1989) 26.22

Mulvihill v. R. (1914), 5 W.W.R. 1229, 19 B.C.R. 197, 22 C.C.C. 354, 18 D.L.R. 189 (C.A.), extension of time for appeal refused (1914), 49 S.C.R. 587, 6 W.W.R. 462, 23 C.C.C. 194, 18 D.L.R. 217 . . . . . 26.13

Murphy v. Lamphier (1914), 31 O.L.R. 287 (H.C.), affirmed 32 O.L.R. 19, 20 D.L.R. 906 (C.A.) 18.1

Myers v. Elman, [1940] A.C. 282 (H.L.) 4.6, 4.17, 24.2, 26.7, 27.5

National Corn Growers Assn. v. Canada (Canadian Import Tribunal), [1990] 2 S.C.R. 1324, 45 Admin. L.R. 161, 114 N.R. 81, 74 D.L.R. (4th) 449, (*sub nom.* American Farm Bureau Federation v. Canadian Import Tribunal) 3 T.C.T. 5303 .... 26.19

Neale v. Lennox, [1902] A.C. 465 (H.L.) 4.8

Nelles v. Ontario, [1989] 2 S.C.R. 170, 69 O.R. (2d) 448 (note), 41 Admin L.R. 1, 37 C.P.C. (2d) 1, 71 C.R. (3d) 358, 49 C.C.L.T. 217, 98 N.R. 321, 35 O.A.C. 161, 42 C.R.R. 1, 60 D.L.R. (4th) 609 .... 26.20

Nelson v. Murphy (1957), 22 W.W.R. 137, 65 Man. R. 252, 9 D.L.R. (2d) 195 (C.A.) 8

Nelson v. State, 346 F. 2d 73 (9th Circ., 1965) 4.11

Neushul v. Mellish & Harkavy (1967), 111 S.J. 399, 117 New L.J. 546, 203 E.G. 27 (C.A.) 14

New Brunswick (Minister of Health) v. G. (J.), [1999] 3 S.C.R. 46 (S.C.C.) 26.2

Newfoundland Telephone Co. v. Newfoundland (Board of Commissioners of Public Utilities), [1994] 1 S.C.R. 623, 134 N.R. 241, 89 D.L.R. (4th) 289, 4 Admin. L.R. (2d) 121, 95 Nfld. & P.E.I.R. 271, 301 A.P.R. 271 .... 26.11

Newfoundland (Treasury Board) v. Newfoundland Association of Public Employees, [1999] N.J. 356 (Nfld. S.C. T.D.) 5.10

Nicholson v. Haldimand-Norfolk (Regional Municipality) Commissioners of Police, [1979] 1 S.C.R. 311, 78 C.L.L.C. 14, 181, 23 N.R. 410, 88 D.L.R. (3d) 671 16

Nine West Division, Re, 78 Bankr. 189 (Bankr. N.D. Ill., 1987) 5.6

Nisbett v. Manitoba (Human Rights Commission), [1992] 3 W.W.R. 582, 9 C.R.R. (2d) 121, 92 C.L.L.C. 17, 036, 90 D.L.R. (4th) 672 (Man. Q.B.) 26.2

Nix v. Whiteside, 470 U.S. 275 (1986) 7.5

Nix v. Whiteside, 475 U.S. 157 (1986) 7.5

Nocton v. Ashburton, [1914] A.C. 932, [1914-15] All E.R. 45 (H.L.) 22.3

Non-Punitive Segregative Inmates v. Kelly, 589 F. Supp. 1339 (U.S.D. Ct., E.D. Pa., 1984) 5.9

Noonan, Re, 102 N.J. 157, 506 A. 2d 722 (1986) 26.17

North Carolina v. Alford, 400 U.S. 25, 91 S. Ct. 160 (1970) 7.7

Northway Chevrolet Oldsmobile Ltd. v. E.A.M. Management Ltd. (1993), 22 C.P.C. (3d) 108, [1994] 3 W.W.R. 314, 117 Sask. R. 237, 110 D.L.R. (4th) 440 (Q.B.) 4.19

Nova Scotia Barristers Society v. Steele, [1995] L.S.D.D. No. 261 (Discipline Sub-committee "A") 26.17

Ocelot Energy Inc. v. Jans, 165 Sask. R. 252, [1998] 8 W.W.R. 708, 31 C.P.C. (4th) 76 (Q.B.) 5.10

O'Connor v. Rentier, [1925] 1 W.W.R. 38, [1925] 1 D.L.R. 398 (Alta. C.A.) 18.2

O'Connor v. Waldron, [1935] A.C. 76, [1934] All E.R. 281 (P.C.) 26.12

O'Dea v. O'Dea (1978), 68 Nfld. & P.E.I.R. 67, 209 A.P.R. 67 (Nfld. U.F.C.) 5.6

O'Donnell, re, reasons of Convocation, September 28, 1995 .... 26.17

Ohralik v. Ohio State Bar Assn., 436 U.S. 447 (1978) 11

Okerman, Re, 310 N.W. 2d 569 (Minn., 1981) 26.17

Oklahoma Bar Assn. v. Porter, 766 P. 2d 958 (1988) 4.23

Oklahoma ex rel. Oklahoma Bar Assn. v. Raskin, 642 P. 2d 262 (1982) 26.17

Old St. Boniface Residents Assn. v. Winnipeg (City), [1990] 3 S.C.R. 1170, 46 Admin. L.R. 161, 2 M.P.L.R. (2d) 217, [1991] 2 W.W.R. 145, 116 N.R. 46, 69 Man. R. (2d) 134, 75 D.L.R. (4th) 385 .... 26.11

Oliver v. Doga, 368 So. 2d 467, reversed on other grounds 384 So. 2d 330 (La. App., 1979) 12

Oliver, Derksen, Arkin v. Fulmyk, [1995] 7 W.W.R. 609, 126 D.L.R. (4th) 123 (Man. C.A.) 5.10

Omenica Enterprises Ltd. v. British Columbia Minister of Forests (1992), 7 Admin. L.R. (2d) 95 (S.C.) 26.18

Ontario Crime Commission, Re (1962), [1963] 1 O.R. 391, [1963] 1 C.C.C. 117, 37 D.L.R. (2d) 382 (C.A.) 4.13, 4.23

Ontario (Human Rights Commission) v. House (1993), 67 O.A.C. 72 (Div. Ct.) 26.6

Ontario New Home Warranty Program v. Campbell (February 10, 1999), Doc. 98-CV-161622 (Ont. Gen. Div.) 5.6

Ontario (Ministry of Transportation & Communications) v. Eat'n Putt Ltd. (1985), 50 O.R. (2d) 503, 12 Admin. L.R. 300 (*sub nom.* Ontario (Min. of Transportation & Communications) v. Eat n' Putt Ltd.; Ontario (Min. of Transportation & Communications) v. Funshine Investments Ltd.; Ontario (Min. of Transportation & Communications) v. 377358 Ont. Ltd.), 7 O.A.C. 389 .... 26.12

Ontario (Securities Commission) v. Greymac Credit Corp. (1983), 41 O.R. (2d) 328, 21 B.L.R. 37, 33 C.P.C. 270, 146 D.L.R. (3d) 73 (Div. Ct.) 3.2

Orchard v. South Eastern Electricity Board, [1987] 1 All E.R. 95, [1987] Q.B. 565 (C.A.) 27.5

Ormingdale Holdings Ltd. v. Ray, Wolfe, Connell, Lightbody & Reynolds (1980), 116 D.L.R. (3d) 346 (B.C. S.C.), affirmed (1982), 36 B.C.L.R. 378 at 390, 135 D.L.R. (3d) 577 (C.A.) 24.6

Osler v. Ford, [1936] O.W.N. 159 (H.C.) 24.6

Ott v. Fleishman, 46 B.C.L.R. 321, [1983] 5 W.W.R. 721, 22 B.L.R. 57 (S.C.) 3.2

P., Re, report adopted by Convocation, September 8, 1989 .... 23.3

Pacific Coast Super 8 Motels Inc. v. Nanaimo Shipyard (1985) Ltd. (1991), 53 B.C.L.R. (2d) 281 (S.C.) 5.10

Pacific Mobile Corp. v. Hunter Douglas Canada Ltd., [1979] 1 S.C.R. 842, 26 N.R. 453 .... 27.5

Panko v. Simmonds, [1983] 3 W.W.R. 158, 42 B.C.L.R. 50 (S.C.) 17.4

Papadopoulos v. Anklewicz (1987), 60 O.R. (2d) 198, 35 M.P.L.R. 105 (H.C.) 24.6

Pari Air Ltd. v. Blue Sky Air Ltd., [1986] 3 W.W.R. 719, 48 Sask. R. 98 (Q.B.) 4.19

Parker, re, order of Convocation, September 29, 1995 .... 26.17

Parker v. Anderson, 667 F. 2d 1204 (5th Cir., 1982), cert. denied 459 U.S. 828, 103 S. Ct. 63 .... 5.12

Parker v. M & T Chemicals Inc., 566 A. 2d 215 (N.J., 1989) 20.1

Parry v. Parry, [1926] 2 W.W.R. 185, 20 Sask. L.R. 577, [1926] 3 D.L.R. 95 (C.A.) 4.19

Parry-Jones v. Law Society, [1968] Ch. 1, [1968] 1 All E.R. 177 (C.A.) 26.4

Parsons, re, order of Convocation, September 26, 1996 .... 26.17

Patry c. Barreau (Québec), [1991] R.J.Q. 2366 (C.S.) 23.1

Patterson v. College of Physicians and Surgeons (British Columbia) (1974), 49 D.L.R. (3d) 219 (B.C. S.C.) 26.16

Pearlman v. Law Society (Manitoba), [1991] 2 S.C.R. 869, 2 Admin. L.R. (2d) 185, (*sub nom.* Pearlman v. Manitoba Law Society Judicial Committee) [1991] 6 W.W.R. 289, 130 N.R. 121, 75 Man. R. (2d) 81, 6 W.A.C. 81, 6 C.R.R. (2d) 259, 84 D.L.R. (4th) 105 .... 26.2, 26.7, 26.10, 26.11, 27.2

Pearson, Re, 70 Bankr. 202 (Bankr. S.D. Fla., 1986) 24.7

Pelky v. Hudson Bay Insurance Co. (1981), 35 O.R. (2d) 97, [1982] I.L.R. 1-1493 (H.C.) 4.18

Pelletier v. Cormier (1981), 35 N.B.R. (2d) 52, 88 A.P.R. 52 (Q.B.) 12

Pender v. Hamilton Street Railway (1917), 12 O.W.N. 262 (Div. Ct.) 4.16

People v. Fife, 392 N.E. 2d 1345 (S.C. Ill., 1979) 4.2

People v. Jackson, 167 Cal. App. 3d 829, 213 Cal. Rptr. 521 (Cal. Ct. of Appeals, 1985) 5.9

People v. Johnson, 26 Cal. 3d 557, 606 P. 2d 738 (1980) 5.8

People v. McGonigle, 198 Colo. 315, 600 P. 2d 61 (1979) 26.8

People v. Nash, 418 Mich. 196 (1983) 7.3

People v. Rhodes, 524 P. 2d 363 (S. Ct. Cal., 1974) 4.2

People v. Salquerro, 433 N.Y.S. 2d 711 (1980) 7.5

People v. Shum, 117 Ill. 2d 317, 512 N.E. 2d 1183 (1987) 6.1

People v. Winkler, 128 A.D. 2d 153, 515 N.Y.S. 2d 488 (1987) 12

People ex rel. Karlin v. Culkin, 248 N.Y. 465 (1928) 26.5

People of the State of Colorado v. Haase, 781 P. 2d 80 (1989) 2.4, 4.6

Percheson v. College of Physicians & Surgeons (Ontario) (1985), 51 O.R. (2d) 91, 10 O.A.C. 76 (Div. Ct.) 26.12

Perini Ltd. v. Toronto Parking Authority (1975), 6 O.R. (2d) 363, 52 D.L.R. (3d) 683 (C.A.) 2.4, 2.11

Perreault, Re, report adopted by Convocation, May 28, 1989 .... 26.17

Peters v. Perras (1909), 42 S.C.R. 244, 13 Alta. L.R. 80 .... 4.14

Petition of Diez-Arguelles, Re, 401 So. 2d 1347 (1981) 23.3

Pettey v. Avis Car Inc. (1993), 13 O.R. (3d) 725, 18 C.P.C. (3d) 50, 103 D.L.R. (4th) 298 (Gen. Div.) 4.21

Phoenix v. Metcalfe, [1974] 5 W.W.R. 661, 48 D.L.R. (3d) 631 (B.C. C.A.) 4.19

Picker International, Inc. v. Varian Associates, Inc., 869 F. 2d 578 (Fed. Cir., 1984) 5.4

Piercy v. Piercy, 48 B.C.L.R. (2d) 145, [1990] 6 W.W.R. 274, 43 C.P.C. (2d) 64, 28 R.F.L. (3d) 1, 75 D.L.R. (4th) 299 (C.A.), reversing 45 B.C.L.R. (2d) 267, [1990] 5 W.W.R. 269, 40 C.P.C. (2d) 194, 26 R.F.L. (3d) 18 (S.C.) 3.4

Pilzmaker, Re, report adopted by Convocation, January 25, 1990 .... 27.1

Pilzmaker and Law Society of Upper Canada, Re (1989), 70 O.R. (2d) 126, 38 Admin. L.R. 185, 36 O.A.C. 244 (Div. Ct.) 26.9

Planned Insurance Portfolios Co. v. Crown Life Insurance Co. (1989), 68 O.R. (2d) 271, 36 C.P.C. (2d) 218, 58 D.L.R. (4th) 106 (H.C.) 4.19

Plant v. Urquhart, [1922] 1 W.W.R. 632, 30 B.C.R. 461, 36 C.C.C. 339, 65 D.L.R. 242 (C.A.) 4.16

Poehler v. Langer (February 4, 1999), Doc. Vancouver C976361, A973386, C976534 (B.C. S.C.) 5.10

Polischuk v. Hagarty (1983), 42 O.R. (2d) 417, 149 D.L.R. (3d) 65 (H.C.), reversed (1984), 49 O.R. (2d) 71, 14 D.L.R. (4th) 446 (C.A.) 17.5

Polk County v. Dodson, 454 U.S. 312, 102 S. Ct. 445 (1981) 7.1

Pool v. Superior Court, 139 Ariz. 988, 677 P. 2d 261 (1984) 6.6

Popowich v. Saskatchewan, [1995] 6 W.W.R. 314, 132 Sask. R. 48 (Q.B.), reversed (1995), [1996] 1 W.W.R. 215, 134 Sask. R. 249, 101 W.A.C. 249 (C.A.) 5.6, 5.10

Posen, Re, report adopted by Convocation, January 21, 1972 .... 26.17

Prandini v. National Tea Co., 557 F. 2d 1015 (1977) 5.12

Prescott v. Law Society (British Columbia), [1971] 4 W.W.R. 433, (*sub nom.* Re Prescott) 19 D.L.R. (3d) 446 (B.C. C.A.) 26.7, 26.11, 26.14, 26.17, 27.5

Princess Auto & Machinery Ltd. v. Winnipeg (City) (1991), 73 Man. R. (2d) 311, 3 W.A.C. 311 (C.A.) 5.6, 5.10

Propp v. Fleming (1968), 64 W.W.R. 13, 67 D.L.R. (2d) 630 (B.C. C.A.) 4.8

Prousky v. Law Society of Upper Canada and Attorney General of Ontario (1987), 61 O.R. (2d) 37, 41 D.L.R. (4th) 465 (H.C.), affirmed (1987), 62 O.R. (2d) 224, 45 D.L.R. (4th) 640 (note) (C.A.) 26.15

Public Accountancy Act v. Stoller. See R. v. Public Accountants Council (Ontario)

Pursey v. R. (1956), 24 C.R. 233, 116 C.C.C. 82 (Que. C.A.) 6.6

R. v. Anders (1982), 67 C.C.C. (2d) 138, 136 D.L.R. (3d) 316 at 335 (Ont. C.A.) .... 4.22(b)

R. v. Askov, [1990] 2 S.C.R. 1199, 75 O.R. (2d) 673, 79 C.R. (3d) 273, 59 C.C.C. (3d) 449, 49 C.R.R. 1, 113 N.R. 241, 42 O.A.C. 81, 74 D.L.R. (4th) 355 .... 26.10

R. v. B. (B.P.) (1992), 71 C.C.C. (3d) 392 (B.C. S.C.) 7.6

R. v. Banks, [1916] 2 K.B. 621, [1916-17] All E.R. 356 (C.C.A.) 6.6

R. v. Barker, 53 C.C.C. (2d) 322, [1980] 4 W.W.R. 202, 20 A.R. 611 (C.A.) .... 4.22(b)

R. v. Basha (1979), 23 Nfld. & P.E.I.R. 286, 61 A.P.R. 286 (Nfld. C.A.) 13

R. v. Bencardino (1973), 2 O.R. (2d) 351, 24 C.R.N.S. 173, 15 C.C.C. (2d) 342 (C.A.) 3.2, 4.14

R. v. Bickerton (1985), 46 C.R. (3d) 286 (Ont. H.C.) .... 4.22(b)

R. v. Boyko (1975), 28 C.C.C. (2d) 193 (B.C. C.A.) 6.6

R. v. Broker-Dealers' Assn. of Ontario, [1971] 1 O.R. 355, 15 D.L.R. (3d) 385 (H.C.) 26.11

R. v. Burkinshaw (1967), 60 D.L.R. (2d) 748 (Alta. T.D.) 5.6

R. v. Carocchia (1972), 14 C.C.C. (2d) 354 (Que. Q.B.), affirmed (1973), 15 C.C.C. (2d) 175 (Que. C.A.) 13

R. v. Chamandy, [1934] O.R. 208, 9 C.B.R. (N.S.) 68, 61 C.C.C. 224, [1934] 2 D.L.R. 48 (C.A.) 6.1

R. v. Charest (1990), 76 C.R. (3d) 63, 28 Q.A.C. 258, 57 C.C.C. (3d) 312 (Que. C.A.) 6.6

R. v. Clarkson, [1986] 1 S.C.R. 383, 69 N.B.R. (2d) 40, 50 C.R. (3d) 289 (*sub nom.* Clarkson v. R.), 25 C.C.C. (3d) 207, 19 C.R.R. 209, 66 N.R. 114, 117 A.P.R. 40, 66 N.R. 114 .... 7.6

R. v. Cohn (1984), 48 O.R. (2d) 65, 42 C.R. (3d) 1, 15 C.C.C. (3d) 150, 10 C.R.R. 142, 13 D.L.R. (4th) 680, 4 O.A.C. 293 (C.A.), leave to appeal to S.C.C. refused (1985), 58 N.R. 160n, 9 O.A.C. 160 (S.C.C.) .... 4.22(b)

R. v. Commissioner of Police of the Metropolis, Ex parte Blackburn, [1967] W.L.R. 902 (C.A.) 6.5

R. v. Courvoisier (1840), 9 C. & P. 362, [1841] 173 Eng. Rep. 869 .... 7.5

R. v. Crneck (1980), 30 O.R. (2d) 1, 17 C.R. (3d) 171, 55 C.C.C. (2d) 1, 116 D.L.R. (3d) 675 (H.C.) 6.5, 7.7

R. v. Daigle (1982), 32 C.R. (3d) 388, 4 C.R.R. 153 (Que. S.C.) 26.5

R. v. Dalke. See Dalke, Re

R. v. Danson. See Danson v. Ontario (Attorney General)

R. v. Dersch, [1990] 2 S.C.R. 1505, (*sub nom.* Dersch v. Canada (Attorney General)) [1991] 1 W.W.R. 231, 80 C.R. (3d) 299, 51 B.C.L.R. (2d) 145, 116 N.R. 340, 43 O.A.C. 256, 60 C.C.C. (3d) 132, 50 C.R.R. 272, 77 D.L.R. (4th) 473, 36 Q.A.C. 258 .... 6.4

R. v. Dubois, (*sub nom.* Dubois v. R.) [1985] 2 S.C.R. 350, [1986] 1 W.W.R. 193, 41 Alta. L.R. (2d) 97, 48 C.R. (3d) 193, 22 C.C.C. (3d) 513, 23 D.L.R. (4th) 503, 18 C.R.R. 1, (*sub nom.* R. v. Dubois) [1986] D.L.Q. 87 (note) 26.15

R. v. Dunbar (1982), 28 C.R. (3d) 324, 138 D.L.R. (3d) 221, 68 C.C.C. (2d) 13 (Ont. C.A.) 22.2

R. v. Dunn (1981), 64 C.C.C. (2d) 253 (Que. C.A.) 6.6

R. v. Durette (1993), [1994] 1 S.C.R. 469, 28 C.R. (4th) 1, 163 N.R. 321, 70 O.A.C. 1, 88 C.C.C. (3d) 1 .... 6.4

R. v. Edwards Books & Art Ltd. See R. v. Videoflicks

R. v. Egger, [1993] 2 S.C.R. 451, 21 C.R. (4th) 186, 45 M.V.R. (2d) 161, 153 N.R. 272, 82 C.C.C. (3d) 193, 103 D.L.R. (4th) 678, 15 C.R.R. (2d) 193, 141 A.R. 81, 46 W.A.C. 81 .... 6.4

R. v. Ensor, [1989] 1 W.L.R. 497 (C.A.) 4.11

R. v. F. (A.) (1996), 30 O.R. (3d) 470 (C.A.) 6.6

R. v. Fontaine (1930), 53 C.C.C. 164, 65 O.L.R. 173 (C.A.) 6.1

R. v. Fosty, [1991] 3 S.C.R. 263, [1991] 6 W.W.R. 673, 8 C.R. (4th) 368, (*sub nom.* R. v. Gruenke) 67 C.C.C. (3d) 289, 75 Man. R. (2d) 112, 130 N.R. 161, 6 W.A.C. 112, 7 C.R.R. (2d) 108 .... 3.2

R. v. Glasner (September 6, 1994), Doc. CA C8879 (Ont. C.A.) 4.22

R. v. Gough, [1993] 2 W.L.R. 883, [1993] A.C. 646 (H.L.) 26.11

R. v. Gratton (1985), 18 C.C.C. (3d) 462, 7 O.A.C. 190 (C.A.), leave to appeal to S.C.C. refused (1985), 18 C.C.C. (3d) 462n, 11 O.A.C. 144n (S.C.C.) 6.6

R. v. Grover, [1991] 3 S.C.R. 387, 67 C.C.C. (3d) 576, 50 O.A.C. 185 .... 6.6

R. v. Gruenke. See R. v. Fosty

R. v. Hawke (1974), 3 O.R. (2d) 210, 16 C.C.C. (2d) 438 (H.C.), reversed (1975), 7 O.R. (2d) 145, 29 C.R.N.S. 1, 22 C.C.C. (2d) 19 (C.A.) 4.14

R. v. Hay (1982), 30 C.R. (3d) 37, 70 C.C.C. (2d) 286, 17 Sask. R. 252 (C.A.) 6.6

R. v. Hayward (1981), 59 C.C.C. (2d) 134 (Nfld. C.A.) 4.19

R. v. Henry, Man. C.A., 1986 (unreported) 13

R. v. Horsham DC, ex. p. Wenman, [1994] 4 All E.R. 681 .... 4.22

R. v. Irwin, [1987] 1 W.L.R. 902 (C.A.) 4.11

R. v. Joanisse (1995), 44 C.R. (4th) 365, 85 O.A.C. 186, 102 C.C.C. (3d) 35 (C.A.), leave to appeal to S.C.C. refused (1997), 99 O.A.C. 79 (note), 208 N.R. 79 (note) (S.C.C.) 4.11

R. v. Jones (1978), 42 C.C.C. (2d) 192 (Ont. C.A.) .... 4.22(b)

R. v. Joubert (1992), 69 C.C.C. (3d) 553, 7 B.C.A.C. 31, 15 W.A.C. 31 (C.A.), application for reconsideration refused (May 7, 1992), Doc. No. CA012513 (B.C. C.A.), leave to appeal to S.C.C. refused (December 10, 1992), Doc. No. 22885 (S.C.C.) 3.2

R. v. Khanzada (February 10, 1992), 15 W.C.B. (2d) 381 (Ont. Gen. Div.) 7.6

R. v. Kienapple (1974), [1975] 1 S.C.R. 729, 26 C.R.N.S. 1, 15 C.C.C. (2d) 524, 44 D.L.R. (3d) 351, 1 N.R. 322 .... 26.2

R. v. Kopyto (1987), 62 O.R. (2d) 449, 61 C.R. (3d) 209, 39 C.C.C. (3d) 1, 24 O.A.C. 81, 47 D.L.R. (4th) 213 (C.A.) 27.6

R. v. Korponey. See Korponey v. Canada (Attorney General)

R. v. Kotapski (1981), 66 C.C.C. (2d) 78 (Que. S.C.) 3.2

R. v. Kuldip, [1990] 3 S.C.R. 618, 1 C.R. (4th) 285, 61 C.C.C. (3d) 385, 1 C.R.R. (2d) 110, 43 O.A.C. 340, 114 N.R. 284 . . . . . 26.15

R. v. L. (T.P.), [1987] 2 S.C.R. 309, 82 N.S.R. (2d) 271, 61 C.R. (3d) 1, 37 C.C.C. (3d) 1, 32 C.R.R. 41, (*sub nom.* R. v. L.) 80 N.R. 161, 207 A.P.R. 271, 44 D.L.R. (4th) 193 . . . . . 26.11

R. v. Labarre (1978), 45 C.C.C. (2d) 171 (Que. C.A.) 6.6

R. v. Law Society of B.C. See Law Society (British Columbia) v. MacKrow

R. v. Lawrie & Pointts Ltd. (1987), 59 O.R. (2d) 161, 48 M.V.R. 189, 32 C.C.C. (3d) 549, 19 O.A.C. 81 (C.A.) 25.9

R. v. Litchfeld, [1993] 4 S.C.R. 333, 14 Alta. L.R. (3d) 1, 25 C.R. (4th) 137, 161 N.R. 161, 86 C.C.C. (3d) 97, 145 A.R. 321, 55 W.A.C. 321 . . . . . 26.12

R. v. Logiacco (1984), 11 C.C.C. (3d) 374, 2 O.A.C. 177 . . . . . 6.1, 26.17

R. v. Lomage (1991), 2 O.R. (3d) 621, 44 O.A.C. 131 (C.A.) 7.1

R. v. McCaw (1971), [1972] 1 O.R. 742, 5 C.C.C. (2d) 416 (C.A.) 7.6

R. v. McDonald (1958), 120 C.C.C. 209 (Ont. C.A.) 6.6

R. v. McKinlay Transport Ltd., [1990] 1 S.C.R. 627, 72 O.R. (2d) 798 (note), 76 C.R. (3d) 283, 55 C.C.C. (3d) 530, 39 O.A.C. 385, 106 N.R. 385, 47 C.R.R. 151, (*sub nom.* Canada v. McKinlay Transport Ltd.) [1990] 2 C.T.C. 103, 68 D.L.R. (4th) 568 . . . . . 26.2, 26.4

R. v. McLoughlin, [1985] 1 N.Z.L.R. 106 (C.A.) 4.11

R. v. Mete, [1973] 3 W.W.R. 709, 22 C.R.N.S. 387 (B.C. C.A.) 4.14

R. v. Murphy (1981), 43 N.S.R. (2d) 676, 58 C.C.C. (2d) 338, 81 A.P.R. 676 (C.A.) 6.6

R. v. Murray (2000), 48 O.R. (3d) 437 (S.C.J.) 3.5

R. v. Murray, 10 Alta. L.R. 275, [1917] 1 W.W.R. 404, 27 C.C.C. 247, 33 D.L.R. 702 (C.A.) 6.1

R. v. Naglik (1991), 3 O.R. (3d) 385, 65 C.C.C. (3d) 272, 46 O.A.C. 81 (C.A.), leave to appeal to S.C.C. granted (December 4, 1991), Doc. Nos. 22490, 22636 (S.C.C.) 7.6

R. v. Naraindeen (1990), 75 O.R. (2d) 120, 80 C.R. (3d) 66, 40 O.A.C. 291 (C.A.), varied on reconsideration (1990), 75 O.R. (2d) 120 at 133, 40 O.A.C. 291 at 301 (C.A.) 6.5

R. v. Nealy (1986), 54 C.R. (3d) 158, 30 C.C.C. (3d) 460, 17 O.A.C. 164 (C.A.) 4.14

R. v. Nova Scotia Pharmaceutical Society. See Canada v. Pharmaceutical Society (Nova Scotia)

R. v. Nugent (1995), 24 O.R. (3d) 295, 100 C.C.C. (3d) 89 (C.A.) 6.6

R. v. Oakes, [1986] 1 S.C.R. 103, 53 O.R. (2d) 719 (headnote only), 50 C.R. (3d) 1, 24 C.C.C. (3d) 321, 65 N.R. 87, 19 C.R.R. 308, 14 O.A.C. 335, 26 D.L.R. (4th) 200 .... 26.16

R. v. Oberkirsch (1999), 176 Sask. R. 230 (Q.B.) 3.2

R. v. O'Connell (1844-5), 7 Ir. L.R. 261 .... 4.2

R. v. Ontario (Racing Commission), [1970] 1 O.R. 458, 8 D.L.R. (3d) 624 (H.C.) 26.12

R. v. Paine (1792), 22 St. Tr. 357 .... 4.2

R. v. Palaramchuk, Ont. Co. Ct., 1984 (unreported) 7.1

R. v. Parsons (1992), 13 C.R. (4th) 248, 72 C.C.C. (3d) 137, 100 Nfld. & P.E.I.R. 260, 318 A.P.R. 260 (Nfld. C.A.) 7.7

R. v. Pinehouse Plaza Pharmacy Ltd., [1988] 3 W.W.R. 705, 38 M.P.L.R. 103, 67 Sask. R. 201 (Q.B.), affirmed [1991] 2 W.W.R. 544, 62 C.C.C. (3d) 321, 4 M.P.L.R. (2d) 1, 89 Sask. R. 47 (C.A.) 10

R. v. Pinx, [1980] 1 W.W.R. 77, 50 C.C.C. (2d) 65, 1 Man. R. (2d) 1, 105 D.L.R. (3d) 43 (C.A.) .... 4.22(b)

R. v. Profit (1992), 11 O.R. (3d) 98, 16 C.R. (4th) 332, 58 O.A.C. 226 (C.A.) 26.17

R. v. Public Accountants Council (Ontario), [1960] O.R. 631, 25 D.L.R. (2d) 410 (*sub nom.* Public Accountancy Act v. Stoller) (C.A.) 26.11

R. v. Quesnel (1985), 53 O.R. (2d) 338, 24 C.C.C. (3d) 78, 12 O.A.C. 165 (C.A.), leave to appeal to S.C.C. refused (1986), 55 O.R. (2d) 543, 16 O.A.C. 80 (note), 68 N.R. 160 (note) (S.C.C.) 26.2

R. v. R. (A.J.) (1994), 20 O.R. (3d) 405 (C.A.) 6.6

R. v. R.B.P. See R. v. B. (B.P.)

R. v. Rapai (1992), 11 O.R. (3d) 47 (Prov. Div.) 7.7

R. v. Roberts (1973), 14 C.C.C. (2d) 368 (Ont. C.A.) 6.6

R. v. Robillard (1986), 28 C.C.C. (3d) 22, 23 C.R.R. 364, 14 O.A.C. 314 (C.A.) 7.6

R. v. Robinson, Ont. H.C., October 24, 1983, *per* Reid J. (unreported) 4.15

R. v. Rooke. See R. v. Saunders

R. v. Rosik (1970), [1971] 2 O.R. 47, 13 C.R.N.S. 129, 2 C.C.C. (2d) 351, 13 Cr. L.Q. 224 (C.A.), affirmed [1971] 2 O.R. 89n, 14 C.R.N.S. 400, 2 C.C.C. (2d) 393n (S.C.C.) 6.6

R. v. Ruddick (1865), F. & F. 497 .... 6.1

R. v. S. (A.) (1996), 28 O.R. (3d) 663 (Gen. Div.) 7.6

R. v. S. (F.) (2000), 47 O.R. (3d) 349 (C.A.) 6.1

R. v. Sask. College of Physicians & Surgeons; Ex parte Sen. See Sen v. College of Physician & Surgeons (Saskatchewan)

R. v. Saunders (1987), 14 B.C.L.R. (2d) 313, 58 C.R. (3d) 83, 35 C.C.C. (3d) 385 (C.A.), affirmed [1990] 1 S.C.R. 1020, 46 B.C.L.R. (2d) 145, 77 C.R. (3d) 397, 56 C.C.C. (3d) 220, (*sub nom.* R. v. Rooke) 108 N.R. 234 .... 4.16

R. v. Savoy (1977), 18 N.B.R. (2d) 489 (C.A.) 6.6

R. v. Shumiatcher. See Shumiatcher, Re

R. v. Silvini (1991), 5 O.R. (3d) 545, 9 C.R. (4th) 233, 68 C.C.C. (3d) 251, 50 O.A.C. 376 (C.A.) 7.6

R. v. Smith (1990), 75 O.R. (2d) 753, 2 C.R. (4th) 253, 61 C.C.C. (3d) 232, 42 O.A.C. 395 (C.A.), affirmed [1992] 2 S.C.R. 915, 15 C.R. (4th) 133, 75 C.C.C. (3d) 257, 139 N.R. 323, 55 O.A.C. 321, 94 D.L.R. (4th) 590 .... 6.6

R. v. Speid (1983), 43 O.R. (2d) 596, 37 C.R. (3d) 220, 8 C.C.C. (3d) 18, 7 C.R.R. 39, 3 D.L.R. (4th) 246 (C.A.) 7.6

R. v. Staranchuk, [1983] 6 W.W.R. 729, 36 C.R. (3d) 285, 48 C.B.R. (N.S.) 6 at 8, 8 C.C.C. (3d) 150, 6 C.R.R. 254, 28 Sask. R. 45, 3 D.L.R. (4th) 574 (C.A.), affirmed [1985] 1 S.C.R. 439, [1985] 4 W.W.R. 544, 47 C.R. (3d) 192, 55 C.B.R. (N.S.) 113, 22 C.C.C. (3d) 512, 19 C.R.R. 31, 68 N.R. 311, 49 Sask. R. 216, 22 D.L.R. (4th) 480 .... 26.15

R. v. Stinchcombe (1991), [1991] 3 S.C.R. 326, 83 Alta. L.R. (2d) 193, [1992] 1 W.W.R. 97, 8 C.R. (4th) 277, 68 C.C.C. (3d) 1, 130 N.R. 277, 120 A.R. 161, 8 W.A.C. 161 .... 2.11, 6.4

R. v. Stork, 31 C.R.N.S. 395, [1975] W.W.D. 127, 24 C.C.C. (2d) 210 (B.C. C.A.) 7.6

R. v. Sussex Justices, Ex Parte McCarthy, [1924] 1 K.B. 256, [1923] All E.R. 233 (D.C.) 5.2

R. v. Swartz, [1977] 2 W.W.R. 751, 34 C.C.C. (2d) 477 (Man. C.A.) .... 4.22(b)

R. v. Sweezey (1987), 39 C.C.C. (3d) 182, 66 Nfld. & P.E.I.R. 29, 204 A.P.R. 29 (Nfld. C.A.) 4.12

R. v. Thomas (No. 2), [1974] 1 N.Z.L.R. 658 (C.A.) 6.1

R. v. Tobin (1992), 9 O.R. (3d) 129, 74 C.C.C. (3d) 508, 56 O.A.C. 354 (C.A.) 6.6

R. v. Turner, [1970] 2 All E.R. 281, [1970] 2 Q.B. 321 (C.A.) 6.5, 7.7

R. v. Vallieres, [1970] 4 C.C.C. 69 (Que. C.A.) 6.6

R. v. Videoflicks Ltd., [1986] 2 S.C.R. 713 (*sub nom.* R. v. Edwards Books & Art Ltd.), 58 O.R. (2d) 442 (note), 55 C.R. (3d) 193, 30 C.C.C. (3d) 385 (*sub nom.* Edwards Books & Art Ltd. v. R.; R. v. Nortown Foods Ltd.), 28 C.R.R. 1, 87 C.L.L.C. 14,001, 19 O.A.C. 239, 71 N.R. 161, 35 D.L.R. (4th) 1 .... 26.2

R. v. W. (W.) (1995), 25 O.R. (3d) 161, 43 C.R. (4th) 26, 100 C.C.C. (3d) 225, 84 O.A.C. 241 (C.A.) 7.6

R. v. Werkman, [1997] 4 W.W.R. 762 (Alta. Q.B.) 7.6

R. v. White (1997), 32 O.R. (3d) 722 (Ont. C.A.) 4.11, 5.9

R. v. Wigglesworth (1987), [1987] 2 S.C.R. 541, [1988] 1 W.W.R. 193, 28 Admin. L.R. 294, 60 C.R. (3d) 193, 37 C.C.C. (3d) 385, 32 C.R.R. 219, 24 O.A.C. 321, 81 N.R. 161, 61 Sask. R. 105, 45 D.L.R. (4th) 235 .... 26.2, 26.4, 26.10, 26.15

R. v. Wilson (1983), 5 C.C.C. (3d) 61 (B.C. C.A.) 4.14, 6.6

R. v. Wyssen (1992), 10 O.R. (3d) 193, 58 O.A.C. 67 (C.A.) 23.3

R.G. Tours and Promotions Ltd. v. Greater Moncton Home Builders Assn. (1992), 126 N.B.R. (2d) 200, 317 A.P.R. 200 (Q.B.) 5.10

R.M.J., Re, 455 U.S. 191 (1982). 10

R. Sherwin Enterprises Ltd. v. Municipal Contracting Services Ltd. (1994), 20 O.R. (3d) 692, 33 C.P.C. (3d) 244 (Gen. Div.) 5.10, 5.14

Racz v. Mission (District) (1988), 22 B.C.L.R. (2d) 70, 28 C.P.C. (2d) 74 (C.A.) 4.8

Rademaker, MacDougall & Co. v. Number Ten Holdings Ltd. (1983), 47 B.C.L.R. 376 (S.C.), reversed (1985), 60 B.C.L.R. 301 (C.A.) 3.2

Radigan, Re, reported adopted by Convocation, April 23, 1982 . . . . 26.17

Rajnauth v. Law Society (Upper Canada) (1993), 13 O.R. (3d) 381, 102 D.L.R. (4th) 443, 63 O.A.C. 212 (Div. Ct.) 23.2

Rak v. British Columbia (Superintendent of Brokers) (1990), 51 B.C.L.R. (2d) 27, 47 Admin. L.R. 243, 74 D.L.R. (4th) 725 (C.A.) 26.16

Rakusen v. Ellis, Munday & Clarke, [1912] 1 Ch. 831, [1911-13] All E.R. 813 (C.A.) 5.6

Ramati, Re, report adopted by Convocation, July 15, 1982 . . . . 26.17

Ramsay, Re, report adopted by Convocation, November 26, 1992 . . . . 25.13

Ramsay v. Toronto (City) Commissioners of Police. See Lang v. Ramsay

Ramsbottom v. Morning (1991), 48 C.P.C. (2d) 177 (Ont. Gen. Div.) 5.6

Rappaport, Re, 558 F. 2d 87 (2nd Cir., 1977) . . . . 25.5(a)

Rayner v. Enright (1993), 20 C.P.C. (3d) 269, 115 Sask. R. 159 (Q.B.) 5.6

Reddall v. College of Nurses (Ontario) (1983), 42 O.R. (2d) 412, 1 Admin. L.R. 278, 149 D.L.R. (3d) 60 (C.A.) 26.14

Rees v. Sinclair, [1974] 1 N.Z.L.R. 180 (C.A.) 4.18, 27.5

Reichmann v. Toronto Life Publishing Co. (1988), 28 C.P.C. (2d) 11 (Ont. H.C.), leave to appeal to Ont. Div. Ct. refused (1988), 29 C.P.C. (2d) 66 (Ont. H.C.) 26.15

Reilly, re, order of Convocation, June 22, 1995 . . . . 26.17

Remus v. United States, 291 F. 501 (6th Cir., 1923) 6.1, 6.6

Republic Steel Corp. v. United States, 572 F. Supp. 275. . . . . 20.1

Reza v. General Medical Council, [1990] 1 A.C. 13 (P.C.) 26.16

Reza v. General Medical Council, [1991] 2 A.C. 182, [1991] 2 All E.R. 796 (P.C.) 26.16

Richmond v. College of Optometrists (Ontario) (1995), 25 O.R. (3d) 448, 85 O.A.C. 379 (Div. Ct.) 26.19

Ringrose v. College of Physicians & Surgeons (Alberta), [1977] 1 S.C.R. 814, [1976] 4 W.W.R. 712, 1 A.R. 1, 9 N.R. 383, 67 D.L.R. (3d) 559 . . . . 26.11

Ringrose v. College of Physicians & Surgeons (Alberta) (No. 2), [1978] 2 W.W.R. 534, 8 A.R. 113, 83 D.L.R. (3d) 680 (C.A.), leave to appeal to S.C.C. refused May 16, 1978 . . . . 26.14, 26.16

River West, Inc. v. Nickel, 188 Cal. App. 3d 1307, 234 Cal. Rptr. 33 (1987) 5.6

Rizzotto, Re, report adopted by Convocation, September 14, 1992 . . . . 23.3

Rizzotto (No. 1), Re, report of admissions committee, June 14, 1991 ....23.3

Rizzotto (No. 2), Re, report of admissions committee, February 3, 1992...........23.3

Robb, Re, report adopted by Convocation, September 23, 1982.................26.17

Robb Estate v. St. Joseph's Health Care Centre (March 10, 1999), Doc. 92-CU-54356, 92-CU-59486, 98-CV-139060 (Ont. Gen. Div.)..................... 4.11.1

Roberge v. Bolduc. See Dorion v. Roberge

Roberts v. College of Nurses of Ontario, [1999] O.J. 2281 (Div. Ct.).............26.11

Roberts v. Pega Capital Corp. (2000), 47 O.R. (3d) 317 (S.C.J.)...................5.9

Robertson Stromberg, Re. See Law Society (Saskatchewan) v. Robertson Stromberg.

Robinson v. College of Physicians & Surgeons (British Columbia) (1986), 9 B.C.L.R. (2d) 36, 32 D.L.R. (4th) 589 (S.C.) 26.10

Rochester (City) v. Chiarella, 86 A.D. 2d 100, 449 N.Y.S. 2d 112 (1982)..........5.12

Rocket v. Royal College of Dental Surgeons (Ontario), [1990] 2 S.C.R. 232, 73 O.R. (2d) 128 (note), 71 D.L.R. (4th) 68, 47 C.R.R. 193, (*sub nom.* Royal College of Dental Surgeons (Ontario) v. Rocket) 111 N.R. 161, 40 O.A.C. 241 ... 10

Rodrigues, Re (1987), 66 Nfld. & P.E.I.R. 54, 204 A.P.R. 54, (*sub nom.* Rodrigues v. Newfoundland Dental Board) 44 D.L.R. (4th) 689 (Nfld. T.D.) 26.11

Romano, Re, 104 N.J. 306, 516 A. 2d 1109 (1986)............................26.17

Romeo v. R., [1991] 1 S.C.R. 86, 110 N.B.R. (2d) 57, 2 C.R. (4th) 307, 62 C.C.C. (3d) 1, 276 A.P.R. 57, 119 N.R. 309 ....6.6

Rondel v. Worsley, [1969] 1 A.C. 191, [1967] 3 All E.R. 993 (U.K. H.L.)...............................2.4, 4.2, 4.14, 4.16, 4.18, 4.23, 27.5

Rooks Rider v. Steel, [1993] 4 All E.R. 716 (Ch.D.)...........................17.5

Rosenbaum v. Law Society (Manitoba), 2 Admin. L.R. 210, [1983] 5 W.W.R. 752, 6 C.C.C. (3d) 472, 22 Man. R. (2d) 260, 150 D.L.R. (3d) 352 (Q.B.), affirmed 7 Admin L.R. 77, [1984] 4 W.W.R. 95, 8 C.C.C. (3d) 256, 25 Man. R. (2d) 154, 3 D.L.R. (4th) 768 (C.A.), leave to appeal to S.C.C. refused (1984), 27 Man. R. (2d) 159n, 55 N.R. 440 (S.C.C.) 26.4, 26.5

Rosenstock v. College of Physicians & Surgeons (Alberta), 64 Alta. L.R. (2d) 193, [1989] 2 W.W.R. 611, 93 A.R. 298, 57 D.L.R. (4th) 106 (Q.B.) 26.3, 26.11

Rosin v. MacPhail (1997), 142 D.L.R. (4th) 304, 85 B.C.A.C. 69, 138 W.A.C. 69, 32 B.C.L.R. (3d) 279 (C.A.) 5.6

Ross v. Caunters (1979), [1980] 1 Ch. 297, [1979] 3 All E.R. 580 (Ch. D.) 18.3

Ross v. Ewachniuk (1986), 9 B.C.L.R. (2d) 216 (S.C.).......................... 12

Roth v. Continental Casualty Co., 676 F. Supp. 816 (N.D. Ill., 1987)...............5.6

Rovet, Re, report adopted by Convocation, January 23, 1992........... 4.22(c), 26.17

Royal Bank v. Lee (1992), 9 C.P.C. (3d) 199, 3 Alta. L.R. (3d) 187, 127 A.R. 236, 20 W.A.C. 236 (C.A.).. 3.2.1

Royal College of Dental Surgeons (Ontario) v. Rocket. See Rocket v. Royal College of Dental Surgeons (Ontario)

Rusonik v. Law Society (Upper Canada) (1988), 28 O.A.C. 57 (Div. Ct.) 26.11, 26.19

Russell v. Law Society (New Brunswick) (1991), 117 N.B.R. (2d) 32, 295 A.P.R. 32, 82 D.L.R. (4th) 278 (C.A.) 26.11

Ryder, Re, 263 F. Supp. 360 (E.D. Va., 1967) 7.3

S. (P.) v. C. (A.J.) (1993), 101 D.L.R. (4th) 345, (*sub nom.* Droit de la famille - 1559) [1993] R.J.Q. 625 (C.A.) 26.11

Sacher v. United States, 343 U.S. 1 (1952) 4.23

Saif Ali v. Sydney Mitchell & Co., [1978] Q.B. 95 (C.A.), reversed on other grounds [1978] 3 All E.R. 1033 (H.L.) 4.4, 4.13, 4.14, 4.18, 4.23

Salter v. St. Jean, 170 So. 2d 94 (Fla. App., 1964) 12

Sandberg v. F., [1945] 4 D.L.R. 446 (B.C. S.C.) (Law Society of B.C. (Visitorial Trib.)) 26.19

Sankey, Re, report adopted by Convocation, January 26, 1984 . . . . . . 26.17

Santobello v. New York, 404 U.S. 257, 92 S. Ct. 495 (1971) 6.5

Satellite Financial Planning v. First National Bank of Washington, 652 F. Supp. 1281 (D. Del., 1987) 5.6

Sawyer v. Ontario (Racing Commission) (1979), 24 O.R. (2d) 673, 99 D.L.R. (3d) 561 (C.A.) 26.18

Schabas v. University of Toronto (1974), 6 O.R. (2d) 271, 52 D.L.R. (3d) 495 (Div. Ct.) 26.11

Schafer v. International Capital Corp. See International Capital Corp. v. Schafer

Scherer, Re, report adopted by Convocation, February 24, 1984 . . . . . . 25.7

Scherer v. Paletta, [1966] 2 O.R. 524 (C.A.) 4.8

Schmidt v. Magnetic Head Corp., 468 N.Y.S. 2d 649 (1983) 5.13

Schware v. Board of Bar Examiners, 353 U.S. 232 (1957) 23.3

Schwisberg v. Perry Krieger & Associates (1997), 33 O.R. (3d) 256 . . . . . . 4.22(a)

Securities and Exchange Commission v. National Student Marketing Corp., 457 F. Supp. 682 (U.S. Dist. Ct., D.C., 1978) 20.5

Selick v. New York Life Insurance Co. (1920), 17 O.W.N. 463 . . . . . . 4.16

Sellers v. Superior Court, 154 Ariz. 281, 742 P. 2d 292 (Ariz. S. Ct., 1987) 5.5

Sen v. College of Physicians & Surgeons (Saskatchewan) (1969), 69 W.W.R. 201, 6 D.L.R. (3d) 520, (*sub nom.* R. v. Sask. College of Physicians & Surgeons; Ex parte Sen) (Sask. C.A.) 26.16

Shane, Re, report adopted by Convocation, October 29, 1982 . . . . . . 26.17

Shapero v. Kentucky Bar Assn., 108 S. Ct. 1916 (1988) 10

Shaughnessy Brothers Investments Ltd. v. Lakehead Trailer Park (1985) Ltd. (1987), 63 O.R. (2d) 225, 23 C.P.C. (2d) 194 (H.C.) 5.2

Shea, Re, report adopted by Convocation, January 16, 1976 . . . . . . 26.8

Shepherd v. Robinson, [1919] 1 K.B. 474 (C.A.) 4.8

Sherman v. Manley (1978), 19 O.R. (2d) 531, 6 C.P.C. 136, 85 D.L.R. (3d) 575 (C.A.) 4.10, 27.4

Shively v. Stewart, 421 P. 2d 65 (1965) 26.6

Shub, Re, report adopted by Convocation, February 25, 1983 . . . . 26.17

Shuckett, No. 2, Re, Man., January 7, 1992 (unreported) 26.17

Shumiatcher, Re, 60 W.W.R. 214, 1 C.R.N.S. 338, [1967] 3 C.C.C. 197, 64 D.L.R. (2d) 24 (*sub nom.* R. v. Shumiatcher) (Sask. Q.B.), varied 64 W.W.R. 743, [1969] 1 C.C.C. 272 (Sask. C.A.) . . . . 4.22(b)

Shumiatcher v. Law Society (Saskatchewan) (1966), 58 W.W.R. 465, 60 D.L.R. (2d) 318 (Sask. C.A.), leave to appeal refused (1967), 61 D.L.R. (2d) 520 (Sask. C.A.) 26.16

Simmonds v. Dalmyn, [1993] 8 W.W.R. 207, 106 D.L.R. (4th) 677, 88 Man. R. (2d) 81, 51 W.A.C. 81 (C.A.) 4.19

Sinclair v. Ridout, [1955] O.R. 167, [1955] 4 D.L.R. 468 (H.C.), time for appealing extended [1955] O.W.N. 633 (C.A.) 5.6, 17.4

Skimming v. Goldberg, [1993] 8 W.W.R. 59, 33 R.P.R. (2d) 203, 89 Man. R. (2d) 27 (Q.B.) 22.2

Smith v. Jones, 169 D.L.R. (4th) 385, (*sub nom.* Jones v. Smith) 60 C.R.R. (2d) 46, 132 C.C.C. (3d) 225, 22 C.R. (5th) 203, 236 N.R. 201, 120 B.C.A.C. 161, 196 W.A.C. 161, [1999] 1 S.C.R. 455, 62 B.C.L.R. (3d) 209, [1999] 8 W.W.R. 364 (S.C.C.) 3.4

Smith v. Robinson (1992), 7 O.R. (3d) 550, 4 C.P.C. (3d) 262, 87 D.L.R. (4th) 360 (Gen. Div.) 4.8

Smith v. Smith, [1952] 2 S.C.R. 312, [1952] 3 D.L.R. 449 . . . . 26.16

Snyder, Re, 472 U.S. 634 (U.S. S. Ct., 1985) 4.23

Solicitor, re, a reasons of Convocation, July 14, 1998 (Ontario) 26.4, 26.5

Solicitor, Re, [1907] 14 O.L.R. 464 (H.C.) 12

Solicitor, Re, [1912] 1 K.B. 302 . . . . 12, 24.2, 26.7

Solicitor, Re (1914), 7 W.W.R. 87, (*sub nom.* Re A.B.) 7 Sask. L.R. 263, (*sub nom.* Re Cole) 20 D.L.R. 502 (S.C.) 26.22

Solicitor, Re (1915), 9 W.W.R. 480, 24 D.L.R. 443 (Alta. C.A.) 26.22

Solicitor, Re (1916), 37 O.L.R. 310, 31 D.L.R. 86 (C.A.) 26.7

Solicitor, Re, [1935] 3 W.W.R. 428 (Sask. C.A.) 26.7

Solicitor, Re, [1956] 3 All E.R. 516 (Q.B.) 26.19

Solicitor, Re, [1992] 2 W.L.R. 552 . . . . 26.16

Solicitor v. Law Society (British Columbia) (1995), 128 D.L.R. (4th) 562, 8 B.C.L.R. (3d) 377, 40 C.P.C. (3d) 67, 33 Admin. L.R. (2d) 314 (S.C.) 26.6

Solicitor "X" v. Nova Scotia Barristers' Society (1998), 171 D.L.R. (4th) 310 (N.S. C.A.) 26.11

Solosky v. Canada, [1980] 1 S.C.R. 821, 16 C.R. (3d) 294, 50 C.C.C. (2d) 495, 30 N.R. 380, 105 D.L.R. (3d) 745 . . . . 3.2

Sonntag v. Sonntag (1979), 24 O.R. (2d) 473, 11 C.P.C. 13 (H.C.)........ 4.17, 4.22(a)

Soriano v. United States, 352 U.S. 270 (1956).................................. 1.1

Soskel v. Texaco, Inc., 94 F.R.D. 201 (S.D.N.Y., 1982) 5.12

Souch, Re, [1938] O.R. 48, [1938] 1 D.L.R. 563 (C.A.)......................... 18.2

South Calgary Properties Ltd. v. J.T. Miller Construction Ltd. (1995), 29 Alta. L.R. (3d) 393, [1995] 8 W.W.R. 146 (*sub nom.* Miller (J.T.) Construction Ltd. v. South Calgary Properties Ltd.) 165 A.R. 361, 89 W.A.C. 361 (C.A.)....... 5.6, 5.10

Southam Inc. v. Lafrance, [1990] R.J.Q. 937, (*sub nom.* Southam Inc. v. La France) 71 D.L.R. (4th) 282 (C.A.) 26.9

Spaulding v. Zimmerman, 116 N.W. 2d 704 (1962) 2.2, 2.5

Spector v. Ageda, [1971] 2 All E.R. 417, 22 P. & C.R. 1002, [1973] Ch. 30 (Ch. D.) 17.4

Speers v. Hagemeister (1974), 52 D.L.R. (3d) 109 (Sask. C.A.) 12

Spence v. Bell, [1982] 6 W.W.R. 385, 22 Alta. L.R. (2d) 193, 39 A.R. 239 (C.A.), leave to appeal to S.C.C. refused (1982), 41 A.R. 305, 46 N.R. 179 (S.C.C.).. 24.6

Spevack v. Klein, 385 U.S. 511 (1967) 26.4

Spicer, Re, report adopted by Convocation, October 3, 1991 .... 23.3

Spicer v. Assn. of Professional Engineers, Geologists & Geophysicists (Alberta) (1989), 95 A.R. 132 (Q.B.) 26.2

Spring v. Law Society (Upper Canada) (1988), 64 O.R. (2d) 719, 30 Admin. L.R. 151, 28 O.A.C. 375, 50 D.L.R. (4th) 523 (Div. Ct.) 26.15, 26.18

Sprung v. Negwer Materials, Inc., 727 S.W. 2d 883 (1987)....................... 8

Squires, Re, report adopted by Convocation, March 21, 1985.................... 26.17

St. Denis v. Thibodeau, [1929] S.C.R. 346 .... 18.2

St. John v. Fraser, [1935] S.C.R. 441, 64 C.C.C. 90, [1935] 3 D.L.R. 465 .... 26.12

Stanbrook, Re, report adopted by Convocation, January 21, 1977 .... 26.17

Stanley v. Douglas, [1952] 1 S.C.R. 260, [1951] 4 D.L.R. 689 .... 4.19

Stanton, Re, 103 N.M. 413, 708 P. 2d 325 (1985) 25.13

State v. Boyd, 160 W. Va. 234, 233 S.E. 2d 710 (1977) 6.6

State v. Henderson, 205 Kan. 231, 468 P. 2d 136 (1970) 7.5

State v. Macumber, 112 Ariz. 569, 544 P. 2d 1084 (1976) 3.1

State v. Olwell, 64 Wash. 2d 828 (1964)...................................... 7.3

State Bar of Nevada v. Raffetto, 183 P. 2d 621 (1947) 11

State of New Mexico v. Valdez, 618 P. 2d 1234 (S. Ct. New Mexico, 1980)......... 3.1

State ex rel. Oklahoma Bar Assn. v. Raskin, 642 P. 2d 262 (Oklahoma, 1982)...... 26.1

Stephen v. College of Physicians & Surgeons (Saskatchewan) (1990), 89 Sask. R. 25, 4 C.R.R. (2d) 373 (Q.B.).. 26.2

Steponaitus, re, order of Convocation, November 25, 1993..................... 26.17

Sterling Rubber Ltd. v. Canadian Imperial Bank of Commerce (June 17, 1991), Doc. No. 9233/86 (Ont. Gen. Div.) . . . 2.3, 2.9

Stevens v. Canada (Prime Minister), (*sub nom.* Stevens v. Canada (Privy Council)) 161 D.L.R. (4th) 85, (*sub nom.* Stevens v. Prime Minister (Can.)) 228 N.R. 142, [1998] 4 F.C. 89, 147 F.T.R. 308 (note), 21 C.P.C. (4th) 327, 11 Admin. L.R. (3d) 169 (Fed. C.A.) . . . 3.2

Stevens v. Canada Privy Council. See Stevens v. Canada (Prime Minister)

Stevens v. Law Society (Upper Canada) (1979), 55 O.R. (2d) 405 (Div. Ct.) . . . 25.2, 26.2, 26.7, 26.12, 26.17

Stevens v. Prime Minister (Can.). See Stevens v. Canada (Prime Minister)

Stevens v. Salt (1995), 22 O.R. (3d) 675 (Ont. Gen. Div.) . . . 4.19

Stewart, Re, report adopted by Convocation, June 25, 1988 . . . 26.17

Stewart, re, order of Convocation, June 27, 1996 . . . 26.17

Stewart v. C.B.C. (June 6, 1997), J. Macdonald J. (Ont. Gen. Div.) . . . 4.11

Stewart v. Canadian Broadcasting Corp. (1997), 150 D.L.R. (4th) 24 (Ont. Gen. Div.), additional reasons at (1997), 152 D.L.R. (4th) 102 (Ont. Gen. Div.) . . . 13,25.2

Stewart v. Speer, [1953] 3 D.L.R. 722 (Ont. C.A.) . . . 4.16

Stickney v. Trusz (1974), 3 O.R. (2d) 538, 28 C.R.N.S. 125, 17 C.C.C. (2d) 478, 46 D.L.R. (3d) 80 (Div. Ct.), affirmed (1974), 3 O.R. (2d) at 539, 28 C.R.N.S. at 126, 17 C.C.C. (2d) at 480, 46 D.L.R. (3d) at 82 (C.A.), leave to appeal to S.C.C. refused (1974), 28 C.R.N.S. at 127 (note) (Ont. C.A.) . . . 26.5

Stivers, Re, 516 N.E. 2d 1066 (1987) . . . 12

Stoangi v. Law Society (Upper Canada) (1978), 22 O.R. (2d) 274, 93 D.L.R. (3d) 204 (H.C.) . . . 26.18

Stoangi v. Law Society (Upper Canada) (No. 2) (1979), 25 O.R. (2d) 257, 100 D.L.R. (3d) 639 (Div. Ct.) . . . 26.17, 26.18

Stone v. Law Society of Upper Canada (1979), 26 O.R. (2d) 166, 102 D.L.R. (3d) 176 (Div. Ct.) . . . 26.2

Stone v. Public Accountants Council (Ontario), [1972] 3 O.R. 801, 29 D.L.R. (3d) 537 (H.C.) . . . 26.11

Stout v. College of Pharmacy (Ontario) (1977), 15 O.R. (2d) 650, 76 D.L.R. (3d) 441 (C.A.) . . . 26.14

Strang v. Beal (1922), 23 O.W.N. 287 (H.C.) . . . 4.7

Stribbell v. Bhalla (1990), 73 O.R. (2d) 748, 42 C.P.C. (2d) 161 (H.C.) . . . 12

Stricklan v. Koella, 546 S.W. 2d 810 (Tenn. Ct. App., 1976) . . . 4.11

Strickland v. Washington, 104 S. Ct. 2052 (1984) . . . 7.6

Strobridge v. Strobridge (1992), 10 O.R. (3d) 540, 42 R.F.L. (3d) 154, 95 D.L.R. (4th) 503 (Gen. Div.) . . . 4.3

Stromberg v. Law Society (Saskatchewan), [1996] 3 W.W.R. 389, 36 Admin. L.R. (2d) 181, 139 Sask. R. 182, 132 D.L.R. (4th) 470 (Q.B.), additional reasons at [1996] 10 W.W.R. 737, 6 C.P.C. (4th) 157, 149 Sask. R. 226, 44 Admin. L.R. (2d) 65 (Q.B.) 26.4, 26.5

Stronghold Investments Ltd. v. Renkema, [1984] 3 W.W.R. 51, 51 B.C.L.R. 189, 4 C.C.L.I. 116, 7 D.L.R. (4th) 427 (S.C.) 24.6

Suchy v. Zurich Insurance Co. (1997), 43 B.C.L.R. (3d) 36, 101 B.C.A.C. 69, 164 W.A.C. 69, [1998] 6 W.W.R. 130 (B.C. C.A.) 5.10

Sue Carpenter, Re, 808 P. 2d 1341 (Kan., 1991) 6.1, 6.6

Sugg and Law Society of Upper Canada, Re, March 30, 1988 (unreported) 26.2

Sun Life Trust Co. v. Bond City Financing Ltd. (1997), 35 O.R. (3d) 83, 26 O.T.C. 200 (Gen. Div. [Commercial List]), additional reasons at (1997), 26 O.T.C. 207 (Gen. Div. [Commercial List]), affirmed (1997), 36 O.R. (3d) 758, 105 O.A.C. 255 (Div. Ct.), leave to appeal refused (March 10, 1998), Doc. CA M21773 (Ont. C.A.) 5.6, 5.10

Sutherland v. Pembroke Hospital (1973), 1 O.R. (2d) 438, 40 D.L.R. (3d) 526 (Div. Ct.) 26.11

Swinfen v. Chelmsford (Lord) (1860), 2 L.J. (N.S.) 406 . . . . 4.2

Sychuk and Law Society of Alberta, Re, [1999] L.S.D.D. 15 (Quicklaw) 26.22

Syndicat des employés de production du Québec & de l'Acadie v. Canada (Canadian Human Rights Commission), [1989] 2 S.C.R. 879, 89 C.L.L.C. 17,022, 11 C.H.r.R. D/1, (*sub nom.* Syndicat des employés de production du Qué. & de l'Acadie v. Comm. canadienne des droits de la personne) 100 N.R. 241 . . . . 26.11

Szarfer v. Chodos (1986), 54 O.R. (2d) 663, 36 C.C.L.T. 181, 27 D.L.R. (4th) 388 (H.C.), affirmed (1988), 66 O.R. (2d) 350, 54 D.L.R. (4th) 383 (C.A.) 3.2, 5.9

Szebelledy v. Constitution Insurance Co. of Can. (1985), 11 C.C.L.I. 140 (Ont. Dist. Ct.) 5.2

Szmuilowicz v. Ontario (Minister of Health) (1995), 24 O.R. (3d) 204, 125 D.L.R. (4th) 688, 82 O.A.C. 183 (Div. Ct.) 26.7

T.C. Theatre Corp. v. Warner Bros. Pictures, Inc., 113 F. Supp. 265 (S.D.N.Y., 1953) 5.6

Tan v. College of Physicians & Surgeons (Saskatchewan) (1985), 39 Sask. L.R. 152 (Q.B.) 26.19

Taylor v. Law Society (British Columbia) (1980), 116 D.L.R. (3d) 41 (B.C. S.C.) 26.13

Taylor v. Mackintosh, [1924] 1 W.W.R. 859, 33 B.C.R. 383, [1924] 1 D.L.R. 877 (S.C.), affirmed [1924] 3 W.W.R. 97, 34 B.C.R. 56, 42 C.C.C. 327, [1924] 3 D.L.R. 926 (C.A.) 12

Taylor v. Murphy (1980), 24 B.C.L.R. 198 (S.C.) 22.3

Taylor v. Taylor (1984), 61 N.B.R. (2d) 116, 43 R.F.L. (2d) 170, 158 A.P.R. 116 (Q.B.) 4.8

Taylor Estate v. Baribeau; Baribeau v. Jakob (1985), 51 O.R. (2d) 541, 4 C.P.C. (2d) 52, 35 M.V.R. 79, 12 O.A.C. 344, 21 D.L.R. (4th) 140 (Div. Ct.) 26.5

Telfer, Re, report adopted by Convocation, January 16, 1981 . . . . 26.8, 26.17

Temoin v. Stanley (1986), 12 C.P.C. (2d) 69 (Ont. Dist. Ct.), reversed in part on other grounds (1987), 7 W.D.C.P. 71 (Ont. H.C.) 4.6

Tencer v. Law Society of Upper Canada, Ont. Div. Ct., July 29, 1985 (unreported) 26.19

Tencer (No. 1), Re, report adopted by Convocation, September 18, 1981 . . . . 26.17

Terrace Developments Ltd. v. Terry, Ont. Ct., Doc. No. 23782/87, May 27, 1992 (unreported) 26.5

Thompson v. Lambton (Board of Education), [1972] 3 O.R. 889, 30 D.L.R. (3d) 32 (H.C.) 26.9

Thomson v. Gough (1977), 17 O.R. (2d) 420, 5 C.P.C. 43, 80 D.L.R. (3d) 598 (H.C.) 4.8

Thomson v. Wishart (1910), 16 C.C.C. 446, 13 W.L.R. 445, 19 Man. R. 340 (C.A.) 12

Thomson Newspapers Ltd. v. Canada (Director of Investigatin & Research), [1990] 1 S.C.R. 425, 72 O.R. (2d) 415 (note), 76 C.R. (3d) 129, 54 C.C.C. (3d) 417, 29 C.P.R. (3d) 97, 39 O.A.C. 161, 106 N.R. 161, 47 C.R.R. 1, 67 D.L.R. (4th) 161 . . . . 26.2, 26.4, 26.15

Thorson v. Jones, [1973] 4 W.W.R. 437, 38 D.L.R. (3d) 312 (B.C. S.C.) 3.2

Threader v. Canada (Treasury Board), [1987] 1 F.C. 41, 68 N.R. 143 (C.A.) 26.12

Toft v. Ketchum, 18 N.J. 280, 113 A. 2d 671, cert. denied 350 U.S. 887 (1955) 26.4

Tombling v. Universal Bulb Co., [1951] 2 T.L.R. 289, [1951] W.N. 247 (C.A.) 4.13

Toronto Dominion Bank v. Leigh Instruments Ltd. (Trustee of) (1997), 32 O.R. (3d) 575 (Ont. Gen. Div. [Commercial List]) 20.1

Trace v. Council of the Institute of Chartered Accountants of Alta. See Trace v. Institute of Chartered Accountants (Alberta)

Trace v. Institute of Chartered Accountants (Alberta) (1988), [1989] 2 W.W.R. 86, 63 Alta. L.R. (2d) 53, 91 A.R. 241, (*sub nom.* Trace v. Council of the Institute of Chartered Accountants) 54 D.L.R. (4th) 82 (C.A.) 26.7, 26.8

Trace v. Institute of Chartered Accountants (Alta.). See Trace v. Institute of Chartered Accountants (Alberta)

Trace v. Institute of Chartered Accountants (Council). See Trace v. Institute of Chartered Accountants (Alberta)

Tracy v. Atkins (1977), 83 D.L.R. (3d) 46 (B.C. S.C.), affirmed (1979), 16 B.C.L.R. 223, 11 C.C.L.T. 57, 105 D.L.R. (3d) 632 (C.A.) 17.4, 22.4, 24.6, 25.3

Transamerica Life Insurance Co. of Canada v. Seward (1997), 33 O.R. (3d) 604 (Gen. Div.) 4.11.1

Trapp, re, order of Convocation, May 23, 1996 . . . . 26.17

Trimm v. Durham Regional Police Force, [1987] 2 S.C.R. 582, 29 Admin. L.R. 106, 37 C.C.C. (3d) 120, 32 C.R.R. 244, 81 N.R. 197, 24 O.A.C. 357, 45 D.L.R. (4th) 276 . . . . . 26.2

Trizec Properties Ltd. v. Husky Oil Ltd. (1997), 200 A.R. 48, 146 W.A.C. 48, (*sub nom. Trizec Properties Ltd. v. Husky Oil Operations, Ltd.*) 148 D.L.R. (4th) 300 (C.A.), additional reasons at (August 19, 1997), Doc. Calgary Appeal 97-176951 (Alta. C.A.) 5.6

Trumbley v. Metropolitan Toronto Police Force, [1987] 2 S.C.R. 577, (*sub nom.* Trumbley v. Fleming) 29 Admin. L.R. 100, 37 C.C.C. (3d) 118, 32 C.R.R. (3d) 118, (*sub nom.* Trumbley v. Toronto Police Force) 81 N.R. 212, 24 O.A.C. 372, 45 D.L.R. (4th) 318 . . . . . 26.2

Trusts & Guarantee Co. v. Hart (1902), 32 S.C.R. 553 . . . . . 22.3

Tukiar v. R. (1934), 52 Commonwealth L.R. 335 . . . . . 7.1

Tunney v. Ohio, 273 U.S. 510, 47 S. Ct. 437 (1927) 26.11

Turner v. Mailhot (1985), 50 O.R. (2d) 561, 28 B.L.R. 222 (H.C.) 5.13

Tweten v. Nichols, 61 B.C.L.R. 225, [1985] 3 W.W.R. 758 (S.C.) 12

Tyler v. Minister of National Revenue (1990), [1991] 2 F.C. 68, 41 F.T.R. 80 (note), 41 F.T.R. 240 (note), [1991] 1 C.T.C. 13, 91 D.T.C. 5022, 120 N.R. 140 (*sub nom.* Tyler v. Canada (Minister of National Revenue)) 4 C.R.R. (2d) 348 (C.A.) 26.4

United States v. Amaral, 488 F.2d 1148 (9th Cir. 1973) 4.12

United States v. Augurs, 427 U.S. 97 (1976) 6.4

United States v. Bagley, 105 S. Ct. 3375 (1985) 6.4

United States v. Blitstein, 626 F. 2d 774 (10th Cir., 1980), cert. denied 449 U.S. 1102, 101 S. Ct. 898 (1981) . . . . . 25.5(a)

United States v. Goodwin, 457 U.S. 368 (1982) 6.5

United States v. Henkel, 799 F. 2d 369 (7th Cir., 1986) 7.5

United States v. Kelly, 543 F. Supp. 1303 (Mass., 1982) 6.6

United States v. Klubock, 639 F. Supp. 117 (1986), affirmed 832 F. 2d 649 (1st Cir., 1987) 6.6

United States v. Schuler, 813 F. 2d 278 (9th Cir., 1987) 6.6

United States v. Socony-Vacuum Oil Co., 310 U.S. 150 (U.S. S. Ct., 1940) 6.6

United States v. Thoreen, 653 F. 2d 1332 (9th Cir., 1981), cert. denied 455 U.S. 938 (U.S. S. Ct., 1982) 4.14

United States v. Wade, 388 U.S. 218 (1967) 7.1

United States v. Young, 470 U.S. 1 (1985) 6.6

United States, ex rel. Wilcox v. Johnson, 555 F. 2d 115 (3rd Cir., 1977) 7.5

United States Steel Corp. v. United States, 569 F. Supp. 870, vacated on other grounds 578 F. Supp. 415 . . . . . 20.1

United States Steel Corp. v. United States, 730 F. 2d 1465 (1984) 20.1

United States Surgical Corp. v. Downs Surgical Canada Ltd. (1982), 68 C.P.R. (2d) 239, 141 D.L.R. (3d) 157 (Fed. T.D.) 5.10

Upjohn v. United States, 449 U.S. 383, 101 S. Ct. 677 (1981) 3.2

Usipuik v. Jensen, Mitchell & Co., [1986] 5 W.W.R. 41, 3 B.C.L.R. (2d) 283, 12 C.P.C. (2d) 74 (S.C.), additional reasons at, 7 B.C.L.R. (2d) 58, [1987] 1 W.W.R. 120, 15 C.P.C. (2d) 251 (S.C.) 12

V., Re, [1924] 3 W.W.R. 552, 20 Alta. L.R. 585, [1924] 4 D.L.R. 852 (C.A.) 26.22

Vadeko International Inc. v. Philosophe (1990), 1 O.R. (3d) 87 (Gen. Div.) 5.13

Vakauta v. Kelly (1989), 87 A.L.R. 633 .... 2.14

Valente v. General Dental Council (1990), 123 N.R. 311 (P.C.) 26.19

Van Haastrecht v. Dunbar (1991), 1 C.P.C. (3d) 57 (Ont. Gen. Div.) 5.10

Vanular, Re, report adopted by Convocation, January 28, 1993 .... 26.17

Vegetable Kingdom Inc. v. Katzen, 653 F. Supp. 917 (N.D.N.Y., 1987) 5.5, 20.5

Venczel v. Assn. of Architects (Ontario) (1989), 74 O.R. (2d) 755, 42 C.L.R. 8, 45 Admin. L.R. 288, 41 O.A.C. 50 (Div. Ct.) 26.18

Vernon v. Bosley No. 2, [1997] 1 All E.R. 614 (C.A.) 4.6

Vernon v. Oliver (1885), 11 S.C.R. 156 .... 4.23

Vespra (Township) v. Ontario (Municipal Board) (1983), 43 O.R. (2d) 680, 7 Admin. L.R. 178, 23 M.P.L.R. 239 (*sub nom.* Vespra v. Barrie), 15 O.M.B.R. 407, 2 D.L.R. (4th) 303 (Div. Ct.) 26.11

Von Richter v. Law Society (New Brunswick) (1991), 116 N.B.R. (2d) 325, 293 A.P.R. 325 (Q.B.) 26.4

Voratovic v. Law Society (Upper Canada) (1978), 20 O.R. (2d) 214, 87 D.L.R. (3d) 140 (H.C.) 26.4

Voutsis v. College of Physicians & Surgeons (Saskatchewan) (1987), 34 C.C.C. (3d) 560, 57 Sask. R. 60, 41 D.L.R. (4th) 378 (Q.B.) 26.5

Vulcan Metals Co. v. Simmons Manufacturing Co., 248 F. 2d 853 (2nd Cir., 1918) 15

W., Re (1979), 27 O.R. (2d) 314, 13 R.F.L. (2d) 381 (Prov. Ct.) 4.3

W.D. Latimer Co. v. Bray (1974), 6 O.R. (2d) 129, 52 D.L.R. (3d) 161 (C.A.) 26.1, 26.11

Wallersteiner v. Moir (No. 2), [1975] Q.B. 373, [1975] 1 All E.R. 849 (C.A.) 12

Warhaftig, Re, 106 N.J. 529, 524 A. 2d 398 (1987) 26.17

Waschuk v. Waschuk, 14 W.W.R. 169, [1955] 1 D.L.R. 686 (Sask. C.A.) 4.19

Wasylyshen v. Law Society (Saskatchewan) (1985), 39 Sask. R. 187 (C.A.) 26.11

Wasylyshen v. Law Society (Saskatchewan), [1987] 3 W.W.R. 289, 53 Sask. R. 232, 36 D.L.R. (4th) 214 (C.A.), leave to appeal to S.C.C. refused [1987] 5 W.W.R. lxiii (note), 80 N.R. 126 (note), 55 Sask. R. 240 (note), 36 D.L.R. (4th) 214 (note) (S.C.C.) 26.11

Watson v. Trace Estate (July 22, 1994), Doc. Barrie G11274 (Ont. Gen. Div.) 5.10

Weare, Re, [1893] 2 Q.B. 439 (C.A.) 25.10, 26.8

Weaver v. United Mine Workers, 492 F. 2d 580 (D.C. Cir., 1973) 5.13

Weisman, re, report to Convocation, January 27, 1997 .... 26.22

Wellman v. General Crane Industries Ltd. (1986), 20 O.A.C. 384 (C.A.) 3.2

Wernikowski v. Kirkland, Murphy & Ain, [1999] O.J. 4812 (C.A.) 4.18

Westinghouse Electric Corp. v. Kerr-McGee Corp., 580 F. 2d 1311 (7th Cir.), cert. denied 439 U.S. 955 (1978) 5.5

Weston v. Central Criminal Courts' Administrator, [1976] 2 All E.R. 875, [1977] Q.B. 32 (C.A.) 27.5

Whittingham v. Crease & Co., [1978] 5 W.W.R. 45, 3 E.T.R. 97, 6 C.C.L.T. 1, 88 D.L.R. (3d) 353 (B.C. S.C.) 18.3

Whyte and Provincial Medical Board (Discipline Committee), Re (1980), 113 D.L.R. (3d) 408 (N.S. T.D.) 26.5

Wilder v. Ontario Securities Commission (2000), 47 O.R. (3d) 361 (Div. Ct.) 27.2

Wilkinson v. Wilkinson (1962), [1963] P. 1, [1962] 1 All E.R. 922 (C.A.) 27.5

Willis, Re, 215 S.E. 2d 771, appeal dismissed (*sub nom.* Willis v. North Carolina State Board of Law Examiners), 430 U.S. 976 (1975) 23.3

Willis v. Barron, [1902] A.C. 271 (H.L.) 18.2

Willy v. Coastal Corp., 647 F. Supp. 116 (S.D. Tex., 1986) 20.1

Wilson, Re, 81 N.J. 451, 409 A. 2d 1153 (1979) 26.17, 26.22

Wilson v. British Columbia (Medical Services Commission) (1988), 30 B.C.L.R. (2d) 1, 34 Admin. L.R. 235, [1989] 2 W.W.R. 1, 41 C.R.R. 276, 53 D.L.R. (4th) 171 (C.A.), leave to appeal to S.C.C. refused [1989] 3 W.W.R. lxxi (note), 36 B.C.L.R. (2d) xxxvii (note), 36 Admin. L.R. xl (note), 92 N.R. 400 (note) (S.C.C.) 26.2

Wilson v. Law Society (British Columbia) (1986), 9 B.C.L.R. (2d) 260, 33 D.L.R. (4th) 572 (C.A.) 26.7, 27.5

Wilson v. Law Society (British Columbia) (No. 2) (1975), 64 D.L.R. (3d) 512 (B.C. S.C.) 26.13

Wilson v. People, 743 P. 2d 415 (Colo., 1987) 6.6

Wilson v. Wilson (1875), 22 Gr. 39 (Ch. D.) 18.1

Wilson P. Abraham Construction Corp. v. Armco Steel Corp., 559 F. 2d 250 (5th Circ., 1977) 5.7

Winter v. Phillips, 56 Alta. L.R. (2d) 382 (*sub nom.* Winter Art Glass Studio Inc. v. Phillips), [1988] 2 W.W.R. 458, 85 A.R. 161, 47 D.L.R. (4th) 309 (Q.B.) 5.6

Withrow v. Larkin, 421 U.S. 35, 95 S. Ct. 1456 (1975) 26.12

Witten, Vogel, Binder & Lyons v. Leung (1983), 25 Alta. L.R. (2d) 257, 46 A.R. 53, 148 D.L.R. (3d) 418 (Q.B.) 17.5

Wong v. Fong, 593 P. 2d 386 (1979) 5.4

Wong v. Thomson, Rogers, [1994] O.J. 1318 (C.A.) 4.18

Wong (Edward) Finance Co. v. Johnson Stokes & Master, [1984] 2 W.L.R. 36, [1984] A.C. 296 (P.C.) 17.5

Wood (No. 2), Re, 489 N.E. 2d 1189 (Ind., 1986) 25.13

World Wide Treasure Adventures Inc. v. Trivia Games Inc. (1987), 16 B.C.L.R. (2d) 135 (S.C.) 27.5

Worrell, Re (1969), [1970] 1 O.R. 184, 8 D.L.R. (3d) 36 (Surr. Ct.) 18.1

Worsley Estate v. Lichong (*sub nom.* Worsley v. Lichong) (1994), 17 O.R. (3d) 615 (Gen. Div.) 4.22

Wright v. Carter, [1903] 1 Ch. 27 (C.A.) 22.3

Wright v. Hearson, [1916] W.N. 216 (D.C.) 4.14

Wyle v. R.J. Reynolds Industries, Inc., 709 F. 2d 585 (9th Cir.) 14

X., Re (1920), 16 Alta. L.R. 542 (T.D.) 26.7

Y. v. Yukon Medical Council, [1998] Y.J. 126 .... 26.9

Yablonski v. United Mine Workers, 448 F. 2d 1175, cert. denied 406 U.S. 906, 92 S. Ct. 1609 (1972) 5.13, 22.4

York Investments Ltd. v. Winnipeg (City). See Princess Auto & Machinery Ltd. v. Winnipeg (City)

Young v. Young (1990), 50 B.C.L.R. (2d) 1, 29 R.F.L. (3d) 113, 75 D.L.R. (4th) 46 (C.A.), leave to appeal to S.C.C. granted (1991), 54 B.C.L.R. (2d) xxxiv (note), 135 N.R. 76 (note), 79 D.L.R. (4th) vi (note) (S.C.C.) 27.5

Zauderer v. Office of Disciplinary Counsel of the Supreme Court of Ohio, 471 U.S. 626 (1985) 10, 11

Zimmerman, Re, 81 Bankr. 296 (1987) 20.5

115 Place Co-operative Housing Association v. Burke (1994), 116 D.L.R. (4th) 657, 94 B.C.L.R. (2d) 60, [1994] 10 W.W.R. 20, 48 B.C.A.C. 181, 78 W.A.C. 181, (*sub nom.* 115 Place Co-operative Housing Assn. v. Burke, Tomchenko, Duprat) (C.A.) 17.5

2747-3174 Québec Inc. c. Québec (Régie des permis d'alcool), [1994] R.J.Q. 2440, 65 Q.A.C. 245, 122 D.L.R. (4th) 553 (C.A.), leave to appeal allowed (1995), (*sub nom.* 2747-3174 Québec Inc. v. Régie des permis d'alcool du Québec) 189 N.R. 160n (S.C.C.), reversed [1996] 3 S.C.R. 919, (*sub nom.* 2747-3174 Québec Inc. v. Québec (Régie des permis d'alcool du Québec)) 205 N.R. 1, 42 Admin. L.R. (2d) 1, 140 D.L.R. (4th) 577 .... 26.18

2747-3174 Québec Inc. v. Québec (Régie des permis d'alcool du Québec. See 2747-3174 Québec Inc. c. Québec (Régie des permis d'alcool)

2747-3174 Québec Inc. v. Régie des permis d'alcool du Québec. See 2747-3174 Québec Inc. c. Québec (Régie des permis d'alcool)

640612 Ont. Inc. v. 253547 Ont. Ltd. (1987), 26 C.P.C. (2d) 93 (Ont. Master) .... 4.22(a)

755568 Ontario Ltd. v. Linchris Homes Ltd. (1990), 1 O.R. (3d) 649, 46 C.P.C. (2d) 157 (Gen. Div.) 26.15

781332 Ontario Inc. v. Mortgage Insurance Co. of Canada (1991), 5 O.R. (3d) 248, 3 C.P.C. (3d) 33 (Gen. Div.) 5.2, 5.10

931473 Ontario Ltd. v. Coldwell Banker Canada Inc. (1992), 5 C.P.C. (3d) 271 (Ont. Gen. Div.) 4.22

Introduction

> If you want to take dough from a murderer for helping him beat the rap you must be admitted to the bar.[1]

Let it be said at the beginning that in the eyes of many members of the public today the legal profession is a self-interested and non-accountable elite that is undeserving of the privilege of self-government.

This professional image persists in spite of many innovations for which the organized bar seldom claims or receives credit — innovations such as legal aid programmes, funded and administered largely by lawyers; clinic funding programmes, lawyer referral services, and other services designed to improve the accessibility and quality of legal services, especially for those unable to afford to retain lawyers privately; mandatory certification by public accountants of lawyers' financial statements as a condition of annual membership renewal; full-time staffs of lawyers, accountants, and investigators who inquire into and prosecute allegations of professional misconduct; public discipline hearings; mandatory errors and omissions insurance coverage (with minimum coverage levels that in Ontario were raised from $50,000 to $1,000,000 during the 1980's); and lawyers' funds for client compensation, which were first established in Alberta in 1939 and in Ontario in 1954, which are fully funded by the profession, and which reimburse claimants who sustain financial losses as a result of lawyers' dishonesty.[2]

There are sound reasons, having to do largely with the independence of the bar, that it is still fundamentally important that the legal profession retain

---

1 This quotation from *In the Best Families* by Rex Stout (Boston: G. K. Hall & Co., 1991, first published 1950) introduces William H. Simon's "The Ideology of Advocacy: Procedural Justice and Professional Ethics" [1978] Wisconsin L.R. 29.

2 See Kenneth E. Howie, "Lawyers Under Fire", Law Society of Upper Canada Gazette, vol. 25, no. 2 (June, 1991), pp. 164-171. The advances of the last quarter century throughout Canada and the United States are vividly illustrated by reading Murray Teigh Bloom's book *The Trouble With Lawyers* (New York: Simon & Schuster, 1969), which depicts a profession indifferent to victims of negligence and dishonesty, without lawyers' funds for client compensation or mandatory professional liability insurance, and with a discipline process that was secretive, casual and ineffective.

the right of self-government.[3] That right is jeopardized by the public's increasingly antagonistic attitude toward lawyers. Most people share Henry Adams' disheartening conclusion that "no priesthood ever reforms itself."[4]

The reasons for lawyers' unfavourable image are complex. To some extent it is a problem shared by professions generally in an age characterized by a sceptical public that has come to embrace George Bernard Shaw's epigram that "every profession is a conspiracy against the laity."[5] It is undoubtedly true that lawyers, who defend others ably, have done a poor job of defending themselves.[6]

A primary reason for this negative image has to do with the public's perception of lawyers' ethics. More than ever before, the qualities associated with lawyers include (among more becoming traits) a preoccupation with money; egocentricity; attitudes variously described as pompous, patronizing, condescending and arrogant; and tendencies to turn everything into a debate to be won, to complicate problems, to make more work and generate higher fees, and to distort or conceal the truth by resorting to technicalities (or worse) in the interest of winning.[7] In the estimation of many, lawyers are far more interested in their clients' interests (and their own) than in the welfare of society. In a decision of the Supreme Court of Canada released in late 1990, Justice Cory wrote of "lawyers soldiering on in the cause of justice."[8] In the view of many members of the public, the soldiers are mercenaries rather than patriots.

I use the term "lawyers' ethics" because it is more comprehensive than either "professional responsibility" or even "legal ethics." For many lawyers, "professional responsibility" has come to connote a rather narrow field of black letter law, whereas "legal ethics" is concerned primarily with lawyers' role morality.[9] Canadian writing in both fields, though particularly the former, has been dominated by a consideration of rules of professional conduct. But rules of professional conduct have only a limited role to play in enhancing public confidence in the profession. The influence that such rules have on

3 These reasons are explored in chapter 27.

4 Quoted by Bloom, *supra*, note 2, p. 351.

5 Quoted by Jacques Barzun in "The Professions Under Siege", Law Society of Upper Canada Gazette, vol. 12, no. 4 (December, 1978), p. 344 at 346.

6 Howie, *supra*, note 2, p. 164.

7 See George A. Reimer, *Ethics: The DRs and Beyond* (Marina Del Ray, California: Josephson Institute of Ethics, 1992), p. 3.

8 *MacDonald Estate v. Martin*, [1990] 3 S.C.R. 1235 at 1270.

9 See Susan Wolf, "Ethics, Legal Ethics, and the Ethics of Law" in David Luban (ed.), *The Good Lawyer: Lawyers' Roles and Lawyers' Ethics* (Totowa, New Jersey: Rowan & Allenhead, 1983), p. 38; Gerald J. Postema, "Self-Image, Integrity, & Professional Responsibility" in the same volume, p. 286 at 310; David Luban, "Calming the Hearse Horse: A Philosophical Research Program for Legal Ethics" (1981) 40 Maryland L.R. 451; and W. Brent Cotter, *Professional Responsibility Instruction in Canada: A Coordinated Curriculum for Legal Education* (Montreal: Conceptcom, 1992), pp. I-6 to I-7.

lawyers' attitudes and behaviour, moreover, is slight. Little real progress is likely to be achieved by continually rewriting those rules.[10]

What is needed in addition to rules of professional conduct is a searching and methodical re-examination by lawyers of their roles in a rapidly changing society.[11] Canadian rules of professional conduct are based for the most part on the traditional model of the sole practitioner who has competent, individual, adult clients in a general practice. To a considerable extent, this traditional model has been overtaken as a result of the great diversity of clients, lawyers, and contexts in which legal services are provided. Corporate clients, government agencies, clients with disabilities, and the poor are unlike the traditional paradigm and are unlike one another. There are few similarities in the practices of high technology law specialists in large Bay Street law firms, lawyers who practise before regulatory and administrative tribunals, storefront general practitioners, lawyers employed by clinics designed to serve low income individuals, lawyers employed by government agencies, lawyers who defend persons charged with serious crimes, lawyers who represent public or special interest groups, lawyers who rub shoulders with influential politicians and sit in on behalf of wealthy corporations at drafting sessions of legislative committees, and lawyers who draft wills, administer estates, and convey property in county towns. The legal profession today is much more pluralistic and heterogenous than ever before.[12]

Indeed, we no longer have a single, unified, legal profession; we have many different subprofessions.[13] For this reason, this text is organized in such a way that the ethical problems of lawyers practising in particular fields, in non-traditional ways, and for non-traditional clients, are dealt with separately. The considerations relevant to whether lawyers have conflicts of interest that may be waived by informed client consent are different if the lawyers are negotiating partnership agreements rather than litigating partnership disputes. They are different again if the lawyers are leaving employment with government agencies to resume private practice in related fields, or if they are acting in class actions for clients whom they have never met. The conflict

---

10 See Stephen Toulmin, "Ethics and Equity: The Tyranny of Principles", Law Society of Upper Canada Gazette, vol. 15, no. 3 (September, 1981), p. 240, particularly at p. 244; Postema, *ibid.*, p. 310; Reed Elizabeth Loder, "Tighter Rules of Professional Conduct: Saltwater for Thirst" (1987-88) 1 Georgetown Journal of Legal Ethics 311 at 333; and R.D. Gibbons, Review of *Professional Conduct for Canadian Lawyers* by B.G. Smith (1990) 69 Can. Bar R. 385 at 387.

11 See Harlan Fiske Stone, "The Public Influence of the Bar" (1934-35) 48 Harvard L.R. 1 at 10; Gibbons, *ibid.*, p. 387.

12 See Charles Wolfram, *Modern Legal Ethics* (St. Paul, Minnesota: West, 1986), pp. 147-148; and Geoffrey C. Hazard, Jr., "Has the Practice the Common Identity to Create a Program of Development?", National Law Journal (November 9, 1992), pp. 15-16.

13 See H.W. Arthurs, "Law, Society and The Law Society", a paper delivered to the Law Society of Upper Canada's Strategic Planning Conference, September 25, 1992, published in Osgoode Hall Law School *Continuum*, vol. 19, no. 1, p. 26 at 26-27 (1993).

of interest problems of criminal defence lawyers who may have to cross-examine former clients are different from those of developers' lawyers who have invested in their clients' projects.

The text is divided into four parts. The first part deals with ethical problems primarily of interest to lawyers who practise before courts and tribunals (though chapters 1, 3 and 8, which deal with the public image of lawyers, confidentiality, and civility respectively are relevant also to lawyers who have not donned their gowns since the day they were called to the bar); the second part deals with such access to justice issues as legal aid, advertising, solicitation, contingency fees, and relations with the media; the third part deals with issues primarily of interest to lawyers who practise in fields that do not usually take them to court (though, again, chapters 14, 15, and 16, which deal with counselling, negotiating, and mediating respectively are relevant to all lawyers); and the final part deals with the regulation of the profession. Separate chapters on conflicts of interest are included in the first and third parts, and the particular conflict of interest problems encountered by lawyers practising in the fields of criminal defence, mediation, real estate, estates, corporate law, and in government service are addressed in chapters 7, 16, 17, 18, 20, and 21 respectively.

It does not follow from the proposition that lawyers' ethics should be considered more broadly than has traditionally been the case in Canada that rules of professional conduct should be neglected in a study of lawyers' ethics. The widespread adoption by law societies of rules of professional conduct is one of the most important developments in the field in the last quarter century. Relevant rules of professional conduct are reviewed and discussed.

All Canadian jurisdictions have adopted rules of professional conduct that are influenced, though to varying degrees, by the Canadian Bar Association's Code of Professional Conduct (C.B.A. Code). The Code was adopted by the Canadian Bar Association's National Council in 1974, and an amended version was adopted by the same body in 1987. In this text, provisions of the 1987 Code (abbreviated as "C.B.A. Code" in each case) have been cited in footnotes wherever relevant, as have provisions of the Rules of Professional Conduct of the Law Society of Upper Canada. Provisions of the rules of professional conduct of other jurisdictions have been cited where they differ significantly from the provisions of the C.B.A. Code. The rules of professional conduct of each jurisdiction have been abbreviated as "Alta. rule", "B.C. rule", etc. References abbreviated as "Que. rule" are references to the code of ethics of advocates of the Barreau du Quebec.

This text makes much more extensive use of American materials than is customary. In the United States the ethics of lawyers has become a subject of intense interest during the last 25 years. In his 1975 book *Lawyers' Ethics in an Adversary System*[14] and in his earlier articles on which it was based[15] Mon-

14 (New York: Bobbs-Merrill, 1975).

15 "Professional Responsibility of the Criminal Defense Lawyer: The Three Hardest Ques-

roe Freedman argued that the duties of loyalty and confidentiality owed to clients in the adversary system may require criminal defence counsel to discredit witnesses they know to be telling the truth, to give clients legal advice when they have reason to believe that the knowledge imparted will tempt their clients to commit perjury, and even in some circumstances to lead testimony they know is false.

Not all of Freedman's controversial conclusions have been widely accepted, but his influence has nevertheless been considerable. He emphasized, perhaps for the first time, the fundamental incompatibility of the various professional duties that are enshrined in rules of professional conduct, and he drew some stark conclusions.[16]

Freedman stimulated debate about the profession's ethics primarily among lawyers, law teachers and law students. At about the same time, Watergate galvanized opinion about the ethics of lawyers among the American public generally. Of the 20 or more central figures in the Watergate scandal all but three[17] were lawyers. Many served jail terms for burglary, obstruction of justice, or perjury, and were disbarred. (Richard Nixon resigned from the California bar under threat of disbarment). The resulting public disdain for the Watergate lawyers' contempt for the law and for ethical standards was tempered somewhat by admiration for the special prosecutors and judges who exposed their corruption.[18]

Americans' heightened interest in the ethics of lawyers has found expression in a rich body of literature. Charles Wolfram's *Modern Legal Ethics*[19] is probably the most comprehensive and useful treatise on the subject ever published anywhere, and is only one of many published over the last 25 years. The Georgetown Journal of Legal Ethics, which has been published quarterly since 1987, is devoted exclusively to issues of the ethics of lawyers. Geoffrey C. Hazard, Jr., a professor at Yale Law School and a prolific writer in the field, and Lawrence A. Dubin, a professor at the University of Detroit School of Law, alternate as bi-weekly columnists on ethical issues for the National Law Journal. Philosophical works such as *The Good Lawyer: Lawyers' Roles and Lawyers' Ethics*[20] and *Lawyers and Justice: An Ethical Study*[21] have

---

tions" (1966) 64 Michigan L.R. 1469; and "Professional Responsibility of the Civil Practitioner: Teaching Legal Ethics in the Contracts Course" (1969) 21 Journal of Legal Education 569. See also Monroe H. Freedman, *Understanding Lawyers' Ethics* (New York: Matthew Bender & Co., 1990).

16 See Luban, *supra*, note 9, p. 10.

17 H.R. Haldeman, Jeb Stuart Magruder and Dwight Chapin were not lawyers.

18 See Martin Garbus and Joel Seligman, "Sanctions and Disbarment: They Sit in Judgment" in Ralph Nader and Mark Green (eds.), *Verdicts on Lawyers* (New York: Thomas Y. Crowell Co., 1976), p. 47; David Riley, "The Mystique of Lawyers" in the same volume, p. 81; Gerry Spence, *With Justice for None* (New York: Random House, 1989), p. 29; and Daniel Novak, "Watergate's Legacy to the Legal Profession", National Law Journal, May 16, 1994, p. A-19.

19 *Supra*, note 12.

20 *Supra*, note 9.

explored in depth themes and issues that were rarely even identified until the 1980's.

In Canada, our literature is embarrassingly sparse by comparison.[22] At least to the extent that it is fair to gauge such matters by reference to scholarly and professional works, the Americans in this field are at least a decade ahead of us. I have accordingly swallowed my anti-continentalism and cited American sources liberally.

One of my purposes in writing this text is to try to contribute in some small way to a critical examination by the profession of the reasons for the deterioration of public confidence in lawyers. I hope that it will be read as well as referred to. It will be kept current with supplements annually. Comments, criticisms, and information about developments in the field from across the country would be greatly appreciated.

Gavin MacKenzie
Unionville, Ontario
May 12, 1993

---

21 David Luban, *Lawyers and Justice: An Ethical Study* (Princeton, New Jersey: Princeton University Press, 1988).

22 The only full length treatises on the subject are Mark Orkin, *Legal Ethics: A Study of Professional Conduct* (Toronto: Cartwright and Sons, 1957) and Beverley G. Smith, *Professional Conduct for Canadian Lawyers* (Toronto: Butterworths, 1989). Articles in the field have appeared in publications that include the Law Society of British Columbia's The Advocate and the Law Society of Upper Canada's Gazette.

PART I

IN COURT

1

Lawyers and Ethics

> Lawyers stride across our social landscape with one hand toward the sky and the other in the gutter.[1]

1.1 THE PUBLIC PERCEPTION OF LAWYERS

The late William Howland, a former Chief Justice of Ontario, said in 1991 that members of the legal profession do not expect to be the subject of praise and are seldom disappointed.[2] Lawyers are in all likelihood the objects of more stinging and unrelenting criticism than are members of any other profession.

Lawyers themselves provide much of the material. Much of the criticism is deserved, and we will examine at least some of the reasons for it. But a balanced account of the public perception of lawyers requires reference to the strange ambivalence that characterizes it.

Even among their harshest critics lawyers, paradoxically, are often envied and, at least for some of their qualities, are respected and even admired. Studies of various professional groups consistently have found that the legal profession ranks among the highest in prestige and status. Many of the profession's critics would be delighted if their children were admitted to law school.[3]

Many of the critics also acknowledge that for all their faults most lawyers are intelligent, logical, and disciplined. Many non-lawyers wish that they could be calm, confident, effectual, rational, and dispassionate even in the

---

1 David Riley, "The Mystique of Lawyers" in Ralph Nader and Mark Green (eds.), *Verdicts on Lawyers* (New York: Thomas Y. Crowell Co., 1976), p. 80 at 93.

2 William Howland, "Reply to a Toast to the Honorees at the Order of Ontario Dinner", Law Society of Upper Canada Gazette, vol. 25, no. 2 (June, 1991), p. 77.

3 Charles Wolfram, *Modern Legal Ethics* (St. Paul, Minnesota: West, 1986) notes that a Roper poll of parents' preferences for children's future careers ranked law (with medicine and teaching) among the first three. Wolfram also draws attention to a social science researcher's survey of the prestige of professions that also ranked lawyers (with university professors and physicians) among the first three.

midst of angry confrontations. Lawyers' education and experience provide unparalleled training in the development of each of these qualities. A good legal education and the practice of law develop articulateness, scepticism, ability to reason, independence of mind, and other intellectual virtues that are of value to clients and to society. Grace under pressure, and the ability to strike a balance between detachment and commitment, are attributes of every good lawyer.[4]

Lawyers are often admired also for their industry. Daniel Webster said that a great lawyer must first become a great drudge.[5] Judge Edward Abbott Parry included "industry" among his "seven lamps of advocacy", and wrote that "the first task of the advocate is to learn to labour and to wait."[6] Most lawyers follow this advice.

The working conditions in which young lawyers have logged long hours have not always been ideal. Many years ago the novelist Louis Auchincloss served as an associate at a leading New York firm long enough to finally earn his own private office, a closet with a tiny window facing into a dark air shaft. A more junior associate who was new to the firm idly asked him whether he often worked at night. "I don't know," Auchincloss answered.[6.1]

Hard work can become addictive. A leading American counsel, Prew Savoy, once argued a case in the Supreme Court while he was in the last stages of lung cancer. He had to fortify himself for the oral argument with blood transfusions. He died within 36 hours. He wanted so badly to work on his case that he argued it on his second last day on earth.[7]

The public's ambivalence toward lawyers is especially marked if we compare to the derision commonly directed toward the profession generally the praise lavished upon individual lawyers. The author of a 1989 bestseller acknowledged the contribution of his lawyer, whom he described as "a man of high principle, great compassion, and profound intelligence, who has elevated the practice of law to the level of moral statement."[8] Not even its most

---

4 See Mark H. McCormack, *The Terrible Truth About Lawyers: What Every Business Person Needs To Know* (London: William Collins and Sons, 1987), pp. 16-17 and 227-228; "A Plague of Lawyers", *The Economist* (August 10, 1991); and Riley, *supra*, note 1, p. 89.

5 Quoted in Law Society of Upper Canada Gazette, vol. 25, no. 2 (June, 1991), p. 222.

6 Edward Abbott Parry, *The Seven Lamps of Advocacy* (New York: Books for Libraries Press, 1923), p. 37.

6.1 Sol M. Linowitz and Martin Mayer, *The Betrayed Profession* (New York: MacMillan, 1994), p. 98.

7 Prew Savoy argued *Soriano v. United States*, 352 U.S. 270, on December 5, 1956. The story of his extraordinary devotion to his case is recounted by one of the judges who presided, Justice William O. Douglas, in the second volume of his memoirs, *The Court Years, 1939-1975* (New York: Random House, 1980), p. 181.

8 Joe McGinniss, *Blind Faith* (New York: Putnam, 1989), p. iv.

avid champions would speak of the profession as a whole in such glowing terms. "Is it not remarkable," Trollope asked rhetorically, "that the common repute we give to lawyers in general is exactly opposite to that which each man gives to his own lawyer in particular?"[9]

There are many possible explanations for this ambivalence. One partial explanation, espoused by John Willis, is that the public's expectations of lawyers generally are different from their expectations of their own lawyers. At least when they are out to get something to which they are not entitled, Willis claimed, clients prefer lawyers "with just a touch of the scoundrel in them."[10]

Another explanation for public ambivalence about lawyers is that the public is not always well-informed about lawyers' work. Portrayals of lawyers in the media typically depict them as either larger-than-life heroes who advise and protect helpless clients against overpowering enemies or as sinister accomplices of criminals. Neither portrayal bears much resemblance to the work of the vast majority of lawyers, who simply provide legal services in a market economy to fee-paying clients, much as do professionals in other fields.[11]

A final explanation is that the public's ambivalence reflects the variety of work that different lawyers do. The types of work that lawyers do today vary widely, and some types are more noble than others. The observation that lawyers' practices have become progressively more specialized over the years is hardly a novelty. In the foreword to his 1957 book on legal ethics Mark Orkin observed that though there may be branches of the law with which many practitioners have little need to be familiar, legal ethics is not one of them. There are no true general practitioners today. The closest thing to a general practitioner today is a lawyer who specializes in small business law or in relatively minor transactions and cases for low or middle-income clients.[12]

It is not altogether clear (and it may not matter a great deal) whether lawyers are currently held in lower esteem than they were historically. It is

---

9 Quoted by Sydney L. Robins, "An Address to New Lawyers", Law Society of Upper Canada Gazette, vol 15, no. 4 (December, 1981), p. 351.

10 John Willis, "What I Like and What I Don't Like About Lawyers", Law Society of Upper Canada Gazette, vol. 4, no. 1 (March, 1970), p. 52.

11 See Charles Wolfram, *Modern Legal Ethics* (St. Paul, Minnesota: West, 1986), pp. 1-4.

12 See Geoffrey C. Hazard, Jr., "Law is Both a Business and a Profession", National Law Journal (October 24, 1988), p. 13, and Wolfram, *ibid.*, p. 1. Some of the most stinging denunciations of lawyers recently have been in the form of jokes. One of the few benign lawyer jokes is about rampant specialization. A lawyer is on holiday. She exchanges pleasantries with another tourist in an adjacent cabin. She learns that he is also a lawyer. She asks where he practises, and learns that he practises in the same city as she. She asks what firm he is with, and learns that he practises in the same *firm* as does she. She asks what type of practice he has, and learns that he practises in the field of real estate — the same field in which she practises. She of course finds this quite amazing, and asks him what sort of real estate work he does. He answers that he limits his practice to vested remainders. "Aha," she says. "That explains it. I specialize in *contingent* remainders."

likely, however, that all professions are less respected today as a result of cynicism about and impatience with authority and elites in the western world generally.[13]

Somehow one doubts that many observers today would subscribe to the views on the American bar that were expressed by Alexis de Tocqueville in the 1830s:

> In America . . . the lawyers form the political upper class and the most intellectual section of society . . . If you ask me where the American aristocracy is found, I have no hesitation in answering that it is not among the rich, who have no common link uniting them. It is at the bar or the bench that the American aristocracy is found . . . When the American people let themselves get intoxicated by their passions or carried away by their ideas, the lawyers apply an almost invisible brake which slows them down . . . Lawyers, forming the only enlightened class not distrusted by the people, are naturally called on to fill most public functions.[13.1]

1.2 LEGAL EDUCATION AND TRAINING

In addition to the traits and intellectual qualities for which lawyers are often admired (as mentioned above), legal education and training may inculcate traits and intellectual qualities of more dubious social value. Aspiring lawyers are expected to become adept in argument and competition. Before they begin law school many students do not have this sort of personality. As a result of their legal education and training they are likely to become confident, assertive, contentious, and cunning, and some may even become arrogant, punitive, and devious. An environment of debate and contest emphasizes winning and Stephen Potter gamesmanship at the expense of collaboration and humility. In short, traditional approaches to legal education and training promote the development of an adversarial turn of mind.[14]

Much progress has been made in legal education, however, over the last 20 years or so. While he was the president of Harvard, Derek C. Bok (who

---

13 See Jacques Barzun, "The Professions Under Siege", Law Society of Upper Canada Gazette, vol. 12, no. 4 (December, 1978), pp. 344-345; Stephen M. Grant, "Sex, Lies, and Legal Ethics", Law Society of Upper Canada Gazette, vol. 24, no. 2 (June, 1990), p. 104; and Wolfram, *supra*, note 11, p. 7.

13.1 Alexis de Tocqueville, *Democracy In America*, translated by George Lawrence, J.P. Mayer (ed.) (New York: Anchor Books, 1969), pp. 268-9.

14 The less attractive qualities common to lawyers, and their origins, are discussed by David Riley, "The Mystique of Lawyers" in Ralph Nader and Mark Green (eds.), *Verdicts on Lawyers* (New York: Thomas Y. Crowell Co., 1976), p. 90; Andreas Eshete, "Does a Lawyer's Character Matter?" in David Luban (ed.), *The Good Lawyer: Lawyers' Roles and Lawyers' Ethics* (Totowa, New Jersey: Rowan & Allenhead, 1983), pp. 271-275; Charles Reich, *The Greening of America* (New York: Random House, 1970) as quoted by Mark H. McCormack, *The Terrible Truth About Lawyers: What Every Businessperson Needs to Know* (London: William Collins and Sons, 1987), p. 34; and American Bar Association, "Legal Education and Professional Development: The Report of the Task Force on Law Schools and the Profession" (Chicago: American Bar Association, 1992), p. 236.

was also a former dean of Harvard Law School) stressed that it is time for the law schools to change their emphases:

> Everyone must agree that the law schools train their students more for conflict than for the gentler arts of reconciliation and accommodation. This emphasis is likely to serve the profession poorly. Over the next generation, I predict, society's greatest opportunity will lie in tapping human inclinations toward collaboration and compromise rather than stirring our proclivities for competition and rivalry.[15]

A related concern has to do with the teaching of lawyers' ethics in law schools. Professor Andrew Kaufman of Harvard Law School, an expert in legal ethics, once remarked that he and Monroe Freedman had been classmates in law school and had, therefore, learned about legal ethics at the same time and place: in practice, of course, because they learned virtually nothing in law school.[16] Robert B. Stevens, while he was the president of Haverford College, wondered whether American law schools produced "analytic giants but moral pygmies."[17]

Most Canadian law schools now offer courses in legal ethics, but the courses are mandatory at only three schools. Bar admission courses have started including mandatory two or three day sections on professional responsibility within the last few years. (For a few years before that, in Ontario, professional responsibility questions were integrated into other courses on the theory that legal ethics should permeate the curriculum and be taught interstitially in each subject). The Federation of Law Societies recently released a commendable report containing recommendations for the development of a coordinated curriculum for the teaching of professional responsibility in Canadian law schools and bar admission courses.[18]

Nevertheless, law school courses on legal ethics still almost invariably start with an explanation that their purpose is not to teach the difference between right and wrong, but rather to consider the often anomalous professional responsibilities of lawyers in their roles as such. Justice Sandra O'Connor of the United States Supreme Court has said that traditional legal education often suggests that law and morality are separated by a wall similar to the one between church and state.[19] What underlies this approach is the

---

15 New York *Times* (April 22, 1983), as quoted in Beverley G. Smith, *Professional Conduct for Canadian Lawyers* (Toronto: Butterworths, 1989), p. 104.

16 Monroe H. Freedman, *Lawyers' Ethics In An Adversary System* (New York: Bobbs-Merrill, 1975), p. vii.

17 Quoted by Gerry Spence in *With Justice for None* (New York: Random House, 1989), p. 51. See also Luban, *supra*, note 14, p. 10.

18 W. Brent Cotter is the author of the report which is titled *Professional Responsibility Instruction in Canada: A Coordinated Curriculum for Legal Education* (Montreal: Conceptcom, 1992).

19 Sandra D. O'Connor, "The Moral Role of the Lawyer" (an address at Fordham University Law School Dedication, New York, October 24, 1984), published in Law Society of Upper Canada Gazette, vol. 19, no. 1 (March, 1985), p. 28 at 29-30.

belief that characters are formed at an early age, long before admission to law school, and that if concerned parents, elementary and secondary school teachers, coaches, other role models, and university teachers have not effectively nurtured the characters of young people by dispensing moral guidance from infancy, the prospect of professional schools succeeding in modifying attitudes is too remote to be worth attempting.[20]

This approach is troubling. As the historian Jacques Barzun has written, explanations of attitudes by reference to childhood determinants leave no room for one of the most easily observed facts, namely the *development* of character.[21] Studies have shown that professional schools *can* influence students' values and moral judgements.[22]

Monroe Freedman has argued persuasively that the historical disregard of questions of professional responsibility in law schools has produced a bar that is largely indifferent to solving them and is indeed often incapable of even recognizing them. "The difficult task of answering hard questions will not be undertaken," he suggests, "until an entire generation of law students is exposed to ethical problems in the classroom in a way that makes it clear to them that these issues are as important as the substantive law relating to damages, anticipatory breach, statutes of limitations and frauds, or written integration of contracts."[23]

Justice O'Connor makes a similar point: "Just as bricks and mortar do not a great law school make so, too, the traditional teaching of only substantive and procedural courses do not a good lawyer make. This is because such instruction does not insure that a lawyer will have an awareness of the social and moral responsibilities of the profession."[24]

What law students learn in professional responsibility courses now is not the main influence on the way most lawyers attempt to resolve ethical questions confronted in practice. After law school, education in lawyers' ethics proceeds almost entirely by example rather than precept. The process of osmosis whereby articling students and junior lawyers learn by observing more senior lawyers in practice influences ethical decisions significantly. The more apprentice-like is the training received by lawyers, the greater is the relative influence of more senior lawyers, compared to the influence of law school, on their professional conduct.[25] Unfortunately, the examples set for beginning

---

20 See Reed Elizabeth Loder, "Tighter Rules of Professional Conduct: Saltwater for Thirst" (1987-88) 1 Georgetown Journal of Legal Ethics 311 at 333.

21 Jacques Barzun, *Clio and the Doctors: Psycho-History, Quanto-History, and History* (Chicago: University of Chicago Press, 1974), p. 69.

22 See Richard A. Salomon, "Shades of Grey and Other Myths" (1987-88) 1 Georgetown Journal of Legal Ethics 463 at 465.

23 Monroe H. Freedman, "Professional Responsibility of the Civil Practitioner: Teaching Legal Ethics in the Contracts Course" (1969) 21 Journal of Legal Education 569 at 581.

24 O'Connor, *supra*, note 19, p. 29.

25 The most thorough and important study that considers the influence of various factors on

lawyers often leave a great deal to be desired; as in law school, an undue emphasis on conflict and gamesmanship is a large part of the problem. An American firm proudly proclaimed in a 1991 brochure that going up against it in court was "a little like encountering Genghis Khan on the Steppes."[26] Such examples are particularly unfortunate when one considers that most aspiring lawyers tend to be idealistic and predisposed to a public service approach to practice.[27]

To be preferred is the kind of training that the late Vincent Foster was talking about in a 1993 commencement address:

> The reputation you develop for intellectual and ethical integrity will be your greatest asset or your worst enemy . . . Treat every pleading, every brief, every contract, every letter, every daily task as if your career will be judged on it. There is no victory, no advantage, no fee, no favour which is worth even a blemish on your reputation for intellect and integrity.[27.1]

1.3 LAWYERS AND COMMERCIALISM

Concerns that the bar has become too commercialized have been common for well over a century, and probably date back into antiquity.[28] In modern times, some lawyers' preoccupation with money has brought much discredit upon the profession.

Shortly after he was called to the bar, a prominent American lawyer, Gerry Spence, was retained by an impoverished claimant in a case in which the other party was clearly at fault. He approached the lawyer for the other party, a wizened veteran of the insurance bar, to beg for an early settlement. The older lawyer laughed knowingly, took Spence to a filing cabinet in his of-

(*Continued on page 1–7*)

---

the process whereby lawyers resolve ethical problems encountered in practice is Frances Zemans and Victor Rosenblum, *The Making of a Public Profession* (Chicago: American Bar Foundation, 1981), particularly at pp. 123-164 and 173-176. See also Geoffrey C. Hazard, Jr., "Instruction in Ethics Never Really Stops", National Law Journal (July 4, 1988), p. 13.

26 See Thomas E. Reid, "Isolated Billing Burns Hamper Legal Profession", *Law Times* (October 28 - November 3, 1991), p. 18.

27 Lawrence K. Hellman, "The Effects of Law Office Work on the Formation of Law Students' Professional Values: Observation, Explanation, Optimization" (1991) 4 Georgetown Journal of Legal Ethics 537; see also Hazard, *supra*, note 25, p. 13.

27.1 Quoted in Sidney Blumenthal, "The Suicide", *The New Yorker* (August 9, 1993), p. 41; see also Rosalie Silberman Abella, "Opening the Courts to Utopia . . . And More", Law Society of Upper Canada Gazette, vol. 27, no. 3-4 (September-December, 1993), p. 165 at 171.

28 Jack L. Sammonds, Jr., "Professing: Some Thoughts on Professionalism and Classroom Teaching" (1989-90) 3 Georgetown Journal of Legal Ethics 609 at 611-612.

fice, opened one drawer slowly after another, and said, "See these files, Spence? Every one of these files is worth a new Cadillac to me. Do you really expect me to give you one of my new Cadillacs?"[29]

Even more recently, during the investigation which culminated in the conviction of Michael Milken for securities offences, the fees of one of the law firms representing Milken totalled two million dollars a month. When the chief executive officer of Milken's employer, Drexel Burnham Lambert, which was paying his fees, questioned the size of the billings, the senior lawyer at the firm who was responsible for the matter, Arthur Liman, flatly refused to reduce them. "The quality of Michael Milken's representation," he said, "will not be affected by Drexel's nickelling and diming their lawyers."[30]

Lawyers practise in a market economy, and the highest bidders in such an economy are wealthy and often powerful. Many lawyers fiddle on the corners where clients throw coins. Access to justice suffers.

The American educator, Jerome Carlin, offered the following assessment more than a quarter century ago: "The best-trained, most responsible lawyers are reserved for the upper reaches of business and society. This leaves the least competent, least well-trained, and least ethical lawyers to the lower income individuals."[31]

There is no evidence that lawyers who act for the wealthy and powerful are any more or less ethical than are those who act for the poor and powerless. Indeed many of the most capable lawyers, with the most highly developed social consciousness, work for public interest groups, governments, and clinics. There is probably still a grain of truth, however, in the belief that on the whole the lawyers retained to act for the wealthy and powerful are likely to be better trained and more skilful than those who act for the poor and powerless. Ralph Nader, a lawyer who has never been accused of being motivated by considerations of personal wealth, recognized in the following passage that in the legal profession he is an exception:

> . . . the best and the brightest labour for the polluters, not the anti-polluters, for sellers, not consumers, for corporations, not citizens, for labour leaders, not the rank and file, for, not against, rate increases, for highway builders, not displaced residents, for, not against, judicial and administrative delay, for preferential business access to government and against equal citizen access to the same government, for agricultural subsidies to the rich but not food stamps for the poor, for tax and quota privileges, not for equity and free trade.[32]

Justice Frank Iacobucci of the Supreme Court of Canada argued in a 1991 address[33] that placing too great an emphasis on the business dimension

29 Gerry Spence, *With Justice for None* (New York: Random House, 1989), p. 151.

30 James B. Stewart, *Den of Thieves* (New York: Simon and Schuster, 1991), p. 429.

31 Jerome Carlin, *Legal Ethics* (New York: Russell Sage Foundation, 1966), p. 177. See also Charles Wolfram, *Modern Legal Ethics* (St. Paul, Minnesota: West, 1986), p. 4.

32 Quoted by Spence, *supra*, note 29, pp. 50-51.

33 "The Practice of Law: Business and Professionalism", The Advocate, vol. 49, part 6 (No-

of the practice of law has many other untoward consequences. First, women and men who would place their professional values before amassing large profits will not be drawn to the profession, resulting in a vicious circle: the more profit-making is emphasized in the practice of law, the more it will be those who put profit before professional values who will become lawyers. Second, the pressure to condone unethical or even unlawful but lucrative acts can be overwhelming; expectations, or requirements, that lawyers will work over 2000 billable hours a year, for example, all but guarantee that some clients will be overcharged. Finally, an undue emphasis on the business dimension of practising law can take a toll on lawyers' humanity. It is easy in such an atmosphere to forget that there is more to life than making money, and that professionals particularly should nurture and develop both their other talents and their relationships with family, friends, and loved ones.[34]

1.4 THE IMPORTANCE OF LAWYERS' ETHICS

Almost all decisions made by lawyers affect others and therefore have ethical implications. In this sense, ethics is part of the everyday life of lawyers.

David Melinkoff wrote that the basic strains on the consciences of lawyers ". . . are not wispy, hypothetical concerns reserved for Sunday or the ivory tower."[35] John Willis wrote that lawyers spend their lives in moral smog, representing clients who frequently are seeking something to which they are not really entitled. The lawyer "does not, like the clergyman, put me off with the vague generalities I remember from the Sunday sermons of my youth . . . Into my smog, and the smogs of all his other clients, he plunges and spends his life trying to find acceptable solutions for the moral problems of real life."[36]

To resolve these moral dilemmas of everyday life requires a peculiar combination of pragmatism and detachment. "This is no life of cloistered ease to which you dedicate your powers," Cardozo wrote. "This is a life that touches your fellow men at every angle of their being, a life that you must live in the crowd, and yet apart from it, man of the world and philosopher by

vember, 1991), p. 859. See also Justice Iacobucci's 1992 address "Striking a Balance: Trying to Find the Happy and Good Life Within and Beyond the Legal Profession", Law Society of Upper Canada Gazette, vol. 25, no. 3 (September-December, 1992), p. 205.

34 *Ibid.*, pp. 861-862. See also Seth Rosner, "Professionalism and Money", American Bar Association Journal (May, 1992), p. 69 at 70; and Peter Megargee Brown, "America's Legal Profession is in Trouble. What Are We Going To Do About It?", New York State Bar Journal (May, 1990), p. 16.

35 David Melinkoff, *The Conscience of a Lawyer* (St. Paul, Minnesota: West, 1973), pp. v, 270-271 and 273-274.

36 John Willis, "What I Like and What I Don't Like About Lawyers", Law Society of Upper Canada Gazette, vol. 4, no. 1 (March, 1970), p. 52.

turns."[37]

Lawyers may thus do great harm. Many years ago, Lord Bolinbroke observed that "the profession of the law, in its nature the noblest and most beneficial to mankind, is in its abuse and abasement the most sordid and pernicious."[38]

For the same reason, however, lawyers are positioned to elevate not only their own conduct but that of others to a higher plane. Brandeis wrote that there is opportunity in the law — "special opportunities for usefulness to your fellow-men."[39] Collectively, lawyers have an opportunity to raise the moral tone of society.[40]

1.5 IMPROVING LAWYERS' ETHICS

We may venture a few tentative suggestions about what lawyers might do to enhance public confidence in the profession. Some of these will be explored further in the chapters that follow.

First, lawyers should upgrade the education and training of law students and junior lawyers by continuing to enhance the teaching of ethics both in law schools and in practice. This will entail a modification of our notions of the qualities that legal education and training should try to cultivate.

Second, lawyers should moderate their scorched earth warrior impulses. We will consider the adversary system in more detail in chapter 2. It will suffice for present purposes to quote Judge Marvin E. Frankel:

> We (lawyers) must alter our prime axiom — that we are combat mercenaries available indifferently for any cause or purpose a client is ready to finance . . . As ministers of justice, we should find ourselves more positively concerned than we now are with the pursuit of truth.[41]

Third, lawyers should enlarge their sense of obligation beyond the unremitting pursuit of narrow client interests to the interests of other stakeholders. Loyalty is a commendable value that often requires the devotion of special efforts on behalf of certain individuals and groups. Other values, such as honesty, fairness, compassion, and empathy, however, have too often been subordinated to it by lawyers.[42] This theme will be explored in chapter 3.

---

37 Quoted by Sydney L. Robins, "An Address To New Lawyers", Law Society of Upper Canada Gazette, vol. 15, no. 4 (December, 1981), p. 349 at 355.

38 Quoted in George Sharswood, *Legal Ethics: An Essay on Professional Ethics*, 5th ed. (Philadelphia: T. and J.W. Johnson & Co., 1884), p. 171.

39 Quoted by David Luban, *Lawyers and Justice: An Ethical Study* (Princeton, New Jersey: Princeton University Press, 1988), pp. xvii-xviii.

40 See George A. Reimer, *Ethics: The DR's and Beyond* (Marina del Ray, California: Josephson Institute of Ethics, 1992), pp. ii-iii and 51; and David Luban (ed.), *The Good Lawyer: Lawyers' Roles and Lawyers' Ethics* (Totowa, New Jersey: Rowan & Allenhead, 1983), p. 20.

41 Quoted in the Washington *Post* (May 7, 1978); see also Reimer, *ibid.*, p. 7.

42 See Paul H. Zalecki, "The Advice of a Business Lawyer: Interplay Between Law and Eth-

Fourth, lawyers when making decisions should treat ethical principles as paramount rather than merely taking them into consideration among other factors.[43]

Finally, lawyers should place greater emphasis on the service dimension of the practice of law, and less on the business dimension.[44] Roscoe Pound wrote that the three hallmarks of a profession are organization, learning, and a spirit of public service; the earning of one's livelihood, he added, is incidental.[45] The decision that every lawyer must make was expressed as follows by Sir Robert Megarry, when he addressed lawyers being called to the Ontario bar in 1983:

> Critics will often poke fun at law and lawyers, and often you will be happy to join them in this: it will be a black day when we cannot laugh at ourselves and our craft. But you will never accept the sneer that lawyers are simply out to make money for themselves; for the essence of the practice of law is that we are there to help others . . . Or you might, I suppose, simply descend into the deplorable ranks of the mere money-grubbing slobs.[46]

---

ics" (1988-89) 2 Georgetown Journal of Legal Ethics 921 at 930; Thomas Shaffer, *American Legal Ethics: Text, Readings, and Discussion Topics* (1985), pp. 175-176; and Reimer, *supra*, note 40, pp. 34-35.

43 See Reimer, *supra*, note 40, p. 14.

44 See Archie Campbell, "Values and Obligations", Law Society of Upper Canada Gazette, vol. 21, no. 2 (June, 1987), p. 162 at 165; and Reimer, *supra*, note 40, p. 7.

45 Roscoe Pound, "What Is A Profession?" (1943-44) 19 Notre Dame L.R. 203 at 204; Roscoe Pound, *The Lawyer from Antiquity to Modern Times* (St. Paul, Minnesota: West, 1953), p. 5.

46 Robert E. Megarry, "Convocation Address", Law Society of Upper Canada Gazette, vol. 17, no. 1 (March, 1983), p. 41 at 45-46.

2

The Adversary System

"Then, there are the lawyers. Their training has schooled them to believe first, last, and always in litigation and the adversary process. They think real advocates don't give ground when their client has a just cause; and that covers almost all cases, and both sides of them."[1]

2.1 INTRODUCTION

Litigation lawyers learn early in their practices that although the adversary system functions tolerably well in many civil cases, its defects are nevertheless extensive and profound. Tactics calculated to delay, distort, obfuscate, obstruct and wear down opponents through frustration and cost are common. Questionable conduct is justified by appeals to the ethics of the adversary system. The consequences are often borne by clients — through increased cost, delay and conflict — and even by lawyers themselves — through stress, fatigue and dissatisfaction with the quality of life that the practice of litigation in our adversary system brings with it.[2]

This loss of conviction in the often-claimed superiority of adversarial procedures is anything but novel. Both a considerable body of feminist analysis and the alternate dispute resolution movement, for example, build on critiques of the adversary system.[3]

The problems remain nevertheless — largely because of the attitudes and expectations that the adversary system engenders. In this chapter we shall examine the source of these attitudes and expectations, consider the ef-

1 M. Rosenberg, "Resolving Disputes Differently: Adieu to Adversary Justice" (1988), 21 Creighton L.R. 801, 816.

2 See Stephen W. Sessums, "Adversarial Co-operation: A Concept that Works", 9 Journal of the American Academy of Matrimonial Lawyers 61 (1992).

3 See Carrie Menkel-Meadow, "Portia in a Different Voice: Speculations on a Women's Lawyering Process" (1985), 1 Berkeley Women's L.J. 39; Marilyn L. Pilkington, "Equipping Courts to Handle Constitutional Issues: The Adequacy of the Adversary System and its Techniques of Proof", [1991] Law Society of Upper Canada Special Lectures 51, 51; and Charles Wolfram, *Modern Legal Ethics* (St. Paul, Minnesota: West, 1986), 568.

ficacy of reforms that have been intended to temper the extravagances of the adversary system, and advance a few proposals that might help to restore public confidence in our system of justice. We will consider the functioning of the adversary system in different fields of practice. As we shall see, different considerations prevail in the criminal law; the reforms we shall consider are designed primarily for non-criminal litigation.

2.2 THE SPORTING THEORY OF JUSTICE

The resemblance between adversarial trials and hearings and athletic contests and other games has frequently been recognized. John Stuart Mill made the observation — which was probably not original even in the nineteenth century — that people speak and act as if they regard a trial "as a sort of game, partly of chance, partly of skill, in which the proper end to be aimed at is not that the truth be discovered, but that both parties may have fair play . . .".[4] In a famous address in 1906, Roscoe Pound identified the pervasiveness of this "sporting theory" as one of the causes of public dissatisfaction with the administration of justice. "The idea that procedure must of necessity be wholly contentious", he asserted, "disfigures our judicial administration at every turn."[5]

Other untoward consequences that have been ascribed to the sporting theory of justice range from a disinclination among lawyers to resolve disputes to the selection of judges based on inappropriate criteria. Professor Roger Fisher of Harvard Law School has imputed the aversion of many lawyers to discharging their ethical responsibility to settle disputes to their love of the contest:

> "They find pleasure in representing a client with the full zeal that the legal canons of ethics call for. For some lawyers, negotiating the settlement of a case being prepared for trial has about as much appeal as negotiating the settlement of a football game or a prize fight would have for the athletes."[6]

A former American judge, Marvin E. Frankel, analogized the practice of selecting judges from among trial lawyers to selecting umpires from among former baseball players: "Reflective people have suggested from time to time

4 Quoted by William F. Buckley, Jr., *Four Reforms* (New York: Putnam's 1973), p. 123.

5 Roscoe Pound, "The Causes of Dissatisfaction with the Administration of Justice", 29 A.B.A. Rep. 395 (reprinted in 57 A.B.A.J. 348 (1971)), 404. See also Rosalie Silberman Abella, "The Civil Litigation Process Under Siege: Roscoe Pound Redux", 28 Law Society of Upper Canada Gazette 213 (1994).

6 Roger Fisher, "He Who Pays The Piper", Advocates' Society Journal (July 1991), 9. Lawyers' professional duty to advise settlement of disputes whenever it is possible to do so on a reasonable basis is expressed in the Canadian Bar Association's Code of Professional Conduct (hereinafter the C.B.A. Code), chapter III, commentary 6, and in the Law Society of Upper Canada Rules of Professional Conduct (hereinafter "Ontario rules"), rule 3, commentary 5.

that qualities of detachment and calm neutrality are not necessarily cultivated by long years of partisan combat."[7]

Our ideas of what qualities of lawyers should be admired are informed by the sporting theory of justice. The performance of John J. Wilson, who represented H.R. Haldeman and John Ehrlichman before the United States Senate Select Committee on Presidential Campaign Activities during the Watergate controversy, was thus described as follows:

> "Wilson was belligerent, insulting (at least to Inouye), formidably well prepared, and a wall-eyed disaster for the committee. He did what a good lawyer is supposed to do for his client: he ate the opposition alive. It was awful to watch, and it was also grand; one began to understand that it was not entirely devotion to the law that made John Adams defend the British soldiers accused of the Boston Massacre. It was also plain love of a good fight that he thought he could win, and he did."[8]

The untoward effects of the adversary system's preoccupation with gamesmanship and contentiousness include forensic excesses, discovery abuse and an often significant discrepancy between lawyers' and non-lawyers' notions of ethical conduct.

2.3 FORENSIC EXCESSES AND THE PRISONER'S DILEMMA

Forensic excesses that are features of litigation in an adversary system include frivolous lawsuits, shotgun pleadings, tactical counterclaims, delay tactics, misstating evidence, *ad hominem* attacks, unfounded objections that are calculated to coach witnesses or break up the flow of examination or argument, and applications to disqualify counsel (often based on supposed conflicts of interest) that are intended to inconvenience opponents.[9] This list is not, of course, exhaustive.

Adversarial tactics such as these tend to escalate despite good intentions. Game theorists have a label for this phenomenon: the "prisoner's dilemma". Lawyers adopt adversarial tactics because to refrain from doing so would put

7 Marvin E. Frankel, "The Search for Truth: An Umpireal View" (a Cardozo lecture) (1975), 123 U. of Pa. L.R. 1031 at 1033. See also former Judge Frankel's book *Partisan Justice* (New York: Hill & Wang, 1980); and Wolfram, *supra*, note 3, 567.

8 George V. Higgins, *The Friends of Richard Nixon* (Boston: Little, Brown, 1975), 226. See also Marvin Joel Huberman, "Advocacy, War, and the Art of Strategy", Law Society of Upper Canada Gazette, vol. 26, no. 2 (June 1992), 122; and Monroe H. Freedman, *Understanding Lawyers' Ethics* (New York: Matthew Bender & Co., 1990), 18, where the author argues that lawyers do not initiate grievances between parties, but rather play an indispensable part in the constructive societal process of channelling such grievances into controlled and non-violent means of dispute resolution.

9 See Stephen G. Coughlan, "The Adversary System: Rhetoric or Reality" (1993), 8 C.J.L.S./R.C.D.S. 139, 140; and R.J. Gerber, "Victory vs. Truth: The Adversary System and Its Ethics" (1987), 19 Arizona St. L.J.3, 6-11.

their clients at a competitive disadvantage relative to the clients of lawyers who show no such restraint. All lawyers may recognize that it would be better for all parties concerned, and for the administration of justice, if none of them adopted such tactics. This recognition is unlikely to induce any of the lawyers to refrain unilaterally from adopting whatever tactics will assist their clients to gain a competitive advantage and win the case. No counsel, moreover, wants others to say of her, "I hope she ends up as counsel for the other side on my next case too". The prisoner's dilemma thus tends to reduce the professional conduct of lawyers to the lowest common denominator.[10]

Despite reforms designed to curtail some of the excesses of the adversary system, the discovery process in civil litigation remains the leading modern example of those excesses, and deserves separate treatment.

2.4 DISCOVERY ABUSE

Techniques employed to frustrate the discovery process include repetitive questions, oppressive requests to compile documents of little if any importance, unsupportable assertions of privilege, frivolous objections, incomplete responses, improper refusals to produce documents, the dogged pursuit of irrelevant details and questioning that is calculated to exhaust or intimidate opponents. In some cases, parties have been inundated with the production of mostly immaterial documents in the hope that damaging documents will pass unnoticed. Impecunious adverse parties have been forced to settle on unfavourable terms due to the prohibitive cost of litigating against well-heeled opponents whose lawyers have exploited their financial disadvantage by building up the costs of discovery.

Abuses abound in the discovery phase of litigation partly because no adjudicator is present to control the counsel. At trial, most lawyers avoid overly aggressive and unfair conduct that is likely to alienate judges and juries. There is less incentive for them to avoid overzealousness on discovery.

Most trial judges are likely to do little about discovery abuses, as they consider the discovery process to be incidental and preliminary. For the judiciary, the trial is everything. Litigation lawyers, on the other hand, realize that a great majority of their cases will be settled prior to trial, generally as a result of discovery, which is accordingly of paramount importance. Litigation lawyers also become inured to the cost and the causticity of discovery excesses.[11]

---

10 David Luban, "Calming the Hearse Horse: A Philosophical Research Program for Legal Ethics" (1981), 40 Maryland L.R. 451 at 460-461; see also Coughlan, *supra* note 9, p. 169.

11 Common types of discovery abuse, and obstacles to remedying the problems, are discussed by Geoffrey C. Hazard, Jr., in "Depositions: Modern-Day Inquisitions", National Law Journal (March 14, 1988), 13; by Wolfram, *supra*, note 3, 594-95; by Michael E. Wolfson, "Addressing the Adversarial Dilemma of Civil Discovery" (1988), 36 Cleveland State L.R. 17 at 42; and by Robert E. Sarazen, "An Ethical Approach to Discovery Abuse" (1991), 4 Georgetown Journal of Legal Ethics 459.

In Canada, rules of professional conduct do not deal specifically with discovery abuse, and disciplinary proceedings have been brought in only a few egregious cases. In the United States, in the last ten years, eleven amendments to the Federal Rules of Civil Procedure and five amendments to the Model Rules of Professional Conduct have been promulgated to curb discovery abuse. The Model Rules, which have been adopted by the bars of a majority of states, expressly prohibit lawyers from making frivolous discovery requests or failing to make reasonably diligent efforts to comply with proper discovery requests of other parties. In a 1989 Colorado case,[12] a lawyer was suspended for six months for withholding on discovery information that an adverse party was entitled to receive. In a 1994 case, a Seattle law firm and its client agreed to pay $325,000 in sanctions for discovery abuse after they misled adverse parties to avoid producing inculpatory documents. The latter case prompted one commentator to write that "the shame of the adversary system has been its degeneration into a pretext for lawyers to hide facts, so as to pervert the truth".[13]

Modern rules of civil procedure dealing with the production of documents exemplify the type of measures that have been taken to modify the adversary system in its pure form. The duty of lawyers to produce documents adverse to their clients is indirect, in the sense that the duty to make full disclosure is imposed on the parties, not their counsel. Lawyers are nevertheless obliged to explain to their clients the necessity of making full disclosure of all documents relevant to the issues in the action as framed by the pleadings, and in some jurisdictions are required to certify to the court that they have done so.[14]

Such practices as producing a critical document in a box car filled with otherwise irrelevant material, and producing relevant documents only when forced to do so, have frequently been condemned by courts and commentators, and occasionally knowing acquiesence by lawyers in their clients' failure to produce relevant documents has been visited with cost sanctions.[15] Again,

---

12 *People of the State of Colorado v. Haase*, 781 P. 2d 80 (1989). In an Ontario case, *Re Balaban*, report adopted by Convocation, May 24, 1984, the Law Society of Upper Canada reprimanded a lawyer publicly for repeatedly making unwarranted, personal and offensive remarks to opposing counsel in an official examiner's office.

13 Stuart Taylor, Jr., "Sleazy in Seattle", *American Lawyer* (April 1994), 5, 79.

14 Rule 30.03(4) of the Ontario Rules of Civil Procedure, R.R.O. 1990, reg. 194, is an example of a provision requiring lawyers to certify that they have explained the obligation of full disclosure to their clients. Rules of civil procedure also, of course, provide remedies and sanctions for the improper conduct of examinations: see, for example, rule 34.14 of the Ontario Rules of Civil Procedure.

15 In *Myers v. Elman*, [1940] A.C. 282 (U.K. H.L.), the House of Lords upheld an order of a trial judge whereby a solicitor who drew an affidavit on production that to the solicitor's knowledge omitted mention of a number of highly relevant documents, was ordered to pay one-third of the successful adverse party's costs. See also *Grossman v. Toronto General Hospital* (1983), 41 O.R. (2d) 457 (H.C.); *Rondel v. Worsley*, [1969] 1 A.C. 191 at 227-28

however, Canadian rules of professional conduct are silent on the subject of a lawyer's duty to disclose relevant documents in civil litigation, and discipline proceedings are rarely initiated as a result of lawyers' failure to disclose.

The fundamental problem, which we will consider below, is that discovery, which constitutes an intentional erosion of the pure adversarial process of the early common law, has been engrafted onto what otherwise remains a thoroughly adversarial process. Full, efficient and meaningful pre-trial disclosure requires co-operation that many lawyers consider to be incompatible with the furtherance of their clients' objectives.[16]

2.5 LEGAL ETHICS AND THE PUBLIC'S ETHICS

Forensic excess and discovery abuse are not the only ethical problems created by the adversary system. Another involves appeals by lawyers to the values of the adversary system to justify conduct that is likely to be regarded as immoral by non-lawyers, thereby compromising public confidence in the administration of justice.

Two examples — both American, both true — illustrate the point:

1. The plaintiff suffers injuries in an automobile accident and brings an action for damages for personal injuries. The lawyer representing the defendant insurance company arranges for a defence medical examination. The doctor conducting the investigation discovers an aortic aneurism, evidently caused by the accident, that the plaintiff's own doctor has not found. The aneurism is life-threatening unless operated upon.

The plaintiff's lawyer serves an offer to settle the claim for $6,500. The insurance company's lawyer knows that if the plaintiff learns of the aneurism — as he will if the report of the defence medical examiner is served before the action is settled — he will insist on a much larger payment. The insurance company's lawyer accepts the offer to settle and does not inform the plaintiff or his lawyer of the aneurism that may cause the plaintiff's death.

The plaintiff learns of the insurance company's lawyer's non-disclosure and brings a motion for an order setting aside the settlement. Although the motion is granted on another basis, the court finds that the defendant's lawyer had no duty to inform the plaintiff of the aneurism while they were in an adversarial relationship.[17]

(U.K. H.L.) per Lord Reid; and Earl A. Cherniak, "The Ethics of Advocacy", Law Society of Upper Canada Gazette, vol. 19, no. 2 (June 1985), 153-54. In a 1991 case, the Law Society of Upper Canada reprimanded a lawyer privately for failing repeatedly to disclose a psychiatric report that he had a duty to disclose to his opponent and to the Court.

16 Wolfson, *supra*, note 11, at 19-20, 48-51.

17 *Spaulding v. Zimmerman*, 116 N.W. 2d 704 (1962). For a more recent, Canadian example, see *Moss v. Chin* (1995), 120 D.L.R. (4th) 406 (B.C.S.C.). See also David Luban, *Lawyers and Justice: An Ethical Study* (Princeton, New Jersey: Princeton University Press, 1988), 149-50; and David Luban, "The Adversary System Excuse" in David Luban (ed.), *The*

2. Two court-appointed lawyers are representing a man charged with murder. The accused man tells the lawyers that he has also killed two other women who have been reported missing. He tells them where the bodies are buried.

The two lawyers search for and find the bodies of the two women — one in a cemetery, one in a mine shaft. One of the lawyers takes pictures of the bodies and moves a skull several feet to locate it near the rest of the remains. They do not report their discovery of the bodies to the police. They do attempt to plea bargain and offer to provide information about two unsolved murders in exchange for leniency.

The father of one of the missing women learns of speculation linking the accused man to his daughter's disappearance. He travels a thousand miles from his home to the accused man's lawyers' office. He meets with the more senior of the two lawyers and pleads with the lawyer to tell him whether he knows if his daughter is dead or alive. The lawyer does not tell the distraught father where his daughter is buried, or even that he knows that she is dead.

Six months after the lawyers' discovery of the women's bodies, the accused man testifies at his trial in support of his defence of insanity that he has been involved in three murders other than the one with which he is charged. He is convicted of the murder with which he is charged and is sentenced to 35 years to life in prison. The lawyers finally reveal their knowledge and the locations of the bodies. They defend their actions at a press conference. The resulting uproar includes calls for their disbarment.

One of the lawyers is charged with violating a public health law requiring prompt burial of deceased persons. He is acquitted on the ground that he had a duty as a lawyer not to disclose what he had learned as a result of what his client had told him.

The lawyers' governing body, similarly, decides that the lawyers not only acted permissibly, but that they could not have disclosed either the murders or the locations of the bodies because they acquired that information as a result of a confidential communication from a client.

Everyone involved in the case, which has become known as the Lake Pleasant Bodies case, was hurt. The pain of the families of the victims was unimaginable. The local tourism-based economy was devastated — people hesitate to go camping where there may be a deranged killer on the loose. The public was appalled. The accused man was convicted and sentenced to 35 years to life and was not aided in the slightest by his lawyers' silence. One of the lawyers was indicted, and the law practices and peace of mind of both were practically ruined.[18]

Good Lawyer: Lawyers' Roles and Lawyers' Ethics (Totawa, New Jersey: Rowan & Allenhead, 1983), 115 (hereinafter "Luban (ed.)").

18 In the Lake Pleasant Bodies case, the accused person, Robert Garrow, was convicted by a jury in July 1974. The lawyer who was indicted, Francis Belge, was acquitted the following year. The case is discussed, among other places, in Jeffrey Frank Chamberlain, "Confiden-

These two cases are unusual, to be sure, but similar ethical problems arise in less unusual cases as well. Let us consider two less sensational examples:

1. A lawyer is retained by a client who has been tried on a charge of aggravated sexual assault. The client is found not guilty by reason of insanity and institutionalized. He wishes to appeal the decision based upon the trial judge's dismissal of his motion to stay the proceedings by reason of an alleged violation of his constitutional right to be tried within a reasonable time.

2. A lawyer is retained by the affluent founder and chief executive officer of what has become a phenomenally successful company. When she was just starting out, the client borrowed $5,000 from a painter who had done some work for her. She has now been sued for the amount of the debt. She wishes to avoid paying the debt by pleading that the claim is statute-barred.[19]

Both lawyers and non-lawyers are likely to conclude that the lawyers' ethical duty in each of these four cases is clear — but they may well mean exactly the opposite of each other. Many non-lawyers are likely to conclude: (i) that it would be unethical to accept the plaintiff's offer to settle and keep secret one's knowledge of the plaintiff's aneurism when his life is at stake; (ii) that it would be unethical to keep secret from a distraught father one's knowledge of the death of his daughter; (iii) that it would be unethical to loose the insane and violent sexual offender on the public; and (iv) that it would be unethical to assist the wealthy executive to renege on her legitimate debt to the impoverished painter. Lawyers are likely to conclude that the lawyer in the four cases has an ethical duty: (i) to maintain in confidence knowledge of the plaintiff's life-threatening aneurism (unless the insurance company, perhaps at the urging of its lawyer, instructs otherwise); (ii) to maintain in confidence the client's confession to murder; (iii) to argue that the client was denied his constitutional right to be tried within a reasonable time; and (iv) to plead the *Limitations Act*.

Lawyers explain their ethics by reference to an adversary system that is poorly understood by others. It is the adversary system — and the principle of confidentiality that is at its heart — that explains the disparity between the reactions of the lawyer and the non-lawyer to these ethical quandaries.

On a conventional view of lawyers' professional responsibilities in an adversary system, lawyers are permitted — indeed required — to raise technical defences to defeat just claims and (as in two of the examples discussed above) to keep information confidential even if doing so may bring helpless third parties to ruin.[20]

---

tiality and the Case of Robert Garrow's Lawyers" (1976), 25 Buffalo L.R. 212; Monroe H. Freedman, *Lawyers' Ethics In An Adversary System* (New York: Bobbs-Merrill, 1975), 1-2; Wolfram, *supra*, note 3, 664-65; and Luban, *supra*, note 17, 53-54.

19 These two examples are adapted from Luban, *supra*, note 10, 456-59.

20 See Luban, *supra*, note 17, 1-2 and 8; and Alan Donegan, "Justifying Legal Practice in the Adversary System" in Luban (ed.), *supra*, note 17, 123-46.

Before considering the adequacy of the traditional justifications for the adversary system, we shall examine briefly the rules of professional conduct that are commonly invoked on behalf of lawyers accused of forensic excesses or conduct regarded as immoral in this sense.

2.6 RULES OF PROFESSIONAL CONDUCT

Rules of professional conduct impose limitations on the competitive conduct of lawyers in an adversary system. Limitations are usually expressed as duties owed by lawyers to the courts. The adversary system requires honesty, courtesy and respect among its participants.[21]

The basic tension between the duty to represent clients resolutely (or "zealously", to use the language of the American Bar Association's model Rules of Professional Conduct) and the duty to treat tribunals and courts with courtesy and respect, is resolved differently in rules of professional conduct in the United States, England, and Canada. The ABA Model Rules[22] emphasize loyalty to one's client as counsel's overriding obligation, a fact that prompted an American judge to observe that the general thrust of the Rules "fosters the attitude that begets gamesmanship at trial".[23] The Code of Conduct of the Bar of England and Wales expressly provides that in cases of conflict between a barrister's duty to the client and the court, the latter duty is paramount.[24] Barristers' courtroom attire reinforces their identification with the court rather than with the client. The following is a description of the English barrister's mode of advocacy:

> "Generally speaking, the barrister representing the accused in England . . . does not proceed upon the notion that his function is to obtain an acquittal by enforcing each and every rule applicable to the trial in the hope that the prosecution will falter. Nor does the defence barrister consider it proper to interject irrelevant matters into the case to confuse the jury, to require witnesses testifying as to uncontested matters to appear in court, to object to break the flow of damaging testimony, to turn the trial into an accusation against the complainant or the police where not called for clearly by the evidence, or to ask the jury to try the prosecutor, the judge, or society rather than the accused."[25]

---

21 See Robert J. Kutak, "The Adversary System and the Practice of Law" in Luban (ed.), *supra*, note 17, 172 at 174-76; and Cherniak, *supra*, note 15, 145 at 147.

22 See, for example, paragraph 7 or the preamble to the Model Rules, which provides in part that "when an opposing party is well represented, a lawyer can be a zealous advocate on behalf of a client and at the same time assume that justice is being done."

23 Thomas L. Steffen, "Truth as second Fiddle: Re-evaluating the Place of Truth in the Adversarial Trial Ensemble", [1988] Utah L.R. 799 at 818.

24 Code of Conduct of the Bar of England and Wales, paragraph 202 (1990).

25 Karen L.K. Miller, "Zip to Nil?", a paper presented to the American Bar Association Section of Litigation, January 13, 1996, quoting Michael H. Graham, *Tightening the Reins of Justice in America* at 236 (1983).

In what many may regard as a classic compromise, Canadian rules of professional conduct give equal prominence to both duties. The Law Society of Upper Canada's *Rules of Professional Conduct*, for example, provide as follows:

> "When acting as an advocate, a lawyer shall represent the client resolutely and honourably within the limits of the law while treating the tribunal with candour, fairness, courtesy, and respect . . .
>
> The lawyer has a duty to the client to raise fearlessly every issue, advance every argument, and ask every question, however distasteful, which the lawyer thinks will help the client's case and to endeavour to obtain for the client the benefit of every remedy and defence authorized by law. The lawyer must discharge this duty by fair and honourable means, without illegality, and in a manner that is consistent with the lawyer's duty to treat the tribunal with candour, fairness, courtesy, and respect and in a way that promotes the parties' right to a fair hearing where justice can be done. Maintaining dignity, decorum and courtesy in the courtroom is not an empty formality because, unless order is maintained, rights cannot be protected . . .
>
> In adversary proceedings the lawyer's function as advocate is openly and necessarily partisan. Accordingly, the lawyer is not obliged (save as required by law or under these rules and subject to the duties of a prosecutor set out below) to assist an adversary or advance matters derogatory to the client's case."[25.1]

2.7 JUSTIFICATIONS OF THE ADVERSARY SYSTEM

Two traditional justifications of the adversary system are frequently advanced. The first concentrates on the belief that truth is most likely to emerge where advocates of adverse positions compete before an impartial tribunal, each testing the merits of the other's position as comprehensively as possible. The adversary system has been described as "our beloved dialectic model of litigation".[26]

The second traditional justification concentrates on the belief that individual rights are better protected in the adversary system. The adversary system symbolizes such democratic ideals as individual liberty, autonomy and dignity. This justification is much more cogent where the example of the criminal trial, and particularly the criminal jury trial, is invoked. Thurman Arnold wrote of this important aspect of the adversary system in his book *The Symbols of Government* more than a half century ago:

> "Much of [the system's] strength is due to the romance and color which is centered in the jury trial. More efficient methods of judicial investigation can easily be imagined, but none more picturesque. When a great government treats the lowliest of criminals as an equal antagonist, strips itself of the executive

---

25.1 Ontario rule 4.01 (1) and accompanying commentary. The C.B.A. Code also gives equal prominence to the two duties: chapter IX, rule, and commentary 1.

26 H. Richard Uviller, "The Advocate, The Truth, and Judicial Hackles: A Reaction To Judge Frankel's Idea" (1975), 123 U. of Pa. L.R. 1067. See also Luban, *supra*, note 17, 69.

power which it possesses, and submits the case to twelve ordinary men, allowing the judge only the authority of an umpire, we have a gesture of recognition to the dignity of the individual which has an extraordinary dramatic appeal. Its claim is on our emotions, rather than our common sense."[27]

It is this second justification that frequently leads lawyers to defend conduct that non-lawyers consider morally questionable. Lawyers' claims that in doing so they are pursuing morally important goals are met with scepticism.[28]

The two traditional justifications of the adversary system are often incompatible. The protection of individual rights often hinders rather than advances the search for truth. Criminal defence lawyers, for example, have a professional responsibility to protect their clients' right, guaranteed by subsection 11(*c*) of the *Charter of Rights and Freedoms,* not to be compelled to be a witness. By invoking the clients' constitutional right, criminal defence counsel place obstacles in the path of truth-finding.[29]

We shall consider these justifications in the context of criminal prosecutions and civil litigation.

2.8 CRIMINAL PROSECUTIONS

Whether or not the adversary system is the most effective way of finding the truth in criminal cases, there can be little doubt that it protects individual rights and cherished democratic values effectively. Particularly in light of the growth of totalitarian regimes, the rights and values that the adversary system protects are so dear to us that we are willing to pay the price of impeding the search for truth to a considerable extent.

The strength and prevalence of the belief that the adversary system is a superior method of protecting individual rights is demonstrated by Italy's decision, in 1989, to adopt adversarial procedures in its criminal justice system.[30] Although the decision was undoubtedly influenced by the inefficiency of the former system — in which even routine cases were frequently delayed for a decade or longer[31] — it was rooted also in Italy's pre-World War II experiment

27 Thurman Arnold, *The Symbols of Government* (New Haven, Connecticut: Yale University Press, 1935), 145. See also Beverley G. Smith, *Professional Conduct for Canadian Lawyers* (Toronto: Butterworths, 1989), 121; and Freedman, *supra*, note 8, 13-14.

28 See Robert J. Kutak, "The Adversary System and the Practice of Law" in Luban (ed.), *supra*, note 17, 174; and Andreas Eshete, "Does a Lawyer's Character Matter?" in Luban (ed.), *supra*, note 17, 270-74.

29 See Monroe H. Freedman, "Professional Responsibility of the Civil Practitioner: Teaching Legal Ethics in the Contracts Course" (1969), 21 Journal of Legal Education 569 at 569-70; and Freedman, *supra*, note 18, 2-3.

30 *Codice Di Procedura Penale*, enacted by Presidential Decree — Law No. 447 of September 22, 1988, No. 250 Gazz. Uff. (October 24, 1988) (effective October 24, 1989).

31 William T. Pizzi and Luca Marafioti, "The New Italian Code of Criminal Procedure: The Difficulties of Building an Adversarial Trial System on a Civil Law Foundation" (1992), 17 Yale Journal of International Law 1, 6.

with fascism, which vividly established how a criminal justice system may become an instrument of the destruction of the political values of a liberal democratic society.[32]

Critics of the adversary system, including Pound, have almost invariably confined their proposals for reform to the administration of civil justice. In criminal cases at least, the second justification for the adversary system is sound.[33]

2.9 CIVIL LITIGATION

The adversary system is almost never discussed except in the context of criminal trials. Conclusions are drawn about the purposes and functioning of the system in civil cases — and even in such processes as negotiation and counselling, which have nothing to do with litigation — based upon the purposes and functioning of the system in criminal cases, often with little if any consideration being given to the different goals of the civil or other processes.[34]

Even in criminal cases, the determination of truth is at least one of the most important objectives of the administration of justice. In civil cases, in which the protection of individual rights from improper encroachment by the state is not normally a factor, the determination of truth must be regarded as by far the most important objective of the process.

Yet, historically we have placed obstacles in the path of truth-finding in civil cases as well. Even today the ethical rule of confidentiality, which is an incident of the adversary system that was developed originally to promote the vindication of individual rights in criminal prosecutions, represents official and deliberate tolerance of the concealment of relevant information from courts and tribunals. Few would find this tolerance objectionable in criminal cases, though it may result in accused persons escaping conviction and punishment for offences that they have committed. Many would find it objectionable in civil cases, in which plaintiffs — such as the plaintiff suffering from the life-threatening aneurism in the example set forth above — may be denied fair compensation for the wrongful acts or omissions of others if all available evidence is not adduced.[35]

---

32 Lawrence J. Fassler, "The Italian Penal Procedural Code: An Adversarial System of Criminal Procedure in Continental Europe", 29 Columbia Journal of Transnational Law 245, 272-73; see also Michael Zander, "From Inquisitorial to Adversarial — the Italian Experiment" (1991), 141 New Law J. 678 and Louis F. DelDuca, "An Historic Convergence of Civil and Common Law Systems — Italy's New Adversarial Criminal Procedure System" (1991), 10 Dickinson Journal of International Law 73.

33 Pound, *supra*, note 5, 349; see also Luban, *supra*, note 17, 58-63; and Edward L. Greenspan, "The Future Role of Defence Counsel", 51 Sask, L.R. 199, 208.

34 See Wolfram, *supra*, note 3, 564.

35 The duty of confidentiality is expressed in the C.B.A. Code, chapter IV and in Ontario rule 2.03; see also Chamberlain, *supra*, note 18, *passim*.

Even apart from the incidents of the adversary system that result in the concealment of relevant facts from the court or tribunal, there are many reasons to be sceptical about the proposition that truth is likely to emerge from a process of partisan combat.

Advocates in the adversary system do not necessarily attempt to convince the court or tribunal to find the truth; they attempt to convince the court or tribunal to find facts favouring their clients' interest. Nor do they necessarily restrict their attempts to convince to the merits of the issues. As we have seen, tactics involving obfuscation, distortion, obstruction and delay are all too frequently adopted. As a result of the phenomenon known as the prisoner's dilemma, as we have also seen, such adversarial tactics tend to escalate, because for lawyers to refrain from adopting them may put their clients at a competitive disadvantage.[36]

The premise that underlies this phenomenon is understood intuitively by lawyers: the adversary system can be effective in determining truth only if the adversaries are equally partisan. A second premise underlying the adversary system, which is also understood intuitively by lawyers, is that the system can be effective in determining truth only if the adversaries are equally competent. A third is that the system can be effective only if the adversaries have equal resources.[37]

In practice, cases in which there are gross disparities in the ability of counsel or the finances of the parties, or both, are common. It has become almost a platitude that if one has a choice of choosing either the better lawyer or the better case one would be well advised to choose the better lawyer. Common sense tells us that there is no reason to believe that if two combative lawyers slug it out in court the client with the better case, rather than the client with the better lawyer, will prevail. The problem is exacerbated where, as is often the case, the party with the more able lawyer also has the financial resources to withstand a sustained battle.[38]

This imbalance, in combination with the pre-eminence of the lawyer's duty to the client, can have serious repercussions. Professor Deborah Rhode of Stanford Law School, a leading American authority on legal ethics, has illustrated the potential of the adversary system to exalt and venerate private

---

36 See text accompanying note 10, *supra*. See also Milton Wessel, *The Rule of Reason* (Reading, Massachusetts: Addison-Wesley, 1976), 9; Virginia Held, "The Division of Moral Labour and the Role of the Lawyer" in Luban (ed.) *supra*, note 17, 60 at 66-71; and Wolfram, *supra*, note 3, 566-67.

37 Murray L. Schwartz discusses the postulates of equal adversariness and equal competence in "The Zeal of the Civil Advocate" in Luban, *supra*, note 17, 150 at 153-154.

38 See David Luban, "The Adversary System Excuse" in Luban (ed.), *supra*, note 17, 99; Wolfram, *supra*, note 3, 568 and 619; David Pannick, *Advocates* (Oxford: Oxford University Press, 1992), 168; and Raymond A. Belliotti, "Our Adversary System: In Search of a Foundation", 1 Canadian Journal of Law and Jurisprudence 19, at 23-24.

self-interest to such an extent that it yields completely unsatisfactory results for many citizens, and in some cases for the public as a whole:

> "Consider what this ethic has brought us. Everyone has favourite candidates, but my own short list begins with some of the lawyers for asbestos manufacturers. Their complicity in continued product distribution without warning of its danger brought premature death and permanent disability to thousands of individuals."[39]

Proponents of the theory that the adversary system is an effective means of discerning truth also contend that lawyers who are motivated by partisanship to seek victory in a trial are stimulated to search out facts diligently and to test effectually through cross-examination evidence adduced by adverse parties. Through this process of proof and challenge to proof, the impartial fact finder, it is said, is best able to ascertain where the truth lies. Extravagant statements on all sides will be exposed and cancelled out, leaving the truth.

By way of contrast, say the proponents of the adversary system, in an inquisitorial or arbitral system — in which judges determine disputes without advocacy from any side — judges are much more likely to posit their own theories. Once judges posit their own theories — often at an early stage of their inquiries — they are likely to resist letting those theories go in order to seriously consider other theories. In short, judges in such a system are much less likely to take a sustained and dispassionate look at a case before forming relatively firm conclusions. On the other hand, it is said, only judges who have had the benefit of vigorous argument from lawyers for all parties feel fully confident of the correctness of their decisions.

Proponents of the adversary system also argue that it is more efficient, as the parties' trained advocates reduce the issues to those that truly divide them. In an inquisitorial system, the argument goes, judges must canvass all possible issues.[40]

These are cogent arguments which, however, do not always hold water in practice. As pointed out above, the effectiveness of the adversary system is largely dependent upon parity among the parties in competence, partisanship and resources. And though the advocacy skills of lawyers can expose inaccuracies and falsehoods in the testimony of opposing witnesses, it is important to remember that in the adversary system lawyers use their skills primarily for the purpose of winning their cases, not necessarily to reveal truth. A lawyer's

---

39 Deborah L. Rhode, "An Adversarial Exchange on Adversarial Ethics: Text, Subtext, and Context", Journal of Legal Education, March 1991, 29, at 36; see also Deborah L. Rhode, "Ethical Perspectives on Legal Practice" (1985), 37 Stan. L.R. 589; and Jeffrey W. Stempel, Review of Stephen Landsman, *Readings on Adversarial Justice: The American Approach to Adjudication* (1988), 55 Brooklyn L.R. 165 (1989), 181.

40 See Wolfram, *supra*, note 3, 566; Smith, *supra*, note 27, 121-22; and Freedman, *supra*, note 8, 13-42.

weapons, in Judge Frankel's words, are "equally lethal for heroes and villains".[41]

As we have seen, the second common justification of the adversary system, the protection of individual rights from incursion by the state, is rarely a requirement in civil cases. There is accordingly little reason in a system of civil justice to compromise the objective of discerning the truth as effectively as possible.

Nor is the argument that the adversary system is more efficient universally accepted. In a 1991 Ontario case,[42] Justice Blenus Wright said that he believes that lawyers generally "are products and captives of an outmoded adversarial system". "Lawyers have a propensity in the adversarial process," he added, "to dredge up every conceivable issue." Little thought is usually given, Justice Wright said, to how cases could be tried more expeditiously.

A final thought, before we consider what should be done about all this:

In the adversary system, truth is sought through a process that is often characterized by absolutes, contradiction, polarization, mutually exclusive and incompatible categories, and binary results. We reason by selecting between dichotomies such as right and wrong, true and false, guilty and innocent, and justice and injustice. Outcomes are treated as wins and losses. What Edward de Bono calls "the sharp polarizations of our dichotomy habit" can bring an unhealthy rigidity to our thinking.[43] Polarization may also have the socially undesirable effect of increasing, rather than diminishing, conflict in society.

2.10 SHOULD WE ABOLISH THE ADVERSARY SYSTEM?

On the basis of this examination of the validity of the traditional justifications of the adversary system in civil litigation, one is tempted to wonder how the system could conceivably have survived for so long. A conclusion that the system should be abolished can nevertheless be drawn only if we are satisfied that an alternative is preferable.

As at least one commentator, Jeffrey Stempel, has observed, whether the adversary system is to be preferred to the usual comparative, namely the inquisitorial or arbitral system, depends very much upon how the question is framed:

---

41 Frankel, *supra*, note 7, at 1039. See also former Judge Frankel's book *Partisan Justice* (New York: Hill & Wang, 1980). Former Judge Frankel's views are discussed by Monroe H. Freedman, "Judge Frankel's Search for Truth" (1975), 123 U. of Pa. L.R. 1060; Judge R.J. Gerber, "Victory vs. Truth: The Adversary System and Its Ethics" (1987), 19 Arizona St. L.J. 3; and Harold See, "An Essay in Legal Ethics and the Search for Truth" (1989-90), 3 Georgetown Journal and Legal Ethics 323.

42 *Sterling Rubber Ltd. v. Canadian Imperial Bank of Commerce* (June 17, 1991), Doc. No. 9233/86 (Ont. Gen. Div.).

43 Edward de Bono, *I Am Right — You Are Wrong* (London: Viking, 1990), particularly at 5, 194-96 and 207; see also Menkel-Meadow, *supra*, note 3.

> "The selected readings seem to suggest that societies wanting an adjudication mechanism for dispute resolution, value articulation, and vindication of individual autonomy can either opt for the adversary mode, in which the judge and the lawyers are independent of the executive and the legislature or they can have a career civil servant who wants to retain his job and advance to higher levels of judging. Society can have lawyers who ferret the facts out or bureaucrats who compile dossiers . . . Of course, the same bipolarism suggests that society must choose between an official, detached, neutral search for truth and the overzealous mud wrestling of many attorneys, resulting in shredded documents, coached testimony, and discovery abuse. When the question is framed this way, adversarialism loses some of its luster."[44]

Despite its defects, the adversary system has developed procedures that are familiar to lawyers and the public alike. Pre-trial motions, examinations for discovery, opening statements, examinations in chief, cross-examinations, objections to the introduction of evidence, final arguments and appeals are all integral parts of a well-developed process that would have to be jettisoned if we were to replace the present system with one less familiar — and quite possibly less acceptable — to the public. At least one Canadian commentator has argued that for this reason improvements to the present system are to be preferred to the adoption of an alternative system.[45]

Similarly, Professor David Luban's conclusion is that although in civil litigation the traditional justifications of the adversary system are inadequate to sustain the argument for its survival, the system's continuance is nevertheless pragmatically justified: we need *some* system of dispute resolution; and the costs of replacing the present system, he argues, would outweigh the benefits to be realized by doing so.[46]

It is important, however, that we not fall into the trap of restricting our alternatives. As Professor Stempel has pointed out, we do not face a starkly bipolar choice "between a highly bureaucratized inquisitorial system and rock-em sock-em adversarialism".[47] A recognization of the deficiencies of the adversary system has brought about many reforms over the years, with the result that the system no longer operates in its pure form.

2.11 THE ADVERSARY SYSTEM TODAY

Civil litigation has undergone many changes over the years which, without altering the fundamental features of the adversary system in the narrow

44 Stempel, *supra*, note 39, at 186. For an engaging debate on the future of the adversary system, see Carrie Menkel-Meadow, "The Trouble with the Adversary System in a Post-modern, Multi-Cultural World", 38 Wm. & Mary L. Rev. 5 (1996) and Monroe H. Freedman, "The Trouble with Postmodern Zeal", 38 Wm. & Mary L. Rev. 63 (1996).

45 Robin S. Sharma, "The Adequacy of the Adversarial System in Charter Litigation" (1993), 3 National Journal of Constitutional Law 99 at 116.

46 David Luban, "The Adversary System Excuse" in Luban (ed.), *supra*, note 17, at 115; see also Joseph Graf Huber and Bernard H. Baumrin, "The Moral Obligations of Lawyers" (1988), 1 Canadian Journal of Law and Jurisprudence 105 at 111-13.

47 Stempel, *supra*, note 39, at 186.

sense, have been designed to temper the extravagances of lawyers whose behaviour is reminiscent of the system's origin in trial by combat.[48]

At one time, lawyers tried to keep hidden from their opponents all they knew about the case, including the identity of witnesses, what the witnesses were expected to say, and what documents were available to prove, or disprove, their case. (In Ontario, until 1975, documents in a party's possession did not have to be produced if they related exclusively to the opposite party's case.[49]) Today, all of this information is available as of right to other parties well before trial. Trials by ambush are for the most part things of the past. Discovery abuses and other forensic excesses may be visited with cost sanctions as well as by disciplinary proceedings, at least in the worst cases.[50]

In a leading 1991 criminal case, the Supreme Court of Canada made the following observation:

> "Production and discovery were foreign to the adversary process of adjudication in its earlier history when the element of surprise was one of the accepted weapons in the arsenal of the adversaries. . . . [I]n civil proceedings this aspect of the adversary process has long since disappeared."[51]

In family law, the *Divorce Act* requires petitioners' lawyers not only to discuss the possibility of reconciliation, but also to advise about such alternatives to litigation as mediation. Lawyers are also obliged to certify to the court that they have complied with this duty.[52]

In spite of the continuing pre-eminence of the lawyers' duty to the client in Canadian and American rules of professional conduct, those rules also place limitations upon the types of conduct that many lawyers consider to be features of an adversary system.

Under Canadian rules of professional conduct, lawyers have a duty to advise and encourage settlement whenever it is possible on a reasonable basis. The fact that this duty is enshrined both in rules governing advising clients and in rules governing advocacy is a clear indication that lawyers have such a duty both before and after litigation is commenced.[53]

---

48 See Coughlan, *supra*, note 9, at 140.

49 The Ontario Court of Appeal held in *Perini Ltd. v. Toronto Parking Authority* (1975), 6 O.R. (2d) 363 (C.A.) that parties have no right to withhold production on such a basis.

50 See, for example, Ontario Rules of Civil Procedure, R.R.O. 1990, reg. 194, rules 30 and 31; see also Richard Wasserstorm, "Roles and Morality" in Luban (ed.), *supra*, note 17, 25 at 36.

51 *R. v. Stinchcombe* (1991), 8 C.R. (4th) 277 at 282; see also Coughlan, *supra*, note 9, 161. Similarly, in the United States, the Federal Rules of Civil Procedure have eliminated the surprise and mystery which, according to one judge were once "as much a part of the procedure as the underlying disputes to be resolved": Thomas D. Lambros, "The Federal Rules of Civil Procedure: A New Adversarial Model for a New Era", 50 U. of Pittsburgh L.R. 789 at 789 (1984).

52 *The Divorce Act*, S.C. 1986, c. 4, s. 9; see also Coughlan, *supra*, note 9, 159.

53 C.B.A. Code, chapter III, commentary 6, and chapter IX, commentary 8; Ontario rule 2.02(2) and (3); British Columbia rules, chapter 1, rule 3(3).

Lawyers also have a duty to discourage the use of adversary proceedings where such proceedings are either useless[54] or, though legal, are motivated by malice.[55] Lawyers are enjoined by the rules to accede to reasonable requests concerning trial dates, adjournments, the waiver of procedural formalities and similar matters that do not prejudice clients' rights.[56] Similarly, lawyers "should not take advantage of or act without fair warning upon slips, irregularities, or mistakes on the part of other lawyers not going to the merits or involving the sacrifice of the client's rights".[57] Finally, lawyers have a duty under the rules of professional conduct to inform the court of any pertinent authority that the lawyer considers to be directly on point that has not been drawn to the court's attention.[58]

Although the improvements that are needed most urgently are improvements in outlook, further reforms to the system in a few particular areas would be welcome.

2.12 PUBLIC LAW, COMMISSIONS OF INQUIRY AND ADMINISTRATIVE TRIBUNAL HEARINGS

The Law Society of Upper Canada's rules of professional conduct specify that the lawyer's duty "to represent the client resolutely" extends not only to court proceedings but also to proceedings before boards, administrative tribunals and other bodies, regardless of their function or the informality of their procedures.[59]

There is of course an immense difference among the purposes and practices of the tribunals that comprise our system of administrative law. Adversarial procedures may be appropriate in some types of proceedings, but are wholly inappropriate in others.

The appropriateness of adversarial procedures in tribunal proceedings will depend in part upon the extent to which the tribunal is empowered to formulate general policy and affect individual rights. Professional discipline tribunals, for example, tend to cluster at the judicial end of the administrative-judicial continuum. They do not formulate policy, except in the sense that common law courts formulate policy incrementally through their judgments in individual cases. A given decision is likely to have a dramatic effect on the reputation and livelihood of the practitioner affected, and virtually no effect on the development of public policy. The proceedings are generally similar in form to criminal proceedings,

54 C.B.A. Code, chapter III, commentary 6; Ontario rule 2.02(2).

55 C.B.A. Code, chapter IX, commentary 2(a); Ontario rule 4.01(1) and (2).

56 C.B.A. Code, chapter XVI, commentary 3; Ontario rule 6.03(2); see also C.B.A. Code, chapter IX, commentary 7; and Ontario rule 4.01(1).

57 C.B.A. Code, chapter XVI, commentary 4; Ontario rule 6.03(3).

58 C.B.A. Code, chapter IX, commentary 2(h); Ontario rule 4.01(2)(h); see also Coughlan, *supra*, note 9, at 164-65.

59 Ontario rule 4.01(1), commentary. The C.B.A. Code contains no equivalent provision, but the fact that the rule creating the lawyer's duty employs the word "tribunal" makes it clear that the duty extends to proceedings before administrative boards.

with pleas of guilty or not guilty, cross-examination of witnesses called by a prosecutor who must discharge a burden of proof that in the most serious cases is similar to the criminal standard, and a penalty if guilt is established that not only may deprive practitioners of their livelihood but that may carry a stigma comparable to the stigma of having a criminal record.

In other types of tribunal proceedings — public inquiries, for example — the effect of the tribunal's decision may have little direct effect on individual rights, but great importance to the formulation of public policy.

There are likely to be significant inequalities among the parties to such proceedings, and many of the parties may not be adversaries in the sense that parties to civil litigation in the courts are adversaries. In such cases, adversarial procedures are unlikely to be conducive to effective decisionmaking.[60]

(*Continued on page 2–19*)

60 See Joan Dwyer, "Overcoming the Adversarial Bias in Tribunal Procedures" (1991), 20 Fed. L.R. 252; Patrick Robardet, "Should We Abandon the Adversarial Model in Favour of the Inquisitorial Model in Commissions of Inquiry?", [1990] Dalhousie L.J. 111; J.C. McRuer, *Report of the Royal Commission of Inquiry into Civil Rights* (Toronto: Queen's Printer, 1968) at 131-32; and Elliott Glicksman, "Judicialization of the Administrative Process: Adversarial Risks for Fairness" (1991), 42 So. Carolina L.R. 345.

Similarly, in the *Charter of Rights* and other public law litigation, as Dean Marilyn Pilkington of Osgoode Hall Law School has argued, the forms of the traditional adversary system may be particularly inappropriate.[61]

2.13 FAMILY LAW

Lawyers with significant experience in family law recognize the particular inappropriateness of adversarial procedures in matrimonial disputes. The parties to such disputes are far more likely than other litigants to continue to have contact with one another after their dispute is disposed of by settlement or judgment. Adversarial court proceedings tend to exacerbate rather than minimize differences.

It is generally possible for both parties to a matrimonial dispute, through negotiation or mediation, to salvage out of their marriage a settlement, within a normal range, of maintenance and access issues that is in the best interest of both parties and their children. Such a resolution is much more likely to be honoured than is a judgment imposed on the parties by a court.[62]

2.14 EXPERT WITNESSES

Judges and tribunal members often find that they are not really assisted by partisan expert opinion. At least one empirical study, perhaps not surprisingly, provides support for the conclusion that in an adversary system, expert witnesses' views may vary depending upon which side retains them.[63] In one case an Australian judge, when told that counsel for an insurer intended to call three named medical experts, responded by referring to the experts as the insurer's "usual panel of doctors who think you can do a full week's work without any arms or legs".[64]

Scepticism about the value of partisan expert evidence is anything but novel. In an article published in the Harvard Law Review in 1901,[65] Learned Hand assailed what he characterized as the "absurd" practice of litigants par-

61 Pilkington, *supra*, note 3, 51; see also Sharma, *supra*, note 45; and A. Chayes, "The Role of the Judge in Public Law Litigation" (1976), 89 Harvard L.R. 1281.

62 See Coughlan, *supra*, note 9, 160-61; and Sessums, *supra*, note 2, 73-74.

63 Randy K. Otto, "Bias and Expert Testimony of Mental Health Professionals and Adversarial Proceedings: A Preliminary Investigation" (1989), 7 Behaviourial Sciences and the Law 267. See also Ralph Slovenko, "The Role of the Expert (With Focus on Psychiatry) In the Adversarial System", Journal of Psychiatry and the Law, Summer 1988, 333; and Dwyer, *supra*, note 60 at 837.

64 *Vakauta v. Kelly* (1989), 87 A.L.R. 633 (Hunt, J.).

65 Learned Hand, "Historical and Practical Considerations Regarding Expert Testimony", 15 Harv. L. Rev. 40 (1901); Hand expressed a similar view 24 years later as a member of the Second Circuit Court of Appeals: *Elyria Iron & Steel Co. v. Mohegan Tube Co.*, 7 F.2d 827 (2d. Cir. 1925); see also Gerald Gunther, *Learned Hand: The Man and the Judge* (New York: Knopf, 1994) at 60, 312.

ading before a lay jury hired experts to testify on complex scientific questions. He advocated instead the appointment by the court of an advisory tribunal of independent experts to assist the court in resolving the contending submissions of the parties.

Such a system would resemble the one in place in German courts. There, a neutral expert is selected. The expert reports to the judge as an officer of the court. The question on which the expert's opinion is sought is formulated by the judge. The expert's opinion may be clarified or challenged by the parties.[66]

In such a system the cost of obtaining expert testimony is likely to be reduced appreciably, which may have the incidental effect of improving access to justice for less well-funded litigants.[67]

2.15 CONCLUSION

The essence of the adversary system is that the parties to litigation, through their counsel, are responsible for leading evidence before a passive adjudicator. To describe the system as adversarial may be a narrow and neutral comment on the proper role of the parties, their counsel, and the judge or tribunal.[68]

In fact, however, to describe the system as adversarial generally carries quite different connotations, and colours the way litigation lawyers perceive their role. To describe the system as adversarial is to describe other parties and their counsel as adversaries — or opponents, or enemies, if you will. In such a system, many lawyers conclude, one's goal is to defeat the enemy, and one's conduct must be abrasive and contentious.[69]

The problem with most reforms designed to temper the extravagances of the adversary system are that they are fundamentally incompatible with most lawyers' conception of their duty to promote their clients' interest. Rules intended to accomplish full, efficient and meaningful discovery, for instance, have done little to reduce the contentious behaviour whereby litigation lawyers make adverse parties fight for everything they seek.[70]

What is needed is a revised understanding of the true meaning of the adversary system. To describe the system as adversarial should not connote contrariness or contentiousness, but rather only that the parties, through their counsel, are responsible for leading evidence before a neutral adjudicator.

Challenging the adversarial culture will not be easy, as it is an ethic that is deeply ingrained.[71] In doing so we need not, however, restrict our choices

66 See J.H. Langbein, "The German Advantage in Civil Procedure" (1985), 52 U. Chicago L.R. 823, 837.
67 Gerber, *supra*, note 9 at 12.
68 See Coughlan, *supra*, note 9, at 143, 170.
69 *Ibid.* 143, 170.
70 Wolfson, *supra*, note 11, at 19-20, 45, 48.
71 *Ibid.* 65.

to the bipolar extremes of European inquisitorial or arbitral systems and the adversary system as it is practised at present in Canada. We should avoid, in other words, the sharp dichotomies that characterize the adversary system itself.

3

Confidentiality

> You will tell nobody, even in the strictest confidence. With your own secrets you may do as you wish; but these professional secrets are not yours, and you must do nothing with them save preserve them inviolate and unused.[1]

> A number of rationales are offered in support. The first harkens back to adolescence: "Friends don't squeal on friends." The rules by which adolescents live hardly ever make good law.[2]

3.1 INTRODUCTION

Almost all of the most intractable problems of legal ethics, including most conflict of interest problems, are at bottom confidentiality problems. The point of divergence between the public's and the profession's conceptions of moral behaviour is the lawyer's duty of confidentiality.

Thus, in one of the cases discussed in chapter 2 the conduct of the defence lawyer who concealed from the plaintiff knowledge of the life-threatening aortic aneurism that might claim the plaintiff's life was held to be justifiable on the ground that the defence lawyer had a duty to his client to maintain that information in confidence. In the Lake Pleasant Bodies Case, also discussed in chapter 2, the conduct of the defence lawyers who concealed from the distraught parent of a woman who had been murdered by their client their knowledge of the woman's death, again, was held to be justifiable on the ground that the defence lawyers had a duty to their client to maintain that information in confidence. The duty of confidentiality is sometimes invoked by lawyers to justify behaviour considered by most non-lawyers to be monstrous.

The lawyer's duty of confidentiality is generally salutary and perhaps even necessary. We value the right to counsel, and believe that it is desirable

---

1 Robert E. Megarry, "Convocation Address", Law Society of Upper Canada Gazette, vol. 17, no. 1 (March, 1983), p. 41 at 43-44.

2 Robert J. Kutak, "The Adversary System and the Practice of Law" in David Luban (ed.), *The Good Lawyer: Lawyers' Roles and Lawyers' Ethics* (Totowa, New Jersey: Rowan & Allenhead, 1983), p. 172 at 181.

that lay people have access to legal expertise. Lawyers cannot responsibly advise clients unless they have a firm grasp of the relevant facts and the clients' objectives as communicated, unreservedly, by the clients. It is therefore assumed (though it has evidently never been proven empirically) that to foster such open communication lawyers must be able to assure clients that their discussions will always remain confidential unless the clients agree that they may be disclosed. To force a client to choose between legal representation without effective communication and legal representation with all secrets revealed publicly is to deprive the client in some cases of the right to counsel.[3]

The troublesome issues that the duty of confidentiality raises have to do with the sufficiency of currently recognized exceptions and the resolution of conflicts with such other responsibilities as the lawyer's duty to be candid with courts and tribunals. Issues in the latter category are dealt with in more detail in chapters 4 and 7.

It should be said here, however, that the lawyer's duty of confidentiality is often an obstacle to the search for truth and, albeit rarely, may result in the conviction of innocent people. In one American case two lawyers were prevented from testifying at a murder trial that a former client, who had since died, had confessed to the murders with which the accused person was charged, as the prosecutor objected that the admission of their evidence would breach solicitor-client privilege.[4] In a similar case, a lawyer was mercifully spared the fate of having to keep his client's admission of murder to himself while another man, serving a death sentence for a murder that he had not committed, was electrocuted.[5]

Rules of professional conduct do not always resolve conflicts among rules. The difficulties created are most acute where the duty of confidentiality conflicts with the duty of candour. Professor Anthony Amsterdam of Stanford Law School has said that these rules are of as much use to the practising lawyer in the courtroom "as a Valentine card would be to a heart surgeon in the operating room."[6]

The Code of Conduct for Lawyers in the European Community puts the lawyer's duty to the courts and the public on an equal footing with the law-

---

3 The policies underlying the duty of confidentiality are discussed, among many other places, in the C.B.A. Code, chapter IV, commentary 2; Ontario rule 4, commentary 2; Charles Wolfram, *Modern Legal Ethics* (St. Paul, Minnesota: West, 1986), pp. 243-245; and L. Ray Patterson, "An Inquiry Into the Nature of Legal Ethics: The Relevance and Role of the Client" (1987-88) 1 Georgetown Journal of Legal Ethics 43.

4 *State v. Macumber*, 112 Ariz. 569 (1976). The accused person's conviction was reversed on other grounds.

5 See David A. Kaplan, "Death Row Dilemma", National Law Journal (January 28, 1988), p. 35. See also *State of New Mexico v. Valdez*, 618 P. 2d 1234 (S. Ct. New Mexico, 1980).

6 Quoted in Monroe H. Freedman, *Lawyers' Ethics In An Adversary System* (New York: Bobbs-Merrill, 1975), p. vii.

yer's duty to the client rather than placing more prominence on the latter duty. It also imposes a higher duty of candour to the courts than do North American rules of professional conduct.[7]

3.2 THE CONFIDENTIALITY RULE

Rules of professional conduct require lawyers to hold in strict confidence all information concerning the business and affairs of clients acquired in the course of a professional relationship. Lawyers must not divulge any such information without the express or implied authorization of their client unless required by law to do so.[8]

The ethical duty of confidentiality is broader than the evidentiary rule of solicitor-client privilege in three ways. First, it requires lawyers to maintain information in confidence, whereas the privilege merely prevents the introduction of confidential information into evidence. Second, it applies not only to confidential communications between clients and lawyers that are exchanged for the purpose of obtaining legal advice, but to all information concerning the clients' affairs acquired from any source during the course of the professional relationship. Third, it applies even though others may share the lawyer's knowledge.[9]

Apart altogether from rules of professional conduct, the Supreme Court of Canada has held that though solicitor-client privilege was originally a rule of evidence, it is now recognized that the client's right to confidentiality gives rise as well to a substantive rule of law that is much broader than the evidentiary privilege. Due to the substantive rule, it is not necessary to wait for an examination for discovery, preliminary inquiry or trial at which a communication is sought to be introduced in evidence to raise the issue of confidentiality. The confidentiality of a communication may be raised, the court held, in any circumstances in which the communication is likely to be disclosed without the client's consent, for example upon the execution of a search warrant.[10]

The Supreme Court of Canada has also held that a lawyer who is called to testify should not be asked questions framed so as to elicit disclosure of confidential communications between lawyer and client unless a waiver of privilege is tendered in evidence. In the absence of such a waiver, the court added, the lawyer witness has a duty to refuse to divulge the confidential information. If the

7 See Geoffrey C. Hazard, Jr., "The European Community's Ethics Code Bears A Family Resemblance to Earlier A.B.A. Codes", National Law Journal (March 30, 1992), p. 13.

8 C.B.A. Code, chapter IV, rule; Ontario rule 2.03; Quebec rule 3.06. The Alberta Rules provide that "A lawyer shall disclose confidential information to the Law Society when required to do so by the Law Society." (Chapter 7, rule 8(a)).

9 C.B.A. Code, chapter IV, commentary 2; Ontario rule 2.03(1) and accompanying commentary. See also David Luban, *Lawyers and Justice: An Ethical Study* (Princeton, New Jersey: Princeton University Press, 1988), p. 201.

10 *Descôteaux v. Mierzwinski*, [1982] 1 S.C.R. 860. See also *Solosky v. Canada*, [1980] 1 S.C.R. 821; and Jeffrey Frank Chamberlain, "Confidentiality and the Case of Robert Garrow's Lawyers" (1976) 25 Buffalo L.R. 212.

lawyer neglects to claim privilege, the court should refuse to receive the confidential information in evidence, whether or not objection is taken.[11]

Just as the common law thus recognizes the existence of a substantive right of clients to insist that communications with their lawyers be maintained in confidence, so too do rules of professional conduct recognize that the purpose of the evidentiary privilege would be defeated if lawyers were free to divulge professional confidences out of court, without clients' consent.[12]

No privilege attaches to documents created in furtherance of a fraud; the privilege is not displaced, however, by a mere allegation of fraud. Although knowledge of the fraud by the solicitors need not be proven, a *prima facie* case that a fraud has occurred must be made out.[12.1]

A substantial body of jurisprudence has developed concerning how the solicitor-client privilege may be extinguished. Generally, disclosure to third parties will constitute an implied waiver of privilege.[13] Once the privilege is waived it is generally irretrievable.

In a 1999 case[13.1] the Saskatchewan Court of Queen's Bench upheld a claim of solicitor-client privilege over notes a client had given her lawyer, in spite of the client's reliance on the contents of the notes in an affidavit she swore in support of the privilege claim. The Court applied the principle that in order to waive privilege a client must not only know of the existence of the right, but must clearly intend to forego it.

The lawyer's duty of confidentiality continues indefinitely, even if the solicitor-client relationship is terminated.[14] A lawyer must not even disclose information received on behalf of a client to the client's new lawyer without the client's consent.

The duty also survives the death of the client; hence the inability of the lawyers in the American case mentioned above to testify at a murder trial that a

---

11 *Bell v. Smith,* [1968] S.C.R. 664. See also Brad Risinger, "Waiver of the Attorney-Client Privilege" (1989-90) 3 Georgetown Journal of Legal Ethics 125.

12 C.B.A. Code, chapter IV, commentaries 1 and 2; Ontario rule 2.03(1) and accompanying commentary. The C.B.A. Code, in commentary 9 to chapter IV, and the Ontario rules, in the commentary to rule 2.03(1), also address the circumstances in which confidential information may be disclosed with the implied authority of the client.

12.1 *Canbook Distribution Corp. v. Borins* (1999), 7 C.B.R. (4th) 121 (Ont. Gen. Div. [Commercial List]), *Goodman & Carr v. Minister of National Revenue,* [1968] 2 O.R. 814 (H.C.). The *Canbook* case also stands for the proposition (articulated previously in *Re Clarkson Co. v. Chilcott* (1984), 48 O.R. (2d) 545 (C.A.)) that an assignee in bankruptcy has no legal right to waive privilege with respect to legal advice given the bankrupt.

13 See, for example, *London Trust & Savings Corp. v. Corbett* (1994), 24 C.P.C. (3d) 226 (Ont.Gen.Div.); *Wellman v. General Crane Industries Ltd.* (1986), 20 O.A.C. 38 (H.C.); and *R. v. Kotapski* (1981), 66 C.C.C. (2d) 78 (Que.S.C.), leave to appeal refused 13 C.C.C. (3d) 185.

13.1 *R. v. Oberkirsch* (1999), 176 Sask. R. 230 (Q.B.).

14 C.B.A. Code, chapter IV, commentary 4; Ontario rule 2.03(1) and accompanying commentary.

former client who had since died had confessed to the murder with which the accused person was charged.[15]

In a 1983 British Columbia case,[16] a woman succeeded in an action against her former lawyer for damages for breach of contract. The action was based upon the lawyer's breach of his duty of confidentiality. The plaintiff had retained the lawyer to institute divorce proceedings. She had also retained a private investigator to obtain evidence of her husband's adultery.

The plaintiff later informed her lawyer that she was having an affair with the private investigator. The lawyer withdrew from the brief and notified the Royal Canadian Mounted Police, which had supervisory jurisdiction over private investigators, and other authorities. The lawyer believed in good faith that the investigator's conduct had been improper. He wished to prevent a possible fraud on the court. The British Columbia Supreme Court held, however, that the lawyer had a duty not to divulge the information, which he had acquired from the plaintiff in his professional capacity. Neither the determination of the retainer nor the lawyer's good intentions relieved him of his duty.

Lawyers must not deal in confidential information by using it for their own benefit or for the benefit of persons other than clients; nor may they use confidential information to the disadvantage of clients.[17] Thus in a 1986 Ontario case,[18] a lawyer was found liable for breaching his fiduciary duty to his client when he had an affair with his client's wife. The court found that the lawyer had learned, while he was acting for the plaintiff in a wrongful dismissal action, that the plaintiff had developed sexual problems, allegedly as a result of the wrongful termination of his employment. The lawyer relied on that information in the wrongful dismissal action to assert a claim for damages for mental distress.

On the evening on which the lawyer completed his written argument in the wrongful dismissal case, he and his client's wife began an affair which lasted for a few weeks. The client alleged, and the court found, that the client suffered compensable anxiety and emotional upset as a result of his discovery of the affair. The court awarded special and general damages to the client. The judgment was upheld on appeal.[19]

The lawyer was also publicly reprimanded for conduct unbecoming a barrister and solicitor as a result of the court's finding.[20]

---

15 *State v. Macumber*, 112 Ariz. 569 (1976).

16 *Ott v. Fleishman* (1983), 46 B.C.L.R. 321 (S.C.). See also *Rademaker, MacDougall & Co. v. Number Ten Holdings Ltd.* (1983), 47 B.C.L.R. 376 (S.C.), reversed (1985), 60 B.C.L.R. 301 (C.A.); and *Guay v. Société Franco-Manitobaine* (1985), 37 Man. R. (2d) 16 (Q.B.).

17 C.B.A. Code, chapter IV, commentary 5; Ontario rule 2.03(6) and accompanying commentary.

18 *Szarfer v. Chodos* (1986), 54 O.R. (2d) 663 (H.C.).

19 (1988), 66 O.R. (2d) 350 (C.A.).

20 *Re Chodos, (No. 1)*, report adopted by Convocation of the Law Society of Upper Canada, November 22, 1986.

Lawyers must not trade in cheap prattle. Thus rules of professional conduct exhort lawyers to avoid indiscreet conversations, even with their spouses and families, about clients' affairs, even if clients are not named or otherwise identified. Apart from the danger that prejudice to clients may result from gossip being overheard, listeners' respect for lawyers is likely, the rules say, to be diminished.[21] Loose lips sink ships — so went the wartime warning.

Not all communications between clients and lawyers are privileged. To be privileged, communications must be made during the course of the clients' seeking legal advice and with the intention that the communications be maintained in confidence. Thus in a 1980 decision,[22] the Supreme Court of Canada ruled that an inmate of a penitentiary was not entitled to a declaration that all correspondence between his lawyer and him was privileged and should therefore be delivered to him unopened.

Similarly, in a 1976 decision,[23] the British Columbia Court of Appeal held that it does not follow from the fact that documents are seized from a lawyer's office that they are necessarily privileged. In a 1992 decision,[24] the same court ruled in a narcotics importing prosecution that the accused persons' lawyers' trust account records, which disclosed transfers of large sums of money suspected to be the proceeds of crime, were not privileged. The court distinguished between real evidence of an accounting nature and confidential communications made in a professional capacity.

Accounts rendered by lawyers to clients, however, may contain privileged information. In a 1998 decision of the Federal Court of Appeal[24.1] the appellant, a former federal cabinet minister, was the subject of an inquiry into conflict of interest allegations arising from certain business dealings. After the inquiry submitted its report to the House of Commons, a report that criticized the appellant, the appellant applied under the *Access to Information Act* for disclosure of the billing accounts and supporting documents of Commission counsel. The appellant sought these documents in support of his allegation that the inquiry's commissioner had allowed commission counsel to write or at least assist in the preparation of the report.

The appellant was provided with 336 pages of legal accounts, receipts and other related documents, but the narrative portions of 73 pages of the disclosed accounts were expurgated on the basis of solicitor-client privilege.

---

21 C.B.A. Code, chapter IV, commentary 7; Ontario rule 2.03(1) and accompanying commentary.

22 *Solosky v. Canada*, [1980] 1 S.C.R. 821. See also *R. v. Bencardino* (1973), 15 C.C.C. (2d) 342 at 349 (Ont. C.A.).

23 *Re B.X. Developments Ltd. and R.* (1976), 70 D.L.R. (3d) 366 (B.C. C.A.).

24 *R. v. Joubert* (1992), 69 C.C.C. (3d) 553 (B.C. C.A.), application for reconsideration refused (May 7, 1992), Doc. No. CA012513 (B.C. C.A.), leave to appeal to S.C.C. refused (December 10, 1992), Doc. No. 22885 (S.C.C.).

24.1 *Stevens v. Canada (Prime Minister)*, (*sub nom. Stevens v. Canada (Privy Council)* 161 D.L.R. (4th) 85 (Fed. C.A.).

On application for judicial review, Justice Rothstein of the Federal Court Trial Division held that the expurgated material was protected by solicitor-client privilege, as it was "directly related to the seeking, formulating or giving of legal advice or assistance."

The Federal Court of Appeal dismissed the appeal. A lawyer's bills of account are at the heart of the solicitor-client relationship, the Court held, as are the terms of the retainer, the arrangements with respect to payment, the types of services rendered, and their cost. A lawyer's bills of account are privileged, while a lawyer's trust account records and other accounting records are not, the Court held, because the former is integral to the seeking, formulating and giving of legal advice, whereas the latter relates to acts done by counsel, which are not protected by solicitor-client privilege. In the present case the narrative portions of the bills of account were communications for the purpose of obtaining legal advice.

The Court also observed that while a government may be more ready than a private party to waive privilege so that is activities will be transparent, it has no higher duty in law to do so. A government is not granted less protection than any other client by the law of solicitor-client privilege.

Finally, the Court distinguished between solicitor-client privilege and a guarantee of confidentiality: the former has evolved from a rule of evidence to become a substantive right; the latter is an ethical or equitable doctrine. The law may in some circumstances compel a person to betray a mere confidence, the Court held, but may not compel someone to reveal something that is the subject of solicitor-client privilege.

The identity of a client may also be both confidential and privileged. Rules of professional conduct stipulate that lawyers should not disclose that they have been consulted or retained by a particular person about a particular matter unless the nature of the matter requires such disclosure.[25] In a 1973 decision of the British Columbia Supreme Court,[26] the name of the client was held to be a privileged communication. There, a driver who had left the scene of a collision disclosed his identity confidentially to his lawyer for the purpose of receiving professional advice. The court held that by virtue of the nature of the matter the essence of the confidential communication was the client's identity.

The same problem was litigated in a widely publicized American case 13 years later. On March 9, 1986, Mark Baltes died as a result of a collision caused

---

25 C.B.A. Code, chapter IV, commentary 3; Ontario rule 2.03(1) and accompanying commentary; British Columbia rules, chapter 5, rule 3. Chapter 7 of rule 2 of the Alberta rules provides that "A lawyer shall not disclose the identity of a client nor the fact of the lawyer's representation".

26 *Thorson v. Jones* (1973), 38 D.L.R. (3d) 312 (B.C. S.C.). See also *Kupferstein v. Gottlieb, Hoffman & Kumer* (1989), 40 C.P.C. (2d) 111 (Ont. Master). The general rule, nevertheless, is that the identity of a client is not protected by solicitor-client privilege unless the client's identity is the essence of the confidential communication: *Ontario (Securities Commission) v. Greymac Credit Corp.* (1983), 41 O.R. (2d) 328 at 338 (Div. Ct.); *Lukas v. Lawson* (1993), 13 O.R. (3d) 447 (Master).

by a driver who left the scene. More than 24 hours later the driver consulted a lawyer. He asked the lawyer to try to negotiate a settlement with the authorities without identifying him. The lawyer retained a second lawyer to act as an intermediary, so that the client's identity would not be discovered by surveillance of the first lawyer's office. The negotiations failed. The first lawyer identified himself as the driver's counsel.

Mr. Baltes' parents were dismayed by the fact that a lawyer who knew who had been responsible for their son's death refused to identify him. They commenced a civil action for damages against John Doe, the unidentified driver, and attempted to subpoena the lawyer to testify on the issue of the driver's identity. The lawyer claimed that the information was privileged, and his claim was upheld by a State Circuit Court judge. A few weeks later the judge rescinded his order so that the issue could be reconsidered. Before the issue was determined, however, the police located the driver of the car.

The case attracted an extraordinary amount of media attention. The New York Times and CBS News were among many news organizations that covered the controversy.

Public opinion was largely critical of the role played by the lawyer. To the extent that that opinion was based upon fear that offenders could avoid detection merely by admitting wrongdoing to lawyers, it was of course misinformed, as the outcome of the case demonstrates.

It is true that if it were not for the solicitor-client privilege the driver of the car which struck Mark Baltes would have been brought to justice sooner. It does not follow that lawyers' duty to protect the public interest requires them to disclose the identity of clients who admit having committed offences. To impose such a requirement would limit access to legal advice and defeat the right to counsel. Without an expectation that his communications with his lawyer would be maintained in confidence, the driver would not have sought his lawyer's advice. Instead he would have realized that approaching a lawyer to ascertain the extent of his possible legal exposure would be tantamount to confessing to the police. In the long term, society would suffer. Lawyers' professional duties should not be equated with those of police officers.[27]

Confidential communications with professionals other than lawyers are also privileged in narrowly defined circumstances. In a 1991 decision,[28] however, the Supreme Court of Canada held that there should not be a recognized class privilege for confidential communications with religious advisors. The policy reasons supporting a class privilege for such communications are less compelling, the court observed, than the reason underlying the class privilege for communications

27 See John R. Przypyszny in "Public Assault on the Attorney-Client Privilege: Ramifications of *Baltes v. Doe*" (1989-90) 3 Georgetown Journal of Legal Ethics 351. See also Robert J. Kutak, "The Adversary System and the Practice of Law" in David Luban (ed.), *The Good Lawyer: Lawyers' Roles and Lawyers' Ethics* (Totowa, New Jersey: Rowan & Allenhead, 1983), p. 172 at 184.

28 *R. v. Fosty*, [1991] 3 S.C.R. 263 (*sub nom. R. v. Gruenke*).

between client and solicitor: namely, that the relationship and the communications between client and solicitor are essential to the effective operation of the legal system. Communications with religious advisors, the court added, are not inextricably linked with the justice system in the same way, despite their social importance.

Thus confidential communications between client and legal advisor are *prima facie* privileged as a class, while confidential communications between individual and religious advisor are *prima facie* non-privileged. Communications in the latter category may nevertheless be protected from disclosure on a case-by-case basis if all four parts of the Wigmore test are satisfied: (i) the communications must originate in a confidence that they will not be disclosed; (ii) this element of confidentiality must be essential to the full and satisfactory maintenance of the relation between the parties; (iii) the relation must be one that in the opinion of the community ought to be sedulously fostered; and (iv) the injury that would inure to the relation by disclosure of the communications must be greater than the benefit thereby gained for the correct disposal of litigation.[29]

It is doubtful whether well-informed non-lawyers would accept that communications between clients and their legal advisors should be *prima facie* privileged while communications between individuals and their spiritual advisors (or between patients and their psychotherapists, among other relationships) should *prima facie* be non-privileged. The distinction raises suspicions of unfair special treatment of the client-lawyer relationship. A case-by-case treatment of confidential communications with all professionals, including lawyers, based upon the Wigmore test — perhaps as modified to weigh interests other than the professional relationship and the correct disposal of litigation — would be preferable to the dichotomy recognized by the law at present.[30] This point is developed in more detail below.

3.2.1 INADVERTENT DISCLOSURE OF CONFIDENTIAL INFORMATION

The courts will exercise their equitable jurisdiction to restrain the publication or use of confidential information improperly or surreptitiously obtained.[30.1] This jurisdiction has also been invoked where privileged documents have inadvertently been disclosed to adverse parties in litigation,[30.2] though the circumstances in

---

29 The Wigmore test is set forth, among many other places, in the judgment of Chief Justice Lamer in the *Fosty* case, *ibid.*, p. 284.

30 See John T. Noonan, Jr., "The Purposes of Advocacy and the Limits of Confidentiality" (1966) 64 Michigan L.R. 1485 at 1485-1486.

30.1 *Ashburton (Lord) v. Pape*, [1913] 2 Ch. 469, [1911-13] All E.R. Rep. 708 (C.A.).

30.2 *Guiness Peat Properties Ltd. v. Fitzroy Robinson Partnership*, [1987] 2 All E.R. 716 (C.A.); *English and American Insurance Co. v. Herbert Smith & Co.*, Lloyd's Maritime Law Newsletter, January 29, 1987; *Royal Bank v. Lee* (1992), 9 C.P.C. (3d) 199, 3 Alta. L.R. (3d) 187, 127 A.R. 236, 20 W.A.C. 236 (C.A.); and *Airst v. Airst* (1998), 37 O.R. (3d) 654 (Gen. Div.).

which this jurisdiction should be exercised has not been settled by the Supreme Court of Canada. Decisions of courts of appeal in Alberta and Manitoba on the point conflict.[30.3]

At present, it is clear that:

(1) Where solicitors to one party to litigation have mistakenly listed, in an affidavit of documents, a document for which they could properly have claimed privilege, the court will ordinarily permit an amendment at any time before the document is inspected by or on behalf of adverse parties;

(2) Where, however, adverse parties or their solicitors have inspected such a document, it will generally be too late for the party seeking to claim privilege to attempt to correct the mistake by applying for injunctive relief; and

(3) Nevertheless, the court will grant injunctive relief to protect the mistaken party where the adverse party or its solicitor either (a) has procured inspection of the document by fraud, or (b) on inspection, realizes that the document was produced only by reason of an obvious mistake.[30.4]

What is unclear is whether there may be other exceptions to the general rule set out in the second enumerated principle. The Manitoba Court of Appeal has expressed the view that, in accordance with general principles of equity, any such exception would necessarily involve an unconscionable use of the document by the party to whom it had been delivered.[30.5] In other cases, courts have held that the privilege has not been waived, and that accordingly injunctive relief will be granted where documents have been produced (and inspected) as a result of a mere mistake.[30.6] In light of the conflicting decisions at the Court of Appeal level, as mentioned above, the question will have to be resolved by the Supreme Court of Canada.

30.3 *Cf. Royal Bank v. Lee, supra*, note 30.2, and *C. (J.M.N.) v. Winnipeg Child and Family Services* (May 26, 1997), AH 97-30-03267 (Man. C.A.).

30.4 *Guiness Peat Properties Ltd. v. Fitzroy Robinson Partnership, supra*, note 30.2, at 730-31.

30.5 *C. (J.M.N.) v. Winnipeg Child and Family Services, supra*, note 30.3, at 10.

30.6 *Royal Bank v. Lee, supra*, note 30.2. See also *Goddart v. Nationwide Building Society*, [1987] Q.B. 670 (C.A.), and British Columbia rules, chapter 5, rule 15, which requires lawyers who come into possession of documents intended for opposing parties to return them unread and uncopied or, if they have read the documents in whole or in part before realizing that they were not intended for them, to cease reading, return the documents uncopied, and inform the opposing party of the extent to which they are aware of the contents and what use they intend to make of the information. See also *Coulombe (Litigation Guardian of) v. Beard* (1993), 22 C.P.C. (3d) 101, (*sub nom. Coulombe v. Beard*) 16 O.R. (3d) 627 (Gen. Div.).

3.3 CONFIDENTIALITY AND THE CORPORATE CLIENT

Neither rules of professional conduct nor the common law differentiate between the duties of confidentiality owed by lawyers to individual and corporate clients.[31] A persuasive case can be made that they should.

Many of the cases that have called into question the desirability of invariably requiring lawyers to maintain in confidence information acquired about clients' affairs have involved powerful and unscrupulous corporations that have committed criminal offences and that have been deserving of little public sympathy.

For example, in an American case a computer leasing firm obtained more than 210 million dollars in fraudulent loans. Its outside counsel, a large firm, was placed in a highly compromising position by its duty of confidentiality. When it was warned that it might be in the midst of a vast fraud, the law firm sought the advice of respected experts in legal ethics. With the experts' approval the firm proceeded to close further loan transactions for the client. When it learned that as a result of these new loans the client had defrauded lenders of more than 60 million dollars the firm withdrew from its representation of the client. Even then, however, it kept its silence, and the client was able to defraud lenders of a further 15 million dollars, using new lawyers.[32]

Proponents of arguments supporting widespread protection of confidentiality usually select as examples of clients in need of the protection powerless individuals charged with criminal offences who are confronting the powerful forces of the state. These clients rely on lawyers as their only champions against mighty and hostile forces. To compel them to select between legal representation without open communication and legal representation with all communications revealed to the prosecution would be to deprive them in some cases of the right to counsel. This would be an affront to human dignity. Hence the client's right, and the lawyer's duty, of confidentiality.

However, arguments appealing to human dignity are inapposite where the client is a corporation or other organization. And it is unrealistic to contend that confidentiality is necessary to safeguard the right to counsel where the clients are corporations that are impelled by circumstances and business necessity to retain lawyers.

This is not to suggest, of course, that corporations should not be entitled as a rule to require their lawyers to maintain solicitor-client communications in confidence. Rather, it is to suggest that the rule should not be applied mechanically, without regard for its rationale. An approach that balances the need for

31 In *Upjohn v. United States*, 101 S. Ct. 677 (1981), the United States Supreme Court made it clear that the client-solicitor privilege extends to communications between corporation lawyers and all employees of the corporation, not just those who are part of a control group. As for the applicability of solicitor-client privilege to in-house counsel, see text accompanying note 1.1 to chapter 20.

32 The case is discussed by Stuart Taylor, Jr., in "Ethics and the Law: A Case History", *New York Times Magazine* (January 9, 1983), p. 31; and by Luban, *supra*, note 27, pp. 11-12.

confidentiality and the need for disclosure might well permit or even require lawyers to disclose corporate illegality.[33] The professional responsibility ramifications of corporate lawyers' whistleblowing are discussed in chapter 20.

3.4 THE FUTURE CRIME OR HARM EXCEPTION

Rules of professional conduct generally provide that lawyers may disclose confidential information in certain circumstances to prevent a crime, or to prevent death or serious bodily harm. The Canadian Bar Association's Code of Professional Conduct[34] provides that disclosure of information necessary to prevent a crime will be justified if the lawyer has reasonable grounds for believing that a crime is likely to be committed. The CBA Code's provision also specifies that such disclosure is mandatory when the anticipated crime is one involving violence. The circumstances in which disclosure is considered justifiable vary considerably among Canadian jurisdictions. New Brunswick has a particularly broad exception, while Ontario has a particularly narrow exception. Each of these exceptions is discussed below.

This exception to the confidentiality rule is based upon the policies that lawyers must not assist clients in planning unlawful acts, and that lawyers have a public responsibility to prevent harm. Except perhaps in cases involving continuing crimes, the exception does no damage to the policy underlying the rule itself, at least in situations in which the rule is explained to clients before they disclose their intention to commit a crime.[35]

The main policy issues are (i) whether disclosure should ever be mandatory and (ii) whether disclosure should be permitted to prevent any crime or only to prevent serious crimes (or harm). In jurisdictions in which the CBA Code has been adopted (as noted above) disclosure is mandatory when the anticipated crime is one involving violence. In Alberta[36] a lawyer must disclose confidential information when necessary to prevent a crime likely to result in death or serious bodily harm, and in New Brunswick disclosure is mandatory if the crime is "serious".[37] In British Columbia[38] and Ontario[38.1] disclosure is never mandatory.

---

33 See Luban, *supra*, note 27, p. 11; David Luban, *Lawyers and Justice: An Ethical Study* (Princeton, New Jersey: Princeton University Press, 1988), pp. 182-183; and Charles Wolfram, *Modern Legal Ethics* (St. Paul, Minnesota: West, 1986), pp. 283-284.

34 Chapter IV, commentary 11.

35 See Lillian S. Hagen, "Client Confidentiality: An Overview and the Crime — Fraud Exception" (1988-89) 2 Georgetown Journal of Legal Ethics 277 at 281; and Bruce M. Landesman, "Confidentiality and the Lawyer-Client Relationship" in Luban, *supra*, note 27, p. 191 at 192, 210 and 213.

36 Alberta rules, chapter 7, rule 8.

37 New Brunswick Professional Conduct Handbook, Part C, rule 5. See also Beverley G. Smith, Professional Conduct for Canadian Lawyers (Toronto: Butterworth's, 1989), p. 177.

38 British Columbia rules, chapter 5, rule 12.

38.1 Ontario rule 2.03 (3).

The CBA Code allows disclosure to prevent any crime, as does the British Columbia rule. The Ontario rule was to the same effect until November 1 2000, when the current, much more restrictive, rule came into force. The wording of the current Ontario rule is derived from a standard articulated by the Supreme Court of Canada in a 1999 case[38.2] in which the Court considered whether solicitor-client privilege may be set aside in the interest of protecting public safety.

An accused was charged with aggravated sexual assault on a prostitute. His counsel referred him to a psychiatrist hoping it would be of assistance in preparing a defence or in mitigation of sentence. Counsel advised that the consultation would be privileged just as a consultation with counsel would be.

The accused described to the psychiatrist in considerable detail his plan to kidnap, rape, and kill prostitutes. The psychiatrist concluded, and informed counsel, that in his opinion the accused was dangerous and would likely commit future offences unless he received treatment.

The accused pleaded guilty to aggravated assault, and the psychiatrist learned that his concerns would not be addressed in the sentencing hearing.

The psychiatrist commenced an action for a declaration that he was entitled to disclose the information in his possession in the interests of public safety.

The Supreme Court of Canada held that in these circumstances the solicitor-client privilege must be set aside for the protection of members of the public.

Three factors should be considered in determining, the majority of the Court held, in determining whether public safety overrides solicitor-client privilege: (1) whether there is a clear risk to an identifiable person or group; (2) whether there is a risk of serious bodily harm or death; and (3) whether the danger is imminent. In the present case, the Court determined, a reasonable observer would consider the potential danger posed by the accused to be clear, serious, and imminent.

The Court ordered that the file be unsealed and that a ban on the publication of the contents of the file be removed, except for portions of the psychiatrist's affidavit that did not fall within the public safety exception.

Lamer, C.J., and Major and Binnie JJ., dissenting, agreed that the danger in the present case was sufficiently clear, serious and imminent to justify a warning to the authorities, but would have limited the scope of the disclosure to permitting the psychiatrist to warn the authorities that the accused poses a threat to prostitutes in a specific area. The psychiatrist should not, in the dissenting justices' opinion, disclose any communication from the accused relating to the circumstances of the offence. This approach would foster a climate in which dangerous individuals would be more likely to seek treatment. As the facts of this case illustrate, the accused was diagnosed and made aware of the possibility of treatment only because he felt secure in confiding to the psychiatrist. The breach of privilege, in the opinion of the dissenting justices, should be as narrow as possible so as to avoid conscriptive evidence, such as the accused's confession, being revealed unnecessarily.

38.2 *Smith v Jones*, [1999] 1 S.C.R. 455.

Thus, the current Ontario rule provides that where a lawyer believes on reasonable grounds that there is an imminent risk to an identifiable person or group of death or serious bodily harm, including serious psychological harm that substantially interferes with health or well-being, the lawyer may disclose confidential information pursuant to judicial order where practicable, where it is necessary to do so in order to prevent the death or harm. The lawyer must not disclose more information than is required.[38.3]

In New Brunswick, the relevant rule of professional conduct goes even further than does the relevant provision of the Canadian Bar Association Code. The New Brunswick rule provides that lawyer-client confidentiality may be breached in relation to "communications relating to criminal or fraudulent transactions unless the lawyer is advising a client who has been charged with a criminal offence. A lawyer is under a duty," the rule adds, "to volunteer information concerning the commission of serious crime."[38.4]

The New Brunswick rule is susceptible of the interpretation that a lawyer has a duty to report crimes admitted by a client with which the client has not been charged. It is also susceptible of the interpretation that a lawyer has a duty to report crimes admitted by a client with which the client *has* been charged in circumstances in which the admissions are made to a lawyer who is representing the client in relation to a matter other than the criminal charge in question.

Neither interpretation would promote the policy underlying the exception, and both interpretations could potentially undermine the purpose of the confidentiality rule itself.

The New York State Bar Association's Committee on Professional Ethics has provided guidance to lawyers who must decide whether to disclose a client's intention to commit a crime. The committee has suggested that six factors should be weighed: the seriousness of potential injury; its likelihood and imminence; the apparent absence of any other feasible way in which the harm can be prevented; the extent to which the client has attempted to involve the lawyer in the prospective crime; the circumstances in which the lawyer acquired the information; and any aggravating or extenuating factors.[38.5]

38.3 Ontario rule 2.03 (3).

38.4 New Brunswick Professional Conduct Handbook, Part C, rule 5. See also Beverley G. Smith, *Professional Conduct for Canadian Lawyers* (Toronto: Butterworths, 1989), p. 177.

38.5 Opinion number 562 (July 19, 1984), referred to in Nancy E. Stuart, "Child Abuse Reporting: A Challenge to Attorney-Client Confidentiality" (1987-88) 1 Georgetown Journal of Legal Ethics 243 at 257. For a discussion of an interesting opinion issued by the Professional Ethics Committee of the Delaware Bar Association in 1988, on the issue whether a lawyer may reveal the fact that a client has AIDS to a person with whom the client has cohabited see Anne L. McBride, "Deadly Confidentiality: AIDS and Rule 1-6(b)" (1991-92) 4 Georgetown Journal of Legal Ethics 435.

3.5 LAWYER SELF-INTEREST EXCEPTIONS

Rules of professional conduct provide that the disclosure of confidential information may be justified in order to defend the lawyer or the lawyer's associates or employees against any allegation of malpractice or misconduct, or in legal proceedings to establish or collect the lawyer's fees. In such cases (and in cases involving other exceptions to the duty of confidentiality), the lawyer must be careful not to divulge more information than is required for the purpose.[39]

Where the disclosure of confidential information is necessary to enable a lawyer to make out a defence to allegations of malpractice or misconduct, such disclosure is permissible regardless of whether the proceedings against the lawyer are initiated by the client. Thus, in a highly publicized Ontario case,[39.1] a lawyer, who was charged with the criminal offence of obstructing justice as a result of his removal (and retention) of videotapes from the home of his client, was permitted to introduce into evidence solicitor-client communications relevant to his defence, including those protected by solicitor-client privilege, notwithstanding the client's opposition to the disclosure of the communications. The Court weighed the possibility of prejudice to the client as a result of disclosure against the possibility of prejudice to the lawyer as a result of non-disclosure. The Court found that the possibility of prejudice to the client was largely theoretical and remote, whereas the lawyer's ability to defend himself, and his right to make full answer and defence, would be threatened, in a case in which his liberty was at stake, if he was not permitted to disclose confidential and privileged communications with his client.

In a 1990 case,[40] the British Columbia Court of Appeal had occasion to consider the implications of allowing disclosure in a proceeding in which a lawyer's fees were in issue while litigation on which the lawyer acted was still before the courts.

In that case, a lawyer acted for a husband in continuing matrimonial litigation. The husband changed lawyers, and his new lawyer arranged for the first lawyer's account to be assessed.

The lawyer for the wife in the continuing matrimonial litigation learned of the assessment and sent a junior lawyer to attend and take notes at the assessment hearing. The junior lawyer identified herself to the husband's first lawyer, who informed the lawyer who represented him at the assessment hearing, who in turn

---

39 C.B.A. Code, chapter IV, commentary 10; Ontario rule 2.03(2). The notes to chapter 5 of the British Columbia rules, however, make it clear that a client who commences a malpractice action, initiates a disciplinary proceeding, or puts legal advice in issue in a proceeding, manifests an intention to waive privilege at least to the extent necessary for the lawyer to mount a defence. The notes also say that there may be some circumstances in which a lawyer charged with a criminal offence may disclose privileged communications.

39.1 *R. v. Murray* (2000), 48 O.R. (3d) 437 (S.C.J.)

40 *Piercy v. Piercy* (1990), 48 B.C.L.R. (2d) 145 (C.A.), reversing (1990), 45 B.C.L.R. (2d) 267 (S.C.).

informed the husband's second lawyer. The husband's second lawyer did not ask the junior lawyer to leave, nor did he ask that the hearing be adjourned or held *in camera.*

At the assessment hearing the husband's first lawyer testified in detail about the steps that he had taken on the husband's behalf, and discussed his settlement and trial strategies. He revealed the husband's final settlement target and testified about the contents of a 28-page opinion letter that he had given the client.

After the assessment hearing the husband retained a third lawyer, who brought a motion for an injunction preventing the wife or her lawyers from further disclosing the information acquired at the assessment hearing, an order requiring the junior lawyer to produce her notes, and an order removing the wife's lawyers as solicitors of record. The injunction requested was granted by a judge in chambers, and the junior lawyer was ordered to produce her notes.

The British Columbia Court of Appeal set aside both orders. The court held that the junior lawyer was entitled to be present at the assessment and that the disclosure of confidential information did not result from any impropriety on her part. There was therefore no basis for an order requiring her to produce her notes or prohibiting her or her firm from communicating the information in relation to which privilege had been waived.

The court added that there may well have been no need for the husband's first lawyer to divulge detailed instructions or the contents of his opinion letter. Responsibility for those disclosures should be visited on either the husband's first lawyer or on his second (for failing to ask the assessment officer to prevent them); however, the junior lawyer who attended the hearing acted neither clandestinely nor improperly.

The case illustrates the problems with the exception. As a result of his decision to challenge his lawyer's fee, the client unwittingly put himself at a severe tactical disadvantage. His settlement target, his lawyer's opinion as to the merits of the case, and his lawyer's trial and settlement strategy were all revealed to his adversary in hotly contested litigation involving the division of valuable matrimonial assets.

The justification for the exception is that fairness should prevent clients from using the confidentiality rule to their lawyers' disadvantage. But the rule may inflict on non-lawyers harm that is often immeasurably greater than the harm inflicted on lawyers who may be unable to prove how much work they have done to earn their fees — witness, again, the case of the plaintiff with the life-threatening aortic aneurism, and the Lake Pleasant Bodies Case. Fairness to the innocent victims of the confidentiality rule in those cases has resulted in the promulgation of no exceptions. The public may be forgiven for suspecting that the legal profession may not be free of self-interest.[40.1]

40.1 See Deborah L. Rhode, "Ethical Perspectives on Legal Practice", 37 Stanford Law Review 589 at 423-424.

Nor for the most part (as mentioned above) have exceptions been recognized in cases involving other confidential professional relationships. A comparison of the solicitor-client and the psychotherapist-patient relationships is particularly telling. Communications by patients to their psychiatrists are also peculiarly sensitive. Successful treatment requires complete self-revelations that are possible only in an environment of inviolate privacy, just as the successful operation of our system of justice is possible only if the confidentiality of clients' communications with their lawyers is respected. Trust is essential in both relationships. One would be hard pressed to devise a convincing reason of policy for allowing lawyers but not psychiatrists (or *vice-versa*) to divulge confidential communications on grounds of self-interest. The inconsistency incites strong suspicions of favouritism.[41]

The British Columbia case also points out the need for greater judicial control over the disclosure of confidential information by lawyers in litigation to which the exception applies. It is clear that the lawyer who represented the client on the assessment should have asked that the proceeding be held *in camera*. It is by no means certain, however, that that request would have been granted. It is also clear that the client's first lawyer, whose account was being challenged, should have been more discreet in divulging confidential information. He had a duty to disclose no more information than was necessary for the purpose of establishing the reasonableness of his fee.

A mechanism whereby the presiding judicial officer, rather than the lawyer — who is of course a party to the fee dispute, with a direct financial interest in the result — determines the need for disclosure, would prevent or at least minimize the problems that the British Columbia case illustrates.

3.6 BALANCING CONFIDENTIALITY AND OTHER INTERESTS

Let us conclude where we began: almost all of the most obstinate problems of professional responsibility are confidentiality problems. Legitimate interests compete with one another — those of the client, the public, the court, and the truth, for example. The competing interests are weighed differently by different constituencies. Few members of the public, for instance, would assign sufficient weight to the interests of the client or the administration of justice in maintaining confidentiality that the jeopardization of the life or well-being of innocent persons would be justified.

The confidentiality rule is for the most part beneficial, and it is essential to the preservation of values that we hold dear. The rule is not absolute; it admits limited exceptions. The real difficulties are, first, that the means of resolving

41 See Wolfram, *supra*, note 33, pp. 308-309; Stuart, *supra*, note 38, p. 263; and John T. Noonan, "The Purposes of Advocacy and the Limits of Confidentiality" (1966) 64 Michigan L.R. 1485.

conflicts between confidentiality and other values have not been adequately addressed; second, that the exceptions are inadequate and sometimes self-serving; and third, that the rule does not allow for the various competing interests to be balanced in individual cases, so that the desirability of maintaining confidentiality may be weighed against the desirability of permitting disclosure. Thus both the rule and the exceptions have generally been applied mechanically, with little heed paid to the harm such a ritualistic approach may cause.[42]

The governing bodies of the legal profession in the countries comprising the European Community have resolved the first of these difficulties by expressly stipulating that "where there is any doubt . . . the strictest rule should be observed — that is, the rule which offers the best protection against breach of confidence."[43] This choice is the same as that made by Monroe Freedman in his controversial works: confidentiality is treated as an absolute value that is uniformly superior to and that therefore takes precedence over such other interests as truth and the well-being of third parties in every case.[44]

That an approach that weighs the competing interests in individual cases is preferable to an approach that invariably prefers the value of confidentiality may be demonstrated by considering two hypothetical clients.

The first client has AIDS. He has taken all reasonable precautions to prevent others from becoming infected. He is particularly vulnerable if the fact he has AIDS becomes known. His personal and business lives could be severely affected. In addition to the stigma of the disease, he may be the subject of false rumours of drug use or homosexuality, and may be fired from his job or lose clients or customers. Because of the significant potential for the infliction of severe damage to the reputation and livelihood of the client and his family, the principle of confidentiality should be strictly adhered to. Most if not all exceptions should be overridden. The fact that a dispute arises over the reasonableness of his lawyer's fees, for example, should not justify public disclosure of the client's condition, even if the work the lawyer did can be explained only by disclosing the client's condition.[45]

The second client is a father who has repeatedly abused his young children in the past, and who is still living with his children. A lawyer is representing him in a matter unrelated to child abuse, but nevertheless learns of the abuse in her professional capacity. The children are virtually certain to be abused repeatedly

---

42 See Landesman, *supra*, note 36, p. 194; and Wolfram, *supra*, note 33, pp. 245-246 and 665-666.

43 Consultative Committee of The Bars and Law Societies of the European Community, "The Declaration of Perugia on the Principles of Professional Conduct of the Bars and Law Societies of the European Community 16. IX. 1977", reproduced in Law Society of Upper Canada Gazette, vol. 14, no. 2 (June, 1980), p. 205.

44 Freedman's theories are most fully developed in his book *Lawyers' Ethics In An Adversary System* (New York: Bobbs-Merrill, 1975).

45 See Robert T. Begg, "Legal Ethics and AIDS: An Analysis of Selected Issues" (1989-90) 3 Georgetown Journal of Legal Ethics 1 at 48.

in the future unless authorities intervene. The abuse is likely to have severe hidden consequences for the children, who are likely to have a distorted notion of society and who may well become abusive parents themselves some day if no one acts to put an end to the abuse and provide counselling. Advising the client to discontinue his criminal acts is ineffective. Here the likely damage to innocent and helpless third parties should weigh heavily. The case for requiring disclosure of the client's continuing crimes is strong, despite the chilling effect of such disclosure on solicitor-client communication in the future.[46]

---

46 See Stuart, *supra*, note 38, *passim*.

4

Advocacy

> The path of the law is strewn with examples of open and shut cases which, somehow, were not; of unanswerable charges which, in the event, were completely answered; of inexplicable conduct which was fully explained.[1]

4.1 THE ETHICS OF ADVOCACY

The sporting theory of justice and the confidentiality rule, discussed in chapters 2 and 3, are at the heart of the ethical problems of litigation lawyers. The basic tensions are between lawyers' duties to represent clients resolutely while maintaining in confidence information that they acquire in the course of the professional relationship, on the one hand, and their duties to treat courts and tribunals with candour, fairness, courtesy, and respect, on the other.[2]

Monroe Freedman has written that these three fundamental professional responsibilities — resolute partisan representation, confidentiality, and candour — create the lawyer's trilemma: the lawyer has a duty to know everything, to keep it in confidence, and to reveal it to the court. Freedman's attempts to come to grips with conflicts among professional responsibilities that are generally not resolved by codes of professional conduct themselves led him to draw some controversial conclusions, as we shall see when we examine the ethical obligations of lawyers in preparing witnesses, leading evidence in chief, and cross-examining.

Freedman's conclusions — that in at least some circumstances it is proper for lawyers to: (i) give clients legal advice when they know that the advice will tempt the clients to commit perjury; (ii) to impeach the credibility of adverse

1 *John v. Rees*, [1970] Ch. 345 at 402, *per* Megarry J.

2 The lawyer's duty to represent clients resolutely is expressed in chapter IX of the C.B.A. Code and Ontario rule 4.01(1). The lawyer's duty to treat courts and tribunals with candour, fairness, courtesy, and respect is expressed in commentary 1 to chapter IX of the C.B.A. Code and Ontario rule 4.01(1) and accompanying commentary. See also Charles Wolfram, *Modern Legal Ethics* (St. Paul, Minnesota: West, 1986), p. 593.

witnesses known to be testifying truthfully; and (iii) to call witnesses who insist on testifying falsely[3] — exemplify the excesses that the adversary system instills.

The confidentiality rule is the basis for each of Freedman's conclusions. But the sporting theory of justice is at least as responsible for such forensic excesses as subterfuge, obfuscation, and delay. In this chapter, we shall examine the ethical responsibilities of lawyers at every stage of the litigation process. Most of these responsibilities apply in civil and criminal proceedings alike, but the responsibilities that are peculiar to prosecutors and criminal defence lawyers are examined in chapters 6 and 7 respectively.

4.2 THE RETAINER AND THE RIGHT TO DECLINE EMPLOYMENT

The relationship between lawyers and their clients is governed by the law of contract for many purposes, but because the relationship is a fiduciary one based upon a high degree of loyalty to the clients' interests, analyses based upon traditional contractual doctrines are at least incomplete. Thus a lawyer who declines to act for a potential client after an initial meeting has a duty to maintain the clients' communications in confidence though no contract has been formed. Similarly, lawyers who have undertaken to represent clients have a duty to do so competently even if they have agreed to act without compensation and there is accordingly no consideration flowing from the clients.[4]

Despite language in the barrister's oath — "You shall neglect no one's interest . . . You shall not refuse cases of complaint reasonably founded . . ." — that seems to import the English cab-rank rule that a barrister is obliged to accept every client, Canadian rules of professional conduct specify that lawyers have a general right to decline a particular employment except when they are assigned as counsel by a court. This general right to decline to act, however, is qualified in two important ways that result in the rules of professional conduct conforming to the injunctions of the barrister's oath. First, the rules provide that the lawyer's right to decline employment, generally speaking, should not be exercised because of the unpopularity of the client or the notoriety of the client's case, because powerful interests or allegations of misconduct or malfeasance are involved, or because of the lawyer's private opinion about the guilt of the accused. Second, the rules provide that the right is to be exercised prudently if the probable result would be to make it very difficult for a person to obtain legal advice or representation. The rules also provide that a lawyer who declines employment should

3 Freedman has discussed the lawyer's trilemma in "Professional Responsibility of the Criminal Defence Lawyer: The Three Hardest Questions" (1966) 64 Michigan L.R. 1469; in *Lawyers' Ethics In An Adversary System* (New York: Bobbs-Merrill, 1975), pp. 27-28; and in *Understanding Legal Ethics* (New York: Matthew Bender & Co., 1990), pp. 109-141.

4 See Beverley G. Smith, *Professional Conduct for Canadian Lawyers* (Toronto: Butterworths, 1989), pp. 16-18; and Wolfram, *supra*, note 2, pp. 145-147 and 495.

assist the client in obtaining the services of another lawyer who is qualified in the field in question and who is able to act.[5]

The English cab-rank rule is based on the idea that it is the duty of barristers, just as it is the duty of priests and surgeons, to serve all those who call on them. The rule is subject to two important qualifications: barristers are bound to accept cases only if they are uncommitted and if their clerks have negotiated appropriate fees with the clients' solicitors. In fixing the fee and reporting upon the barristers' availability there is in practice ample room for clerks to protect barristers against unwanted briefs.

The rule is nevertheless at the heart of the democratic ideals exemplified by the ethics of advocacy. A lawyer has a duty not to refuse to act on the basis of the unpopularity of the client or the cause, or the personal opinion of the lawyer. This central principle is closely allied with the principle that lawyers do not express their own opinions, but make submissions on behalf of their clients. A third central principle of advocacy is that the performance of this function is essential to both public access to justice and the judicial determination, after a full and fair trial, of the parties' rights and duties. All these principles apply in civil and criminal cases alike.[6]

Lawyers who choose among potential clients based upon the acceptability of their conduct and opinions associate themselves with their clients and their clients' causes and provide a personal endorsement to submissions they make on their clients' behalf. This is dangerous, because once we associate some lawyers with their clients and their clients' causes, and treat their submissions as expressions of personal opinion, we are likely to fall into the trap of associating all lawyers with their clients and their clients' causes, and to treat all submissions of lawyers as expressions of personal opinion. If we associate lawyers with unpopular clients and causes, it will become difficult for unpopular clients to obtain competent representation.

In 1976, an editorial in the London *Times* commented on the difficulty of obtaining convictions in obscenity cases when the defence was represented by the English barrister (and novelist) John Mortimer, because of his "passionate devotion to defence of the freedom of pornography." Mortimer wrote a letter to the editor of the *Times*:

> Any barrister's duty is to be "passionately devoted" to the defence of his client. It would be a sad day if a defendant charged with an alleged crime could not be defended without his counsel being accused of devotion to murder or robbing banks.[7]

5 C.B.A. Code, chapter XIV, commentary 6; Ontario rule 3.01 and accompanying commentary. See also *Demarco v. Ungaro* (1979), 21 O.R. (2d) 673 at 694 (H.C.).

6 See *Rondel v. Worsley*, [1969] 1 A.C. 191 at 227 (H.L.), *per* Lord Reid; and David Pannick, *Advocates* (Oxford: Oxford University Press, 1992), pp. 132 and 140-142.

7 London *Times* (January 30 and February 3, 1976), as quoted by Pannick, *ibid.*, pp. 132-133.

Apart altogether from considerations of the unpopularity of clients and their causes, lawyers should be disinclined to refuse to represent clients based upon their assessment of the likelihood of success in litigation. As discussed below, lawyers have a duty to advise clients competently, honestly, and fully, based upon adequate investigation of the facts of the case and applicable legal principles. An experienced Canadian counsel said in 1971 that an advocate "must always remember, however, that he is not a judge and, even against his advice, the client is entitled to the advocate's services so long as the matter does not involve fraud or deceit or is plainly frivolous."[8]

That the lawyer "is not a judge" is only a partial explanation for the cab-rank rule's bias against turning away clients. Not only is it the task of the judge, not the lawyer, to decide the client's rights, it is a task that cannot be performed until the case has been argued, and a task that can be performed properly only if the competing arguments for each side are made by competent counsel.[9]

Lord Pearce wrote in a 1969 judgment of the House of Lords that in many cases "the unpleasant, the unreasonable, the disreputable and those who have apparently hopeless cases turn out after a full and fair hearing to be in the right."[10] A prominent American lawyer, Lloyd Cutler, said that "the essence of the adversary process is that judgments of right and wrong are to be made after the process is completed, not before it begins."[11]

Lawyers who are obliged not to refuse to act for clients will not always be persuaded personally by the submissions they make on behalf of their clients. As we have seen, lawyers need not endorse their clients' positions, and should not be identified with their clients or their clients' beliefs; they need only believe that the truth is more likely to be revealed, and mistakes and prejudices to be avoided, if the issues in the case are rationally debated by the presentation of divergent points of view.[12]

In the United States, it is clear that lawyers have no duty to represent any client, except perhaps if the client would otherwise be unable to obtain counsel. The English cab-rank rule is nevertheless sometimes disingenuously invoked by American lawyers to explain how, with freedom to choose among clients, they sometimes act for such disagreeable ones. American lawyers' supposed adoption of the English rule as a personal moral view may in fact be a straight rationalization

---

8 John T. Weir, "Advocacy Before Administrative Tribunals", 1971 Law Society of Upper Canada Special Lectures, p. 349.

9 See Pannick, *supra*, note 6, p. 149.

10 *Rondel v. Worsley, supra*, note 6, p. 275.

11 Book Review (1970) 83 Harvard L.R. 1746 at 1750.

12 See Pannick, *supra*, note 6, pp. 148-149.

for (in Charles Wolfram's words) "acquiring a personal fortune representing rich but odious clients."[13]

In a 1974 decision,[14] the Supreme Court of California reversed an accused person's conviction on the ground that he was represented at trial by a lawyer who at the time of trial also served as a prosecuting City Attorney. The court expressed concern that there was a serious risk that a defence lawyer who contemporaneously served as a prosecutor would not provide "vigorous and determined advocacy" on the client's behalf, and that "public confidence in the integrity of the criminal justice system could be adversely affected."[15]

The English experience would seem to demonstrate that these concerns are ill-founded. That English barristers accept briefs regularly on behalf of both the prosecution and the accused in criminal cases, and on behalf of both plaintiffs and defendants in civil cases, has not noticeably resulted in either a reduction in partisanship or a deterioration in the quality of justice. An appreciation of the perspective of one's adversary cannot help but sharpen a lawyer's skills. One suspects also that objectivity is more conducive to effective advocacy than is emotional attachment.[16]

The notion that lawyers should be mouthpieces for clients has frequently been repudiated. Chief Baron Pollock said "I will be my client's advocate, not his agent."[17] Justice Crampton likened the position of a barrister to that of a legislator: a representative, but not a delegate.[18]

Lawyers must nevertheless guard against the preference of some clients, at the opposite end of the spectrum, to rely on lawyers (and other experts) to make decisions that the clients should make themselves. In the division of responsibilities it is for clients to decide upon the ends they wish to achieve, whereas it is for lawyers to decide upon the means by which those ends are attempted. It is for clients to decide whether to sell a home, obtain a divorce, buy a business, or settle a lawsuit.

Even among competent clients, the degree of autonomy appropriately exercised by lawyers will vary depending upon the sophistication of the client. With the client's approval, some decisions that should be made by executives of a client that is a public corporation may appropriately be made by the lawyer of a

---

13 Charles Wolfram, *Modern Legal Ethics* (St. Paul, Minnesota: West, 1986), p. 571. Wolfram compares the English and American rules and discusses how they work in practice at pp. 571-572 of the same work. The most frequently quoted justification for the English rule is from Thomas Erskine's speech in *R. v. Paine* (1792), 22 St. Tr. 357: "From the moment that any advocate can be permitted to say, that he *will* or will *not* stand between the Crown and the subject arraigned in the Court where he daily sits to practise, from that moment the liberties of England are at an end . . .".

14 *People v. Rhodes*, 524 P. 2d 363 at 367 (1974). *People v. Fife*, 392 N.E. 2d 1345 (S.C. of Ill., 1979) is to the same effect.

15 *Ibid.*, p. 367.

16 See David Pannick, *Advocates* (Oxford: Oxford University Press, 1992), p. 140.

17 *Swinfen v. Chelmsford (Lord)* (1860) 2 L.J. (N.S.) 406 at 413.

18 *R. v. O'Connell* (1844-5), 7 Ir. L.R. 261 at 312.

client who is inexperienced in business and who is distraught because of the recent death of a spouse.

What is at least important, however, as the ultimate decision is the process by which the decision is made. Trust, respect, and communication between lawyer and client are essential.[19]

4.3 CHILDREN AND CLIENTS UNDER A DISABILITY

The relationship between lawyer and client cannot function in the usual way where the client is not legally competent to instruct counsel, for example, due to age or disability.

In 2000 the Law Society of Upper Canada's *Rules of Professional Conduct* were amended to address, for the first time, the lawyer's professional duties in these circumstances. The rule[19.1] provides that when a client's ability to make decisions is impaired because of minority, mental disability, or any other reason, the lawyer has a duty, as far as reasonably possible, to maintain a normal lawyer and client relationship. Commentary to the rule makes it clear that the lawyer also has an ethical obligation to ensure that the client's interests are not abandoned.

Rules of court generally require children, mental incompetents, and absentees to be represented by litigation guardians, who in turn (unlike other human parties) must be represented by lawyers. Additional protection is provided by provisions requiring judicial approval of settlements involving parties who are not legally competent.[20]

Some legislation affecting children, including, for example, the *Young Offenders Act*, expressly provides that children subject to the legislation are entitled to legal representation. Some legislation governing child protection proceedings empowers the court to direct that legal representation be provided where such representation is desirable to protect the interest of the child.[21]

Where litigation guardians are appointed to represent incompetent persons' interests, their lawyers are bound to follow their instructions to the same extent as they would be bound to follow the instructions of competent clients. If a lawyer believes that a litigation guardian of a child client is not acting in the child's best

19 See Wolfram, *supra*, note 13, p. 156; American Bar Association Model Rules of Professional Conduct, Model Rule 1-2(a); and Monroe H. Freedman, *Understanding Lawyers' Ethics* (New York: Matthew Bender & Co., 1990), pp. 60-64.

19.1 Ontario rule 2.02 (6).

20 For an example of provisions designed to protect the interest of incompetent parties in litigation see rule 7 of the Ontario Rules of Civil Procedure, R.R.O. 1990, reg. 194.

21 Statutes that enshrine the right of affected children to legal representation include the *Young Offenders Act*, R.S.C. 1985, c. Y-1 (s. 11(1)) and the *Children's Law Reform Act*, R.S.O. 1990, c. C.12 (s. 65(4)). For an example of legislation empowering the court to direct that legal representation be provided in child protection proceedings, see s. 38 of the *Child and Family Services Act*, R.S.O. 1990, c. C.11.

interest, the lawyer generally is precluded from taking steps to alter the litigation guardian's decisions, partly because of the confidentiality rule.[22]

The duty of the lawyer for a child in such litigation as child protection proceedings, in which no litigation guardian is appointed to instruct the lawyer, is more complicated. If in such cases the children are too young to participate in the decision as to what is in their best interest or are ambivalent in their wishes, their lawyer must make the decision that the children would make if they were capable of making an informed decision.

Older children, though not of the age of majority, may nonetheless be competent to make certain decisions concerning their best interest. Their lawyers in such cases generally have a duty to inform the court of the children's wishes and to adduce evidence and make submissions designed to advance what the children consider to be in their best interest as if the children were competent adults, even if the lawyers' personal views of what is in the children's best interest differs. It is for the court, not the children's lawyer, to decide what is in the children's best interest.[23]

In a 1980 Ontario Provincial Court (Family Division) decision,[24] however, the court observed that though lawyers representing children in child welfare proceedings should ordinarily advocate the children's preferences, where to do so would expose them to a dangerous situation lawyers owe a duty to protect the children by informing the court of the danger.

It is nevertheless clear that this possible qualification to the general rule that lawyers should advocate the preferences of clients who are children does not justify the disclosure of information imparted to lawyers by the children in confidence. Nor will withdrawal from the brief normally be justified by differences of opinion between lawyers and their child clients. Withdrawal solves only the lawyers' problem, and may be prejudicial to the children's interest.

Similarly, in proceedings under the *Young Offenders Act* lawyers for young persons, in the traditions of the adversary system, have a duty to seek to obtain the best possible results for their clients. This duty may require them, for example, to seek to exclude evidence that they know is accurate. The Act recognizes that young persons have the rights and freedoms guaranteed by the *Canadian Charter of Rights and Freedoms* among other rights. The Act specifically provides that a young person has the right to retain and instruct counsel without delay at any

22 See Charles Wolfram, *Modern Legal Ethics* (St. Paul, Minnesota: West, 1986), p. 160.

23 *Strobridge v. Strobridge* (1992), 10 O.R. (3d) 540 (Gen. Div.). The duties of lawyers representing children in proceedings in which no litigation guardians are appointed are also discussed by Ontario Provincial Court Judge Rosalie Abella (as she then was) in *Re W.* (1979), 27 O.R. (2d) 314; by George M. Thomson in "Eliminating Role Confusion in the Child's Lawyer: The Ontario Experience" (1983) 4 Can. J. Fam. L. 125; by James W. Eayrs, "Some Problems of Professional Ethics in the Legal Representation of Minors", Law Society of Upper Canada Gazette, vol. 20, no. 1 (March, 1986), p. 106; and by Wolfram, *ibid.*, pp. 161-162.

24 *Re J.C. and S.C.* (1980), 31 O.R. (2d) 53 (Prov. Ct.).

stage of proceedings. All the provisions of the *Criminal Code* apply in respect of offences alleged to have been committed by young persons except to the extent that they are inconsistent with or are excluded by the Act.[25]

Lawyers must, of course, be alert to possible conflicts of interest if they are representing one or both parents as well as one or more children. This aspect of the problem is dealt with in more detail in chapter 5.

4.4 ADVISING CLIENTS CONCERNING POSSIBLE LITIGATION

Rules of professional conduct require a lawyer who is consulted about possible litigation to give the client a competent opinion based on a sufficient knowledge of the relevant facts, an adequate consideration of the applicable law, and the lawyer's own experience and expertise. The advice must clearly disclose what the lawyer honestly thinks about the merits of the case and probable results.[26] The lawyer must try to correct any apparent misunderstanding of the client as to what the litigation is likely to involve.[27]

The lawyer should articulate the facts, circumstances, and assumptions upon which the opinion is based. If, for example, the lawyer obtains instructions not to do a comprehensive investigation because such an expense is not justified in the circumstances, the lawyer's opinion should so state. Unless the client instructs otherwise, the lawyer should investigate the facts in sufficient detail to be able to express an opinion rather than merely comment with many qualifications.[28] The lawyer should avoid bold and confident assurances of success, particularly where the lawyer's retainer may depend upon optimism inspired by the lawyer's advice.[29]

In a 1978 decision of the Court of Appeal in England,[30] Lord Denning said that "in giving his opinion beforehand [the lawyer] must only advise proceedings if there is a reasonable case to be made — putting away from himself, like the plague, any thought of the extra fees which would come to him if the case was fought — and remembering the hardship on the other side if harassed unfairly."

---

25 The provisions of the *Young Offenders Act*, R.S.C. 1985, c. Y-1, that are referred to are s. 3(1)(e) (applicability of *Charter* and other rights to young persons), s. 11 (right to counsel), and s. 51 (application of *Criminal Code*). In *Re Gault*, 87 S. Ct. 1428 (1967), the United States Supreme Court held that due process requires that young offender proceedings follow many of the adversarial system guarantees mandated for the criminal trial of adults, including the right to counsel.

26 C.B.A. Code, chapter III, commentary 1; Ontario rule 2.02(1) and accompanying commentary; British Columbia rules, chapter 1, rule 3(1).

27 C.B.A. Code, chapter III, commentary 2; Ontario rule 2.01(1) and accompanying commentary.

28 C.B.A. Code, chapter III, commentary 3; Ontario rule 2.01(1) and accompanying commentary.

29 C.B.A. Code, chapter III, commentary 4; Ontario rule 2.01(1) and accompanying commentary.

30 *Saif Ali v. Sydney Mitchell & Co.*, [1978] Q.B. 95 at 103 (C.A.), affirmed [1980] A.C. 198 (H.L.).

Lord Denning also emphasized that a lawyer "must not allow a charge of fraud to be made unless there is evidence to support it."[31]

Before the client discloses the facts on which the lawyer's advice is sought, the lawyer should discuss the confidentiality principle with the client. A statement to the effect that "everything that you say to me is confidential" is inadequate in that it is likely to be understood by clients to mean something different than it means to lawyers, who are aware of the numerous instances in which the duty of confidentiality is inapplicable, legal or ethical rules override the duty of confidentiality, or the lawyer is entitled to use information acquired about the client's affairs against the client. A client is entitled to be able to make an informed choice about what information should be disclosed to a lawyer.

One commentator has suggested that lawyers provide to clients a one or two page summary of the duty of confidentiality and its limitations. Such a summary might mention, for example, that confidential information may be disclosed to other members or employees of the lawyer's firm, but that disclosure to those people may be limited if the client wishes.[32]

4.5 MEDICAL-LEGAL REPORTS

A particular confidentiality problem that arises from time to time in actions for damages for personal injuries involves the obligation of lawyers who receive medical-legal reports containing opinions or findings that may cause harm or injury to their clients if disclosed to them.

The problem is specifically addressed by Ontario's rules of professional conduct, which provide that when lawyers receive medical-legal reports containing such opinions or findings they should attempt to dissuade their clients from seeing the reports. If the clients insist on seeing the reports, however, lawyers are duty-bound to produce them.[33]

The Ontario rule also provides that lawyers who receive medical-legal reports that are accompanied by a proviso that they not be shown to clients must return the reports immediately to their authors unless they have received specific instructions to accept the reports on that basis.[34]

The commentaries to the Ontario rule suggest that lawyers can avoid some of the problems anticipated by the rule by having a full and frank discussion with physicians who are asked to prepare reports, preferably before reports are prepared. Such an exchange will serve to inform the physicians of the lawyers' duties respecting disclosure of medical-legal reports to clients.[35]

---

31 *Ibid.*, p. 103.

32 Roy M. Sobelson, "Lawyers, Clients and Assurances of Confidentiality: Lawyers Talking Without Speaking, Clients Hearing Without Listening" (1987-88) 1 Georgetown Journal of Legal Ethics 703 particularly at pp. 703-704 and 712-713.

33 Ontario rule 2.02(8).

34 Ontario rule 2.02(7).

35 Ontario rule 2.02(7) and accompanying commentary.

The commentaries also suggest that in the event that clients insist on seeing medical-legal reports about which lawyers have reservations because of concerns that disclosure of the findings or opinions might cause harm or injury to their clients, lawyers should advise their clients to attend at their physician's office to see the reports in order that the clients will have the benefit of the physicians' expertise in understanding the significance of the physicians' conclusions.[36]

4.6 DISCOVERY

Although reforms to the discovery process in civil litigation have modified some of the excesses of the adversary system, the process remains the leading modern example of those excesses. Though designed to promote settlement and shorten trials by narrowing issues, the discovery process is too often manipulated to frustrate those objectives.

The techniques employed to frustrate the process include repetitive questions, oppressive requests to compile documents of little if any importance, unsupportable assertions of privilege, frivolous objections, incomplete responses, improper refusals to produce documents, the dogged pursuit of irrelevant details, and questioning that is calculated to exhaust or intimidate the opponent. In some cases, parties have been inundated with the production of mostly immaterial documents in the hope that damaging documents will pass unnoticed. Impecunious adverse parties have been forced to settle on unfavourable terms due to the prohibitive cost of litigating against well-healed opponents whose lawyers have exploited their financial disadvantage by building up the costs of discovery.

The main reason that abuses abound in the discovery phase of litigation is that no adjudicator is present to control the counsel. At trial, most lawyers avoid overly aggressive and unfair conduct that is likely to alienate judges and juries. There is less incentive for them to avoid overzealousness on discovery.

Most trial judges are likely to do little about discovery abuses, as they consider the discovery process to be incidental and preliminary, if not irrelevant. For the judiciary, the trial is everything. Litigation lawyers, on the other hand, realize that a great majority of their cases will be settled prior to trial, generally as a result of discovery, which is accordingly of paramount importance. Litigation lawyers also become inured to the cost and the occasional savagery of discovery excesses.[37]

Until 2000, when the Law Society of Upper Canada's *Rules of Professional Conduct* were amended to specifically address the lawyer's professional obligations in the discovery process, Canadian rules of professional conduct did not

---

36 Ontario rule 2.02(7) and accompanying commentary.

37 Common types of discovery abuse, and obstacles to remedying the problems, are discussed by Geoffrey C. Hazard, Jr., in "Depositions: Modern-Day Inquisitions", National Law Journal (March 14, 1988), p. 13; by Charles Wolfram, *Modern Legal Ethics* (St. Paul, Minnesota: West, 1986), pp. 594-595; and by Robert E. Sarazen, "An Ethical Approach to Discovery Abuse" (1991) 4 Georgetown Journal of Legal Ethics 459.

deal specifically with discovery abuse, and disciplinary proceedings were brought only in a few egregious cases. The Ontario rules now impose a duty on lawyers, where the rules of the court or tribunal require the parties to produce documents or attend on examinations for discovery, to explain to their clients (i) the necessity of making full disclosure of all documents relating to any matter in issue and (ii) the duty to answer to the best of their knowledge, information and belief, any proper question relating to any issue in the action or made discoverable by the rules of court or the rules of the tribunal. Lawyers are also required to assist their clients in fulfilling their obligations to make full disclosure. Finally, lawyers are prohibited from making frivolous requests for the production of documents and from making frivolous demands for information on examinations for discovery.[37.1]

In the United States, in the last ten years, 11 amendments to the Federal Rules of Civil Procedure and five amendments to the Model Rules of Professional Conduct have been promulgated to curb discovery abuse. The Model Rules, which have been adopted by the bars of a majority of states, expressly prohibit lawyers from making frivolous discovery requests or failing to make reasonably diligent efforts to comply with proper discovery requests of other parties. In a 1989 Colorado case,[38] a lawyer was suspended for six months for withholding on discovery information that an adverse party was entitled to receive. In a 1994 case, a Seattle law firm and its client agreed to pay $325,000 in sanctions for discovery abuse after they misled their adversaries to avoid producing inculpatory documents. The latter case prompted one commentator to write as follows:

> The shame of the adversary system has been its degeneration into a pretext for lawyers to hide facts, so as to pervert the truth. It's time for those who care about the system to make it clear that the duty of zealous advocacy neither requires nor permits lawyers to be cover-up artists.[38.1]

Modern rules of civil procedure dealing with the production of documents exemplify the type of measures that have been taken to modify the adversary system in its pure form. The duty of lawyers to produce documents adverse to their clients is indirect, in the sense that the duty to make full disclosure is imposed on the parties, not their counsel. Lawyers are nevertheless obliged to explain to their clients the necessity of making full disclosure of all documents relevant to

37.1 Ontario rule 4.01 (4).

38 *People of the State of Colorado v. Haase*, 781 P. 2d 80 (1989). In an Ontario case, *Re Balaban*, report adopted by Convocation, May 24, 1984, the Law Society of Upper Canada reprimanded a lawyer publicly for repeatedly making unwarranted, personal and offensive remarks to opposing counsel in an official examiner's office.

38.1 Stuart Taylor, Jr., "Sleazy in Seattle", *American Lawyer* (April 1994), p. 5, 79.

the issues in the action as framed by the pleadings, and in some jurisdictions are required to certify to the court that they have done so.[39]

Such practices as producing a critical document in a box car of otherwise irrelevant material and producing relevant documents only when forced to do so have frequently been condemned by courts and commentators, and occasionally knowing acquiesence by lawyers in their clients' failure to produce relevant documents has been visited with cost sanctions.[40] Again, however, Canadian rules of professional conduct are silent on the subject of a lawyer's duty to disclose relevant documents in civil litigation, and discipline proceedings are rarely initiated as a result of lawyers' failure to disclose.

Issues of relevance are determined by the pleadings. If, in a product liability case, the plaintiff has pleaded negligent manufacture but has raised no issue concerning the design of the product, the defendant has no duty to produce damaging memoranda relating to design as long as the memoranda are not relevant to any other pleaded issue.

Where a claim of privilege is asserted, the documents must be described sufficiently to enable a determination of the claim of privilege to be made, but no details need be given that would enable adverse parties to discover indirectly the contents.[41]

In a 1996 decision,[41.1] the Ontario Court of Justice (General Division) refused to allow evidence on discovery to be read into the record at trial on the ground that, under the Law Society of Upper Canada's *Rules of Professional Conduct*,[41.2] counsel may not delegate to a law clerk or other non-lawyer the conduct of an examination for discovery.

---

39 Rule 30.03(4) of the Ontario Rules of Civil Procedure, R.R.O. 1990, reg. 194, is an example of a provision requiring lawyers to certify that they have explained the obligation of full disclosure to their clients. Rules of civil procedure also, of course, provide remedies and sanctions for the improper conduct of examinations: see, for example, rule 34.14 of the Ontario Rules of Civil Procedure.

40 In *Myers v. Elman*, [1940] A.C. 282, the House of Lords upheld an order of a trial judge whereby a solicitor who drew an affidavit on production that to the solicitor's knowledge omitted mention of a number of highly relevant documents, was ordered to pay one-third of the successful adverse party's costs. See also *Grossman v. Toronto General Hospital* (1983), 41 O.R. (2d) 457 (H.C.); *Rondel v. Worsley*, [1969] 1 A.C. 191 at 227-228 (H.L.), *per* Lord Reid; *Vernon v. Bosley No. 2*, [1997] 1 All E.R. 614 (C.A.); and Earl A. Cherniak, "The Ethics of Advocacy", Law Society of Upper Canada Gazette, vol. 19, no. 2 (June, 1985), pp. 153-154. In a 1991 case, the Law Society of Upper Canada reprimanded a lawyer privately for failing repeatedly to disclose a psychiatric report that he had a duty to disclose to his opponent and to the court.

41 See Ontario Rules of Civil Procedure, R.R.O. 1990, reg. 194, rule 30.03 (2)(b); *Brampton Engineering Inc. v. Alros Products Ltd.* (1986), 8 C.P.C. (2d) 48 (Ont. Master); and *Temoin v. Stanley* (1986), 12 C.P.C. (2d) 69 (Ont. Dist. Ct.), reversed in part on other grounds (1987), 7 W.D.C.P. 71 (Ont. H.C.).

41.1 *Dumais v. Zarnett* (1996), 30 O.R. (3d) 431, 6 O.T.C. 264 (Gen. Div.); see also *Atamanchuk v. DeBruin* (1992), 14 C.P.C. (3d) 259, 106 Sask. R. 288 (Q.B.).

41.2 Ont. rule 16(2)(d)(iii).

4.7 OTHER LAWYERS

Charles Wolfram has written that Shakespeare's notion that adversaries in law "strive mightily, but eat and drink as friends" describes either strife or friendship in a peculiar way. In fact many lawyers make lasting enemies of other lawyers.[42]

Lawyers should deal with one another courteously and in good faith.[43] If they behave otherwise they do a disservice to their clients. Ultimately, unfair and discourteous behaviour impairs the ability of lawyers to perform their function properly and it is antagonistic to the public interest, which demands that matters entrusted to lawyers be dealt with effectively and expeditiously.[44]

Lawyers acting as counsel in litigation should never allow acrimony between their clients to influence their conduct and demeanour toward either each other or the parties. Personal animosity between lawyers may cause their judgment to be clouded and hinder the proper resolution of the dispute.[45]

Hence, lawyers should accede to reasonable requests for adjournments and the waiver of procedural formalities that do not prejudice their clients' rights.[46] They should not take advantage of or act without fair warning upon slips, irregularities, or mistakes on the part of other lawyers that do not go to the merits or involve the sacrifice of the client's rights.[47]

In an address on legal ethics delivered in 1905, Chancellor Boyd said that what is required of a lawyer is "truth and not trickery, simplicity and not duplicity, candour and not craftiness in the conduct of legal affairs."[48] Justice Rose, in a

---

42 Shakespeare's oft-quoted observation is from *The Taming of the Shrew*, act 1, scene ii. Wolfram's comment is from *Modern Legal Ethics*, *supra*, note 37, p. 609.

43 C.B.A. Code, chapter XVI, rule; Ontario rule 6.03(1). Under the Ontario rules that came into force on November 1, 2000, this duty is owed not only to other lawyers and persons lawfully representing themselves, as was formerly the case, but to all persons with whom lawyers have dealings in the course of their practice.

44 C.B.A. Code, chapter XVI, commentary 1; Ontario rule 6.03(1) and accompanying commentary.

45 C.B.A. Code, chapter XVI, commentary 2; Ontario rule 6.03(1) and accompanying commentary.

46 C.B.A. Code, chapter XVI, commentary 3; Ontario rule 6.03(1) and accompanying commentary.

47 C.B.A. Code, chapter XVI, commentary 4; Ontario rule 6.03(3). In *Chrysler Credit Canada Ltd. v. 734925 Ontario Ltd.* (1991), 5. O.R. (3d) 65 (Gen. Div.) a master held that the refusal of a lawyer to approve a draft order, based on instructions from a client, where there are no proper grounds to withhold approval, contravenes the lawyer's duties to the court and to other lawyers under rules 10 and 14 of the Law Society of Upper Canada's rules of professional conduct (now Ontario rules 4.01 and 6.03).

48 4 Can. L. Rev. 85. Justice Middleton said in *Arthur v. Meaford (Town)* (1915), 34 O.L.R. 231 at 233-234 (H.C.), that it is no part of the duty of a professional person "to build up a client's case on the slips of an opponent."

similar address, said that in the conduct of litigation, counsel should try the merits of the cause, and not try each other.[49]

If a party to litigation is represented by a lawyer, lawyers for other parties may not communicate directly with the party about the litigation except with the consent of the parties' lawyer.[50] The prohibition against communicating with represented parties applies even where lawyers have reason to believe that settlement offers have not been forwarded to adverse parties by their counsel. Lawyers in this situation can only suggest a settlement meeting with clients present.[51]

If a represented party approaches directly a lawyer representing another party, the lawyer should refuse to negotiate with the party personally.[52]

The rule against communicating with represented parties also extends to preventing lawyers from causing their employees and others under their control — such as investigators and even clients — to communicate directly with represented parties.[53] The rule does not prohibit communications with employees of corporate parties who have information relevant to the issues in litigation, and who are not themselves parties who are represented by the corporate party's counsel. Nor does the rule prevent a client from obtaining a second opinion. Parties who are dissatisfied with a lawyer's representation, for instance, may consult a second lawyer without terminating the first lawyer's retainer or even obtaining the first lawyer's consent.

Where parties are not represented by lawyers, it will of course be necessary for lawyers for other parties to deal with them directly. In communicating with unrepresented parties lawyers have the same duties of courtesy and good faith as they have toward other lawyers.[54] They also have a duty not to either overreach or misstate their representational role. Lawyers must be sensitive to the danger that unrepresented parties may rely to their detriment on advice that is not disinterested.[55]

4.8 THE DUTY TO SETTLE

The great American lawyer Elihu Root said that "about half the practice of a decent lawyer consists in telling would-be clients that they are damned fools

49 (1900) 20 C.L. Times 59. See also *Strang v. Beal* (1922), 23 O.W.N. 287 (H.C.), in which the court observed that official examiners also are entitled to be treated with courtesy and respect.

50 C.B.A. Code, chapter XVI, commentary 8; Ontario rule 6.03(7); New Brunswick rules, Part D, rule 3.

51 See Geoffrey C. Hazard, Junior, "Contacts With The Opponent", National Law Journal (May 15, 1989), p. 13.

52 *Bank of Montreal v. Wilson* (1867), 2 Ch. 117; New Brunswick rules, Part D, rule 3.

53 See Charles Wolfram, *Modern Legal Ethics* (St. Paul, Minnesota: West, 1986), pp. 611-613.

54 C.B.A. Code, chapter XVI, commentary 10; Ontario rule 6.03(1).

55 See Wolfram, *supra*, note 53, pp. 616-617.

and should stop."[56] He was not the first to advise other lawyers to settle out of court. Abraham Lincoln stated:

> Discourage litigation. Persuade your neighbours to compromise whenever you can. Point out to them how the nominal winner is often a real loser — in fees, expenses, and waste of time. As a peacemaker, the lawyer has a superior opportunity of being a good man. There will be business enough.[57]

Charles Dickens also advised litigants to stay out of court, and to stay away particularly from the Court of Chancery: "Suffer any wrong that can be done you, rather than come here."[58]

In Canadian rules of professional conduct the duty to advise and encourage settlement whenever it is possible to do so on a reasonable basis is enshrined in both rules governing advising clients and rules governing advocacy — a clear indication that lawyers have such a duty both before and after litigation is commenced. It warrants emphasis that to encourage clients to resolve disputes at either juncture is more than just sensible and wise advice: lawyers have a professional duty to do so.[59]

The duty is twice qualified, once by the words "whenever it is possible to do so on a reasonable basis", and second by the words "whenever the case can be fairly settled." Hence lawyers of course have no duty to encourage clients to accept unreasonable or unfair settlement offers. Lawyers do, however, have a duty to inform their clients of settlement proposals and to explain such proposals properly.[60]

Counsel for other parties to litigation are entitled to assume that offers of settlement that are communicated by counsel are authorized by counsel's client. A lawyer has apparent authority to compromise a claim unless the lawyer's retainer limits the lawyer's authority to do so, and that limitation is known to the lawyer for the other party.[61]

---

56 Quoted in David Shrager and Elizabeth Frost (eds.), *The Quotable Lawyer* (New York: Facts on File Publications, 1986), p. 189.

57 The Lincoln quotation is the epigraph to Mark H. McCormack's book *The Terrible Truth About Lawyers: What Every Business Person Needs to Know* (London: William Collins & Sons, 1987).

58 Charles Dickens, *Bleak House* (Harmondsworth, Middlesex, England: Penguin Books, 1971, first published 1853).

59 C.B.A. Code, chapter III, commentary 6 and chapter IX, commentary 8; Ontario rule 2.02(2); British Columbia rules, chapter 1, rule 3(3). The New Brunswick rules, Part C, rule 3, qualify the duty by making it clear that the lawyer is not the judge of the client's case, and that if there is a reasonable prospect of success the lawyer is justified in proceeding to trial.

60 C.B.A. Code, chapter III, commentary 7(j); Ontario rule 2.02(2). See also *Karpenko v. Paroian, Courey, Cohen & Houston* (1980), 117 D.L.R. (3d) 383 (Ont. H.C.); *Maillet v. Haliburton* (1983), 55 N.S.R. (2d) 311 (T.D.); and *Taylor v. Taylor* (1984), 61 N.B.R. (2d) 116 (Q.B.).

61 *Scherer v. Paletta*, [1966] 2 O.R. 524 at 526 (C.A.). See also *Propp v. Fleming* (1968), 67 D.L.R. (2d) 630 (B.C. C.A.); and *Canada (A.G.) v. Veinotte* (1987), 81 N.S.R. (2d) 356 (T.D.), affirmed (June 7, 1989), Doc. No. S.C.A. 02014 (N.S. C.A.).

However, in a 1983 decision,[62] the British Columbia Court of Appeal refused to enforce a settlement agreement completed by counsel under a misapprehension as to the severity of injuries sustained by the plaintiff. The plaintiff's counsel had made a settlement offer that had been accepted by the defendant. The offer was made without express instructions. The plaintiff's counsel's general retainer imposed no limitation on his authority to settle the plaintiff's claim.

The plaintiff repudiated the settlement and provided substantial evidence concerning the nature and extent of the injuries, which were more serious than the lawyer had believed when the settlement offer was made and accepted. The defendant brought a motion for an order staying the plaintiff's action and enforcing the settlement.

The Court of Appeal held that a judge may refuse to order a stay that is requested on the ground that an action has been settled in four circumstances: (i) where there was a limitation on counsel's authority to settle that was communicated to the opposite party; (ii) where there was a misapprehension by the lawyer of the client's instructions or of the facts, of a type that would result in injustice or make it unreasonable or unfair to enforce the settlement; (iii) where there was fraud or collusion; or (iv) where there is an issue to be tried as to whether there was such a limitation, misapprehension, fraud or collusion in relation to the settlement. The Court of Appeal upheld the judge's order refusing a stay because the circumstances fell within the second category, in that the plaintiff's lawyer had made the settlement offer in question on the basis of a misapprehension as to the true extent of the plaintiff's injuries.

The dangers implicit in lawyers purporting to settle litigation without express instructions from clients is demonstrated also by two 1988 cases. In one,[63] a judge of the Supreme Court of Ontario found a lawyer negligent where the lawyer had settled the plaintiff's claim for an inadequate amount without instructions from the plaintiff. In the second case,[64] the British Columbia Court of Appeal set aside a consent, signed by the plaintiff's lawyer, to dismiss an action where the consent was signed without the client's authority.

In a 1992 decision,[65] the Ontario Court of Justice (General Division) dismissed a plaintiff's motion for judgment that was based on the plaintiff's acceptance of an offer to settle that had been served on behalf of the defendants three years earlier. The defendants had instructed their lawyers to withdraw the offer, but their lawyers had neglected to do so. The defendants' lawyers' want of authority to leave the offer open for acceptance was brought to the court's attention before judgment. There was no issue between the client and its lawyers as to the scope of the lawyers' authority; thus the prohibition against embarking upon an inquiry as to whether a limitation of authority was imposed by the client upon its

---

62 *Hawitt v. Campbell*, [1983] 5 W.W.R. 760 (B.C. C.A.).

63 *Coulombe v. Horner*, Ont. S.C., 1988 (unreported).

64 *Racz v. Mission (District)* (1988), 22 B.C.L.R. (2d) 70 (C.A.).

65 *Smith v. Robinson* (1992), 7 O.R. (3d) 550 (Gen. Div.).

lawyer did not apply. In these circumstances, Justice Ferrier held, the court may refuse to grant judgment in accordance with an accepted offer.[66]

The proposition that a lawyer's general retainer authorizes the lawyer to settle the client's claim in the absence of a limitation preventing the lawyer from doing so, is an anachronism that will no doubt be judicially abrogated explicitly in due course. It is important not to confuse the proposition that counsel for other parties are entitled to rely upon a lawyer's *apparent* authority to compromise a claim with the proposition that, as between the client and the lawyer, the lawyer's retainer permits the lawyer to settle the claim without express authority. The latter proposition is incompatible with the reasonable expectations of the parties. Prudent lawyers not only obtain specific instructions to make or accept a particular settlement offer, but obtain the clients' written instructions to settle the claim, if possible by arranging for the client to sign the settlement agreement.

Where litigation, or potential litigation, cannot be settled lawyers should explore the possibility of resolving the issues by arbitration or some other means of alternative dispute resolution. Although it may be premature to elevate consideration of alternative dispute resolution to an ethical duty, such options as a mini-trial may cost only one-quarter of what a lawsuit would cost. To charge ahead with an action without exploring such options is incompatible with the duty to settle.[67]

4.9 THE LAW'S DELAY

The law's delays have long been a common reason for public dissatisfaction. Shakespeare wrote that the plodding pace of legal procedures is one of the "slings and arrows" that might drive a person to despair or even suicide. In Hamlet's "To be or not to be" soliloquy, "the law's delay" ranks with "the oppressor's wrong" and "the pangs of dispriz'd love" among the irritations "that make calamity of so long life."

Only occasionally are delays caused by lawyer self-interest; even where lawyers' fees are based on hourly charges they are subject to review by assessment officers who will consider the necessity of interlocutory proceedings and reduce accounts for work that is not efficiently performed.

More often, litigation is delayed because of procrastination or the pressure of lawyers' other work. This too, however, is likely to instill anxiety and suspicion in clients. Lawyers' explanations for delay tend to be thin. The Advocate repeat-

---

66 See also *Holt v. Jesse* (1876), 3 Ch. D. 177; *Neale v. Lennox*, [1902] A.C. 465 (H.L.); *Shepherd v. Robinson*, [1919] 1 K.B. 474 (C.A.); *Thomson v. Gough* (1977), 17 O.R. (2d) 420 (H.C.); *Bank of Montreal v. Arvee Cedar Mills Ltd. (No. 2)*, [1979] 1 W.W.R. 219 (B.C. S.C.); and *Fabian v. Bud Mervyn Construction Ltd.* (1981), 35 O.R. (2d) 132 (Div. Ct.).

67 See Beverley G. Smith, *Professional Conduct for Canadian Lawyers* (Toronto: Butterworths, 1989), pp. 109-110. See also the final report of the Law Society of Upper Canada's Dispute Resolution Subcommittee (Toronto: Law Society of Upper Canada, 1993).

edly tells K in Kafka's novel *The Trial* that "progress had always been made, but the nature of the progress could never be divulged."[68]

In these cases also the lawyers who are responsible are in breach of their professional obligations: rules of professional conduct require lawyers to perform work that they undertake "in a conscientious, diligent and efficient manner", and to inform clients if they can reasonably foresee undue delay in providing advice or services.[69]

The more troublesome problems involving delay arise in litigation in which delay is in the client's interest. In most litigation, delay can be employed as a tactic by at least one party (usually a defendant) in whose interest it is to postpone the day of judgment. The renowned American trial lawyer, Edward Bennett Williams, used to warn eager clients with dubious cases that "he who seeks justice may catch it."[70]

In the United States, the American Bar Association's Model Rules of Professional Conduct, which have been adopted by most state bar associations, impose a duty on lawyers to "make reasonable efforts to expedite litigation consistent with the interests of the client." The test for resolving the tension between expediting litigation and promoting the client's interest is "whether a lawyer acting in good faith would regard the course of action as having some substantial purpose other than delay. Realizing financial or other benefit from otherwise improper delay in litigation is not a legitimate interest of the client." Hence delay in litigation cannot be justified merely by invoking the client's interest.[71]

In Canadian jurisdictions, the obligation of the lawyer is not quite as clear, though the same principles are expressed. Rules of professional conduct provide that "it is desirable that the lawyer should avoid and discourage the client from . . . tactics which will merely delay or harass the other side", as "such practices can readily bring the administration of justice and the legal profession into disrepute."[72] Judges, moreover, have emphasized that lawyers have a duty to respect, and a duty not to impede, the directions of judges concerning trial lists.[73]

68 Franz Kafka, *The Trial* (1925) (London: Penguin, 1953), p. 138.

69 C.B.A. Code, chapter II, rule, paragraph (b) and commentary 8; Ontario rule 2.01(1) and accompanying commentary.

70 Evan Thomas, *The Man To See: Edward Bennett Williams — Ultimate Insider; Legendary Trial Lawyer* (New York: Simon & Schuster, 1991), p. 420.

71 The model rule quoted is rule 3.2. The text that is quoted is from the commentary to the same rule. See also Charles Wolfram, *Modern Legal Ethics* (St. Paul, Minnesota: West, 1986), p. 599.

72 C.B.A. Code, chapter IX, commentary 7; Ontario rule 4.01(1) and accompanying commentary. The New Brunswick rules, in Part A, rule 2(g), include "the bringing of proceedings solely for the purpose of delay" in a list of examples of conduct that is prohibited as a result of lawyers' duty not to assist clients to break or subvert the law.

73 *Adcock v. Algoma Steel Corp.*, [1970] 3 O.R. 560 (H.C.), *per* Wright J.

4.10 WITHDRAWAL AS COUNSEL

The client-lawyer relationship is terminable at will by the client. The client does not need grounds to terminate the lawyer's retainer, and is not required to give notice. If the lawyer is discharged, the lawyer has no further responsibility or right to proceed with the representation, and the court and other parties to the litigation cannot continue to recognize the discharged lawyer over the client's objections.[74]

The lawyer, however, has no right to terminate the retainer by withdrawing services except for good cause and upon notice appropriate in the circumstances. When the lawyer is retained, the lawyer undertakes to complete the services that are the subject of the retainer except in cases involving justifiable cause for terminating the relationship. Even then (and, indeed, when the lawyer is discharged) the lawyer has a duty to minimize expense and avoid prejudice to the client, and to do all that can reasonably be done to facilitate the orderly transfer of the matter to the client's new lawyer.[75]

These rules recognize the significance of the consequences to the client if the lawyer withdraws from a brief. The termination of the retainer by the lawyer can hamper the ability of the client to obtain a favourable result in litigation by settlement or judgment, and can cause both economic and psychological damage.[76]

Cases in which lawyers have good cause for withdrawal can be divided into two categories. In some circumstances lawyers have a duty to withdraw. In addition to cases in which they are discharged by the client, lawyers have a duty to withdraw in the following circumstances: (i) if they are instructed by their client to do something that is inconsistent with their duty to the court and, despite explanation, their client persists in giving such instructions; (ii) if their client is guilty of dishonourable conduct in the proceedings or is taking a position solely to harass or maliciously injure another; (iii) if it becomes clear that their continued employment will lead to a breach of one or more other rules of professional

---

74 C.B.A. Code, chapter XII, commentary 1; Ontario rule 2.09(1) and accompanying commentary; see also *Sherman v. Manley* (1978), 85 D.L.R. (3d) 575, in which the Ontario Court of Appeal held that the court has no power to interfere with a party's right to discharge counsel, subject to the narrow exception that if parties collude to defeat a lawyer's right to costs, the court may interfere at the lawyer's instance to prevent that purpose from being carried into effect. See also Wolfram, *supra*, note 71, pp. 546-547.

75 C.B.A. Code, chapter XII, rule, and commentaries 1 and 2; Ontario rule 2.09(1) and accompanying commentary and 2.09(8); Yukon rules, part one, rule 21; Quebec rules, sections 3.03.04, 3.03.05, and 4.02.01 (j); British Columbia rules, chapter 10. In *Mans v. State Farm Mutual Insurance Company* (1996), 32 O.R. (3d) 786 (Gen. Div.) the Court emphasized that the mantle of solicitor of record may not be discarded except in accordance with rules of civil procedure, and ordered a law firm to pay costs thrown away when it caused costs to be incurred unnecessarily by failing to bring a motion to be removed from the record in a timely way.

76 See Beverley G. Smith, *Professional Conduct for Canadian Lawyers* (Toronto: Butterworths, 1989), p. 146.

conduct, such as the conflict of interest rule; and (iv) if they are not competent to handle the matter.[77]

In cases in which there has been a serious loss of confidence between client and lawyer, lawyers are entitled to withdraw — as always, upon notice appropriate in the circumstances — but they do not invariably have a duty to do so. Such a serious loss of confidence may result from their client's attempting to deceive them or may be indicated by their client's refusing to accept the lawyer's advice on a significant point.[78] In some cases, as for instance where their client accuses them of fraud, the loss of confidence may be so acute that withdrawal is obligatory. In a 1946 decision,[79] the Ontario Court of Appeal held that in such a case it would be improper for a lawyer to continue to act. Lawyers should not in any case use the threat of withdrawal as a device to force a hasty decision by their client on a difficult question.

Withdrawal will also be justified, unless serious prejudice to the client would result, where the client has failed to provide funds on account of disbursements or fees after reasonable notice.

A lawyer's belief that the client is likely to be unsuccessful is not cause for withdrawal in itself, though situations in which a serious loss of confidence between client and lawyer will result from such a belief can readily be imagined.[80]

What period of notice is appropriate in the circumstances will be determined by statutory provisions or rules of court where applicable. In other situations the governing principle is that lawyers should protect their client's interests to the best of their ability and should not desert their client at a critical stage of a matter or at a time when withdrawal would put their client in a position of disadvantage or peril.[81]

Because, in Canada, the legal relationship between lawyers and their clients is essentially contractual, the question whether a lawyer should withdraw is to be determined by the lawyer, not by the court before whom the lawyer is appearing. In a 1985 British Columbia criminal case,[82] a defence counsel informed the court at the beginning of the second day of trial that he was withdrawing as counsel. When the judge asked why, the lawyer initially refused to answer, then responded that the accused person had failed to instruct him. The judge asked the accused

---

77 C.B.A. Code, chapter XII, commentary 4; Ontario rule 2.09(7); B.C. Rules, chapter 8, rules 7 and 8. For cases dealing with the circumstances in which courts will remove solicitors of record on conflict of interest grounds, see chapter 5. See also Wolfram, *supra*, note 71, pp. 656-657.

78 C.B.A. Code, chapter XII, commentary 5; Ontario rule 2.09(2) and accompanying commentary.

79 *Collison v. Hurst*, [1946] O.W.N. 668 at 671 (C.A.).

80 The New Brunswick rules, Part C, rule 6, specify that "good cause" justifying the lawyer in terminating the client-lawyer relationship does not include a belief that the client is likely to be unsuccessful.

81 C.B.A. Code, chapter XII, commentary 7; Ontario rule 2.09(1) and accompanying commentary.

82 *Leask v. Cronin*, [1985] 3 W.W.R. 152 (B.C. S.C.).

person if he had any objection to the lawyer continuing to act for him. The accused person answered that he did not. The judge thereupon ordered that the lawyer continue to act. The lawyer, however, refused to cross-examine a Crown witness, and the judge said that he intended to cite the lawyer for contempt. The trial was concluded in the lawyer's absence.

The lawyer brought a motion for an order prohibiting the issuance of a citation for contempt. In granting the motion, Justice McKay held that trial judges have no right in law to order lawyers to continue in the defence of accused persons after lawyers inform the court that they have decided to withdraw. Judges may urge counsel to reconsider and to try to reconcile their differences with their clients, Justice McKay added, but if counsel stand firm, the judge may go no further.

Justice McKay qualified his remarks by pointing out that lawyers could be cited for contempt or exposed to disciplinary proceedings if they withdraw as a ploy to delay or hinder the trial process. Because there was no evidence that the moving party in the case before the court withdrew for that reason, Justice McKay granted the order of prohibition — a lawyer may not be cited for contempt of an order that is unlawful. Justice McKay also held that lawyers should not be asked about their reasons for withdrawing in the absence of a proper waiver of privilege.[83]

A few years later, the British Columbia Court of Appeal adopted the principles articulated by Justice McKay, and held that those principles are equally applicable in civil litigation.[84]

The duty of lawyers upon withdrawal to minimize expenses and avoid prejudice to their client, and to facilitate the orderly transfer of the matter to their client's new lawyer, entails the following requirements: (i) lawyers should deliver to or to the order of their client, all papers and property to which their client is entitled; (ii) lawyers should give their client all information that may be required in connection with the case; (iii) lawyers should account for all client funds that they are holding or have previously dealt with, including refunding any remuneration not earned during the employment; (iv) lawyers should promptly render an account for outstanding fees and disbursements; and (v) lawyers should cooperate with their client's new lawyer.[85]

---

83 *Ibid.*, pp. 164-165.

84 *Luchka v. Zens* (1989), 37 B.C.L.R. (2d) 127 (C.A.). The C.B.A. Code makes no distinction between civil and criminal cases in its rules governing withdrawal. The Ontario rules do make such a distinction. The rules governing withdrawal in criminal cases in that jurisdiction are discussed in chapter 7.

85 C.B.A. Code, chapter XII, commentary 8; Ontario rule 2.09(9) and accompanying commentary.

Where a lawyer who has been acting for two or more clients ceases to act for one or more of them, the lawyer has a duty to co-operate with the successor lawyer or lawyers, and to avoid any unseemly rivalry, whether real or apparent.[86]

These duties affect lawyers' right to claim a lien against their client's papers and property for unpaid fees and disbursements. Lawyers have a duty not to enforce a solicitor's lien if the result would be to prejudice materially their client's position in any uncompleted matter. Lawyers who neglect or refuse to turn over their client's documents in circumstances in which serious damage to their client may result are subject to discipline. Except where lawyers are discharged without cause and their client's interests will not be prejudiced by the assertion of a solicitor's lien, lawyers would be well-advised to disregard the possibility.[87]

The duties of successor lawyers are also worthy of consideration. Before accepting employment, the successor lawyer should be satisfied that the former lawyer approves, or has withdrawn or been discharged by the client. It is proper for the successor lawyer to urge the client to settle or take reasonable steps to settle or secure the former lawyer's outstanding account, especially if the former lawyer withdrew for good cause or was discharged without good cause. Even in these latter cases, however, the client's interest comes first: if a trial or hearing is in progress or imminent, or if the client would otherwise be prejudiced, the fact that the former lawyer has an outstanding account should not be allowed to interfere with the successor lawyer acting for the client.[88]

The successor lawyer has no duty to persuade the client not to abandon the former lawyer, or to offer to attempt to bring about a reconciliation between the client and the former lawyer. Although M.H. Ludwig suggested more than 80 years ago that successor lawyers had such duties, the suggestion is incompatible with the client's right to be represented by counsel of choice.[89]

The dissolution of a law firm will result in the termination of the client-lawyer relationship insofar as at least some of the lawyers in the firm are concerned. The decision whether to continue to retain any of the lawyers from the dissolved firm rests, of course, with the client. The lawyers who are no longer retained should act in accordance with the rules referred to above, particularly the rule requiring former lawyers to act in such a way as to minimize expense

86 C.B.A. Code, chapter XII, commentary 10; Ontario rule 2.09(9) and accompanying commentary.

87 C.B.A Code, chapter XII, commentary 11; Ontario rule 2.09(9) and accompanying commentary. See also *Re Gladstone*, [1972] 2 O.R. 127 at 128 (C.A.), *per* McGillivray J.A.; and Charles Wolfram, *Modern Legal Ethics* (St. Paul, Minnesota: West, 1986), pp. 543-544.

88 C.B.A. Code, chapter XII, commentary 12; Ontario rule 2.09(10) and accompanying commentary.

89 See Mark Orkin, *Legal Ethics: A Study of Professional Conduct* (Toronto: Cartwright & Sons, 1957), pp. 93-94, commenting on Ludwig's article, "Practical Ethics of a Lawyer" (1909) 29 C.L. Times 253.

and avoid prejudice to the client, and to facilitate the orderly completion of the matter.[90]

4.11 DUTY TO FOLLOW INSTRUCTIONS

Before his appointment as a justice of the Ontario Court of Appeal, G. Arthur Martin likened lawyers taking instructions from clients to surgeons taking instructions from patients: "The defence counsel is not the *alter ego* of the client. The function of defence counsel is to provide professional assistance and advice. He must, accordingly, exercise his professional skill and judgment in the conduct of the case and not allow himself to be a mere mouthpiece for the client."[91]

Courts have generally granted lawyers the authority, even over their clients' objections, to make such tactical decisions as agreeing to adjournments, agreeing upon facts that are not in dispute, calling or declining to call witnesses, agreeing to the introduction of evidence introduced by adverse parties, and raising, refusing to raise, or abandoning positions or defences.[92]

In a 1997 decision,[92.1] the Ontario Court of Appeal considered the extent of control defence counsel should have in a criminal case. One ground of appeal was the alleged incompetence of defence counsel. The allegation was based in part on counsel's failure to call certain witnesses.

In declining to give effect to this ground of appeal, the Court affirmed[92.2] that considerable deference should be accorded to counsel in such a case because of the broad spectrum of professional judgment that might be considered reasonable, bearing in mind that advocacy is a highly individualized art. The Court added that the decision whether to call a particular witness is generally that of counsel, not the client.

In a decision released a few months later,[92.3] the Ontario Court of Justice (General Division) emphasized that though the right to control the case in court gives counsel the right to decide how the case is conducted despite the client's

90 C.B.A. Code, chapter XII, commentary 13; Ontario rule 2.09(7) and accompanying commentary.

91 Mr. Martin made these remarks in an address to the Advocates Society in 1970 that is quoted in part by George D. Finlayson (later Justice Finlayson of the Ontario Court of Appeal) in "The Lawyer As A Professional", Law Society of Upper Canada Gazette, vol. 14, no. 3 (September, 1980), p. 229 at 232. See also *Batchelor v. Pattison and Makersy* (1876), 3 R. 914 at 918 (Scot. Ct. of Sess.); and Arthur Maloney, "The Role of the Independent Bar", 1979 Law Society of Upper Canada Special Lectures, p. 49.

92 See Maloney, *ibid.*, p. 49; *Jones v. Barnes*, 463 U.S. 745 (1983); *Nelson* v. *State*, 346 F. 2d 73 at 81 (9th Cir., 1965); *Stricklan v. Koella*, 546 S.W. 2d 810 (Tenn. Ct. App., 1976); and David Luban, *Lawyers and Justice: An Ethical Study* (Princeton, New Jersey: Princeton University Press, 1988), p. 159.

92.1 *R. v. White* (1997), 32 O.R. (3d) 722.

92.2 Citing *R. v. Joanisse* (1995), 44 C.R. (4th) 365, 85 O.A.C. 186, 102 C.C.C. (3d) 35 (C.A.), leave to appeal to S.C.C. refused (1997), 99 O.A.C. 79 (note), 208 N.R. 79 (note) (S.C.C.).

92.3 *Stewart v. C.B.C.*, (June 6, 1997), J. Macdonald J. (Ont. Gen. Div.) at 65-6.

wishes (subject to exceptions discussed below), that right carries with it the duty to exercise control in accordance with reasonable professional standards.

Some strategic decisions are so fundamental that lawyers have a duty to defer to their clients' instructions in preference to their own judgment. Lawyers cannot, for example, commence civil proceedings without specific instructions to do so. In criminal cases, although lawyers have a duty to advise their clients fully about the ramifications of the decisions, the decisions whether to plead guilty or not guilty and whether to testify are the clients' alone.[93]

Some decisions as to what defences to raise are also so fundamental that lawyers cannot act contrary to their clients' instructions. Thus in a 1985 case,[94] the New Zealand Court of Appeal set aside a conviction for rape and ordered a new trial where the accused person's counsel, contrary to the client's instructions, ignored an alibi defence and raised a defence that the complainant had consented to sexual intercourse. The court ruled that "following any advice he thought it proper to give to his client, [the lawyer's] duty was to either act on the instructions he then received or to withdraw from the case . . . Counsel may not take it upon himself to disregard his instructions and to then conduct the case as he himself thinks best."[95]

Generally, however, the courts will proceed on the basis that lawyers' tactical decisions are made pursuant to authority impliedly granted by clients who have instructed them to act on their behalf, and will intervene only in cases in which the courts have lurking doubts that litigants may have suffered injustice as a result of flagrantly incompetent advocacy.[96] Lawyers are responsible for their conduct of cases, and may not justify incompetent or unprofessional conduct on the ground that it was in accordance with clients' instructions.

4.11.1 COMMUNICATING WITH REPRESENTED PARTIES AND WITH WITNESSES PRIOR TO TRIAL

Lawyers must not approach a party who is adverse in interest and who is represented by a lawyer except through, or with the consent of, the party's lawyer.[96.1] Lawyers may, however, seek information from a potential witness who is not a party (whether or not the potential witness is under subpoena) so long as they disclose their interest and take care not to subvert or suppress evidence or to procure the witness to stay out of the way.[96.2]

93 See chapter 7.

94 *R. v. McLoughlin*, [1985] 1 N.Z.L.R. 106 (C.A.). See also *R. v. Irwin*, [1987] 1 W.L.R. 902 (C.A.), which is to the same effect.

95 *Ibid.*, p. 107.

96 *R. v. Ensor*, [1989] 1 W.L.R. 497 at 502 (C.A.). See also David Pannick, *Advocates* (Oxford: Oxford University Press, 1992), pp. 91-92, 98.

96.1 C.B.A. Code, chapter IX, commentary 6; Ontario rule 4.03(2).

96.2 C.B.A. Code, chapter IX, commentary 6; Ontario rule 4.03(1).

Rules of professional conduct have not generally addressed the applicability of these principles to corporate or organizational parties. In 2000, however, the Law Society of Upper Canada's *Rules of Professional Conduct* were amended to specify which employees or agents of the corporation or other organization should be treated as parties, rather than mere witnesses, for the purpose of the rule. The Ontario rule[96.3] provides that where a corporation or other organization has retained a lawyer on a matter, another lawyer seeking information about that matter must not, without the consent of the lawyer representing the corporation or other organization, approach or deal with (a) directors, officers, or persons likely involved in the decision-making process concerning the matter, or (b) employees and agents of the corporation or organization whose acts or omissions in connection with the matter are in issue or whose acts or omissions may expose the corporation or organization to civil or criminal liability.

The effect of the Ontario rule may be illustrated with an example. If the plaintiff in a medical malpractice action alleges that the plaintiff has sustained damage as a result of the negligence of a nurse in the operating room, for which the defendant hospital is responsible in law, the plaintiff's lawyer will be prohibited (without the consent of the hospital's lawyer) from interviewing directors, officers and others likely involved in the decision-making process concerning the matter, and will be prohibited also from interviewing the nurse against whom allegations of negligence are made, regardless of whether the nurse is personally joined as a party. Nevertheless, the plaintiff's lawyer may, without the consent of the hospital's lawyer, interview other nurses who were present in the operating room against whom no allegations of negligence are made, as they are treated as mere witnesses rather than as parties.

Commentary to the Ontario rule makes it clear that if a lawyer for a corporation or other organization is asked also to represent employees of the corporation or organization, the lawyer must comply with rules governing the avoidance of conflicts of interest, and must not represent that the lawyer represents the employees unless the lawyer has complied with those requirements. The commentary adds that a lawyer retained by a corporation or other organization must not be retained by an employee solely for the purpose of sheltering factual information from another party.

Commentary to the Law Society of Alberta's *Code of Professional Conduct*[96.4] provides that if an opposing party is an organization such as a corporation, association or government department, a lawyer is prohibited from communicating about the matter with directors and officers of the organization and management-level personnel having decision making authority. The Alberta rules do not prohibit a lawyer from communicating directly with a non-managerial level employee whose acts or omissions may expose the corporation or organization to civil or criminal liability, as do the Ontario rules.

96.3 Ontario rule 4.03 (3) and accompanying commentary.

96.4 Alberta rules, chapter 4, rule 6, commentary 6.

The limits of these principles have been tested at the superior court level in three Canadian cases.

In a 1992 decision[96.5] Justice Oliver of the British Columbia Supreme Court was called upon to consider the propriety of an unannounced visit by the defendants' counsel to a pulp mill owned and operated by the plaintiff. While a motion was pending for an order requiring the plaintiff to permit the defendants' lawyers and technical consultants to inspect the pulp mill, the defendants' lawyers and a technical consultant made arrangements for a public tour of the mill without informing the plaintiffs' counsel of the intended visit.

On their arrival at the mill, the lawyers and technical consultant were met by a summer student who regularly conducted public tours. When the student learned that the visitors were lawyers and that they seemed to be more familiar with pulp mills than most members of the public would be, she spoke with a manager of the mill, who decided to meet with the visitors personally because he found the visit peculiar. The manager spoke with the visitors for about half an hour, answering questions about such things as the mill's relationship with regulatory agencies and its program for dealing with asbestos at the mill, subjects that were relevant to the litigation. When the discussion concluded, the summer student escorted the visitors on a tour of the facilities.

The Court found that the manager knew that he was speaking to lawyers who were not associated with his employer, who had an unusual knowledge and interest in pulp mill operations, and who had aroused the tour guide's suspicion. The Court also found that at no time did the lawyers ask a question that gave the manager the feeling that in answering he was imparting information that he would not have imparted to members of the public. Finally, the Court found that the lawyers had not asked for an opportunity to speak to the manager; rather, their discussion began at the manager's initiative, and was entirely voluntary.

The Court held[96.6] that though it had no jurisdiction to discipline for professional misconduct, it may nevertheless consider whether an allegation of misconduct has been established for the limited purpose of determining whether judicial intervention in the proceedings is warranted. Judicial intervention will be warranted, however, only where a breach is so grave that it raises a real hazard of injustice or, in other words, that a just result in the proceeding may be threatened. "The question that the court must answer is not: did the respondent lawyers in fact breach a rule of professional conduct", Justice Oliver wrote, "but rather: are the actions alleged to constitute that breach of such a serious nature, from the perspective of fairness in the proceedings of the underlying action, as to require judicial intervention?"[96.7]

The Court held that in order to justify the drastic remedy of removal of a solicitor, the moving party must show not only an appearance of impropriety but

---

96.5 *MacMillan Bloedel Ltd. v. Freeman & Co.* (1992), 78 B.C.L.R. (2d) 325 (S.C.).

96.6 At 329.

96.7 At 332, 336.

also a "probability of mischief", a standard that was not satisfied on the evidence. Observing that the manager had not specified any statements that he was concerned about having made, the Court concluded that a fair-minded and reasonably informed member of the public would not believe that the proper administration of justice required the removal of the defendants' solicitors.[96.8]

The second case in which the courts have considered the limits of the principles relating to pre-trial communications with represented parties and witnesses is a 1997 decision of Justice Brennan of the Ontario Court of Justice (General Division).[96.9] The plaintiff had brought an action for damages against a company that had managed a mortgage portfolio on the plaintiff's behalf. Appraisals of certain properties on which the plaintiff had mortgages were provided by appraisers named Seward and Shaw.

On discovery, the plaintiff learned that a company controlled by Seward had received a large payment from one of the borrowers whose property he had appraised at the request of the defendant. The plaintiff's solicitors retained investigators to pursue suspicions arising out of the payment.

The plaintiff also commenced a second action, framed in negligence, against Seward. The statement of claim was issued to protect against the possible expiry of a limitation period, but was not served immediately.

The investigators retained by the plaintiff's solicitors interviewed Seward and Shaw, who were not told that an action had been commenced against Seward or that an action against Shaw was being considered. The plaintiff's solicitors used information obtained during the interviews to amend the statement of claim in the action that had been commenced against Seward, to commence a second action against Seward, and to commence an action against Shaw. Seward and Shaw brought a motion for an order removing the plaintiff's solicitors in the actions that had been commenced against them.

Justice Brennan dismissed the motion, and held that the interviews breached no obligation imposed on the plaintiff's counsel by rules of professional conduct, in light of the fact that Seward and Shaw were not represented by counsel. "A lawyer may direct an investigator, and may use the fruits of the investigation, notwithstanding that the investigator has not disclosed the interest of the lawyer in the information so obtained,"[96.10] Justice Brennan wrote.

Justice Brennan also made the following observations,[96.11] which summarize the courts' approach in these two cases to disqualification motions based upon allegedly improper communications with adverse parties:

1. Matters of professional conduct are better left to the Law Society except where they affect the rights of parties before the court, in which case the

---

96.8 At 339.

96.9 *Transamerica Life Insurance Co. of Canada v. Seward* (1997), 33 O.R. (3d) 604 (Gen. Div.).

96.10 At 609.

96.11 At 613.

court ought to consider and respect the rules promulgated by the Society and other professional bodies such as the Canadian Bar Association.

2. The integrity of the justice system would be ill-served if the court too readily disqualified counsel at the suggestion of adverse parties.

The third case in which the courts have considered the prohibition against communicating with a represented party who is adverse in interest is a 1999 decision[96.12] of Justice Ellen Macdonald, also of the Ontario Court of Justice (General Division). The case raised the issue of the application of the prohibition to counsel who wishes to interview a witness who is employed by the federal government, where the Crown in Right of Canada is a party represented by counsel employed by the Department of Justice. The Court held that the witness, who was not separately represented, could be approached for an interview only through counsel from the Department of Justice.

The Court also considered the question of whether *former* employees of parties to the litigation could be approached directly for interviews, and held that any such persons must be informed that they are entitled to have a lawyer present during such interviews, but that the lawyer must not be employed or retained by any party to the litigation because of the risk that the lawyer for a party may have a conflict of interest.

4.12 PREPARING WITNESSES

In the preparation of witnesses to testify, lawyers confront some of their most troublesome practical ethical problems. Differing conceptions of the goals of the adversary system and how they can be achieved, the reach and implications of the confidentiality rule, and the conflict between resolute partisanship and the lawyer's duty to the court, are again at the heart of the difficulty.

Although some types of behaviour are clearly improper — subornation of perjury is the obvious example — the great grey area in which the fine and fuzzy distinction between zealous advocacy and the improper tailoring of a witness's evidence tests the honour of even the most noble advocate.

Rules of professional conduct require counsel to "represent the client resolutely and honourably within the limits of the law."[97] This duty requires the lawyer to "raise fearlessly every issue, advance every argument, and ask every question, however distasteful, which the lawyer thinks will help the client's case and to endeavour to obtain for the client the benefit of every remedy and defence authorized by law."[98] The rules recognize that in adversary proceedings "the lawyer's function is necessarily partisan" and that, generally, "the lawyer is not

---

96.12 *Robb Estate v. St. Joseph's Health Care Centre* (March 10, 1999), Doc. 92-CU-54356, 92-CU-59486, 98-CV-139060 (Ont. Gen. Div.).

97 C.B.A. Code, chapter IX, rule; Ontario rule 4.01(1); Quebec rules, section 2.

98 C.B.A. Code, chapter IX, commentary 1; Ontario rule 4.01(1) and accompanying commentary; Quebec rules, section 3.02.01.

obliged . . . to assist an adversary or advance matters derogatory to the client's case."[99]

The rules qualify this duty of resolute partisanship, however, by providing that the lawyer must discharge it in a manner consistent with the lawyer's duty to treat the tribunal with candour.[100] The lawyer must not knowingly attempt to deceive a tribunal "or influence the course of justice", the rules say, by "suppressing what ought to be disclosed." The lawyer must "take care not to subvert or suppress any evidence."[101]

Where the witness in question is the lawyer's client, the difficulty often goes beyond giving appropriate weight to sometimes conflicting duties to client and court, for what the client tells the lawyer as the lawyer prepares the client to testify is likely to be confidential. The lawyer often has a *duty* to suppress evidence, and a duty *not* to be candid with the court, to the extent that the client wishes to maintain in confidence communications with the lawyer. The lawyer's duty in such cases is not to disclose those communications, directly or indirectly, though the lawyer must not mislead the court.

Before grappling with the central problems, let us identify the types of lawyer conduct that are clearly proper and those that are as clearly improper.

Lawyers have a responsibility to their clients to interview witnesses prior to trial. To call a witness whom neither the lawyer nor the lawyer's junior, student, clerk, or investigator has interviewed prior to trial will be actionable negligence in some circumstances,[102] and may in egregious cases be a violation of the lawyer's duty to serve the client in a conscientious, diligent and efficient manner and, therefore, be professional misconduct.[103] Rules of professional conduct make it clear that lawyers may seek information from any potential witness, whether under subpoena or not, but should disclose the lawyer's interest and take care not to subvert or suppress any evidence or procure the witness to stay out of the way. Witnesses who are parties, and who are represented by counsel, should

99 C.B.A. Code, chapter IX, commentary 15; Ontario rule 4.01(1) and accompanying commentary.

100 C.B.A. Code, chapter IX, commentary 1; Ontario rule 4.01(1)) and accompanying commentary.

101 Ontario rules, 4.01(2)(e) and 4.03(1).

102 *Fawell v. Atkins* (1981), 28 B.C.L.R. 32 (S.C.) is an example of a successful solicitor's negligence action that was based on the lawyer's failure to interview a material, independent witness.

103 The lawyer's duty to serve the client in a conscientious, diligent and efficient manner is articulated in the C.B.A. Code, chapter II, rule (b), and in Ontario rule 2.01(1)(e).

not be approached or dealt with except through or with the consent of their lawyer.[104]

In interviewing witnesses, the lawyer is not required to play a purely passive role, or to be a mere scribe. The rule of thumb that a lawyer may advise a witness how to testify, but must refrain from advising the witness what to say, oversimplifies the problem, but at least recognizes that the lawyer may honourably play an active role in preparing witnesses to give evidence, both in chief and in cross-examination.

Lawyers may advise witnesses on proper courtroom attire, and how to address the judge, the lawyers, and the parties. Lawyers may also advise witnesses about their demeanour and tone of voice, and may advise them not to volunteer information that is not responsive to questions asked, all for the purpose of assisting the witnesses to testify in a straightforward and effective way.

It is also proper for lawyers to direct the witnesses' attention to relevant issues, to probe in an attempt to refresh their memories by suggesting and referring to known facts or other evidence, even if an effect of so doing is to prompt answers that witnesses might not have volunteered without such prodding. Lawyers may prepare witnesses to meet a hostile cross-examination.

In cases in which techniques such as these do not have the effect of inducing witnesses to misrepresent material facts, either explicitly through actual testimony or implicitly through demeanour, both of the lawyer's duties — resolute partisanship and candour to the court — are discharged. The effective preparation of witnesses serves not only the client's interest, but also the interest of the effective and efficient administration of justice.[105]

At the opposite end of the spectrum, it is clear that the lawyer must not suborn perjury, knowingly attempt to deceive the court or tribunal by offering false testimony or relying upon a false or deceptive affidavit, or otherwise assist in any fraud, crime, or illegal conduct. The lawyer must not try to persuade witnesses to avoid lawful subpoenas or to absent themselves from trial. (In the United States, courts have held that lawyers may not advise witnesses whom they

---

104 C.B.A. Code, chapter IX, commentary 6; Ontario rule 4.03(1) and accompanying commentary; British Columbia rules, chapter 8, rules 11-12. In *Everingham v. Ontario* (1992), 8 O.R. (3d) 121 the Divisional Court dismissed an appeal from an order disqualifying a lawyer who had a coincidental, innocent, and unprejudicial meeting with an adverse party who was committed to a mental hospital on a Lieutenant Governor's warrant. Although the court held that the lawyer did not contravene commentary 14 to rule 10 (now rule 4.03(2)) because the words "approached or dealt with" in that commentary mean approached or dealt with in relation to the subject matter or process of the litigation itself, the court also held that the lawyer's disqualification was required due to an objective appearance of unfairness and deprivation of counsel.

105 See Earl A. Cherniak, "The Ethics of Advocacy", Law Society of Upper Canada Gazette, vol. 19, no. 2 (June, 1985), pp. 148-149; Joseph D. Piorkowski, Jr., "Professional Conduct and the Preparation of Witnesses for Trial: Defining the Acceptable Limitations of "Coaching"" (1987-88) 1 Georgetown Journal of Legal Ethics 389 at 389-392; and Charles Wolfram, *Modern Legal Ethics* (St. Paul, Minnesota: West, 1986), p. 648.

are not representing of the witnesses' right to refuse to testify on the ground of self-incrimination if the advice is given with the intent of protecting the lawyer's client rather than the interests of the witness.) Lawyers must not obstruct access to witnesses by other parties. Nor may lawyers knowingly permit witnesses to be presented in a false or misleading way, or to impersonate other persons.[106]

Rules of professional conduct stipulate that lawyers must neither needlessly inconvenience nor "needlessly abuse, hector or harass a witness."[107] The quoted words may be read restrictively, as being limited to lawyers' conduct toward witnesses testifying in court; the rules use the term "potential witness" in providing for limitations on lawyers' conduct in interviewing prior to trial. Potential witnesses are nevertheless entitled to be free from misrepresentations, invasions of privacy, and other improper investigative techniques. The Canadian Bar Association's Code of Professional Conduct proscribes the use of a tape recorder by a lawyer to record a conversation except where the lawyer has disclosed an intention to do so.[108] The Law Society of Upper Canada's rules of professional conduct proscribe only the surreptitious recording of conversations with clients and other lawyers.[109] One may infer that in Ontario lawyers may secretly record conversations with witnesses, at least where to do so cannot be characterized as harassment or abuse.

It is generally accepted that lawyers must not attempt improperly to influence witnesses' testimony. The identification of the indistinct boundary separating proper and improper influences is the chief problem in the great grey area of difficulty. Is it proper for the lawyer to elicit answers by means of leading questions? Is it proper to provide the client with legal advice if the advice may tempt the client to commit perjury? To what extent may the lawyer modify a witness's use of speech or demeanour for the purpose of influencing reaction to the witness's testimony?

Monroe Freedman has pointed out the extent to which the witness's memory of events may, without dishonesty, be influenced by the form and content of the lawyer's questions. Psychological learning about memory has shown that the process of "remembering" events involves more reconstruction than recollection. Much of what is said to be perceived is in fact inferred. Recollection is influenced significantly by the witness's personality, prior experiences, and interest. Even honest witnesses suppress and invent facts, both supplementing and falsifying the data of perception, without realizing that they are doing so.

Even straightforward questions may play a strong part in inducing the witness to introduce detail into the process of remembering. Studies have shown that when leading questions are deliberately used to induce error, they do so to a

106 C.B.A. Code, chapter IX, commentary 2(e), (i), and (j); Ontario rule 4.02(2)(e), (i), and (j); Wolfram, *ibid.*, pp. 646-647; and *Meek v. Fleming*, [1961] 3 All E.R. 148.

107 C.B.A. Code, chapter IX, commentaries 2(k) and (l), and 6; Ontario rule 4.01(2)(k) and (m).

108 C.B.A. Code, chapter XIV, commentary 5.

109 Ontario rule 6.03(4).

remarkable extent. In one American study, witnesses' estimates of the speed of a car they observed in a collision varied depending upon the verb used by the questioner in describing the impact: when the car "contacted" another, its speed averaged 31.8 miles per hour; when it "hit" it, its speed was 34.0 miles per hour; when it "bumped" the other car its speed increased to 38.1 miles per hour; when it "collided" with the other car it was travelling 39.3 miles per hour; and, finally, when it "smashed" into the other car it did so at a 40.8 mile per hour clip. Thus the verb used by the questioner may mean the difference between due care and attention and negligence. In the same study, twice as many witnesses reported seeing non-existent broken glass on the ground when the questioner used the word "smashed" rather than "hit."

Thus the process of remembering is a process of active reconstruction, a process that is significantly influenced by the form and content of the questions asked as well as what witnesses believe to be in their own interest even when, on a conscious level, they are answering as honestly as they can.[110]

The conscientious lawyer's dilemma will be evident, as most witnesses cannot be expected to relate all that is relevant without considerable direc-

(*Continued on page 4–27*)

110 See Monroe H. Freedman's books, *Lawyers' Ethics In An Adversary System* (New York: Bobbs-Merrill, 1975), pp. 64-69 and *Understanding Lawyers' Ethics* (New York: Matthew Bender & Co., 1990), pp. 152-160. Freedman quotes from F.C. Bartlett, *Remembering: A Study in Experimental and Social Psychology*. The study on the effect on recollection of the words used by a questioner was conducted by Elizabeth Loftus and reported in the Decem-

tion. Important facts can be lost and undeveloped if the lawyer relies on narrative statements unassisted by questions designed to elicit important facts. An inarticulate victim of an automobile collision may say only that "it hurts bad." Such a client may, and should, be helped to express what the pain is like, and how it interferes with work, family life, sleep and recreation. On the other hand, by telling the witnesses that a particular fact is important, and why, the lawyer may induce the client to "remember" the fact even though it did not occur.[111]

To probe the witness's memory by directing the witness's attention to other evidence is entirely consistent with each of the lawyer's duties. To elicit answers by means of leading questions is to court the accusation that the lawyer is improperly influencing the witness's evidence. Apart altogether from ethical considerations, the extent to which the witness has been "woodshedded" is a proper subject of cross-examination. Leading questions should be avoided in interviewing, and saved for cross-examining.

An even more troublesome problem is the extent to which, if at all, the lawyer may provide the client with legal advice in circumstances in which the advice may tempt the client to commit perjury. The problem may be illustrated by a fictional example.

In the 1958 play *Anatomy of a Murder* (which was written pseudonymously by Judge Richard Traver, and which was made into a popular movie in 1959) a lawyer whose client has just provided an inculpatory account of murder in the first degree says to the client, "If the facts are as you have stated them, you have no legal defence and you will probably be electrocuted. On the other hand, if you acted in a blind rage, there is a possibility of saving your life. Think it over and we will talk about it tomorrow."

Almost everyone would agree that this advice is improper, as the lawyer is clearly attempting to induce the client to give perjured evidence.[112] The lawyer is not just advising the client about the law, but is actively participating in (and, indeed, initiating) a perjurious case. Monroe Freedman eventually came to this conclusion, after initially justifying the lawyer's advice on the following rationale.

The lawyer has given the client legal advice that might induce the client to testify falsely, but the advice consists of information that the lawyer him-

---

ber, 1974 edition of *Psychology Today*. See also Elizabeth Loftus, *Memory* (Cambridge, Mass.: Harvard University Press, 1980); and Michael Owen Miller, "Working with Memory", Litigation, vol. 19, no. 4 (Summer, 1993), p. 10. In *United States v. Amaral*, 488 F. 2d 1148 (9th Cir., 1973) the court outlined the rules governing the admissibility of expert psychological testimony, and affirmed the exclusion of expert evidence on the frailties of memory.

111 Freedman, *Lawyers' Ethics In An Adversary System, ibid.*, p. 69; Freedman, *Understanding Lawyers' Ethics, ibid.*, p. 149.

112 Cherniak, *supra*, note 105, p. 149, says that most counsel would agree that the advice of the lawyer in *Anatomy of a Murder* "goes far beyond the mark."

self would have if he were in the client's position. The client is entitled to have this information about the law and to make her own decision how to act upon it. To hold that the lawyer must refrain from providing the advice, Freedman argued, would not only penalize less well-educated clients and witnesses, but would also disadvantage the client because of her initial truthfulness in confiding in her lawyer.[113]

Ultimately Freedman formed the view that this rationale was not sound on the facts of the *Anatomy of a Murder* example. The lawyer did more than merely provide legal advice — he created a defence that he knew was false. Though the client was originally truthful in relating the facts in confidence to her lawyer, confidentiality would not have been breached if the lawyer had simply declined to create a false defence for the client.[114]

It does not follow from the impropriety of the lawyer's interviewing technique in the *Anatomy of a Murder* example that lawyers must refrain from providing legal advice in every case in which the result of their advice may be that the witness will testify falsely. What makes it clear in the *Anatomy of a Murder* example that the lawyer has acted improperly is that the lawyer knew the client's unaided recollection of the facts before providing advice. If, before hearing the client's account, the lawyer had provided to the client information about possible defences to charges of first degree murder, and circumstances that might have the effect of reducing a charge of first degree murder to second degree murder or manslaughter, it would be much more difficult to conclude that the lawyer had improperly attempted to influence the client to testify falsely. As we have seen, most people, entirely honestly, recollect facts in a way that favours their interests. To require a client to commit to a version of events without benefit of legal advice and without understanding what is in the client's interest is to prejudge the client as a perjurer.[115]

Let us consider a more common example. Lawyers routinely tell clients in fatal accident actions that remarriage is likely to reduce significantly the damages awarded, that the client's prospects of remarriage are likely to be investigated, and that the client may be the object of surveillance for that reason. No one would seriously argue that that is advice that the client should not have. But the lawyer's intention, and the circumstances in which the advice is given, will affect its propriety. If the lawyer provides the advice immediately after being introduced to the client's fiancé, at a meeting to prepare the client to testify at her examination for discovery, the irresistible inference

---

113 Freedman explained his original justification of the lawyer's advice in "Professional Responsibility of the Criminal Defence Lawyer: The Three Hardest Questions" (1966) 64 Michigan L.R. 1469.

114 Freedman re-examined his original rationale in *Lawyers' Ethics In An Adversary System, supra*, note 110, p. 73. See also Freedman, *Understanding Lawyers' Ethics, supra*, note 110, pp. 156-158. (New York: Bobbs-Merrill, 1975), p. 73.

115 Freedman, *Lawyers' Ethics In An Adversary System, supra*, note 110, pp. 59-76.

will be that the lawyer's purpose in providing the advice is to suggest to the client the answer that will be most beneficial.[116]

An English barrister, John Mathew Q.C., expressed the view at a Canadian advocacy symposium in 1984 that it is permissible for lawyers to say to clients that their stories are so incredible that no jury would believe them, but that it is not permissible for lawyers to suggest more plausible alternatives. This would suggest that the fictional barrister in *Anatomy of a Murder* may not have crossed the line if he had stopped after telling the client that if the facts were as she had stated them she would probably be electrocuted, without adding that if she had acted in a blind rage her life might be saved. However, any lawyer would know that to go even that far would tempt the client to perjure herself, which is precisely what lawyers must avoid. Lawyers are well-advised to heed the shop-worn maxim: If you have to ask whether you are crossing the line, then you are probably standing too close to it.

It is a recognition of the danger that witnesses may adopt the advocate's version of events rather than their own version that lies behind the English rule that barristers are not to interview witnesses.[116.1]

To summarize: Lawyers may provide legal advice to their client for the purpose of directing the client's mind to facts about which the client may testify. Lawyers should not normally assume that the client will make unlawful use of their lawyer's advice. In some cases, notably when they already know the client's unaided recollection of the facts, it will be evident to lawyers that to provide certain advice will tempt their client to commit perjury. In these cases, lawyers should keep this advice to themselves.

To what extent may lawyers modify witnesses' demeanour or use of speech? It is clearly proper for lawyers to advise witnesses to avoid technical jargon so that their evidence is intelligible to the judge (and jury, if any). It is also proper for lawyers to advise witnesses to avoid vulgar and even colloquial expressions out of respect for the court and a sense of decorum. Nor is it improper for lawyers to advise witnesses to avoid habitual prefatory phrases such as "I would have" where it is clear that the witness, in fact, has a specific recollection of what the witness did or perceived.

As far as advice about witnesses' demeanour is concerned, as noted above, it is clearly proper for lawyers to provide to witnesses such information as how the judge, the lawyers, and the parties should be addressed.

---

116 See Earl A. Cherniak, "The Ethics of Advocacy", Law Society of Upper Canada Gazette, vol. 19 (June, 1985), pp. 148-149.

116.1 See the comments of Michael Hill in "Ethics Forum and Debate: Rules of Conduct for Counsel and Judges: A Panel Discussion on English and American Practices", Georgetown Journal of Legal Ethics, vol. 7, no. 4 (Spring 1994) p. 865 at 869. In *R. v. Dye* (1992), Criminal Law Rev. 449 the Court of Appeal allowed an appeal from conviction where the defence learned after trial that all the key prosecution witnesses, prior to trial, had taken part in a planned television programme in which the producers staged a mock trial of the persons accused in the case. The Court of Appeal held that the defence should

At the other end of the scale, again, lawyers must not advise witnesses to alter their diction or syntax where the effect of the alteration is to modify their intended meaning. In the illustration cited above, to suggest that a witness to a car accident substitute the word "contacted" for the words "smashed into" would be improper. Similarly, it would be improper for a lawyer to advise a witness to appear surprised if a particular event is mentioned in cross-examination.

A more difficult issue is whether lawyers may encourage witnesses to substitute words that do not alter the witnesses' intended meaning but that modify the potential emotional impact of their words. For instance, if a witness says that the lawyer's client repeatedly thrust the knife into the victim's heart, is it proper for the lawyer to suggest that the witness say that she saw the lawyer's client stab the victim several times in the chest? If the witness's meaning is left intact, the court is not misled, and the evidence is neither subverted nor suppressed, current rules of professional conduct do not prohibit such a practice. Bearing in mind again that the way in which a witness has been prepared may properly be explored in cross-examination, to suggest such changes in diction is nonetheless dangerous.

Another difficult question is whether it is proper for lawyers to advise witnesses to appear confident. If the circumstances are that the witness is testifying to facts about which the witness in fact lacks confidence, it is likely that the lawyer's advice would be construed as an attempt to mislead the court, though the lawyer may have done nothing to advise the witness to alter the substance of the evidence.[117]

In summary, lawyers must not coach or assist witnesses so as to distort the evidence that they would give if unaided. These limitations follow from the lawyer's duty not to use false evidence in presenting a case. The issue whether lawyers have subverted witnesses' evidence will usually be determined by reference to the lawyers' intention. For instance, lawyers who inform witnesses about desired testimony before seeking their own version of events may or may not be guilty of deliberately distorting the witnesses' testimony, depending upon the witnesses' foreseeable reaction to the lawyers' information.[118]

Rules of professional conduct do not address the propriety of compensating witnesses for their testimony. It is of course proper to pay attendance

---

have been informed that the witnesses had rehearsed their evidence before actors playing the parts of counsel and judge.

117 Joseph D. Piorkowski, Jr., discusses the extent to which lawyers may properly advise witnesses to modify their demeanour and speech in "Professional Conduct and the Preparation of Witnesses for Trial: Defining the Acceptable Limits of Coaching" (1987-88) 1 Georgetown Journal of Legal Ethics 389 at 391-407.

118 See Charles Wolfram, *Modern Legal Ethics* (St. Paul, Minnesota: West, 1986), p. 648.

money as provided for by rules of court. It is also generally considered proper to pay reasonable amounts to witnesses to compensate them for travel expenses and wages lost as a result of their attendance in court.[118.1]

Expert witnesses may be paid a proper professional fee for their services. Although, again, the practice is not explicitly prohibited by rules of professional conduct, an expert witness fee — or a payment to any other witness — should not be contingent upon the result of the case, as such an arrangement may appear to create an improper inducement to the witness to shade or falsify testimony in order to earn a higher fee. Again, the basis of witnesses' compensation is a proper subject matter for cross-examination.[119]

British Columbia's rules of professional conduct prohibit lawyers from questioning an opposing party's expert on matters protected by the doctrine of legal professional privilege unless the privilege has been waived.[120] The British Columbia rules also require lawyers to notify counsel for opposing parties who have retained an expert of their intention to communicate with the expert.[121] The rules add that when lawyers communicate with an opposing party's expert they must disclose for whom they are acting and make it clear

(*Continued on page 4–31*)

118.1 For an American perspective, see Michael R. Koval, "Living Expenses, Litigation Expenses, and Lending Money to Clients", Georgetown Journal of Legal Ethics, vol. 7, no. 4 (Spring 1994), p. 1117.

119 *Ibid.*, pp. 651-652.

120 British Columbia rules, chapter 8, rule 14.

121 British Columbia rules, chapter 8, rule 15.

that they are not acting for the party who retained the expert.[122] They must also raise with the expert the question of whether they are accepting responsibility for payment of any fee charged by the expert arising out of the lawyers' communication with the expert.[123]

As mentioned above, a lawyer must not approach a witness who is a party who is represented except through the witness's counsel.[124] Lawyers may of course seek information from any potential witness, whether under subpoena or not, but they should disclose their interest and take care not to subvert or suppress any evidence or procure the witness to stay out of the way.[125] British Columbia's rules of professional conduct provide that lawyers must not advise potential witnesses not to communicate with opposing parties or their counsel.[126]

In addition to disciplinary sanctions, lawyers should keep in mind that excessive zeal in the counselling of witnesses may also have criminal implications. In a 1987 Newfoundland case,[127] a lawyer who had counselled a witness to be forgetful and evasive was convicted of wilfully attempting to obstruct justice and sentenced to 18 months' imprisonment. The sentence was reduced to one year by the Newfoundland Court of Appeal.

4.13 LEADING EVIDENCE: THE PERJURY PROBLEM

In 1991, in New York, Morris Eisen, a lawyer whose personal injury firm had been among the most successful in the city, was sentenced to almost five years in jail upon his conviction for racketeering. His conviction resulted from his falsification of evidence and subornation of perjury in personal injury claims against the City of New York. His fraudulent acts took place over a number of years and resulted in nine million dollars in awards and settlements.

Eisen was caught when the chief of the tort division of the city corporation counsel's office recalled that one of the litigation lawyers on his staff had telephoned him several months earlier about a development in a trial in Queens. "He said the plaintiffs had put on a great witness, a guy who said he was at the very location two weeks before the accident occurred, and he remembered this pothole. And then he just happened to have been there when the accident took place." The city settled the case for $650,000.

About eight months latter, the chief of the tort division received another call, this time from another lawyer on his staff who was acting as counsel in a trial in

122 British Columbia rules, chapter 8, rule 16(a).

123 British Columbia rules, chapter 8, rule 16(a).

124 C.B.A. Code, chapter IX, commentary 6, chapter XVI, commentary 8; Ontario rule 4.03(1) and (2). As mentioned above (see text accompanying note 96.2), the Ontario rules were amended in 2000 to address the applicability of these principles to corporate and organizational parties.

125 C.B.A. Code, chapter IX, commentary 6; Ontario rule 4.03(1).

126 British Columbia rules, chapter 10, rule 18.

127 *R. v. Sweezey* (1987), 66 Nfld & P.E.I.R. 29 (Nfld. C.A.).

the Bronx. "He says he is not doing so well. A witness came in and said he saw the pothole two weeks ago and he happened to be going by when he witnessed the accident . . . I said, Gee, that sounds familiar." The witnesses in Queens and the Bronx turned out to be the same person. The witness had been in jail on the day he claimed to have witnessed the accident in the Bronx.[128]

To suborn perjured evidence, in civil and criminal proceedings, in Canada as in the United States, is of course not only unprofessional, but criminal. This is so whether or not the perjured evidence is in fact tendered; if it is, the lawyer will be a party to the client's perjury; if it is not, the lawyer will be subject to prosecution for counselling the offence.[129]

In civil proceedings, the only problematic issues are, first, when does the lawyer "know" that a witness will give perjured evidence if called; and, second, what should the lawyer do if a witness whom the lawyer has called, unexpectedly testifies falsely. (The problems for criminal defence lawyers are more complex, and are dealt with in chapter 7).

Rules of professional conduct provide that lawyers must discharge their duty to their clients by fair and honourable means, without illegality and in a manner consistent with their duty to treat tribunals with candour, fairness, courtesy, and respect; and that the lawyer must not knowingly assist or permit the client to do anything that the lawyer considers to be dishonest or dishonourable, or knowingly attempt to deceive a tribunal by offering false evidence, presenting or relying upon a false or deceptive affidavit, suppressing what ought to be disclosed, or otherwise assisting in any fraud, crime, or illegal conduct.[130]

The rules add that if a client wishes to adopt a course that would involve a breach of these duties, the lawyer must refuse and do everything reasonably possible to prevent it. If the client persists in such a course, the rules say, the lawyer should, subject to rules governing withdrawal, withdraw or seek leave to do so.[131] British Columbia's rules expressly provide that lawyers who withdraw in such circumstances must not disclose to the court or tribunal, or to any other person, the fact that their withdrawal was occasioned by their client's insistence on offering false testimony.[132]

Finally, the rules provide that a lawyer who has unknowingly done or failed to do something that, if done or omitted knowingly, would have been in breach of the lawyer's duties as an advocate, has a duty to the court, subject to rules

---

128 Marcia Chambers, "Why Lawyers Must Police Themselves", National Law Journal (November 11, 1991), p. 13.

129 *Criminal Code*, R.S.C. 1985, c. C-46, as amended, ss. 21, 22, 131, 132 and 464.

130 C.B.A. Code, chapter IX, commentaries 1, 2(b), and 2(e); Ontario rule 4.01(1) and accompanying commentary and 4.01(2); Quebec rules, section 4.02.01 (c), (e), and (g).

131 C.B.A. Code, chapter IX, commentary 4; Ontario rule 4.01(5) and accompanying commentary; British Columbia rules, chapter 8, rules 2 and 3.

132 British Columbia rules, chapter 8, rule 4.

governing confidentiality, to disclose the error or omission and to do all that can reasonably be done in the circumstances to rectify it.[133]

The footnotes to the rules provide some additional guidance: A 1939 decision of the House of Lords[134] is cited for the proposition that a lawyer who has innocently put on the record an affidavit that the lawyer later determines to be "certainly false" has a duty to the court "to put the matter right at the earliest date if he continues to act."[135] A 1962 decision of the Ontario Court of Appeal[136] is cited to the same effect.

New Brunswick's rules of professional conduct provide that upon learning of fraudulent testimony participated in by the lawyer's client, the lawyer has a duty to withdraw from the case and to inform the court and adverse parties of the fraud.[137]

An Ontario lawyer who has considerable experience as counsel in civil proceedings has suggested an alternative to disclosing the falsity of evidence to the court and opposing counsel: the lawyer may continue, perhaps asking previously unanticipated questions designed to elicit answers that will correct the false evidence, but without otherwise making reference to the false evidence until the lawyer advises the court in argument, without explanation, that the evidence cannot be relied upon. To ask leave to withdraw in these circumstances is wholly unsatisfactory, not only because withdrawal is unlikely to be permitted (if only because it would enable a perjurious party to delay the litigation repeatedly) but also because it merely shifts the problem to another lawyer if one is retained, or permits the false evidence to remain part of the record and possibly be repeated if one is not.[138]

British Columbia's rules of professional conduct deal with the perjury problem more directly and in more detail than do those of other jurisdictions. The British Columbia rules provide that where a lawyer is informed by a client that the client intends to offer false testimony, the lawyer has a duty to explain that if the client insists on offering, or in fact does offer, false testimony, the lawyer will have a professional duty to withdraw.[139] The rules explicitly add that a lawyer must not call as a witness in a proceeding persons who have informed the lawyer that they intend to offer false testimony.[140]

---

133 C.B.A. Code, chapter IX, commentary 3; Ontario rule 4.01(5).

134 *Myers v. Elman*, [1940] A.C. 282 at 293-294 (H.L.), *per* Viscount Maugham.

135 *Ibid.*, pp. 293-294.

136 *Re Ontario Crime Commission* (1962), 37 D.L.R. (2d) 382 at 391 (Ont. C.A.), *per* McLennan J.A.

137 New Brunswick Professional Conduct Handbook, Part B, rule 8.

138 Bryan Finlay, "The Conduct of Lawyers in the Litigious Process: Some Thoughts" in Eric Gertner (ed.), *Studies In Civil Procedure* (Toronto: Butterworths, 1979), pp. 27-28. See also Beverley G. Smith, *Professional Conduct for Canadian Lawyers* (Toronto: Butterworths, 1989), pp. 141-143.

139 British Columbia rules, chapter 8, rule 2.

140 British Columbia rules, chapter 8, rule 5.

Unlike the rules of other Canadian jurisdictions, the British Columbia rules specifically address the question of in what circumstances lawyers can be said to "know" that a witness will give false testimony if called. Mere inconsistency in a client's or a witness's statements or testimony or between two preferred defences is insufficient to support the conclusion that the person will offer or has offered false testimony, the rules say. Lawyers have a duty, however, the rules add, to explore the inconsistency with the client or witness at the first available opportunity. If, based on that enquiry, the lawyer is certain that the client or witness intends to offer or has offered false testimony, the lawyer has a duty to comply with the provisions of the rules governing the lawyers' duties when they know that a client or witness intends to offer or has offered false testimony. Otherwise, the lawyer is entitled to proceed, leaving it to the court or tribunal to assess the truth.[141]

American rules of professional conduct are even more elaborate. It is clear in most American jurisdictions that if a lawyer has actual knowledge of the falsity of testimony favourable to a client's position that the client or a witness proposes to give, the lawyer has a duty to remonstrate with the client or witness in an attempt to persuade the client or witness not to give or, if it is presented, to correct, the false testimony. The remonstrance should cover the facts that perjury is a serious criminal offence, that it is likely to be detected by adverse parties and exposed by cross-examination and impeachment evidence, that it is vital to the administration of justice that evidence adduced be truthful, and that the lawyer may have a duty to disclose the falsity of the evidence to the court or tribunal.

American rules of professional conduct also make it clear that the lawyer controls access to the witness box and has a duty not to call a witness who will testify falsely. The lawyer may, however, call a witness who will testify truthfully in response to some questions but falsely in response to others, provided that the lawyer does not put to the witness questions in the latter category.

In argument, an American lawyer is prohibited from urging the fact finder to accept, as credible, evidence that the lawyer knows is false.

In jurisdictions governed by the American Bar Association's Model Rules of Professional Conduct, the lawyer is required to disclose the falsity of evidence in cases in which the lawyer learns of the deception after the evidence is introduced and in cases in which the false evidence is given unexpectedly. Disclosure, either to adverse parties or to the court or tribunal, is required even if the perjury is that of the lawyer's own client and even if the lawyer knows of the perjury as a result of what would otherwise be a confidential communication. The lawyer has no duty to disclose the intention of a client or witness to commit perjury in the future; the duty of disclosure is triggered only if evidence that the lawyer knows is false is actually given. Lawyers have no duty to disclose false testimony if they learn of it only after the court or tribunal has rendered final judgment, even if the false testimony has materially affected the outcome of the case.

---

141 British Columbia rules, chapter 8, rule 6.

Such disclosure is almost certain, of course, to have disastrous consequences for the client where it is the client's perjury that is disclosed. Criminal prosecution, the loss of the case, and feelings of betrayal by the lawyer are likely to be among the consequences. The alternative, however, is the acquiescence of the lawyer in the deception of the court or tribunal and, accordingly, in the subversion of the truth-finding process.

It warrants emphasizing that the American rules of professional conduct requiring remonstrating with the witness, refraining from calling the witness or asking the witness questions that may elicit false evidence, and taking remedial measures including disclosing the falsity of testimony, all come into play only where the lawyer has certain knowledge of the falsity of the expected or actual evidence. The lawyer has a discretion, but not a duty, to decide not to offer evidence that the lawyer reasonably believes to be false. It is no part of the lawyer's responsibility to make findings of credibility that will deprive the client of the client's day in court. Lawyers are entitled to assume that witnesses will not give false evidence, despite their previously stated intention to do so, if the witnesses have been informed subsequently of the lawyer's duty to disclose perjury to the tribunal.[146]

Canadian rules of professional conduct concerning the lawyer's duties to prevent the introduction of perjured evidence and to correct perjured evidence if offered, as referred to above, are for the most part consistent, though less explicit, than their American equivalents. The following guidelines, though based in large part on the American rules, may nevertheless be helpful to Canadian lawyers:

(1) The lawyer should bear in mind the fact that clients are entitled to have issues of credibility assessed by a duly-constituted court or tribunal. Lawyers have no professional duty to refuse to call evidence except where they have actual knowledge of its falsity.

(2) Where lawyers have actual knowledge of the falsity of evidence favourable to their client's position that their client or a witness proposes to give, lawyers should remonstrate with their client or the witness for the purpose of dissuading the client or witness from testifying falsely. The fundamental importance to our system of justice of evidence that is adduced being truthful, the possibility of criminal prosecution for perjury, the likelihood that the falsity of the evidence will be exposed on cross-examination or otherwise, possible cost consequences, and the duties of lawyers to refrain from calling false evidence and to expose perjury in many circumstances, should all form part of the remonstrance.

146 See American Bar Association Model Rules of Professional Conduct (1983), rule 3.3; American Bar Association Model Code of Professional Responsibility (1969), DR 7-102; American Bar Association Formal Opinion 87-853; Charles Wolfram, *Modern Legal Ethics* (St. Paul, Minnesota: West, 1986), pp. 653-660; Monroe H. Freedman, "Legal Ethics and the Suffering Client" (1987) 36 Cath. U.L. Rev. 319; and Monroe H. Freedman, *Understanding Lawyers' Ethics* (New York: Matthew Bender & Co., 1990), pp. 127-132.

(3) The effects of remonstrating for this purpose are likely to include the termination of the lawyer's retainer if the client or witness is not convinced. Withdrawal may be necessary, if permitted by the court, even though it may accomplish little except to shift the problem to another lawyer or to encourage the client or witness to be less candid with the next lawyer, and to disclose the witness's perjury to the court and other parties in many cases.

(4) Lawyers acting as counsel in civil cases should not call witnesses who, to the lawyers' knowledge, will testify falsely. Lawyers may, however, call witnesses who will testify truthfully on some points but falsely on others if the lawyers' questions are confined to the evidence in the former category.

(5) If false evidence is introduced unexpectedly, or if the lawyer learns of the falsity of evidence after it is introduced, the lawyer should take reasonable steps to correct it. This should be done by urging the client or witness to correct the evidence if possible, either privately or by asking questions designed to enable the truth to emerge. If the client or witness does not correct the evidence, the lawyer should do so. This may be accomplished by informing the court or tribunal in argument, without explanation, that the evidence in question cannot be relied upon. Anything short of that, including silence, is inadequate, as lawyers cannot know what weight a court or tribunal will place on the false evidence even if lawyers make no use of it.[147]

These guidelines will have to be adapted to take into account differences in the rules among jurisdictions. The British Columbia and New Brunswick rules, for example, deal differently with the question of the lawyer's obligation to disclose client perjury.[148]

There is no reason in principle to restrict this duty of disclosure to evidence introduced in response to a lawyer's examination in chief. Lawyers should have the same duty where false evidence is elicited in cross-examination from witnesses called by them. Lawyers must neither participate nor acquiesce in the introduction of evidence that they know to be false. The duty of resolute partisanship in an adversarial system has nothing to do with the matter. It is no part of a lawyer's duty to assist a client to mislead the court.[149]

Lawyers' duty to be candid with the court extends beyond their responsibility not to lead evidence that they know to be false. Lawyers must neither deceive nor knowingly or recklessly mislead the court either on the facts or on the law.[150] In a 1961 English action for damages for alleged assault and false imprisonment, the plaintiff's appeal was allowed on the ground that the defendant's counsel had

---

147 See *Holowaty v. Holowaty*, [1949] 1 W.W.R. 1064 (Sask. K.B.); and Mark M. Orkin, *Legal Ethics: A Study of Professional Conduct* (Toronto: Cartwright & Sons, 1957), pp. 53-55.

148 See text accompanying notes 132 and 137, *supra*.

149 See David Pannick, *Advocates* (Oxford: Oxford University Press, 1992), pp. 161-162; and Wolfram, *supra*, note 146, pp. 641-644.

150 *Tombling v. Universal Bulb Co.*, [1951] 2 T.L.R. 289 at 297 (C.A.), *per* Denning L.J.

not made known to the court that the defendant, a police officer, had been reduced in rank from Chief Inspector due to his deception of a court in another case. The case turned on the credibility of the parties. Both the plaintiff's counsel and the trial judge referred to the defendant as "Chief Inspector." Lord Justice Holroyd Pearce, for the Court of Appeal, said that in his judgment "the duty to the Court was here unwarrantably subordinated to the duty to the client."[151]

The principle that lawyers must not mislead the court is not contravened in criminal cases, however, where defence lawyers "passively stand by and watch the court being misled by reason of its failure to ascertain facts" that are within the lawyers' knowledge.[152] Criminal defence lawyers are of course entitled to put the Crown to the proof of its case, a point developed in chapter 7.

4.14 CROSS-EXAMINATION

Canadian rules of professional conduct, in dealing with the ethics of cross-examination, apart from the general guiding principle referred to above ("The lawyer has a duty to . . . ask every question, however distasteful, which the lawyer thinks will help the client's case . . .") specify only that the lawyer must not needlessly abuse, hector, or harass a witness.[153] Lawyers are often in a position to humiliate or hurt witnesses, to damage reputations, and to pry publicly into private concerns. Although lawyers sometimes have a duty to ask questions having one or more of these effects, they should nevertheless exercise their privileges fairly and with restraint.

Lawyers must be sufficiently firm and strong in cross-examination to insist upon receiving responsive answers to their questions. (An effective alternative to insisting in some cases is to say to the witness, "I have asked that question three times and each time you have talked about something else. Would you prefer that I drop the question?") There is a difference, however, between being firm and being a bully. Apart altogether from ethical considerations, answers extracted from terror-stricken witnesses who have been frightened into submission are likely to be given less weight than the same answers elicited by gentler means.

Particularly with honest witnesses, a friendly, courteous, and conversational tone is likely to extract more candid responses than is a belligerent one. Lawyers' duties to their clients require them to vary their manner as circumstances require, and at times lawyers must ask questions in a way that would rightly be regarded as discourteous on social occasions. They should abandon courtesy, however, only when and to the extent necessary to discharge their duty properly. It is improper to belittle a witness who has done nothing to deserve contempt.

Lawyers must not interrupt witnesses who are about to give damaging evidence. An interruption may be necessary if it is clear that the witness has mis-

151 *Meek v. Fleming*, [1961] 2 Q.B. 366 at 379-380 (C.A.).

152 *Saif Ali v. Sydney Mitchell & Co.*, [1980] A.C. 198 at 220 (H.L.).

153 C.B.A. Code, chapter IX, commentary 2(k); Ontario rule 4.01(2)(k).

understood the question or is for some other reason giving a lengthy answer that is irrelevant, but even then the witness can be interrupted politely: "Excuse me — you are talking about what happened before the meeting. I wanted to know what happened after it." "Excuse me — I didn't ask you what furniture was in the building. Let me repeat the question: how large was the utility room?"

In cross-examination, lawyers are not confined to questions relevant strictly to the issues between the parties. They may also ask questions relevant to the witness's credibility, subject to the court's discretion to prevent abuse. Lawyers have an ethical responsibility, however, to refrain from attacking witnesses' character or morality in cases in which their credibility is not really in issue. To ask witnesses whether they have been convicted of a crime in such cases is improper.

Even where the witness's credibility is in issue, lawyers have no licence to pry into witnesses' private affairs except to the extent that the questions are genuinely material to credibility. Whether the witness is married to the person with whom he or she shares a home is not relevant to credibility. Nor are witnesses' religious beliefs, political affiliations, or sexual preferences.[154]

Lawyers should not ask questions that are intended only to irritate or insult witnesses or other persons. Even where credibility is in issue, lawyers should refrain from asking questions that are intended to impeach credibility in the absence of sufficient grounds for believing that the suggestions made are true. In a 1969 decision of the House of Lords, Lord Reid said that a lawyer "must not lend himself to casting aspersions on the other party or witnesses for which there is no sufficient basis in the information in his possession."[155] A decade later, Lord Diplock acknowledged that "questions of considerable nicety may arise as to what constitutes sufficient foundation or relevance to justify the particular aspersion which his client wants him to make."[156]

Extra judicial statements of people who have not been and will not be witnesses should not be put to witnesses unless they are receivable in evidence on some ground, and are to be proven. Thus, if a witness claims not to have attended a particular function, the lawyer cannot say, "But the Bishop has said that he saw you there. I cannot call him as a witness because he is abroad, but he is positive that he saw you there. Are you suggesting that the Bishop is lying?" Adverse parties, and the witness, are perfectly entitled to object that unless the

---

154 At pp. 12-23 of his book *Cross-Examination: A Practical Handbook* (Cape Town: Juta & Co., 1970), George Colman Q.C., a former judge of the Supreme Court of South Africa, includes a chapter on the ethics of cross-examination. Many of the principles and illustrations referred to here are adapted from Judge Colman's work. See also Francis L. Wellman, *The Art of Cross-Examination* (New York: MacMillan, 1903); Charles L. Dubin, "Cross-Examination Before Juries", Law Society of Upper Canada Special Lectures 1959 (Toronto: Richard de Boo Ltd., 1959); and Roger E. Salhany, *Cross-Examination: A Practical Handbook* (Toronto: Butterworths, 1988).

155 *Rondel v. Worsley*, [1969] 1 A.C. 191 at 227 (H.L.).

156 *Saif Ali v. Sydney Mitchell & Co., supra*, note 152, p. 220.

Bishop comes to court to testify, they do not accept that he made any such statement.

The Judicial Committee of the Privy Council[157] and the Ontario Court of Appeal,[158] in decisions rendered in 1960 and 1973 respectively, have held that in cross-examination lawyers may make allegations that they cannot prove, the penalty for doing so being that they will be left with a denial that they will be helpless to refute if the witness does not admit the allegation. In more recent decisions, however, the British Columbia Court of Appeal[159] and the Ontario Court of Appeal[160] have made it clear that though not every suggestion made in cross-examination must necessarily be proven directly, any imputation conveyed must be well-founded, and must not be based on information received from witnesses who are so unreliable that counsel would not call them. In a 1989 decision[160.1] the Supreme Court of Canada held that, in cross-examining an expert, counsel must not put as a fact (or even as a hypothetical fact) that which is not and will not become part of the case as admissible evidence.

That an adverse party is free to object to a question is no justification for asking it. Lawyers should not impart to the court information that might influence it, and that to the lawyers' knowledge the court should not receive. It is improper for a lawyer to ask any question, knowing that it will rightly be objected to, because the lawyer hopes the question will have some effect upon the court or the witness.

It is particularly important in jury trials that lawyers refrain from frustrating the rules of evidence by obtruding inadmissible information before an objection can be made. The fact is that supposedly curative instructions are likely to have the opposite effect and "serve only the mnemonic function of giving vividness to the memory trace the jurors are requested to erase."[161]

It is also improper to misquote or distort evidence that the witness has given either on an earlier occasion or earlier in the same examination. Adversaries are likely to have a tendency, quite unintentionally, to paraphrase vague answers favourably to the position for which they are contending, or to forget troublesome qualifications. It is for that very reason that lawyers have an ethical responsibility to take care that a witness's evidence is accurately quoted or summarized.

The lawyer has a duty to put to a witness in cross-examination what witnesses called by the lawyer will say if it conflicts with the witness's evidence. This must be done in such a way that the witness has a fair opportunity to explain the

---

157 *Fox v. General Medical Council*, [1960] 1 W.L.R. 1017 at 1023 (P.C.).

158 *R. v. Bencardino* (1973), 15 C.C.C. (2d) 342 at 346 (Ont. C.A.).

159 *R. v. Wilson* (1983), 5 C.C.C. (3d) 61 at 85 (B.C. C.A.).

160 *R. v. Nealy* (1986), 30 C.C.C. (3d) 460 (Ont. C.A.). See also *Fletcher & Son v. Jubb*, [1920] 1 K.B. 275 (C.A.); and *Wright v. Hearson*, [1916] W.N. 216 (D.C.).

160.1 *Howard v. The Queen* (1989), 48 C.C.C. (3d) 38 at 46.

161 R.E. Schofield, "Psychology, Law, and the Expert Witness" (1956) 11 American Psychologist 1 at 3, quoted by Charles Wolfram, *Modern Legal Ethics* (St. Paul, Minnesota: West, 1986), p. 621.

apparent conflict. It must also be done it such a way that the witness is not misled into thinking that the lawyer is in a position to contradict the witness if the evidence to do so either does not exist or is unavailable.[162]

In criminal cases in which the identity of an accused person is in issue, lawyers must not substitute other persons at the counsel table or elsewhere in court for the purpose of provoking a misidentification.[163]

All of these examples illustrate the principles that cross-examination must be fair, and that the witness must not be misled. It does not follow, however, that lawyers must always divulge the purpose of their questions to witnesses. Questions framed in such a way that the witness does not know which answer the lawyer would prefer are often the ones most likely to reveal the truth. Nor does it follow from the lawyer's duty of fairness that it is necessarily the lawyer's duty to extract a truthful answer from every witness to every question asked. There is nothing improper about framing questions in such a way as to encourage untruthful witnesses to add to or magnify their falsehoods. In addition to witnesses who are lying, some witnesses give evidence that is unreliable because of their forgetfulness, vanity, prejudice, bias, or inability to differentiate between observation and inference, or between reality and imagination. The court or tribunal that is charged with the responsibility of assessing the evidence of such witnesses should be aware of their traits and frailties. Thus questions designed to demonstrate those traits and frailties ultimately assist the court or tribunal to ascertain the truth, though the answers that the lawyer deliberately elicits may be exaggerated, inaccurate, or untruthful.[164]

In chapter 7, we shall see that there is general agreement among commentators that because of the purposes of the criminal justice system, it is proper for criminal defence lawyers to cross-examine witnesses whom they know to be telling the truth in such a way as to persuade the court not to believe the witnesses. There is no basis for extending the acceptability of the practice to either civil proceedings or to the prosecution in criminal proceedings.[165]

4.15 COMMUNICATING WITH WITNESSES GIVING EVIDENCE

It is universally considered improper for a lawyer who calls a witness to have any conversation with that witness about the witness's evidence or relating

162 *Browne v. Dunn* (1893), 6 R. 67 (H.L.); *Peters v. Perras* (1909), 42 S.C.R. 244; *R. v. Hawke* (1974), 3 O.R. (2d) 210 at 225 (H.C.), reversed (1975), 7 O.R. (2d) 145 (C.A.). It does not follow that a presumption of truth attaches to the evidence of a witness who is not cross-examined: *R. v. Mete*, [1973] 3 W.W.R. 709 (B.C. C.A.).

163 *United States v. Thoreen*, 653 F. 2d 1332 (9th Cir., 1981), cert. denied 455 U.S. 938 (U.S. S. Ct., 1982).

164 For an interesting illustration of a lawyer's use of questions framed so as to encourage an untruthful witness to magnify his falsehoods see Alan M. Dershowitz, *The Best Defence* (New York: First Vintage Books, 1983), pp. 52-66.

165 Wolfram, *supra*, note 161, p. 651.

to any issue in the proceeding, except with leave of the court, while the witness is under cross-examination.[166] In Ontario, the Law Society has promulgated more comprehensive rules[167] concerning the propriety of communicating with witnesses giving evidence. Those rules read as follows:

> 4.04 Subject to the direction of the tribunal, the lawyer shall observe the following rules respecting communication with witnesses giving evidence:
>
> (a) during examination-in-chief, the examining lawyer may discuss with the witness any matter that has not been covered in the examination up to that point,
>
> (b) during examination-in-chief by another lawyer of a witness who is unsympathetic to the lawyer's cause, the lawyer not conducting the examination-in-chief may discuss the evidence with the witness,
>
> (c) between completion of examination-in-chief and commencement of cross-examination of the lawyer's own witness, the lawyer ought not to discuss the evidence given in chief or relating to any matter introduced or touched on during the examination-in-chief,
>
> (d) during cross-examination by an opposing lawyer, the witness's own lawyer ought not to have any conversation with the witness about the witness's evidence or any issue in the proceeding,
>
> (e) between completion of cross-examination and commencement of re-examination, the lawyer who is going to re-examine the witness ought not to have any discussion about evidence that will be dealt with on re-examination,
>
> (f) during cross-examination by the lawyer of a witness unsympathetic to the cross-examiner's cause, the lawyer may discuss the witness's evidence with the witness,
>
> (g) during cross-examination by the lawyer of a witness who is sympathetic to that lawyer's cause, any conversations ought to be restricted in the same way as communications during examination-in-chief of one's own witness, and
>
> (h) during re-examination of a witness called by an opposing lawyer, if the witness is sympathetic to the lawyer's cause the lawyer ought not to discuss the evidence to be given by that witness during re-examination. The lawyer may, however, properly discuss the evidence with a witness who is adverse in interest.

Commentary to the Ontario rule makes it clear that these rules apply with necessary modifications to examinations out of court.

If any question arises whether the lawyer's behaviour may violate these rules, it will often be appropriate to obtain the consent of the opposing lawyer or

166 C.B.A. Code, chapter IX, commentary 16.
167 Ontario rule 4.04.

leave of the court or tribunal before engaging in conversations that may be considered improper.[167.1]

Local rules and practices concerning communicating with witnesses about their evidence at various stages of a proceeding vary among jurisdictions. For example, in Nova Scotia, it has for many years been considered improper for a lawyer to communicate with a witness called by the lawyer either during examination-in-chief or during cross-examination.[168] The former dean of the Ontario bar, John Robinette, however, has said that there is nothing improper in saying to one's own witness during a recess while the witness is testifying in chief, "I asked you why you said what you said and you gave reason X. Were there any other reasons?"[169]

Judges often caution witnesses that they should not discuss the case with anyone while their examination is continuing. If a lawyer wishes to discuss the witness's evidence with the witness in circumstances permitted by the guidelines, the lawyer may have to ask the judge to qualify an overgeneralized caution.[170]

Lawyers must not discuss with witnesses who have been excluded, evidence that has been introduced in their absence. In a 1983 Ontario case,[171] Justice Reid emphasized that courts must rely heavily on counsel as officers of the court to ensure that orders excluding witnesses are carried out. Lawyers must inform witnesses who were not present when the order was made of the order's existence and meaning. They should also instruct witnesses not to allow themselves to become familiar, directly or indirectly, with testimony already given.

A lawyer may nevertheless question a witness who has been excluded and who has not yet testified, about facts in evidence and the contents of documents that have been marked as exhibits, as long as the lawyer does not disclose what was said in court. In other words, the lawyer is precluded only from divulging evidence already introduced, not from preparing witnesses to testify.[172]

4.16 ARGUMENT

In argument, lawyers must not knowingly misstate the contents of documents, the testimony of witnesses, the substance of arguments, or the provisions of legislation.[173] They must not knowingly assert something for which there is no reasonable basis in evidence.[174] Lawyers must inform the court or tribunal of

---

167.1 See commentary accompanying Ontario rule 4.04.

168 See also C.B.A. Code, chapter IX, note 28.

169 Quoted by Earl A. Cherniak in "The Ethics of Advocacy", Law Society of Upper Canada Gazette, vol. 19, no. 2 (June, 1985), pp. 150-151.

170 *Ibid.*, p. 152.

171 *R. v. Robinson*, Ont. H.C., October 24, 1983 (unreported), *per* Reid J.

172 Cherniak, *supra*, note 169, pp. 152-153.

173 C.B.A. Code, chapter IX, commentary 2(f); Ontario rule 4.01(2)(f).

174 C.B.A. Code, chapter IX, commentary 2(g); Ontario rule 4.01(2)(g); New Brunswick rules, Part B, rule 7(a).

authorities that bear on the issues, whether or not the authorities advance the position for which the lawyer contends.[175]

Justice Lawton pointed out in an English case[176] that for lawyers to discharge this last duty may require them "to face the embarrassment of bringing to the attention of the court authorities of which their opponents have been ignorant and which they know will lose the case for the client who has paid their fees."[177] On appeal to the House of Lords,[178] Lord Pearce added that it can be difficult for a lawyer "to explain to a client why he is indulging in what seems treachery to his client because of an abstract duty to justice and professional honour."[179]

To inform the court or tribunal of relevant authorities, however, is good advocacy as well as being a professional responsibility. Drawing attention to adverse authority before an adversary does so, while distinguishing or criticizing it, or both, not only takes the wind out of the adversary's sails, but also instills judicial confidence in the quality and thoroughness of the lawyer's submission. If the court or tribunal learns of the adverse authority independently, it may infer that the lawyer would not have suppressed it unless the lawyer considered it to be especially damaging.[180]

It is universally recognized that lawyers should not assert their personal belief in the justice of their clients' causes, or as to any of the facts involved in the case, whether they are appearing before a judge alone or a judge and jury. In a 1955 decision,[181] the Supreme Court of Canada commented upon the impropriety of counsel for either the Crown or the accused in a criminal trial expressing an opinion as to the guilt or innocence of the accused.

There are at least five reasons for this rule. First, lawyers' opinions are irrelevant; cases must be decided on the evidence and the law. Second, expressions of personal opinion would not be admitted as evidence if tendered by a witness who was under oath and subject to cross-examination; *a fortiori* they should not be received from counsel in the absence of such safeguards. Third, if expressions of lawyers' personal opinions were permitted, more weight may be given to the opinions of more prominent lawyers than to those of relatively unknown lawyers, with the result that the court would try the case based upon the lawyers' promi-

---

175 C.B.A. Code, chapter IX, commentary 2(h); Ontario rule 4.01(2)(h); New Brunswick rules, Part B, rule 2.

176 *Rondel v. Worsley*, [1967] 1 Q.B. 443 (C.A.).

177 *Ibid.*, p. 469.

178 [1969] 1 A.C. 191 (H.L.).

179 *Ibid.*, p. 272. See also *Glebe Sugar Refining Co. Ltd. v. Greenock Port & Harbour Trustees*, [1921] 2 A.C. 66 (H.L.); *Plant v. Urquhart*, [1922] 1 W.W.R. 632 at 638-639 (B.C. C.A.), *per* McPhillips J.A.; and *Giacomelli v. O'Reilly* (1979), 9 C.P.C. 65 (Ont. Master), in which a party was deprived of costs of a motion because of a failure to bring a relevant authority to the attention of the court.

180 See Charles Wolfram, *Modern Legal Ethics* (St. Paul, Minnesota: West, 1986), pp. 681-682.

181 *Boucher v. R.*, [1955] S.C.R. 16. The duty is expressed in the C.B.A. Code, chapter IX, commentary 5; Ontario rule 10, commentary 16(b); Yukon rules, part 3, rule 3; New Brunswick rules, Part C, rule 11; and in the British Columbia rules, chapter 1, rule 2(3).

nence rather than on the merits.[182] Fourth, if statements of belief are permitted, their absence in a case will be particularly adverse. Finally, lawyers might be discouraged from representing those whom they cannot endorse if it were not for the rule.

Lawyers have been disciplined only rarely for forensic excesses in argument. In a 1986 Florida case,[183] however, a lawyer was publicly reprimanded and ordered to pay costs because, among other things, the lawyer had hinted in arguing a case before a jury, without an evidentiary basis and in circumstances in which it was irrelevant, that his client might be suicidal.

Admonishments from the bench are more common. In a 1987 decision,[184] for example, the British Columbia Court of Appeal criticized defence counsel in a criminal jury trial for saying both in opening and in argument that the evidence of a person who was not called as a witness would have absolved his clients.

New trials have been ordered in cases in which lawyers have brazenly appealed to jurors' emotions. In a 1953 Ontario case,[185] for example, a plaintiff's lawyer asked jurors rhetorically, "If any of your wives manifested the symptoms that have been manifested to you today, do you think money would compensate?" On appeal, Hogg J.A. said that this was "an appeal to the jury to fix the amount of damages upon an appraisement governed by emotion and not by reason based upon the evidence", and characterized it as going "beyond the ordinary and legitimate use of rhetoric."[186]

In an earlier action for damages for personal injuries,[187] the plaintiff's lawyer told the jury that the defendant, an insurance company, was a "soulless corporation" that hustles for insurance all over the world and takes people's money and then refuses to pay them. A new trial was ordered on appeal from the jury's verdict in the plaintiff's favour.[188]

4.17 COSTS

Canadian rules of professional conduct admonish lawyers not to abuse the process of the court or tribunal by instituting or prosecuting proceedings that,

182 See Mark M. Orkin, *Legal Ethics: A Study of Professional Conduct* (Toronto: Cartwright & Sons, 1957), pp. 105-106.

183 *Florida Bar v. Newhouse*, 498 So. 2d 935 (1986).

184 *R. v. Saunders* (1987), 14 B.C.L.R. (2d) 313 at 321 (C.A.), affirmed [1990] 1 S.C.R. 1020.

185 *Stewart v. Speer*, [1953] 3 D.L.R. 722 (Ont. C.A.).

186 *Ibid.*, pp. 725-727.

187 *Selick v. New York Life Insurance Co.* (1920), 17 O.W.N. 463.

188 *Ibid.*, pp. 464-465. See also *Dale v. Toronto Railway Co.* (1915), 34 O.L.R. 104 (C.A.); *Pender v. Hamilton Street Railway* (1917), 12 O.W.N. 262 (Div. Ct.); *Gage v. Reid* (1917), 38 O.L.R. 514 (C.A.); and *Cousineau v. Vancouver (City)*, [1926] 3 D.L.R. 265 (B.C. C.A.). New Brunswick's rules (Part B, rule 7(b)) expressly provide that counsel should avoid inflammatory statements designed to mislead or distort the judgment of a judge or jury.

although legal in themselves, are clearly motivated by malice on the part of the client and are brought solely for the purpose of injuring the other party.[189]

Lawyers are rarely disciplined, however, for violations of this rule. Perhaps because the mischief that the rule seeks to avoid includes the creation of unnecessary costs of litigation, violations of the rule have been punished primarily by cost awards, including awards of costs against lawyers personally. Such orders are made to discipline lawyers whose professional conduct during litigation falls below acceptable standards, in the exercise of the court's inherent jurisdiction to control its own process.[190]

In civil proceedings in Ontario, the court may make orders: disallowing costs between lawyers and clients; directing lawyers to repay to clients money paid on account of costs; directing lawyers to reimburse clients for any costs that clients have been ordered to pay to any other party; and requiring lawyers personally to pay the costs of any party. These orders may be made where a lawyer for a party has caused costs to be incurred without reasonable cause or money to be wasted by undue delay, negligence or other default.[191]

Costs have been awarded against lawyers personally in cases in which they have: commenced or continued proceedings without authority;[192] unduly interfered with the conduct of an examination;[193] made irresponsible and unfounded allegations about the integrity and good faith of an executive;[194] deprived clients of an opportunity to advance certain claims as a result of their inept handling of litigation;[195] failed to attend in chambers on applications that they have initiated;[196] litigated abstract legal issues contrary to the client's express wishes because of their strong personal beliefs;[197] and causing a mistrial by providing to the court a without prejudice settlement offer from the opposite party's counsel.[197.1]

4.18 COUNSEL'S LIABILITY IN NEGLIGENCE

In addition to discipline proceedings, cost sanctions, and contempt of court citations, the professional conduct of lawyers may be called into question in negligence litigation.

---

189 C.B.A. Code, chapter IX, commentary 2(a); Ontario rule 4.01(2)(a).

190 See Neil Gold, "The Court's Authority to Award Costs Against Lawyers" in Eric Gertner (ed.), *Studies In Civil Procedure* (Toronto: Butterworths, 1979), p. 68; *Myers v. Elman*, [1940] A.C. 282 (H.L.); and *Danson v. Ontario (Attorney General)* (1987), 19 C.P.C. (2d) 249 (Ont. C.A.), affirmed [1990] 2 S.C.R. 1086. See also chapter 27, *infra*, part 5.

191 Ontario Rules of Civil Procedure, R.R.O. 1990, reg. 194, rule 57.07.

192 *Evans v. Savarin Ltd.* (1980), 27 O.R. (2d) 705 (H.C.).

193 *Sonntag v. Sonntag* (1979), 24 O.R. (2d) 473 (H.C.).

194 *Re Bisyk (No. 2)* (1980), 32 O.R. (2d) 281 (H.C.), affirmed (1981), 32 O.R. (2d) 28 (C.A.).

195 *Dobud v. Herbertz* (1985), 50 C.P.C. 283 (Ont. Dist. Ct.).

196 *Martin v. Martin* (1987), 19 C.P.C. (2d) 97 (Sask Q.B.).

197 *Burke v. Burke*, 425 N.W. 2d 550 (Mich. App., 1988).

197.1 *Lynch v. Checker Cabs Ltd.*, [1999] A.J. No. 782 (Alta. Q.B.).

In 1969 the House of Lords ruled[198] that barristers — and solicitors acting as advocates — are absolutely immune from suit at the instance of clients for negligence in the conduct of clients' cases in court. The High Court of Australia came to the same conclusion in a 1988 decision.[199]

These authorities have not been followed in Ontario, however,[200] and in 2000 the House of Lords effectively overruled its earlier decision and abolished the immunity of advocates from suits cast in negligence.[201] Although at least one Canadian decision at the court of appeal level[202] stands for the proposition that advocates still enjoy "a limited degree of immunity" for decisions made in the conduct of litigation in court, the fact that even the House of Lords has now ruled that advocates enjoy no such immunity makes it unlikely that the immunity will be recognized by Canadian courts in the future. The issue has not been settled, however, by the Supreme Court of Canada.

It is difficult to defend the proposition that lawyers should enjoy even a limited immunity from civil consequences that is not enjoyed by any other profession. This difficulty was recognized by Justice Krever, then a member of the Ontario High Court of Justice, in what has come to be regarded as the leading Canadian authority on point: "It has not been, is not now, and should not be, public policy in Ontario to confer exclusively on lawyers engaged in court work an immunity possessed by no other professional person." Justice Krever added that decisions made by lawyers in the conduct of a case in court are unlikely to be held to be negligence as opposed to mere errors in judgment unless the errors are egregious.[207]

Although the barrister's immunity in England was explained on the basis of the lack of privity of contract between client and barrister, the principal justification advanced by the House of Lords was the barrister's divided loyalties: though barristers owe duties to their clients, they have overriding duties to the courts and the public. The latter duties sometimes conflict with the former. Lord Reid feared that liability for negligence might make lawyers less willing to perform their duty to the court when that duty conflicts with their duty to their client.[208]

---

198 *Rondel v. Worsley*, [1969] 1 A.C. 191 (H.L.).

199 *Giannarelli v. Wraith* (1988), 62 A.L.J.R. 611.

200 *Demarco v. Ungaro* (1979), 21 O.R. (2d) 673 (H.C.), *per* Krever J.; *Karpenko v. Paroian, Courey, Cohen & Houston* (1980), 117 D.L.R. (3d) 383 (Ont. H.C.), *per* Anderson J.; and *Pelky v. Hudson Bay Insurance Co.* (1981), 35 O.R. (2d) 97 (H.C.), *per* Catzman J.; *Wong v. Thomson, Rogers*, [1994] O.J. 1318 (C.A.); *Boudreau v. Benaiah*, [2000] O.J. 278 (C.A.); *Wernikowski v. Kirkland, Murphy & Ain*, [1999] O.J. 4812 (C.A.).

201 *Arthur J.S. Hall & Co. v. Simons*, [2000] H.L. J. 43.

202 *Garrant v. Moskal* (1985), 40 Sask. R. 155 (C.A.).

207 *Demarco v. Ungaro* (1979), 21 O.R. (2d) 673 at 693 (H.C.). Justice Krever's decision was cited with approval by three of the law lords in *Arthur J.S. Hall & Co. v. Simons*, [2000] H.L. J. 43.

208 *Rondel v. Worsley*, *supra*, note 206, p. 228.

As Lord Morris pointed out, however, lawyers know that courts would immediately accept that "any refusal to depart at the behest of the client from accepted standards of propriety and honest advocacy would not be held to be negligence."[209] In California, where lawyers enjoy no immunity from action, the Supreme Court held in 1978 that to found an action for negligence "the attorney's choice to honour the public obligation must be shown to have been so manifestly erroneous that no prudent attorney would have done so."[210] Lawyers who deliberately violate their duty to the court to advance their clients' interests may also be vulnerable to contempt of court citations and disciplinary sanctions.[211] Immunity, in short, is unnecessary to give effect to the lawyer's duties to the court and to the public. Indeed, the very fact that the lawyer was discharging such duties would be a complete answer to an action brought by a client.

None of the other justifications advanced by the House of Lords in its 1969 decision justify an immunity for lawyers. These justifications include a fear that if lawyers were vulnerable to being sued by their clients they would become unduly prolix for fear that their clients may allege that they omitted to argue points that the lawyers considered to be without merit. But lawyers know that in advocacy prolixity is ineffective as a tool of persuasion. They also know that a court is unlikely to rule that a choice among points to be argued amounts to more than an error in judgment, even if the court would have chosen differently.

A third justification advanced by the House of Lords was that the law gives broad immunities against defamation actions to all who participate in court proceedings in the interest of the discovery of truth and the effective administration of justice. That policy of the law, however, is irrelevant to the particular immunity under consideration, namely the immunity from legal action for negligent acts and omissions, an immunity that has little or no role to play in furthering the cause of freedom of expression in court.

A fourth justification was that it may be considered unfair to make lawyers liable in negligence in circumstances in which they are obliged to act for any person who chooses to retain them for a proper professional fee in an area of law in which they practise. Apart altogether, however, from the fact that Canadian lawyers have greater freedom to decline to act in particular cases than do English barristers, it is difficult to understand why the English cab-rank rule should justify immunity for lawyers from actions in negligence when people in many other lines of work (including, for example, operators of public transportation systems, taxi drivers, and innkeepers) who generally cannot refuse to accept customers may nevertheless be liable in negligence. Moreover, as Lord Diplock pointed out in a 1979 decision of the House of Lords,[212] this justification does not warrant de-

209 *Rondel v. Worsley*, *supra*, note 206, p. 251.

210 *Kirsch v. Duryea*, 578 P. 2d 935 at 939 (1978) (Clark J.).

211 David Pannick, *Advocates* (Oxford: Oxford University Press, 1992), p. 200.

212 *Saif Ali v. Sydney Mitchell & Co.*, [1980] A.C. 198 at 221 (H.L.).

priving all clients of any possibility of a remedy for negligence, however obvious the lawyer's error or omission may be.

A final justification for immunity was that if lawyers were liable for errors and omissions in the conduct of litigation in court, court calendars would abound with suits against lawyers instigated by disgruntled litigants who wish merely to relitigate cases in which they have been unsuccessful, necessitating endless reconsideration of the merits of trials. Courts are unlikely, however, to tolerate collateral attacks on their decisions disguised as claims based upon the negligence of lawyers. Ontario courts have hardly been overwhelmed by negligence actions against lawyers based upon their work in court since the suggestion of immunity was rejected in 1979.[213]

To the extent that there is substance to some of the justifications for immunity, the justifications must be weighed against the arguments favouring the imposition of liability on lawyers for negligence in the conduct of litigation in court. Three principal arguments may be advanced, two of which are closely related to each other.

First, the imposition of liability is likely to have the effect of raising professional standards, just as the imposition of tort liability in any other field of endeavour is widely assumed to serve as a deterrent to carelessness and intentional misconduct.

Second, it is wrong in principle that victims of professional negligence, no matter how flagrant, should have no remedy. In a 1988 decision, the High Court of Australia followed the 1969 decision of the House of Lords by holding that lawyers are immune from actions framed in negligence for work done in court. Justice Deane, dissenting, said that the justifications advanced by the House of Lords do not "outweigh or even balance the injustice and consequent public detriment involved in depriving a person, who is caught up in litigation and engages the professional services of a legal practitioner, of all redress under the common law for in court negligence, however gross and callous in its nature or devastating in its consequences."[214]

The third, related, argument for refusing to give lawyers immunity for negligence in court is the most convincing: it is essential to the reputation of the legal profession and indeed the legal system that lawyers be free of any taint or reasoned suspicion of favouritism. As the English barrister, David Pannick, has written, "[t]he immunity of lawyers from actions for negligence for their performance in Court contributes to the cynicism and distrust expressed by laymen for lawyers."[215]

---

213 The justifications for immunity are critically examined by David Pannick in *Advocates, supra*, note 211, pp. 203-204 and by Gene Anne Smith in "Liability for the Negligent Conduct of Litigation: The Legacy of *Rondel v. Worsley*" (1983) 47 Sask. L.R. 211.

214 *Giannarelli v. Wraith* (1988), 62 A.L.J.R. 611 at 627.

215 Pannick, *supra*, note 211, pp. 205-206.

Counsel for the aggrieved client argued in the House of Lords in 1969 that the peculiar characteristics of the professional work of lawyers are relevant to the *standard* of care that the law should impose, but should not result in the denial of the *existence* of a duty of care.[216] The submission did not find favour with their Lordships at that time, but it did 31 years later. One hopes that appeal courts throughout Canada will follow Ontario's lead and make the same choice.

4.19 LAWYERS AS WITNESSES

A lawyer should not act as counsel and be a witness in the same proceeding. Thus, in a proceeding in which a lawyer is acting as counsel the lawyer should neither submit the lawyer's own affidavit nor testify, except as permitted by rules of civil procedure, or as to purely formal or uncontroverted matters.[217]

A further corollary of the rule that one should not simultaneously serve as counsel and be a witness is that the lawyer should not express personal opinions or beliefs, or assert as facts anything that is properly subject to legal proof, cross-examination, or challenge. The lawyer must not in effect become an unsworn witness or put the lawyer's own credibility in issue.

In cases in which a lawyer is a necessary witness the lawyer should testify and entrust the conduct of the case to another lawyer. A lawyer who has given evidence also should not appear as counsel on appeal.

There are no restrictions on counsel's right to cross-examine another lawyer. Thus a lawyer who appears as a witness should expect no special treatment as a result of professional status.

The Canadian Bar Association's Code of Professional Conduct provides that, generally speaking, a lawyer's partners and associates should not testify in proceedings except as to merely formal matters.[218] This portion of the Canadian Bar Association Code has not been adopted in Ontario, in which the Law Society has also added a provision to the effect that each of the requirements referred to above are at all times subject to any contrary provisions of the law or the discretion of the tribunal before which the lawyer is appearing.[219] In a 1993 decision,[220] the Ontario Divisional Court held it is not the case that when a lawyer is expected

216 *Rondel v. Worsley*, [1969] 1 A.C. 191 at 196 (H.L.). See also Charles Wolfram, *Modern Legal Ethics* (St. Paul, Minnesota: West, 1986), p. 217.

217 See *Eastholme Realty Ltd. v. Grundy*, [1954] O.W.N. 583 (C.A.); *Parry v. Parry*, [1926] 2 W.W.R. 185 (Sask. C.A.); *Cairns v. Cairns*, [1931] 3 W.W.R. 335 at 345 (Alta. C.A.), *per* McGillivray J.A.; *Waschuk v. Waschuk* (1955), 14 W.W.R. 169 (Sask. C.A.); *Stanley v. Douglas*, [1951] 4 D.L.R. 698 (S.C.C.); and *R. v. Hayward* (1981), 59 C.C.C. (2d) 134 (Nfld. C.A.).

218 C.B.A. Code, chapter IX, commentary 5. See also Quebec rules, section 3.05.06; British Columbia rules, chapter 8, rule 9; the Alberta rules provide that "A lawyer must not act as counsel in any proceeding in which it is likely that the lawyer will give evidence that will be contested.": Chapter 10, rule 10.

219 Ontario rule 4.02.

220 *Essa (Township) v. Guergis* (1993), 15 O.R. (3d) 573 (Div. Ct.).

to testify in a lawsuit the lawyer's firm must always be prevented from acting as counsel. Courts should adopt a flexible approach, the Divisional Court observed, and should be particularly reluctant to make what may be premature orders preventing lawyers from continuing to act. Factors that the court should consider include the stage of the proceedings; the likelihood that the witness will be called; the good faith (or otherwise) of the party making the application; the significance of the evidence to be led; the impact of removing counsel on the party's right to be represented by counsel of choice; whether trial is to be by judge or jury; the likelihood of a real conflict arising or that the evidence will be "tainted"; who will call the witness; and the connection or relationship between counsel, the prospective witness and the parties involved in the litigation.[221] Flexibility is desirable to prevent the rule from being used as a tactical device by parties who wish to delay or cause unfair prejudice to their opponents by depriving them of counsel of their choice.[222]

In a 1980 Ontario case, a judge of the High Court of Justice wrote that a lawyer who is called to give expert evidence in a solicitor's negligence action has a duty to be as familiar with the case as was the lawyer whose act or omission is in question.[223]

4.20 *EX PARTE* PROCEEDINGS

In adversary proceedings the lawyer's function is openly and necessarily partisan, and lawyers generally have no duty to assist adversaries or advance matters derogatory to their client's case. In situations in which opposing interests are not represented (for example, in *ex parte* or uncontested proceedings) and in other situations in which the full proof and partisan advocacy generally inherent in the adversary system cannot obtain, lawyers must be particularly careful to be

---

221 *Ibid.*, 583. See also *Phoenix v. Metcalfe*, [1974] 5 W.W.R. 661 (B.C.C.A.); *Bilson v. University of Saskatchewan*, [1984] 4 W.W.R. 238 (Sask. C.A.); *Pari Air Ltd. v. Blue Sky Air Ltd.*, [1986] 3 W.W.R. 719 (Sask. Q.B.); and *Planned Insurance Portfolios Co. v. Crown Life Insurance Co.* (1989), 68 O.R. (2d) 271 (H.C.); *Simmonds v. Dalmyn*, [1993] 8 W.W.R. 207 (Man. C.A.); *Northway Chevrolet Oldsmobile Ltd. v. E.A.M. Management Ltd.*, [1994] 3 W.W.R. 314 (Sask. Q.B.), in which the respondent's counsel was ordered removed from the record prior to examinations for discovery; *Harvard Investments Ltd. v. Winnipeg (City)*, [1994] 6 W.W.R. 127 (Man. Q.B.), in which the court required the examination of counsel's colleague to be conducted by counsel unaffiliated with the witness and *Stevens v. Salt* (1995), 22 O.R. (3d) 675 (Ont. Gen. Div.), in which the defendant's counsel, whose colleague had represented the defendant on the real estate transaction that gave rise to the litigation, was ordered removed from the record in circumstances in which the case was likely to be won or lost on the evidence of the colleague.

222 See *Comden v. Superior Court*, 20 Cal. 3d 906, cert. denied 99 S. Ct. 568 (1978); and Wolfram, *supra*, note 216, pp. 378-388.

223 *Karpenko v. Paroian, Courey, Cohen & Houston* (1980), 30 O.R. (2d) 776 at 783 (H.C.), *per* Anderson J.

accurate, candid and complete in presenting their client's case so as to ensure that the court is not misled.[224]

This disclosure obligation is imposed to correct deficiencies in the adversary system in cases in which a premise underlying the effective functioning of the system — that each party will be represented by counsel of roughly equivalent competence in the proof and refutation of facts, and in argument — is faulty.[225]

Ontario's rules of civil procedure codify the common law requirement that where a motion or application is made without notice, the moving party or applicant must make full and fair disclosure of all material facts. A failure to do so is itself sufficient ground for setting aside any order obtained on the motion or application.[226]

4.21 AGREEMENTS GUARANTEEING RECOVERY (MARY CARTER AGREEMENTS)

In civil proceedings, lawyers have a duty not to mislead the court as to the position of their clients in the adversary process. Thus, a lawyer representing a party to litigation who has made or is party to an agreement made before or during the trial whereby a plaintiff is guaranteed recovery by one or more parties notwithstanding the judgment of the court, must immediately reveal the existence and particulars of the agreement to the court and to all parties to the proceedings.[227]

In a 1993 decision,[227.1] Justice Ferrier of the Ontario Court of Justice (General Division) upheld the validity of a Mary Carter agreement in dismissing a motion brought by the defendants who were not privy to the agreement, for an order staying the action on the grounds that the agreement was an abuse of process and void as against public policy. The agreement guaranteed the plaintiffs recovery in a specified amount while "capping" the contracting defendants'

(*Continued on page 4–53*)

224 C.B.A. Code, chapter IX, commentary 15; Ontario rule 4.01(1) and accompanying commentary; British Columbia rules, chapter 8, rule 21.

225 Wolfram, *supra*, note 216, pp. 679-680.

226 Ontario Rules of Civil Procedure, R.R.O. 1990, reg. 194, subrule 39.01 (6). See also *Herman v. Klig*, [1938] O.W.N. 270 (H.C.); *Launch! Research & Development Inc. v. Essex Distributing Co.* (1977), 4 C.P.C. 261 (Ont. H.C.); *J. & P. Goldfluss Ltd. v. 306569 Ontario Ltd.* (1977), 4 C.P.C. 296 (Ont. H.C.); *Merker v. Leader Terrazzo Tile Mosaic Ltd.* (1983), 43 O.R. (2d) 632 (H.C.); and *Hess v. Mandzuk* (1984), 44 C.P.C. 179 (Ont. H.C.).

227 C.B.A. Code, chapter IX, commentary 17; Ontario rule 10, commentary 4. See also *J. & M. Chartrand Realty Ltd. v. Martin* (1981), 22 C.P.C. 186 (Ont. H.C.). The term "Mary Carter agreement" is derived from a Florida case, *Booth v. Mary Carter Paint Co.*, 202 So. 2d 8 (Fla. 1967).

227.1 *Pettey v. Avis Car Inc.* (1993), 13 O.R. (3d) 725 (Gen. Div.).

exposure. The plaintiffs were at liberty to continue their claims against the non-contracting defendants, and the contracting defendants were at liberty to pursue their cross-claims for indemnity against the non-contracting defendants.

Because the agreement was promptly disclosed to the court, Justice Ferrier ruled, the court was able to control its process with full knowledge of all relevant circumstances. A result of the agreement, however, was that it was in the interest of the contracting defendants that the plaintiffs' damages be assessed as high as possible. Accordingly, the court held, procedural safeguards should be introduced to prevent any distortion of the process. Thus, the contracting defendants were prohibited from cross-examining on issues concerning the quantum of damages except with the leave of the court.[227.2]

4.22 CONTROL OF ADVOCACY

Excesses in advocacy are subject to formal control in three ways: first, by direct judicial intervention in the form of contempt citations and orders requiring lawyers personally to pay costs; second, by indirect judicial intervention in the form of procedural and evidentiary rulings and orders requiring parties to pay costs, all of which may influence advocacy by influencing the outcome of litigation; and, third, by disciplinary sanctions imposed by law societies.

The second means of control is by far the most significant. Most competent judges go through an entire judicial career without imposing a contempt sanction on a lawyer, and though orders requiring lawyers to pay costs personally have become more common in recent years, such sanctions are generally imposed only in egregious cases. Disciplinary sanctions, except in cases involving the falsification of evidence or attempts to obstruct justice, have been exceedingly rare.

The rarity of direct intervention to control excesses, either by courts or law societies, reflects tolerance for lapses that are inevitable in the emotionally heated atmosphere of adversarial trials, and recognition of the fact that more subtle means of control are available. Courts and law societies appreciate, too, that contempt citations and disciplinary sanctions may have the effect of inhibiting the vigorous partisan advocacy that is required in an adversary system.[228]

(a) Cost Sanctions Against Lawyers

In a 1963 case in England, the Court of Appeal allowed an appeal brought by a solicitor from an order requiring him to pay 15 guineas toward the costs of a prosecution in Magistrates' Court in which he acted for the accused person. The magistrate's order was made on the ground that the solicitor had

227.2 *Ibid*. at 742.

228 Charles Wolfram, *Modern Legal Ethics* (St. Paul, Minnesota: West, 1986), pp. 620 and 625-626.

taken a bad point. In the Court of Appeal, Lord Denning affirmed that it was the solicitor's duty "to take any point which he believed to be fairly arguable on behalf of his client. An advocate is not to usurp the province of the judge." He added that a lawyer "only becomes guilty of misconduct if he is dishonest. That is, if he knowingly takes a bad point and thereby deceives the court." Lord Harmon, concurring, added that "even if a legal proposition is untenable, counsel may properly urge it in good faith; he may do so even though he may not expect to be successful, provided of course that he does not resort to deceit or to wilful obstruction of the orderly processes."[229]

Rules of civil procedure that came into effect in Ontario in 1985 empower courts (among other things) to require lawyers to pay costs personally where they have caused costs to be incurred without reasonable cause or to be wasted by undue delay, negligence or other default.[230] Even before the rule came into force, lawyers were ordered to pay costs personally in cases in which they initiated or continued proceedings without authority,[231] initiated ill-conceived proceedings,[232] unduly interfered with examinations,[233] failed to be frank with the court,[234] and made irresponsible and unfounded allegations against the integrity and good faith of an executive.[235]

Since the rule came into force, orders requiring lawyers to pay costs personally have been made fairly infrequently. In one case, a lawyer was ordered to pay the costs of a motion where part of the relief sought was completely unfounded and the balance of the relief sought was premature.[236] A judge of the Ontario Supreme Court had held that awards of costs against lawyers personally are justified only in cases in which the lawyers have failed to carry out their professional duty or have been guilty of gross negligence. Something more than mere negligence is required on the part of counsel, the court held, before the court will order costs against a lawyer personally.[237] Similarly, in a 2000 decision,[237.1] the British Columbia Court of Appeal held that an order for costs against a lawyer personally cannot be made on the basis of a mere error

229 *Abraham v. Jutsun*, [1963] 2 All E.R. 402 (C.A.).

230 Ontario Rules of Civil Procedure, R.R.O. 1990, reg. 194, subrule 57.07(1).

231 *Evans v. Savarin Ltd.* (1980), 27 O.R. (2d) 705 (H.C.).

232 *Re Consiglio (No. 2)*, [1973] 3 O.R. 329 (C.A.).

233 *Sonntag v. Sonntag* (1979), 24 O.R. (2d) 473 (H.C.).

234 *Supra*, note 231.

235 *Re Bisyk (No. 2)* (1980), 32 O.R. (2d) 281 (H.C.), affirmed (1981), 32 O.R. (2d) 281n (C.A.).

236 *640612 Ont. Inc. v. 253547 Ont. Ltd.* (1987), 26 C.P.C.(2d) 93 (Ont. Master).

237 *Cini v. Micallef* (1987), 60 O.R. (2d) 584 (H.C.). See also *931473 Ontario Ltd. v. Coldwell Banker Canada Inc.* (1992), 5 C.P.C. (3d) 271 (Ont. Gen. Div.).

237.1 *Kent v. Waldock*, [2000] 7 W.W.R. 10 (B.C. C.A.). The Court added that the lawyer's conduct, though an affront to the dignity of the plaintiff, did not result in costs incurred or wasted, and as such was not the proper subject of an order that a lawyer pay costs personally.

or even the occurrence of negligence, but rather only on the basis of conduct that is reprehensible or that amounts to an abuse of process.

In two 1994 decisions, however, judges of the Ontario Court of Justice (General Division) rejected that position in awarding costs against lawyers personally. In the first case,[237.2] a lawyer was ordered to pay the costs of a motion to set aside her client's notice of readiness for trial. The purpose of the motion was to enable the lawyer to conduct examinations for discovery. Her only explanation for serving a notice of readiness and setting the action down for trial before discoveries was that she did not know that the rules of civil procedure prohibited discovery after an action is set down. The court expressed dismay that counsel could be unaware of such a fundamental aspect of the rules.

In the second case,[237.3] costs were awarded personally against a lawyer who failed to appear when an action in which he was acting as counsel was called for trial. The court held that the lawyer was negligent in failing to monitor the progress of the action, and ordered him to pay personally the costs of his (successful) motion to set aside the judgment.

In a 1997 decision,[237.4] the Ontario Court of Appeal reversed an order requiring a lawyer to pay the costs of a motion seeking a contempt order against the lawyer's client. The costs order was based upon the fact that the lawyer had advised the client that an order directing an interim receiver to take immediate possession of the client's books and records imposed no positive obligation on the client to package up the books and records and send them to the receiver.

The Court of Appeal held that there was no basis for finding that the lawyer had acted in bad faith, and that his interpretation of the order was reasonable and may have been correct. The Court also emphasized that the rules of civil procedure permit an order requiring a lawyer to pay costs personally only if the lawyer is given a reasonable opportunity to make representations to the court. Moreover, the liability of the lawyer to pay costs personally should have been dealt with after the contempt proceedings were concluded, the Court added. Otherwise the client could be seriously prejudiced, as the lawyer in defending himself might have been required to advance arguments that were inconsistent with the client's interest and that might have required disclosure of privileged communications.

237.2 *Worsley Estate v. Lichong* (1994), 17 O.R. (3d) 615 (Gen. Div.).

237.3 *Faber-Castell Canada Ltd. v. Woods*, Ont. Gen Div., Matlow J., March 14, 1994 (unreported); see also *Mireau v. Saskatchewan (Minister of Justice)*, [1995] 4 W.W.R. 389 (Sask. C.A.); *Filmlab Systems International Ltd. v. Pennington*, [1994] 4 All E.R. 673; and *R. v. Horsham DC, ex.p. Wenman*, [1994] 4 All E.R. 681. In *Mans v. State Farm Mutual Insurance Company* (1996), 32 O.R. (3d) 786 a law firm was required to pay costs that it caused to be incurred by its failure to bring a motion to be removed as solicitors of record in a timely way.

237.4 *Schwisberg v. Perry Krieger & Associates* (1997), 33 O.R. (3d) 256.

In a 1999 decision of the Alberta Court of Queen's Bench,[237.5] a lawyer was ordered to pay costs of $25,000 for causing a mistrial by providing to the Court a without prejudice settlement offer from counsel for the opposite party. The Court applied the principle that costs may be awarded on a solicitor-client scale in cases of misconduct or default or negligence of a serious character. It would be inequitable, the Court added, to require either the plaintiffs or the defendants to bear any of wasted costs incurred solely as a result of the conduct of counsel, bearing in mind that the object of imposing personal liability for costs on counsel is not to punish the lawyer but to protect the client. Even if one were to accept counsel's dubious explanation that he lost his senses in the heat of battle, the Court concluded, his conduct in passing up to the judge the defendants' offer to settle was a fundamental breach of one of the most basic tenets of civil procedure, and met the test for costs payable personally.

(b) Contempt of Court

The *Criminal Code* preserves the authority of courts to impose punishment for contempt of court, but does not define the offence.[238] In a 1984 case,[239] the Ontario Court of Appeal defined the term "contempt of court" in such a way as to include words or acts "which are intended or likely to interfere with or obstruct the fair administration of justice." The Law Reform Commission of Canada in its report on contempt of court identified four types of contempts:

(1) Disruption of judicial proceedings, including conduct in the courtroom that is offensive or disorderly, as well as disobedience to orders made concerning the conduct of judicial proceedings.

(2) Defiance of judicial authority, including disobedience to court orders amounting to outright defiance, and public challenges to judicial authority.

(3) Affronts to judicial authority, including conduct calculated to insult a court, and attacks on the independence, impartiality, or integrity of a court or of the judiciary.

(4) Interference with pending judicial proceedings, including the publication of information that the publisher knows or ought to know may interfere with the proceedings.[240]

237.5 *Lynch v. Checker Cabs Ltd.* (June 30, 1999), Doc. Calgary 9701-16341 (Alta. Q.B.).

238 *Criminal Code*, R.S.C. 1985, c. C-46, as amended, ss. 8 and 9.

239 *R. v. Cohn* (1984), 15 C.C.C. (3d) 150 at 156 (Ont. C.A.), leave to appeal to S.C.C. refused (1985), 9 O.A.C. 160 (S.C.C.).

240 Law Reform Commission of Canada Report number 17, "Contempt of Court" (1988). See also Beverley G. Smith, *Professional Conduct for Canadian Lawyers* (Toronto: Butterworths, 1989), pp. 132-133.

Convictions of lawyers for contempt of court, as mentioned above, are rare. In a 1981 case,[241] the British Columbia Supreme Court held that for a lawyer to criticize a judge's conduct in a particular case or to criticize any particular decision of the courts does not amount to contempt of court (and, indeed, is entirely proper) if the criticism is free of abuse and aspersions on the court's motives. In a 1977 decision,[242] the Manitoba Court of Appeal drew a distinction between a lawyer deliberately frustrating the due carrying on of court proceedings by wilfully refusing to attend in court, and a lawyer impulsively reacting to an adverse ruling by attempting to withdraw. In the latter case, the Court of Appeal held, the lawyer is not guilty of contempt, but only of an error in judgment.

In a 1978 decision,[243] the Ontario Court of Appeal held that a lawyer's failure to attend in court due to inadvertence, even if the lawyer has been negligent, does not amount to contempt of court unless the lawyer's conduct

(*Continued on page 4–57*)

241 *Re Dalke* (1981), (*sub nom. R. v. Dalke*) 21 C.R. (3d) 380 (B.C. S.C.).

242 *R. v. Swartz* (1977), 34 C.C.C. (2d) 477 (Man. C.A.).

243 *R. v. Jones* (1978), 42 C.C.C. (2d) 192 (Ont. C.A.).

reflects indifference to the lawyer's duty to the court. The court added that a lawyer's *deliberate* failure to attend in court will generally be treated as a contempt of court.

Four years later, the same court upheld a finding of contempt of court against a lawyer whose failure to appear in court showed a serious indifference to his responsibilities to his client and the court. The lawyer, having failed to attend when his case was called, had failed again to attend court on the following day as directed by the judge.[244]

In three cases involving the practice of double booking, courts, while deploring the practice, have declined to make or uphold findings of contempt of court. In one of the cases, a lawyer's appeal from a conviction for contempt was allowed by the Manitoba Court of Appeal for procedural reasons, but the court said that a lawyer's failure to attend at a scheduled hearing because the lawyer has arranged to appear as counsel in another court may amount to a contempt of court in some circumstances.[245] In the second case, the Chief Justice of the Ontario High Court of Justice held that the lawyer's conduct did not cross the "rather vague and uncertain line" between discourtesy and contempt of court.[246] In the third case,[246.1] the Ontario Court of Appeal, by a two-to-one majority, allowed a lawyer's appeal from conviction, holding that to support a conviction for contempt of court against a lawyer who fails to attend in court because of double booking the court must be satisfied that the lawyer has been reckless in her or his responsibilities to the court.

In a much earlier case, Justice Riddell of the Supreme Court of Ontario (Appellate Division) criticized the "mischievous practice of some counsel . . . of employing inflammatory language in addressing juries." He characterized the practice as an abuse of the privilege of counsel and added that, if persisted in, the practice may amount to contempt of court.[247]

In a 1969 decision, the Saskatchewan Court of Appeal upheld a finding that for a lawyer to engage "in the regrettable practice of needling the court in the hope that something may be said or done which would ensure a new trial, if one became necessary" amounts to contempt of court.[248]

In recent years, however, courts of appeal have emphasized the undesirability of trial courts invoking their contempt powers to punish lawyers for comments made in court in advancing their client's case. In 1984, the High Court of Australia allowed a lawyer's appeal from his conviction for contempt of court for saying to the jury in his closing address at a criminal trial that the judge had favoured the prosecution's case. The High Court said that a judge "should be slow to hold

---

244 *R. v. Anders* (1982), 67 C.C.C. (2d) 138 (Ont. C.A.).

245 *R. v. Pinx* (1980), 50 C.C.C. (2d) 65 (Man. C.A.).

246 *R. v. Bickerton* (1985), 46 C.R. (3d) 286 (Ont. H.C.).

246.1 *R. v. Glasner* (1994), 19 O.R. (3d) 739 (C.A.).

247 *Dale v. Toronto Railway Co.* (1915), 34 O.L.R. 104 (C.A.).

248 *Re Shumiatcher* (1967), 64 D.L.R. (2d) 24 at 31 (Sask. Q.B.), fine reduced an appeal from $1000 to $500 [1969] 1 C.C.C. 272 (Sask. C.A.).

that remarks made during the course of counsel's address to the jury amount to a wilful insult to the judge, when the remarks may be seen to be relevant to the case which counsel is presenting to the jury on behalf of his client." The High Court added that although the lawyer's conduct was "extremely discourteous, perhaps offensive, and deserving of rebuke, it was not punishable as contempt."[249]

In a 1980 case,[250] the Alberta Court of Appeal also observed that mere discourtesy or the use of uncomplimentary remarks to the court will not always amount to contempt of court. Nevertheless, the Court of Appeal held, a lawyer's repeated refusal to answer a proper question put by the presiding judge will normally constitute contempt.

Finally, in 1957, the Supreme Court of Canada convicted a lawyer of contempt of court where he objected, without any reasonable basis, to a particular judge sitting on the court hearing an appeal in which the lawyer was acting as counsel.[251]

(c) Law Society Disciplinary Sanctions

Rules of professional conduct provide that lawyers' professional obligations to be courteous and civil to the court and to those engaged on the other side are not co-extensive with the obligations the breach of which are punishable as contempt of court. A consistent pattern of rude, provocative or disruptive conduct by a lawyer, the rules provide, even though unpunished as contempt, might well merit discipline.[252]

Discourtesy in litigation has nevertheless been visited with disciplinary sanctions only rarely. In a 1984 case,[253] the Law Society of Upper Canada reprimanded publicly a lawyer who had interfered with the orderly administration of justice by repeatedly making offensive remarks to opposing counsel and deliberately spilling coffee on opposing counsel's notes during a cross-examination on an affidavit in an official examiner's office. Two years later, the same lawyer was suspended from practice for three months as a result of his repeated refusal to stand when addressing the court in a criminal case.[254]

Attempts to mislead courts or tribunals, or to obstruct justice, are somewhat more frequently the basis of disciplinary proceedings. In another 1984 Ontario case,[255] a lawyer was suspended for one month for making false submissions in speaking to sentence on behalf of a client charged with being an inmate in a common bawdy-house. The lawyer told the court that the accused was a divorced single parent who was supporting two young children, and who had resorted to

---

249 *Lewis v. Ogden* (1984), 53 A.L.R. 53 at 57 and 60 (H.C.).

250 *R. v. Barker* (1980), 53 C.C.C. (2d) 322 (Alta. C.A.).

251 *Re Duncan* (1957), 11 D.L.R. (2d) 616 at 618 (S.C.C.).

252 C.B.A. Code, chapter IX, commentary 14; Ontario rule 4.01(6) and accompanying commentary.

253 *Re Balaban*, report adopted by Convocation, May 24, 1984.

254 *Re Balaban (No. 2)*, report adopted by Convocation, September 25, 1986.

255 *Re Dubinsky*, report adopted by Convocation, September 21, 1984.

prostitution because she was in desperate financial trouble. In fact, the accused had never been married, was not supporting any children, had given up her only child for adoption ten years earlier, and had no serious financial difficulties at the relevant time.

In a 1985 case,[256] the Law Society of Upper Canada suspended for one year a lawyer who had been convicted in the criminal courts for conspiring to obstruct justice by "fixing" traffic tickets. In a 1992 case,[257] the Law Society of Upper Canada suspended for one year a lawyer who (among other things) had made a false statement of fact in writing in a submission to a labour relations board. (Because the lawyer had voluntarily withdrawn from practice six months before his suspension, the effective length of his suspension was 18 months.)

4.23 LAWYERS AND JUDGES

When he was a young lawyer, the great English barrister F.E. Smith (later Lord Birkenhead) was retained by a tram company that had been sued for damages on behalf of an injured boy. Smith appeared at trial before a Judge Willis, who said of the plaintiff, in the jury's presence, "Poor boy, poor boy. Blind. Put him in that chair so the jury can see him." The following exchange ensued:

> *Smith* (sardonically): Perhaps Your Honour would like to have the boy passed around the jury box.
>
> *Judge Willis* (glaring): That is a most improper remark!
>
> *Smith*: It was provoked by a most improper suggestion.
>
> *Judge Willis* (pausing to gain control of his temper): Mr. Smith, have you ever heard of a saying by Bacon — the great Bacon — that youth and discretion are ill-wed companions?
>
> *Smith*: Indeed I have, Your Honour; and has Your Honour ever heard of a saying by Bacon — the great Bacon — that a much-talking judge is like an ill-tuned cymbal?
>
> *Judge Willis* (livid with fury): You are extremely offensive, young man!
>
> *Smith*: As a matter of fact we both are. The only difference between us is that I am trying to be and you can't help it. I have been listened to with respect by the highest tribunal in the land and I have not come down here to be browbeaten!

On another occasion, Judge Willis asked rhetorically, "What do you suppose I am on the bench *for*, Mr. Smith?"

"It is not for me, Your Honour," replied Smith, "to attempt to fathom the inscrutable workings of Providence."[258]

---

256 *Re May*, report adopted by Convocation, January 24, 1985.

257 *Re Rovet*, report adopted by Convocation, January 23, 1992.

258 Both F.E. Smith anecdotes are recounted in John Train (ed.), *Wit: The Best Things Ever Said* (New York: Harpercollins, 1991), pp. 17-18.

The fundamental tension in the ethics of advocacy is between the lawyer's duty of resolute partisanship and the lawyer's duty to treat the court or tribunal with candour, fairness, courtesy, and respect.[259] It is the right and duty of the lawyer fearlessly to pursue (in the words of Lord Pearce) "an approach which is as biased in favour of his client's contentions as public considerations allow."[260] Lawyers have a right of audience and a duty to insist on being heard. They also have a right to make objections to questions and arguments of opposing counsel and to make objections to the judge's charge to the jury. Freedom of expression is critical to the effective administration of justice.

Judges are generally careful to avoid penalizing lawyers for remarks that they (judges) may find offensive but that in the judgment of counsel are made in pursuit of the client's interest. In a 1952 decision of the United States Supreme Court, Justice Jackson said that courts should "unhesitatingly protect counsel in fearless, vigorous and effective performance of every duty pertaining to the office of advocate on behalf of any person whatsoever." He added that one must not, however, "equate contempt with courage or insults with independence."[261] In other words, lawyers can and should be firm and strong without being discourteous or disrespectful to the opposing parties or the judiciary. It is inevitable that in an adversarial process feelings among litigants will run high, and judges wield power over lawyers and litigants alike and must sometimes be challenged boldly, particularly on the infrequent occasions when their power is abused. Lawyers must rise above the rancour that may characterize their clients' attitude so that their relations with the court are not contaminated by animosity.[262]

Because the process is competitive, litigants and lawyers are often tempted to vent publicly their disappointment over unfavourable decisions. To prohibit adverse criticism of judicial decisions would of course be an unthinkable invasion of freedom of expression. The United States Supreme Court said in 1978 that the law gives "judges as persons and courts as institutions . . . no greater immunity from criticism than other persons or institutions."[263]

Lawyers must bear in mind, however, that in order to preserve the appearance of impartiality judges have traditionally refused to be drawn into public contro-

259 C.B.A. Code, chapter IX, rule, and commentaries 1 and 15; Ontario rule 4.01 and accompanying commentary.

260 *Rondel v. Worsley*, [1969] 1 A.C. 191 at 274 (H.L.).

261 *Sacher v. United States*, 343 U.S. 1 at 13-14 (1952). See also *Re Snyder*, 472 U.S. 634 at 646-647 (U.S. S. Ct., 1985); David Pannick, *Advocates* (Oxford: Oxford University Press, 1992), pp. 76 and 82-83; and Mark Orkin, *Legal Ethics: A Study in Professional Conduct* (Toronto: Cartwright & Sons, 1957), pp. 37-38 and 44.

262 See Justice Anglin's speech "Relations of Bench and Bar", 29 C.L. Times 1, quoted by Orkin, *ibid.*, p. 33; Charles Wolfram, *Modern Legal Ethics* (St. Paul, Minnesota: West, 1986), p. 600; M. Naeem Rauf, "Judicial Misbehaviour: How Should a Lawyer Handle It?", Law Society of Upper Canada Gazette, vol. 25, no. 3 (September-December 1992), p. 285.

263 *Landmark Communications Inc. v. Virgina*, 435 U.S. 829 at 839 (1978) quoting from the dissenting judgment of Justice Frankfurter in *Bridges v. California*, 314 U.S. 252 at 289 (1941).

versies about their actions, and are hence helpless to defend themselves against ill-founded allegations. This imposes two duties on lawyers: (i) to ensure that any criticisms they level against judges are fair and balanced; and (ii) to defend judges who are unjustly accused.[264]

In considering the scope of the former duty it is important to bear in mind that the public interest requires that the shortcomings of certain judges be exposed, and that because of their training and experience lawyers are uniquely situated to comment on those shortcomings. Lawyers should not be reticent about calling the attention of the authorities and the public to judicial incompetence and corruption.

Thus, the Supreme Court of Oklahoma held in a 1988 decision that ethical rules governing lawyers' conduct should not "shield the judiciary from the critique of that portion of the public most perfectly situated to advance knowledgeable criticism." The court declined to discipline a lawyer who said of a judge who had found the lawyer's client guilty, "He showed all the signs of being a racist . . . I've never tried a case before him that I felt I got an impartial trial out of him." Crucial to the court's holding was its finding that the lawyer's statements were made in good faith. The first amendment would not protect such a statement, the court said, if it were made in bad faith for the purpose of spreading falsehoods against a judge.[265]

Judges have repeatedly emphasized the fundamental importance of candour, integrity, and fairness on the part of lawyers in their relations with judges in court. Sir John Donaldson, the Master of the Rolls, said in a 1986 judgment that a "requirement of absolute probity" is imposed on advocates in the public interest.[266] Lord Morris said in a 1969 decision of the House of Lords that "to a certain extent every advocate is an amicus curiae."[267] Lord Denning said in a 1978

---

264 See Wolfram, *supra*, note 262, pp. 600-601. See also Justice Gerald V. La Forest's speech "Integrity in the Practice of Law", Law Society of Upper Canada Gazette, vol. 21, no. 1 (March, 1987), p. 42 at 44; Geoffrey C. Hazard, Jr., "A Crumbling Judicial Base Hurts the Bar", National Law Journal (November 19, 1990), p. 13; and Monroe H. Freedman, "The Threat to Judicial Independence by Criticism of Judges — A Proposed Solution to the Real Problem", 25 Hofstra Law Review 729 (1997).

265 *Oklahoma Bar Association v. Porter*, 766 P. 2d 958 (1988). See also Lawrence Dubin, "Can Lawyer Call Judge a Racist?", National Law Journal (March 6, 1989), p. 13. In *Vernon v. Oliver* (1885), 11 S.C.R. 156 the Supreme Court of Canada ordered that the appellant's *factum* be stricken from the court's files on the ground that it was framed "in such a virulent and malignant spirit of invective" directed at the judgments of the courts below as to disgrace the court.

266 *Abse v. Smith*, [1986] Q.B. 536 at 545 (C.A.).

267 *Rondel v. Worsley*, [1969] 1 A.C. 191 at 247 (H.L.). A similar point is made by Lord Upjohn at p. 282. See also La Forest, *supra*, note 264, pp. 43-44, and Justice Anglin's speech "Relations of Bench and Bar", 29 C.L. Times 1, quoted by Orkin, *supra*, note 261, p. 26.

decision that the lawyer "must be independent of the wishes of the client, no matter how pressing and no matter how high the fee."[268]

Other professional responsibilities imposed on lawyers in their relations with judges are designed to promote judicial neutrality. Lawyers are forbidden from appearing before judges (or judicial officers) when they, their associates, or their clients have business or personal relationships with the judge that give rise or might reasonably appear to give rise to pressure, influence or inducement affecting the judge's impartiality.[269] Nor may lawyers endeavour or allow anyone else to endeavour, directly or indirectly, to influence the decision or action of a court or tribunal or any of its officials in any case or matter by any means other than open persuasion as an advocate.[270]

The latter admonition enjoins lawyers from discussing pending cases with the presiding judge in the absence of opposing counsel.[271] The purposes of the prohibition are to prevent the communicating party from gaining an unfair advantage (or appearing to do so) and to assure all parties a fair hearing, including the right to hear and respond to all evidence and argument offered by an adversary.

Some *ex parte* communications are, of course, authorized by law. An interlocutory injunction may be obtained without notice in a very limited range of cases where, for example, it would be impossible to give notice to the respondents without defeating the purpose of the motion.[272] Such cases are, of course, exempt from the prohibition in the rules of professional conduct, as are consent matters. Every trip to the courthouse need not be duplicated by a lawyer for the opposite party if the matter is not in dispute.

The prohibition extends to jurors as well as judges: lawyers must not communicate with jurors outside of the trial itself. If a juror attempts to engage a lawyer in any conversation other than a perfunctory greeting, the lawyer should politely but firmly decline.[273]

4.24 LAWYERS AND JURORS

Lawyers' relations with jurors have not generally been a subject filled in Canadian rules of professional conduct. This void was addressed by the Law

268 *Saif Ali v. Sydney Mitchell & Co.*, [1978] Q.B. 95 at 103 (C.A.), reversed on other grounds [1978] 3 All E.R. 1033 (H.L.). See also *Re Ontario (Crime Commission)* (1962), 37 D.L.R. (2d) 382 at 391 (Ont. C.A.).

269 C.B.A. Code, chapter IX, commentary 2(c), and chapter XIX, commentary 5; Ontario rule 4.01(2)(c).

270 C.B.A. Code, chapter IX, commentary 2(d); Ontario rule 4.01(2)(d); Quebec rules, section 4.02.01(b).

271 *Allinson v. General Medical Council*, [1844] 1 Q.B. 750 at 758-759, *per* Esher M.R.

272 See, for example, *Launch! Research & Development Inc. v. Essex Distributing Co.* (1977), 4 C.P.C. 261 (Ont. H.C.).

273 See Charles Wolfram, *Modern Legal Ethics* (St. Paul, Minnesota: West, 1986), pp. 604-606; and *Re Delgado*, 306 S.E. 2d 591 (1983), cert. denied 464 U.S. 1057 (1984).

Society of Upper Canada in 2000, however, when a new rule titled "Relations with Jurors" was added to the Ontario rules.

The Ontario rule provides that before trial a lawyer must not communicate with (or cause another to communicate with) anyone that the lawyer knows to be a member of the jury panel for that trial.[274] The lawyer may investigate a prospective juror to ascertain any basis for challenge, provided that the lawyer does not directly or indirectly communicate with the juror or any member of the juror's family, but the lawyer should not directly or indirectly conduct a vexatious or harassing investigation of either a member of the jury panel or a juror.[275]

The Ontario rule also requires lawyers to disclose to the judge or opposing counsel any information of which the lawyer is aware that a juror or prospective juror has or may have a direct or indirect interest in the outcome of the case, or is acquainted with or connected in any manner with the presiding judge, or any counsel, litigant, or witness.[276] Lawyers are also required to disclose to the court any information that they have about improper conduct by a member of a jury panel or by a juror toward another member of the jury panel, another juror, or to the members of a juror's family.[277]

Except as permitted by law, lawyers acting as advocates must not directly or indirectly communicate with jurors during trial.[278]

Lawyers who are not connected with a case before the court are also prohibited from directly or indirectly communicating with jurors, though this prohibition applies only to communications about the case.[279] The restrictions on communications with jurors and potential jurors also apply to communications with or investigations of members of their families.[280]

274 Ontario rule 4.05 (1).
275 Ontario rule 4.05 (1) and accompanying commentary.
276 Ontario rule 4.05 (2).
277 Ontario rule 4.05 (3).
278 Ontario rule 4.05 (4).
279 Ontario rule 4.05 (5).
280 Ontario rule 4.05 (5) and accompanying commentary.

5

Conflicts of Interest in Litigation

5.1 INTRODUCTION

Conflicts of interest are pervasive in the practice of every litigation lawyer. The problems that arise involve competing considerations of variable importance, and their resolution is often intricate and difficult.

Canadian rules of professional conduct are of little assistance in resolving the most troublesome conflict of interest problems that confront lawyers in a litigation practice. The rules provide more guidance to lawyers who carry on a solicitor's practice, and are considered in that context in chapter 22. Particular problems that lawyers are likely to encounter in the fields of criminal defence, mediation, real estate, estates, corporate law, and government practice are considered in chapters 7, 16, 17, 18, 20, and 21 respectively.

Conflict of interest problems arise in a litigation practice as a result of relationships involving lawyers, their partners and associates, their current and former clients, adverse parties, co-parties, witnesses, and judges and other adjudicators. Specialized litigation including class actions, shareholder derivative actions, indemnity insurance claims, and matrimonial disputes, among others, introduce specialized conflict of interest issues.

In struggling with the great variety of complications that such an array of relationships and circumstances presents, courts have frequently resolved conflict of interest problems on the basis of assumed appearances of impropriety. Although sound reasons of policy justify judicial intervention despite an absence of evidence of actual misconduct in some cases, it is likely that the appearance of impropriety standard has been invoked in many other cases as a superficially attractive but in fact simplistic alternative to a thoroughgoing analysis of the many relevant factors that should be weighed in each case. This has impeded the development of a coherent jurisprudence and has sometimes resulted in clients suffering quite unfair consequences.

5.2 APPEARANCES OF IMPROPRIETY

Plutarch said that Caesar's wife must be above suspicion; Lord Goddard wrote that justice must not only be done, but must manifestly be seen to be done.[1] Both aphorisms have been invoked in cases of alleged conflicts of interest in support of the proposition that lawyers must not only be innocent of actual misconduct, but must be innocent also of even an appearance of misconduct.[2]

The maintenance of public confidence in the administration of justice and the ethical standards of the legal profession is generally cited as the foundation for the appearance of impropriety standard.[3] The practical difficulty of determining whether actual misconduct has occurred where that determination may require the revelation of confidential information that forms the very basis of an alleged conflict has also induced courts to resort to appearances.[4]

Both of these concerns are genuine and substantial. The latter, however, can be and generally has been accommodated by means of a presumption that confidential information has been imparted to the lawyer.[5] As for the former concern, it is by no means clear that an appearance of impropriety standard is the most effective way of maintaining public confidence, particularly in cases in which the application of such a standard has resulted in unfairness.

To determine whether a lawyer's representation of a party to litigation gives rise to an appearance of impropriety, the courts have invented a fictitious person to whom they have delegated the task of deciding whether the questioned lawyer's conduct is acceptable. Little has been said of the qualities of the fictitious person. It is safe to conclude that she is not a lawyer. She is usually described as being reasonably informed, and one assumes that she herself is honourable. The judge's attempt to read her mind, however, can amount to little more than guesswork. The result of using such a device is unlikely to differ from the result of the judge using his or her own impression of the propriety of the lawyer's representation. The fictitious person is likely to contribute little more than an illusion of objectivity to the process.[6]

Even if it were possible for judges to divine the fictitious person's reaction to a lawyer's representation of a client, it is by no means clear that that reaction

---

1 *R. v. Sussex Justices ex Parte McCarthy*, [1924] 1 K.B. 256 (D.C.). See also John Sopinka, "Conflicts of Interest: To What Extent Are We Governed By Appearance", an address to a joint meeting of the Civil Litigation and Insurance Subsections of the Canadian Bar Association (Ontario Branch), June 25, 1991, p. 1.

2 See, for example, *MacDonald Estate v. Martin*, [1990] 3 S.C.R. 1235 at 1243 and 1265; *Szebelledy v. Constitution Insurance Co. of Canada* (1985), 11 C.C.L.I. 140 at 156 (Ont. Dist. Ct.); *Shaughnessy Brothers Investments Ltd. v. Lakehead Trailer Park (1985) Ltd.* (1987), 63 O.R. (2d) 225 (H.C.); *781332 Ontario Inc. v. Mortgage Insurance Co. of Canada* (1991), 5 O.R. (3d) 248 (Gen. Div.); and *Laidlaw Environmental Services (Sarnia) Ltd. v. Ontario (Minister of Environment and Energy)* (1997), 32 O.R. (3d) 795 (Gen. Div.). In the United States, the American Bar Association rejected the appearance of impropriety standard when it promulgated its Model Rules of Professional Conduct in 1983.

3 See, for example, *MacDonald Estate v. Martin*, *ibid.*, pp. 1247-1252 and 1258.

4 *Ibid.*, p. 1260.

5 See Sopinka, *supra*, note 1, p. 1; and Charles Wolfram, *Modern Legal Ethics* (St. Paul, Minnesota: West, 1986), p. 320.

6 See Wolfram, *ibid.*, pp. 320-321.

should be determinative. Public reaction to lawyers' acting for most persons accused of criminal offences is likely to be unfavourable, but neither the courts nor the profession would think of allowing adverse public opinion to play a role in determining the propriety of the representation. It is possible, of course, to endow the fictitious person with qualities that enable her to analyze the problem dispassionately and to balance all relevant considerations before formulating an opinion. But what, then, does her opinion add?[7]

The determination of conflict of interest issues based on appearances can result in unfairness. To deprive clients, who may have invested a great deal of time, energy and money in litigation, of counsel of their choice is a necessary — though often disruptive and expensive — consequence of a process that must ensure that other parties are protected against such improprieties as disloyalty and breaches of confidentiality. To deprive clients of the right to be represented by counsel of their choice — and in some cases to inflict on them the burdens of disruption, duplication of effort, and added expense — based on a mere appearance of impropriety that does not in fact exist, may be intolerable.[8]

Motions for disqualification orders may not always be sought for the purest of motives. Many such motions are undoubtedly brought by reason of genuine concerns about lawyers' loyalty or breaches of confidence. Others may be brought, however, to gain a tactical advantage by burdening a less well-financed adversary with additional costs, or by depriving the adversary of the services of a lawyer who is known to be effective in a particular type of case.[9]

The appearance of impropriety standard creates no incentive to avoid improprieties: actual misconduct can be controlled by refraining from it; an appearance of misconduct may be unpreventable. Indeed an appearance of impropriety standard may expose lawyers to disqualification — and may expose their clients to potential duplication, disruption, and expense — based on speculation and even innuendo.[10]

The chief difficulty with the appearance of impropriety standard, however, is that its application tends to result in decisions that, though clothed in objectivity, are in fact arbitrary. It does not follow that public perceptions should be disregarded, or that the importance of maintaining public confidence in both the administration of justice and the ethical standards of lawyers should be minimized. Standards can be developed that are much less likely than an appearance of impropriety test to lead to arbitrary and unfair results, while fully taking into account the necessity of maintaining public confidence in the process.

We will turn, then, to a consideration of those standards. They differ, of course, depending on both the types of relationships and the types of cases involved.

7 See Sopinka, *supra*, note 1, p. 2.
8 See Wolfram, *supra*, note 5, p. 318.
9 See Sopinka, *supra*, note 1, pp. 1-2.
10 See Wolfram, *supra*, note 5, pp. 322-323.

5.3 ACTING FOR ADVERSE PARTIES IN SAME LITIGATION

The most obvious conflict of interest is the representation of parties who are adverse in interest in the same litigation. Canadian rules of professional conduct provide that lawyers must not advise or represent both sides of a dispute.[11]

Occasionally, parties who in fact have only common interests may be named as opposing parties for purely formal reasons. In a 1977 case,[12] the United States Court of Appeals for the Fifth Circuit held that joint representation of the formal adversaries in such cases is permissible. It is not proper, however, for a lawyer to act for both spouses in an uncontested divorce proceeding unless all issues relating to custody, access, maintenance, and the division of the parties' property have already been determined as a result of negotiations or litigation in which each party has been independently represented. The reason for this was explained in a 1966 California case:[13]

> The attorney's professional obligations do not permit his descent to the level of a scrivener. The edge of danger gleams if the attorney has previously represented the husband. A husband and wife at the brink of division of their marital assets have an obvious divergence of interests. Representing the wife in an arm's length divorce, an attorney of ordinary professional skill would demand some certification of the husband's financial statement; or, at the minimum, inform the wife that the husband's statement was unconfirmed, that wives may be cheated, that prudence called for investigation and verification. Deprived of such disclosure, the wife cannot make a free and intelligent choice. Representing both sides in an uncontested divorce situation (whatever the ethical implications), the attorney's professional obligations demand no less. He may not set a shallow limit on the depth to which he will represent the wife.[14]

In a 1996 decision,[14.1] a lawyer was disqualified from representing the plaintiffs in an action brought against an accounting firm of which the lawyer was a former partner. Although he was not involved in the transactions that gave rise to the litigation while with the accounting firm, the plaintiffs' lawyer would be exposed to financial liability if the plaintiffs' action were successful. On behalf of his clients, the Court held, the plaintiffs' lawyers had in effect sued himself.

Although the plaintiffs had waived the apparent conflict, the Court was unwilling to give effect to the waiver in the absence of evidence that the plaintiffs

---

11 C.B.A. Code, chapter V, rule; Ontario rule 2.04(2); New Brunswick rules, Part C, rule 9.

12 *Brown & Williamson Tobacco Corp. v. Daniel International Corp.*, 563 F. 2d 671 at 673-674 (1977).

13 *Ishmael v. Millington*, 50 Cal. Rptr. 592 (1966).

14 *Ibid.*, pp. 596-597. See also John De P. Wright, "The Duty of an Advocate", Law Society of Upper Canada Gazette, vol. 17, nos. 3 and 4 (September and December, 1983), p. 327 at 344-345.

14.1 *Moffat v. Wetstein* (1996), 135 D.L.R. (4th) 298, 5 C.P.C. (4th) 128, 4 O.T.C. 364, 29 O.R. (3d) 371 (Gen. Div.).

had received independent legal advice with respect to the waiver and fully comprehended the nature of the conflict.

The Court declined to disqualify the law firm in which the plaintiffs' lawyer had been a partner. By the time the disqualification motion was heard, the plaintiffs' lawyer had withdrawn from the firm that was the solicitor of record of the plaintiffs and had become a partner in another law firm. Although the new firm could not act because of the lawyer's conflict, the Court held, his former firm was no longer at odds with the interests of its clients. It was important to this aspect of the decision that the source of the conflict was personal to the lawyer, and that the basis of the conflict was not the risk of disclosure or misuse of confidential information, but the lawyer's duty of undivided loyalty as a fiduciary.[14.2]

5.4 ACTING AGAINST CURRENT CLIENTS IN UNRELATED LITIGATION

Potential conflicts of interest also arise in the representation of clients who are adverse in interest in different but contemporaneous litigation. The propriety of such representations has not been determined conclusively by Canadian courts. It is evident that even if the two actions are entirely unrelated, and if there is accordingly little if any danger of confidential information being improperly used, for a lawyer (or firm) to simultaneously oppose in one action a person whom the lawyer (or firm) is representing in another may adversely affect the lawyer's (or firm's) loyalty to the client.[15]

Thus, in a 1966 American case,[16] a lawyer who had acted for a client in several minor matters continued to represent him in a collection claim while other lawyers in the firm brought an action for damages for assault against him. The court characterized the firm's representation in the latter action as a "reprehensible breach of loyalty."[17]

Twelve years later, the United States Court of Appeals for the Second Circuit granted another motion for an order disqualifying a law firm from acting against a client on whose behalf the firm was then acting in unrelated litigation.[18] The court rejected an argument that the motion should be dismissed on the ground that there was no substantial relationship between the two cases, and therefore no risk that confidential information would be used to the detriment of the client. Although whether there is a substantial relationship between matters is important in cases involving *former* clients, the court held, when the case involves current clients the lawyer's duty of loyalty is paramount: "The propriety of this conduct

14.2 At 384-92.

15 See C.B.A. Code, chapter V, commentary 1; Ontario rule 2.04(3) and accompanying commentary. See also Charles Wolfram, *Modern Legal Ethics* (St. Paul, Minnesota: West, 1986), pp. 351-352.

16 *Grievance Committee v. Rottner*, 203 A. 2d 82 (1964).

17 *Ibid.*, p. 85.

18 *Cinema 5, Ltd. v. Cinerama, Inc.*, 528 F. 2d 1384 (1976).

must be measured not so much against the similarities in litigation, as against the duty of undivided loyalty which an attorney owes to each of his clients."[19]

The court declined to go so far as to hold that the simultaneous representation of clients with adverse interests in unrelated matters should be prohibited absolutely, though it made it clear that a law firm must bear a heavy burden if it wishes to attempt to rebut the presumption of impropriety that the court will draw in such circumstances.[20] In a 1981 decision,[21] the same court held that the burden that a lawyer or firm must bear to rebut the presumption of impropriety is "so heavy that it will rarely be met."[22]

In some American cases,[23] however, courts have adopted a more flexible approach and have balanced the potential harm caused by allowing simultaneous adverse representations in unrelated matters against the potential harm caused to the client whose lawyer will be disqualified if the motion is granted. In these cases, the courts have recognized: that disqualification orders have immediate adverse effects on clients by separating them from counsel of their choice; that such motions are often brought for tactical reasons; and that even when they are brought in good faith such motions cause avoidable delay.[24] The weight that should be attributed to each of these factors will vary from case to case. More weight should be given to the removal of counsel of choice, for example, if the case is about to be called for trial than if the law firm has just been retained.

Balanced against these considerations are the risks that confidential information will be misused and that clients will not receive from their counsel the loyal and resolute representation to which they are entitled. Due to the risk of misuse of confidential information, where there is a substantial relationship between the matters the lawyer should not be allowed to continue to act in the absence of the free and fully informed consent of the client.

In an important 1998 decision[24.1] the House of Lords stated, *obiter dicta*, that in the absence of client consent a firm may not in any circumstances act

19 *Ibid.*, p. 1386.

20 *Ibid.*, p. 1387.

21 *Glueck v. Jonathan Logan, Inc.*, 653 F. 2d 746 (1981).

22 *Ibid.*, p. 749. See also *I.B.M. Corp. v. Levin*, 579 F. 2d 271 (3rd Cir., 1978); and *Picker International, Inc. v. Varian Associates, Inc.*, 869 F. 2d 578 (Fed. Cir., 1984) to the same effect.

23 *Board of Education v. Nyquist*, 590 F. 2d 1241 (2nd Cir., 1979); *Wong v. Fong*, 593 P. 2d 386 (1979); *Bodily v. Intermountain Health Care Corp.*, 649 F. Supp. 468 (Utah, 1986); *Aerojet Properties Inc. v. New York*, 530 N.Y.S. 2d 624 (N.Y. App., 1988); and see the dissenting judgment of Judge Archer in *Picker International Inc. v. Varian Associates, Inc.*, *ibid.*

24 *Board of Education v. Nyquist*, *ibid.*, p. 1246.

24.1 *Bolkiah v. KPMG* (1998), [1999] 2 W.L.R. 215 (U.K. H.L). Although the *Bolkiah* case involved accountants engaged in forensic work, the House of Lords acted on the accounting firm's concession that for the purposes of the case it must be treated in the same way as a firm of solicitors. The case dealt primarily with the firm's duty not to act against a former client in a related matter, and is considered in some detail in the text accompanying notes 48.1 through 48.5, *infra*.

against a current client, as it would be a breach of its fiduciary duty to do so. The House of Lords would thus reject the balancing test adopted in some of the American cases. In a 1999 decision the Ontario Divisional Court[24.2] quoted the House of Lords' dictum with approval and held that "in the unique circumstances of this case, there is a reasonable basis to believe that the [firm's fiduciary] duty may be sufficiently broad to prohibit" the firm from acting on a matter directly adverse to a continuing client. The Court found that for the purpose of a motion for an interlocutory injunction "the scope of the duty and whether there has been a breach are serious issues to be tried."[24.3]

Where the matters are unrelated, whether the lawyer should be disqualified should depend on the risk of compromised loyalty. This risk too is likely to vary significantly from case to case. If one lawyer in the Vancouver office of a national firm that was recently formed by a merger is taking instructions from the general counsel of a corporate client while another lawyer practising in the Montreal office of the firm is handling a wrongful dismissal action in which she must examine for discovery the director of human resources of a different division of the same corporation, the potential risk of diminished loyalty may be quite slight. If a lawyer is representing an individual in one action while representing an adverse party in another case in which the lawyer will be required to cross-examine vigorously the same individual to impeach his credibility, the potential for disharmony is almost certain to be dispositive.[25]

24.2 *Drabinsky v. KPMG* (1999), 10 C.B.R. (4th) 130 (Ont. Div. Ct.).

24.3 In *Moffat v. Wetstein* (1996), 135 D.L.R. (4th) 298 (Ont. Gen. Div.), leave to appeal refused (1997), 144 D.L.R. (4th) 188, 29 O.T.C. 65 (Gen. Div.) the Court based a disqualification order on the risk of the plaintiff's lawyer breaching his fiduciary duty of undivided loyalty. The Court did not disqualify the law firm, however, in which the lawyer had been a partner, in spite of the fact that it had acted for the defendant in the past and indeed was acting on its behalf on unrelated matters at the time of the motion. The Court treated the issue of the firm's possible disqualification strictly as an issue of whether was a risk of disclosure or misuse of confidential information, and was not satisfied on the evidence that there was such a risk. The issue of whether the firm would be in breach of its duty of loyalty in acting against a current client was not considered by the Court. The issue of whether a law firm has a duty of loyalty that prevents it from acting against a current client in an unrelated matter must be treated as unsettled in Canada in light of the facts that (i) the issue was not considered, though it was raised, in *Moffatt v. Wetstein*, and (ii) the conclusion reached by the Divisional Court in *Drabinsky v. KPMG* was on an appeal from an order on an interlocutory injunction motion, and the Court was accordingly required only to consider whether the possibility of such a duty raised a serious question to be tried.

25 See Nathan M. Crystal, "Disqualification of Counsel for Unrelated Matter Conflicts of Interest" (1990) 4 Georgetown Journal of Legal Ethics 273 at 291-294. See also Thomas D. Morgan, "Suing a Current Client" (1996), 9 Georgetown Journal of Legal Ethics 1157. Rule 1.7(a) of the American Bar Association's *Model Rules of Professional Conduct* provides that: "A lawyer shall not represent a client if the representation of that client will be directly adverse to another client, unless . . . the lawyer reasonably believes the representation will not adversely affect the relationship with the other client; and . . . each client consents after consultation."

Clients are free to consent to their lawyers representing adverse parties in unrelated contemporaneous litigation. However, as mentioned above, in a 1996 decision[26] on a motion to remove a lawyer who represented the plaintiffs in an action against an accounting firm in which the lawyer was a former partner, the Ontario Court of Justice (General Division) refused to give effect to the plaintiffs' waiver of the apparent conflict in the absence of evidence that the plaintiffs had received independent legal advice with respect to the waiver and fully comprehended the nature of the conflict. The consent must be fully informed and freely given.[26.1]

Again, the effectiveness of such a consent will vary depending on the circumstances. Most courts would be loath to find that a proferred client consent is both free and fully informed in a case in which a lawyer is simultaneously acting in different actions on behalf of and against the same individual client. Where different lawyers in the same firm are simultaneously acting for and against a large company with in-house counsel in completely unrelated matters, there is likely to be little reason not to give effect to the company's consent if the consent is based on adequate disclosure.

In the absence of Canadian authority,[26.2] either in the form of jurisprudence or in the form of rules of professional conduct, one is free to choose either of the approaches adopted by American courts. The more flexible balancing approach, which can give due weight to the many and variable factors represented in each case with a view to preventing unfairness to all interested parties, would be the wiser choice.

5.5 ACTING FOR CO-PARTIES IN SAME LITIGATION

The rule that a lawyer must not advise or represent both sides of a dispute[27] disqualifies lawyers from representing co-defendants and other co-parties where one or more of them has filed a cross-claim against another.

The issue of whether a lawyer is disqualified from acting for co-parties cannot always be determined, however, merely by determining from the pleadings whether the co-parties are formally aligned against each other as adversaries. Lawyers who are asked to represent co-parties have a duty to consider the possibility that each of the co-parties may have a claim against the other. If one co-party for whom the lawyer has been asked to act may have a reasonable cause of action against the other, the lawyer should proceed no further with the joint

26 *Moffat v. Wetstein* (1996), 135 D.L.R. (4th) 298, 5 C.P.C. (4th) 128, 4 O.T.C. 364, 29 O.R. (3d) 371 (Gen. Div.). See text accompanying note 14.1, *supra*.

26.1 C.B.A. Code, chapter V, rule; Ontario rule 2.04(3) and accompanying commentary.

26.2 See notes 24.1 through 24.3, *supra*, and accompanying text.

27 C.B.A. Code, chapter V, rule; Ontario rule 2.04(2).

representation unless each co-party freely consents on the basis of adequate disclosure.[28]

Whether or not it is evident at the outset that one co-party whom the lawyer is asked to represent may be entitled to assert a cross-claim against another, a lawyer asked to act for more than one client in such a situation has a duty to advise the potential clients that the lawyer has been asked to act for both or all of them, that no information received in connection with the matter from one can be treated as confidential so far as any of the others are concerned and that, if a conflict develops that cannot be resolved, the lawyer cannot continue to act for both or all of them and may have to withdraw completely.[29] If one of the co-parties is a person with whom the lawyer has a continuing relationship and for whom the lawyer acts regularly, that fact should be revealed to the other or others at the outset with a recommendation that they obtain independent representation.[30] If, after this disclosure is made the co-parties are content that the lawyer act, the lawyer should obtain the written consent of each co-party, or record their consent in a separate letter to each. Even where both or all co-parties whom the lawyer has been asked to represent are willing to consent to the same lawyer representing them, the lawyer should decline to act for more than one co-party where it is reasonably obvious that an issue contentious between them may arise or that their interests, rights or obligations will diverge as the matter progresses.[31]

Canadian rules of professional conduct recognize that fully informed clients may wish to be represented by the same lawyer despite the existence or possibility of a conflicting interest. "As important as it is to the client that the lawyer's judgment and freedom of action on the client's behalf should not be subject to other interests, duties or obligations," the rules provide, "in practice this factor may not always be decisive. Instead it may be only one of several factors that the client will weigh when deciding whether to give the consent referred to in the rule. Other factors might include, for example, the availability of another lawyer of comparable expertise and experience, the extra cost, delay and inconvenience involved in engaging another lawyer and the latter's unfamiliarity with the client and the client's affairs. In the result, the client's interest may sometimes be better served by not engaging another lawyer."[32] To the rule's list of examples may be added the avoidance of future discord and the opportunity of providing a united front.[33]

---

28 See C.B.A. Code, chapter V, rule, and commentary 4; Ontario rule 2.04(3) and accompanying commentary; and Charles Wolfram, *Modern Legal Ethics* (St. Paul, Minnesota: West, 1986), p. 353.

29 C.B.A. Code, chapter V, commentary 5; Ontario rule 2.04(6).

30 *Ibid.*

31 *Ibid.*

32 C.B.A. Code, chapter V, commentary 4; Ontario rule 2.04(3) and accompanying commentary.

33 See *Sellers v. Superior Court*, 742 P. 2d 292 at 297 (Ariz. S. Ct., 1987); and Julia Reynolds, "Conflicts of Interest: Disclosure, Consent, and Related Issues" (1988-89) 2 Georgetown Journal of Legal Ethics 143.

Unless the co-parties and the lawyer have agreed at the outset that the lawyer may continue to represent one of them in the event that an issue contentious between them arises, the lawyer should refer both or all co-parties whom he represents to other lawyers in that event.[34]

If co-parties freely consent, based on adequate disclosure, to their joint representation by the same lawyer, a motion for an order disqualifying the lawyer from acting will be granted only if an actual conflict of interest arises.[35]

In a 1994 Ontario case,[35.1] the Divisional Court (by a two-to-one majority), however, upheld a coroner's ruling disqualifying a lawyer from representing more than one party at an inquest, despite the fact that all of his clients were content that he act.

The inquest involved the death of a person shot by a police officer during an arrest. The Metropolitan Toronto Police Services Board, which was responsible for the operation of the police force, and five officers who had been involved in the incident retained the same lawyer to represent them.

The majority in the Divisional Court observed that whereas the police board had a duty to the public to attempt to determine whether a similar tragedy might be avoided in the future by such measures as improved training of police officers or changes in the operations of the police force, the chief interest of the police officers lay in preserving their reputations within the police force and in the community. The majority held that the coroner was justified in finding that the lawyer could not properly serve the interests of both the board and the officers. The majority endorsed the coroner's view that the lawyer had both an actual and an apparent conflict of interest.

In a 1996 decision,[35.2] the British Columbia Court of Appeal reversed an order requiring each of four defendants represented by the same counsel, who was appointed by the defendants' insurer, to appoint separate counsel. The plaintiffs had commenced proceedings in which they claimed damages for personal

---

34 C.B.A. Code, chapter V, commentary 6; Ontario rule 2.04(9) and accompanying commentary. The Ontario rule qualifies this obligation by adding that where no legal advice is required and the clients are sophisticated, the clients may settle the contentious issue by direct negotiation in which the lawyer does not participate.

35 As mentioned above, in *Moffat v. Wetstein* (1996), 135 D.L.R. (4th) 298, 5 C.P.C. (4th) 128, 4 O.T.C. 364, 29 O.R. (3d) 371 (Gen. Div.), the Ontario Court of Justice (General Division) refused to give effect to the plaintiffs' waiver of a conflict of interest in the absence of evidence that the plaintiffs had received independent legal advice with respect to the waiver and fully comprehended the nature of the conflict. See text accompanying notes 14.1 and 26, *supra*. See also *Vegetable Kingdom Inc. v. Katzen*, 653 F. Supp. 917 (N.D.N.Y., 1987); *cf. Hill v. Berkshire Farm Center and Service for Youth*, 521 N.Y.S. 2d 358 (N.Y.S. Ct., 1987).

35.1 *Booth v. Huxter* (1994), 16 O.R. (3d) 528 (Div. Ct.). See also Paul M. Perell, "Classifying Conflicts of Interest", Law Society of Upper Canada Gazette, vol. 28, no. 1 (March 1994), p. 11 at 17-21.

35.2 *Mara (Guardian ad litem of) v. Blake*, 134 D.L.R. (4th) 716, [1996] 10 W.W.R. 277, (*sub nom. Mara v. Blake*) 74 B.C.A.C. 296, 121 W.A.C. 296, 23 B.C.L.R. (3d) 225 (C.A.).

injuries sustained in four separate accidents. All four defendants were insured by the same insurer, who appointed the same counsel to act in all four actions.

The defendants in three of the actions admitted liability but pleaded contributory neglience. The defendant in the fourth action denied liability. The actions were ordered to be tried together.

The order requiring each of the defendants to appoint separate counsel was issued by the trial judge after a meeting in chambers immediately before the trial was scheduled to begin. The insurer objected to the trial judge's order because of the additional expense involved.

The Court of Appeal pointed out that the regulations to the province's *Insurance (Motor Vehicle) Act* grant to insurers the exclusive right to control and conduct the defence to actions against insured persons.

The Court added that while a court is always free to point out to counsel any perceived conflicts, it should exercise its inherent jurisdiction to interfere with a litigant's choice of counsel "with the highest level of restraint", and only where the administration of justice is threatened, particularly in the absence of objection by either the insured or the plaintiffs.

The issue of the propriety of a lawyer representing co-parties often arises when an employer as well as employees are named as co-defendants. In such cases a lawyer who is asked to act for both the employer and the employees should consider the possibilities that the employer may seek to escape liability by showing that the employees acted outside the scope of their authority, and that the employees may seek to shift responsibility to their employer by showing that they acted in good faith in accordance with policies established by the employer. If the employer acknowledges that the employees were acting within the scope of their employment and the employees have a binding indemnification agreement, joint representation is permissible with the informed consent of the employees.[36] The courts are reluctant to make what may be premature orders preventing lawyers from continuing to act, and accordingly will remove solicitors of record in such circumstances only in cases of actual conflict, for example where one or more defendants implicate others.[36.1]

Lawyers should be alert to the possibility of conflicts of interest among potential co-parties even before litigation is commenced, and even where they have no intention of representing more than one party. An example will illustrate the need for such caution.

A lawyer receives a telephone call from a municipality that her firm regularly represents. The municipality has just received a notice of a civil claim against it that is being asserted by a motorist who says that she was stopped for a traffic

36 See *Chapman v. 3M Canada Inc.* (1995), 25 O.R. (3d) 658, 43 C.P.C. (3d) 142 (Gen. Div.); and *Wolfram, supra*, note 28, p. 354.

36.1 *Chapman v. 3M Canada Inc.* (1995), 25 O.R. (3d) 658, 43 C.P.C. (3d) 142 (Gen. Div.); see also *Laidlaw Environmental Services (Sarnia) Ltd. v. Ontario (Ministry of Environment and Energy)* (1997), 32 O.R. (3d) 795 (Gen. Div.).

violation by a police officer employed by the municipality's police force, and that the officer used unnecessary force and racial epithets. The municipality asks the lawyer to act for it, and the lawyer arranges to meet that afternoon with the police officer to begin a preliminary investigation.

The lawyer tells the officer upon meeting him that she has been asked by the municipality to defend the claim. During the meeting, the officer acknowledges that he pushed the motorist against the trunk of the officer's car and used a racial slur in an attempt to intimidate the motorist into compliance.

Shortly thereafter, the lawyer realizes that the interests of the municipality and the officer are not entirely congruent and telephones the officer to make it clear to him that she cannot act for him. The next day, the lawyer receives a call from a lawyer who has been retained by the officer. The officer's lawyer says that when the officer met with the municipality's lawyer he did so on the basis of his understanding that she was acting for both the municipality and him, and that he disclosed confidential information to her based on that belief. The officer's lawyer threatens to bring a motion for an order disqualifying the municipality's lawyer from acting if necessary.[37]

It is probably reasonable on these facts for the police officer to believe that the lawyer was representing him, though she did not say so or intend to do so. The officer's meeting with the lawyer resembled an initial meeting between a client and his lawyer, and the lawyer did not disabuse the officer of the idea that what he told her would remain confidential.

Although it may seem absurd to suggest that a lawyer may acquire a client unintentionally, it is not unfair to impose on the lawyer in such a case the onus of making it clear that she has agreed to act only for the municipality, that she cannot act for the officer if his interest and that of the municipality diverge, that what he tells her will not be privileged if she does not act for him, that what he tells her will be divulged to her client, the municipality, in any event, that he is not required to answer any of her questions, and that he should consider retaining an independent lawyer.[38]

Unless a discussion along these lines takes place, the lawyer risks disqualification.[39] It is clear that the solicitor-client privilege extends to protect persons who meet with a lawyer with the intention of retaining the lawyer to act for them, whether or not the lawyer is ultimately retained.[40]

37 The example is from Debra Bassett Perschbacher and Rex R. Perschbacher, "Enter At Your Own Risk: The Initial Consultation and Conflicts of Interest" (1989-90) 3 Georgetown Journal of Legal Ethics 689 at 689-690.

38 See C.B.A. Code, chapter V, commentary 5; Ontario rule 2.04(6), (7) and (8) and accompanying commentary; and Perschbacher, *ibid.*, pp. 704-705.

39 See C.B.A. Code, chapter V, rule; Ontario rule 2.04(3).

40 *Westinghouse Electric Corp.* v. *Kerr-McGee Corp.*, 580 F. 2d 1311 at 1319 (7th Cir.), cert. denied 439 U.S. 955 (1978).

5.6 ACTING AGAINST FORMER CLIENTS

Canadian rules of professional conduct provide that a lawyer who has acted for a client in a matter should not thereafter act against the client (or against persons who were involved in or associated with the client in that matter) in the same or any related matter, or take a position where the lawyer might be tempted or appear to be tempted to breach the rule relating to confidential information. The rule also provides that it is not, however, improper for the lawyer to act against a former client in a fresh and independent matter wholly unrelated to any work the lawyer has previously done for that person.[41]

As a result of an amendment in 2000, the Law Society of Upper Canada's *Rules of Professional Conduct* now permit the partner or associate of a lawyer who has acted for a former client and obtained relevant confidential information, to act in a new matter against the former client if the law firm establishes that it is in the interests of justice that it act in the new matter having regard to all relevant circumstances, including (i) the adequacy and timing of the measures taken to ensure that no disclosure of the former client's confidential information to the lawyer having carriage of the new matter will occur, (ii) the extent of prejudice to any party, (iii) the good faith of the parties, (iv) the availability of suitable alternative counsel, and (v) issues affecting the public interest.[41.1]

A person may be a client for the purpose of this rule even if the lawyer chooses not to act for the person after a brief consultation. The same result may follow if the lawyer participates in a "beauty contest" in which a potential client interviews a number of lawyers about the prospect of their acting as counsel on a matter, even where the client chooses not to retain the lawyer. The question in each case is whether the person seeking disqualification has demonstrated that the consultation was such as to create a presumption that the lawyer received confidential information relevant to the matter.[41.2]

Similarly, a lawyer (or firm) may be precluded from acting against a former executive of a corporate client where the former executive has imparted information to the lawyer (or firm) and has a reasonable expectation that the information will be maintained in confidence.

In a 1995 Alberta case,[41.3] however, the Court of Appeal dismissed a motion to disqualify a law firm from acting for a longstanding corporate client in an action against a former principal of the company based upon an alleged diversion

41 C.B.A. Code, chapter V, commentary 8; Ontario rule 2.04(4) and accompanying commentary.

41.1 Ontario rule 2.04(5) and accompanying commentary.

41.2 See *Popowich v. Saskatchewan* (1995), [1996] 1 W.W.R. 215 (Sask. C.A.), reversing [1995] 6 W.W.R. 314 (Sask. Q.B.); *Holizki v. Reeves* (1997), 10 C.P.C. (4th) 63 (Sask. Q.B.); and *Ainsworth Electric Co. v. Alcatel Canada Wire Inc.* (1998), 40 O.R. (3d) 123 (Master).

41.3 *Gainers Inc. v. Pocklington* (1995), 29 Alta. L.R. (3d) 323 (Alta. C.A.). The Saskatchewan Court of Appeal came to the same conclusion on similar facts in *International Capital Corp. v. Schafer* (*sub nom. Schafer v. International Capital Corp.*), [1997] 8 W.W.R. 412 (Sask. C.A.).

of assets of the company. Although the principal had consulted with the law firm and discussed his business philosophy nine years earlier, he had his own personal lawyers at all times. The Court held that the principal did not have a reasonable expectation that what he told the law firm would be kept secret from the company, and concluded that the possibility of harm resulting from the law firm continuing to act was unlikely.

In a 1997 decision of the Ontario Court of Justice (General Division),[41.4] counsel for the petitioner in matrimonial proceedings was removed from the record on the ground that his wife had represented the respondent in the past. Although there was no solicitor-client relationship between the petitioner's counsel himself and the respondent, the Court held that a reasonably informed person would believe that confidential information provided to the petitioner's counsel's wife would be used in the current retainer.

The crucial question in cases in which the propriety of lawyers acting against former clients is in issue is whether the new matter is "related" to the former representation. The issue of whether the lawyer might be tempted or appear to be tempted to breach the rule relating to confidential information will generally be co-extensive with the issue of whether the current and former representations are related: a lawyer generally will not be precluded from acting against a former client in an unrelated matter if the only confidential information the lawyer received in the former representation is irrelevant to the new matter.[42]

In fact, the authorities make it clear that the very purpose of inquiring into whether former and current representations are related is to avoid having to inquire into whether the lawyer acquired from the client confidential information that could be misused. The latter inquiry should be avoided because its determination is likely to require the revelation of the confidential information for which the client seeks protection, thereby defeating the whole purpose of the application. To determine the issue based on a lawyer's bare denial in circumstances in which the client is helpless to contradict the denial is an unsatisfactory alternative.[43]

Nevertheless, a bald assertion by the former client that the lawyer it seeks to remove has had access to documents that may be relevant to the current retainer, is insufficient to discharge the onus on the applicant of showing that the matters are related. Thus, in a 1996 case,[43.1] a defendant asserted that in acting for it previously, the plaintiffs' law firm had access to insurance policies, partnership

---

41.4 *Goldstein v. Friedmann* (1997), 32 O.R. (3d) 212 (Gen. Div.).

42 The Ontario rule (rule 2.04(4) and accompanying commentary) makes this clear; *Messinger v. Bramalea Ltd.* (1989), 35 C.P.C. (2d) 260 (Ont. H.C.), in which solicitors were removed from the record on the ground that they had previously prepared a will for a party adverse in interest in unrelated litigation is contrary to the weight of authority.

43 *MacDonald Estate v. Martin*, [1990] 3 S.C.R. 1235 at 1260-1261, *per* Sopinka J. See also *Analytica, Inc. v. NPD Research, Inc.*, 708 F. 2d 1263 (7th Cir., 1983); and *T.C. Theatre Corp. v. Warner Bros. Pictures, Inc.*, 113 F. Supp. 265 (S.D.N.Y., 1953).

43.1 *Moffat v. Wetstein* (1996), 29 O.R. (3d) 371, 135 D.L.R. (4th) 298, 5 C.P.C. (4th) 128, 4 O.T.C. 364 (Gen. Div.).

agreements, and its litigation philosophy. The Ontario Court of Justice (General Division) held that though confidential information of this type could in some cases justify disqualification, in light of the drastic nature of such a remedy the court should require cogent and compelling evidence that the prior relationship is sufficiently related to the present retainer to justify the denial of a party's *prima facie* right to be represented by counsel of its choice. Although an applicant need not divulge the specifics of the confidential information it seeks to protect, it should at least describe how the law firm acquired the information and why it is related to the new matter, so that the court is not left to guess at the type of documents and information to which the firm has been privy.[43.2] The Alberta Court of Appeal came to a similar conclusion in a 1997 decision.[43.3]

The Ontario Court of Justice (General Division) in a 1999 case[43.4] was also unwilling to grant a disqualification motion in the absence of cogent evidence that confidential information gained by a lawyer in the past may be, or

(*Continued on page 5–15*)

43.2 At 400-01.

43.3 *Trizec Properties Ltd. v. Husky Oil Ltd.* (1997), 200 A.R. 48, 146 W.A.C. 48, (*sub nom. Trizec Properties Ltd. v. Husky Oil Operations, Ltd.*) 148 D.L.R. (4th) 300 (C.A.), additional reasons at (August 19, 1997), Doc. Calgary Appeal 97-176951 (Alta. C.A.).

43.4 *Ontario New Home Warranty Program v. Campbell* (February 10, 1999), Doc. 98-CV-161622 (Ont. Gen. Div.).

may be perceived to be, impartial. The Court was unwilling to find a relationship sufficient to justify disqualification despite the fact that the lawyer had acted as exclusive outside counsel to the moving party for 17 years.

From 1977 until 1994 the defendant had acted as exclusive outside counsel to the plaintiffs. For three years after that he had continued to act for the plaintiffs on some matters, though not on an exclusive basis. In 1998 he ceased to act for the plaintiffs.

The defendant then sent two form letters and a newsletter to residential home builders, a group likely to be involved in litigation against the plaintiffs. The newsletter included statements in which the defendant challenged the practices, policies and legal authority of the plaintiffs in their dealings with builders. The letters and newsletter were communications designed to solicit new clients based upon the defendant's representation that he had acquired expertise through acting as counsel to the plaintiffs. Some of the language and content was at least inappropriate, particularly as the comments related to a former client.

The defendant accepted retainers from a number of builders who retained him to act in proceedings in which the plaintiffs were adverse in interest. The plaintiffs commenced the present action and brought a motion for an interlocutory injunction to restrain the defendant from acting in matters in which the plaintiffs were adverse in interest on the ground that to do so would place the defendant in a conflict of interest.

The plaintiffs put their case on the basis that the defendant was necessarily in a conflict of interest in every case in which he acted for a party adverse in interest to the plaintiffs. The plaintiffs introduced evidence that they had discussed with the defendant all the most sensitive legal issues affecting them, and that the defendant was familiar with their strategies in and approach to litigation, and the issues the plaintiffs felt should be resolved through negotiation. The plaintiffs also introduced evidence that the defendant had become acquainted not only with the personnel employed by the plaintiffs who made decisions about litigation and settlement, but also with technical personnel whom he had prepared to testify. The plaintiffs asserted that the defendant's knowledge of the individual strengths and weaknesses of these employees gave him an unfair advantage.

There was a conflict in the evidence on the question of what confidential information the defendant had acquired that may be relevant to his new retainers. The defendant's evidence was that he was retained on a file-by-file basis and this opinions were case specific. The plaintiffs' evidence was that many of the issues on which the defendant's advice was sought were issues of a general nature that would equally pertain to many files past, present and in the future. To preserve privilege, the plaintiffs properly avoided references to specific confidential communications in the affidavit filed in support of their motion. When invited by the Court to provide further affidavit evidence subject to a confidentiality order, however, the plaintiffs declined to do so.

The Court dismissed the plaintiffs' motion. It did not necessarily follow from the extent of the parties' prior professional relationship alone, the Court held, that the defendant has acquired confidential information relevant to virtually any current or future matter involving the plaintiffs. To establish that the previous relationship is sufficiently related to the present matters to imply that confidential information may be (or may be perceived to be) imparted required cogent evidence of the confidential information acquired in the past as it relates to the present matters. The broad generalities in the evidence introduced by the plaintiffs was inadequate to satisfy the requirements established both by the case law and by commentary 13 to rule 5 of the Law Society of Upper Canada's *Rules of Professional Conduct*, namely, that to justify disqualification the former client must show that the lawyer acquired information that was both confidential and related to the present matter.

Once it is shown that the former representation is related to the present representation, courts will generally presume that confidential information was imparted to the lawyer. In a 1997 Ontario case[43.5] however, the Court found that though the prior retainer was indirectly related to the lawyer's new retainer, the lawyer received no confidential information relevant to the new matter. The Court also found that the previous relationship was not "sufficiently" related to the new matter to justify a presumption that confidential information was imparted to the lawyer.

In cases in which the court presumes from the relationship of the former matter to the new matter that confidential information has been imparted to the lawyer, the Supreme Court of Canada has now made it clear that the presumption is rebuttable. The burden on the lawyer is a most difficult one to discharge, however, as the lawyer must satisfy the court that no information was imparted during the prior representation that could be relevant, without disclosing the specifics of any confidential communications that were exchanged. It is likely that any doubts regarding the alleged disclosure of confidential information will be resolved in favour of the former client. This heavy burden may be discharged, however, in cases in which it is established beyond any reasonable doubt that no confidential information relevant to the current matter was disclosed, as for example where the applicant client admits on cross-examination that that is the case.[44]

43.5 *Sun Life Trust Co. v. Bond City Financing Ltd.* (1997), 35 O.R. (3d) 83 (Gen. Div. [Commercial List]), additional reasons at (1997), 26 O.T.C. 207 (Ont. Gen. Div. [Commercial List]), affirmed (1997), 36 O.R. (3d) 758 (Div. Ct.), leave to appeal refused (March 10, 1998), Doc. CA M21773 (Ont. C.A.).

44 *MacDonald Estate v. Martin*, *ibid.*, pp. 1260-1261. See also *Re Columbia Realty Associates Ltd.*, 71 Bankr. 804 at 810 (Bankr. N.D. Ill., 1987). In a number of American cases, courts have held that this presumption is irrebuttable: see, for example, *Kempner v. Oppenheimer & Co.*, 662 F. Supp. 1271 at 1277 (S.D.N.Y., 1987). See also *Aptowitzer v. Ontario* (1995), 23 O.R. (3d) 315 (Gen. Div.).

In a 1987 American case,[45] the court held that the presumption was rebutted where the evidence was that the lawyer in question during the prior representation had been an associate at a large firm that had acted for the applicant in complex litigation in which the associate's role was confined to summarizing depositions and cataloguing discovery that was turned over to the opposite party. The associate had devoted 350 hours to those tasks. It is doubtful that a Canadian court would find the presumption rebutted on such evidence based upon the heavy onus that the lawyer must discharge, as described by the Supreme Court of Canada.

Traditionally, to obtain an order disqualifying a lawyer from acting for an adversary based on the lawyer's prior representation of a client, the applicant was required to show "that there is a real mischief and real prejudice which in all human probability will result if the solicitor is allowed to act."[46] The "mischief" contemplated was the possible misuse of confidential information by the lawyer against a former client.[47]

The Supreme Court of Canada has now made it clear, however, that the probability of real mischief test imposes an unduly onerous burden on the former client, and that once it is established that the former and current matters are related, the court need only be satisfied that there is a mere "possibility of real mischief."[48]

The House of Lords also repudiated the probability of real mischief test in a leading 1998 decision.[48.1] Because the decision may influence significantly the approach that will be adopted by Canadian courts in future, it is worthwhile to consider it in some detail.

In this case the House of Lords considered for the first time the question of whether, and if so in what circumstances, a professional firm that has provided litigation support services to a former client may be enjoined from

---

45 *Roth v. Continental Casualty Co.*, 676 F. Supp 816 (N.D. Ill., 1987); *cf. Crawford W. Long Memorial Hospital of Emory University v. Yerby*, 373 S.E. 2d 749 (S. Ct. Ga., 1988).

46 *Rakusen v. Ellis, Munday & Clarke*, [1911-13] All E.R. 813 at 814 (H.L.), *per* Cozens-Hardy M.R., followed in *Mercator Enterprises Ltd. v. Harris* (1978), 29 N.S.R. (2d) 703 (T.D.); *Christo v. Bevan* (1982), 28 R.F.L. (2d) 197 at 200 (Ont. H.C.); *Aldrich v. Struk* (1986), 26 D.L.R. (4th) 352 (B.C. S.C.); *O'Dea v. O'Dea* (1987), 68 Nfld. & P.E.I.R. 67 (Nfld. U.F.C.); *Winter v. Phillips*, [1988] 2 W.W.R. 458 (Alta. Q.B.); *Landru v. Landru*, [1989] 3 W.W.R. 705 (Sask. C.A.); *Dalfen's Ltd. v. Bay Roberts Shopping Centre Ltd.* (1989), 78 Nfld. & P.E.I.R. 128 (Nfld. T.D.); *Barry v. Law Society (New Brunswick)* (1989), 100 N.B.R. (2d) 245 (Q.B.); *Farm-Rite Equipment Ltd. (Receiver of) v. Robinson Alamo Sales Ltd.* (1989), 78 Sask. R. 161 (C.A.); and *Brar v. Brar*, [1990] 3 W.W.R. 495 (Sask. Q.B.), among other cases.

47 *MacDonald Estate v. Martin*, [1990] 3 S.C.R. 1235 at 1260-1261.

48 *Ibid.*, pp. 1259-1263. See also *Carson v. Law Society (Saskatchewan)* (1975), 61 D.L.R. (3d) 652 at 672 (Sask. C.A.); *Canada Southern Railway v. Kingsmill, Jennings* (1978), 8 C.P.C. 117 at 120 (Ont. H.C.); *Christo v. Bevan* (1982), 28 R.F.L. (2d) 197 at 200 (Ont. H.C.); and *Princess Auto & Machinery Ltd. v. Winnipeg (City)* (1991), 73 Man. R. (2d) 311 (C.A.).

48.1 *Bolkiah v. KPMG* (1998), [1999] 2 W.L.R. 215 (U.K. H.L.).

undertaking work for another client with an adverse interest. The professional firm affected, KPMG, conceded that an accounting firm that provides litigation support services of the kind it provided to its former client must be treated for purposes of this case in the same way as solicitors. The House of Lords acted on this concession, though Lord Millett (in a speech in which each of the other members of the House of Lords joined) added that the duties of accountants in other circumstances may be less exacting than those of solicitors, in that information relating to clients' affairs in a solicitor's possession is usually privileged as well as confidential.

KPMG had been retained to perform the annual audit of the Brunei Investment Agency (BIA) since its establishment in 1983. Over a period of 18 months between 1996 and 1998, KPMG was also retained by the plaintiff Prince Jefri Bolkiah to undertake a significant investigation in connection with major litigation in which he was personally involved. Prince Jefri was the Chair of BIA at that time. The investigation was given the code name Project Lucy.

Project Lucy involved KPMG's forensic accounting department in tasks usually undertaken by solicitors, including interviewing witnesses, communicating and meeting with counsel, drafting subpoenas, and preparing ideas for cross-examination. KPMG acquired extensive confidential information concerning Prince Jefri's assets and financial affairs.

Members of the team who worked on Project Lucy were instructed that the assignment was exceptionally confidential and should not be discussed outside the team. Team members were forbidden from taking work home to avoid the risk of documents being stolen or mislaid.

The litigation was settled in March 1998. In July 1998 the Government of Brunei appointed a Task Force to investigate the activities of BIA. KPMG was instructed to assist. It became clear at that time that the assignment would be at least in part adverse to Prince Jefri's interests, and may indeed lead to civil and even criminal proceedings against Prince Jefri. Prince Jefri was removed as Chair of BIA.

The further assignment was given the code name Project Gemma. Project Gemma was to be undertaken by members of the forensic accounting department. At least some of the confidential information obtained by KPMG in the course of Project Lucy was or might be relevant to Project Gemma.

KPMG did not inform Prince Jefri about Project Gemma, or seek his consent to the firm's acceptance of the new retainer.

KPMG employed 50 people on Project Gemma. Eleven of these had previously been engaged on work for Prince Jefri, but KPMG contended that none of the 11 was in possession of information confidential to Prince Jefri.

When KPMG accepted instructions on Project Gemma an information barrier (popularly known as a "Chinese Wall") was put in place within the forensic accounting department. Staff were selected to work on Project Gemma in a way intended to ensure that no one in possession of information confidential to Prince Jefri would be permitted to work on the new assignment. Staff who had done work of a minor administrative nature on Project Lucy were permitted to work on Project Gemma but only after KPMG satisfied itself that they were not in possession of information confidential to Prince Jefri.

The House of Lords observed that until the present case the controlling authority in England was a 1912 decision of the Court of Appeal[48.2] that stood for two propositions: (i) that there is no absolute rule of law that a solicitor may not act in litigation against a former client; and (ii) that a solicitor may be restrained from acting if such a restriction is necessary to avoid a significant risk of the disclosure or misuse of confidential information belonging to the former client.

The House of Lords affirmed that the basis of the court's jurisdiction to intervene on behalf of a former client is the protection of confidential information, not the avoidance of any perception of possible impropriety. It added that is is otherwise where the court's intervention is sought by an existing client: a fiduciary cannot act at the same time both for and against the same client. In such a case disqualification has nothing to do with the confidentiality of client information; it is based on the inescapable conflict of interest inherent in the situation. Clients nevertheless may consent to their solicitors or accountants acting against them, and in some situations consent may be inferred.

Where the court's intervention is sought by a former client the court's jurisdiction is not based on either real or perceived conflict of interest, for there is none, Lord Millett observed. The fiduciary relationship between solicitor and client comes to an end with the termination of the retainer. Thereafter the solicitor has no obligation to defend and advance the interests of the former client. The only duty to the former client that survives the termination of the client relationship is a continuing duty to preserve the confidentiality of information imparted during its subsistence.

The burden is on the plaintiff in such a case to establish (i) that the solicitor is in possession of information that is confidential to the client and (ii) that the information is or may be relevant to the new matter in which the interest of the other client is or may be adverse. Lord Millett added that this burden is not a heavy one.

The House of Lords held that, given the basis on which the court's jurisdiction is exercised, there is no need to impute the knowledge of one partner to others. In this regard, the House of Lords chose not to follow the jurisprudence of the United States.

The duty to preserve confidentiality, the House of Lords also held, is unqualified. It is a duty to keep the information confidential, not merely to take all reasonable steps to do so. A former client is entitled to prevent a

48.2 *Rakusen v. Ellis*, [1912] 1 Ch. 831 (Eng. C.A.).

solicitor from exposing him or her to any avoidable risk, including the increased risk of the use of the information to his or her prejudice as a result of the acceptance of instructions to act for another client with an adverse interest in a matter to which the information is or may be relevant.

For this reason, the House of Lords rejected the Court of Appeal's statement of the applicable test in 1912, *i.e.* that the court will not intervene unless it is satisfied that there is a "real probability of real mischief." Such a test would place an unfair burden on former clients, expose them to potential and avoidable risks to which they have not consented, and fail to give them a sufficient assurance that their confidences will be respected.

The House of Lords also held that the court should intervene unless it is satisfied that there is no risk of disclosure. The risk must be real, and not just fanciful or theoretical, but it need not be substantial.

A balancing test, such as that adopted by the Court of Appeal in the present case, is inappropriate, the House of Lords held. No solicitor should, without the consent of the former client, should accept instructions unless, viewed objectively, doing so will not increase the risk that information that is confidential to the former client may come into the possession of a party with an adverse interest.

Once the former client has discharged the burden of establishing that the defendant firm is in possession of information that was imparted in confidence and that the firm is proposing to act for another party adverse in interest in a matter to which the confidential information is relevant, the evidential burden shifts to the defendant firm to show that there is no risk that the information will come into the possession of those now acting for the other party. There is no rule of law that Chinese Walls are insufficient to eliminate the risk, but the starting point must be that unless special measures are taken information moves within a firm. The House of Lords cited Justice Sopinka's statement in the leading Canadian case on conflicts of interest in the legal profession,[48.3] that the court should restrain the firm from acting "unless satisfied on the basis of clear and convincing evidence that all reasonable measures have been taken to ensure that no disclosure will occur", and adopted this formulation of the test with the substitution of the word "effective" for the words "all reasonable".

Finally, the House of Lords held that an effective Chinese Wall needs to be an established part of the organizational structure of the firm, rather than created *ad hoc* and dependent on the acceptance of evidence sworn for the purpose by members of staff engaged on the relevant work. It emphasized that established institutional arrangements designed to prevent the flow of information between separate departments of a firm are much more likely to be found to be effective by the courts than arrangements put in place within the same department in a particular case.

48.3 *MacDonald Estate v. Martin*, (*sub nom. Martin v. Gray*) [1990] 3 S.C.R. 1235.

The House of Lords was not satisfied that KPMG had discharged the heavy burden of showing that there was no risk that information in its possession that was confidential to Prince Jefri may unwittingly come to the notice of those working on Project Gemma. The appeal was accordingly allowed and an injunction granted.

It will be interesting to see whether Canadian courts adopt a number of aspects of this important judgment. Four aspects of the judgment bear watching in future.

First is the House of Lords' distinction between the bases for disqualification where the application is brought by a former client rather than a current one. In the latter case the basis of disqualification is the duty of loyalty. In the former case the basis of disqualification, however, is not the duty of loyalty or indeed conflict of interest at all; it is, rather, the duty to maintain former clients' confidences. Canadian rules of professional conduct deal with duties to former clients in commentaries to conflict of interest rules.[48.4] Rules of professional conduct treat the duty of confidentiality, as well as the duty of loyalty, to underlie conflict of interest rules.

Second, the House of Lords clearly suggests, *obiter dicta*, that in the absence of client consent a firm may not in any circumstances act against a current client. This issue has not been definitively settled in Canada, and American decisions conflict.[48.5]

Third, the extent to which accountants are made subject to a standard less exacting than that applicable to lawyers in cases involving accountants doing work other than forensic accounting or litigation support, remains to be determined.

Finally, the unqualified nature of the duty to maintain confidentiality, and the strictness of the standard applied by the House of Lords as a result, if followed in Canada, would make it difficult for firms to satisfy the courts that Chinese Walls are effective to prevent the disclosure or use of confidential information in any case in which a disqualification motion is brought by a former client. Virtually all Chinese Walls in Canadian law firms are erected *ad hoc* to respond to concerns arising in particular cases. Chinese Walls between departments are not normally "an established part of the organizational structure of the firm."

The decision of the House of Lords is of particular interest in Canada because it was released within a few weeks of a well-publicized decision of the Ontario Court of Justice (General Division)[48.6] in a case which, coincidentally, involved the same accounting firm, KPMG, as did the case decided by the House of Lords.

48.4 See, for example, *C.B.A. Code*, chapter V, commentary 8, and Ontario rules 2.04(4) and (5) and accompanying commentary.

48.5 The subject of acting against current clients in unrelated litigation is dealt with in section 5.4 *supra*.

48.6 *Drabinsky v. KPMG* (1998), 41 O.R. (3d) 565 (Gen. Div.), leave to appeal allowed (November 4, 1998), Doc. Toronto 664/98 (Ont. Div. Ct.), affirmed (1999), 10 C.B.R. (4th) 130 (Ont. Div. Ct.).

The Court followed the decision of first instance that was ultimately upheld by the House of Lords (after having been reversed by the Court of Appeal).

The plaintiff brought a motion for an interlocutory injunction restraining KPMG from further participating in a pending investigation into financial records of Livent Inc., a company of which the plaintiff had been a senior officer, on the ground that KPMG had acted as the plaintiff's tax advisor for many years, in which capacity it had obtained confidential information from the plaintiff. The motion was granted.

The Court held that the fiduciary duty between a client and professional advisor, either a lawyer or accountant, imposed duties beyond the duty not to disclose confidential information, including a duty of loyalty and good faith and a duty not to act against the interests of the client.

The Court held that accountants offering forensic services were subject to obligations similar to those imposed on solicitors. It left open the question whether accountants offering other services (including audits) stand in a different position.

The Court ruled that the question whether KPMG absolved itself of any breach of fiduciary duty by erecting a Chinese Wall to prevent the disclosure of confidential information to its investigative team, was a question to be determined at trial.

Accordingly, the Court ordered that KPMG be restrained from undertaking any further investigative work pursuant to Livent's retainer; that KPMG deliver to the plaintiff a draft report of its investigation containing only the results of objective fact finding without expressions of opinion or conclusion; that the plaintiff be given five business days thereafter to satisfy himself that the draft complies with the court order or to apply to the court for a determination of that question; and that KPMG be restrained from disclosing any of the plaintiff's confidential information.

The decision was upheld on appeal by the Divisional Court,[48.7] which quoted with approval the *obiter dictum* of the House of Lords in the decision discussed at length above (which had by then been released) to the effect that a fiduciary cannot act at the same time both for and against the same client. The Divisional Court found that the fiduciary duty *may* be sufficiently broad to protect KPMG from acting adverse to its continuing client, the plaintiff, and that the scope of the duty and whether there was a breach were serious issues to be tried.

In most cases, the question whether the former and current representations are related presents little difficulty. In an 1987 American decision,[49] the court developed a three-stage procedure. First, the court must undertake a factual reconstruction of the scope of the prior legal representation. Second, the court must determine whether it is reasonable to infer that the confidential information allegedly disclosed would have been disclosed to a lawyer representing a client in

48.7 *Drabinsky v. KPMG* (1999), 10 C.B.R. (4th) 130 (Ont. Div. Ct.).

49 *Re Nine West Division*, 78 Bankr. 189 (Bankr. N.D. Ill., 1987).

those circumstances. Finally, the court must determine whether that information

(*Continued on page 5-17*)

is relevant to the issues raised in the litigation in which the former client is now a party.[50]

The rule that lawyers must not act against former clients in related matters without the informed consent of the former clients is designed to protect clients not only against breaches by lawyers of their duty of confidentiality, but also against breaches by lawyers of their duty of loyalty. Thus, courts have consistently decided that in litigation arising out of a transaction in which a lawyer acted for both parties, the lawyer must not act for one of the parties against the other.[51] It is no answer to a motion for a disqualification order for the lawyer to say that both parties agreed that no information received from either of them could be treated as confidential so far as the other was concerned.[52]

There are at least two reasons that lawyers should be enjoined from acting against former clients in related matters even if there is no risk of confidential information being misused. The first is the danger that in the original representation the lawyer might consciously or subconsciously fail to protect one client's interest adequately due to a desire to leave the door open to future representations of the other, perhaps more affluent, client.[53] The second reason focuses not on the former client but the surviving or succeeding client. The danger is that the client for whom the lawyer acts in the second matter may receive a less vigorous representation than that to which all clients are entitled because the lawyer may (again, consciously or subconsciously) "go easy" on the former client. Most lawyers, for example, are likely to find it more difficult to cross-examine aggressively a former client than a stranger.[54]

A disqualification motion brought on behalf of a former client may be dismissed despite proof that the prior representation is related to the present representation if the former client delays bringing the motion. In a 1991 Ontario case,[55] the court refused to remove the defendant's solicitors, though their removal would otherwise have been warranted, because the former client delayed more than two years before bringing the motion. It would be unfair to require a party

---

50 *Ibid.*, p. 190.

51 See, for example, *Eastholme Realty Ltd. v. Grundy*, [1954] O.W.N. 583 (C.A.); *Sinclair v. Ridout*, [1955] O.R. 167 (H.C.); *R. v. Burkinshaw* (1967), 60 D.L.R. (2d) 748 (Alta. T.D.); *MTS International Services Inc. v. Warnat Corp.* (1980), 31 O.R. (2d) 221 (H.C.); *Goldberg v. Goldberg* (1982), 141 D.L.R. (3d) 133 (Ont. Div. Ct.); *Flynn Developments Ltd. v. Central Trust Co.* (1985), 51 O.R. (2d) 57 (H.C.); and *Bow Valley Energy Inc. v. San Diego Gas and Electric Co.* (1995), 36 Alta. L.R. (3d) 269, 43 C.P.C. (3d) 384, [1996] 4 W.W.R. 115, 179 A.R. 75 (Q.B.), affirmed (1996), 38 Alta. L.R. (3d) 116, 181 A.R. 261, 116 W.A.C. 261, 48 C.P.C. (3d) 99 (C.A.).

52 The issue was squarely raised and decided in *E.F. Hutton & Co. v. Brown*, 305 F. Supp. 371 (S.D. Tex., 1969). See also C.B.A. Code, chapter V, commentaries 5 and 8, and Ontario rules 2.04(4) and (6) and accompanying commentary.

53 See Charles Wolfram, *Modern Legal Ethics* (St. Paul, Minnesota: West, 1986), p. 362.

54 *Ibid.*, p. 362.

55 *Ramsbottom v. Morning* (1991), 48 C.P.C. (2d) 177 (Ont. Gen. Div.).

to give up the right to be represented by counsel of the party's choice after having been represented by that counsel for such an extended period, the court held.[55.1]

Similarly, in a 1987 decision,[56] the California Court of Appeals developed a narrow exception to the usual rule in a case in which the moving party knew of the conflict of interest for at least three years before bringing a motion to disqualify the opposing party's counsel. During the three year period, the opposing party's counsel had engaged in "over 3000 hours of litigation effort at a cost of $387,000."[57]

Canadian courts have repeatedly affirmed that solicitors of record should not be removed where a disqualification motion is brought not because of a genuine concern about the possible breach of a lawyer's duties of confidentiality or loyalty, but because of a desire to frustrate or delay an opponent or otherwise secure a tactical advantage in litigation.[57.1] Thus in a 1992 decision[57.2] the Chief Justice of the British Columbia Supreme Court stated as follows:

> "Until very recently, applications to remove lawyers were so rare an event that, at least in this jurisdiction, few judges or lawyers seemed to be more than vaguely aware that such a remedy existed. Nor, so far as I am aware, was there any general feeling of discontent on the part of the public arising from the possibility of conflict. But there was and is a rising tide of discontent with the length, complexity and cost of proceedings. Since *MacDonald Estate v. Martin*, the application to disqualify has become a growth area as it began to do 20 or so years ago in the United States where it seems to have reached the stage of being a common feature of major litigation. No doubt, some of those applications are brought to prevent a risk of real mischief. But can there be any doubt that many are brought simply because an application to disqualify has become a weapon which can be used, amongst many others, to discomfit the opposite party by adding to the length, cost and agony of litigation? If that becomes a regular feature of our litigation it would not likely do much to improve the profession's standards in an area in which there seem to have been few serious problems. But it could do much to further reduce the court's ability to get judgment in a timely way."

Similarly, in a 1993 decision of the Saskatchewan Queen's Bench[57.3], the Court observed as follows:

55.1 The Alberta Court of Appeal reached the same conclusion in *South Calgary Properties Ltd. v. J.T. Miller Construction Ltd.* (1995), 29 Alta. L.R. (3d) 393.

56 *River West, Inc. v. Nickel*, 234 Cal. Rptr. 33 (1987).

57 *Ibid.*, pp. 43-44.

57.1 See, for example, *Moffat v. Wetstein* (1996), 29 O.R. (3d) 371, 135 D.L.R. (4th) 298, 5 C.P.C. (4th) 128, 4 O.T.C. 364 (Gen. Div.) at 408-409; and *Trizec Properties Limited v. Husky Oil Limited* (1997), 200 A.R. 48, 146 W.A.C. 48, (*sub nom. Trizec Properties Ltd. v. Husky Oil Operations, Ltd.*) 148 D.L.R. (4th) 300 (Alta. C.A.), additional reasons at (August 19, 1997), Doc. Calgary Appeal 97-176951 (Alta. C.A.).

57.2 *Manville Canada Inc. v. Ladner Downs*, 88 D.L.R. (4th) 208, 63 B.C.L.R. (2d) 102, [1992] 2 W.W.R. 323 (S.C.), affirmed 76 B.C.L.R. 121, 43 W.A.C. 121 (C.A.).

57.3 *Rayner v. Enright* (1993), 20 C.P.C. (3d) 269, 115 Sask. R. 159 (Q.B.).

> "Concerns have been expressed that motions such as these have become a standard tactic in litigation in recent years. The courts must be vigilant to confine the principle to those cases where a litigant's interests are threatened or at least reasonably appear to be threatened as any expansion of the principle beyond the present guidelines will make the delivery of legal services to the public by law firms of large or medium size extremely difficult. Such is not a concern only for the lawyers; the expense and inconvenience to a litigant required to obtain new counsel cannot be overlooked in assessing the impact of judicial decisions in this area."

Again, in a 1993 decision[57.4] the Ontario Divisional Court remarked that such motions are not always brought based upon the purest of motives.

These decisions underline the desirability of balancing the interests of the succeeding client against those of the former client as advocated above in relation to simultaneous unrelated matter conflicts of interest. The protection of the confidences of former clients is essential, but the strategic use of disqualification motions to delay litigation or to hinder an adversary unfairly should be discouraged.[58]

The client affected may of course waive the conflict of interest. In a 1996 Ontario case,[58.1] a disqualification motion was brought not by the client affected but by a minority shareholder of the client who had brought an oppression action against the client and certain of its directors and officers. The motion was dismissed on the basis that the client and the directors and officers named as parties chose to be represented by law firms who had conflicts of interest after considering all relevant information and having had the benefit of independent legal advice.

In cases in which the prior representation was the responsibility not of the lawyers who have carriage of the current matter, but rather their partners or associates, confidentiality screens or "Chinese walls" erected in accordance with Law Society rules and Canadian Bar Association guidelines may provide a complete response to a disqualification motion. In a 1996 decision of the Ontario Court of Justice (General Division),[58.2] the Court held that Law Society rules and Canadian Bar Association guidelines applicable to cases in which lawyers transfer between firms ought to be read *pari passu* as being applicable also to cases in which law firms act against former clients where different lawyers have carriage of the new matter.[58.3] Such a screen, however, must be put in place from the

---

57.4 *Essa (Township) v. Guergis* (1993), 15 O.R. (3d) 573, 52 C.P.R. (3d) 372, (*sub nom. Heck v. Royal Bank*) 22 C.P.C. (3d) 63 (Div. Ct.).

58 See *Satellite Financial Planning v. First National Bank of Washington*, 652 F. Supp. 1281 at 1283 (D. Del., 1987); and Rick R. Rothman, "Conflicts of Interest: Subsequent Adverse Representations" (1988-89) 2 Georgetown Journal of Legal Ethics 119 at 127-128.

58.1 *Algonquin Mercantile Corporation v. Cockwell* (1996), 2 C.P.C. (4th) 231, 3 O.T.C. 97 (Gen. Div.).

58.2 *Ford Motor Company of Canada, Limited v. Osler, Hoskin & Harcourt* (1996), 27 O.R. (3d) 181, 24 B.L.R. (2d) 217, 43 C.P.C. (3d) 156, 131 D.L.R. (4th) 419 (Gen. Div. [Commercial List]).

58.3 At page 200.

outset of the retainer.[58.4] The complications arising in cases of imputed conflicts of interest are explored in section 5.10 below.

5.7 ACTING AGAINST FORMER CO-CLIENTS AND CO-PARTIES

As pointed out above,[59] the rules of professional conduct[60] that prohibit lawyers from acting against former clients in related matters are framed in language that makes it clear that the prohibition extends to situations in which the lawyer represents more than one client in the original matter or transaction. It is no answer for the lawyer to say that the former client agreed that information divulged to the lawyer could not be treated as confidential so far as the other client was concerned,[61] as the former client rule is designed to protect not only confidentiality interests, but also loyalty interests.

A related issue may arise when two or more co-parties are represented by separate counsel, but agree to share information to advance their common interest. It is likely that a lawyer who acquired confidential information in such circumstances would be enjoined from acting against his or her client's co-party in the same or a related matter. Rules of professional conduct provide that the prohibition against acting against a former client in a related matter extends also to protect "persons who were involved in or associated with the client in that matter."[62] The pooling of confidential information to further the co-parties' common interest in litigation does not result in a general waiver of privilege.[63] It is likely that a person who imparts confidential information to a co-party's lawyer would be held to be a person who was involved in or associated with the lawyer's client in the matter, at least where the person has not waived confidentiality.

There is no reason in principle that a lawyer should be prohibited from acting against a client or former client's co-party if the co-party was separately represented in the original proceeding and no confidential information was shared. The lawyer in such circumstances would be bound neither by principles of confidentiality nor by principles of loyalty to refrain from acting against the co-party. American courts have held that lawyers may properly act for clients against former co-parties of the clients in related matters, so long as no confidential information

---

58.4 At page 185. However, in *Canadian Southern Petroleum v. Amoco Canada Petroleum Ltd.*, [1997] 5 W.W.R. 395, 193 A.R. 273, 135 W.A.C. 273, 144 D.L.R. (4th) 30, 48 Alta. L.R. (3d) 382, 7 C.P.C. (4th) 26 (C.A.), leave to appeal to S.C.C. refused (1997), 216 N.R. 159 (note) (S.C.C.) the Alberta Court of Appeal upheld a decision not to disqualify a law firm though no screen was put into place until 18 months after the conflict arose. See text accompanying note 107.3, *infra*.

59 See text accompanying notes 46 through 49.

60 C.B.A. Code, chapter V, commentary 8; Ontario rule 2.04(4).

61 See C.B.A. Code, chapter V, commentary 5; Ontario rule 2.04(6); and Charles Wolfram, *Modern Legal Ethics* (St. Paul, Minnesota: West, 1986), pp. 373-374.

62 C.B.A. Code, chapter V, commentary 8; Ontario rule 2.04(4).

63 See Wolfram, *supra*, note 61, p. 374.

was in fact shared in the original representation.[64] In such cases, the courts have refused to presume that confidential information was shared.

It is not entirely clear that the applicable Canadian rules of professional conduct are susceptible of an interpretation that varies depending on whether confidential information has been shared by co-parties. In other words, can a co-party be considered a person who was involved in or associated with a lawyer's client in a matter if confidential information was shared, but not be so considered if confidential information was not shared? In principle, the answer should be yes. It would be preferable, of course, if the rules were amended to make this clear.

5.8 ISSUE AND PROCEDURAL CONFLICTS BETWEEN CLIENTS

Conflicts of interest may also arise in a litigation practice as a result of differing interests of clients whom a lawyer represents in unrelated proceedings. Lawyers may be disqualified, for example, if they argue a point of law in one action which, if decided in their client's favour, will be prejudicial to the interest of another client in a different pending proceeding.[65] A similar conflict of interest may arise if two clients, or two courts, are pressing a lawyer to start different trials at the same or conflicting times.[66]

The lawyer has a conflict of interest in each of these cases, as the lawyer is placed in the position of having to prefer the interests of one client to the interests of another.[67] In each case, lawyers may continue to act only if the clients freely consent on the basis of adequate disclosure.[68]

5.9 LAWYER-CLIENT CONFLICTS OF INTEREST

Essentially the same considerations that apply where a conflict of interest arises by reason of the lawyer's duties to another client apply also where a conflict

64 See *Wilson P. Abraham Construction Corp. v. Armco Steel Corp.*, 559 F. 2d 250 at 253 (5th Cir., 1977); and Wolfram, *supra*, note 61, p. 374.

65 See *Estates Theatres, Inc. v. Columbia Pictures Industries, Inc.*, 345 F. Supp. 93 (S.D.N.Y., 1972); Wolfram, *supra*, note 61, p. 355; and Monroe H. Freedman, *Understanding Lawyers' Ethics* (New York: Matthew Bender & Co., 1990), pp. 179-180.

66 See *People v. Johnson*, 26 Cal. 3d 557 (1980); and Wolfram, *supra*, note 61, pp. 355-356.

67 See C.B.A. Code, chapter V, commentary 1; Ontario rule 2.04(1).

68 C.B.A. Code, chapter V, rule; Ontario rule 2.04(3).

of interest arises by reason of the personal interest of the lawyer or the lawyer's spouse, children, partner or other associate.[69]

Conflicts that arise as a result of lawyers' personal interest are discussed in more detail, in the context of solicitors' practices, in chapter 22. Most such conflicts arise in situations in which lawyers enter into business transactions with clients, and accordingly have a personal financial interest that might compromise the lawyer's judgment or objectivity.

In a 2000 case[69.1] a lawyer who was a plaintiff personally was disqualified from acting as counsel for his co-plaintiffs in an action arising out of the failure of an agreement to provide financing to the plaintiffs for the purchase of real estate. The Court held that there was a significant risk that the line between the lawyer's personal interest in the litigation and his duties as counsel would become blurred, particularly in light of the fact that one of the co-plaintiffs had suggested that the lawyer may bear some responsibility for the plaintiffs' losses.

It is not only lawyers' personal *financial* interests, however, that engage conflict of interest rules. In a 1986 Ontario case,[70] a former client of the defendant lawyer succeeded in recovering substantial damages based on an alleged breach of the lawyer's fiduciary duty where the lawyer had an affair with the plaintiff's wife. The lawyer had acted for the plaintiff in a wrongful dismissal action in which the plaintiff asserted a claim for damages for mental distress. In connection with his damage claim, the plaintiff confided to the lawyer that as a result of the stress caused by his dismissal he suffered from impotency. The court found that the lawyer preferred his own interests to those of his client by using this confidential information for his own benefit and to the disadvantage of the plaintiff. The lawyer was also reprimanded publicly for conduct unbecoming a barrister and solicitor.[71]

Similarly, in a 1990 decision of the Wisconsin Supreme Court[72] a lawyer was publicly reprimanded for acting in a matrimonial proceeding in which he had a conflict of interest as a result of a personal relationship with one of the parties. The lawyer had been approached by a man for whom he had previously acted in real estate and business matters, who wanted to discuss the fact that his wife

---

69 See C.B.A. Code, chapter VI, rule, paragraph (c), and commentary 3; Ontario rule 2.04(1) and accompanying commentary. See also *R. v. White* (1997), 32 O.R. (3d) 722, in which the Ontario Court of Appeal declined to give effect to a ground of appeal based upon an alleged conflict of interest that arose as a result of a business relationship that deteriorated around the time the appellant's trial began. Where a client first alleges on appeal that his lawyer had a conflict of interest at trial, the Court held, the client must demonstrate both that the lawyer had an actual (as opposed to apparent) conflict of interest and that the conflict adversely affected the lawyer's representation of the client.

69.1 *Roberts v. Pega Captial Corp.* (2000), 47 O.R. (3d) 317 (S.C.J.).

70 *Szarfer v. Chodos* (1986), 27 D.L.R. (4th) 388 (Ont. H.C.), affirmed (1988), 54 D.L.R. (4th) 383 (Ont. C.A.).

71 *Re Chodos (No. 1)*, Law Society of Upper Canada, report adopted by Convocation, November 22, 1986.

72 *Disciplinary Proceedings Against Webster*, 452 N.W. 2d. 374 (S. Ct. Wisconsin, 1990).

wanted a divorce. The man wanted to reconcile. He told the lawyer that he thought that his wife should not have joint custody if she was having an affair, and asked the lawyer whether he had any information linking his wife romantically with any other men. The lawyer replied that the custody issue would not be determined on the basis of his wife's possible infidelity. Unbeknownst to the client, the lawyer had himself recently commenced an intimate relationship with the client's wife.

In due course, the lawyer was approached to act for both the husband and the wife in the resolution of the issues arising out of the termination of their marriage. The lawyer told them that he would not act for either of them because he knew them both, but that he would be willing to act as a "scrivener" in the preparation of legal documents memorializing arrangements that they would make independently of him. The husband and wife signed a retainer agreement acknowledging that he would not represent the separate interests of either of them against those of the other in an adversarial manner and that he would withdraw if a dispute arose between them that could not be resolved. They jointly signed the divorce petition.

Before the matter was completed, however, the husband learned of the intimate personal relationship between his wife and the lawyer. He dismissed the lawyer, and both he and his wife retained new counsel. The lawyer was not compensated by either for his legal services.

In disciplinary proceedings against the lawyer the court upheld a finding that though the lawyer had neither caused nor encouraged the divorce in any way, he had acted in circumstances in which he had a conflict of interest in that his intimate romantic interest in the wife was directly adverse to the husband's desire for reconciliation. This adversity of interests was evidenced by the lawyer's withholding of information when he was asked by the husband whether he knew whether his wife was having an affair.

An issue that has received little attention in Canada to date is whether lawyers who are married to each other — or who are engaged, cohabiting or dating — are permitted to act for parties adverse in interest in litigation.[72.1] Canadian rules of professional conduct, however, stipulate that a lawyer must not act for a client where the lawyer's duty to the client "and the personal interests of the lawyer or

72.1 However, in *Goldstein v. Friedmann* (1996), 32 O.R. (3d) 212 (Gen. Div.) the Ontario Court of Justice (General Division) ordered the petitioner's lawyer removed from the record where the lawyer's wife had formerly represented the respondent. See text accompanying note 41.3, *supra*.

an associate" are in conflict.[73] The term "associate" is defined in such a way as to include the lawyer's spouse, but not (for example) a person unrelated to the lawyer who is cohabiting with the lawyer.[74]

In litigation in which a lawyer's spouse represents a party adverse in interest the personal interests of an associate of the lawyer (*viz.*, the lawyer's spouse) conflict with the lawyer's duty to the client. It would seem to follow that in such an action the lawyer may act only if the lawyer's client consents based upon adequate disclosure.[75] A lawyer who is engaged to, cohabiting with or dating a lawyer who is acting for a party adverse in interest to the lawyer's client would also be well advised to disclose that fact to the client and to seek the client's consent to the representation, though it is not clear that in such circumstances any of these relationships give rise to conflicts of interest as the rules are framed at present.

In the United States, the American Bar Association's Model Rules of Professional Conduct provide that a lawyer related to another lawyer as parent, child, sibling, or spouse must not represent a client in a representation directly adverse to a person who is represented by the other lawyer except with the consent of the client after consultation regarding the relationship.[76] Like its Canadian counter-

---

73 C.B.A. Code, chapter VI, rule, paragraph (c); see also Ontario rule 2.04(1) and accompanying commentary to the same effect. The Alberta rules provide that "A lawyer must not *personally* represent a party to a dispute when a related person is acting for an opposing party." (emphasis added): Chapter 6, rule 6(a). The code also provides that "Unless all parties consent, a lawyer must not *personally* represent a party to a matter when a related person is representing another party to the matter and those parties are in a conflict or potential conflict situation." (emphasis added): Chapter 6, rule 6(b). The code also provides that "A lawyer must not act *personally* in a matter when the lawyer's objectivity is impaired to the extent that the lawyer would be unable to properly and competently carry out the representation." (emphasis added): Chapter 6, rule 8. Finally, the code provides that "If a relationship exists that does not . . . prevent a lawyer from acting in a matter but that raises a reasonable apprehension of impropriety the lawyer must disclose the relationship to the client.": Chapter 6, rule 6(c). The commentary to chapter 6 of the code makes it clear (as do the words emphasized above) that the prohibitions in rules 6(a), 6(b) and 8 apply only to the lawyer having the relationship and not to other members of the lawyer's firm.

74 C.B.A. Code, chapter VI, commentary 3. In the Ontario rules, the term "associate" is defined to include lawyers who are employees of law firms and non-lawyer employees of multi-discipline practices (rule 1.02), but family members as well as law partners are also mentioned by way of examples in the commentary to rule 2.04 (1). The Alberta rules define the term "related person" as used in rule 6(a) and (b) of chapter 6 (and as quoted in note 73, *supra*) to mean "the spouse, child, sibling, parent, grandchild or grandparent of a lawyer, and any person who is a member of the lawyer's household". The commentary to rule 6(c) of chapter 6 of the code (which is also quoted in note 73, *supra*, and which requires disclosure to the client but not withdrawal) provides the following examples of relationships that must be disclosed to the client: (i) where the lawyer is married to the secretary of opposing counsel; (ii) where the lawyers on opposing sides of a matter are cousins or close friends; and (iii) where opposing counsel is a member of a small firm in which the lawyer's spouse also practises.

75 See C.B.A. Code, chapter VI, commentary 1 and chapter V, rule; Ontario rule 2.04(3).

76 Model Rule 1-8(i).

part, the model rule is silent about fiancés, cohabiting lawyers, and lawyers who are dating.

Most American jurisdictions have chosen not to adopt the American Bar Association's model rule. Some jurisdictions, including Illinois and the District of Columbia, have absolutely prohibited spouses from opposing each other in criminal cases, even with client consent. None, however, have promulgated rules to govern the representation of clients whose interests are adverse by lawyers who are engaged, cohabiting, or dating.[77]

5.10 IMPUTED DISQUALIFICATION

The simple fact that lawyers practise together — in law firms or variants thereof, and in government departments, corporate law departments, and other organizations — brings about many of the most difficult conflict of interest problems that arise in litigation. Lawyers who practise together are permitted by law to share confidential information, and may have ready access to one another's files. They are bound together also by ties of finance, friendship, and loyalty.[78]

In rules of professional conduct[79] and judicial decisions on disqualification motions,[80] lawyers' conflicts of interest have been imputed to their partners and associates. In general, if a lawyer has a conflict of interest, every other lawyer in his or her firm has a conflict of interest too. Hence partners cannot advise or represent both sides of a dispute, and lawyers who have conflicts of interest cannot cure them by shifting responsibility for advising or representing clients to their partners or associates. Lawyers may be disqualified on grounds of imputed con-

---

77 See *Blumenfeld v. Borenstein*, 247 Ga. 406 (S. Ct. Ga., 1981); *Non-Punitive Segregative Inmates v. Kelly*, 589 F. Supp. 1339 (U.S.D. Ct., E.D. Pa., 1984); *People v. Jackson*, 167 Cal. App. 3d 829 (1985); and Stacy DeBroff, "Lawyers As Lovers: How Far Should Ethical Restrictions on Dating or Married Attorneys Extend?" (1987-88) 1 Georgetown Journal of Legal Ethics 433.

78 See Charles Wolfram, *Modern Legal Ethics* (St. Paul, Minnesota: West, 1986), p. 391. The question of whether a lawyer's conflict of interest may be imputed to the lawyer's spouse is considered below. See the text accompanying note 112.1.

79 See C.B.A. Code, chapter V, commentary 9; and Ontario rules 1.02 (definition of "client") and 2.04(5) and accompanying commentary. The Alberta rules contain detailed rules governing the circumstances in which law firms may continue to act when a lawyer who has relevant information about a matter transfers to another firm that represents a client in the same or a related matter: Chapter 6, rule 4. Alberta was thus the first province to promulgate a rule as a consequence of *MacDonald Estate v. Martin*, [1990] 3 S.C.R. 1235 (see text accompanying notes 83 to 93 below).

80 See, for example, *United States Surgical Corp. v. Downs Surgical Canada Ltd.* (1982), 141 D.L.R. (3d) 157 (Fed. T.D.); *Morton v. Asper*, [1988] 1 W.W.R. 47 (Man. Q.B.), affirmed, [1988] 2 W.W.R. 317 (Man. C.A.); *MacDonald Estate v. Martin*, [1990] 3 S.C.R. 1235; and *Calgas Investments Ltd. v. 784688 Ontario Ltd.* (1991), 4 O.R. (3d) 459 (Gen. Div.), leave to appeal to Div. Ct. refused (1991), 4 O.R. (3d) 459n (Gen. Div.).

flicts of interest in both simultaneous and subsequent adverse representation cases.[81]

Unless confined to situations in which there is a realistic danger that principles of confidentiality or loyalty will be violated, the imputation of conflicts of interest to all lawyers associated in practice with an affected lawyer may unfairly deprive clients of their right to be represented by counsel of their choice. In extreme cases, clients may be compelled by an overly broad application of the imputation rule to choose between abandoning litigation in

(*Continued on page 5–21*)

81 See C.B.A. Code, chapter V, rule; Ontario rules 2.04(2), (3) and (4). See also Wolfram, *supra*, note 78, p. 391; and Christopher J. Bellini, "Vicarious Disqualification: Second-Hand Taint" (1988-89) 2 Georgetown Journal of Legal Ethics 129 at 130. See, however, *Sun Life Trust Co. v. Bond City Financing Ltd.* (1997), 35 O.R. (3d) 83 (Gen. Div. [Commercial List]), additional reasons at (1997), 26 O.T.C. 207 (Ont. Gen. Div. [Commercial List]), affirmed (1997), 36 O.R. (3d) 758 (Div. Ct.), leave to appeal refused (March 10, 1998), Doc. CA M21773 (Ont. C.A.) in which the Court held that where the lawyer in fact had no confidential information and the prior retainer was not "sufficiently" related to the new matter to justify a presumption that confidential information was imparted to the lawyer, no such presumption should be drawn. See text accompanying note 43.5, *supra*.

which they have invested years of effort and enormous expense, and duplicating much of that effort and expense as a result of having to retain counsel who are unfamiliar with the case. Unless confined to cases in which breaches of confidentiality or loyalty principles is a realistic danger, the imputation of conflicts of interest may impose severe restrictions on the mobility of lawyers within the profession. An undue emphasis on the imputation of conflicts of interest to lawyers who are in fact without confidential information or ties of loyalty could result in an entire firm of hundreds of lawyers inadvertently being disqualified from representing one or more longstanding clients as a result of the hiring of a new junior associate.[82]

The competing considerations are illustrated by the leading Canadian case, a 1990 decision of the Supreme Court of Canada.[83]

The plaintiff in a complex civil action involving a claim for an accounting retained a leading counsel, A. Kerr Twaddle, Q.C., in 1983. A junior lawyer, Kristen Dangerfield, actively worked with Twaddle on the case, and was privy to confidential communications and information.

Twaddle was appointed to the bench in 1985. Dangerfield joined another firm at that time. In 1987, Dangerfield was among eight of the 11 members of her firm who then joined Thompson, Dorfman, Sweatman, who were the solicitors for the defendant in the case in which Dangerfield juniored to Twaddle, which was still pending. Both Dangerfield and senior members of Thompson, Dorfman, Sweatman swore affidavits to the effect that Dangerfield had not and would not discuss the case with her new colleagues.

The plaintiff brought a motion for a declaration that Thompson, Dorfman, Sweatman were ineligible to continue to act. Although the Manitoba Court of Appeal,[84] by a two to one majority, had held that the motion should be dismissed, the Supreme Court of Canada unanimously allowed the appeal and ordered that Thompson, Dorfman, Sweatman be disqualified.

In the Manitoba Court of Appeal, Justice Huband for the majority held that the only absolute rule in such cases is that confidential information exchanged between clients and lawyers must be maintained in confidence even after the solicitor-client relationship is determined. Beyond that, the Court of Appeal majority held, each case must be decided on its own facts. In light of the complexity of the litigation, the sense of confidence that had developed between the defendant and his solicitors as a result of their relationship of six years' duration, and the fact that there was "no real danger of prejudice or impropriety", the majority would have allowed the relationship to continue.[85]

---

82 Wolfram, *supra*, note 78, pp. 318 and 393.

83 *MacDonald Estate v. Martin*, [1990] 3 S.C.R. 1235.

84 *MacDonald Estate v. Martin*, [1989] 3 W.W.R. 653 (Man. C.A.).

85 *Ibid.*, p. 668.

In the Supreme Court of Canada, majority and minority judgments were also delivered, though the court was unanimously of the view that Thompson, Dorfman, Sweatman should be disqualified. Justice Sopinka, for the majority, observed that in such cases the court is concerned with at least three competing values: (i) the maintenance of high ethical standards by the legal profession and the integrity of our system of justice; (ii) the principle that litigants should not be deprived of their choice of counsel without good cause; and (iii) the desirability of permitting reasonable mobility within the legal profession. Justice Sopinka recognized the pre-eminence of the first consideration (as did the minority, to an even greater degree)[86] and emphasized that the other considerations must not be accommodated by slackening the standard of what constitutes a conflict of interest.[87]

The difference of opinion between the majority and minority judgments centred on the fact that bare assurances (even under oath) that confidential information has not been and will not be shared among colleagues are likely to be considered to be unconvincing. The minority went so far as to hold (as had some courts in prior cases)[88] that the presumption that the knowledge of one member of the firm is shared with all other members of the firm is irrebuttable. The majority (as had other courts in prior cases)[89] held that the presumption that confidences are shared by colleagues may be rebutted by evidence sufficient to reassure reasonably well-informed persons that effective measures had been taken to isolate the affected lawyer. The majority urged the Canadian Bar Association and law societies to take the lead in determining whether such institutional devices as Chinese walls (in which affected lawyers are screened, to prevent communication between other members of the firm and them) and cones of silence (in which affected lawyers provide solemn undertakings not to divulge confidential information) are effective, and in developing uniform national standards for the use of such institutional devices.[90]

---

86 *MacDonald Estate v. Martin*, *supra*, note 83, pp. 1265-1266.

87 *MacDonald Estate v. Martin*, *supra*, note 83, pp. 1243-1244.

88 See, for example, *Fisher v. Fisher* (1986), 76 N.S.R. (2d) 326 (C.A.); *Davey v. Woolley, Hames, Dale & Dingwall* (1982), 35 O.R. (2d) 599 (C.A.), leave to appeal to S.C.C. refused (1982), 37 O.R. (2d) 499n (S.C.C.); *Morton v. Asper*, [1988] 1 W.W.R. 47 (Man. Q.B.), affirmed [1988] 2 W.W.R. 317 (Man. C.A.).

89 See, for example, *United States Surgical Corp. v. Downs Surgical Canada Ltd.* (1982), 141 D.L.R. (3d) 157 (Fed. T.D.); and *Law Society (Manitoba) v. Giesbrecht* (1983), 24 Man. R. (2d) 228 (C.A.).

90 *MacDonald Estate v. Martin*, [1990] 3 S.C.R. 1235 at 1259-1263. In *Bolkiah v. KPMG* (1998), [1999] 2 W.L.R. 215 (U.K. H.L.), the House of Lords adopted Justice Sopinka's statement in *MacDonald Estate v. Martin* that the court should restrain a firm from acting "unless satisfied on the basis of clear and convincing evidence that all reasonable measures have been taken to ensure that no disclosure will occur", but added that it would substitute the adjective "effective" for "all reasonable" in this formulation of the applicable test. The *Bolkiah* case is discussed in detail in the text accompanying notes 48.1 to 48.5, *supra*. See also *Drabinsky v. KPMG* (1998), 41 O.R. (3d) 565 (Gen. Div.), leave to appeal allowed (November 4, 1998), Doc. Toronto 664/98 (Ont. Div. Ct.), affirmed (1999), 10 C.B.R. (4th) 130 (Ont. Div. Ct.), which is discussed in the text accompanying note 48.6 *supra*.

Justice Sopinka, for the majority, wrote that though he was not prepared to say that a court should never accept the use of such devices as sufficient evidence of effective screening until the governing bodies have approved of them and adopted rules with respect to their operation, he would foresee a court doing so only in exceptional circumstances. *A fortiori* mere undertakings and conclusory statements in affidavits, the majority held, are inadequate.[91]

Justice Sopinka was motivated to confine the application of the presumption that the knowledge of one member of a firm is the knowledge of all in part because the unlimited application of the presumption would result in firms being disqualified from acting not only where lawyers have been personally involved on the opposite side of litigation handled by their new firm, but also where other lawyers in their former firm are acting on matters related to matters on which lawyers in their new firm are acting. In other words, the presumption, if unconfined, must be applied to both firms with which the moving lawyer is associated, and irrespective of whether the moving lawyer had any personal involvement in or knowledge of the case.[92] The minority, whose reasons for judgment were written by Justice Cory, said that the issue whether a lawyer who has not personally been involved in any way with the client on the matter in issue and who moves to a firm acting for the opponent of the client, should also be irrefutably presumed to have received and imparted confidential information to the new firm, should be left for another occasion on which the issue is squarely raised.[93]

Since its release in December, 1990, the Supreme Court of Canada's decision has been considered in a surprising number of decisions[94] and

91 *Ibid.*, p. 1263.

92 *Ibid.*, p. 1261.

93 *Ibid.*, p. 1271.

94 See, for example, *Princess Auto & Machinery Ltd. v. Winnipeg (City)* (1991), 73 Man. R. (2d) 311 (C.A.); *Van Haastrecht v. Dunbar* (1991), 1 C.P.C. (3d) 57 (Ont. Gen. Div.); *Calgas Investments Ltd. v. 784688 Ontario Ltd.* (1991), 4 O.R. (3d) 459 (Ont. Gen. Div.), leave to appeal to Div. Ct. refused (1991), 4 O.R. (3d) 459n (Gen. Div.); *781332 Ontario Inc. v. Mortgage Insurance Co. of Canada* (1991), 5 O.R. (3d) 248 (Ont. Gen. Div.); *Asian Video Movies Wholesaler Inc. v. Mathardoo* (1991), 36 C.P.R. (3d) 29 (Fed. T.D.); *Chin v. Wong* (1991), 53 B.C.L.R. (2d) 288 (S.C.); *Pacific Coast Super 8 Motels Inc. v. Nanaimo Shipyard (1985) Ltd.* (1991), 53 B.C.L.R. (2d) 281 (S.C.); *Re Markovina* (1991), 57 B.C.L.R. (2d) 73 (S.C.); *Manville Canada Inc. v. Ladner Downs*, [1992] 2 W.W.R. 323 (B.C. S.C.); *Chief Industries v. Equisource Corp.*, Ont. Gen. Div., July, 1992 (unreported), *per* Chapnick J.; *Champlain Lending Corp. v. Orillia (City)*, July, 1992 (unreported), Master Peterson; *Merck & Co. v. Interpharm Inc.* (1992), 44 C.P.R. (3d) 440 (Fed. T.D.); *Atlantic Shipping Ltd. v. Payne* (1992), 122 N.B.R. (2d) 211 (Q.B.); *R.G. Tours & Promotions Ltd. v. Greater Moncton Home Builders Assn.* (1992), 126 N.B.R. (2d) 200 (Q.B.); *Lasch v. Annapolis (County)* (1992), 118 N.S.R. (2d) 418 (Co. Ct.); *Ashburton Oil Ltd. v. Sharp* (1992), 67 B.C.L.R. (2d) 64 (S.C.); *Princess Auto & Machinery Ltd. v. Winnipeg (City)* (1991), 73 Man. R. (2d) 311 (C.A.); *Michel v. Lafrentz* (1992), 85 Alta. L.R. 1 (C.A.); *Essa (Township) v. Guergis* (1993), 15 O.R. (3d) 573 (Div. Ct.); *Chippewas of Kettle & Stony Point v. Canada (Attorney General)* (1993), 17 C.P.C. (3d) 5 (Ont. Gen. Div.), affirmed (1993), [1994] 2 C.N.L.R. 33 (Ont. Div. Ct.); *Feherguard Products Limited v. Rocky's of B.C. Leisure Ltd.*, [1993] 3 F.C. 619 (C.A.); *Manville Canada Inc. v. Ladner Downs*, [1993]

articles.[95] It is generally accepted that all members of the court agreed on a standard more rigorous than that applied in most earlier cases. One commentator, who deplores the burden on the loyalty owed to clients represented by such phenomena as billable hour targets and other norms of productivity measurements, hailed the decision as "a major effort to establish ethical limits in the face of economic pressure."[96] Others are troubled by the possible implications of the decision in circumstances that were not squarely before the court and that remain to be considered in the light of the Supreme Court of Canada's decision.[97]

---

5 W.W.R. 36 (B.C. C.A.); *Watson v. Trace Estate* (July 22, 1994), Doc. Barrie G11274 (Ont. Gen. Div.); motion for leave to appeal to Divisional Court dismissed by Hogg J., October 11, 1994; *GM&A Advertising Ltd. v. Chubb Insurance Company of Canada* (1994) Lawyers Weekly Reports, vol. 2, no. 5, p. 17 (Ont. Gen. Div.); *R. Sherwin Enterprises Ltd. v. Municipal Contracting Services Ltd.* (1994), 20 O.R. (3d) 692 (Gen. Div.); *Choukalos Woodburn McKenzie Maranda Ltd. v. Smith, Lyons, Torrance, Stevenson & Mayer*, [1995] 1 W.W.R. 3 (B.C. S.C.); *Baumgartner v. Baumgartner* (1995), 2 B.C.L.R. (3d) 126 (B.C. C.A.); *Aptowitzer v. Ontario* (1995), 23 O.R. (3d) 315 (Gen. Div.); *Popowich v. Saskatchewan*, [1995] 6 W.W.R. 314 (Sask. Q.B.); *McRory v. Anderson*, [1995] 6 W.W.R. 600 (Alt. Q.B.); *Gainers Inc. v. Pocklington*, [1995] 7 W.W.R. 413 (Alta. C.A.); *Colborne Capital Corp. v. 542775 Alberta Ltd.*, [1995] 30 Alta. L.R. (3d) 127 (Q.B.); *Oliver, Derksen, Arkin v. Fulmyk*, [1995] 7 W.W.R. 609 (Man. C.A.); *South Calgary Properties Ltd. v. J.T. Miller Construction Ltd.*, [1995] 8 W.W.R. 146 (Alta. C.A.); *G. (D.L.) v. Wood* (1995), 125 D.L.R. (4th) 712 (N.S. C.A.); *Montreal Trust Co. of Canada v. Basinview Village Ltd.* (1995), 126 D.L.R. (4th) 61, 39 C.P.C. (3d) 200, 142 N.S.R. (2d) 337, 407 A.P.R. 337 (C.A.); *Hermanns v. Ingle* (1996), 80 O.T.C. 23 (Gen. Div.); *Suchy v. Zurich Insurance Co.*, [1998] 6 W.W.R. 130 (B.C. C.A.); *Davies, Ward & Beck v. Baker and McKenzie* (1998), 40 O.R. (3d) 257 (C.A.); *Canadian Pacific Railway v. Aikins, MacAulay & Thorvaldson*, [1998] 6 W.W.R. 351 (Man. C.A.); *Millennium (Diagnostic) Corp. v. Canadian Blood Bank Corp.* (1998), 168 Nfld. & P.E.I.R. 168 (Nfld. T.D.).

95 See, for example, W. Brent Cotter, "The Supreme Court of Canada Speaks on Lawyers' Conflicts of Interest" (1991) 17 Nova Scotia Law News 125; Patrick Glenn, "Case Comment: *MacDonald Estate v. Martin*" (1991) 70 Can. Bar Rev. 351; Rodney Massel, "Case Comment: *MacDonald Estate v. Martin* and Subsequent Decisions in British Columbia Courts" (1991) 50 The Advocate 251; I.M. Steele, "Imputing Knowledge from One Member of a Firm to Another" (1991) 13 Advocates' Quarterly 90; Archie J. Rabinowitz and Neil S. Rabinovitch, "More About Imputing Knowledge from One Member of a Firm to Another" (1991) 13 Advocates' Quarterly 370; Joyce Harris, "Status Report on Conflict of Interest Post-*Martin v. Gray*", a paper delivered to the Advocates' Society (Ontario) fall conference, October, 1992; and Paul M. Perell, "Classifying Conflicts of Interest", Law Society of Upper Canada Gazette, vol. 28, no. 1 (March 1994), p. 11. Articles that antedate the Supreme Court of Canada's decision but remain of value include: Paul R. Taskier and Alan H. Casper, "Vicarious Disqualification Because of Taint" (1987-88) 1 Georgetown Journal of Legal Ethics 155; Richard Burke and Leslie Rosenberg, "Conflicts of Interest: Vicarious Disqualification" (1989-90) 3 Georgetown Journal of Legal Ethics 165; M. Peter Moser, "Chinese Walls: A Means of Avoiding Law Firm Disqualification When a Personally Disqualified Lawyer Joins the Firm" (1989-90) 3 Georgetown Journal of Legal Ethics 399; and I.M. Steele, "Imputing Knowledge From One Member of a Law Firm to Another: 'Lead Us Not Into Temptation' " (1990) 12 Advocates' Quarterly 46.

96 Glenn, *ibid.*, pp. 357-358.

97 See Steele, *supra*, note 95, p. 90 at 97; and Rabinowitz and Rabinovitch, *supra*, note 95, pp. 377-381. The major unresolved questions are identified below.

Since the Supreme Court of Canada's decision was released, both the Canadian Bar Association and the Federation of Law Societies of Canada have established special committees to consider the effectiveness and acceptability of screening devices, as suggested in Justice Sopinka's opinion.

The Canadian Bar Association task force recommended in an interim report that screening mechanisms be allowed to rebut the presumption that confidential information will be shared among colleagues at the moving lawyer's new firm.[98] In reaching this conclusion, the task force adopted the three competing values referred to by the court, but added a fourth, namely, the discouragement of the use of disqualification motions as tactical weapons.[99]

(*Continued on page 5–25*)

98 Canadian Bar Association, "Draft Discussion Paper on *Martin v. Gray* Conflicts", October, 1991.

99 *Ibid.*, pp. 22-34.

The task force weighed the advantages to the new firm's clients of allowing screening devices — advantages that include the ability to employ counsel of their choice and the avoidance of unnecessary costs and delay — against the advantages to the former firm's clients of disallowing screening devices, advantages that include the uncertainty whether any screen can always be effective and the consequential restiveness that clients might undergo.

The task force concluded that an effective screen should consist of both physical and non-physical elements. Physical elements include the prevention of oral communications, the isolation of the lawyers and staff working on the matter in question, the isolation of the affected lawyer's office, and the isolation of files.[100] Non-physical elements include the dissemination of a written policy, affidavits providing undertakings of adherence to the policy, efforts to obtain the former client's informed consent to the new firm's representation based on independent legal advice, and the non-participation of the affected lawyer in fees generated by the case.[101] The task force devised 11 rules in all, seven of which it considered essential to the effective functioning of a screen and the remaining four of which it recommended whenever possible.[102]

In its final report, in February 1993, the C.B.A. task force refined its 11 rules into 13 guidelines, only the first three of which the task force considered essential to the success of a screen:

(1) The screened lawyer should not participate in the current representation.

(2) The screened lawyer should not disclose confidential information relating to the prior representation.

(3) No member of the new firm should disclose confidential information relating to the current matter or the prior representation with the screened lawyer.

(4) The current client matter should be discussed only within the limited group working on the matter.

(5) The files of the current client, including computer files, should be physically separated from the regular filing system, specifically identified, and accessible only to those lawyers and support personnel in the firm who are working on the matter (or require access for other specifically identified and approved reasons).

(6) No member of the new firm should show the screened lawyer any documents relating to the current client matter.

(7) The measures taken by the firm to screen the lawyer should be stated in a written policy explained to all lawyers and support staff in the firm, with an

100 *Ibid.*, pp. 41-44.
101 *Ibid.*, pp. 44-48.
102 *Ibid.*, pp. 49-51, and schedule "A". See also Harris, *supra*, note 95, pp. 11-14.

admonition that violation of the policy will result in sanctions, up to and including dismissal.

(8) Affidavits and undertakings, whichever are appropriate to the circumstances, should be provided by the relevant firm members, setting out that they have adhered to, and that they will continue to adhere to, all elements of the screen.

(9) The current and former clients should be informed that the screened lawyer is now with the firm representing the current client.

(10) The current and former clients should be informed of the measures adopted by the firm to ensure that there will be no misuse of the confidential information.

(11) The screened lawyer's office should be located away from the offices of those working on the current matter.

(12) The screened lawyer should work with associates and support personnel different from those working on the current client matter.

(13) Every effort should be made to obtain the former client's informed consent to the new firm's representation.[103]

The task force's report — which was adopted at the Canadian Bar Association's annual meeting in August 1993 — has been criticized for considering as mandatory only three elements of a screen that in fact go no further than lawyers' existing professional duties to maintain the confidences of clients and former clients. At least one commentator has suggested that the ten other guidelines should be mandatory in almost every case.[104]

As a result of the efforts of the special committee struck by the Federation of Law Societies, a detailed new rule entitled "Conflicts Arising as a Result of Transfer Between Law Firms" has been adopted in some jurisdictions. The rule in Ontario[105] is set forth in full below. Noteworthy features of the rule include the following:

1. The rule deals only with lawyers (and articling law students) who have actual confidential information about a client matter. Imputed knowledge does not give rise to disqualification.

2. The term "law firm" is defined broadly, and includes, in addition to lawyers practising in partnerships and sole proprietorships, lawyers practising in associ-

---

103 Canadian Bar Association, "Final Report of Task Force on *Martin v. Gray* Conflicts", February 1993.

104 See the comments of Professor Marilyn Pilkington and Peter Kryworuk in Tom Onyshko, "Conflict of Interest: The Legal Profession Debates How Law Firms Should Deal With a Difficult Ethics and Practice Issue", The Lawyers Weekly (April 2, 1993), p. 12.

105 Ontario rule 2.05.

ation for the purpose of sharing common expenses who are otherwise independent practitioners, and lawyers practising in professional law corporations, government, Crown corporations or other public bodies, and in corporations or other private organizations.

3. Where the transferring lawyer actually possesses relevant information respecting a client of her or his former firm, the new firm generally must cease its representation of its client in that matter. The new firm may continue to act, however, either if the client of the former firm consents, or if the new firm establishes that it is in the interests of justice that its representation of its client continue having regard to such considerations as the adequacy of screening measures, the extent of prejudice to any party, and the availability of suitable alternative counsel.

The rule and commentary provide as follows:

2.05 CONFLICTS FROM TRANSFER BETWEEN LAW FIRMS

Definitions

2.05 (1) In this rule

"client" includes anyone to whom a member owes a duty of confidentiality, whether or not a solicitor-client relationship exists between them,

"confidential information" means information obtained from a client that is not generally known to the public, and

> Commentary
>
> The duties imposed by this rule concerning confidential information should be distinguished from the general ethical duty to hold in strict confidence all information concerning the business and affairs of the client acquired in the course of the professional relationship, which duty applies without regard to the nature or source of the information or to the fact that others may share the knowledge.

"matter" means a case or client file but does not include general "know-how" and, in the case of a government lawyer, does not include policy advice unless the advice relates to a particular case.

Application of Rule

(2) This rule applies where a member transfers from one law firm ("former law firm") to another ("new law firm"), and either the transferring member or the new law firm is aware at the time of the transfer or later discovers that

(a) the new law firm represents a client in a matter that is the same as or related to a matter in which the former law firm represents its client ("former client"),

(b) the interests of those clients in that matter conflict, and

(c) the transferring member actually possesses relevant information respecting that matter.

(3) Subrules (4) to (7) do not apply to a member employed by the federal, a provincial, or a territorial Attorney General or Department of Justice who, after transferring from one department, ministry, or agency to another, continues to be employed by that Attorney General or Department of Justice.

> Commentary
>
> The purpose of the rule is to deal with actual knowledge. Imputed knowledge does not give rise to disqualification.
>
> Lawyers and support staff - This rule is intended to regulate members of the Society and articled law students who transfer between law firms. It also imposes a general duty on members to exercise due diligence in the supervision of non-lawyer staff, to ensure that they comply with the rule and with the duty not to disclose confidences of clients of the member's firm and confidences of clients of other law firms in which the person has worked.
>
> Government employees and in-house counsel - The definition of "law firm" includes one or more members of the Society practising in a government, a Crown corporation, any other public body, and a corporation. Thus, the rule applies to members transferring to or from government service and into or out of an in-house counsel position, but does not extend to purely internal transfers in which, after transfer, the employer remains the same.
>
> Law firms with multiple offices - The rule treats as one "law firm" such entities as the various legal services units of a government, a corporation with separate regional legal departments, an inter-provincial law firm, and a legal aid program with many community law offices. The more autonomous each unit or office is, the easier it should be, in the event of a conflict, for the new firm to obtain the former client's consent or to establish that it is in the public interest that it continue to represent its client in the matter.

Law Firm Disqualification

(4) Where the transferring member actually possesses relevant information respecting the former client that is confidential and that, if disclosed to a member of the new law firm, may prejudice the former client, the new law firm shall cease its representation of its client in that matter unless

(a) the former client consents to the new law firm's continued representation of its client, or

(b) the new law firm establishes that it is in the interests of justice that it act in the matter, having regard to all relevant circumstances, including,

(i) the adequacy and timing of the measures taken to ensure that no disclosure to any member of the new law firm of the former client's confidential information will occur,

(ii) the extent of prejudice to any party,

(iii) the good faith of the parties,

(iv) the availability of suitable alternative counsel, and

(v) issues affecting the public interest.

Commentary

The circumstances enumerated in subrule (4)(b) are drafted in broad terms to ensure that all relevant facts will be taken into account. While clauses (ii) to (iv) are self-explanatory, clause (v) addresses governmental concerns respecting issues of national security, cabinet confidences, and obligations incumbent on Attorneys General and their agents in the administration of justice.

(5) For greater certainty, subrule (4) is not intended to interfere with the discharge by an Attorney General or his or her counsel or agent (including those occupying the offices of Crown Attorney, Assistant Crown Attorney, or part-time Assistant Crown Attorney) of their constitutional and statutory duties and responsibilities.

Transferring Lawyer Disqualification

(6) Where the transferring member actually possesses relevant information respecting the former client but that information is not confidential information which, if disclosed to a member of the new law firm, may prejudice the former client,

(a) the member shall execute an affidavit or solemn declaration to that effect, and

(b) the new law firm shall

(i) notify its client and the former client, or if the former client is represented in that matter by a member, notify that member of the relevant circumstances and its intended action under this rule, and

(ii) deliver to the persons referred to in (i) a copy of any affidavit or solemn declaration executed under (a).

(7) A transferring member described in the opening clause of subrule (4) or (6) shall not, unless the former client consents,

(a) participate in any manner in the new law firm's representation of its client in that matter, or

(b) disclose any confidential information respecting the former client.

(8) No member of the new law firm shall, unless the former client consents, discuss with a transferring member described in the opening clause of subrule

(4) or (6) the new law firm's representation of its client or the former law firm's representation of the former client in that matter.

Determination of Compliance

(9) Anyone who has an interest in, or who represents a party in, a matter referred to in this rule may apply to a tribunal of competent jurisdiction for a determination of any aspect of this rule.

Due Diligence

(10) A member shall exercise due diligence in ensuring that each member and employee of the member's law firm, each non-member partner and associate, and each other person whose services the member has retained

(a) complies with this rule, and

(b) does not disclose

(i) confidential information of clients of the firm, and

(ii) confidential information of clients of another law firm in which the person has worked.

Commentary

MATTERS TO CONSIDER

When a law firm considers hiring a lawyer or articled law student ("transferring member") from another law firm, the transferring member and the new law firm need to determine, before the transfer, whether any conflicts of interest will be created. Conflicts can arise with respect to clients of the law firm that the transferring member is leaving and with respect to clients of a firm in which the transferring member worked at some earlier time. The transferring member and the new law firm need to identify, first, all cases in which

(a) the new law firm represents a client in a matter that is the same as or related to a matter in respect of which the former law firm represents its client,

(b) the interests of these clients in that matter conflict, and

(c) the transferring member actually possesses relevant information respecting that matter.

When these three elements exist, the transferring member is personally disqualified from representing the new client, unless the former client consents.

Second, they must determine whether, in each such case, the transferring member actually possesses relevant information respecting the former client that is confidential and that, if disclosed to a member of the new law firm, may prejudice the former client. If this element exists, the transferring member is disqualified unless the former client consents, and the new law firm is disqualified unless the former client consents or the new law firm establishes that its continued representation is in the public interest.

In determining whether the transferring member possesses confidential information, both the transferring member and the new law firm need to be very careful to ensure that they do not, during the interview process itself, disclose client confidences.

MATTERS TO CONSIDER BEFORE HIRING A POTENTIAL TRANSFEREE

After completing the interview process and before hiring the transferring member, the new law firm should determine whether a conflict exists.

A. Where a conflict does exist

If the new law firm concludes that the transferring member does actually possess relevant information respecting a former client that is confidential and that, if disclosed to a member of the new law firm, may prejudice the former client if the transferring member is hired, the new law firm will be prohibited from continuing to represent its client in the matter unless

(a) the new law firm obtains the former client's consent to its continued representation of its client in that matter, or

(b) the new law firm complies with subrule (4)(b), and, in determining whether continued representation is in the interests of justice, both clients' interests are the paramount consideration.

If the new law firm seeks the former client's consent to the new law firm continuing to act, it will in all likelihood be required to satisfy the former client that it has taken reasonable measures to ensure that no disclosure to any member of the new law firm of the former client's confidential information will occur. The former client's consent must be obtained before the transferring member is hired.

Alternatively, if the new law firm applies under subrule (9) for a determination that it may continue to act, it bears the onus of establishing the matters referred to in subrule (4)(b). Ideally, this process should be completed before the transferring person is hired.

B. Where no conflict exists

Although subrule 2.05(6) does not require that the notice required by that subrule be in writing, it would be prudent for the new law firm to confirm these matters in writing. Written notification eliminates any later dispute about whether notice has been given and about its timeliness and content.

The new law firm might, for example, seek the former client's consent to the transferring member acting for the new law firm's client in the matter because, in the absence of such consent, the transferring member may not act.

If the former client does not consent to the transferring member acting, it would be prudent for the new law firm to take reasonable measures to ensure that no disclosure will occur to any member of the new law firm of the former client's confidential information. If such measures are taken, it will strengthen the new law firm's position if it is later determined that the transferring member did in fact possess confidential information which, if disclosed, may prejudice the former client.

A transferring member who possesses no such confidential information puts the former client on notice by executing an affidavit or solemn declaration and delivering it to the former client. A former client who disputes the allegation of no such confidential information may apply under subrule (9) for a determination of that issue.

C. Where the new law firm is not sure whether a conflict exists

There may be some cases where the new law firm is not sure whether the transferring member actually possesses confidential information respecting a former client that, if disclosed to a member of the new law firm, may prejudice the former client. In such circumstances, it would be prudent for the new law firm to seek guidance from the Society before hiring the transferring member.

REASONABLE MEASURES TO ENSURE NON-DISCLOSURE OF CONFIDENTIAL INFORMATION

As noted above, there are two circumstances in which the new law firm should consider the implementation of reasonable measures to ensure that no disclosure will occur to any member of the new law firm of the former client's confidential information:

(a) where the transferring member actually possesses confidential information respecting a former client that, if disclosed to a member of the new law firm, may prejudice the former client, and

(b) where the new law firm is not sure whether the transferring member actually possesses such confidential information, but it wants to strengthen its position if it is later determined that the transferring member did in fact possess such confidential information.

It is not possible to offer a set of "reasonable measures" that will be appropriate or adequate in every case. Instead, the new law firm that seeks to implement reasonable measures must exercise professional judgment in determining what steps must be taken "to ensure that no disclosure will occur to any member of the new law firm of the former client's confidential information."

In the case of law firms with multiple offices, the degree of autonomy possessed by each office will be an important factor in determining what constitutes "reasonable measures." For example, the various legal services units of a government, a corporation with separate regional legal departments, an inter-provincial law firm, or a legal aid program may be able to demonstrate that, because of its institutional structure, reporting relationships, function, nature of work, and geography, relatively fewer "measures" are necessary to ensure the non-disclosure of client confidences. If it can be shown that, because of factors such as the above, lawyers in separate units, offices, or departments do not "work together" with other lawyers in other units, offices or departments, this shall be taken into account in the determination of what screening measures are "reasonable."

The guidelines at the end of this Commentary, adapted from the Canadian Bar Association's Task Force report entitled *Conflict of Interest Disqualification: Martin v. Gray and Screening Methods* (February 1993), are intended as a checklist of relevant factors to be considered. Adoption of only some of the guidelines may be adequate in some cases, while adoption of them all may not be sufficient in others.

In cases where a transferring lawyer joining a government legal services unit or the legal department of a corporation actually possesses confidential information respecting a former client that, if disclosed to a member of the new "law firm", may prejudice the former client, the interests of the new client (Her Majesty or the corporation) must continue to be represented. Normally, this will be effected by instituting satisfactory screening measures, which could include referring the conduct of the matter to counsel in a different department, office or legal services unit. As each factual situation will be unique, flexibility will be required in the application of subrule (4)(b), particularly clause (v). Only in those situations where the entire firm must be disqualified pursuant to subrule (4) will it be necessary to refer conduct of the matter to outside counsel.

GUIDELINES

1. The screened member should have no involvement in the new law firm's representation of its client.

2. The screened member should not discuss the current matter or any information relating to the representation of the former client (the two may be identical) with anyone else in the new law firm.

3. No member of the new law firm should discuss the current matter or the previous representation with the screened member.

4. The current matter should be discussed only within the limited group that is working on the matter.

5. The files of the current client, including computer files, should be physically segregated from the new law firm's regular filing system, specifically identified, and accessible only to those lawyers and support staff in the new law firm who are working on the matter or who require access for other specifically identified and approved reasons.

6. No member of the new law firm should show the screened member any documents relating to the current representation.

7. The measures taken by the new law firm to screen the transferring member should be stated in a written policy explained to all lawyers and support staff within the firm, supported by an admonition that violation of the policy will result in sanctions, up to and including dismissal.

8. Undertakings should be provided by the appropriate law firm members setting out that they have adhered to and will continue to adhere to all elements of the screen.

9. The former client, or if the former client is represented in that matter by a member, that member, should be advised

(a) that the screened member is now with the new law firm, which represents the current client, and

(b) of the measures adopted by the new law firm to ensure that there will be no disclosure of confidential information.

10. The screened member's office or work station and that of the member's support staff should be located away from the offices or work stations of lawyers and support staff working on the matter.

11. The screened member should use associates and support staff different from those working on the current matter.

12. In the case of law firms with multiple offices, consideration should be given to referring conduct of the matter to counsel in another office.[106]

In two 1993 decisions[107] that pre-dated the adoption of the Canadian Bar Association task force's report at the Canadian Bar Association's annual meeting in August 1993, arrangements involving confidentiality screens were held to be inadequate to rebut the presumption that colleagues share confidences, in part because the Canadian Bar Association guidelines had not been adopted and made binding on the profession in a formal way. In a 1994 decision of the Ontario Court of Justice (General Division),[107.1] however, the court relied upon a law firm's substantial compliance with the Canadian Bar Association guidelines among other factors in dismissing a motion to disqualify the law firm.

106 See also Alberta rules, chapter 6, rule 4.

107 *Chippewas of Kettle & Stony Point v. Canada, supra,* note 94; and *Feherguard Products Limited v. Rocky's of B.C. Leisure Ltd., supra,* note 94.

107.1 *Watson v. Trace Estate, supra,* note 94.

In a 1997 decision,[107.2] the same Court made it clear that a confidentiality screen that would satisfy a reasonably informed person that no confidential information will be used or disclosed, inadvertently or otherwise, will be sufficient to protect a firm from disqualification if it is in place from the outset of the retainer or transfer.

In a decision released the same year,[107.3] the Alberta Court of Appeal upheld a decision not to disqualify counsel despite the fact that no screen was put in place until 18 months after the transferring lawyer had joined the defendants' law firm. The Court recognized that the transferring lawyer was not directly involved in the lawsuit and that the lawyers who had carriage of the litigation acted promptly to establish a confidentiality screen after they discovered the conflict that had in fact arisen much earlier. The Court also considered the fact that the transferring lawyer was in the Toronto branch of the defendants' law firm whereas the litigation counsel with carriage of the action were situated in Calgary.

The Ontario rule addresses a number of issues that remained unresolved in the wake of the Supreme Court of Canada's decision. These include: (1) the fundamental question whether the use of screening devices may rebut the presumption that a lawyer who charges firms shares confidential information with the new colleagues (under the Ontario rule, it may); (ii) the equally fundamental question whether firms may be subject to double imputation, that is, whether migrating lawyers with imputed but not actual confidential information may subject their new firms to disqualification (under the Ontario rule, they may not); (iii) the question whether the presumption that lawyers share confidences extends to such support staff as paralegals, clerks and secretaries (under the Ontario rule, it does not, though it extends to articling students); and (iv) the question whether the principles articulated by the Supreme Court of Canada apply to government lawyers,[108] lawyers employed by corporations and other organizations, and law-

107.2 *Ford Motor Company of Canada Limited v. Osler, Hoskin & Harcourt* (1996), 27 O.R. (3d) 181, 24 B.L.R. (2d) 217, 43 C.P.C. (3d) 156, 131 D.L.R. (4th) 419 (Gen. Div. [Commercial List]). See text accompanying notes 58.2 to 58.4, *supra*. In the *Ford* case the Court held that the screen was not effective to protect the *Osler* firm from disqualification because it was not put in place until several months after the firm was retained. The British Columbia Supreme Court reached the same conclusion in *Poehler v. Langer* (February 4, 1999), Doc. Vancouver C976361, A973386, C976534 (B.C. S.C.), in which no institutional measures were put in place for five months after a lawyer who had articled with a firm representing defendants accepted a position upon completion of his articles with the firm representing the plaintiff in the same action. The Court reached this conclusion despite uncontradicted evidence that the lawyer and his new firm had agreed orally at the outset that he must not discuss or be involved in the matter, and put effective institutional measures in place immediately upon receiving a letter from the defendants' solicitors demanding the firm cease to act. The bar has been set high, the Court observed, but no higher than is justified by the need to ensure utmost confidence in the legal system.

107.3 *Canadian Southern Petroleum v. Amoco Canada Petroleum Ltd.*, [1997] 5 W.W.R. 395, 193 A.R. 273, 135 W.A.C. 273, 144 D.L.R. (4th) 30, 48 Alta. L.R. (3d) 382, 7 C.P.C. (4th) 26 (C.A.), leave to appeal to S.C.C. refused (1997), 216 N.R. 159 (note) (S.C.C.).

108 See Steele, *supra*, note 95, page 97.

yers who share common expenses but are otherwise independent practitioners (under the Ontario rule, they do).

Although the rule applies only to lawyers and articling students who transfer between law firms, the commentary to the rule makes clear that lawyers have a general duty to exercise due diligence in the supervision of non-lawyer support staff, to ensure that they comply with the rule and with the duty not to disclose confidences of clients of their employer's firm and confidences of clients of other law firms in which they have worked. In two 1998 decisions law firms were disqualified upon the transfer between firms of non-lawyer support staff who had worked on litigious matters on the opposite side before changing employment. In one case[109] the transferring employee was a secretary; in the other,[110] a law clerk. In neither case were reasonable institutional measures taken in a timely way to ensure that there would be no disclosure to any member of the new law firm of confidential information of the former employer's client.

One hopes that heightened awareness of the danger of imputed disqualification will result in firms maintaining more effective conflict information systems. This is particularly important in transactional practices. The minimum mechanical requirements include a new matter form that all lawyers are required to submit to a central source, and a computerized index system through which clients, matters, parties to litigation, opposing counsel, and (if and when available) corporate officers, affiliated companies, and beneficiaries can be correlated.[111]

In two 1999 cases[112] courts in British Columbia and Newfoundland considered (evidently for the first time in Canada) the issue of whether a lawyer's conflict of interest should be imputed to the lawyer's spouse. Both courts concluded that it should not.

In the British Columbia case, an alleged bankrupt brought a motion to have a law firm removed as counsel to a court-appointed interim receiver on the ground that one of the lawyers on the counsel team representing the interim receiver was married to one of the lawyers on the counsel team representing the petitioning creditors. The alleged bankrupt submitted that the fact that a husband and wife are active members of the counsel teams advising different parties to litigation raises a perception that confidential information will be communicated between those parties. No actual wrongdoing was alleged.

The Court rejected the alleged bankrupt's submission and dismissed the motion. The Court emphasized that both public attitudes toward marriage and the

---

109 *Ocelot Energy Inc. v. Jans*, [1998] 8 W.W.R. 708 (Sask. Q.B.).

110 *Cartledge (Litigation Guardian of) v. Brown* (1998), 41 O.R. (3d) 376 (Gen. Div.).

111 See Geoffrey C. Hazard, Jr., "Close Watch Must Be Kept for Conflicts", National Law Journal (September 26, 1988), p. 13; Patrick Glenn, "Case Comment: *MacDonald Estate v. Martin* (1991) 70 Can. Bar Rev. 351 at 359; and Joyce Harris, "Status Report on Conflict of Interest Post-*Martin v. Gray*", a paper delivered to the Advocates' Society (Ontario) fall conference, October, 1992, p. 18.

112 *Re Down*, [1999] B.C.J. No. 1809 (B.C. S.C.); and *Newfoundland (Treasury Board) v. Newfoundland Association of Public Employees*, [1999] N.J. 356 (Nfld. S.C.T.D.).

laws relating to marriage have changed significantly: the concept of a husband and wife being one person in the eyes of the law, for example, is no more. Perhaps more importantly, the Court observed that advertent disclosures of a client's confidences by a lawyer to his or her spouse would violate the lawyer's professional duty to maintain such confidences, whether or not the spouse is also a lawyer. A court should not presume that a lawyer will breach fundamental professional duties by disclosing confidential information to a spouse.

In the Newfoundland case, the Court granted an application to set aside an award of an arbitration board. The spouse of the employer's representative on the board had provided legal advice to the employer in an unrelated matter in the past. The board had held that this gave rise to a reasonable apprehension of bias on the part of the union.

The Court disagreed. Both the courts and the public may safely assume, the Court held, that a person bound by professional ethics will operate fairly and with complete independence. The contrary view, the Court added, may have its roots in the lack of independence of spouses during the earlier part of the twentieth century; "the time has come," the Court concluded, "for the courts to show clearly that [that view] has no place in today's jurisprudence."

5.11 PAYMENT OF FEES BY NON-CLIENTS

In most litigation practices, situations in which the lawyer's fee is paid by someone other than the client are common. Parents often pay fees for legal work performed for children, for example, and employers often retain lawyers to represent employees.

Lawyers must be vigilant in such cases to ensure that their loyalty to their clients is not compromised by loyalty to the interests of the persons who are paying their fees. The lawyer's duty is such cases is to pursue the client's interests singlemindedly. To pursue the interests of the party who is paying the lawyer's fee to the detriment of the client would be improper.[113]

In some cases, for instance where an employer and employee are co-defendants, as pointed out above,[114] lawyers may have no alternative but to disqualify themselves if they would otherwise be constrained to represent parties adverse in interest.

5.12 CLASS ACTIONS

Neither Canadian nor American rules of professional conduct address the particular conflict of interest problems of lawyers who act for plaintiffs in class actions. These include most notably conflicts that surface where class representatives have interests or objectives that differ from those of represented but absent class members. In some extreme American cases class representatives have re-

113 See Charles Wolfram, *Modern Legal Ethics* (St. Paul, Minnesota: West, 1986), pp. 443-445.

114 See part 5.5, *supra*.

jected favourable offers to the class in efforts to exact from defendants an offer providing greater benefits to the class representatives.[115]

Conflicts may also arise because of the existence of subclasses with differing interests. Where the interests of subclasses are in conflict, different lawyers must be designated to represent each subclass.[116]

As we have seen, a potential conflict of interest between lawyer and client is present in almost every representation of any type because the client's financial interest in minimizing the lawyer's fee conflicts with the lawyer's financial interest in maximizing it. This potential conflict is much more likely to become real in class actions in which class representatives are the class lawyers themselves, because independent class representatives can help protect against overreaching by class lawyers. The risk has been minimized in the American federal courts, which have held that if lawyers bring an action as plaintiffs on behalf of a class, neither the named lawyers nor any lawyers associated with them in practice may act as counsel in the litigation.[117]

In a 1977 case,[118] the United States Court of Appeals for the Third Circuit imposed a rule that in class actions lawyers could not negotiate their fee until after the court has approved any negotiated settlement of the merits of the action. It has been suggested that fees in class actions should always be submitted to the court for determination.[119]

The Ontario courts have held[119.1] that for class counsel to simultaneously negotiate a settlement of the action and an agreement respecting class counsel's fee involves no disqualifying conflict of interest where the fee agreement is negotiated at arm's length by experienced counsel, the payment is not to be made from the same fund as the settlement and accordingly would not diminish the recovery of the class members, and the fee arrangement is subject to the scrutiny of the court.

---

115 See *Parker v. Anderson*, 667 F. 2d 1204 at 1211 (5th Cir., 1982) cert. denied 103 S. Ct. 63; and *Soskel v. Texaco, Inc.*, 94 F.R.D. 201 (S.D.N.Y., 1982); and see also Wolfram, *supra*, note 113, p. 492.

116 See *Rochester (City) v. Chiarella*, 449 N.Y.S. 2d 112 (1982); and Wolfram, *supra*, note 113, p. 492.

117 See, for example, *Kramer v. Scientific Control Corp.*, 534 F. 2d 1085 (3rd Cir., 1976), cert. denied 97 S. Ct. 90 (1976); and see also Wolfram, *supra*, note 113, p. 493; and Michael D. Ricciuti, "Equity and Accountability in the Reform of Settlement Procedures in Mass Tort Cases: The Ethical Duty to Consult" (1987-88) 1 Georgetown Journal of Legal Ethics 817.

118 *Prandini v. National Tea Co.*, 557 F. 2d 1015 (1977).

119 B.V. Calhoun, "Attorney-Client Conflicts of Interest and the Concept of Non-Negotiable Fee Awards Under 42 U.S.C. S. 188" (1984) 55 U. Colo. L. Rev. 341. Under the *Class Proceedings Act, 1992*, S.O. 1992, c. 6, fee agreements must be approved by the court prior to certification of the action as a class proceeding, so that at least the basis of the calculation is endorsed by the court.

119.1 *Dabbs v. SunLife Assurance Co. of Canada* (1997), 35 O.R. (3d) 708 (Gen. Div.), leave to appeal dismissed 36 O.R. (3d) 770 (Gen. Div.).

5.13 DERIVATIVE PROCEEDINGS

Business corporations legislation generally provides a mechanism whereby shareholders may apply to the court for leave to bring an action on a corporation's behalf.[120] Such applications are usually based on allegations of impropriety on the part of directors and officers who control the corporation.

The principal ethical issue that arises on such applications is whether the same lawyer or law firm may represent both the corporation and the directors and officers who are alleged to be guilty of wrongdoing. A related issue is who in the corporation should engage and instruct the lawyer or firm representing the corporation where that task would ordinarily be the responsibility of one or more directors or officers who is alleged to be a wrongdoer.

In Canada, neither rules of professional conduct nor the decided authorities provide specific assistance in the resolution of these problems.[121] American authorities make it clear that the filing of a derivative proceeding in itself does not necessitate the separate representation of the corporation and the directors or officers who are named as respondents; the claims asserted and the relief sought must be scrutinized for the purpose of determining whether a conflict of interest is likely. Thus where applicants bring proceedings that are patently spurious, that do not allege serious wrongdoing on the part of directors or officers, or that will give rise to only minor relief even if successful, separate representation may not be required.[122]

Nevertheless, the clear trend in the United States over the last 20 years or so has been to require separate representation on the basis of a conflict of interest between the corporation and its directors and officers who are accused of improprieties.[123] The requirement of separate representation does not, however, necessarily require the individual directors and officers to bear the expense of paying their own lawyers. The corporation may fund their defence so long as their lawyers discharge their responsibilities to treat the directors and officers, and only the directors and officers, as their clients.[124]

The types of conflicts of interest that arise in derivative proceedings cannot be cured by the directors who are named as respondents voting the corporation's consent to common representation of themselves and the corporation. Loyalties

---

120 See, for example, *Business Corporations Act*, R.S.O. 1990, c. B.16, s. 246.

121 See *Turner v. Mailhot* (1985), 50 O.R. (2d) 561 (H.C.); and *Vadeko International Inc. v. Philosophe* (1990), 1 O.R. (3d) 87 (Gen. Div.).

122 *Schmidt v. Magnetic Head Corp.*, 468 N.Y.S. 2d 649 (1983). See also Charles Wolfram, *Modern Legal Ethics* (St. Paul, Minnesota: West, 1986), pp. 425-426 and the cases cited there.

123 See *Cannon v. United States Acoustic Corp.*, 532 F. 2d 1118 (7th Cir., 1976), affirming in relevant part 398 F. Supp. 209 (N.D. Ill., 1975). See also Wolfram, *ibid.*, p. 425 and cases cited there.

124 Wolfram, *ibid.*, p. 426.

among directors may call into question the validity of the votes on the issue of consent of directors who are not named as parties.[125]

Generally the problems may be overcome by the assignment of the responsibility of retaining counsel for the corporation — and, if necessary, for the directors and officers who are parties — to a committee of outside directors who are not named as parties. This committee can provide instructions to the corporation's counsel as required as the litigation continues.[126] If this solution is impractical (as it would be, for example, if all the corporation's directors and officers were named as parties, or if there were no independent directors), it may be necessary to involve the court in the selection of independent counsel for the corporation.[127]

Similar problems arise in the context of unincorporated entities such as, most notably, labour unions. As in the case of derivative proceedings, in cases arising as a result of dissension within a union the critical factor is likely to be whether it is alleged that officers who are named as parties were complicit in unlawful or improper acts that caused damage to the union or other entity. If so, the same lawyer or firm should not represent both the entity and the officers; if not, joint representation is likely to be appropriate.[128]

In a leading American case, a 1971 decision of the District of Columbia Circuit Court of Appeals,[129] a senior officer of a union was alleged to have been guilty of wrongdoing. The court allowed an appeal from an order dismissing a motion to disqualify from acting for both the union leader and the union a law firm that had acted for both the union, as its general counsel, and for the union leader personally during a time when the union leader was the union's dominant figure. The court held that counsel for the union in such a case must be able to analyze objectively the true interests of the union as an institution without being hindered by allegiance to an incumbent office holder who was said to have committed improprieties. The court found illuminating the analogy of the position of a corporation and its individual officers when confronted with a shareholder derivative proceeding.[130]

5.14 INDEMNITY INSURANCE LITIGATION

Liability insurance policies generally require the insurer to pay any judgment for damages obtained against the insured and to bear the costs (including legal

---

125 *Ibid.*, pp. 426-427.

126 *Ibid.*, p. 427.

127 *Ibid.*

128 *Weaver v. United Mine Workers*, 492 F. 2d 580 at 583 (D.C. Cir., 1973). See also Wolfram, *ibid.*, pp. 427-428.

129 *Yablonski v. United Mine Workers*, 448 F. 2d 1175, cert. denied 406 U.S. 906, 92 S. Ct. 1609 (1972).

130 *Ibid.*, pp. 1179-1181. See also Geoffrey C. Hazard, Jr., "Triangular Lawyer Relationships: An Exploratory Analysis" (1987-88) 1 Georgetown Journal of Legal Ethics 15 at 19-21.

fees) of defending claims against the insured. Such policies generally reserve to the insured the rights to control the defence of the action and to decide whether to settle claims. This arrangement frequently spawns conflict of interest problems for lawyers retained and instructed by insurers to represent insured persons. The most common conflict is between the insurer's interest in limiting its coverage and the insured's interest in maximizing it. The financial interest of the lawyer will usually lie in favouring the insurer who will pay the lawyer's fee and who may send future work to the lawyer. The lawyer's professional duty, however, is conscientiously and resolutely to protect and advance the interest of the lawyer's client, the insured.[130.1]

Again, Canadian rules of professional conduct do not deal specifically with conflicts of interest that arise in this particular type of proceeding. The general conflict of interest rules, which require adequate disclosure and the informed consent of both the insurer and the insured before a lawyer may act in a case involving an actual or possible conflict of interest, are applicable.[131]

A lawyer retained by an insurer to represent an insured may not continue to represent the insured while simultaneously preparing a defence for the insurer (and against the insured) on a potential or actual claim for coverage. If the insurer learns of grounds that may justify a denial of coverage, the lawyer retained by the insurer should preface any interviews with the insured concerning that aspect of the matter with an express warning that the questions the lawyer is about to ask pertain to the issue of whether the policy provides coverage and that the insured's answers cannot be maintained in confidence insofar as the insurer is concerned. The lawyer must not elicit answers that support a denial of coverage by the insurer on the pretext that the lawyer is furthering the interests of the insured.[132]

If the issue of coverage cannot be resolved, the insurer may defend the action on the basis of a non-waiver agreement whereby the insurer preserves its right to contest coverage if a judgment is obtained against the insured. Under most policies, the insurers' duties to defend and to provide coverage are not co-extensive. The insurer is likely to be obligated to bear the expense of defending claims against the insured even if it is entitled to deny coverage. If the insurer contests coverage or if a conflict of interest otherwise arises, the insured is not required to consent to be represented by a lawyer of the insurer's choice. The insured is entitled to retain an independent lawyer at the insurer's expense.[133]

130.1 *R. Sherwin Enterprises Ltd. v. Municipal Contracting Services Ltd.* (1994), 20 O.R. (3d) 692 (Gen. Div.). See Douglas R. Richmond, "Lost in the Eternal Triangle of Insurance Defence Ethics", 9 Georgetown Journal of Legal Ethics 475 (1996).

131 See C.B.A. Code, chapter V, rule, and commentaries 1 and 4; and Ontario rules 2.04(3) and (6) and accompanying commentary. See also Charles Wolfram, *Modern Legal Ethics* (St. Paul, Minnesota: West, 1986), pp. 428 and 430.

132 Wolfram, *ibid.*, pp. 431-432.

133 *Ibid.*, p. 431.

In many cases, for instance where the insured is related to the plaintiff, the insured may hope that the plaintiff is successful, as any damages will be paid by the insurer. The lawyer who is retained and instructed by the insurer to protect the insured's interest may nevertheless oppose the plaintiff's claim.[134] The lawyer should advise the insured of the risks of collusion with the plaintiff, and indeed of admitting liability, which may result in forfeiture of the insurance protection as a breach of the insured's contractual responsibility to co-operate with the insurer in defending claims.[135]

A lawyer who is retained by an insurer may be instructed to represent more than one insured. For example, the insurer's duty to defend under an automobile insurance policy may extend to non-owner drivers of the insured vehicle. To all of these persons the lawyer owes a duty to minimize their personal risk of loss. Accordingly, such a lawyer could not without the consent of a driver admit that the driver was operating the vehicle without the owner's permission, or take any other position that may protect the insurer and the main insured but may expose an additional insured to personal liability.[136]

As discussed above,[136.1] in a 1996 decision[136.2] the British Columbia Court of Appeal reversed an order requiring each of four defendants represented by the same counsel, who was appointed by the defendants' insurer, to appoint separate counsel. The court's inherent jurisdiction to interfere with a litigant's (or insurer's) choice of counsel should be exercised with "the highest level of restraint", the Court held, and only where the administration of justice is threatened.

A common conflict of interest between insurer and insured arises where the claim is in an amount in excess of the policy limits, but the insurer has an opportunity to settle the case for an amount within the policy limits. If an insurer receives a reasonable settlement offer at or near the policy limits, the insurer may be tempted to decide that it has little to lose by rejecting the offer, in that a judgment in an amount significantly in excess of the policy limits will cost the insurer little more than would the acceptance of the settlement offer, whereas a judgment for an amount significantly lower than the settlement offer would result in a substantial saving. Refusals by insurers to settle in such cases have given rise to liability to the insured in the amount of the liability imposed on the insured in excess of the policy limits. Lawyers retained by insurers to represent insureds have also been found liable in damages to their clients in such circumstances on the theory that they have acted in bad faith.[137]

---

134 See *Buchanan v. Buchanan*, 99 Cal. App. 3d 587 (1979).

135 See Wolfram, *supra*, note 131, p. 432.

136 Wolfram, *supra*, note 131, p. 432.

136.1 See text accompanying note 35.2.

136.2 *Mara (Guardian ad litem of) v. Blake*, 134 D.L.R. (4th) 716, [1996] 10 W.W.R. 277, (*sub nom. Mara v. Blake*) 74 B.C.A.C. 296, 121 W.A.C. 296, 23 B.C.L.R. (3d) 225 (C.A.).

137 *Betts v. Allstate Insurance Co.*, 154 Cal. App. 3d 688 (1984). See also Wolfram, *supra*, note 131, pp. 432-433.

Lawyers and insurers have the same duty to act in good faith to protect the interests of the insured when settlement offers are received that are in excess of policy limits.[138] Most lawyers retained by insurers advise insured persons to retain their own lawyer where an amount in excess of the policy limits is claimed.

138 *Bell v. Commercial Insurance Co.*, 280 F. 2d 514 (3rd Cir., 1990).

6

Prosecuting

> It is the task of prosecuting counsel to present the facts in a neutral manner and not to try to score a victory. This duty (not always carried out, I may say, by those who habitually persecute down at the Old Bailey) takes the fun out of the art of advocacy. There are many adjectives which might be used to describe Rumpole at work, but neutral is not among them. It is a sad but unmistakable fact that as soon as I buckle on the wig and gown and march forth to war in the courtroom, the old adrenalin courses through my veins and all I want to do is win.[1]

6.1 DOING JUSTICE

The ethical principles that govern prosecutors are all variations of the same rule of professional conduct: the prosecutor's duty is not to seek a conviction, but to see that justice is done.[2] As Rumpole realizes, it is not a role with which lawyers trained in the adversary system's sporting theory of justice feel entirely comfortable.

Norman Schwartz, a former prosecutor, describes the tension that prosecutors must try to resolve:

> The advocate in you says you should do everything you can to convict someone you believe is guilty. Yet you have a duty to do justice, to help the other side, even to tear down your own case. The potential is there for terrible conflict.[3]

Not all prosecutors succeed in resolving the conflict. "This "innocent until proven guilty' business doesn't hold with a prosecutor," says an American assistant district attorney featured in James Mills's book *The Prosecutor*. "In court

---

1 Horace Rumpole in John Mortimer, *Rumpole À La Carte* (London: Viking, 1990), pp. 204-205.

2 C.B.A. Code, chapter IX, commentary 9; Ontario rule 4.01(3) and accompanying commentary; Yukon rules, part three, rule 12; New Brunswick rules, part C, rule 12; and British Columbia rules, chapter 8, rule 18.

3 James B. Stewart, *The Prosecutors* (New York: Simon & Schuster, 1987), p. 225.

it's an adversary system — for me he's guilty and I'm out to make twelve other people agree with me."[4]

Examples of such unreconstructed adversarial spirit abound. In a 1987 Illinois case, a prosecutor in closing argument called the accused person a "mutant from hell."[5] In a 1991 case,[6] a prosecutor was censured publicly by the Supreme Court of Kansas for failing to personally confirm the truth of a statement that she had made to a jury in a rape trial. The prosecutor had said to the jury that the accused person had transmitted gonorrhoea to the victim. In fact there was no evidence that the victim either contracted or was treated for gonorrhoea.

In a 2000 Ontario case,[6.1] Crown counsel stated in his closing address that his job was to obtain a conviction and ensure that justice was done for the complainant; that he was an honest and just person and that if the jury was not convinced of the accused's guilt it was because he had failed to do his job successfully; and that if the accused were not convicted "we would have to live with the sad result." (The accused's appeal from conviction was allowed on the ground that the cumulative effect of Crown counsel's improprieties was seriously prejudicial to the accused.)

Such cases demonstrate that Professor Alan M. Dershowitz was right when he wrote that many prosecutors reverse the motto on the wall of the United States Justice Department. The motto proclaims that the government "wins its point whenever justice is done." Many prosecutors believe, wrote Dershowitz, that justice is done whenever the government wins its point.[7]

The prosecutor's duty has been expressed in many different ways. The best known Canadian statement is that of Justice Rand in a 1955 decision of the Supreme Court of Canada:

> The role of prosecutor excludes any notion of winning or losing; his function is a matter of public duty than which in civil life there can be none charged with greater personal responsibility. It is to be performed with an ingrained sense of the dignity, the seriousness and the justness of the judicial proceedings.[8]

In the same case, Justice Taschereau added that the prosecutor's role is quasi-judicial.[9]

---

4 James Mills, *The Prosecutor* (New York: Farrar, Straus and Giroux, 1968), p. 5.

5 *People v. Shum*, 117 Ill. 2d 317 (1987). The Supreme Court of Illinois declined to reverse the accused person's conviction on this ground, holding that the trial judge had taken sufficient steps to remedy any possible prejudice.

6 *Re Sue Carpenter*, 808 P. 2d 1341 (Kan., 1991). See also Lawrence Dubin, "Criminal Trial is Not Just Sporting Event", National Law Journal (July 22, 1991), p. 13.

6.1 *R. v. S. (F.)* (2000), 47 O.R. (3d) 349 (C.A.).

7 Alan M. Dershowitz, *The Best Defence* (New York: First Vintage Books, 1983), p. xvi.

8 *Boucher v. R.*, [1955] S.C.R. 16 at 23-24.

9 *Ibid.*, p. 21. The prosecutor's role has also been described as quasi-judicial, or as being more akin to that of a judge than that of a partisan advocate, by Justice Blackburn in *R. v. Berens*, 4 F. & F. 842 (followed in *R. v. Murray*, [1917] 1 W.W.R. 404 (Alta. C.A.)); and by Charles Wolfram in *Modern Legal Ethics* (St. Paul, Minnesota: West, 1986), p. 759.

These two themes have been repeated continually. Prosecutors who keep them in mind are unlikely to violate their responsibilities: prosecutors must not allow themselves to be betrayed by feelings of rivalry or competitiveness, and should approach their responsibilities with the even-handedness of a judge rather than with the partisan spirit of an advocate. The duty of fairness applies even in cases in which the prosecutor believes in good faith that the accused person is guilty.

Thus in a 1934 decision of the Ontario Court of Appeal, Justice Riddell said as follows:

> . . . a criminal prosecution is not a contest between the State and the accused in which the State seeks a victory, but being an investigation, it is the duty of prosecuting counsel . . . to lay all the facts before the jury, those favourable to the accused as those unfavourable to him.[10]

The leading American authority is a decision of the United States Supreme Court that was released the following year, in which Justice Sutherland wrote as follows:

> The United States Attorney is the representative not of an ordinary party to a controversy, but of a sovereignty whose obligation to govern impartially is as compelling as its obligation to govern at all; and whose interest, therefore, in a criminal prosecution is not that it shall win a case, but that justice shall be done. As such, he is in a peculiar and very definite sense the servant of the law, the two-fold aim of which is that guilt should not escape or innocence suffer. He may prosecute with earnestness and vigor — indeed, he should do so. But, while he may strike hard blows, he is not at liberty to strike foul ones. It is as much his duty to refrain from improper methods calculated to produce a wrongful conviction as it is to use every legitimate means to bring about a just one.[11]

In the same vein, Justice Douglas of the United States Supreme Court wrote in a dissenting judgment in a 1974 case that the prosecutor's function is "not to tack as many skins of victims as possible to the wall." Rather, he added, a prosecutor is required to vindicate the rights of people as expressed in the law and to give those accused of crime a fair trial.[12] "A trial is not a sporting event where one should concern themselves with notches in their belt," said the Supreme

---

10 *R. v. Chamandy*, [1934] O.R. 208 at 211 (C.A.). See also *R. v. Ruddick* (1865), 4 F. & F. 497 at 499 (Crompton J.).

11 *Berger v. United States*, 55 S. Ct. 629 at 635 (1935).

12 *Donnelly v. De Christoforo*, 416 U.S. 637 at 648-649 (1974). See also *R. v. Thomas (No. 2)*, [1974] 1 N.Z.L.R. 658 at 659 (N.Z. C.A.), *per* Wild C.J.; and *R. v. Fontaine* (1930), 53 C.C.C. 164 (Ont. C.A.) (Riddell J.).

Court of Kansas in the 1991 case referred to above, "but instead is a fundamental method used by our society to determine the truth."[13]

One of the reasons for this significant modification of the adversary system is that prosecutors play a dual role. Prosecutors are not just advocates who are responsible for obtaining convictions of guilty accused persons; they are also administrators of justice who are responsible for seeing that innocent persons are not prosecuted, convicted, or punished.[14] Their role is one of considerable power. Studies have shown that the outcome of more cases is determined by prosecutors' decisions than by the decisions of any other component of the criminal justice system.[15] A former Attorney General of the United States, Robert H. Jackson, wrote that the prosecutor "has more control over life, liberty, and reputation than any other person in America."[16]

It does not follow from the prosecutor's duty to see that justice is done that the prosecutor must avoid advocacy. Chief Justice Kerwin of the Supreme Court of Canada wrote in the leading Canadian case that counsel for the Crown is entitled to examine all the evidence and ask the jury to come to the conclusion that the accused is guilty as charged.[17] The prosecutor may present the government's position "in forcible and direct language", so long as the language is not inflammatory.[18] In a 1925 judgment of Judge Learned Hand, the court rejected an accused person's attempt to confine a prosecutor to an impartial statement of the evidence. The prosecutor, Judge Hand wrote, "is an advocate, and it is entirely proper for him as earnestly as he can to persuade the jury of the truth of his side."[19] Justice Cory, while a member of the Ontario Court of Appeal, added that "the Crown prosecutor must proceed courageously in the face of threats and attempts at intimidation".[19.1]

It is the prosecutor's dual role that creates the conflict referred to above. James Mills wrote that "a prosecutor's handling of a case can involve forbidding, godlike decisions that leave him tossing in his bed, questioning his beliefs, fer-

---

13 *Re Sue Carpenter*, *supra*, note 6. For a brief discussion of the fairness principle's application to the role of counsel to the Law Society in disciplinary proceedings see Gavin MacKenzie, "Lawyer Discipline and the Independence of the Bar: Can Lawyers Still Govern Themselves?", 24 Law Society of Upper Canada Gazette, part 4 (December, 1990), p. 319 at 325-326.

14 William F. McDonald, "The Prosecutor's Domain" in William F. McDonald (ed.), *The Prosecutor* (Beverly Hills: Sage, 1979), p. 15; Wolfram, *supra*, note 9, p. 759.

15 Thomas F. Eagleton, Preface to William F. McDonald, *ibid.*, p. 8.

16 Robert H. Jackson, "The Federal Prosecutor", 24 Journal of the American Judicature Society 18. See also William F. Wessell, "From Cracker Barrel to Supermarket: Taking the Country Out of Prosecution Management" in William F. McDonald (ed.), *supra*, note 14, p. 137.

17 *Boucher v. R.*, [1955] S.C.R. 16 at 19.

18 *Remus v. United States*, 291 F. 501 at 511 (6th Cir., 1923).

19 *DiCarlo v. United States*, 6 F. 2d 364 at 368 (2nd Cir., 1925). In *Liani v. The Queen* (1980), 13 M.P.L.R. 161 (Ont. Div. Ct.), the Court observed that while it is of course the duty of the Crown to be fair and honest, in the adversary system it is also the duty of the Crown to put the case for the prosecution as strongly as possible consistent with such fairness and honesty.

19.1 *R. v. Logiacco* (1984), 11 C.C.C. (3d) 374 at 378 (Ont. C.A.).

reting his brain for bias."[20] Charles Wolfram has characterized "maintaining the justice — oriented stance that the dual role implies" as "one of the most psychologically difficult tasks that lawyers are asked to perform."[21]

The contrast between the function of prosecutors and the function of lawyers representing parties in civil proceedings is dramatic. Yet in a speech that he delivered to the Canadian Bar Association in 1922, Sir John Simon (later Lord Simon) said that "fundamentally the position of a barrister who is prosecuting a criminal [case] is a mere example and epitome of the kind of honour and the sort of conscience which ought to be shown in all branches of the advocate's work."[22] Reforms in civil procedure, as mentioned in chapters 2 and 4, have gone part way toward achieving this ideal, but we have a long way to go before it is fully realized.

6.2 WHO IS THE CLIENT?

Prosecutors often make decisions that, in civil litigation, would be made by clients rather than lawyers.[23] Their duty is to serve the public interest. They do not have clients in the conventional sense.

Prosecutors do, however, have constituencies. These include, most importantly, the police, victims of crime, other government officials, and the judiciary. Each of these constituencies attempts to influence prosecutorial decisions in much the same way clients attempt to influence the decisions that must be made in any litigation. None, however, can accurately be described as the prosecutor's client.

Prosecutors in subordinate roles should regard the prosecutor to whom they report as their client in relation to matters on which policies have been established or specific directions given. Subject to that qualification, the prosecutor's client is the public.[24]

6.3 THE CHARGING DECISION

In three Canadian jurisdictions, namely British Columbia, Quebec, and New Brunswick, Crown Attorneys decide whether criminal prosecutions should be initiated. In all other Canadian jurisdictions, this decision is made by the police.[25] In all jurisdictions, the decision whether to continue a prosecution or ask that charges be stayed, withdrawn, or dismissed, is made by prosecutors.

Each of these decisions has important consequences. Because the process becomes public when a charge is laid, the charging decision is particularly crucial.

20 James Mills, *The Prosecutor* (New York: Farrar, Straus and Giroux, 1968), p. 25.

21 Charles Wolfram, *Modern Legal Ethics* (St. Paul, Minnesota: West, 1986), pp. 759-760.

22 25 Law Notes 228 at 231, quoted by Mark Orkin, *Legal Ethics: A Study in Professional Conduct* (Toronto: Cartwright & Sons, 1957), p. 120.

23 Monroe H. Freedman, *Lawyers' Ethics In An Adversary System* (New York: Bobbs-Merrill, 1975), p. 79.

24 Wolfram, *supra*, note 21, pp. 759-760.

25 Stephen Owen, *Report of the Discretion to Prosecute Inquiry (the Owen Report)*, vol. 1 (Vancouver: British Columbia Ministry of the Attorney General, 1990), p. 29.

A public announcement that a person has been charged with an offence often causes as much damage to that person as does a conviction. The expense of defending a criminal case can be considerable, but in most cases, considerations of cost pale in significance in comparison to the personal trauma and damage to reputation sustained by the accused person.[26]

In British Columbia, the sole function of some Crown Attorneys is to review investigative reports to decide whether charges recommended by the police should be approved. The Crown Attorneys who perform this function have been directed as a matter of policy to approve charges only if they are satisfied on the evidence available (including evidence reflecting the likely defence, if available) that (i) there is a substantial likelihood of conviction and (ii) it is in the public interest that a prosecution should be undertaken.

The Ministry of the Attorney General policy in which this two-pronged test is articulated makes it clear that the substantial likelihood of conviction standard is significantly stricter than either the *Criminal Code*'s reasonable and probable grounds test or a *prima facie* case test. Factors that the policy requires the Crown Attorney to weigh in considering the second prong of the test include the nature and seriousness of the allegations, the personal circumstances of the accused (including his or her criminal record), the likelihood of achieving the desired result by means other than a criminal prosecution (such as an established diversion process), the harm suffered by the victim, and the cost of the prosecution compared to the social benefit to be gained by it.[27]

Proponents of the traditional system, which remains in place in most other provinces, contend that the British Columbia charge approval system erodes the independence of the police. Proponents of the British Columbia system argue that the damage caused by publication of a charge can be sufficiently harsh that the process should not become public unless and until it is clear that there is a likelihood of conviction. The British Columbia system is thus fairer to accused persons. It is also more objective — police officers who have expended considerable time and energy investigating a possible offence may feel that their efforts have been wasted if charges are not laid. Finally, though perhaps least importantly, the British Columbia system is more efficient than the traditional system.[28]

In 1987, Justice Thomas G. Zuber, in his capacity as author of the Report of the Ontario Court Inquiry, recommended that Crown prosecutors should be involved in the determination of what charge should be laid to a far greater degree than has been the case in the past.[29]

In a 1990 working paper, the Law Reform Commission of Canada emphasized the necessity of consistency and fairness in the determination of both which

---

26 *Ibid.*, p. 25.

27 *Ibid.*, pp. 13-15.

28 *Ibid.*, pp. 20-27.

29 Thomas G. Zuber, *Report of the Ontario Court Inquiry (The Zuber Report)* (Toronto: Ontario Ministry of the Attorney General, 1987), p. 227.

prosecutions should be commenced and which should be discontinued. The Commission recommended: that the advice of a public prosecutor be sought by the police before a charge is laid; that guidelines be issued by Attorneys-General so that the basis of charging decisions is less obscure than was formerly the case; that the guidelines require prosecutors to weigh the available evidence rather than merely decide whether there is a *prima facie* case; that the guidelines require prosecutors to conclude that a prosecution is justified in the public interest before advising that a charge be laid; and that the standard for commencing a prosecution should not be so strict as to discourage prosecutions that are in the public interest though the likelihood of conviction may be somewhat less than "substantial."[30]

Later in 1990, British Columbia's Ombudsman, Stephen Owen, acting in his capacity as Inquiry Commissioner on the province's Discretion to Prosecute Inquiry, issued a report in which he reviewed the British Columbia charge approval system, among other things. Commissioner Owen concluded that the charging decision should remain a prosecutorial responsibility. He also recommended that the two-pronged test should be maintained. Commissioner Owen was persuaded by the Law Reform Commission's analysis that Crown Attorneys should require only a "reasonable" rather than a "substantial" likelihood of conviction, in order to give more flexibility to proceed with charges for offences of grave public concern that, for instance, may involve evidentiary complications, as in sexual assault and child abuse cases.[31]

It is likely, and, for the reasons expressed above, it is desirable, that Canadian prosecutors in the future will play an increasingly direct and important role in deciding whether charges should be laid and, if so, what those charges should be. At present, rules of professional conduct do not specifically address the prosecutor's professional responsibility in laying charges or discontinuing proceedings. The rules say simply that "the prosecutor exercises a public function involving much discretion and power, and must act fairly and dispassionately."[32]

In the United States, prosecutors frequently become involved not only in deciding what charges should be laid, but in deciding what or who should be investigated. The power to make such decisions, like the power to decide who should be charged, is a dangerous one, raising questions of selective and arbitrary enforcement and favouritism.

While Robert Kennedy was the Attorney General of the United States, there was a group in the Justice Department that was actually called the "get-Hoffa-squad." Jimmy Hoffa, the Teamsters' leader, had become an enemy of Kennedy previously. The Justice Department brought more prosecutions against Hoffa and other Teamsters' officials than there were civil rights cases in the entire country.

---

30 Law Reform Commission of Canada, *Controlling Criminal Prosecutions: The Attorney General and the Crown Prosecutor* (Working Paper 62) (Ottawa: Law Reform Commission of Canada, 1990), pp. 76-83.

31 Owen, *supra*, note 25, pp. 98-105.

32 C.B.A. Code, chapter IX, commentary 9; Ontario rule 4.01(3) and accompanying commentary; British Columbia rules, chapter 8, rule 18.

The Justice Department's investigative and prosecutorial strategy was one of target law enforcement: upon being selected as targets people had no choice but to resign themselves to merciless investigation, reinvestigation, indictment, reindictment, trial, and retrial, until the Government obtained one or more guilty verdicts. The "get-Hoffa-squad" was led by a lawyer named Walter Sheridan. When Hoffa disappeared in 1976, Hoffa's daughter said that she wished that the government had a Walter Sheridan working on *that* case. Monroe Freedman wrote that when Robert Kennedy became Attorney General, satisfying his grudge against Jimmy Hoffa became the public policy of the United States.[33]

The involvement of prosecutors in the process before charges are laid has led to another phenomenon in the United States, namely the prosecutor's press conference announcing an accused person's indictment. Some American prosecutors justify such press conferences on the basis of the public's right to know. That purpose, however, can as effectively be served by simply making the indictment (or, in Canada, the information) a public document. Press conferences in which charges are announced can result in both the defamation of an accused person who is presumed (and who may later be found) to be innocent, and difficulty in empanelling an unbiased jury.[34]

One is tempted to surmise that the calling of the press conference may have more to do with the prosecutor's desire to influence public opinion than with any proper purpose. Particularly when the prosecutor is an elected official, one may be forgiven for speculating that the prosecutor may be motivated by personal ambitions. As the English barrister, David Pannick, has written, aspiring prosecutors would be well advised to avoid as a role model the district attorney in Tom Wolfe's 1988 novel *The Bonfire of the Vanities* who "never went near a courtroom. He didn't have time. There were only so many hours in the day for him to stay in touch with channels 1, 2, 4, 5, 7 and 11 and the New York *Daily News*, the *Post*, the *City Light*, and the *Times*."[35]

As Canadian prosecutors become involved at an earlier stage in the process, we should be vigilant to avoid such excesses. The central problem in Canada, however, remains the control of abuses of decisions to charge suspects with crimes and to continue prosecutions initiated by the police.

The problem may be illustrated with an example. An elderly white person is suddenly grabbed from behind in a poorly lighted stairwell by a black youth with a knife who takes the victim's wallet. The incident lasts less than 30 seconds. A week or so later the victim sees someone in the same neighbourhood whom he believes is the assailant. The victim informs the police, who arrest the suspect. There is nothing unusual about the suspect's appearance. The suspect has an alibi;

---

33 Monroe H. Freedman, *Lawyers' Ethics In An Adversary System* (New York: Bobbs-Merrill, 1975), pp. 81-83. See also George V. Higgins, *The Friends of Richard Nixon* (Boston: Little, Brown, 1975), p. 261; and Steven Brill, *The Teamsters* (New York: Simon & Schuster, 1978), pp. 39-40 and 44.

34 Freedman, *ibid.*, p. 94.

35 David Pannick, *Advocates* (Oxford: Oxford University Press, 1992), p. 120.

his mother says that he was home watching television with her at the time. The victim had never seen the suspect previously, and acknowledges that he knows few black people personally. He remains confident, however, in his identification.[36]

A police officer could swear that he or she has reasonable and probable grounds to believe that the suspect is guilty of armed robbery. There is clearly a *prima facie* case that would justify the accused person's committal for trial. Even the British Columbia substantial (or reasonable) likelihood of conviction test may well require that the suspect be charged. The frailties of identification evidence are not well understood by juries and many judges would also convict on the basis of the elderly victim's positive identification. In light of the seriousness of the offence it would be difficult to justify a decision not to charge the suspect on public interest grounds. Many would accuse a prosecutor who decides not to charge the suspect or continue the prosecution with usurping the function of the trier of fact.

Yet the issue is not free of difficulty. Can prosecutors ethically initiate charges or continue prosecutions if they are not personally satisfied beyond a reasonable doubt of the accused person's guilt? Unlike most jurors, the prosecutor knows the fallibility of identification evidence and recognizes that there is a real possibility that the suspect will be unjustly convicted if the case proceeds to trial. Does the conviction vindicate the prosecutor's decision that a charge should be laid or that the prosecution should be continued? Are prosecutors exonerated of ethical responsibility in such cases?

A prosecutor who authorized the laying of a charge on these facts would not be in breach of current Canadian rules of professional conduct. The rules should, however, require prosecutors to refuse to approve charges and to refuse to continue prosecutions when a foreseeable result of their doing so is the wrongful conviction of an accused person. Even the British Columbia substantial (or reasonable) likelihood of conviction test is inadequate. The approval of a charge, and the continuance of a prosecution, should require the prosecution to be satisfied after reviewing the admissible evidence of each of the following:

(1) that there is a reasonable likelihood of conviction;

(2) that a fair-minded person would be satisfied beyond a reasonable doubt of the suspect's guilt;[37] and

---

36 The example is adapted from Professor Richard Uviller's article "The Virtuous Prosecutor or In Quest of an Ethical Standard: Guidance from the American Bar Association" (1973) 71 Michigan L.R. 1145 at 1157-1159. See also Freedman, *supra*, note 33, pp. 84-88.

37 See Freedman, *supra*, note 33, pp. 84-88. See also *Gregg v. Georgia*, 428 U.S. 153 at 225 (1976), *per* Justice White; Charles Wolfram, *Modern Legal Ethics* (St. Paul, Minnesota: West, 1986), pp. 762-765; and Ellen S. Podgor and Jeffrey S. Weiner, "Prosecutorial Misconduct: Alive and Well and Living in Indiana?" (1989-90) 3 Georgetown Journal of Legal Ethics 657.

(3) that it is in the public interest that the prosecution be brought or continued.

Similar considerations are relevant to the selection of charges and the addition and withdrawal of charges; all are acts of virtually unchallenged discretion that are susceptible to possible abuse.

A practice of overcharging, or laying multiple counts that cumulatively are more serious than are warranted by the incident giving rise to the prosecution, should be discouraged. Most prosecutors do not engage in a practice of overcharging in an extreme form partly because (for the reasons discussed above) it would not be responsible to do so, and partly because without evidence prosecutors lack leverage to induce a plea. What does occur is that accused persons are sometimes charged with every conceivable offence of which they may be guilty, without regard to what charge is really warranted by the circumstances, in the hope that a plea bargain will thereby be facilitated. Where admissible evidence supports each of the charges laid and proceeded with, prosecutors are not in violation of any current rule of professional conduct, unless with the complicity of unscrupulous defence counsel they are participating in misleading accused persons into believing that favourable plea bargains have been negotiated on their behalf when in fact the lawyers on both sides know that the accused persons are pleading guilty to what they should have been charged with in the first place.[38]

6.4 DISCLOSURE

Canadian rules of professional conduct do address expressly the prosecutor's duty of disclosure by requiring that prosecutors "to the extent required by law and accepted practice, should make timely disclosure to the accused or defence counsel (or to the court if the accused is not represented) of all relevant facts and known witnesses, whether tending to show guilt or innocence, or that would affect the punishment of the accused."[39]

Because the prosecutor's obligation is qualified by the words "to the extent required by law and accepted practice" this rule cannot, of course, be read in isolation from the authorities. In a 1991 decision,[40] the Supreme Court of Canada considered the extent of the prosecutor's duty of disclosure in cases in which the accused person is charged with an indictable offence. On behalf of a unanimous seven judge court, Justice Sopinka wrote that in serious criminal cases, prosecutors are duty-bound to disclose information obtained by police that might help the defence: "The fruits of the investigation are not the property of the Crown for

---

38 See Jay A. Sigler, "The Prosecutor: A Comparative Functional Analysis" in William F. McDonald (ed.), *The Prosecutor* (Beverly Hills: Sage, 1979), p. 53; Pamela J. Utz, "Two Models of Prosecutorial Professionalism", at pp. 105 and 110 of the same volume; and Freedman, *supra*, note 33, p. 88.

39 C.B.A. Code, chapter IX, commentary 9; Ontario rule 4.01(3) and accompanying commentary (the last nine words quoted are deleted from the Ontario rule.). See also *Milgaard v. Kujawa*, [1995] 2 W.W.R. lixv (note) (Sask. C.A.).

40 *R. v. Stinchcombe*, [1991] 3 S.C.R. 326.

use in securing a conviction, but the property of the public to be used to ensure that justice is done."[41]

The court quashed the conviction of the appellant on the ground that he had not been provided with disclosure of statements made to the police that were potentially favourable to him. The appellant knew that the potential witness, his former secretary, had made statements to the police, but did not know what she had said. On the third day of the trial, the appellant was told that his former secretary would not be called as a Crown witness because the prosecutor had formed the view that she was not a credible witness.[42] Justice Sopinka observed that it was not up to the prosecutor to decide whether a potential witness is credible; that is a decision for the judge.

The court went on to add that disclosure should be the general rule and that there should be very few exceptions. The identity of informants or other people who need to be protected from injury or harassment might be excepted, as might information that is "clearly irrelevant" to the case. Information may be withheld temporarily if disclosure would jeopardize continuing investigation.[43]

Any decisions made by a prosecutor to withhold information are subject to review by the courts, so that the courts may satisfy themselves that the information that is not disclosed falls within one of the exceptions. Generally, Justice Sopinka added, disclosure should be made before the accused person is required to enter a plea.[44] Justice Sopinka also wrote that possibly the same principles should be applied to summary conviction proceedings, but that a decision on that issue should be deferred until the issue is before the court.[45]

In later decisions, the Supreme Court of Canada has held that the full disclosure requirement applies with equal vigour to both factual and procedural defences,[45.1] and that an accused person is not required to make a preliminary showing of potential prejudice from lack of access (to edited material, in the case in question) as a condition of entitlement to disclosure.[45.2]

The United States Supreme Court has also held that prosecutors have a constitutional duty, created by the due process clauses of the fifth and fourteenth amendments, to disclose to accused persons all materially favourable evidence.[46]

---

41 *Ibid.*, p. 333.

42 *Ibid.*, pp. 329-331.

43 *Ibid.*, pp. 339-340.

44 *Ibid.*, pp. 340-343.

45 *Ibid.*, p. 342.

45.1 *R. v. Egger* (1993), 103 D.L.R. (4th) 678 (S.C.C.).

45.2 *R. v. Durette* (1993), 88 C.C.C. (3d) 1 (S.C.C.); see also *R. v. Dersch* (1990), 77 D.L.R. (4th) 473 (S.C.C.).

46 *Brady v. Maryland*, 373 U.S. 83 (1962); *United States v. Augurs*, 427 U.S. 97 (1976); and *United States v. Bagley*, 105 S. Ct. 3375 (1985). See also Terrence J. Galligan, "The Prosecutor's Duty to Disclose Exculpatory Evidence After *United States v. Bagley*" (1987-88) 1 Georgetown Journal of Legal Ethics 213; and Charles Wolfram, *Modern Legal Ethics* (St. Paul, Minnesota: West, 1986), pp. 768-769.

6.5 PLEA BARGAINING

Canadian rules of professional conduct that address the responsibility of lawyers in plea bargaining consider the issue primarily from the perspective of the defence counsel. The C.B.A. Code makes it clear, however, that the public interest must not be compromised by agreeing to a guilty plea,[47] an admonition that would appear to be directed at least equally to prosecutors. Ontario's rules provide, somewhat more specifically, that "the public interest must not . . . be sacrificed in pursuit of an apparently expedient means of disposing of doubtful cases."[48]

For overworked prosecutors a plea bargain means less work, more time to devote to other cases, and perhaps fewer nights and weekends at the office. Most prosecutors are paid not by the hour, but by the year. When working for a fixed fee, defence counsel also may have a financial incentive to negotiate a plea bargain: it takes far less time to bargain most cases than to try them.[49]

Negotiated pleas can and usually do result in just dispositions of cases, and can contribute also to the efficient use of scarce prosecutorial and judicial resources. It is important that pleas not be negotiated for reasons of expedience where such dispositions are not in the public interest and, particularly, where it is not clear that the accused is in fact guilty.

A trial judge has jurisdiction to refuse to accept a plea to a lesser offence, despite the concurrence of the prosecutor, where on the agreed facts the accused is guilty of the offence charged. Thus in a 1990 decision,[50] the Ontario Court of Appeal held that a trial judge did not err in refusing to accept a plea bargain whereby the accused pleaded guilty to common assault where the facts as stated by the Crown Attorney supported a finding of assault with a weapon. The court observed that trial judges in most cases do, and should, give great weight to the decision of counsel for the prosecution, as a representative of the public interest, to accept a plea of guilty to an included or lesser offence. The court added that its decision should not be taken as a holding that a trial judge would be wrong in accepting a plea to an included or lesser offence even though the facts might indicate that the full offence was committed where a case is made out that the result reflects a reasonable exercise of prosecutorial discretion having regard to the public interest in the effective administration of justice.[51]

---

47 C.B.A. Code, chapter IX, commentary 12. See also *R. v. Turner*, [1970] 2 All E.R. 281 at 285 (C.A.).

48 Ontario rule 4.01(9) and accompanying commentary.

49 Alan M. Dershowitz, *The Best Defence* (New York: First Vintage Books, 1983), pp. 132-133.

50 *R. v. Naraindeen* (1990), 75 O.R. (2d) 120 (C.A.), varied on reconsideration (1990), 75 O.R. (2d) 120 at 133 (C.A.).

51 *Ibid.*, pp. 128-129. On the issue of whether courts may become involved in the exercise of prosecutorial discretion to withdraw charges see *R. v. Commissioner of Police of the Metropolis, Ex parte Blackburn*, [1967] W.L.R. 902 (C.A.); and William F. McDonald, "The Prosecutor's Domain" in William F. McDonald (ed.), *The Prosecutor* (Beverly Hills: Sage, 1979), p. 27.

If a plea bargain is made, the Crown has a duty to uphold it. In a 1980 decision[52] Justice Krever, who was then a member of the Ontario High Court of Justice, had occasion to consider whether the court should allow a prosecutor to repudiate an agreement entered into by a prosecutor who formerly had carriage of the case on the ground that the agreement was not in the public interest. One of three co-accused had entered into an agreement with the prosecution whereby she agreed to give a statement to the police and to testify against one of her co-accused in exchange for immunity from prosecution. She had fulfilled the first of the two obligations that she had undertaken — by providing an inculpatory statement to the police — when a second prosecutor who had been assigned responsibility for the case repudiated the agreement.

Justice Krever granted a motion for an order staying the proceedings against the accused person who had entered into the agreement, holding that there was considerable merit in her submission that the Crown's repudiation of the plea bargain "undermines the administration of justice and brings the entire system of the administration of justice into disrepute." Moreover, Justice Krever added, if permitted to withdraw from the agreement, the Crown would have caused serious prejudice to the applicant in her defence.[53]

The United States Supreme Court has also held that though a prosecutor is under no obligation to enter into a plea bargain, once an agreement has been reached the prosecutor has a duty to fulfil it.[54]

The United States Supreme Court has also considered the propriety of a prosecutor threatening to cause an accused person to be reindicted and subjected to a harsher potential sentence if the accused person does not accept a proffered plea agreement. In the case before the court the accused person chose not to plead guilty to a charge of issuing a forged instrument, knowing that the prosecutor would recommend a five-year sentence if he would plead guilty, but that if he did not plead guilty the prosecutor would proceed to reindict him under habitual criminal legislation, thereby subjecting him to possible life imprisonment. By a majority, the Supreme Court ruled that plea bargaining is an important component of the criminal justice system, involving give and take. Because the accused person had full knowledge of the possible consequences of a decision not to plead guilty, the court held, he could not complain of the prosecutor's arranging for his reindictment. The majority did not regard the prosecutor's conduct as unilateral action taken in retaliation for the exercise by the accused person of his constitutional rights. An accused person must show actual vindictiveness by a prosecutor, the court held, to succeed in obtaining a stay or dismissal of proceedings in such a case.[55]

---

52 *R. v. Crneck* (1980), 30 O.R. (2d) 1 (H.C.).

53 *Ibid.*, pp. 12-13.

54 *Santobello v. New York*, 92 S. Ct. 495 (1971); *Blackledge v. Allison*, 97 S. Ct. 1621 (1977).

55 *Bordenkircher v. Hayes*, 98 S. Ct. 663 (1978). See also *Blackledge v. Perry*, 417 U.S. 21 (1974); and *United States v. Goodwin*, 457 U.S. 368 (1982).

6.6 IMPERMISSIBLE TACTICS

As a result of their duty to approach their responsibilities with quasi-judicial fairness rather than in a partisan spirit, prosecutors' advocacy must be much more restrained than that of lawyers representing either persons accused of criminal offences or parties to civil proceedings. Limitations imposed on all advocates in the interest of discouraging forensic excesses apply *a fortiori* to prosecutors, and prosecutors are subject to limitations that do not apply to advocates for private parties who are discharging their duty of resolute partisanship. Thus it is particularly important that prosecutors do not express personal opinions concerning the guilt of the accused person[56] or the credibility of witnesses,[57] or make other prejudicial or inflammatory remarks to the court.[58] It is also important that prosecutors refrain from speaking to witnesses called by them who are being cross-examined.[59]

The prosecutor's duty to ensure that an accused person receives a fair trial heightens the prosecutor's duty of care. Prosecutors must take reasonable steps to assess the truth or falsity, and not just the plausibility, of evidence that they

---

56 *Boucher v. R.* [1955] S.C.R. 16 at 19 and 26, *per* Kerwin C.J.C. and Locke J.; *Romeo v. R.* (1991), 62 C.C.C. (3d) 1 (S.C.C.); *R. v. Murphy* (1981), 58 C.C.C. (2d) 338 (N.S. C.A.); *R. v. Wilson* (1983), 5 C.C.C. (3d) 61 (B.C. C.A.); *R. v. McDonald* (1958), 120 C.C.C. 209 (Ont. C.A.); *Pursey v. R.* (1956), 116 C.C.C. 82 (Que. C.A.); *Greenberg v. United States*, 280 F. 2d 472 at 475 (1st Cir. 1960); and *United States v. Socony-Vacuum Oil Co.*, 310 U.S. 150 at 264 (U.S. S. Ct., 1940), *per* Roberts J. In *Liani v. The Queen* (1980), 13 M.P.L.R. 161, the Ontario Divisional Court held that the breach of this rule where the trial is before a judge alone is unlikely to be prejudicial to the accused's right to a fair trial.

57 *R. v. Boyko* (1975), 28 C.C.C. (2d) 193 (B.C. C.A.); *Wilson v. People*, 743 P. 2d 415 at 418 (Colo., 1987).

58 In *R. v. Tobin* (1992), 9 O.R. (3d) 129 the Ontario Court of Appeal held that the conduct of Crown counsel in advising the jury to dismiss the accused person's claimed amnesia on the ground that the very first thing that the Crown counsel had learned in law school was that a blackout is the first refuge of a guilty mind, did not lead to a miscarriage of justice. See also *R. v. Nugent* (1995), 24 O.R. (3d) 295 (C.A.); *R. v. Grover* (1991), 67 C.C.C. (3d) 576 (S.C.C.); *R. v. Smith* (1990), 61 C.C.C. (3d) 232 (Ont. C.A.), affirmed [1992] 2 S.C.R. 915; *R. v. Charest* (1990), 57 C.C.C. (3d) 312 (Que. C.A.); *R. v. Gratton* (1985), 18 C.C.C. (3d) 462 (Ont. C.A.), leave to appeal to S.C.C. refused (1985), 18 C.C.C. (3d) 462n (S.C.C.); *R. v. Dunn* (1981), 64 C.C.C. (2d) 253 (Que. C.A.); *R. v. Labarre* (1978), 45 C.C.C. (2d) 171 (Que. C.A.); *R. v. Roberts* (1973), 14 C.C.C. (2d) 168 (Ont. C.A.); *R. v. Rosik* (1970), 2 C.C.C. (2d) 351 (Ont. C.A.), affirmed [1971] 2 O.R. 89n (S.C.C.); *R. v. Vallieres*, [1970] 4 C.C.C. 69 (Que. C.A.); *Dupuis v. R.* (1967), 3 C.R.N.S. 75 (Que. C.A.); *R. v. Banks*, [1916] 2 K.B. 621; *Remus v. United States*, 291 F. 501 at 511 (6th Cir., 1923); *Commonwealth v. D'Amato*, 514 Pa. 471 (1987); and see Monroe H. Freedman, *Lawyers' Ethics In An Adversary System* (New York: Bobbs-Merrill, 1975), p. 95.

59 In *R. v. Savoy* (1977), 18 N.B.R. (2d) 489 (C.A.) the trial judge had granted to counsel for the Crown, permission to speak to a witness whom the Crown had called, while the witness was under cross-examination. The Court of Appeal said that such a discussion should not have been permitted, but did not allow an appeal brought by the accused person on this ground because no objection was made by defence counsel at trial, and the answer to the only question asked after the discussion occurred was consistent with the witness's previous answers.

lead; they must not lead evidence that they know, or ought to know, is false.[60] They must personally confirm the truth of statements that they make to the court. Prosecutors who are reckless as to the truth of such statements violate their duty to do justice.[61]

It should be no answer to allegations of prosecutorial misconduct for prosecutors to say that they are merely "fighting fire with fire", or responding to provocation in the form of impermissible tactics on the part of the defence. The same rules do not apply to prosecution and defence counsel, who play dramatically different roles in the process. The impediment to a fair trial is the same whether or not the prosecutor is provoked. The proper course for a prosecutor to follow if defence counsel exceed the limits of acceptable advocacy is to object and ask the trial judge to intervene. They should not respond in kind.[62]

Like all lawyers, prosecutors have a duty not to communicate directly with persons who are represented by counsel except with counsel's consent.[63] Prosecutors also have a duty, as, again, do all lawyers, to deal in good faith with lay persons who are lawfully representing others or themselves.[64] Both duties must be observed particularly scrupulously by prosecutors. It would be highly improper for a prosecutor to attempt to obtain directly from an accused person a waiver of such rights as the right to remain silent, the right to counsel, and the right to a preliminary inquiry.[65]

Although, again, the practices are not explicitly prohibited by current Canadian rules of professional conduct, prosecutors should ensure that arrangements that they make with witnesses do not risk influencing the witnesses' testimony. Arrangements whereby accomplices' sentences are deferred until after they testify

---

60 *United States v. Kelly*, 543 F. Supp 1303 at 1309-1310 (Mass., 1982). See also Charles Wolfram, *Modern Legal Ethics* (St. Paul, Minnesota: West, 1986), p. 767.

61 In *R. v. Hay* (1982), 70 C.C.C. (2d) 286 (Sask. C.A.), a new trial was ordered because the prosecutor stated that the accused person and the owner of a motor vehicle were the same person, though the prosecutor was aware that the police investigation had revealed that they were not. See also *Re Sue Carpenter*, 808 P. 2d 1341 (Kan., 1991).

62 *Commonwealth v. Kozec*, 505 N.E. 2d 519 at 522 (Mass. Sup. Jud. Ct., 1987); *United States v. Schuler*, 813 F. 2d 978 (9th Cir., 1987); but see *United States v. Young*, 470 U.S. 1 (1985), in which the United States Supreme Court, by a bare majority, found no unfairness sufficient to justify reversing an accused person's conviction where the prosecutor expressed a personal opinion that the accused person was guilty as charged in response to the defence counsel's expression of the opposite opinion. *Gridley v. United States*, 44 F. 2d 716 at 739 (6th Cir., 1930), cert. denied 283 U.S. 827 (U.S. S. Ct., 1931) is to the same effect. David Pannick suggests that these decisions are wrong in *Advocates* (Oxford: Oxford University Press, 1992), pp. 118-119.

63 C.B.A. Code, chapter XVI, commentary 8 and chapter IX, commentary 6; Ontario rules 6.03(7) and 4.03(1) and (2).

64 C.B.A. Code, chapter XVI, commentary 10; Ontario rule 6.03(1).

65 The American Bar Association's Model Rules of Professional Conduct, which have been adopted by 37 states, provide that a prosecutor "shall . . . not seek to obtain from an unrepresented accused a waiver of important pretrial rights such as the right to a preliminary hearing." See also Wolfram, *supra*, note 60, p. 618.

at the trials of other alleged parties to their offences enable prosecutors to maintain strong and coercive holds over witnesses, and may well risk influencing the witnesses to testify falsely in the hope that they will be rewarded with more lenient sentences.[66]

Other tactics that, at least in some circumstances, may violate the prosecutor's duty to act fairly and dispassionately include: issuing subpoenas to defence counsel;[67] using accused persons' criminal records to impeach credibility in situations in which the prejudicial effect of doing so outweighs the asserted justification of casting doubt on credibility;[68] unnecessarily interrupting defence counsel's examination of witnesses;[69] adopting a belligerent attitude toward accused persons, defence counsel, or defence witnesses;[70] and pursuing lines of questioning or argument that are clearly irrelevant or otherwise impermissible, such as cross–examination of an accused person that suggests that he or she has previously been suspected of another crime.[71]

In a 1996 decision,[71.1] the Ontario Court of Appeal ordered a new trial on charges of gross indecency and indecent assault in part because of improper and abusive cross-examination of the accused and other defence witnesses. The accused and his wife were asked repeatedly why the complainant, their daughter, would fabricate her allegations, and were called upon to comment on the credibility of the complainant. The court held that these questions not only put the accused and his wife in the invidious position of having to call their own daughter a liar, but suggested that there was an onus on the accused to provide a motive for the complainant's testimony, thereby undermining the fundamental principle of the presumption of innocence. "We think it is unfortunate that Crown counsel persist in this kind of unfair questioning in the face of the many judgments of this Court that such questioning is improper," the Court added.[71.2]

Although for reasons discussed in chapter 7 defence counsel may ethically cross-examine prosecution witnesses to make them appear to be inaccurate or untruthful, even though the defence counsel knows that the witnesses are testifying accurately and truthfully, none of the reasons justify prosecutors in

---

66 See Monroe H. Freedman, *Lawyers' Ethics In An Adversary System* (New York: Bobbs-Merrill, 1975), pp. 89-90; and Wolfram, *supra*, note 60, p. 651.

67 See *United States v. Klubock*, 639 F. Supp. 117 (Mass., 1986), affirmed 832 F. 2d 649 (1st Cir., 1987); and Peter C. Sheridan, "Grand Jury Subpoenas to Criminal Defense Attorneys: Massachusetts Restrains the Federal Prosecutor Through an Ethical Rule" (1988-89) 2 Georgetown Journal of Legal Ethics 485.

68 See Freedman, *supra*, note 66, p. 90.

69 *State v. Boyd*, 160 W. Va. 234 (1977).

70 *R. v. R. (A.J.)* 1994), 20 O.R. (3d) 405 (C.A.); *Pool v. Superior Court*, 677 P. 2d 261 (1984); and Wolfram, *supra*, note 66, p. 766.

71 See Wolfram, *supra*, note 66, p. 766.

71.1 *R. v. F. (A.)* (1996), 30 O.R. (3d) 470 (C.A.).

71.2 At 471.

making defence witnesses appear to be testifying inaccurately or untruthfully when the prosecutors know that they are not.[72]

6.7 THE MAGISTERIAL PROSECUTOR

Prosecutors come in two models: the adversarial model and the magisterial model.[73]

The adversarial model of prosecutor promotes law enforcement values to the exclusion of all others. Accused persons are consistently overcharged, as aggressive and indiscriminate charging is one of many legitimate weapons in the prosecutor's arsenal in a legal contest with the defence.[74]

The adversarial prosecutor will exploit the laxity, inexperience, or incompetence of defence counsel because to do so is consistent with the prosecutor's combative approach. Game-like bargaining and the pursuit of maximum sentences are also characteristic of the adversarial model's approach, which can be summarized in a word as "zealous."[75]

The magisterial model of prosecutor (the adjective is derived from the noun "magistrate") exemplifies a professional ethic that rejects lawyerly partisanship and rivalry. The claims of both law enforcement and fundamental justice are considered objectively.[76] The magisterial model's approach is quasi-judicial and moderated. Ensuring the fairness of accused persons' trials is as important a goal as the protection of the public.

A less aggressive formulation of charges reflects not a policy of leniency but a careful evaluation of the practical likelihood of proving the charges, and of what result is truly warranted on the available, and admissible, evidence.[77]

Other distinguishing qualities of the magisterial model of prosecutor include a willingness to make full and prompt disclosure and a repudiation of questionable trial tactics, in combination with appropriate firmness.

The adversarial model of prosecutor has no place in our process. The line should be discontinued. Prosecutors should come only in the magisterial model.

---

72 See Monroe H. Freedman, *Understanding Lawyers' Ethics* (New York: Matthew Bender & Co., 1990), p. 214.

73 Pamela J. Utz, "Two Models of Prosecutorial Professionalism" in William F. McDonald (ed.), *The Prosecutor* (Beverly Hills: Sage, 1979), pp. 103-114.

74 *Ibid.*, pp. 103-109.

75 *Ibid.*, pp. 103-109. See also Jerome Frank, *Courts on Trial* (New York: Athenium, 1963); James B. Stewart, *The Prosecutors* (New York: Simon & Schuster, 1987), pp. 287 and 351-355; and Kenneth Bresler, "'I Never Lost a Trial': When Prosecutors Keep Score on Criminal Convictions", 9 Georgetown Journal of Legal Ethics 537 (1996).

76 Utz, *supra*, note 73, pp. 109-114.

77 Utz, *supra*, note 73, pp. 109-114.

7

Criminal Defence

7.1 THE ETHICS OF THE CRIMINAL DEFENCE LAWYER

The criminal defence bar has an image problem. Its predicament is not new. Jeremy Bentham considered criminal lawyers who successfully defended accused persons whom they believed to be guilty to be little better than accessories after the fact.[1] More recently, the prominent American trial lawyer Gerry Spence overheard someone talking about him in a restaurant. "He's worse than the criminals he represents," the person said. "*He* knows better."[2] When Professor John M. Burkoff told friends and colleagues that he was writing a book about criminal defence ethics they would often respond with sarcasm. "Criminal defence ethics," they would snicker. "It must be a pretty short book."[3]

Lawyers who defend criminal cases have often been regarded by non-lawyers and sometimes even by other lawyers as being somewhat on the shady side of the practice of law.[4] There are two related reasons for this persistent belief. First, many lay people wrongly associate lawyers with their clients; and, as the American jurist Edward G. Ryan observed, "It is not the saints of the world who chiefly give employment to our profession."[5] Second, the role of the defence lawyer in the criminal justice process is widely misunderstood. The standards of professional ethics that criminal defence lawyers are bound to maintain are no less exacting than those by which prosecutors are bound,[6] but they are quite different.

1 Walter Schroeder, "Some Ethical Problems in Criminal Law", 1963 Law Society of Upper Canada Special Lectures (Toronto: Law Society of Upper Canada, 1963), p. 87 at 89.

2 Gerry Spence, *With Justice For None* (New York: Random House, 1989), p. 31.

3 Samuel Dash, Book Review of John M. Burkoff's *Criminal Defense Ethics* (New York: Clark Boardman, 1986) (1987-88) 1 Georgetown Journal of Legal Ethics 641.

4 *Ibid.*, p. 641.

5 David Shrager and Elizabeth Frost (eds.), *The Quotable Lawyer* (New York: Facts on File, 1986), p. 197.

6 See *Jackson v. United States*, 297 F. 2d 195 at 198 (D.C. Cir., 1961) in which Judge Warren E. Burger, as he then was, wrote in a concurring opinion that "it must be remembered that there is not a dual standard of conduct, one for the prosecutor and one for the defense counsel." See also David G. Bress, "Professional Ethics in Criminal Trials: A View of the Defense Counsel's Responsibility" (1966) 64 Michigan L.R. 1493.

Criminal defence lawyers have no generalized duty to do justice. By striving to prevent the conviction of clients whom they know or believe to be guilty, criminal defence lawyers are upholding, not contravening, their professional duty, a duty that is fundamental to the achievement of the goals of the criminal justice process in a democracy.

Canadian rules of professional conduct provide that when defending an accused person, the lawyer's duty is to protect the client as far as possible from being convicted except by a tribunal of competent jurisdiction and upon legal evidence sufficient to support a conviction for the offence with which the client is charged. Thus, the rules add, notwithstanding the lawyer's private opinion as to credibility or the merits, the lawyer may properly rely upon any evidence or defences including so-called technicalities not known to be false or fraudulent.[7]

The ethics of attempting to obtain acquittals for accused persons known by their lawyers to be guilty is understood at some level by non-lawyers for whom the question, "how can you defend someone you know is guilty?" nevertheless remains valid and troubling. For the most part, criminal defence lawyers themselves consider the question boring and irrelevant. "The fundamental mindset of most criminal defense lawyers toward defending the guilty is one of staggering indifference to the question," Professor Barbara Babcock of Stanford Law Society has written.[8] Martin Erdmann, the former head of the Supreme Court branch of New York City's Legal Aid Society — who is said to have defended more persons accused of crimes than anyone else in the world — once said "I have nothing to do with justice. Justice is not even part of the equation."[9]

Martin Erdmann also said that "myths are very important in this business."[10] An appreciation of the symbolic importance of the criminal trial in a democracy is essential to understanding the reason that the high ethical duties of prosecutors and criminal defence lawyers are so dramatically different.

An American lawyer, Thurman Arnold, wrote that the criminal trial is "the center of ideals of every Western government" in that it embodies the "great principles which give dignity to the individual" as well as those "which not only make of the state a great righteous protector but at the same time keep it in its place."[11] "The notion that every man however lowly is entitled to a trial and an impartial hearing is regarded as the cornerstone of civilized government," he added. "Even a criminal caught in the act is still entitled to present his 'defense'

---

7 C.B.A. Code, chapter IX, commentary 10; Ontario rule 4.01(1) and accompanying commentary; Quebec rules, section 2.04; Yukon rules, part three, rule 6; see also British Columbia rules, chapter 1, rule 3(6).

8 Barbara Allen Babcock, "Defending the Guilty", Cleveland State Law Review, vol. 33, no. 2 (1985), quoted in Evan Thomas, *The Man To See: Edward Bennett Williams — Ultimate Insider; Legendary Trial Lawyer* (New York: Simon & Schuster, 1991), p. 120.

9 James Mills, "I Have Nothing To Do With Justice", *Life* Magazine (July, 1973), p. 57.

10 *Ibid.*, p. 60.

11 Thurman Arnold, *The Symbols of Government* (New Haven, Connecticut: Yale University Press, 1935), p. 128.

to a tribunal which must be ignorant of the event. This ideal is as old as Western civilization, and its significance in our culture is tremendous. It involves the humanitarian notion that the underdog is always entitled to a chance."[12]

For the underdog to be entitled to a chance, the right to counsel is essential. Resolute partisan advocacy on behalf of those accused of crimes is the greatest safeguard against encroachment by the state.[13] The right to counsel is essential whether or not the accused person is guilty. To suggest that defence counsel represent only people who are innocent (or any other category of people) is to open the door to a system in which the government decides who is, and who is not, entitled to a defence.[14]

Jesse Berman, in an article about the Cuban popular tribunals, wrote that "the first job of a revolutionary lawyer is not to argue that his client is innocent, but rather to determine if his client is guilty and, if so, to seek the sanction which will best rehabilitate him."[15] In Western democracies, however, it is no part of defence lawyers' function to determine whether their clients are guilty. Dr. Samuel Johnson's statement that "a lawyer has no business with the justice or injustice of the cause which he undertakes . . . The justice or injustice of the cause is to be decided by the judge"[16] is universally accepted. Thus Baron Bramwell observed in an 1871 decision[17] that "a man's rights are to be determined by the court, not by his advocate or counsel . . . A client is entitled to say to his counsel, "I want your advocacy, not your judgment: I prefer that of the court'."

A longtime justice of the Ontario Court of Appeal once said that it is no more proper to level a charge of insincerity or duplicity against lawyers who defend persons whom they believe to be guilty than it would be to level such a charge against members of debating clubs who have been assigned the task of supporting the affirmative or negative side of arguments on subjects not of their

---

12 *Ibid.*, pp. 134-135.

13 See *Canadian Charter of Rights and Freedoms*, Part I of the *Constitution Act, 1982*, being Schedule B of the *Canada Act 1982* (U.K.), 1982, c. 11, s. 10(b); *Gideon v. Wainwright*, 372 U.S. 335 (1963); and David Luban, *Lawyers and Justice: An Ethical Study* (Princeton, New Jersey: Princeton University Press, 1988), p. 58.

14 Alan M. Dershowitz, *The Best Defence* (New York: First Vintage Books, 1983), pp. 415-416.

15 Jesse Berman, "The Cuban Popular Tribunals" (1969) 69 Columbia L.R. 1317 at 1341.

16 James Boswell, *Life of Johnson*, vol. 5 (London: Murray, 1876), pp. 28-29 (quoted by Mark Orkin, *Legal Ethics: A Study in Professional Conduct* (Toronto: Cartwright & Sons, 1957), p. 111.

17 *Johnson v. Emerson and Sparrow* (1871), L.R. 6 Ex. 329 at 367. See also *Tukiar v. R.* (1934) 52 Commonwealth L.R. 335; *Polk County v. Dodson*, 454 U.S. 312 at 318 (1981), *per* Powell J.; and *Re Griffiths*, 413 U.S. 717 at 724 (1973), *per* Powell J..

choosing and on sides that may not appeal to them. Moreover, he added, experience shows us that improbable stories can be and are true.[18]

The rules of professional conduct referred to above recognize that the criminal defence counsel's duty of resolute partisan advocacy must be discharged irrespective of the lawyer's personal opinion as to the credibility of witnesses and the merits of the case.[19]

The realization of the anti-totalitarian goals of preserving individual liberty and dignity sometimes frustrates the realization of other goals of the criminal justice process, including efficiency, and the ascertainment of truth.[20] It is the professional responsibility of defence counsel in many cases to prevent the whole truth from coming out by all lawful means. Defence lawyers have a professional responsibility to object to the admission of improperly obtained evidence, even if they know it to be truthful. Nor, of course, is it improper for defence counsel to advise clients to invoke their constitutionally guaranteed rights and refuse to make statements to the police or testify at trial.[21]

If a Crown Attorney mistakenly tells the court that an accused person has no criminal record, the accused person's lawyer has no duty to disclose prior convictions and, indeed, has a duty not to do so. If asked by the court to confirm the Crown's statement, the defence counsel may say "I understand that the Crown is not relying on a prior record" but should avoid saying "I do not contest the Crown's statement", as that might be considered misleading. If pressed further, the defence counsel should refuse to answer on the grounds that the proof of prior convictions is the responsibility of the Crown, and that it is not for an accused person's own lawyer to prove or disprove the accused person's record.[22]

In a 1967 opinion Justice White of the United States Supreme Court differentiated the ethical duties of criminal defence lawyers from those of prosecutors:

> Law enforcement officers have the obligation to convict the guilty and to make sure they do not convict the innocent. They must be dedicated to making the

---

18 Walter Schroeder, "Some Ethical Problems in Criminal Law" 1963 Law Society of Upper Canada Special Lectures (Toronto: Law Society of Upper Canada, 1963), pp. 89 and 91. Justice Schroeder also said (at p. 92 of the same lecture) that if a client confesses but insists on pleading not guilty, the lawyer should withdraw if time permits, because "it is highly doubtful if he could plead the case effectively and affect "warmth for his client' without being plagued by his conscience that he is acting the role of a base dissembler."

19 See rules cited *supra*, note 7.

20 Thurman Arnold, *The Symbols of Government* (New Haven, Connecticut: Yale University Press, 1935), pp. 129 and 134-135; Monroe H. Freedman, *Lawyers' Ethics In An Adversary System* (New York: Bobbs-Merrill, 1975), p. 8.

21 *Charter of Rights and Freedoms*, s. 11(c) and (d). See also Dershowitz, *supra*, note 14, p. xix; and Freedman, *ibid.*, p. 79.

22 See Earl A. Cherniak, "The Ethics of Advocacy", Law Society of Upper Canada Gazette, vol. 19, no. 2 (June, 1985), p. 145 at 155. See also *R. v. Palaramchuk*, Ont. Co. Ct., 1984 (unreported), which purports to impose on defence counsel a duty to be candid in disclosing the circumstances of prior convictions in plea discussions with the Crown that are initiated by defence counsel.

> criminal trial a procedure for the ascertainment of the true facts surrounding the commission of the crime . . . But defence counsel has no comparable obligation to ascertain or present the truth. Our system assigns to him a different mission. He must be and is interested in preventing the conviction of the innocent, but . . . we also insist that he defend his client whether he is innocent or guilty. The State has the obligation to present evidence. Defence counsel need present nothing, even if he knows what the truth is. He need not furnish any witnesses to the police, or reveal any confidences of his client, or furnish any other information to help the prosecution's case. If he can confuse a witness, even a truthful one, or make him appear at a disadvantage, unsure or indecisive, that will be his normal course. Our interest in not convicting the innocent permits counsel to put the State to its proof, to put the State's case in the worst possible light, regardless of what he thinks or knows to be the truth. Undoubtedly there are some limits which defense counsel must observe but more often than not, defense counsel will examine a prosecution witness, and impeach him if he can, even if he thinks the witness is telling the truth, just as he will attempt to destroy a witness who is lying. In this respect, as part of our modified adversary system, and as part of the duty imposed on the most honourable defense counsel, we countenance or require conduct which in many instances has little, if any, relation to the search for truth.[23]

In a 1991 decision the Ontario Court of Appeal emphasized the critical role played by defence counsel in criminal trials. Courts should be slow to second guess such tactical decisions of defence counsel as declining to object to evidence or deciding not to call an accused person to testify: "We must never forget that ours is an adversarial system and the role of defence counsel is every bit as important as that of any other party to the proceedings, including that of the judge" wrote Justice Finlayson. "When we minimize the failure of counsel to object to evidence which he clearly saw as being to his client's advantage, we diminish the role of defence counsel."[24]

The year after Confederation the Honourable John H. Cameron was retained to represent Patrick James Whelan, who was charged with the murder of Thomas D'Arcy McGee. It was what today would be described as a "high-profile case"; the trial was of national interest. It is reported that at the trial, Cameron went to extraordinary lengths to defend himself for having taken on the difficult task of defending Whelan. His apology was undoubtedly harmful to his client. Many years later the author of *Famous Canadian Trials* wrote that "Mr. Cameron's eloquent and vehement apology for embarking upon this famous case was taken by thousands of people, and very likely the jury as well, to imply a disbelief in the innocence of the prisoner."[25]

---

23 *United States v. Wade*, 388 U.S. 218 at 256-258 (1967). Justice White, joined by Justices Harlan and Stewart, concurred in part and dissented in part.

24 *R. v. Lomage* (1991), 2 O.R. (3d) 621 at 630 (C.A.).

25 Albert R. Hassard, *Famous Canadian Trials* (Toronto: Carswell, 1924), pp. 146-147 [quoted by Beverley G. Smith, *Professional Conduct for Canadian Lawyers* (Toronto: Butterworths, 1989), p. 175].

No apology was necessary. The defence of persons accused of crimes, whether or not they are in fact guilty, is among the most honourable and important enterprises that lawyers can pursue.

7.2 CONFIDENTIALITY AND TRUTH

As is the case in all areas of practice, the most difficult ethical problems of criminal defence lawyers involve the resolution of conflicting professional responsibilities. Criminal defence lawyers have a duty, as do all lawyers serving as advocates, to be candid with the court.[26] They also have a duty to hold in strict confidence all information concerning the business and affairs of clients acquired in the course of professional relationships,[27] and a duty to protect clients as far as possible from being convicted except upon legal evidence sufficient to support a conviction for the offences with which they are charged.[28]

As we have seen, the discharge of the latter duty often frustrates the truth-finding function of the criminal justice process. It is only during the last 25 years or so, however, that the full implications of the conflicts among criminal defence lawyers' professional responsibilities have become evident, primarily as a result of the writings of Monroe Freedman, who emphasized the importance and the consequences of criminal defence lawyers' duty of confidentiality.

The right to counsel, as we have seen, is fundamental to the realization of such values of the criminal justice system as individual dignity: no person should be required to defend a criminal charge, prosecuted by the State with its frightening power, without the assistance of an advocate trained in the law.

Freedman argued that the advocate can serve effectively, however, only if fully informed by the accused person about the facts of the case. Accused persons cannot be expected to reveal to their lawyers all potentially relevant facts — including incriminating facts — unless they are assured that their lawyers will maintain those facts in confidence. To allow lawyers, without client consent, directly or indirectly, to divulge information disclosed by clients during the course of the professional relationship would destroy the benefits to be derived by accused persons from professional assistance. Accused persons should not be expected to know what facts it is in their interest to reveal to their lawyers; nor should accused persons be encouraged to conceal or falsify facts in discussing their cases with their counsel. The right to counsel would be meaningless if accused persons were not free to communicate fully with their lawyers.[29]

26 C.B.A. Code, chapter IX, commentary 1; Ontario rule 4.01(1).

27 C.B.A. Code, chapter IV, rule; Ontario rule 2.03(1).

28 C.B.A. Code, chapter IX, commentary 10; Ontario rule 4.01(1) and accompanying commentary; Quebec rules, section 2.04.

29 Freedman, *supra*, note 20, pp. 4-5 and 8. See also William H. Simon, "The Ideology of Advocacy: Procedural Justice and Professional Ethics", [1978] Wisconsin L.R. 29 at 34-35; and Alan Donagan, "Justifying Legal Practice in the Adversary System" in David Luban (ed.), *The Good Lawyer: Lawyers' Roles and Lawyers' Ethics* (Totowa, New Jersey: Rowan & Allenhead, 1983), p. 123 at 144.

The duty to be candid with the court is obviously in conflict with the duty to maintain in confidence information disclosed by clients. This conflict creates what Freedman called the lawyer's trilemma: the lawyer has a duty to know everything, to hold it in confidence, and to reveal it to the court.[30] For the reasons outlined above, however, to interpret the duty of candour to require lawyers to divulge admissions made by accused persons would be to deprive accused persons of the benefit of professional assistance, an essential right. The duty of candour to the court, Freedman argued, should thus be interpreted more narrowly, so as not to interfere with the lawyer's duty not to disclose confidential information obtained from clients, directly or indirectly.[31]

The conclusions that Freedman drew concerning the practical consequences of this choice of values were unpalatable to most non-lawyers and to many lawyers as well. As a result of the duty of confidentiality, Freedman concluded, it is proper for lawyers to cross-examine for the purpose of discrediting the reliability or credibility of witnesses whom they know to be telling the truth. It is also proper in some circumstances, Freedman concluded, for lawyers to call their clients as witnesses knowing that they will commit perjury.

If criminal defence lawyers were to refuse to cross-examine witnesses whom they knew, based upon information provided by their clients, to be telling the truth, the clients would rightly feel betrayed, Freedman argued. If lawyers had a duty not to cross-examine only because clients, based upon explicit or implied assurances that their candour would not prejudice them, have been candid, clients would quickly discern that the assurances are empty and the duty of confidentiality a sham. Such a result, Freedman concluded, would inevitably impair the freedom of consultation that is essential to the administration of justice.[32]

Similarly, Freedman concluded, lawyers who prevent clients from testifying only because the clients have confided their guilt to them violate the duty of confidentiality by acting upon information disclosed in confidence in a way that will seriously harm the clients' interest.[33]

We shall examine each of these problems in more detail. First, however, we will consider the implications of the duty of confidentiality on the question whether lawyers have a responsibility not to destroy or actively conceal from the police and the Crown physical evidence that may incriminate their clients.

30 Freedman, *supra*, note 20, pp. 27-28; Monroe H. Freedman, "Professional Responsibility of the Criminal Defence Lawyer: The Three Hardest Questions" (1966) 64 Michigan L.R. 1469 at 1470-1474.

31 Freedman, *supra*, note 20, pp. 1-8; Freedman, *supra*, note 30, pp. 1470-1474.

32 Freedman, *supra*, note 20, pp. 43-45; Freedman, *supra*, note 30, pp. 1474-1475.

33 Freedman, *supra*, note 20, pp. 40-41; Freedman, *supra*, note 30, pp. 1475-1478.

7.3 THE DUTY NOT TO DESTROY OR CONCEAL PHYSICAL EVIDENCE

Freedman made it clear that it does not follow from the duty of confidentiality that lawyers may participate in concealing or destroying evidence.[34] On this point there is universal agreement.

An experienced Canadian counsel has written that if a lawyer is given a bloody piece of clothing or a weapon that the lawyer knows or suspects will be evidence on a pending charge, the lawyer has a duty to turn over the clothing or weapon to the police without comment. Any confidential discussions between the lawyer and the client about the evidence must not be divulged. In most such cases the lawyer will not be in a position to continue to act, as the lawyer will be a witness to the existence and continuity of the evidence.[35]

If the client tells the lawyer that the client will destroy the evidence rather than leave it with the lawyer if the lawyer is going to turn it over to the police, the lawyer has a duty to advise the client that he would be guilty of obstructing justice if he were to do so. The lawyer should not, however, attempt to prevent physically the client from leaving the lawyer's office with the evidence and should, again, treat the communication with the client as confidential.[36]

Thus in a 1967 Virginia case,[37] a lawyer was suspended for 18 months for removing from his client's safe deposit box to his own safe deposit box a sawed off shotgun that had been used and money that had been stolen during a robbery. In a 1981 California case,[38] a defence counsel found a victim's wallet in the trash as a result of confidential disclosures by his client. The court ruled that client-lawyer confidentiality did not have the effect of preventing disclosure to the jury of the location of the wallet when found, as the removal of the wallet prevented the prosecution from discovering material evidence.

The criminal defence lawyer's duty to preserve physical evidence and to turn it over to the prosecution is limited to the apparent instrumentalities of crime — such as weapons — and the apparent products of crime — such as stolen

34 Freedman, *supra*, note 20, p. 6.

35 See Earl A. Cherniak, "The Ethics of Advocacy", Law Society of Upper Canada Gazette, vol. 19, no. 2 (June, 1985), p. 147.

36 *Ibid.*, p. 147. In the 1969 Special Lectures of the Law Society of Upper Canada, Justice E. Patrick Hartt, Judge Lloyd Graburn, Joseph Sedgwick Q.C. and G. Arthur Martin Q.C. (as he then was) discussed the defence counsel's obligation in these circumstances.

37 *Re Ryder*, 263 F. Supp. 360 (E.D. Va., 1967). See also *Commonwealth v. Steinhach*, 514 A. 2d 114 (Penn., 1986); and Monroe H. Freedman, *Lawyers' Ethics In An Adversary System* (New York: Bobbs-Merrill, 1975), p. 6.

38 *California v. Meredith*, 29 Cal. 3d 682 (1981). In two other American cases, *State v. Olwell*, 64 Wash. 2d 828 (1964) and *People v. Nash*, 418 Mich. 196 (1983), the courts held that the lawyers in question had a duty to turn over the instrumentalities or proceeds of crime to the prosecution, but prohibited disclosure of the source of the evidence (i.e., the defence counsel) to the jury. See also Lawrence Dubin, "A Legal Duty to Turn Over the Evidence", National Law Journal (July 18, 1988), p. 13.

money or property. Neither lawyers nor non-lawyers have either a general duty to co-operate with the police in an investigation into possible criminal wrongdoing or a duty to make disclosure of documents relevant to a criminal charge. Lawyers who merely keep to themselves information or documents provided by clients in confidence that may evidence criminal wrongdoing do not act improperly. It is the destruction or active concealment of physical evidence consisting of the instrumentalities or proceeds of crime that is proscribed. Even in these cases the lawyer's information about the source of the incriminating evidence will be protected from disclosure if that source is the lawyer's client.[39]

An American lawyer has suggested that a system preferable to one in which lawyers have a duty to turn over apparent instrumentalities or proceeds of crime directly to the police or prosecution would be a system in which lawyers have a duty to turn over such physical evidence to their governing body, which would have a duty to turn it over to the police or prosecution without disclosing its source. Such a system would minimize the possibility of revelation of the original source of the evidence and would maintain the confidentiality of client-lawyer communications while ensuring the availability of cogent physical evidence of criminal misconduct.[40]

7.4 CROSS-EXAMINING THE TRUTHFUL WITNESS

As mentioned above, Monroe Freedman argued that criminal defence lawyers should be entitled to cross-examine for the purpose of discrediting witnesses who, because of admissions made to them by their clients, they know to be telling the truth.[41]

He illustrated his argument with an enlightening hypothetical example. A person accused of robbery admits to his lawyer that only a few minutes before the robbery was committed he was a block away from the scene. He did not, however, commit the crime. The accused person has a criminal record.

The prosecution has two witnesses. The first honestly but mistakenly identifies the accused person as the person who committed the crime. The second witness is an elderly woman whose vision is poor, who testifies, accurately, that she observed the accused person in the immediate vicinity of the occurrence within minutes of the time at which the victim says the offence occurred.

The first witness is and appears to be honest. His evidence, though mistaken, cannot be shown to be so. His identification of the accused person may, however, be inadequate to prove guilt beyond a reasonable doubt unless the evidence of the other witness called by prosecution is accepted.

---

39 See Cherniak, *supra*, note 35, pp. 147-148; Charles Wolfram, *Modern Legal Ethics* (St. Paul, Minnesota: West, 1986), p. 645; and *Morrell v. State*, 575 P. 2d 1200 (Alaska, 1978).

40 Nancy Alyse Jacobson, "Is Silence Really Golden?" (1989-90) 3 Georgetown Journal of Legal Ethics 377.

41 See part 7.2, *supra*.

That witness's evidence, though truthful, is vulnerable. The witness saw the person whom she identified as the accused from a distance in a poorly lighted area, and the witness's vision is poor. The witness is easily confused.

To prohibit the defence counsel from discrediting the truthful evidence of this witness, Freedman argues, would not only breach the lawyer's duty to maintain in confidence facts provided by the client, but would probably result also in a serious miscarriage of justice. To say that the lawyer's duty to be candid with the court prohibits impeachment of the credibility of a witness who is known to be telling the truth seems absurd where a result of the lawyer's failure to cross-examine is the wrongful conviction of an accused person.[42]

The facts of hypothetical cases, however, can colour our views of lawyers' ethical responsibilities. Another American lawyer who has a special interest in legal ethics, Harry I. Subin, tells of defending a man charged with rape who had admitted to him that he was guilty. The complainant's evidence, though true, was implausible in some respects. "I was prepared to stand before the jury posing as an officer of the court in search of the truth," Subin wrote many years later, "while trying to fool the jurors into believing a wholly fabricated story, that is, that the woman had consented when in fact she had been forced at gunpoint to have sex with the defendant. I was also prepared to demand an acquittal because the State had not met its burden of proof when, if it had not, it would have been because I made the truth look like a lie. If there is any redeeming social value in permitting an attorney to do such things," he concluded, "I frankly cannot discern it."[43]

The traditional answer to this concern is based upon the criminal defence lawyer's different mission, as described in the judgment of Justice White that is quoted above.[44] Defence counsel's function is not limited to protecting the innocent from wrongful conviction, but includes also protecting those who are in fact guilty against overreaching by the State. Both to protect the innocent and to protect individual autonomy, the criminal justice system permits the State to intrude into the life of an individual citizen only if it is able to establish legal guilt by discharging the onus of proving allegations of criminal wrongdoing beyond a reasonable doubt.[45] Subin eventually was convinced that to preclude defence counsel from attacking a truthful case against an accused person may be incompatible with the defence counsel's responsibility to ensure that the prosecution meets its high burden of proof at trial. Even though they know that the prosecution's evidence is true, he concluded, defence counsel may suggest alternative

42 Monroe H. Freedman, "Professional Responsibility of the Criminal Defence Lawyer: The Three Hardest Questions" (1966) 64 Michigan L.R. 1469 at 1474.

43 Harry I. Subin, "The Criminal Lawyer's "Different Mission': Reflections On The "Right' To Present A False Case" (1987-88) 1 Georgetown Journal of Legal Ethics 125 at 135.

44 *Supra*, part 7.5.

45 Subin, *supra*, note 43, p. 143; John B. Mitchell, "Reasonable Doubts Are Where You Find Them: A Response to Professor Subin's Position on the Criminal Lawyer's 'Different Mission"' (1987-88) 1 Georgetown Journal of Legal Ethics 339 at 342 and 346. See also Geoffrey C. Hazard, Jr., "Quis Custodiet Ipsos Custodes?" (1986) 95 Yale L.J. 1523 at 1529.

explanations of the facts for the purpose of assisting the court to assess the weight of the evidence.[46]

Canadian rules of professional conduct are less clear on the issue than one would like. After providing that admissions made by accused persons to their lawyers may impose strict limitations on the conduct of the defence, that the accused persons should be made aware of this, and that lawyers to whom such admissions are made must not call evidence that in light of the admissions they believe to be false, the rules add that "such admissions will also impose a limit upon the extent to which the lawyer may attack the evidence for the prosecution" and that though "the lawyer is entitled to test the evidence given by each individual witness for the prosecution and argue that the evidence taken as a whole is insufficient to amount to proof that the accused is guilty of the offence charged", nevertheless, "the lawyer should go no further than that."[47]

The obvious questions that are left unanswered by this formulation of the rule are, what is the "limit" imposed on the extent to which the lawyer may attack the prosecution's evidence? and, specifically, whether the lawyer's licence to "test" the evidence of each witness allows the lawyer to impeach the credibility of a witness the lawyer knows to be telling the truth? In view of the affirmation in the immediately preceding rule[48] that the defence lawyer's duty is to protect the client from being convicted except upon legal evidence sufficient to support a conviction for the offence with which the client is charged, one is impelled to conclude that clearer language would be required to alter the traditional view that it is entirely proper for criminal defence counsel to discredit or impeach the evidence of witnesses whom they know are testifying truthfully and accurately.

7.5 THE PERJURIOUS CLIENT

As mentioned above,[49] Monroe Freedman's analysis of the competing professional responsibilities of the criminal defence lawyer led him to conclude that it is proper in some circumstances for criminal defence lawyers to call their clients as witnesses even if they know that the clients will commit perjury. If lawyers were to prevent accused persons from testifying only because of an admission of guilt, Freedman argued, they would be violating their duty of confidentiality by acting upon information disclosed in confidence in a way that would seriously

46 Harry I. Subin, "Is This Lie Necessary? Further Reflections On the Right To Present A False Defense" (1987-88) 1 Georgetown Journal of Legal Ethics 689 at 689-690. See also Monroe H. Freedman, *Lawyers' Ethics In An Adversary System* (New York: Bobbs-Merrill, 1975), pp. 43-46.

47 C.B.A. Code, chapter IX, commentary 11; Ontario rule 4.01(1) and accompanying commentary. These rules are based on Lord MacMillan's essay "The Ethics of Advocacy" in *Law and Other Things* (London: Sweet & Maxwell, 1937), p. 181, as are the rules cited in note 48, *infra*.

48 C.B.A. Code, chapter IX, commentary 10; Ontario rule 4.01(1) and accompanying commentary.

49 *Supra*, part 7.2.

harm the clients' interests. They would, in effect, be disclosing the facts learned from their clients that form the basis for their conclusion that their clients intend to perjure themselves. Clients who confide in their lawyers would also be deprived of their right not to incriminate themselves in such circumstances.

Each of the alternatives to leading and relying upon the perjured evidence, Freedman contended, are unsatisfactory. If the lawyer withdraws from the case, the client will approach another lawyer, realizing that the obligation of confidentiality is not what it is said to be, and withhold incriminating information from the new lawyer. The identical perjured evidence will be presented, and the new lawyer will be in no position to attempt to dissuade the client from presenting it.[50]

For the lawyer to explain the ethical problem to the judge is equally unsatisfactory. A request for a mistrial is likely to be denied because otherwise accused persons would be able to cause a series of mistrials in the same way. The lawyer would violate the duty of confidentiality and rather than resolving the ethical problem would be transferring it to the judge. The accused person would be at risk of being tried before and sentenced by a judge who has been informed of the accused person's guilt by the accused person's own lawyer.

Nor, Freedman argued, is it satisfactory for the lawyer to allow the client to testify falsely without the lawyer's participation,[51] then to omit reference to the client's testimony in argument. To do so is to inform the court of the falsity of the client's evidence.

The only alternative, Freedman concluded, is to put the client on the stand to be examined in the usual way, and to argue the case based upon the client's evidence. Before clients testify falsely, their lawyers have a duty to discourage them from doing so on grounds of law, morality, and results. Perjured testimony is likely to be exposed as such, and may result in the client's prosecution for

---

50 While criminal cases are pending in court, withdrawal requires judicial approval, which will often be denied if the reason is to avoid involvement with client perjury: see, for example, *State v. Henderson*, 205 Kan. 231 at 239 (1970); *People v. Salquerro*, 433 N.Y.S. 2d 711 at 715 (1980). See also Norman Lefstein, "Client Perjury in Criminal Cases: Still in Search of an Answer" (1987-88) 1 Georgetown Journal of Legal Ethics 521 at 525-526.

51 Other commentators support the option of asking the accused person to make a narrative statement to the fact finder respecting parts of the accused person's testimony that the lawyer knows to be false: see Warren E. Burger, "Standards of Conduct for Prosecution and Defense Personnel: A Judge's Viewpoint", Federal Bar Association Symposium (1966) 5 Am. Crim. L.Q. 8; and Lefstein, *ibid.*, pp. 522-523. This alternative was ultimately rejected in the American Bar Association's Model Rules of Professional Conduct (1983) on the ground that it would deprive accused persons of their constitutional right to the effective assistance of counsel, a right not forfeited by their perjury: see *Ferguson v. Georgia*, 365 U.S. 570 (1961); *Lowery v. Cardwell*, 575 F. 2d 727 at 730 (9th Cir., 1978); and Monroe H. Freedman, *Understanding Lawyers' Ethics* (New York: Matthew Bender & Co., 1990), p. 117.

perjury among other consequences. The decision, Freedman wrote, must nevertheless be the client's.[52]

By proceeding in this way, Freedman added, the lawyer is not suborning perjury. Subornation requires the wilful procuring of false evidence, which is not what happens where a lawyer dissuades a witness from testifying falsely on grounds of illegality among others, but then accepts the client's decision.[53]

Freedman's arguments are difficult to answer, though many have tried,[54] but his conclusion has nevertheless been universally rejected in both Canada and the United States. Some early responses to Freedman's analysis were more visceral than analytical.[55] Perhaps the most convincing counter-argument is that the assumption that lawyers cannot be expected to ascertain all the relevant facts unless they are able to assure clients of unlimited confidentiality is unsound in cases involving accused persons who are innocent; and that though accused persons who are in fact guilty are entitled to invoke their right not to incriminate themselves, they have no legal or moral right to enlist professional help in deceiving the court through their false evidence. The right against self-incrimination is a right to keep silent, not a right to lie; both involve non-co-operation with the prosecution, but there the resemblance ends.[56] Though accused persons have a right to testify, they have no right to testify falsely.[57]

In other words, Freedman's arguments are based on an indefensible premise. The duty of confidentiality, like the client-lawyer privilege, does not extend to clients' intentions to commit crimes. For policy reasons, moreover, lawyers should not have any duty to assist clients to carry out their expressed intentions to commit

52 Monroe H. Freedman, "Professional Responsibility of the Criminal Defence Lawyer: The Three Hardest Questions" (1966) 64 Michigan L.R. 1469 at 1475-1478; Freedman, *supra* note 46, pp. 40-41.

53 Freedman, *supra*, note 46, p. 31.

54 See, for example, John T. Noonan, Jr., "The Purposes of Advocacy and the Limits of Confidentiality" (1966) 64 Michigan L.R. 1485; David G. Bress, "Professional Ethics in Criminal Trials: A View of Defence Counsel's Responsibility" (1966) 64 Michigan L.R. 1493. See also William H. Simon, "The Ideology of Advocacy: Procedural Justice and Professional Ethics", [1978] Wisconsin L.R. 29; Edward L. Kimball, "When Does A Lawyer "Know' Her Client Will Commit Perjury?" (1988-89) 2 Georgetown Journal of Legal Ethics 579; and David Luban, *Lawyers and Justice: An Ethical Study* (Princeton, New Jersey: Princeton University Press, 1988), p. 198. In *Maddox v. State*, 613 S.W. 2d 275 at 279 (1981), the Texas Court of Appeals said that "the problem of the perjurious defendant is one that has attracted the attention of a small army of . . . commentators."

55 See, for example, Burger, *supra*, note 51. See also Freedman, *supra*, note 46, pp. 44-45.

56 See Alan Donagan, "Justifying Legal Practice In the Adversary System" in David Luban (ed.), *The Good Lawyer: Lawyers' Roles and Lawyers' Ethics* (Totowa, New Jersey: Rowan & Allenhead, 1983), p. 123 at 146; Bruce M. Landesman, "Confidentiality and the Lawyer-Client Relationship" in David Luban (ed.), *The Good Lawyer: Lawyers' Roles and Lawyers' Ethics* (Totowa, New Jersey: Rowan & Allenhead, 1983), p. 191 at 210; and Luban, *supra*, note 54, pp. 200-201.

57 *Nix v. Whiteside*, 475 U.S. 157 at 173 (1986).

crimes. To require lawyers to do so is to corrupt the appropriate role of criminal defence lawyers in the administration of criminal justice.[58]

Canadian rules of professional conduct require lawyers to inform their clients that admissions they make to their counsel may impose strict limitations on the conduct of the defence. If an accused person clearly admits to the lawyer the factual and mental elements necessary to constitute the offence, the accused person's lawyer — if convinced that the admissions are true and voluntary — must not call any evidence that, because of the admissions, the lawyer believes to be false.[59] The rules also expressly prohibit lawyers from knowingly attempting to deceive courts and tribunals by offering false evidence or otherwise, and from knowingly assisting or permitting clients to do anything that the lawyers consider to be dishonest or dishonourable.[60]

The Canadian rules also spell out the lawyer's duty upon learning of a client's intention to commit perjury. Lawyers in these circumstances are required to do everything possible to prevent the client from doing so. Despite Freedman's concerns about the ineffectiveness of such a course, the rules provide that if the client persists, subject to rules governing withdrawal, the lawyer should withdraw or seek leave to do so.[61]

Finally, the rules address (albeit obliquely) the lawyer's duty where the client unexpectedly testifies falsely. In such circumstances the lawyer should, subject to rules governing confidentiality, make disclosure to the court and do all that can reasonably be done to rectify the problem.[62] It is of course the qualification ("subject to rules governing confidentiality") that creates the dilemma.

Although the last rule, particularly, is not a model of clarity, the footnotes to it make it tolerably clear (as pointed out in chapter 4)[63] that a lawyer who has innocently introduced false evidence has a duty to correct the false evidence as soon as possible even if the lawyer knows of the falsity of the evidence as a result of a confidential communication with the client.

The relevant American rules, which are consistent with but more explicit than their Canadian counterparts, are summarized in chapter 4.[64] Insofar as the lawyer's duty to correct false evidence is concerned, neither Canadian nor Amer-

58 See Lefstein, *supra*, note 50, pp. 524-525.

59 C.B.A. Code, chapter IX, commentary 11; Ontario rule 4.01(1) and accompanying commentary.

60 C.B.A. Code, chapter IX, commentary 2(b) and (e); Ontario rule 4.01(2)(b) and (e); see also Quebec rules, section 3.02.01.

61 C.B.A. Code, chapter IX, commentary 4; Ontario rule 4.01(5) and accompanying commentary.

62 C.B.A. Code, chapter IX, commentary 3; Ontario rule 4.01(5).

63 Part 4.13, *supra*.

64 Part 4.13, *supra*.

ican rules, or cases, differentiate between the lawyer's duty in civil and criminal cases.[65]

It should again be stressed that the lawyer's duties not to lead false evidence and to correct false evidence if it is unexpectedly given, apply only to evidence that the lawyer *knows* to be false. The lawyer's knowledge of the falsity of evidence must generally be based upon admissions that the lawyer is convinced are true and voluntary, though a newly discovered alibi that cannot be explained as a failure of recollection is an example of a case in which the lawyer may be sure the evidence is false despite the absence of an explicit admission.[66] There must be no doubt about the falsity of the evidence, however, for the lawyer's duty to be triggered. Even the fact that the client has told the lawyer different stories is not consistent only with the falsity of the second version.[67] Criminal defence lawyers often harbour suspicions about the veracity of their clients, but the validity of those suspicions is for the court to judge. As Sir Robert Megarry has said, often criminal defence lawyers neither believe nor disbelieve their clients, but are instead in the neutral state of non-belief.[68] To lead evidence they suspect is false while in such a state is entirely proper. It must be said, however, that this leaves a broad opening for counsel to avoid the ethical issue.

7.6 CONFLICTS OF INTEREST

Lawyers' professional responsibilities in situations involving conflicts of interest are dealt with in detail in chapter 22, and the duties of lawyers as advocates in such situations are considered in chapter 5. It is essential that conflicts of interest encountered by criminal defence lawyers also be considered separately because Canadian courts now recognize that persons accused of criminal offences

---

65 See American Bar Association Model Rules of Professional Conduct, Model Rules 3.3(a)(4) and 3.3(b); *Nix v. Whiteside*, 470 U.S. 275 (1986); Charles Wolfram, *Modern Legal Ethics* (St. Paul, Minnesota: West, 1986), pp. 660-663; and David Luban, *Lawyers and Justice: An Ethical Study* (Princeton, New Jersey: Princeton University Press, 1988), pp. 198-199. Monroe H. Freedman criticizes the Model Rules' approach to the problem in *Understanding Lawyers' Ethics* (New York: Matthew Bender & Co., 1990), pp. 136-137, on the basis that it requires defence counsel who have established a relationship of trust and confidence with their clients to become agents of the state.

66 *Commonwealth v. Alderman*, 437 A. 2d 36 (1981). See also Norman Lefstein, "Client Perjury in Criminal Cases: Still in Search of an Answer" (1987-88) 1 Georgetown Journal of Legal Ethics 521 at 529-530.

67 *United States, ex rel. Wilcox v. Johnson*, 555 F. 2d 115 at 122 (3rd Cir., 1977); *Butler v. United States*, 414 A. 2d 844 (D.C. App., 1980); and see *United States v. Henkel*, 799 F. 2d 369 (7th Cir., 1986); and Lefstein, *ibid.*, pp. 528-538.

68 Robert E. Megarry, "Convocation Address", Law Society of Upper Canada Gazette, vol. 17, no. 1 (March, 1983), p. 41 at 42-43. In his book *The Conscience of a Lawyer* (St. Paul, Minnesota: West, 1973) David Mellinkoff discusses in detail the ethical dilemma encountered by Sir Charles Phillips in *R. v. Courvoisier* (1840), [1841] 173 Eng. Rep. 869. Phillips' client admitted his guilt to Phillips in the midst of the trial, and instructed Phillips to continue the defence based upon his not guilty plea nevertheless.

have a right, protected through section 7 of the *Charter of Rights and Freedoms*, to the effective assistance of a counsel who is unencumbered by a conflict of interest.[69] Thus, in criminal cases, conflicts of interest now have a constitutional dimension.

The constitutionally guaranteed right of an accused person in a joint trial to the effective assistance of a counsel who is not burdened with a conflict of interest was recognized in a 1991 decision of the Ontario Court of Appeal.[70] In that case the appellant, who had been convicted at trial of conspiracy to traffic in heroin, was represented by the same lawyer as was his co-accused, who was also convicted at trial. The co-accused had discharged the lawyer shortly before the trial was scheduled to begin, but renewed the retainer after the trial judge permitted a brief adjournment to allow the co-accused to decide whether he would proceed without counsel or be represented by the lawyer.

Until the opening of trial the co-accused had planned to plead guilty and to testify in the appellant's defence that the appellant was not involved in the alleged conspiracy. The co-accused in fact pleaded not guilty and did not testify. The lawyer did not apply for severance.

The Court of Appeal accepted the appellant's submission that his lawyer's effectiveness was seriously impaired. The lawyer could not compel the co-accused to testify, and was unable to advise the co-accused whether to testify without potentially harming the interests of one of his clients. The lawyer was also unable to cross-examine Crown witnesses and argue to the jury in such a way as to show that the case against the co-accused was much stronger than the case against the appellant, as such a strategy would compromise the co-accused's position. Finally, the lawyer was unable in argument to contrast the appellant's conduct in taking the witness stand and denying his guilt with the co-accused's refusal to testify.[71] In short, because of his lawyer's conflict of interest, the legitimate and often effective strategy of shifting the blame to one's co-accused was unavailable to the appellant.

Prior to the enactment of the *Charter of Rights and Freedoms*, the Ontario Court of Appeal recognized that accused persons jointly charged with others and represented by the same counsel in a joint trial may be prejudiced in their defence and, as a result, may be deprived of their statutory and common law rights to make full answer and defence.[72]

---

69 *R. v. Silvini* (1991), 5 O.R. (3d) 545 (C.A.).

70 *Ibid.* The case is discussed by David Littlefield in "*Silvini*: Divided Loyalty" (1992), 9 C.R. (4th) 250 and by Alan D. Gold in "Full Answer and Defence — Effective Assistance of Counsel" (1992) 34 Crim. L.Q. 155.

71 Subsection 4(6) of the *Canada Evidence Act*, R.S.C. 1985, c. C-5, prohibits only the judge and Crown counsel from commenting on the failure of an accused person to testify. See *R. v. Naglik* (1991), 3 O.R. (3d) 385 at 393-397 (C.A.), leave to appeal to S.C.C. granted (December 4, 1991), Doc. Nos. 22490, 22636 (S.C.C.).

72 *R. v. McCaw* (1971), 5 C.C.C. (2d) 416 (Ont. C.A.). See also *R. v. Speid* (1983), 43 O.R. (2d) 596 (C.A.); *R. v. Robillard* (1986), 28 C.C.C. (3d) 22 (Ont. C.A.); *R. v. Silvini, supra*, note 69, p. 551; and *R. v. B. (B.P.)* (1992), 71 C.C.C. (3d) 392 (B.C. S.C.).

Similarly, in a 1975 decision[73] the British Columbia Court of Appeal allowed two appellants to withdraw pleas of guilty where their counsel at trial had also represented a third accused person who had paid the lawyer a substantial fee to represent the appellants and himself. The Crown withdrew the charge against the third accused person who had paid the lawyer's fee, in exchange for pleas of guilty by the appellants. The Court of Appeal held that the lawyer was "in a position of hopeless conflict of interest" and that there was an appearance of unfairness in the lawyer's influencing two of the three co-accused whom he represented to plead guilty.

In a 1995 decision[73.1], the Ontario Court of Appeal dismissed an appeal from conviction that was based upon an allegation that trial counsel had a conflict of interest in representing a husband and wife who were jointly charged with sexual assaults. The complainant was the male accused's niece, and the defence of both accused was a denial of her allegations.

The Court of Appeal held that where an appellant alleges that joint representation resulted in a miscarriage of justice, he or she must demonstrate both an actual conflict of interest and an impairment of counsel's ability to represent effectively the interests of the appellant as a result of the conflict.

The Court noted that the accused were advised of their right to separate representation but made it clear that they both wished to be represented by their trial counsel, who had successfully cross-examined the complainant in connection with another matter. The Court also noted that the defence of both accused was identical: both denied that the sexual assaults had occurred. While it was suggested that trial counsel's representation of the husband prevented him from negotiating a favourable plea bargain on behalf of the wife (who was less culpable), in dismissing the appeal the Court observed that plea negotiations on behalf of the wife were not an available option, as she denied that the assaults ever occurred.

It would be impossible to catalogue every conceivable way in which the defence of accused persons may be prejudicially affected in cases in which their lawyers also represent co-accused who are jointly charged. In addition to the ways mentioned in the cases already referred to, courts have recognized that in cases of joint representations lawyers may or may appear to avoid exploring plea negotiations that might result in agreements to testify for the prosecution in exchange for the prosecution withdrawing charges, proceeding on lesser charges, or making more favourable sentence recommendations.[74] Courts have also rec-

73 *R. v. Stork* (1975), 24 C.C.C. (2d) 210 (B.C. C.A.).

73.1 *R. v. W. (W.)* (1995), 25 O.R. (3d) 161, 43 C.R. (4th) 26, 100 C.C.C. (3d) 225, 84 O.A.C. 241 (C.A.).

74 *Holloway v. Arkansas*, 98 S. Ct. 1173 at 1181 (U.S. S. Ct., 1978), *per* Burger C.J.

ognized that in such cases lawyers may or may appear to challenge the admissibility of evidence prejudicial to one client but favourable to another.[75]

In light of the risk of conflict of interest inherent in virtually every joint representation, one wonders whether criminal defence lawyers can ever justify acting for more than one co-accused or more than one target of a police investigation. In exceptional cases the expense of co-accused persons' retaining separate counsel will be a significant factor. Moreover, particularly in the early stages of investigations of possible white-collar crimes, there may be compelling strategic reasons for a defence counsel to represent as many people as possible who were involved in the activities under investigation. The fewer such people who are unrepresented, or who are represented by counsel who may adopt a different strategy, the more control the defence counsel exercises over the release of potentially damaging information to the police or prosecution. Representing as many potential accused persons as possible to avoid disclosure of damaging information to the prosecution was a standard strategy of the renowned American lawyer Edward Bennett Williams who used to say that "this defence works as long as everyone locks arms."[76] At some point in many such investigations and prosecutions, however, the interests of the clients diverge, in that the best strategy for one or more, but not all, will be to co-operate with the police or prosecution in exchange for more favourable treatment.

As in other areas of legal practice, clients may consent to lawyers' acting for them despite potential or actual conflicts of interest, just as clients may choose to represent themselves if they wish. As in other areas of practice, however, in order to be effective the client's consent must be based upon disclosure that is adequate to enable the client to make an informed decision.[77]

In criminal cases, because of the severity of the potential consequences of an accused person's consenting to representation by a lawyer encumbered by a conflict of interest, courts are particularly loath, especially in the face of a joint representation with disastrous consequences, to find that an accused person knowingly and voluntarily waived the right to conflict-free assistance of counsel. In the 1991 decision of the Ontario Court of Appeal referred to above,[78] the court applied a standard articulated by the Supreme Court of Canada in the context of an alleged implicit waiver of the right to counsel. The Supreme Court of Canada

---

75 *Glasser v. United States*, 62 S. Ct. 457 (1942); *Holloway v. Arkansas*, *ibid.*, p. 1181 *per* Burger C.J. Other leading American cases in which the dangers of joint representations are discussed include *Camera v. Fogg*, 658 F. 2d 80 (2nd Cir., 1981); *Strickland v. Washington*, 104 S. Ct. 2052 (1984); and *Burger v. Kemp*, 107 S. Ct. 3114 (1987).

76 Evan Thomas, *The Man To See: Edward Bennett Williams — Ultimate Insider; Legendary Trial Lawyer* (New York: Simon & Schuster, 1991), pp. 141 and 404; Jesse Kornbluth, *Highly Confident* (New York: William Morrow & Co., 1992), p. 128. See also Charles Wolfram, *Modern Legal Ethics* (St. Paul, Minnesota: West, 1986), pp. 417-418.

77 C.B.A. Code, chapter V, rule, and commentaries 4, 5 and 6; Ontario rules 2.04(3) and (6) and accompanying commentary.

78 *R. v. Silvini* (1991), 5 O.R. (3d) 545 at 553 (C.A.).

held that the validity of any waiver "... is dependent upon it being *clear and unequivocal that the person is waiving the procedural safeguard and is doing so with full knowledge of the rights the procedure was enacted to protect and of the effect the waiver will have on those rights in the process.*"[79] (Emphasis in original).

Before embarking upon the defence of two or more jointly accused persons, the lawyer should discuss separately with each client each of the following points:

(1) The nature and source of all foreseeable conflicts of interest.

(2) The fact that no information received in connection with the case can be treated as confidential insofar as any of the other clients are concerned.

(3) The consequences of sharing confidential information in this way.

(4) Whether the lawyer has a continuing relationship with or acts regularly for one or more of the co-accused persons.

(5) The range of trial strategy options both in the event of joint representation and in the event of separate representation.

(6) The potential consequences of the clients' possibly divergent objectives insofar as plea bargaining, and the possible withdrawal of charges or other more favourable treatment in exchange for co-operation in the prosecution are concerned.

(7) The potential consequences if one or more co-accused persons withdraw consent or if the lawyer is constrained to withdraw.

(8) The right of each accused person to be represented by a lawyer who is unburdened by a conflict of interest.

(9) The right of each eligible accused person to legal aid.[80]

Lawyers should act for more than one of the accused persons after such a discussion only if they are convinced that each client fully understands each point and nevertheless unambiguously and voluntarily consents to the joint represen-

---

79 *Korponey v. Canada (Attorney General)*, [1982] 1 S.C.R. 41 at 49, applied in *R. v. Clarkson*, [1986] 1 S.C.R. 383 at 394. In *R. v. Robillard* (1986), 14 O.A.C. 314 (C.A.) the Court of Appeal upheld an order disqualifying a lawyer from acting for an accused person in circumstances in which the lawyer had previously acted for a Crown witness. The disqualification order, which was obtained on a motion brought by the Crown, was upheld despite the fact that the Crown witness had signed a waiver discharging the lawyer from any duty of confidentiality. As Paul M. Perrell had pointed out in his article "Classifying Conflicts of Interest", Law Society of Upper Canada Gazette, vol. 28, no. 1 (March 1994), p. 11 at p. 20, the case shows that loyalty rather than confidentiality is the predominant feature of cases involving lawyers who have acted for multiple parties. See also *R. v. B. (B.P.)* (1992), 71 C.C.C. (3d) 392 (B.C. S.C.), and Wolfram, *supra*, note 76, pp. 417-19.

80 See C.B.A. Code, chapter V, commentary 5; Ontario rules 2.04(6) and (7) and accompanying commentary; and Wolfram, *supra*, note 76, p. 419.

tation. The discussions should be summarized in writing and signed by the clients who consent. Even where two or more co-accused persons consent, lawyers should decline to act for more than one if it is reasonably obvious that an issue that is contentious between them may arise or that their interests will diverge as the matter progresses.[81]

Different problems arise where a possible conflict of interest is raised by a prosecutor. The prosecutor's motives may or may not be honourable. The prosecutor may be genuinely concerned that the interests of one co-accused are being sacrificed by an unscrupulous defence counsel who is preferring the interests of another client. It is also legitimately in the Crown's interest that a reversal of conviction on grounds of conflict of interest on the part of defence counsel be avoided.

On the other hand, the prosecutor may be motivated by an illegitimate desire to drive a wedge between two accused persons to gain a partisan advantage. Although there is little jurisprudence on the issue, it has been suggested that if the court, at the request of the prosecutor, has assured itself that an accused person has waived the right to a conflict-free representation voluntarily and based upon full disclosure of the possible consequences, the court should not interfere in the accused person's decision. It must not be made to appear to accused persons that the prosecution can influence or dictate their choice of counsel.[82]

Conflicts of interest may also arise in a criminal defence practice where counsel has formerly represented a person who is a Crown witness. In a 1996 decision,[82.1] the Ontario Court of Justice (General Division) ordered the disqualification of counsel for the accused where counsel's firm had previously represented a person who was an important Crown witness. The defence counsel had a duty, the Court held, not to take an adversarial position against his firm's former client in a related matter.

7.7 PLEA BARGAINING

Criminal defence lawyers will often realize a more favourable result for clients by plea bargaining than by trying cases. Indeed, because of the potential for more favourable outcomes, defence lawyers have a duty to attempt to negotiate a plea bargain in appropriate cases. In a 1983 case,[83] the United States Court of Appeals for the Sixth Circuit allowed an appeal from conviction on the ground

---

81 *Ibid.*

82 See *R. v. Khanzada* (February 10, 1992), 15 W.C.B. (2d) 381 (Ont. Gen. Div.); *R. v. Rapai* (1992), 11 O.R. (2d) 47 (Prov. Div.); *R. v. Parsons* (1992), 72 C.C.C. (3d) 137 (Nfld. C.A.); and *Laidlaw Environmental Services (Sarnia) Ltd. v. Ontario (Minister of Environment and Energy)* (1997), 32 O.R. (3d) 795 (Ont. Ct. (Gen. Div.)). See also Wolfram, *supra*, note 76, p. 420.

82.1 *R. v. S. (A.)* (1996), 28 O.R. (3d) 663 (Gen. Div.). See also *R. v. Speid* (1983), 43 O.R. (2d) 596 (C.A.) and *R. v. Werkman*, [1997] 4 W.W.R. 762 (Alta. Q.B.).

83 *Martin v. Rose*, 717 F. 2d 295 (1983).

of ineffective assistance of counsel where the accused person's lawyer at trial had made no effort to negotiate a plea bargain. The court regarded attempts to negotiate plea bargains to be reflective of basic competence.

Criminal defence lawyers must nevertheless be vigilant to ensure that their clients' right to put the Crown to the proof of its case is not sacrificed for the sake of expediency. Professor Alan Dershowitz has pointed out that in many cases both prosecutors and defence counsel have incentives to negotiate plea agreements — incentives that may tempt them to breach their duties to the public and their clients respectively if they are not conscientious. Defence counsel who receive flat fees for cases may be tempted to bargain as many cases as possible. Thus if a lawyer receives $5,000 for a case, and is able to negotiate a plea bargain in ten hours, the lawyer will earn $500 an hour. If it takes the lawyer 100 hours to try the case, the lawyer will earn $50 an hour — which may not be enough to pay the overhead.[84]

"I'd be suspicious," Dershowitz has written, "of lawyers who *always* bargain. They generally get the worst deals for their clients, since the prosecutors know that they are bluffing when they threaten to go to trial. The best deals are generally secured by those lawyers who rarely bargain; by those lawyers who litigate and win many of their cases. Those are the lawyers whom the prosecutors most fear; and these are the lawyers to whom they are prepared to give the most to eliminate the risk of being beaten."[85]

Although in the mid-1970's the Law Reform Commission of Canada recommended the abolition of plea bargaining on the ground that the practice can be justified only on grounds of efficiency,[86] Canadian rules of professional conduct recognize the legitimacy of the practice, provided that certain safeguards are observed. Criminal defence lawyers may ethically discuss a possible disposition of a case with the prosecutor where, following investigation:

(1) the lawyer concludes in good faith and advises the client that an acquittal of the offence charged is uncertain or unlikely;

(2) the client is prepared to admit the necessary factual and mental elements of the offence;

(3) the lawyer fully advises the client of the implications and possible consequences, and particularly of the detachment of the court; and

(4) the client so instructs the lawyer, preferably in writing.

---

84 See Alan M. Dershowitz, *The Best Defence* (New York: First Vintage Books, 1983), pp. 132-133. See also chapter 6, *supra*, part 6.5.

85 See Dershowitz, *ibid.*, p. 133. Emphasis in original.

86 See Beverley G. Smith, *Professional Conduct For Canadian Lawyers* (Toronto: Butterworths, 1989), p. 182.

The rules add that the public interest and the client's interests must not be sacrificed in pursuit of an apparently expedient means of disposing of doubtful cases.[87]

In a 1970 decision of the Court of Appeal in England, Chief Justice Parker considered the circumstances in which the courts should sanction plea bargaining, and issued the following admonitions on behalf of the court:

(1) the accused person must have complete freedom of choice whether to plead guilty or not guilty;

(2) there must be freedom of access between counsel and judge;

(3) the judge should never indicate the sentence that the judge is minded to impose, but may indicate that no matter what the plea of the accused, the sentence will or will not take a particular form, for example, probation, fine, or incarceration; and

(4) where any discussion on sentence has taken place between the judge and counsel, the defence lawyer should disclose it to the client and inform the client of what took place.[88]

Once completed, plea bargains are binding on the Crown.[89] Although they are not binding on the court, they are rightly given considerable weight. In a 1988 decision,[90] the Nova Scotia Court of Appeal allowed an appeal from a sentence of 18 months' imprisonment imposed upon the appellant's conviction for indecent assault on the ground that the trial judge was unaware of a plea bargain whereby the appellant agreed to plead guilty in exchange for the Crown's agreement not to seek a term of imprisonment. The Court of Appeal substituted a sentence of probation for one year.

The wording of the rules of professional conduct referred to above do not necessarily preclude a defence counsel from discussing a plea bargain in cases in which the client maintains innocence. They require, rather, only that the lawyer in good faith conclude, following investigation, that an acquittal is "uncertain or unlikely", that the client "is prepared to admit" the necessary factual and mental elements of the offence, and that the lawyer enters into discussions with the prosecutor on the client's instructions. A plea may be accepted by the court, moreover, where the accused person admits facts on the basis of which a jury could find guilt.[91] Ultimately, again, legal guilt is for the client and the court to determine.[92]

---

87 C.B.A. Code, chapter IX, commentary 12; Ontario rule 4.01(9) and accompanying commentary. There are a few differences between the wording of the C.B.A. rule and the Ontario rule. Perhaps most notably, the Ontario rule omits any reference to the client's interest in the concluding sentence.

88 *R. v. Turner*, [1970] 2 All E.R. 281 (C.A.).

89 *R. v. Crneck* (1980), 30 O.R. (2d) 1 (H.C.). See chapter 6, *supra*, at part 6.5.

90 *Baker v. R.*, N.S. C.A., 1988 (unreported).

91 *North Carolina v. Alford*, 91 S. Ct. 160 (1970).

92 See Charles Wolfram, *Modern Legal Ethics* (St. Paul, Minnesota: West, 1986), pp. 591-592.

7.8 WITHDRAWAL AS COUNSEL

The circumstances in which lawyers have a duty to withdraw as counsel or may be permitted to do so by the court are discussed in part 4.10, *supra*. The Canadian Bar Association Code draws no distinction between criminal and civil cases in its rules governing withdrawal.

In Ontario, the issue of withdrawal is governed by the same considerations generally in both criminal and civil cases, but the benchers have added a series of rules and commentary that apply only in criminal proceedings.[93] They read as follows:

> **Withdrawal from Criminal Proceedings**
>
> (4) Where a lawyer has agreed to act in a criminal case and where the interval between a withdrawal and the trial of the case is sufficient to enable the client to obtain another lawyer and to allow such other lawyer adequate time for preparation, the lawyer who has agreed to act may withdraw because the client has not paid the agreed fee or for other adequate cause provided that the lawyer
>
> (a) notifies the client, preferably in writing, that the lawyer is withdrawing because the fees have not been paid or for other adequate cause,
>
> (b) accounts to the client for any monies received on account of fees and disbursements,
>
> (c) notifies Crown counsel in writing that the lawyer is no longer acting, and
>
> (d) in a case when the lawyer's name appears on the records of the court as acting for the accused, notifies the clerk or registrar of the appropriate court in writing that the lawyer is no longer acting.
>
> Commentary
>
> A lawyer who has withdrawn because of conflict with the client should not indicate in the notice addressed to the court or Crown counsel the cause of the conflict or make reference to any matter that would violate the privilege that exists between lawyer and client. The notice should merely state that the lawyer is no longer acting and has withdrawn.
>
> (5) Where a lawyer has agreed to act in a criminal case and where the date set for trial is not far enough removed to enable the client to obtain another lawyer or to enable another lawyer to prepare adequately for trial and an adjournment of the trial date cannot be obtained without adversely affecting the client's interests, the lawyer who agreed to act may not withdraw because of non-payment of fees.

93 Ontario rule 2.09(4) to (6) and accompanying commentary.

(6) Where the lawyer is justified in withdrawing from a criminal case for reasons other than non-payment of fees and there is not a sufficient interval between a notice to the client of the lawyer's intention to withdraw and the date when the case is to be tried to enable the client to obtain another lawyer and to enable such lawyer to prepare adequately for trial, the first lawyer, unless instructed otherwise by the client, should attempt to have the trial date adjourned and may withdraw from the case only with the permission of the court before which the case is to be tried.

Commentary

Where circumstances arise that in the opinion of the lawyer require an application to the court for leave to withdraw, the lawyer should promptly inform Crown counsel and the court of the intention to apply for leave in order to avoid or minimize any inconvenience to the court and witnesses.

not sufficiently far removed to enable the client to obtain another lawyer or to enable such other lawyer to prepare adequately for trial.

A lawyer who has agreed to act may withdraw from a criminal case because the client has not paid the agreed fee where the interval between the withdrawal and the trial of the case is sufficient to enable the client to obtain another lawyer and to allow such other lawyer adequate time for preparation, provided that the lawyer:

(a) notifies the client, preferably in writing, that the lawyer is withdrawing because the fees have not been paid;

(b) accounts to the client for any monies received on account of fees and disbursements;

(c) notifies Crown Counsel in writing that the lawyer is no longer acting;

(d) notifies the clerk or registrar of the appropriate court in writing that the lawyer is no longer acting in a case when the lawyer's name appears on the records of the court as acting for the accused.

The requirement contained in subparagraph (d) has not previously been considered necessary. This may have been due, in part, to the fact that in all counties in Ontario, except the Judicial District of York, the Crown Attorney is also the Clerk of the Peace who has by law the custody of certain documents relating to criminal cases. It is considered, however, that such a requirement is desirable as a courtesy to the court and, indeed, to protect the lawyer from unwarranted criticism by the court, and to prevent the consequential loss of public confidence in the profession if Crown Counsel were not in a position to inform the court that the lawyer had given timely notification of the withdrawal.

The lawyer who has undertaken the defence of a criminal case may withdraw from the case for adequate cause, other than the non-payment of fees, where the interval between the time of withdrawal and the trial of the case is sufficient to allow the client ample time to obtain another lawyer and to permit such other lawyer to prepare adequately for trial. Such withdrawal shall be subject to the same requirements of notice to the client, accounting for monies received, notice to Crown Counsel and notice to the court as apply where the lawyer desires to withdraw because of non-payment of fees.

The lawyer who has withdrawn because of conflict with the client should not under any circumstances indicate in the notice addressed to the court or Crown Counsel the cause of the conflict, or make reference to any matter which would violate the privilege that exists between lawyer and client. The notice should merely state that the lawyer is no longer acting and has withdrawn.

Where the lawyer is justified in withdrawing from a criminal case for reasons other than non-payment of fees, and there is not a sufficient interval between the notice to the client of the lawyer's intention to withdraw and the date when the case is to be tried to enable the client to obtain another lawyer and to enable such lawyer to prepare adequately for trial, the first lawyer may withdraw from the case only with the permission of the court before which the case is to be tried.

Where circumstances arise which in the opinion of the lawyer require an application to the court for leave to withdraw, the lawyer should promptly inform Crown Counsel and the court of the intention to apply for leave in order to avoid or minimize any inconvenience to the court and witnesses. See also *Dunkley v. R.*, [1995] 1 All E.R. 279 (P.C.).

8

Civility

> Stupidity you may be born with, but nobody is born with bad manners. They are acquired, and can be "unacquired' — except it's a lot harder.[1]

A frequent complaint of experienced lawyers is that civility is on the decline. Often the evidence of incivility is adduced on examinations for discovery.[2] A leading American expert on legal ethics has accurately observed that civil litigation is often uncivil.[3]

Whether standards of civility today are lower than formerly might be debated. There is no shortage of anecdotal evidence that the standards of a few decades ago were wanting as well. In 1955, a Toronto magistrate who published a book titled *Legal Etiquette and Court-Room Decorum*[4] found it necessary to issue the following injunctions in a list of transgressions that, the author asserted, were perpetrated by counsel every day:

> Do not address the court or examine witnesses with your hands in your pockets.
>
> Do not put pencils, cigarettes, etc., over your ear.
>
> Do not read newspapers, magazines, etc., in court.
>
> Do not work out crossword puzzles at the counsel table.
>
> Do not comb your hair, trim your fingernails . . . [or] arrange lipstick in court. . .
>
> Remove topcoats or overcoats before addressing the courts . . .
>
> Do not use terms like "found-ins", "drunks" or "vags" in magistrates courts. Every human being is entitled to be treated with dignity. If these unfortunates must be referred to as a class, they should be referred to as: those charged with (convicted of) being found in. . .

---

1 John D. Arnup, "Advocacy", Law Society of Upper Canada Gazette, vol. 13, no. 1 (March, 1979), p. 27 at 35.

2 See chapter 4, *supra*, part 4.6.

3 Geoffrey C. Hazard, Jr., "The Prospect of Rule 11 Gives Pause", National Law Journal (May 13, 1991), p. 17 at 18.

4 S. Tupper Bigelow, *Legal Etiquette and Court-Room Decorum* (Toronto: Carswell, 1955).

> It is not good manners to put your feet on the courtroom chairs while addressing the court or examining witnesses, or use the chairs in any other unconventional way, such as leaning back in them, straddling them backward, and so on. Half-standing, half-sitting on the counsel table is not correct in any circumstances.
>
> It is not proper to chew gum, eat candy or peanuts or suck lozenges in court.
>
> . . . the court should not be addressed or a witness asked a single question while you are seated.[5]

A legendary American trial lawyer, Vincent Hallinan (who died at the age of 95 in 1992) claims to have had 28 fist fights with opposing counsel in courtroom hallways. He called this "settling out of court." He used to dismiss witnesses at the completion of his cross-examinations by saying, "That is all. You can crawl down off the witness stand now."[6]

Whether or not today's standards of civility and etiquette are lower than those of the past, few would argue that they are as high as they should be.[7] The difficult issues are whether it is within the province of the organized bar to regulate civility and, if so, what should be done to elevate standards.

Ethics and etiquette share a common concern, namely, respect for the interests and dignity of others. Both have as their goal the fostering of a civilized common life. The field of ethics tends to be concerned more with larger issues and long term objectives, whereas etiquette is concerned mainly with the here and now. The difference, however, is one of degree rather than quality.[8] Felix Frankfurter said that "morals are three-quarters manners."[9] One may forgive the hyperbole in the assertion of the character in playwright Tom Stoppard's *Professional Foul* that "the history of human calumny is largely a series of breaches of good manners."[10]

No one is likely to urge law societies to emulate the curious preoccupation of some judges with such irrelevancies as the length or colour of barristers' skirts or pants. (An English judge in the late nineteenth century said that he always found difficulty "in appreciating the arguments of counsel whose legs are encased in light-coloured trousers").[11] Canadian rules of professional conduct already

---

5 *Ibid.*, pp. 67-68.

6 Michael Checchio, "Vincent Hallinan Still Roars", National Law Journal (May 20, 1991), p. 34.

7 See Geoffrey C. Hazard, Jr., "Change Rules to "Civilize' the Profession", National Law Journal (April 17, 1989), p. 13.

8 See Thomas Hurka, "The Difference Between Etiquette and Morality? It's a Question of Degree", Toronto *Globe and Mail* (April 23, 1991), p. A-16.

9 David Shrager and Elizabeth Frost (eds.), *The Quotable Lawyer* (New York: Facts on File Publications, 1986), p. 223.

10 Tom Stoppard, "Every Good Boy Deserves Favour" and "Professional Foul" (London: Faber and Faber, 1978), p. 54.

11 David Pannick, *Judges* (Oxford: Oxford University Press, 1987), p. 203. See also David Pannick, *Advocates* (Oxford: Oxford University Press, 1992), pp. 179-180.

require lawyers to treat other lawyers,[12] lay persons lawfully representing others and themselves,[13] and the court,[14], with courtesy. As a result of amendments that came into effect in 2000, the Law Society of Upper Canada's *Rules of Professional Conduct* now extend this duty of courtesy to all persons with whom the lawyer has dealings in the course of the lawyer's practice.[14.1] "A consistent pattern of rude, provocative or disruptive conduct by the lawyer," the rules say, ". . . might well merit disciplinary action."[15] The rules make it clear that the concern addressed is not the maintenance of traditions that have become obsolete, but rather the effective and expeditious completion of legal services in the public interest. Lawyers who behave discourteously or unfairly do a disservice to the client, the rules say, and neglect of the rule that lawyers' conduct toward each other should be characterized by courtesy and good faith will impair the ability of lawyers to perform their function properly.[16]

Rules of professional conduct also caution lawyers against becoming contaminated by ill feelings that frequently characterize the attitudes of their clients toward each other. "The presence of personal animosity between lawyers involved in a matter may cause their judgment to be clouded by emotional factors and hinder the proper resolution of the matter", the rules provide. "Personal remarks or references between them should be avoided. Haranguing or offensive tactics interfere with the orderly administration of justice and have no place in our legal system."[17]

The rules explicate the content of the duty of courtesy toward other lawyers in several ways. Lawyers should accede to reasonable requests for trial dates, adjournments, waivers of procedural formalities and similar matters that do not prejudice clients' rights.[18] A lawyer who knows that another lawyer has been consulted by a party adverse in interest to the lawyer's client should not proceed

---

12 C.B.A. Code, chapter XVI, rule; Ontario rule 6.03(1); Yukon rules, part two, rule 1 and 2.

13 C.B.A. Code, chapter XVI, commentary 10; Ontario rule 6.03(1).

14 C.B.A. Code, chapter IX, rule, and commentary 1; Ontario rule 4.01(1) and accompanying commentary; New Brunswick rules, Part B, rule 3; British Columbia rules, chapter 1, rule 2(1).

14.1 Ontario rule 6.03(1). See also Ontario rule 4.01(6), which requires lawyers to be courteous, civil, and act in good faith to the court or tribunal and with all persons with whom the lawyer has dealings in the course of litigation.

15 C.B.A. Code, chapter IX, commentary 14; Ontario rule 4.01(6) and accompanying commentary.

16 C.B.A. Code, chapter XVI, commentary 1; Ontario rule 6.03(1) and accompanying commentary; Quebec rules, section 4.03.03.

17 C.B.A. Code, chapter XVI, commentary 2; Ontario rule 6.03(1) and accompanying commentary.

18 C.B.A. Code, chapter XVI, commentary 3; Ontario rule 6.03(2).

with default proceedings without warning.[19] Lawyers should avoid sharp practice and not take advantage of or act without fair warning upon slips, irregularities or mistakes of other lawyers not going to the merits or involving any sacrifice of clients' rights.[20] Lawyers should not use tape recorders to tape conversations with clients or other lawyers, even if lawful, without informing the other person of their intention to do so.[21]

The rules add that lawyers should answer with reasonable promptness all professional letters and communications from other lawyers that require answers, and should be punctual in fulfilling all commitments.[22] Lawyers should not give undertakings that cannot be fulfilled, and should fulfil every undertaking given.[23]

The rules also stipulate that lawyers should not communicate with or attempt to negotiate directly with a party who is represented by a lawyer except with that lawyer's consent.[24] Finally, while lawyers should be willing to advise and represent clients in complaints involving other lawyers, they should avoid ill-considered or uninformed criticism of the competence, conduct, advice, or charges of other lawyers.[25]

From time to time lawyers are required to appear before discipline committees as a result of discourteous conduct. Most complaints are dealt with by way

---

19 C.B.A. Code, chapter XVI, commentary 3; British Columbia rules, chapter 17, rule 8. In *Sprung v. Negwer Materials, Inc.*, 727 S.W. (2d) 883 (1987), the Missouri Supreme Court was divided on the issue of whether lawyers' duty of professional courtesy to other lawyers requires them to inform lawyers acting for a defendant during a one-month period prescribed by statute for contesting a default judgment, that a default judgment had been obtained against their client. One member of the court held that the lawyers had a duty to follow their client's instructions not to disclose the default judgment. A second judge held that the lawyers' duty to zealously pursue their client's objectives is not violated by avoiding offensive tactics, or by treating with courtesy other persons involved in the legal process.

20 C.B.A. Code, chapter XVI, commentary 4; Ontario rule 6.03(3); Yukon rules, part two, rule 5. See also *Arthur v. Meaford (Town)* (1915), 34 O.L.R. 231 at 233-234 (H.C.), *per* Middleton J.; and *Meadwell Enterprises Ltd. v. Clay & Co.* (1983), 44 B.C.L.R. 188 at 200 (S.C.). The Law Society of Alberta's code of professional conduct provides that "A lawyer must not take advantage of a mistake on the part of another lawyer if to do so would obtain for the lawyer's client a benefit to which the client has no *bona fide* claim or entitlement." (Chapter 4, rule 3)

21 C.B.A. Code, chapter XVI, commentary 5; Ontario rule 6.03(4); British Columbia rules, chapter 11, rule 14. The commentary in the C.B.A. Code includes, in addition to clients and other lawyers, "anyone else." The Ontario counterpart provision is restricted to clients and other lawyers. The British Columbia rule is restricted to other lawyers, and provides for an exception where the lawyer has reason to believe that another lawyer will, during the conversation, commit or indicate an intention to commit an indictable offence. See also Mark Koehn, "Attorney, Participant Monitoring, and Ethics: Should Attorneys be Able to Surreptitiously Record Their Conversations?" (1991) 4 Georgetown Journal of Legal Ethics 403.

22 C.B.A. Code, chapter XVI, commentary 6; Ontario rule 6.03(6).

23 C.B.A. Code, chapter XVI, commentary 7; Ontario rule 6.03(8) and accompanying commentary.

24 C.B.A. Code, chapter XVI, commentary 8; Ontario rule 6.03(7). See also *Nelson v. Murphy* (1957), 9 D.L.R. (2d) 195 at 213 (Man. C.A.), *per* Tritschler J.A.

25 C.B.A. Code, chapter XVI, commentary 9; Ontario rule 6.03(1) and accompanying commentary.

of informal invitations to attend before the committee (which do not result in the acquisition of a discipline record) or by unpublished reprimands. Breaches of undertakings are sometimes visited with harsher sanctions, depending on the consequences of the breach and other circumstances of the case.

At least one lawyer has been publicly disciplined twice for persistent discourtesy. In the first case, the lawyer led off a cross-examination of a witness whom he was representing by saying to the lawyer who was conducting the cross-examination, "You can start now, Dumbo." He then spilled coffee on the opposing counsel's notes three times during the cross-examination, which terminated with the lawyer telling the opposing counsel that he could "crawl back into [his] hole now." The lawyer was publicly reprimanded.[26] In the second case, the lawyer was suspended for three months when he refused to stand when addressing the court, despite the judge's repeated insistence that he do so.[27]

In an English case, a solicitor was struck from the roll for writing an offensive letter to the Secretary-General of the Law Society. The letter read as follows:

> I thank you for your letter of the 11th instant and think it may well help you and any other jumped up prat who has to consider matters, if I first put one or two things straight.
>
> H is a bent little git and T as useless a pillock as I have ever encountered.
>
> They have breached their duty to the court, made it make two stupid orders through different judges with about as much integrity as a cow pat.
>
> Attached is a page from the Salvation Army songbook that I inspired them or they chose to use on Sunday night. Sort yourself out, laddie.

A year earlier, the solicitor had been fined £2000 after a discipline hearing, also for writing offensive letters. He had refused to pay the fine. At his second hearing, he refused to apologize for his conduct. His right to practise was revoked after 22 years as a solicitor, perhaps because he had proven himself ungovernable.[28]

---

26 *Re Balaban*, Law Society of Upper Canada, discipline committee report adopted by Convocation, May 24, 1984.

27 *Re Balaban (No. 2)*, Law Society of Upper Canada, discipline committee report adopted by Convocation, September 25, 1986.

28 London *Evening Standard* (April 13, 1991). In *Li v. College of Pharmacists* (1994), 116 D.L.R. (4th) 606, 95 B.C.L.R. (2d) 153, 49 B.C.A.C. 115, 80 W.A.C. 115 (C.A.), the British Columbia Court of Appeal, by a two-to-one majority, upheld a decision quashing an order of the disciplinary committee of the respondent College finding the appellant guilty of professional misconduct for dealing with several customers in a rude, belligerent and unprofessional way. The majority of the Court observed that "civility is not amenable to regulation" and is not reasonably connected to any objective embodied in the governing legislation. The case can readily be distinguished from those involving lawyers who have been disciplined for such lapses on the basis that rules of professional conduct expressly require lawyers to treat clients, other lawyers, and the court with courtesy (see notes 12 through 14, *supra*).

More problematic are instances of discourtesy that litigation lawyers encounter regularly. These include truculence and attempts to humiliate witnesses and lawyers for adverse parties. Some lawyers negotiate as if they believed that trying to understand another party's position would weaken the strength of their resolve in bargaining.[29]

Many explanations have been offered for these belligerent attitudes: the bar has grown impersonal as it has multiplied in size; there is greater competition for clients and cases; as society itself has become more contentious, civility has come to be equated with servility and weakness.[30]

Codes of professional civility have been considered in several American jurisdictions. In 1992, the United States Court of Appeal for the Seventh Circuit adopted a recommendation that all lawyers seeking to practise before it first certify that they have read and will abide by a newly approved civility code.[31] Should law societies try to eliminate the problems of abusive language and tactics by adopting such a code?

Although the severity of the problem is apparent, it is not apparent that another code will help to remedy it. At least one American commentator, Geoffrey Hazard, has suggested that a code of civility is likely, on the contrary, to intensify conflict over "professionalism."[32] "True civility" he says, "involves an element that eludes legislative prescription."[33]

What is required is the sense to follow a good example. Professions, like families, have pride and traditions. Our greatest advocates have been renowned for their courtesy. A former Chief Justice of Canada, John Cartwright, has been described as having the characteristics of "gentlemanliness, fairness, reasonableness, candour, magnanimity, and complete integrity." He has also been described as the most effective counsel of his time.[34] A former Chief Justice of the United States, similarly, has written that:

> There are some lawyers who scoff at the idea that manners and etiquette form any part of the necessary equipment of the courtroom advocate. Yet if one were to undertake a list of the truly great advocates of the last one hundred years, I

---

29 See Lord Hailsham, *A Sparrow's Flight: The Memoirs of Lord Hailsham of St. Marylebone* (London: Collins, 1990), p. 362; Geoffrey C. Hazard, Jr., "Change Rules to Civilize the Profession", National Law Journal (April 17, 1989), p. 13; and John Honsberger, "Civility Within the Profession", Law Society of Upper Canada Gazette, vol. 25, no. 2 (June, 1991), p. 176 at 177-179.

30 Hazard, *ibid.*, p. 13; Honsberger, *ibid.*, p. 179.

31 Martha Middleton, "Seventh Circuit OK's Rules On Civility", National Law Journal (January 11, 1993), p. 14. See also Geoffrey C. Hazard, Jr., "Civility Code May Lead to Less Civility", National Law Journal (February 26, 1990), p. 13.

32 Hazard, *ibid.*, p. 13.

33 Hazard, *supra*, note 29, p. 13.

34 Honsberger, *supra*, note 29, p. 177. See also John J. Robinette, "John Robert Cartwright", Law Society of Upper Canada Gazette, vol. 14, no. 3 (September, 1980), p. 214 at 216, in which the author recalls the school motto of Winchester School, William of Wykeham's Foundation, and Chief Justice Cartwright's precept: "Manners Maketh Man."

> suggest he would find a common denominator: They were all intensely individualistic, but each was a lawyer for whom courtroom manners were a key weapon in his arsenal. Whether engaged in the destruction of adverse witnesses or undermining damaging evidence or in final argument, the performance was characterized by coolness, poise, and graphic clarity, without shouting or ranting, without baiting witnesses, opponents or the judge.[35]

There are limits to what codes of conduct and the disciplinary process should be expected to accomplish. Improved training in advocacy skills, concentrating on the models of the great advocates of the past and present, and combined with a collective "that's not done"[36] may be the most effective remedy for incivility.

---

35 Warren E. Burger, Lecture, Fordham University Law School, December 28, 1973, quoted in David Shrager and Elizabeth Frost (eds.), *The Quotable Lawyer* (New York: Facts on File Publications, 1986), p. 194. See also the quotation from former Chief Justice Burger's address to the American Law Institute, May 24, 1971, appearing at p. 193 of the same volume; and W. Gibson Gray, "Expectations of Courts", Law Society of Upper Canada Gazette, vol. 15, no. 2 (June, 1981), p. 129 at 131.

36 See Thomas Hurka, "The Difference Between Etiquette and Morality? It's a Question of Degree", Toronto *Globe and Mail* (April 23, 1991), p. A-16.

PART II

ACCESS TO JUSTICE

9

How Much Justice Can You Afford?[1]

If you are to keep our democracy, there must be one commandment: Thou shalt not ration justice.[2]

The United States Supreme Court observed in a 1974 decision[3] that we live in a society in which the availability of legal assistance, like the availability of most other goods and services, is regulated mainly by the dynamics of free enterprise. The gap between the need for legal services and the ability to pay for it seems perpetually to be widening.[4]

The poor have a greater need for legal assistance, partly because even the uniform application of the law produces injustice. "The law, in its majestic equality," wrote Anatole France, "forbids the rich as well as the poor to sleep under bridges, to beg in the streets and to steal bread."[5]

The access to justice problem is fundamentally a problem of access to competent legal representation. In 1902, Clarence Darrow said to the assembled prisoners in Chicago's Cook County jail that nine-tenths of them were in jail because they did not have a good lawyer, and that they did not have a good lawyer

---

1 This title is from a New Yorker cartoon in which a distinguished looking lawyer is speaking to an anxious prospective client. The caption reads: "You have a pretty good case, Mr. Pitkin. How much justice can you afford?" It is quoted in Mark Green, "The Gross Legal Product: How Much Justice Can You Afford?" in Ralph Nader and Mark Green (eds.), *Verdicts on Lawyers* (New York: Thomas Y. Crowell Co., 1976), p. 65.

2 Learned Hand, Address to Legal Aid Society of New York, February 16, 1951, quoted in William O. Douglas, *The Court Years 1939-1975: The Autobiography of William O. Douglas* (New York: Random House, 1980), p. 384.

3 *Fuller v. Oregon*, 94 S. Ct. 2116 as 2124 (1974).

4 See Sandra D. O'Connor, "The Moral Role of the Lawyer", an address delivered at Fordham University, Law School Dedication, New York, New York, October 24, 1984, published in Law Society of Upper Canada Gazette, vol. 19, no. 1 (March, 1985), p. 28 at 30.

5 Quoted by Justice Samuel G. McD. Grange of the Ontario Court of Appeal in "Justice and the System", one of the David B. Goodman Memorial Lectures, Faculty of Law, University of Toronto, March, 1985, reproduced in the Law Society of Upper Canada Gazette, vol. 19, no. 2 (June, 1985), p. 125 at 138.

because they did not have enough money to pay one.[6] The democratic ideals of equal opportunity and the equal benefit of the law require equal access to competent counsel.[7]

Legal aid plans, financed by governments and the legal profession, have alleviated the inequities to a considerable extent. Increases in government funding have often lagged behind rates of inflation, however. The result has been that the original intention of legal aid plans—that the poor receive legal representation of the same quality as persons of modest means—has not always been realized.

Canadian rules of professional conduct recognize that lawyers have a general duty to break down barriers to equal access to legal services, but fall far short of prescribing such specific duties as acting for reduced or no fees to accomplish that objective. Thus, while lawyers are enjoined to "encourage respect for and try to improve the administration of justice",[8] to have "a basic commitment to the concept of equal justice for all",[9] and to "make legal services available to the public in an efficient and convenient manner",[10] the rules make it clear that lawyers have a general right to decline a particular employment,[11] and that whether they wish to participate in legal aid plans and other programmes designed to provide legal representation or public education or advice is entirely up to them.[12] The only qualifications to the lawyer's right to decline employment that are relevant to the access to justice problem are that lawyers, first, are required to act when assigned as counsel by a court (an exceedingly rare occurrence); second, are to exercise the right "prudently" if the probable result would be to make it very difficult for a person to obtain legal advice or representation;[13] and third, should assist, generally without charge, in obtaining the services of another lawyer who is qualified and able to act.[14]

Many lawyers believe that lawyers have a moral duty to provide services on legal aid certificates and, where legal aid is unavailable, at reduced fees or *pro bono* as necessary to ensure equality of access to competent legal assis-

---

6 Arthur Weinberg (ed.), *Attorney for the Damned* (New York: Simon & Schuster, 1957), p. 7, quoted in David Mellinkoff, *The Conscience of a Lawyer* (St. Paul, Minnesota: West, 1973), p. 179.

7 See s. 15 of the *Canadian Charter of Rights and Freedoms*, Part I of the *Constitution Act, 1982*, being Schedule B of the *Canada Act 1982* (U.K.), 1982, c. 11; and Clayton Ruby, "Law and Society", Toronto *Globe and Mail* (August 11, 1992), p. A-20.

8 C.B.A. Code, chapter XIII, rule; Ontario rule 4.06(1).

9 C.B.A. Code, chapter XIII, commentary 1; Ontario rule 4.06(1) and accompanying commentary.

10 C.B.A. Code, chapter XIV, rule; Ontario rule 3.01.

11 C.B.A. Code, chapter XIV, commentary 6; Ontario rule 3.01 and accompanying commentary.

12 C.B.A. Code, chapter XIV, commentary 5; Ontario rule 3.01 and accompanying commentary.

13 C.B.A. Code, chapter XIV, commentary 6; Ontario rule 3.01 and accompanying commentary.

14 C.B.A. Code, chapter XIV, commentaries 4 and 6; Ontario rule 3.01 and accompanying commentary.

tance. Justice Samuel Grange of the Ontario Court of Appeal was encouraging observance of such a duty when he said that "You cannot tailor the cloth of your labours entirely to your client's purse."[15]

Because legal aid payments have lagged behind rates of inflation, in many fields only a small proportion of legal aid services are provided by lawyers with significant experience in those fields. The disparity in the quality of legal services provided to the well-to-do and to the poor is narrowed, but hardly eliminated, by legal aid. To approach equality of access to justice, and discard the notion that the affluent are entitled to expect first class legal representation while the less fortunate must take what they can get, senior lawyers must be willing to take on with enthusiasm a significant amount of legal aid, reduced fee, and *pro bono* work.[16]

The most famous *pro bono* case in history was *Gideon v. Wainwright*, the 1963 United States Supreme Court decision in which Abe Fortas, of the Washington firm then called Arnold, Fortas & Porter, argued the appeals of a drifter who had been convicted of a crime in a trial in which he was not represented by counsel. The court set aside the conviction and established a rule that all persons on trial for felonies are constitutionally entitled to counsel, and that if they cannot afford counsel themselves the state must pay for counsel to represent them. Neither Fortas nor his firm was paid for either their time or the expenses they incurred in working on the case. It is both apt and comforting that the case that perhaps contributed more than any other to the advancement of equal justice for all benefitted from the tradition of leading lawyers working on behalf of those who cannot afford representation.[16.1]

Like their Canadian counterparts, American rules of professional conduct commend *pro bono* work, but require none.[17] Nevertheless, by 1987, seven American jurisdictions had initiated mandatory *pro bono* programs. In Orange County, Florida, and El Paso, Texas, lawyers are required to take at least two

---

15 *Supra*, note 5, p. 139.

16 See David Luban, *Lawyers and Justice: An Ethical Study* (Princeton, New Jersey: Princeton University Press, 1988), p. 277; and Charles Wolfram, *Modern Legal Ethics* (St. Paul, Minnesota: West, 1986), pp. 932-953. See also Jack W. Londen, "The Impact of Pro Bono Work on Law Firm Economics" (1996), 9 Georgetown Journal of Legal Ethics 925, and Garth C. Grissom, "Pro Bono and the Transaction Lawyer" (1996), 9 Georgetown Journal of Legal Ethics 929. By doing a high volume of some types of legal aid work, experienced lawyers can and do earn large incomes. These types of work are typically those in which lawyers are paid a block fee rather than an hourly rate, for example, for negotiating a guilty plea and speaking to sentence in criminal cases. Some critics charge that this type of compensation arrangement creates a financial incentive for lawyers to urge clients to plead guilty in cases in which their guilt might not be provable. At any rate, the fact that experienced lawyers are willing for other than altruistic reasons to take on some types of profitable cases at legal aid rates does not assist in the slightest in narrowing the access to justice gap in the vast majority of cases.

16.1 See Sol M. Linowitz and Martin Mayer, *The Betrayed Profession* (New York: MacMillan, 1994), pp. 145-46.

17 American Bar Association Model Rules of Professional Conduct, Model Rule 6.1.

civil cases a year *pro bono*. Programmes of this type, however, involve fewer than 8000 lawyers, a small proportion of the American profession.[18]

Legal benefits plans similar to medical and dental insurance have also become popular in the United States, where more than 50 million people are covered. Plans of the same type are in their infancy in Canada. They generally cover routine services, such as the preparation of wills and residential real estate conveyancing, rather than such extraordinary services as defences to serious criminal charges or representation in medical malpractice claims. Because of the restrictions in the types of services covered, and because legal benefits plans do not generally assist people who are in truly necessitous circumstances, they are unlikely to narrow appreciably the access to justice gap.

Critics have often argued that lawyers have contributed to inequities in the availability of legal services by promulgating and enforcing restrictive rules governing advertising, solicitation, contingency fees, and relations with the media. Each of these subjects deserves special treatment, and is dealt with in a separate chapter below.

---

18 Luban, *supra*, note 16, pp. 277-279. See also Jerry L. Anderson, "Court-Appointed Counsel: The Constitutionality of Uncompensated Conscription" (1989-90) 3 Georgetown Journal of Legal Ethics 503 at 505; and Suzanne Bretz, "Why Mandatory Pro Bono is a Bad Idea" (1990) 3 Georgetown Journal of Legal Ethics 623. As Justice Major of the Supreme Court of Canada pointed out in the keynote address to a national conference on the legal profession and ethics in 1994, however, the American bar has proven itself more willing to recognize and respond to its obligation to do *pro bono* work than has its Canadian counterpart. In large American firms it is not uncommon for lawyers to be assigned to do only *pro bono* work, and some firms contribute more than 40,000 *pro bono* hours a year.

10

Advertising

The best way to select a lawyer is to watch late night t.v., which is where your top legal minds advertise.[1]

In the debate over advertising by lawyers, strong feelings are aroused by factors that have little or nothing to do with public access to legal services. These factors vary from assertions of lawyers' rights of commercial freedom of expression on the one side to assertions of the need to protect the image of the profession on the other.

Until relatively recently, advertising was generally prohibited. Canadian rules of professional conduct banned advertisements containing biographical detail[2] and concerned themselves with such minutiae as the size of lettering on law office signs.[3] As recently as the early 1980's, a commentary that read in part as follows was included in the Law Society of Upper Canada's rules of professional conduct:

> Promotional advertising is not in the interest of the public or the profession. Such advertising has for good reason been prohibited by all professions. It would be likely to encourage self-aggrandizement at the expense of truth and could mislead the uninformed and arouse unattainable hopes and expectations resulting in the distrust of legal institutions and lawyers. Moreover, there are sound economic reasons for not allowing promotional advertising, quite apart from the traditional reasons for which the professions have rejected it. There is the risk that such advertising would tend to increase the cost of legal services and in the course of time would tend to bring about a concentration of legal services in large firms that could afford to advertise freely to the detriment of the medium size and small firm, thereby unduly limiting the choice of persons seeking independent legal representations.[4]

---

1 Dave Barry, *Guide To Life* (New York: Wings Books, 1991), p. 83.

2 Law Society of Upper Canada Professional Conduct Handbook, 1964, ruling 18(a).

3 *Ibid.*, ruling 10(c).

4 Law Society of Upper Canada Professional Conduct Handbook, 1978, rule 13, commentary 4.

The "traditional reasons" for proscribing promotional advertising were not all as legitimate as some of those referred to in this commentary: they included the Victorian snobbery which denigrated any calling that besmirched itself by taking on the trappings of a trade, and the desire of established lawyers to limit competition.[5]

Canadian rules of professional conduct today allow advertising in any medium, subject to restrictions designed in large part to ensure that advertisements are neither false nor misleading.[6] Ontario's rules, however, which are quite typical, still require lawyers' advertisements to be "in good taste and not such as to bring the profession or the administration of justice into disrepute",[7] and specify that advertisements must not compare services or charges with other lawyers or firms.[8] Commentary to the Ontario rules provides that the means by which a lawyer seeks to make legal services more readily available to the public must be consistent with the public interest and must not detract from the integrity, independence, dignity, or effectiveness of the legal profession.[9]

Although the Canadian Bar Association's Code of Professional Conduct explains the reversal in policy to allow advertising on the basis of the desirability of improving access to the legal system,[10] it is likely that constitutional protections of freedom of expression have played a greater role. The United States Supreme Court ruled in 1977 that broad prohibitions against lawyer advertising are unconstitutional restraints on lawyers' freedom of speech.[11] The court found "the postulated connection between advertising and the erosion of true professionalism to be severely strained."[12] Since then the court has held that blanket mailings by lawyers to the general population,[13] print advertising geared to people with specific legal problems (for example, those who have used a product that has caused harm),[14] and mailings targeted to people with specific legal problems,[15] cannot constitutionally be absolutely prohibited.

---

5 Charles Wolfram, *Modern Legal Ethics* (St. Paul, Minnesota: West, 1986), p. 776.

6 C.B.A. Code, chapter XIV, commentaries 1 and 2 (which allow advertising where local rules permit in the interest of increasing access to the legal system, and which recognize that consideration must be given to the clientele to be served by the advertising). See generally Ontario rule 3.04(1); Alberta rules, Part One, rule 3; Manitoba rule 72; Quebec rules, section 4.02.01(v); New Brunswick rules, Part F, rule 2; Newfoundland rules, sections 8.05 and 8.11; and British Columbia rules, chapter 14.

7 Ontario rule 3.04(1)(b).

8 Ontario rule 3.04(1)(c); see also British Columbia rules, chapter 14, rule 5(c)(i) and (d).

9 Ontario rule 3.04 and accompanying commentary.

10 *Supra*, note 6.

11 *Bates v. Arizona State Bar*, 433 U.S. 350 (1977).

12 *Ibid.*, p. 368

13 *Re R.M.J.*, 455 U.S. 191 (1982).

14 *Zauderer v. Office of Disciplinary Counsel of the Supreme Court of Ohio*, 471 U.S. 626 (1985).

15 *Shapero v. Kentucky Bar Association*, 108 S. Ct. 1916 (1988). See also Debra Antzis, "Pro-

In a series of decisions released between 1988 and 1990,[16] the Supreme Court of Canada held that the right of freedom of expression, guaranteed by subsection 2(b) of the *Charter of Rights and Freedoms*, protects commercial speech such as advertising, which fosters informed economic choices. In the most recent of the decisions,[17] the court struck down regulations that allowed dentists to advertise only their name, address, telephone number and, on business cards, their office hours. The regulations offended subsection 2(b), the court held, and were not saved by section 1 of the *Charter*, as the means used in the regulations to promote professionalism and prevent irresponsible and misleading advertising on matters not susceptible of verification did not impair freedom of expression as little as possible. Many examples of expression not falling within the exceptions to the absolute prohibition on advertising, the court ruled, should clearly be permitted.

Several years earlier, the Manitoba Court of Appeal had upheld a rule of the Law Society of Manitoba that required pre-screening of print advertisements. Such a requirement, the court ruled, was a reasonable limit on freedom of expression that can be demonstrably justified in a free and democratic society.[18]

In practice, lawyers are rarely if ever disciplined for publishing advertisements unless they are misleading. The genre is characterized by self-congratulation and boastfulness that is in questionable taste, but lawyers who brag that they are the country's premier practitioners in a specialized field of practice, for example, are unlikely to be charged with professional misconduct, difficult though that claim may be to verify.

---

fessionalism, the First Amendment, and Targeted Direct Mailing by Attorneys" (1988-89) 2 Georgetown Journal of Legal Ethics 561.

16 *Quebec (Attorney General) v. Ford*, [1988] 2 S.C.R. 712; *Irwin Toy Ltd. v. Quebec (Attorney General)*, [1989] 1 S.C.R. 927; *Rocket v. Royal College of Dental Surgeons (Ontario)*, [1990] 2 S.C.R. 232. See also *Merchant v. Law Society (Saskatchewan)* (1972), 32 D.L.R. (3d) 178 (Sask. C.A.); *Law Society (British Columbia) v. Canada (Attorney General)*, [1982] 2 S.C.R. 307 (*sub nom. British Columbia (Attorney General) v. Jabour*); *Klein v. Law Society (Upper Canada)* (1985), 50 O.R. (2d) 118 (Div. Ct.); *Ebert Howe & Associates v. Optometric Assn. (British Columbia)*, [1985] 6 W.W.R. 394 (B.C. C.A.); *Grier v. Alberta Optometric Assn.*, [1987] 5 W.W.R. 539 (Alta. C.A.); *Maroist v. Barreau du Québec*, [1987] R.J.Q. 2322 (C.A.); *R. v. Pinehouse Plaza Pharmacy Ltd.*, [1988] 3 W.W.R. 705 (Sask Q.B.), affirmed [1991] 2 W.W.R. 544 (Sask. C.A.); *Griffin v. College of Dental Surgeons (British Columbia)* (1989), 40 B.C.L.R. (2d) 188 (C.A.); Velon L. John, "Legal Advertising: A Matter of Ethics", Law Society of Upper Canada Gazette, vol. 11, no. 3 (September, 1977), p. 206; George D. Finlayson, "Professional Advertising — The Fine Line Between Informational and Promotional", Law Society of Upper Canada Gazette, vol. 13, no. 2 (June, 1979), p. 93; Phyllis Weiss Haserot, "Promotion and Ethics May Clash", National Law Journal (July 15, 1991), p. 15; and Margot A. Metzner, "Strategies That Break the Rules", National Law Journal (July 15, 1991), p. 16.

17 *Rocket v. Royal College of Dental Surgeons (Ontario)*, *ibid.*

18 *Law Society (Manitoba) v. Savino*, [1983] 6 W.W.R. 538 (Man. C.A.).

It is largely due to matters of taste, however, that lawyers' advertising was restricted in the first place. In the 1890's, an Arizona lawyer named Major Hopkins placed an advertisement that read as follows:

> Come to Major Hopkins to get full satisfaction. I win nine-tenths of my cases. If you want to sue, if you have been sued, I am the man to take your case. Embezzlement, highway robbery, felonious assault, arson and horse stealing, don't amount to shucks if you have a good lawyer behind you. My strong point is weeping as I appeal to the jury, and I seldom fail to clear my man. Out of eleven murder cases last year, I cleared nine of the murderers. Having been in jail no less than four times myself, my experience cannot fail to prove of value to my clients. Come early and avoid the rush.[19]

In its landmark 1977 decision, the United States Supreme Court said that "special problems of advertising on the electronic broadcast media will warrant special consideration",[20] and the court has yet to elaborate on what that means. State bars took up the invitation to tighten regulations governing advertising by lawyers on television only in 1991 and 1992, when at least 20 states took steps toward working out new rules.[21] Many traditionalists believe that the advertisements that have been produced over the last 15 years have provided ample provocation.

A lawyer in Madison, Wisconsin, named Kenneth Hur, wore striped pyjamas for a television advertisement in which he played a convict whose final words from the electric chair were that he wished he had called Mr. Hur's legal clinic. Vincent Trantolo of Hartford, Connecticut, won a permanent place in legal ethics conferences for a television commercial that featured an actor taking a chain saw to furniture while a narrator talked about better ways of dividing matrimonial property. A Miami lawyer, David Singer, sponsored a television advertisement in which a barber warns a little boy that if he does not sit still, he will lose an ear. "You do that," the boy snaps back into the camera, "and I'll call David Singer."[22]

The Singer advertisement has never been shown, as it ran afoul of the Florida State Bar's 1991 rules banning jingles, testimonials, actors, dramatizations, and real or simulated sirens. Former Florida Bar President James F. Miller has explained the reason for the rules in part as follows: "I don't think the practice of law is enhanced by having the Supremes in the background going Doo-wah, doo-wah." Proponents of lawyers' advertising, on the other hand, talk about the need to be accessible to lower income people who do not routinely rub shoulders with lawyers. They also point out ironically that if

---

19 Murray Teigh Bloom, *The Trouble With Lawyers* (New York: Simon & Schuster, 1969), p. 100.

20 *Bates v. Arizona State Bar*, 433 U.S. 350 at 384 (1977).

21 Gail Diane Cox, "Battle On Legal Ads Comes Down To Class", National Law Journal (August 10, 1992), pp. 1 and 44.

22 *Ibid.*

they were marching with Nazis, other lawyers would line up to defend their right of freedom of expression.[23]

It is likely that the *Charter of Rights and Freedoms'* guarantee of freedom of expression and heightened awareness of the exigencies of access to justice will result in lawyers' advertising in the future being scrutinized only for truth, and not for taste. As much as we may hope for the triumph of professionalism over the forces of those who see the law as just another business, we cannot attain that goal by imposing restrictions that may obstruct the flow of useful information to those most in need of it.[24]

A preferable way of promoting good taste in advertising is to emphasize aspirational goals. At its 1992 annual meeting, the American Bar Association presented its first annual dignity award to a Texas law firm that produced a series of advertisements titled "Let's Get Involved." The series extolled jury duty, deplored homelessness, and avoided telephone numbers.[25]

---

23 *Ibid.*, pp. 1, 44 and 45.

24 See Debra Antzis, "Professionalism, the first Amendment, and Targeted Direct Mailing by Attorneys" (1988-89) 2 Georgetown Journal of Legal Ethics 561 at 562.

25 Cox, *supra*, note 21, p. 44.

11

Solicitation

Rules of professional conduct prohibiting the solicitation of professional employment — like rules prohibiting advertising — sacrifice public access to legal representation to considerations of dignity and taste. Regulation that proscribes lawyers from exploiting or invading the privacy of the vulnerable is commendable; regulation that prevents lawyers from advising the vulnerable of their legal rights, or that otherwise inhibits the ability of the public to vindicate those rights, is to be deplored.

Lawyers who have sought out potential clients have often been guilty of overreaching and misrepresentation, and the profession's image has been tarnished when these forms of vexatious conduct have come to light. The prohibition of solicitation itself, however, rather than the prohibition of the unscrupulous practices that often accompany it, limits access to justice, frustrating one of the primary functions of lawyers, and causing greater harm to the profession in the long run.

The solicitation of potential clients probably has a history as long as that of the profession itself. Lawyers who have solicited potential clients include Abraham Lincoln, who once wrote to both a municipality and a railway in an attempt to attract legal work while litigation brewed between them.[1]

In the twentieth century, the solicitation of potential clients by lawyers has grown in proportion to the significance of the automobile in modern life. The variety of techniques designed to attract legal business that are often generically described as "ambulance chasing" were originated in the early 1900's in New York, primarily by a negligence law pioneer named Abraham Gatner.

In 1907 Gatner was an 18-year-old whose formal education had ended after two years of high school. Manhattan then had only a few hundred automobiles, but that was more than enough for an energetic ambulance chaser. (In 1905 there were only two automobiles in Kansas City, but they

---

1 Charles Wolfram, *Modern Legal Ethics* (St. Paul, Minnesota: West, 1986), pp. 785-786.

somehow managed to crash into each other.) Gatner persuaded a law firm to give his idea a chance.

His idea was to hang around police headquarters at nine o'clock in the morning, to pay a dollar to a newspaper reporter in exchange for a list of the previous day's accidents, to approach the accident victims whose names and addresses were on the list, and to sell those victims on the idea of signing an agreement to retain his employer. It was Gatner who called his work "ambulance chasing." In fact, in the early days, he did not reach the victims until hours after the ambulance left.

In time, predictably, Gatner had competitors. Through his use of another new technological innovation, the telephone, he was able to stay a few steps ahead of his rivals. Gatner had the first telephone on his block. He arranged for a clerk in the police department to call him at two o'clock in the morning to give him the accident list. He was out hustling retainers three hours later.

Eventually Gatner was able to get even fresher information. He promised to pay police officers three dollars for every tip on an accident, provided that the police officers would deliberately change some minor detail in the injured person's address when wiring in reports to the police telegraph bureau. Thus Gatner not only had the initial advantage of obtaining information on accident victims sooner, but had the additional advantage that his competitors wasted time trying to track down victims at the wrong addresses carried on the police telegraph bureau line.

Gatner also cultivated physicians who were in a position to refer accident victims to him. Often he was able to persuade accident victims who had signed a retainer that they really needed three, four, or five visits, for each of which the physician was paid 50 cents.

In 1928, when he was 39 years old, as a result of one of the earliest of New York's periodic investigations into ambulance chasing, Abraham Gatner was found guilty of defrauding one of the lawyers with whom he was associated, and was sentenced to a brief jail term. Thus ended the career of the inventor of ambulance chasing, fee splitting, and the medical build-up. The innovator of techniques still used today by some lawyers to attract plaintiffs' personal injury work disappeared unheralded from history.[2]

The profession's distaste for the solicitation of prospective clients is unsurprising, for other accounts of the solicitation of accident victims over the years are, if anything, even less edifying. In 1947 a lawyer in Las Vegas was suspended for six months for paying money to taxi drivers who brought prospective divorce clients directly from the airport to his office.[3] After the crash of a Northwest airplane in Detroit on August 16, 1987, a man posing as a Catholic priest appeared on the scene, ostensibly to console the families of the victims. He hugged grieving parents and children, talked of God's re-

2 The Abraham Gatner story is told in Murray Teigh Bloom, *The Trouble With Lawyers* (New York: Simon & Schuster, 1969), pp. 118-122.

3 *State Bar of Nevada v. Raffetto*, 183 P. 2d 621 (1947).

wards in the hereafter, and cried along with the stunned families. Then he passed out the business cards of a Florida lawyer whom he urged them to call.[4]

Even some cases that do not feature referral fees or misrepresentations sometimes involve unseemly persistence that may amount to an invasion of privacy. After the Arrow Air disaster in Gander, Newfoundland on December 12, 1985, one widow reported that she had been telephoned at least 50 times by lawyers whom she did not know. Another reported that she had received calls from lawyers on Christmas Day.[5]

Mass disasters on this scale epitomize the solicitation problem. Those who are being solicited are as a rule genuinely in need of legal assistance, particularly if the accident scene is populated by insurance company representatives.[6] The potential financial rewards, however, tempt some lawyers to unethical conduct.

The first American lawyer on the scene of the 1984 Union Carbide India Limited chemical plant toxic gas disaster induced 60,000 potential plaintiffs to sign retainers. According to his Indian translator, the lawyer made contact with the mayor, who "hinted as to how the system works", and who was paid at least $20,000 and provided with several all expense paid trips to the United States. "We got a hell of a deal," said the opportunistic lawyer later in defending the payments to the mayor. "He put us in touch with *everybody*." The lawyer was dismissed as an ambulance chaser by many members of the plaintiffs' bar who had less effective travel agents.[7]

It is to be expected, then, that rules of professional conduct would be promulgated to proscribe solicitation based on considerations of undue pressure, dignity, and taste, among others. The Canons of Legal Ethics approved by the Canadian Bar Association in 1920 provided that solicitations "lower the tone of the lawyer's high calling, and should not be tolerated."[8] The 1987 Canadian Bar Association Code of Professional Conduct prohibits solicitations that "detract from the integrity, independence or effectiveness of the legal profession", that "mislead the uninformed or arouse unattainable hopes and expectations", and that are "so undignified, in bad taste or otherwise offensive as to be prejudicial to the interests of the public or the legal profession."[9] Until 2000, Ontario's rules of professional conduct stipulated that "a lawyer may not solicit professional employment from a prospective client with whom the lawyer has no prior professional relationship, by mail, in person or otherwise, when a significant motive for the lawyer's so doing is to be retained in a particular matter." Lawyers in Ontario were permitted to send letters or advertising circulars to persons not known to need legal services in a particular matter, but who are so situated that they might

---

4 See Eric S. Roth, "Confronting Solicitation of Mass Disaster Victims" (1988-89) 2 Georgetown Journal of Legal Ethics 967 at 972.

5 *Ibid.*, pp. 971-972. See also *Matter of Anis*, 126 N.J. 448 (1992).

6 *Ibid.*, p. 977.

7 John A. Jenkins, *The Litigators* (New York: St. Martin's, 1991), pp. 63-113.

8 C.B.A. Canons of Legal Ethics, 1920, Canon 5(3).

9 Chapter XIV, commentary 3. See also New Brunswick rules, Part F, rule 1.

in general find such services useful, provided that such materials, are clearly marked "advertisement" on each page.[10] The American Bar Association's Model Rules of Professional Conduct, similarly, prohibit in person solicitation "when a significant motive for doing so is the lawyer's pecuniary gain."[11]

However, it is important that these concerns about whether the tone of the profession is lowered by bad taste and whether lawyers seeking employment are motivated by a desire to be retained in a particular matter not be permitted to obscure or undermine their responsibility to make legal services accessible to the public. Monroe Freedman, the chief exponent of the view that anti-solicitation rules should be relaxed, has pointed out that lawyers deduct membership fees in country clubs and other "business development" and "client entertainment" expenses on the express ground that they are a means of soliciting business. Problems of propriety are likely to arise, Freedman says, only when lawyers seek to represent members of socio-economic groups who are least likely to know that they need a lawyer, and least able to find one, at a time when they need a lawyer the most.[12]

Freedman has cited a number of examples over the years to illustrate his point. The following three will suffice.

In a 1961 case,[13] a five-year-old boy was seriously injured in an automobile accident as a result of negligent driving. Shortly thereafter an insurance adjuster employed by the negligent driver's insurer visited the boy's mother. He told her that it would be unnecessary for her to retain a lawyer, as his employer would settle the claim as soon as her son was out of a doctor's care. If she was not satisfied with the settlement offered by the insurance company, she could retain a lawyer then to bring an action. Twenty-three months later, immediately after the boy was released from a doctor's care, his mother repeatedly tried unsuccessfully to reach the insurance adjuster. She then retained a lawyer, who promptly commenced an action. The action was dismissed, however, because the lawyer for the insurance company successfully pleaded a two-year limitation period.

If a lawyer, motivated by a desire to be retained in the particular case for pecuniary gain, and not as a public service, had approached the boy's mother at any time before the limitation period expired the mother would have been in-

10 Former Ontario rule 12(4); see also British Columbia rules, chapter 14, rule 5. The current Ontario rule is discussed below (see text accompanying note 25).

11 Model Rule 7.3. Louise L. Hill, "A Lawyer's Pecuniary Gain: The Enigma of Impermissible Solicitation" (1991) 5 Georgetown Journal of Legal Ethics 393 at 421-422 has suggested that it is illogical to qualify the permissibility of lawyers communicating with potential clients on whether the lawyers' motivation is financial. See also Steven P. Handler, Steven F. Pflaum, and Jane M. Cozad, "The Ethics of Solicitation of Business from Corporate Clients" (1991) 5 Georgetown Journal of Legal Ethics 423 at 432-433, in which the authors suggest that since the purpose of limitations on solicitation is the protection of unsophisticated consumers of legal services, there should be no restrictions on communicating with corporate counsel provided that such communications are true.

12 Monroe H. Freedman, *Lawyers' Ethics In An Adversary System* (New York: Bobbs-Merrill, 1975), pp. 116-117.

13 *Gunn v. Washek*, 405 Pa. 521 (1961).

formed of her family's rights. Either the claim would have been settled fairly or an action would have been commenced in a timely way. In either event, the boy would have received compensation for pain and suffering and the cost of his future care.

The insurance company's lawyer, who had no prior knowledge of the adjuster's actions, did nothing wrong, and would not be disciplined. If a lawyer had solicited employment by the family, protected their rights, and obtained an adequate settlement or award on their behalf, that lawyer would be vulnerable to a complaint of professional misconduct. "The thrust of bar discipline," Freedman says, "has been directed toward restricting lay persons' knowledge of their rights and their access to legal redress." Former United States Attorney General Ramsey Clark once pointed out that "A citizen who is unaware of his rights is hard to distinguish from a subject who has none."[14]

In a 1974 case,[15] a woman arrived at an intimidating metropolitan courthouse holding a small boy by the hand. She spoke almost no English at all. She was frightened and confused. All she knew was that she was supposed to be somewhere in that building because her landlord was trying to evict her family. People brushed by her, concerned with their own problems. Then a man appeared. He smiled at her, and asked her in her own language what he could do to help her. He introduced her to his employer, whom she retained to guide her to the proper place and represent her interests, for a fee. "In my view," says Freedman, "that lawyer should have been given a citation as attorney of the year." Instead, he was subjected to disciplinary proceedings and censured by the court for soliciting business.[16]

At a 1987 American Bar Association Conference on Professionalism, Freedman presented a hypothetical case in which the protagonist is a sole practitioner in a large city. An acquaintance, who is a social worker, mentions to the lawyer the appalling conditions he has witnessed at a privately-owned nursing home. He tells of filth, contaminated food, and neglect. One resident actually has maggots growing in her flesh. The residents are elderly, poor, and bedridden, and are seldom visited by anyone. The staff seems indifferent. He suspects that health ministry inspectors have been bribed. He seems resigned to the fact that nothing can be done.

With the social worker's assistance, the lawyer attends at the nursing home, explains to the residents the possibility of her suing on their behalf, and asks several of the residents to sign a retainer requiring them to pay a contingency fee. She neither misleads nor pressures the residents; she simply ensures that they are fully informed about what can be done. She soon becomes their counsel.

---

14 Freedman, *supra*, note 12, pp. 113-114; and Monroe H. Freedman, *Understanding Lawyers' Ethics* (New York: Matthew Bender & Co., 1990), pp. 237-240.

15 *Re Solomon Cohn*, New York Law Journal (February 19, 1974), pp. 1:6-7, 3:3.

16 Freedman, *supra*, note 12, p. 118.

After much manoeuvring and a dramatic trial, the lawyer obtains a substantial money judgment against the nursing home. She also obtains an order protecting the residents from further neglect. She obtains a contingency fee of one-third of the judgment, which is customary and proper in her jurisdiction.

Disciplinary proceedings are initiated against the lawyer. She candidly admits that the potential fee was a substantial motive for her seeking to be retained, as was the prospect of widespread publicity. She emphasizes that she could not possibly have afforded to act *pro bono* in such a difficult and time-consuming case. She also acknowledges, with equal candour, that though she would prefer to represent the nursing home residents in such a case, she would have been willing to act for the owner of the nursing home instead; she believes in the English barrister's ethic of taking the next client in line.

The lawyer is clearly in breach of the rules of professional conduct quoted above. She has sought professional employment, motivated substantially by a wish to be retained in a particular case for pecuniary gain, not as a public service. Yet she has provided legal help to persons who needed it desperately and who probably would not have gotten it were it not for her. She is a good lawyer who has won her case, leaving her clients far better off than she found them. She did so without sacrificing the financial well-being on which depends her ability to do such good work for clients again. She has exemplified the ideals that lawyers should embrace — serving and benefitting others — though she has done so by means the organized bar has repudiated. As Freedman has suggested, the policy of the anti-solicitation rules that the lawyer has breached is evidently that it is "better to have maggots feeding on your flesh than to have a lawyer sitting at your bedside."[17]

It is important to distinguish between cases in which potential clients who are solicited would not otherwise be represented, on the one hand, and cases in which potential clients who are solicited would be represented by *some* lawyer in any event. In the latter type of case the solicitation itself is ethically neutral, though if the solicitation is fraudulent or amounts to an invasion of privacy, disciplinary sanctions are appropriate. In the former case, in which the solicited potential client is ignorant of the law or may lose valuable legal rights (for instance, by signing a release prepared by an insurance adjuster in exchange for inadequate compensation for personal injuries) solicitation serves a valuable social function, whether or not the soliciting lawyer is motivated more by a wish to be retained in a particular matter than by a wish to perform a public service.[18]

---

17 Monroe H. Freedman, *Understanding Lawyers' Ethics* (New York: Matthew Bender & Co., 1990), pp. 252-253. See also Michael Davis, "Professionalism Means Putting Your Profession First" (1988-89) 2 Georgetown Journal of Legal Ethics 341 at 348-349.

18 See Charles Wolfram, *Modern Legal Ethics* (St. Paul, Minnesota: West, 1986), p. 787; and Eric S. Roth, "Confronting Solicitation of Mass Disaster Victims" (1988-89) 2 Georgetown Journal of Legal Ethics 967 at 979-980.

In a ruling[19] that post-dated by only a year its decision that prohibitions against advertising by lawyers are unconstitutional,[20] the United States Supreme Court held in 1978 that states may constitutionally prohibit in-person solicitation. The court acknowledged that solicitation may serve some of the same purposes as advertising by lawyers, but added that unlike advertising, in-person solicitation is not visible to public scrutiny and may expose potentially vulnerable people in an emotionally weakened state to risks of undue influence, intimidation, or overreaching.[21]

The difficulty with prohibiting soliciting, however, is that as a result of doing so the same vulnerable and emotionally weakened people may not learn of their rights in an atmosphere in which insurance company representatives are communicating with them for the purpose of advancing their employer's conflicting interest. To prohibit undue influence, intimidation, overreaching, and invasion of privacy — difficult though they may be to police — would be preferable to prohibiting solicitation itself.

Another suggestion worth considering is a prohibition against both lawyers and insurers communicating with accident victims or their families for a specified time.[22] Unless solicitation is permitted upon the expiry of the time period, however, some victims will make decisions contrary to their interests and in ignorance of their rights whenever the insurance company's representative attempts to settle the claim. In other words, to adopt such a suggestion may only postpone an injustice.

A more effectual means of preventing overreaching by either lawyers or insurers, at least in mass disasters, may be for the organized bar to provide on the scene assistance. After a 1988 plane crash in Texas one of the first support groups on the scene was the Texas State Bar, which set up an emergency office. Three representatives of the state bar's general counsel's office were available there to answer questions from victims and their families. There were no reports of solicitation by lawyers or intimidation by insurers. Unfortunately, all three of the lawyers returned to private practice within a week.[23]

After a major disaster two groups rush to the site: the lawyers and the media. Each group is there to further fundamental rights—the right to petition the courts for the redress of grievances, and freedom of the press—and each has a financial interest in doing so. Sometimes reporters ask offensive and intrusive questions: "How did you feel when you learned that your child burned to death on the school

19 *Ohralik v. Ohio State Bar Assn.*, 436 U.S. 447 (1978).

20 *Bates v. Arizona State Bar*, 97 S. Ct. 2691 (1977).

21 *Ohralik*, *supra*, note 19, pp. 454-456 and 464-466. See also Roth, *supra*, note 18, pp. 977-978; Debra Antzis, "Professionalism, the First Amendment, and Targeted Direct Mailing by Attorneys: *Shapero v. Kentucky Bar Association* [108 S.Ct. 1916(1988)]" (1988-89) 2 Georgetown Journal of Legal Ethics 561 at 563-565; *Re Primus*, 436 U.S. 412 (1978); and *Zauderer v. Office of Disciplinary Counsel of the Supreme Court of Ohio*, 471 U.S. 626 (1985).

22 Roth, *supra*, note 18, pp. 981-983.

23 Roth, *supra*, note 18, pp. 983-984.

bus?" After they have covered the main story the media often criticize the way in which lawyers invade the privacy of the victims and their families by offering them legal services.[24]

Most of the barriers to lawyer advertising have fallen. One hopes that the barriers to solicitation will not be too far behind. Amendments to the Law Society of Upper Canada's *Rules of Professional Conduct* in 2000 represent a significant change to the traditional approach. The governing principles underlying the current Ontario rules are, first, that it is in the public interest that the people of Ontario be made aware of their legal rights and the legal services that are accessible to them; and, second, that what should be regulated or prohibited are means of solicitation that are exploitive or reprehensible, or that bring the profession or the administration of justice into disrepute. The Ontario rule provides that a lawyer may offer professional services to a prospective client by any means other than means (a) that are false or misleading, (b) that amount to coercion, duress, or harassment, (c) that take advantage of a person who is vulnerable or who has suffered a traumatic experience and has not yet had a chance to recover, (d) that are intended to influence a person who has retained another lawyer for a particular matter to change his or her lawyer for that matter, unless the change is initiated by the person or the other lawyer, or (e) that otherwise bring the profession or the administration of justice into disrepute.[25]

---

24 Freedman, *supra*, note 17, p. 253.

25 Ontario rule 3.06 and accompanying commentary.

12

Contingency Fees

The legal profession should ease, rather than impede, access to the courts. Lawyers' fees that are conditional on the result of civil litigation should be allowed in Ontario, as they are in every other Canadian and American jurisdiction. The arguments in favour of allowing contingency fees, subject to regulation by the courts, are compelling. The arguments in favour of prohibiting contingency fees altogether have hardly any validity at all.

Before we examine these arguments, we should be clear about just what a contingency fee is. Although contingency fees are usually calculated as a percentage of recovery, that feature of a fee agreement is not determinative of whether the fee is contingent. What is crucial is the question whether the lawyer risks receiving no fee in the event that when the agreed services are completed the result is unfavourable to the client.

Thus a percentage fee need not be contingent. Fees for residential real estate transactions or for probating estates may be based upon a percentage of the purchase price or the value of the estate respectively without being contingent in any realistic sense. Conversely, a fixed fee could be made contingent by providing that the lawyer would receive it only upon accomplishing a specified result.[1]

Contingency fees were allowed in the frontier colonies that became British

---

1 See *Desmoulin v. Blair* (1994), (*sub nom. Desmoulin (Committee of) v. Blair)* 21 O.R. (3d) 217, 76 O.A.C. 1, 120 D.L.R. (4th) 700 (C.A.); *Stribbell v. Bhalla* (1990), 73 O.R. (2d) 748, 42 C.P.C. (2d) 161 (H.C.); and *Kenyeres (Litigation Guardian of) v. Cullimore* (1992), 13 C.P.C. (3d) 385 (Ont. Gen. Div.), in which a fee arrangement was approved by the Court though the amount to be paid was dependent upon the result of the litigation in that the arrangement called for the plaintiff's counsel's fees to be substantially reduced if the action were dismissed (because of the plaintiff's inability to pay) but greater than the party-and-party costs available in the event of success. See also Charles Wolfram, *Modern Legal Ethics* (St. Paul, Minnesota: West, 1986), p. 526.

Columbia and Manitoba from their early beginnings.[2] As noted above, they are now permitted by the laws of every Canadian province and territory except Ontario.[3] In England and Wales, barristers and solicitors are prohibited from charging contingency fees, though in a green paper presented to Parliament in 1989 the Lord Chancellor recommended that the restrictions against contingency fees at least be relaxed.[4] In Scotland, there is a long tradition of lawyers acting on a "speculative" basis, which enables them to receive costs as assessed by the court if the client is successful, but nothing if the client is unsuccessful.[5] In many American states, contingency fees were prohibited at one time. The last state to prohibit contingency fees was Maine, which repealed its statutory prohibition in 1965.[6]

The Canadian Bar Association's Code of Professional Conduct provides that except where prohibited by the laws of the jurisdiction in which the lawyer practises, it is not improper for the lawyer to enter into an arrangement with the client for a contingent fee, provided such fee is fair and reasonable and the lawyer adheres to any rules of court or local practice relating to such an arrangement.[7] In Ontario, the *Solicitors Act* expressly allows written agreements between clients and lawyers for the payment for services by a commission or percentage in conveyancing or other non-contentious matters, but specifies that nothing in the provisions of the *Act* that allow such agreements gives validity to an agreement by which a lawyer stipulates for payment only in the event of success or where

---

2 See Barbara D. Holman,"Background Paper on Contingency Fees" (Appendix A to first report of Law Society of Upper Canada's special committee on contingency fees, May 27, 1988) (Toronto: Law Society of Upper Canada, 1988), p. 2; *Thomson v. Wishart* (1910), 19 Man. R. 340 (C.A.); and *Taylor v. Mackintosh*, [1924] 3 W.W.R. 97 (B.C. C.A.), *per* McPhillips J.A.

3 See Alberta Rules of Court, Alta. Reg. 390/68, Rules 613(f) to 621; Law Society of British Columbia Rules, rule 1050; *Law Society Act*, R.S.M. 1987, c. L-100, s. 58 (adopting 1974 C.B.A. Code); *Judicature Act*, S.N.B. 1973, c. J-2, s. 72.1 as amended by S.N.B. 1978, c. 32, s. 32; s. 61 of the regulations enacted pursuant to the *Barristers' Society Act*, S.N.B. 1973, c. 80, s. 41 (adopting 1974 C.B.A. Code); Rules of Barristers' Society of New Brunswick, rule E-2; Rules of the Supreme Court (Newfoundland), 1986, rules 55.16 to 55.19; Northwest Territories Rules of Court, rules 551(f), 553 to 558(l), and 559; Nova Scotia Civil Procedure Rules, rules 63.16 to 63.22; Prince Edward Island Rules of Civil Procedure, rules 7317 and 6322; *Bar Act*, R.S.Q. 1977, c. B-1, s. 126(3); *Tariff of Certain Extrajudicial Fees of Advocates*, R.R.Q. 1981, c. B-1, rule 14; *Legal Profession Act*, R.S.Y.T. 1986, c. 100, ss. 68, 7(8) (adopting 1974 C.B.A. Code); rules enacted pursuant to Yukon *Legal Profession Act*, s. 224(a) and (b) (adopting 1974 CBA Code) and Code of Professional Conduct - Pt. I, rule 12.

4 Lord Chancellor's Department, *Contingency Fees* (Green Paper presented to Parliament by the Lord High Chancellor, January, 1989) (London: Her Majesty's Stationery Office, 1989), p. 14. The English courts' reasons for refusing to permit compensation of counsel on a contingent basis are explained in *Re Solicitor*, [1912] 1 K.B. 302 and *Wallersteiner v. Moir (No. 2)*, [1975] 1 Q.B. 373 (C.A.).

5 Lord Chancellor's Department, *ibid.*, pp. 3 and 10; David Pannick, *Advocates* (Oxford: Oxford University Press, 1992), pp. 189-190.

6 Wolfram, *supra*, note 1, pp. 526-527.

7 C.B.A. Code, chapter XI, commentary 10.

the amount to be paid is a percentage of the value of property recovered or dependent on the result of the proceeding. The Law Society of Upper Canada's *Rules of Professional Conduct* provide that: "A lawyer shall not enter into an arrangement with the client for a contingent fee except in accordance with the *Solicitors Act* . . .."[8]

It is likely that the Ontario prohibition will be abrogated within the foreseeable future. Legislation governing class actions that came into force in

(*Continued on page 12–3*)

8 R.S.O. 1990, c. S.15, s. 28. Section 16 of the Act allows written agreements between clients and lawyers for the payment for services by a commission or percentage in conveyancing or other non-contentious matters. Rule 2.08(4) of the Ontario rules provides that it is improper for a lawyer to enter into an arrangement with a client for a contingent fee except in accordance with the *Solicitors Act*. Ontario lawyers often act for plaintiffs in cases in which their clients will be unable to pay their fees and disbursements if their actions are dismissed, a practice that has been characterized as an informal or *de facto* contingency system: see Herbert M. Kritzer, "Fee Arrangements and Fee Shifting: Lessons from the Experience in Ontario" (1984) 47 Law and Contemporary Problems 125 at 130-133; and Law Society of Upper Canada's Special Committee on Contingency Fees, First Report, May 27, 1988 (Toronto: Law Society of Upper Canada, 1988), p. 1, respectively. In *Bergel & Edson v Wolf* (2000), 50 O.R. (3d) 777 Justice Spiegel of the Ontario Superior Court of Justice held that neither section 28 of the *Solicitors Act* nor former commentary 10 to rule 9 (now rule 2.08 (4)) of the Ontario rules invalidate contingent fee agreements in contentious matters.

January, 1993, allows contingency fees in that type of proceeding.[9] Convocation in May, 1988, approved in principle a recommendation of a special committee on contingency fees that the provincial government be urged to permit contingency fee arrangements.[10] The special committee has since then reported back to Convocation on two occasions, most recently in July, 1992. At that time Convocation passed a more specific proposal that called upon the government to adopt a cost-plus-percentage method of calculating contingency fees. At present the government is considering the Law Society's recommendation.[11]

The most compelling reason for permitting contingency fees is that they provide a means of access to justice for persons of modest means who cannot otherwise afford the high cost of litigation. Contingency fees are great equalizers of legal resources between rich and poor. Means tests applied by legal aid plans make ineligible for assistance a great many middle class people who cannot finance a lawsuit. Contingency fees enable such people to use the present economic value of their possible future recovery to hire a lawyer, and thereby satisfy the perceived need for greater accessibility to legal services by the middle class.[12]

Certain secondary reasons for permitting contingency fees are also worthy of mention. To permit contingency fees is to promote freedom of contract: competent clients of modest means or otherwise should be free to choose to compensate their lawyers by means of a contingency fee if that option is mutually beneficial.[13] Contingency fees also reduce uncertainty and enhance client satisfaction. Clients are likely to regard "nothing, if we lose" to be a more satisfactory answer to the valid question almost invariably posed at the first interview — how much will this cost me? — than the inevitably

9 *Class Proceedings Act, 1992*, S.O. 1992, c. 6.

10 Law Society of Upper Canada's Special Committee on Contingency Fees, *supra*, note 8.

11 Third Report of Law Society of Upper Canada's Special Committee on Contingency Fees, February 28, 1992 (Toronto: Law Society of Upper Canada, 1992). See also the remarks of the chair of the special committee, Kenneth E. Howie Q.C. in the Proceedings of Convocation of the Law Society of Upper Canada, vol. R.1, no. 10, July 10, 1992, pp. 26-30.

12 Barbara D. Holman, "Background Paper on Contingency Fees" (Appendix A to first Report of Law Society of Upper Canada's special committee on contingency fees, May 27, 1988) (Toronto: Law Society of Upper Canada, 1988), pp. 11-12; Charles Wolfram, *Modern Legal Ethics* (St. Paul, Minnesota: West, 1986), p. 528; Law Society of Upper Canada, *supra*, note 8, p. 2; Canadian Bar Association (Ontario Branch), "Opening Doors or Stirring Up Strife: The Implementation of Contingency Fees In Ontario" (Toronto: Canadian Bar Association (Ontario Branch), 1988), p. 41; and Lord Chancellor's Department, *supra*, note 4, pp. 1-2.

13 Michael A. Dover, "Contingent Percentage Fees: An Economic Analysis" (1985-86) 51 Journal of Air Law and Commerce 531 at 535; Holman, *ibid.*, p. 13; Canadian Bar Association (Ontario Branch), *ibid.*, p. 42.

vague response necessitated by an hourly rate approach. Fees are not payable where legal representation results in no client gain.[14]

Many arguments have been advanced to support a ban against contingency fees. Most are without merit, and have not proven out in jurisdictions in which contingency fees are permitted. Others justify regulation but, in the absence of a satisfactory alternative that will equalize access to the courts, cannot sustain the burden of justifying an absolute prohibition.

Arguments based on ancient taboos against champerty and maintenance hold little attraction today. What once was regarded as the stirring up of litigation is now likely to be considered as a means of facilitating the enforcement of legal rights. Contingency fee contracts can easily be structured to avoid difficulties created by lawyers acquiring an interest in clients' causes of action.[15]

It has often been suggested that if contingency fees are permitted, the number of unmeritorious lawsuits will increase. Research done in Ontario for the Law Society's special committee on contingency fees disclosed that Canadian jurisdictions in which contingency fees have been permitted have experienced no increase in unmeritorious claims.[16] This may well be attributable in part to the Canadian cost system, in which plaintiffs with unsuccessful claims are generally required to pay successful defendants' costs, a significant economic disincentive to the pursuit of claims of dubious merit. Indeed, the fact that plaintiffs' lawyers must bear the risk of not recovering the value of their time and disbursements itself is a real disincentive to the prosecution of unmeritorious litigation. Lawyers who will be paid an hourly rate for their time are far more likely to accept instructions to bring questionable litigation for clients than are lawyers who will be paid nothing if such litigation is unsuccessful. It is not realistic to expect that lawyers will take on cases in which there is little prospect of success.[17]

A third argument is that if lawyers have a direct financial interest in the outcome of litigation they may try to enhance their clients' chances of success by misleading the court, suppressing damaging evidence, or other unfair or unworthy means.[18] This argument is both insulting to lawyers and dismissive

---

14 B.J. Birrell, "Contingency Fees — A Viable Alternative" (1981) 55 Australian L.J. 333 at 335; Holman, *ibid.*, pp. 12-13.

15 *Goodman v. R.*, [1939] S.C.R. 446; *Amacher v. Erickson*, [1963] 42 W.W.R. 348 (B.C. S.C.); Wolfram, *supra*, note 12, p. 529; Holman, *ibid.*, pp. 3-4.

16 Law Society of Upper Canada's Special Committee on Contingency Fees, First Report, *supra*, note 8, p. 1.

17 Ronald McIsaac, "The Contingent Fee" (1979) 37 The Advocate 41 at 43; Holman, *supra*, note 12, p. 4; Canadian Bar Association (Ontario Branch), *supra*, note 12, pp. 53-54; Lord Chancellor's Department, *Contingency Fees* (Green paper presented to Parliament by the Lord High Chancellor, January 1989) (London: Her Majesty's Stationery Office, 1989), p. 7.

18 See *Re Solicitor*, [1907] 14 O.L.R. 464 (H.C.), *per* Boyd C; *Wallersteiner v. Moir (No. 2)*,

of the abilities of law societies and the courts to sanction professional misconduct. Nor is it logical. Lawyers compensated on the basis of a flat fee or an hourly rate also want to succeed, partly because they will not be retained in the future if they have a reputation for losing, but more importantly because they are bound to fulfil clients' expectations that they are fully committed to a successful outcome. Wanting success cannot be wrong in itself in an adversary system, and the adversary system requires lawyers to attempt to succeed within the rules. Lawyers are subject to stringent codes of professional conduct, serious violations of which may result in their losing their right to practise their profession, with the loss of livelihood and reputation that would follow. As the Lord Chancellor's Department maintained in its 1989 green paper, to assume that lawyers will abandon their professional responsibilities because of their financial interest in the outcome of litigation is to assume an unreasonably low standard of conduct for the profession as a whole. There is no evidence to justify such an assumption.[19]

Other arguments raise legitimate concerns which, however, can be accommodated by requiring contingency fees to be approved by the court and by other regulatory measures. A basic problem is that lawyers have a conflict of interest both in negotiating the contingency fee agreement and in conducting their clients' cases. Lawyers are in a position to overreach clients who are poorly equipped to understand the complexities of risk in litigation, by using their greater knowledge and experience to set their fees at levels that bear little relationship to the time and money they must risk. Lawyers also have a financial incentive to settle cases at points that maximize their own hourly return rather than that of their clients. Often it will be in the lawyer's interest to settle the claim as soon as possible rather than spending many additional hours on the case, possibly for only a marginal increase in the fee. It may well be in the interest of the client, who is not required to compensate the lawyer on a time basis, for the lawyer to work many more hours to maximize the client's recovery.[20]

These inherent conflicts of interest are not grounds for prohibiting contingency fees, as lawyers paid on the basis of an hourly rate (or on any other basis) have similar conflicts of interest. Because the fees of lawyers who are

---

[1975] Q.B. 373 at 402 (C.A.), *per* Buckley L.J. See also Clayton Ruby, "Want to Line a Lawyer's Pocket? Contingency Fees Can Help You", Toronto *Globe and Mail* (June 16, 1992), p. A-22.

19 Lord Chancellor's Department, *supra*, note 17, pp. 1 and 5. See also Stewart Jay, "The Dilemmas of Attorney Contingent Fees" (1988-89) 2 Georgetown Journal of Legal Ethics 813 at 883-884; Holman, *supra*, note 12, pp. 6-7; McIsaac, *supra*, note 17, p. 42; David Pannick, *Advocates* (Oxford: Oxford University Press, 1992), p. 189; and Canadian Bar Association (Ontario Branch), *supra*, note 12, pp. 48-49 and 111-112.

20 Lynn E. Busath, "The Contingent Fee: Disciplinary Rule, Ethical Consideration, or Free Competition" (1979) 3 Utah L.R. 547 at 561-562; Holman, *supra*, note 12, p. 7; Wolfram, *supra*, note 12, p. 529; Canadian Bar Association (Ontario Branch), *supra*, note 12, pp. 47-48; and Lord Chancellor's Department, *supra*, note 17, pp. 1 and 5.

paid by the hour increase in direct proportion to the time spent on the case, there is little incentive for lawyers to be efficient. It is often in the lawyer's interest to work as many hours as possible, whereas it is in the client's interest that the lawyer work only the number of hours necessary to maximize the client's net recovery. The type of regulatory measures that have been taken in jurisdictions allowing contingency fees to minimize the undesirable effects of lawyers' conflicts of interest include safeguards to protect clients' unfettered right to accept or reject settlement offers, and lawyers' right to recover their fees where court awards are in amounts lower than reasonable but rejected settlement offers.[21]

Another argument advanced by opponents of contingency fees is that when lawyers' fees are based on a percentage of their clients' recovery, they may not be commensurate with the time, skill, and experience required, and often may overvalue lawyers' services. A final, and related, argument is that contingency fees encourage juries to inflate damage awards because jurors recognize that a substantial portion of awards must be paid to plaintiffs' lawyers, and they compensate by increasing awards accordingly.[22]

Although lawyers working on a percentage may be overcompensated for their time in some cases, contingency fees compensate lawyers not only for their time but also for their assumption of risk; if there is a real risk that the client will realize no recovery and the lawyer will in such an eventuality receive no fee, a premium is entirely proper in the event of a successful outcome.[23] Lawyers paid on an hourly basis would also be overcompensated in some cases were it not for the supervisory jurisdiction of the courts over lawyers' fees, a jurisdiction that is a feature also of contingency fee regimes.

Examples of measures that have been taken to prevent lawyers from exacting excessive fees include limiting percentages recoverable by lawyers and the modification or cancellation of contingency fee agreements where lawyers have not taken appropriate steps to ascertain information important to determining the likelihood of the action succeeding (for example, whether liability is in issue) before establishing a percentage fee.[24] In some jurisdictions contingency fees are fixed on the basis of sliding scales, so that the percentages of recoveries to which lawyers are entitled are dependent upon the amount of the recovery or the stage of the action at which the claim is resolved. A one-third contingency fee may be reasonable if a claim is settled on the courtroom steps for $75,000. A one-third contingency fee may be quite

21 Dover, *supra*, note 13, pp. 7-9.

22 Lord Chancellor's Department, *supra*, note 17, p. 1; Holman, *supra*, note 12, pp. 8-11.

23 *Deck v. Rody*, [1977] 2 C.P.C. 348 (Sask Q.B.); *Deans v. Armstrong* (1983), 149 D.L.R. (3d) 295 at 307 (B.C. S.C.); Dover, *supra*, note 13, p. 550; Holman, *supra*, note 12, pp. 9-10; and Canadian Bar Association (Ontario Branch), *supra*, note 12, p. 50.

24 *Usipuik v. Jensen, Mitchell & Co.*, [1986] 3 B.C.L.R. (2d) 283 (S.C.), *per* Southin J.

unreasonable if the same claim is settled for $750,000 before an action is commenced.[25]

Measures have also been taken to prevent excessive awards. These include caps on non-pecuniary damages, for example.[26] There is no empirical evidence that contingency fees unduly inflate jury verdicts in any event.[27] The Lord Chancellor's green paper, which was presented to Parliament in 1989, concluded that the other differences between litigation in the United States and the United Kingdom were such that the worst excesses of American litigation would not develop in the United Kingdom if contingency fees were permitted. The other differences in American litigation that were referred to included the greater prevalence of punitive damages, the availability of treble damages in anti-trust cases, and the greater propensity of the American public to resolve disputes by resorting to the courts.[28]

Jurisdictions that allow contingency fees impose restrictions on the type of cases in which contingency fees are permitted. In such jurisdictions lawyers are generally prohibited on policy grounds from charging a contingency fee in either matrimonial or criminal cases. In matrimonial cases the fear is that to provide lawyers with such an economic incentive to win might prevent the reconciliation of estranged spouses, thus offending the public policy favouring the maintenance of marriages.[29] A second reason for prohibiting contingency fees in matrimonial cases is that the parties' emotional state will often be a barrier to their ability to appreciate the meaning, consequences, and possible alternatives to contingency fee contracts.[30]

Where the matrimonial relationship is already severed but the division of property remains in issue, neither justification for the prohibition retains its force. In some American cases in which only the division of property has been in issue, an exception to the prohibition against contingency fees has

---

25 See Barbara D. Holman, "Background Paper on Contingency Fees" (Appendix A to first report of Law Society of Upper Canada's special committee on contingency fees, May 27, 1988) (Toronto: Law Society of Upper Canada, 1988), p. 11; Canadian Bar Association (Ontario Branch), "Opening Doors or Stirring Up Strife: The Implementation of Contingency Fees In Ontario" (Toronto: Canadian Bar Association (Ontario Branch), 1988), p. 72.

26 See, for example *Arnold v. Teno*, [1978] 2 S.C.R. 287; and Holman, *ibid.*, p. 8.

27 Holman, *ibid.*, p. 8; Jay, *supra*, note 19, pp. 883-884.

28 Lord Chancellor's Department, *Contingency Fees* (Green Paper presented to Parliament by the Lord High Chancellor, January, 1989) (London: Her Majesty's Stationery Office, 1989), p. 9.

29 See Law Society of Upper Canada Special Committee on Contingency Fees, First Report, May 27, 1988 (Toronto: Law Society of Upper Canada, 1988), pp. 3-4 and 6; R.C.A. White, "Contingency Fees: A Supplement to Legal Aid?" (1978) 41 Modern L.R. 286 at 291; Holman, *supra*, note 25, p. 15; Canadian Bar Association (Ontario Branch), *supra*, note 25, pp. 91-92; American Bar Association Model Rules of Professional Conduct, Model Rule 1.5 (d); and Charles Wolfram, *Modern Legal Ethics* (St. Paul, Minnesota: West, 1986), pp. 538-539.

30 Wolfram, *ibid.*, p. 541.

been recognized on the ground that in such circumstances a contingency fee is unobjectionable.[31]

The prohibition against contingency fees in criminal cases is often explained on the basis of the danger of corrupting justice. This is an inadequate explanation, however, unless one assumes that members of the criminal defence bar are more likely to violate their professional responsibilities than are lawyers who act as counsel in civil cases.[32]

A second explanation for the prohibition is that a lawyer whose contingency fee is payable only upon an acquittal has an economic incentive to forego plea bargaining that may lead to a favourable result based on a plea to a lesser offence. Such an incentive could easily be removed, however, by providing for a sliding scale of payments based upon various possible results.[33]

More satisfactory explanations for the prohibition are that there is simply less need for contingency fees in criminal cases, and that unlike in civil cases no *res* is created from which a contingency fee can be paid. Modern legal aid plans ensure that persons accused of serious criminal offences who are unable to afford counsel will have competent counsel provided for them. Competent counsel are less accessible through legal aid plans to the vast majority of people who are unable to finance civil litigation. Few people who could afford to pay a lawyer on a contingency basis to defend a criminal case would be unable to privately retain the same lawyer on the basis of a more conventional arrangement.[34]

The Canadian fee shifting cost system, whereby unsuccessful parties to litigation are generally required to pay a significant portion of the legal costs and disbursements of successful parties, introduces a complication not normally present in American jurisdictions. As mentioned above,[35] in Ontario the Law Society's special committee on contingency fees has recommended that Ontario lawyers be permitted to charge a comparatively low percentage (20 percent) of the client's recovery in addition to costs awarded by the court. In Manitoba and Quebec contingency fee contracts may provide for remuneration in lieu of or in addition to the costs awarded, whereas in British Columbia lawyers are prohibited from being paid both a percentage of the recovery

31 *Salter v. St. Jean*, 170 So. 2d 94 (Fla. App., 1964); *Burns v. Stewart*, 290 Minn. 289 (1971); and *Oliver v. Doga*, 368 So. 2d 467, reversed on other grounds 384 So. 2d 330 (La. App., 1979); and see Wolfram, *ibid.*, p. 541.

32 See Wolfram, *ibid.*, pp. 537-538.

33 *Ibid.*

34 See Law Society of Upper Canada Special Committee on Contingency Fees, First Report, May 27, 1988, *supra*, note 29, pp. 4-5; Canadian Bar Association (Ontario Branch), "Opening Doors or Stirring Up Strife: The Implementation of Contingency Fees In Ontario" (Toronto: Canadian Bar Association (Ontario Branch), 1988), pp. 91-92; Wolfram, *supra*, note 29, pp. 536-538; *Re Stivers*, 516 N.E. 2d 1066 (Indiana, 1987); *People v. Winkler*, 515 N.Y.S. 2d 488 (1987); and Doug Lowell, "Contingent Fees" (1988-89) 2 Georgetown Journal of Legal Ethics 233.

35 *Supra*, p. 12-3.

and the costs awarded.[36] In Saskatchewan, rules of professional conduct discourage the practice of lawyers taking a contingency fee in addition to taxable costs.[37]

In Ontario, the Law Society recommended that contingency fees be limited to a specified maximum percentage of the client's recovery only with some reluctance. The committee's reluctance was attributable to its belief that most lawyers would charge the maximum percentage in all cases, regardless of the risk involved, so that the maximum percentage would in practice become a minimum percentage as well.[38] The only Canadian province that currently imposes a ceiling on contingency fees is Quebec, where the maximum permissible fee is 30 percent of the amount recovered in addition to the costs paid by the opposing party.[39] In some American jurisdictions, maximums are stipulated based on sliding scales. The *Federal Tort Claims Act*,[40] for example, establishes a 25 percent limit on contingency fees paid out of judgments awarded by courts after trials, and a 20 percent limit on settlements. In Massachusetts lawyers may charge a maximum of 40 percent of the first $150,000 recovered, 33 1/3 percent of the next $150,000, 30 percent of the next $200,000, and 25 percent of any amount by which the recovery exceeds $500,000.[41]

Legislated maximum limits alone, however, are inadequate as a means of balancing the various considerations involved; it is not possible to establish a fair fee based upon an arbitrary percentage of the amount recovered.[42] Requirements that contingency fee agreements be filed with the court, that contingency fees be reviewed by the court for reasonableness upon the completion of the case, or that complaints of clients about contingency fees be mediated (or some combination of these requirements) are accordingly features of most regulatory schemes.[43]

In jurisdictions in which contingency fee contracts are subject to review by the court the lawyer must bear the onus of demonstrating that the fee is reasonable, as the lawyer has a fiduciary duty to the client and is in a position

---

36 *Law Society Act*, R.S.M. 1987, c. L100, s. 49(1); *Tariff of Certain Extrajudicial Fees of Advocates*, R.R.Q. 1981, c. B-1, r. 14; *Legal Profession Act*, S.B.C. 1987, c. 25, s. 78.

37 Saskatchewan Professional Conduct Ruling 17.

38 Law Society of Upper Canada, Special Committee on Contingency Fees, Second Report, September, 1990 (Toronto: Law Society of Upper Canada, 1990), p. 5.

39 *Tariff of Certain Extrajudicial Fees of Advocates*, R.R.Q. 1981, c. B-1, rule 14, s. 3.

40 28 U.S.C. (1982), s. 2 678.

41 *General Law of Massachusetts*, c. 231, s. 601, as amended by c. 351 (1986), s. 27.

42 See John F. Grady, "Some Ethical Questions About Contingency Fees" (1975-76) 2 Litigation 20 at 52; Barbara D. Holman, "Background Paper on Contingency Fees" (Appendix A to first report of Law Society of Upper Canada's special committee on contingency fees, May 27, 1988) (Toronto: Law Society of Upper Canada, 1988), p. 18; and Law Society of Upper Canada, Special Committee on Contingency Fees, Second Report, *supra*, note 38, p. 5.

43 See Holman, *ibid.*, pp. 19-21.

to assess more accurately what constitutes a reasonable contingency fee.[44] The reasonableness of the fee should of course be assessed by reference to the risk as it appeared at the time the agreement was negotiated, and not as of the time of the assessment, when it may falsely appear with the benefit of hindsight that the risk of failure was minimal all along.[45] In Ontario, the Law Society's Special Committee on Contingency Fees has also suggested that the fee should be reduced if the fee, though reasonable at the time of negotiation, is unconscionably high for the amount of work required, as where an apparently complex case is settled after a few phone calls.[46]

Although the main justification for allowing contingency fees is that they enable persons who may otherwise be unable to obtain redress for legal wrongs to finance litigation, only one Canadian jurisdiction (New Brunswick) stipulates that contingency fee contracts are impermissible where clients are able to pay for the legal services required.[47] In most jurisdictions, concerns about clients who have the financial wherewithal to pay lawyers based on affordable hourly rates entering into contingency fee agreements that are not in their best interests, have been addressed less intrusively through mandatory disclosure requirements. New Brunswick's rules of professional conduct require that the client be given an opportunity to retain the lawyer on the basis of a fee-for-service arrangement.[48] As a special committee of the Ontario Branch of the Canadian Bar Association wryly pointed out in its 1988 report on the implementation of contingency fees in Ontario, in practice the number of clients who have the means to pay counsel on anything but a speculative

44 See Law Society of Upper Canada, Special Committee on Contingency Fees, Second Report, *supra*, note 38, p. 3; *Commonwealth Investors Syndicate Ltd. v. Laxton* (1994), 117 D.L.R. (4th) 382 (B.C.C.A.); *Tweten v. Nichols* (1985), 61 B.C.L.R. 225 (S.C.); *Taylor v. Mackintosh*, [1924] 1 W.W.R. 859 (B.C.S.C.), affirmed, [1924] 3 W.W.R. 97 (B.C.C.A.); *Usipuik v. Jensen, Mitchell & Co.*, [1986] 3 B.C.L.R. (2d) 283 (S.C.); and *Macfarlane v. MacLaughlin*, [1975] 1 W.W.R. 764 (B.C.S.C.).

45 *Speers v. Hagemeister* (1974), 52 D.L.R. (3d) 109 (Sask. C.A.); and Law Society of Upper Canada, Special Committee on Contingency Fees, Second Report, *supra*, note 38, p. 3. Contingency fees of 40 percent were reduced by the court on the basis of the relatively small risk of failure in *MacFarlane v. MacLaughlin*, *ibid.*; and *Ross v. Ewachniuk* (1986), 9 B.C.L.R. (2d) 216 (S.C.), *per* McKay J. See also *Deans v. Armstrong* (1983), 149 D.L.R. (3d) 295 (B.C. S.C.); and *Re Commonwealth Investors Syndicate Ltd. v. Laxton* (1990), 50 B.C.L.R. (2d) 186 (C.A.), leave to appeal to S.C.C. refused (1991), 54 B.C.L.R. (2d) xxxiv (note) (S.C.C.).

46 Law Society of Upper Canada, Special Committee on Contingency Fees, Second Report, *supra*, note 38, pp. 3-4.

47 *Judicature Act*, S.N.B. 1978, c. J-2, s. 72.1 (2) and (3). See *Pelletier v. Cormier* (1981), 35 N.B.R. (2d) 52 (Q.B.); Loraine Minish, "The Contingent Fee: A Re-Examination" (1979) 10 Man. L.J. 65 at 72; and John Y. Taggart, "Comment: Are Contingency Fees Ethical Where the Client is Able to Pay a Retainer?" (1959) 20 Ohio State L.J. 329.

48 New Brunswick rules, Part E, rule 2; Barbara D. Holman, "Background Paper on Contingency Fees" (Appendix A to First Report of Law Society of Upper Canada's Special Committee on Contingency Fees, May 27, 1988) (Toronto: Law Society of Upper Canada, 1988), pp. 24-25.

basis is not great.[49] In the same report the C.B.A.O. committee suggested that it would be an unnecessary restraint on freedom of contract to prevent more affluent clients from negotiating a contingency fee agreement after they have been fully informed of the alternatives.[50]

Regulatory regimes must also address the thorny issue of the lawyer's right to compensation where a contingency fee agreement is terminated before the litigation is disposed of. The timing and amount of the lawyer's compensation should vary depending on the reasons for the termination of the agreement. The Canadian Bar Association (Ontario Branch) committee recommended in its 1988 report that if clients wish to determine contracts because they have negotiated lower percentage fees with other lawyers they must be permitted to do so, but they should be required to pay the fees of their first lawyer immediately after assessment. Lawyers, on the other hand, the committee suggested, should be allowed to terminate a contingency fee contract prior to the resolution of the claim only on the basis that they will receive no fees.[51]

In Ontario, the Law Society's Special Committee on Contingency Fees recommended in its second report in 1990 that where a lawyer is dismissed and the client's claim is settled or brought to trial by another lawyer, the first lawyer's fee should be resolved by agreement between the lawyers or, failing agreement, by arbitration. Where lawyers are unreasonably discharged or clients abandon claims against their lawyers' advice, the committee added, lawyers should be entitled to recover on a *quantum meruit* basis.[52]

The issue was considered by the British Columbia Court of Appeal in a 1983 case.[53] In that case a lawyer had been discharged without cause from a contingency fee contract that was silent on the subject of termination before the resolution of litigation. The court held that though the client's obligation to pay arises upon discharge, the parties to the contract must await the resolution of the litigation that is the subject matter of the contract before the lawyer's fees are assessed and paid, because the result obtained in the litigation will be a factor in fixing the lawyer's fees on a *quantum meruit* basis. It would be unfair, the court observed, to force a client to choose between discontinuing litigation and continuing litigation represented by a lawyer in

---

49 Canadian Bar Association (Ontario Branch), "Opening Doors or Stirring Up Strife: The Implementation of Contingency Fees in Ontario" (Toronto: Canadian Bar Association (Ontario Branch), 1988), pp. 92-93.

50 *Ibid.*, p. 93.

51 *Ibid.*, pp. 86-89.

52 Law Society of Upper Canada, Special Committee on Contingency Fees, Second Report, September, 1990 (Toronto: Law Society of Upper Canada, 1990), p. 6. The Saskatchewan Court of Queen's Bench allowed recovery on a *quantum meruit* basis in *Graham v. Conroy* (1983), 29 Sask. R. 13 (Q.B.) where clients had changed lawyers prior to trial. See also W.B. Williston, "The Contingency Fee In Canada" (1968) 6 Alta. L. R. 184.

53 *McQuarrie v. Foote*, [1983] 2 W.W.R. 283 (B.C. C.A.), reversing [1982] 1 W.W.R. 359 (B.C. S.C.).

whom the client has lost confidence. To force a client to make such a choice would be to defeat the purpose of contingency fees.[54]

54 See also Holman, *supra*, note 48, p. 33.

13

The Media

Until the early 1980's, lawyers were as a rule enjoined from speaking to the media about matters on which they were retained. Although this traditional prohibition has been relaxed, the two principal reasons for imposing restrictions on lawyers' freedom to speak unreservedly to the media remain valid and continue to limit both the circumstances in which lawyers may speak to the media at all and what they may say to the media when such communications are permissible.

Those two reasons are, first, the lawyer's duty to maintain in strict confidence all information about the business and affairs of the client acquired in the course of the professional relationship; and, second, the lawyer's duty to avoid conduct that might be interpreted as an attempt to influence a court or tribunal in a pending proceeding.[1]

The traditional restrictions have been relaxed largely because of the media's increased interest in legal matters, particularly since the enactment of the *Charter of Rights and Freedoms* in 1982. At the same time, the legal profession has increasingly recognized that the public interest is served better by openness rather than secrecy about legal affairs.

Thus, in situations in which a lawyer is asked by the media for information or comment about a matter that is not then before a court or tribunal and in relation to which the lawyer is not representing a client — as for instance when a lawyer is approached by the media for information or comment about pending legislation because of the lawyer's expertise in the field — it is proper for the lawyer to respond to the media's requests.[2] Indeed, in an address to the 1984 annual meeting of the Canadian Bar Association the then Chief Justice of Canada, the Right Honourable Brian Dickson, urged lawyers and judges alike to provide to the media "comprehensive answers in response to genuine requests for information." "The success of the legal system in a democracy," the Chief Justice said, "depends upon an educated and enlightened citizenry. Bench and bar can promote that

---

1 See Beverley G. Smith, *Professional Conduct for Canadian Lawyers* (Toronto: Butterworths, 1989), p. 89.

2 C.B.A. Code, chapter XVIII, commentaries 6 and 7; Ontario rule 6.06(1) and accompanying commentary.

objective", he added, "by taking the time to make sense of legal issues of current interest."[3]

Even where the media's inquiries do not relate to a pending proceeding and the lawyer is not representing a client whose interests are affected by the subject matter of the inquiry, the lawyer should bear relevant professional responsibilities in mind, including: (i) the lawyer's duty, where possible, to encourage public respect for and try to improve the administration of justice; and (ii) the lawyer's duty to treat other lawyers, the courts, and tribunals with respect, integrity, and courtesy.[4]

In addition to these professional duties, lawyers should be conscious of the fact that they will ordinarily have no control over any editing that may follow, the context in which their comments may be used, or under what headline they may appear.[5] Public communications should not be used for the purpose of publicizing the lawyer and should be free from any suggestion that the lawyer's real purpose is self-promotion or self-aggrandizement.[6]

Subject to the same qualifications, lawyers may comment publicly in any of the following situations, all of which involve improving public awareness about our system of justice or otherwise contributing to the community: (i) when called upon to comment on the effectiveness of existing statutory or legal remedies or the effect of particular legislation or decided cases, or to offer an opinion with respect to cases that have been or are about to be commenced;[7] (ii) when involved as an advocate for special interest groups whose objective it is to bring about changes in legislation or government policy or to heighten public awareness about certain issues;[8] and (iii) in a non-legal setting, to publicize such things as community, charitable, or political organizations, programs of public institutions, or racial, religious or other special interest groups.[9]

The qualifications listed above also apply where the lawyer is asked to comment on a matter in which the lawyer is representing a client and which is before a court or tribunal. More importantly, however, before making a public statement concerning a client's affairs, a lawyer should obtain the client's instructions to do so. Before making such a statement, the lawyer must be satisfied that any communication is in the interests of the client and within the scope of the retainer. The lawyer owes a duty to the client to be qualified to represent the client

---

3 Former Chief Justice Dickson's remarks are referred to in Smith, *supra*, note 1, p. 90.

4 C.B.A. Code, chapter XVIII, commentary 4; Ontario rule 6.06(1) and accompanying commentary.

5 C.B.A. Code, chapter XVIII, commentary 12; Ontario rule 6.06(1) and accompanying commentary.

6 Ontario rule 21, commentary 5; New Brunswick rules, Part F, rule 2(3)(b).

7 C.B.A. Code, chapter XVIII, commentary 9; Ontario rule 6.06(1) and accompanying commentary.

8 C.B.A. Code, chapter XVIII, commentary 10; Ontario rule 6.05(2) and accompanying commentary.

9 C.B.A. Code, chapter XVIII, commentary 8; Ontario rule 6.05(1) and accompanying commentary.

effectively before the public and not to permit any personal interest or other cause to conflict with the client's interests.[10] The lawyer should refrain from expressing the lawyer's personal opinions as to the merits of a client's case.[11]

The lawyer's duty will of course vary from case to case. In some cases, the lawyer should have no contact with the media. In others, for example, where a tribunal is an instrument of government policy and influenced by public opinion, the lawyer may have a specific duty to contact the media to properly serve the client.[12]

Rules of professional conduct in most Canadian jurisdictions are silent on the subject of the lawyer's duty to make no public comment that may influence a court or tribunal in a pending proceeding in which the lawyer is representing a client. This duty is now recognized, however, by the Law Society of Upper Canada's *Rules of Professional Conduct* which, as a result of an amendment in 2000, provide that a lawyer must not communicate information to the media or make public statements about a matter before a court or tribunal if the lawyer knows or ought to know that the information or statement will have a substantial likelihood of materially prejudicing a party's right to a fair trial or hearing. This duty has also been recognized by Canadian courts.[12.1]

In a 1979 decision,[13] the Newfoundland Court of Appeal declared its intention to bring to the attention of the Director of Public Prosecutions the fact that counsel participated in a media programme about the case while the matter was *sub judice*, so that a decision could be made whether contempt proceedings should be instituted. The courts have repeatedly stressed that they do not pay attention to media reports when considering the merits of cases, but rather base their decisions solely on the evidence. Such an assurance was given by the Manitoba Court of Appeal in a 1986 decision.[14] Counsel who represented a teenager who had been convicted of a brutal sexual assault said to the court that such cases attract media attention, and that there is great deal of public pressure put on the court system to punish criminals. In addition to assuring counsel that the court ignores media reports, the court told counsel that he was close to contempt.

Fourteen years earlier, however, the Quebec Court of Queen's Bench had asserted that any judge could only be conscious of media pressure. "The danger", the court observed, "is that unknowingly the judge would react against one or the other of the parties involved. I would add that the parties suffering from prejudice

10 C.B.A. Code, chapter XVIII, commentary 2; Ontario rule 6.06(1) and accompanying commentary; British Columbia rules, chapter 14, rule 6(b); Newfoundland rules, section 8.09(1).

11 C.B.A. Code, chapter XVIII, commentary 3; Ontario rule 4.01(1) and accompanying commentary.

12 C.B.A. Code, chapter XVIII, commentary 11; Ontario rule 6.06(1) and accompanying commentary.

12.1 Ontario rule 6.06 (2) and accompanying commentary.

13 *R. v. Basha* (1979), 23 Nfld. & P.E.I.R. 286 (Nfld. C.A.).

14 *R. v. Henry*, Man. C.A., 1986 (unreported).

would not necessarily be the ones suffering damaging publicity."[15] In other words, a judge is likely to respond to statements by lawyers in the media that the judge considers to have been calculated to influence the court by bending over backwards to demonstrate impartiality.

The dangers of speaking to the media about a pending case were vividly illustrated in a 1995 decision of the Supreme Court of Canada.[15.1] The Court upheld an award of $300,000 general damages for libel in an action brought by a Crown Attorney against a criminal defence counsel and the latter's client, the Church of Scientology. (The Court also upheld an award of $500,000 aggravated damages and $800,000 punitive damages against the Church of Scientology.) The criminal defence counsel, in his barrister's gown, had held a press conference outside the courthouse, at which he read from a notice of motion he was bringing to commit the Crown Attorney for contempt of court. In the notice of motion the Crown Attorney was alleged to have misled the Court and to have breached orders whereby documents belonging to the Church of Scientology were sealed — allegations that were ultimately found to be untrue.

A 1997 decision of Justice John Macdonald of the Ontario Court of Justice (General Division)[15.2] illustrates the dangers of lawyers making public appearances or statements about cases in which they have acted as counsel, even long after their retainer has come to an end. In that case, a prominent lawyer served as narrator and host of a television programme that featured realistic depictions of criminal cases. One case that was selected for re-enactment was a case in which the lawyer who served as host and narrator had acted as defence counsel on sentencing and on appeal (the accused had been convicted after a trial at which he had been represented by other counsel). By the time the episode was broadcast, the lawyer's former client had served his sentence and had re-established himself. The former client objected to the case being re-enacted on television.

Justice Macdonald accepted that the lawyer could not have prevented the programme from being produced or broadcast, though the lawyer could have withdrawn as the programme's host and narrator. Justice Macdonald also found that the lawyer had abided by his duty to maintain confidentiality; the script had been prepared from trial transcripts and other public documents.

Justice Macdonald found, however, that the lawyer's primary purpose in involving himself in the production was self-promotion, and that he accordingly

15 *R. v. Carocchia* (1972), 14 C.C.C. (2d) 354 at 363 (Que. Q.B.), affirmed (1973), 15 C.C.C. (2d) 175 (Que. C.A.). See also *Manitoba (Attorney General) v. Groupe Quebecor Inc.*, [1987] 5 W.W.R. 270 (Man. C.A.); Beverley G. Smith, *Professional Conduct for Canadian Lawyers* (Toronto: Butterworths, 1989), pp. 96-100; New Brunswick rules, Part F, rule 2(c) and (d); British Columbia rules, chapter 14, rule 6(a).

15.1 *Hill v. Church of Scientology of Toronto*, [1995] 2 S.C.R. 1130, (*sub nom. Hill v. Church of Scientology*) 30 C.R.R. (2d) 189, 25 C.C.L.T. (2d) 89, 184 N.R. 1, 126 D.L.R. (4th) 129, 24 O.R. (3d) 865*n*, 84 O.A.C. 1

15.2 *Stewart v. Canadian Broadcasting Corp.* (1997), 150 D.L.R. (4th) 24 (Ont. Gen. Div.), additional reasons at (1997), 152 D.L.R. (4th) 102 (Ont. Gen. Div.)

ran afoul of the requirement of the Ontario rules of professional conduct that "[p]ublic communications should not be used for the purpose of publicizing the lawyer and should be free from any suggestion that the lawyer's real purpose is self-promotion or self-aggrandizement."[15.3] More importantly, Justice Macdonald held that rules of professional conduct are not an exhaustive code of lawyers' professional obligations; lawyers of course owe fiduciary duties to their clients, and rules of professional conduct do not diminish by implication the rights and protections that the common law and equity afford to clients. By appearing as host and narrator of the programme, Justice Macdonald held, the lawyer breached his fiduciary duty of loyalty to his client by favouring his own interests over those of his client.

In a 1991 decision,[16] the United States Supreme Court was called upon to rule on the constitutionality of a disciplinary rule that limited what lawyers could say about pending litigation in which they are acting as counsel. The appellant, a Las Vegas criminal defence lawyer, had held a press conference the day after his client was indicted based on allegations of theft of drugs and money from a warehouse that he owned. The press conference occurred six months before trial. The lawyer's purpose in calling the press conference was to counter what he believed to be the "tremendous imbalance" created by the prosecution's use of the media "to set up a presumption of guilt for over a year." The constitutionality of the disciplinary rule that the lawyer allegedly breached was challenged on first amendment grounds.

At the press conference, the lawyer said that the evidence at trial would not only prove the innocence of his client, but would prove also that the person who was in the most direct position to have stolen the drugs and money was a police officer, whom he named. He added that four of the "so-called other victims" were known drug dealers and money launderers.

The majority of the court held that the disciplinary rule in question, which prohibited lawyers from making extra-judicial public statements that will have a substantial likelihood of materially prejudicing an adjudicative proceeding, was void for vagueness. The court emphasized that comments such as those made by the lawyer, which were critical of the exercise of the State's power, lay at the very heart of the First Amendment. Justice Kennedy made the following observation:

> An attorney's duties do not begin inside the courtroom door. He or she cannot ignore the practical implications of a legal proceeding for the client. Just as an attorney may recommend a plea bargain or civil settlement to avoid the adverse consequences of a possible loss after trial, so too an attorney may take reasonable steps to defend a client's reputation and reduce the adverse consequences of indictment, especially in the face of a prosecution deemed unjust or commenced

---

15.3 Ontario rule 6.06(1) and accompanying commentary.

16 *Gentile v. State Bar of Nevada*, 111 S. Ct. 2720 (1991). See also Marcia Coyle, "When Can A Lawyer Speak Out?", National Law Journal (April 15, 1991), p. 1.

> with improper motives. A defense attorney may pursue lawful strategies to obtain a dismissal of an indictment or reduction of charges, including an attempt to demonstrate in the court of public opinion that the client does not deserve to be tried.[17]

The majority of the court found that there was no support for the conclusion that the lawyer's statement created a likelihood of material prejudice or of any harm of sufficient magnitude or imminence to support a punishment for speech.

The court also made it clear, however, that a more carefully worded prohibition of media comment that may prejudice the fairness of pending court proceedings may well survive constitutional scrutiny. The difficulty with the Nevada prohibition under review, in the view of the majority of the court, was that it failed to provide fair notice to those to whom it was directed what types of comments would be subject to disciplinary sanctions.

The use of publicity to bolster the image of a party in a high profile case can thus raise troubling ethical questions. While acting on behalf of Michael Milken on an appeal of his ten year sentence for securities offences, Harvard law professor Alan Dershowitz placed full page newspaper advertisements in the New York *Times* and devoted a series of media interviews to sullying the reputation of Milken's leading media critic, James Stewart, who had written an incriminating bestseller, *Den of Thieves*,[18] about Milken's activities. Dershowitz called Stewart everything from an anti-semite to a liar.

Milken's team of high-powered lawyers and public relations advisers had at their disposal a budget that in some months reached two million dollars. They put it to use by portraying their client as a visionary who had revolutionized finance, though he had inadvertently broken a few technical securities laws to help his clients.[19] As we have seen, it is not clear that Canadian judges and juries will tailor their decisions to satisfy public opinion as shaped by such publicity campaigns. It is likely that a Canadian lawyer who took such a direct role in attempting to influence a court in a pending proceeding would at least be criticized by the court if not disciplined, though (as in the United States Supreme Court case referred to above[20]) the fact that the purpose of a publicity campaign is to counter an imbalance created by the lawyer's adversary is likely to be regarded as an important extenuating circumstance.

Alan Dershowitz's use of the media in the Milken case also points out the lawyer's duty to the client to be qualified to represent the client in the media, a skill that not all capable trial lawyers possess. While it is not uncommon for parties to sensitive litigation to hire public relations advisers, as Professor Stephen

---

17 *Gentile v. State Bar of Nevada, ibid.*, pp. 2728-2729.

18 (New York: Simon & Schuster, 1991).

19 Jacquie McNish, "Milken's Lawyer Wages P.R. Battle With Critics", *Globe & Mail Report on Business* (October 26, 1991), pp. B-1, B-4.

20 *Supra*, note 16. See also Clayton Ruby, "Law and Society", Toronto *Globe and Mail* (May 4, 1993), p. A-22.

Gillers of New York University Law School observed of Dershowitz, "with Alan it's one-step shopping."[21]

21 McNish, *supra*, note 19, p. B-4.

PART III

OUT OF COURT

14

Counselling

In litigation, the resolute partisanship required of lawyers is tempered by their duties to courts and tribunals. All interested parties are protected to a significant extent from partisan excesses by rules designed to promote procedural fairness, by their right to engage their own counsel, and by the fact that the result of the litigation is determined by a neutral adjudicator.[1]

Interested parties other than a lawyer's client who may be harmed as a result of a lawyer's advice in a non-litigious matter are much more vulnerable. They are much less likely to have legal representation of their own, and indeed may be unaware that the lawyer and client are considering a course that may adversely affect their interests. Their rights are not protected by a court, tribunal, or other disinterested intermediary.[2]

Canadian rules of professional conduct impose professional duties on lawyers in advising clients.[3] The rules generally do not differentiate between lawyers' duties in barristers' work and solicitors' work. Except to the extent that lawyers are forbidden from knowingly assisting or encouraging dishonesty, fraud, crime, or illegal conduct,[4] the rules are designed to protect lawyers' clients rather than other interested parties.

The rules require lawyers to be honest and candid when advising clients.[5] The lawyer's duty is to give the client a competent opinion based on sufficient knowledge of the relevant facts, adequate consideration of the applicable law, and the lawyer's own experience and expertise. The advice must be open and undisguised, and it must clearly disclose what the lawyer honestly thinks about

---

1 See, generally, chapter 4, *supra*. See also C.B.A. Code, chapter IX, rule, and commentaries 1, 2, and 15; Ontario rule 4.01(1) and accompanying commentary; and Charles Wolfram, *Modern Legal Ethics* (St. Paul, Minnesota: West, 1986), pp. 688-689.

2 See Wolfram, *ibid.*, pp. 688-689; and Paul H. Zalecki, "The Advice of a Business Lawyer: Interplay Between Law and Ethics" (1988-89) 2 Georgetown Journal of Legal Ethics 921.

3 C.B.A. Code, chapter 3; Ontario rule 2.02(1); British Columbia rules, chapter 1, rule 3; Quebec rules, section 3.02.04.

4 C.B.A. Code, chapter 3, commentary 7; Ontario rule 2.02(5).

5 C.B.A. Code, chapter III, rule; Ontario rule 2.02(1).

the merits and probable results.[6] The lawyer must not remain silent if it is obvious that the client is rushing into an imprudent decision.[7]

The rules specify that whenever it becomes apparent that the client has misunderstood or misconceived what is really involved, the lawyer should explain as well as advise, so that the client is informed of the true position and is fairly advised about the real issues involved.[8] The lawyer should clearly indicate the facts, circumstances and assumptions upon which the opinion is based. This is particularly important where the circumstances do not warrant the client's incurring the expense of a comprehensive investigation. Unless instructed otherwise by the client, however, the rules say, the lawyer should investigate the matter in sufficient detail to be able to express an opinion rather than merely make comments with many qualifications.[9]

The rules caution that lawyers should be wary of bold and confident assurances to the client, especially where the lawyer's employment may depend on advising in a particular way.[10] If the client wishes, the lawyer should assist in obtaining a second opinion.[11]

Often lawyers are asked for advice on non-legal questions. For example, lawyers are often asked for business advice, or may be asked which of several alternatives the client should choose. The rules recognize that in many cases the lawyer's advice on such matters will be of real benefit to the client. The lawyer should, however, point out any lack of experience or other qualification in the particular field, and should clearly distinguish legal advice from other advice.[12] Where acting in their professional capacity lawyers provide non-legal advice, they owe a duty of care to their clients. Unless they meet the standard of the reasonably competent lawyer, lawyers are vulnerable in professional negligence actions. Thus, in a 1983 Manitoba case,[13] a lawyer was found liable for providing negligent investment advice to a client.

The duty to give honest and candid advice requires the lawyer to inform the client promptly upon discovering that a mistake that is or may be damaging to the client and that cannot readily be rectified, has been made in connection with a matter for which the lawyer is responsible. When informing the client the lawyer

---

6 C.B.A. Code, chapter III, commentary 1; Ontario rule 2.01(1) and accompanying commentary.

7 *Neushul v. Mellish & Harkavy* (1967), lll Sol. Jo. 399 (C.A.), *per* Lord Danckwerts.

8 C.B.A. Code, chapter III, commentary 2; Ontario rule 2.01(1) and accompanying commentary.

9 C.B.A. Code, chapter III, commentary 3; Ontario rule 2.01(1) and accompanying commentary.

10 C.B.A. Code, chapter III, commentary 4; Ontario rule 2.01(1) and accompanying commentary.

11 C.B.A. Code, chapter III, commentary 5.

12 C.B.A. Code, chapter III, commentary 10; Ontario rule 2.01(1) and accompanying commentary.

13 *Brumer v. Gunn*, [1983] 1 W.W.R. 424 at 433 (Q.B.). See also *Eckstein v. Law Society (Manitoba)*, [1981] 1 W.W.R. 566 (Man. Q.B.), reversed on other grounds [1981] 3 W.W.R. 171 (Man. C.A.); *Lockhart v. MacDonald* (1980), 118 D.L.R. (3d) 397 (N.S. C.A.), varied on other grounds (1980), 44 N.S.R. (2d) 261 (C.A.), leave to appeal to S.C.C. denied (1980), 118 D.L.R. (3d) 397n; and Beverley G. Smith, *Professional Conduct for Canadian Lawyers* (Toronto: Butterworths, 1989), pp. 48-49.

should be careful not to prejudice any rights of indemnity that either the lawyer or the client may have, for example, by admitting liability in breach of the lawyer's errors and omissions insurance policy. The lawyer should recommend that the client obtain legal advice from an independent lawyer about any rights that the client may have arising from the mistake, and whether it is appropriate for the lawyer to continue to act.[14]

Lawyers also have a duty to give prompt notice of any potential claim to the lawyer's insurers so that any opportunity that the client may have to recover from that source is not prejudiced. Unless the client objects, the lawyer should co-operate with the insurer to the extent necessary to enable any claim that is made to be dealt with promptly. If the lawyer is not indemnified, or to the extent that the lawyer's insurance does not fully cover the claim, the lawyer should deal expeditiously with any claim that may be made, and must not in any circumstances take unfair advantage that might defeat or impair the client's claim. In cases in which liability is clear and the insurer is willing to pay its portion of the claim, the lawyer has a duty to arrange for payment of the balance.[15]

In some types of transaction (for example, where they have a financial interest), lawyers have a duty to insist or advise that clients be independently represented or at least have independent legal advice.[16] Canadian rules of professional conduct require that lawyers who undertake to represent or advise the clients of other lawyers in such transactions take the obligation seriously, as such an undertaking is not to be lightly assumed or perfunctorily discharged. The lawyer's duty to the client is the same as in any other lawyer and client relationship and ordinarily extends to the nature and result of the transaction.[17]

As mentioned above, the rules also stipulate that when advising clients, lawyers must never knowingly assist in or encourage any dishonesty, fraud, crime or illegal conduct (including disobedience of court orders), or instruct clients on how to violate the law and avoid punishment. The rules add that lawyers should be on guard against becoming a tool or dupe of unscrupulous clients or persons associated with such clients.[18] Lawyers may, however, advise and represent clients who in good faith and on reasonable grounds wish to challenge or test a law, where the test can most effectively be made by means of a technical breach

14 C.B.A. Code, chapter III, commentary 11; Ontario rule 6.09(1).

15 C.B.A. Code, chapter III, commentary 11; Ontario rule 6.09(2) through (5).

16 See, for example, C.B.A. Code, chapter VI, commentary 2, and Ontario rule 2.06(2) and accompanying commentary.

17 C.B.A. Code, chapter III, commentary 12. The Ontario rules do not include this provision, perhaps on the assumption that it goes without saying.

18 C.B.A. Code, chapter III, commentary 7; Ontario rule 2.02(5) and accompanying commentary. See also John Honsberger, "Legal Rules, Ethical Choices and Professional Conduct", Law Society of Upper Canada Gazette, vol. 21, no. 2 (January, 1987), p. 113 at 116-118; and Geoffrey C. Hazard Jr., "Lawyers and Client Fraud: They Still Don't Get It" (1993), 6 Georgetown Journal of Legal Ethics 701.

giving rise to a test case, so long as no injury to the person or violence is involved in the breach.[19]

The prohibition against knowingly assisting in or encouraging illegal conduct raises the difficult question of the extent to which it is proper for lawyers to advise on the limits of the law. Monroe Freedman[20] cites as a hypothetical illustration of the problem the owner of an appliance store in a border town, whose competitors across the border are able lawfully to be open for business on Sundays, who seeks legal advice about what risk she would run if she were to open her store on Sunday in violation of the law. Her lawyer tells her that the maximum penalty is 25 dollars for each violation, and that the courts have interpreted the term "violation" in this context to mean each day that business is done rather that each sale made. The client, predictably, uses the lawyer's advice as her basis for deciding to break the law by opening for business the following Sunday. Has the lawyer encouraged illegal conduct?

In trying to answer this question, Freedman quotes a respected and experienced practitioner and law teacher who has said that if he were asked what countries have no extradition treaty with his country, he would answer the question because "in that situation I am only a law book."[21] "It seems absurd," Freedman adds, apropos the Sunday closing law hypothetical example, "to hold broadly that a lawyer cannot tell a client what is in a public statute and in relevant decisions of courts."[22]

But what if a lawyer is asked whether the maximum sentence for robbery is greater if an automatic weapon is used rather than an imitation?[23] Although the "I am just a law book" response seems inadequate where it is apparent that the lawyer's advice may form the basis for a client's decision to rob a bank with an automatic weapon, rules of professional conduct do not draw distinctions among cases based on the seriousness of the offence that the client may be tempted to commit as a result of the lawyer's advice. Because the words "knowingly assist in or encourage" seem to refer to active participation in clients' unlawful acts (going beyond mere advice as to what the law is), it is likely that a lawyer who provides such advice in either of the hypothetical cases posited above has not

---

19 C.B.A. Code, chapter III, commentary 8; Ontario rule 2.02(5) and accompanying commentary.

20 Monroe H. Freedman, *Lawyers' Ethics In An Adversary System* (New York: Bobbs-Merrill, 1975), p. 59.

21 *Ibid.*, p. 60.

22 *Ibid.*, p. 59.

23 It is not: ss. 302 and 303 of the *Criminal Code*, R.S.C. 1985, c. C-46. This example also comes from Freedman, *supra*, note 20, p. 60.

offended the rule.[24] This interpretation is compatible with a policy of expanding and equalizing access to the law.

Lawyers who advise or otherwise participate in client projects that they know to be fraudulent or unlawful not only violate rules of professional conduct, but are parties to their clients' offences, subject themselves also to whatever sanctions are provided for violations of the law.[25] Lawyers who advise their clients, correctly, that planned transactions contravene the criminal law, but who then proceed to prepare documents or otherwise assist their clients to carry out the transaction, are vulnerable to criminal prosecution. In criminal prosecutions lawyers are entitled to be given the benefit of reasonable doubts that they entertained about their clients' possible non-criminal implementation of their advice.[26] This is an evidentiary matter, however. Lawyers who are ignorant of readily accessible facts only because they have consciously avoided them are likely to be held to have the functional equivalent of knowledge of those facts.[27] Charles Wolfram has written that lawyers may not avoid the bright light of clear facts simply by averting their eyes.[28]

Similarly, the lawyer's duty to be honest and candid when advising clients requires the lawyer to exercise sound professional judgment about the limits of the law. Although the limits of the law may be ill-defined, the lawyer must not strain to discover "wished-for" ambiguities in a one-sided search for validation of clients' questionable enterprises.[29] Lawyers' functions include serving as gatekeepers for the legal system. They have a duty to keep others out of places they should not go.[30] This function can be discharged only by lawyers who have a sense of objectivity and detachment from their clients.

Lawyers whose practices involve them in transactional work are often asked by clients to provide legal opinions for the eyes of third parties. For instance, a corporation that is selling assets or obtaining financing by issuing securities may be required by purchasers or underwriters to provide legal opinions concerning the state of the corporation's title or the legality or tax consequences of the transaction.

---

24 Freedman reached the same conclusion in interpreting the American Bar Association's Model Code of Professional Responsibility's Disciplinary Rule 7-102 (A)(7), which provides that a lawyer "shall not . . . counsel or assist [a] client in conduct that the lawyer knows to be illegal." He suggests, however, that the rules *should* distinguish among cases on the basis of the seriousness of the offence that the client may be encouraged by the lawyer's advice to commit. Lawyers should be prohibited from giving advice on the basis of which the client may foreseeably be encouraged to commit a crime involving violence or moral turpitude, Freedman says. See Freedman, *supra*, note 20, p. 61.

25 *Criminal Code*, R.S.C. 1985, c. C-46, s. 21.

26 Charles Wolfram, *Modern Legal Ethics* (St. Paul, Minnesota: West, 1986), p. 693.

27 *Wyle v. R.J. Reynolds Industries, Inc.*, 709 F. 2d 585 at 590 (9th Cir., 1983).

28 *Supra*, note 26, p. 696.

29 *Supra*, note 26, pp. 696-697.

30 Geoffrey C. Hazard, Jr., "Transactional Lawyers As Gatekeepers", National Law Journal (June 25, 1990), p. 13.

Canadian rules of professional conduct are silent on the lawyer's duty to the non-clients whose decisions will be affected by the lawyer's opinion. The duties to be honest and candid when providing advice and to provide competent opinions based on sufficient knowledge of relevant facts and adequate consideration of the applicable law, on their face apply only to opinions provided to clients. There is no reason in principle, however, for any less exacting standard to be applied where lawyers know that their opinions are to be relied on by non-clients. Persons expected to rely on opinions are entitled to expect independent professional judgment.[31]

Lawyers should provide such opinions, of course, only with their clients' informed consent, and only where doing so is compatible with their other duties to their clients.[32]

31 See Wolfram, *supra*, note 26, pp. 706-710.

32 See American Bar Association's Model Rules of Professional Conduct, Model Rule 2.3; and Wilfred M. Estey, *Legal Opinions in Commercial Transactions* (Toronto: Butterworths, 1989), at pp. 4-5, 10.

15

Negotiation

Official efforts to curb the excesses of the adversary system in litigation have not altered the ethics of negotiation in the slightest. The advocate's duty of resolute partisanship is tempered by such limitations as the duty to treat courts and tribunals with candour,[1] the duty not to suppress what ought to be disclosed,[2] and the duty to inform the tribunal of adverse authorities that are on point.[3] Canadian rules of professional conduct generally impose no comparable duties on lawyers, however, to make disclosure of that which may be detrimental to their clients, or even to refrain from misrepresentations. False statements abound about such matters as the lawyer's authority to compromise and the estimated value of property being sold or offered as security. Even active and deliberate misrepresentations may be minimized by being described as mere puffery, and be permitted. Bluffing in negotiation is considered to be akin to bluffing in poker.[4] "To conceal one's true position, to mislead an opponent," wrote one realistic if cynical commentator, "is the essence of negotiation."[5]

The bar's laissez-faire approach to the ethics of negotiation has been justified on several grounds. The first has its roots (as do so many aspects of the ideology of the legal profession) in the adversary system. A just bargain is assumed to result when professional negotiators clash on a battlefield of contentions. To impose a widespread disclosure obligation on lawyers, it is said, would be inimical to the adversarial premise that each side is responsible for marshalling its own factual contentions. Lawyers would in effect be co-opted into the service of the opposite party. "If the lawyer's competence is deployed for the benefit of the opposing party, where does the deployment properly stop," a leading American

---

2 C.B.A. Code, chapter IX, commentary 2(e); Ontario rule 4.01(2)(e).

3 C.B.A. Code, chapter IX, commentary 2(h); Ontario rule 4.01(2)(h).

4 See Charles Wolfram, *Modern Legal Ethics* (St. Paul, Minnesota: West, 1986), pp. 720-721; and Thomas Hurka, "Principles", Toronto *Globe and Mail* (June 4, 1991), p. A-20.

5 James White, "Machiavelli and the Bar: Ethical Limitations on Lying in Negotiation", 1980 American Bar Foundation Res. J. 926 at 928.

expert on legal ethics asks rhetorically, "short of a takeover of the transaction and assumption of the responsibility for the interests of both parties?"[6]

A second justification for forgoing truth in negotiating obligations is the lack of consensus about the types of disclosure that should be required, and the types of representations that should be proscribed. Where does one draw the line between permissible negotiation tactics and impermissible concealment or deception?[7]

Next, excesses in negotiating are controlled by the substantive law. The extent to which one may avoid disclosure of material facts or make representations that are exaggerated or untrue is governed by criminal laws prohibiting false pretences and fraud, and by principles of deceit, misrepresentation, and mistake in tort and contract.[8]

Finally, it is said that if rules of professional conduct hinder lawyers in negotiating in ways in which clients are not hindered, some clients will dispense with legal representation, and bargaining inequality will result. Ultimately, lawyers will routinely disregard the rules, in which case promulgating the rules in the first place is futile.[9]

None of these grounds, alone or in combination, are adequate to justify the complete absence of rules of professional conduct designed to promote truth in negotiating. The hard edges of the adversary system in litigation, as mentioned above, have been softened by reforms intended to foster fairness and truth — reforms such as the imposition of obligations to make full disclosure of documents — which are universally regarded as progressive, and which have not had any perceptible adverse effects.

The difficulty in drawing the line between permissible and impermissible conduct is common to all problems of professional responsibility and cannot legitimately be invoked to justify a failure to require ethical conduct in negotiating — let alone a failure to proscribe even egregious improprieties — any more than it could legitimately be invoked to justify a failure to regulate, say, conflicts of interest.

Nor is the fact that the substantive law governs the subject a reason for rules of professional conduct to be silent. The substantive law of privilege deals with the confidentiality of communications between clients and lawyers, but that neither does nor should prevent law societies from urging or requiring lawyers to

---

6 Geoffrey C. Hazard, Jr., "The Lawyer's Obligation To Be Trustworthy When Dealing With Opposing Parties" (1981) 33 S.C.L. Rev. 181 at 194. See also Gary Tobias Lowenthal, "The Bar's Failure to Require Truthful Bargaining By Lawyers" (1988-89) 2 Georgetown Journal of Legal Ethics 411 at 431-436.

7 See Lowenthal, *ibid.*, p. 411.

8 See Wolfram, *supra*, note 4, p. 719.

9 Wolfram, *supra*, note 4, p. 714. See also Lowenthal, *supra*, note 6, pp. 441-442.

observe even more exacting professional duties to hold information concerning clients' affairs in strict confidence.[10]

Finally, the danger of clients electing to forgo legal representation if lawyers are obligated to be more truthful and forthcoming than clients is at best speculative, and is of course no reason at all to avoid requiring lawyers to be as truthful and forthcoming as clients are required to be. Unless rules of professional conduct impose standards that lawyers generally regard as unworthy of respect, the prospect of widespread violation is minimal.

The issue is important because there are many opportunities in bargaining for lawyers to take advantage of trusting or credulous people. Most negotiation takes place in private, and no record is usually kept of representations made. The temptation to hide or distort information can be strong.[11]

The Law Society of Alberta's code of professional conduct contains a separate chapter titled "The Lawyer As Negotiator".[11.1] It provides that "A lawyer must not lie to or knowingly mislead an opposing party".[11.2] The Alberta rules add that, subject to their duty of confidentiality, lawyers must immediately correct misinformation on the part of an opposing party that has resulted from the lawyer or the client having misled the opposing party.[11.3] The duty to correct misinformation applies also where the lawyer has made a material misrepresentation to an opposing party that was accurate when made but which has become inaccurate due to a change in circumstance.[11.4]

The American Bar Association's Model Rules of Professional Conduct prohibit lawyers from making false statements of material fact or law to third persons. They also require lawyers to disclose material facts if disclosure is necessary to avoid assisting in criminal or fraudulent acts of clients.[12]

Commentaries to the American Bar Association model rule make it clear that although lawyers are required to be truthful when dealing with others on clients' behalf, they do not have an affirmative duty to inform opposing parties of relevant facts except where the clients are attempting to perpetrate frauds. The commentaries also make it clear that under generally accepted conventions in negotiation, certain types of statements ordinarily are not taken as statements of material facts. This category includes estimates of the price or value placed on the subject of a transaction and statements about parties' intentions concerning acceptable settlement figures.[13]

---

10 C.B.A. Code, chapter IV, rule, and commentary 2 thereto; Ontario rule 2.03(1) and accompanying commentary.

11 See Lowenthal, *supra*, note 6, p. 411.

11.1 Chapter 11.

11.2 Chapter 11, rule 1.

11.3 Chapter 11, rule 2(a) and (b).

11.4 Chapter 11, rule 2(c).

12 American Bar Association, Model Rules of Professional Conduct, Model Rule 4-1.

13 *Ibid.*, comment to Model Rule 4-1.

Critics of the Model Rules' approach contend that the lawyer's duty to disclose material facts should be extended, and that generally accepted conventions of negotiation are an inadequate justification for condoning false statements by lawyers.[14] The lawyer's purpose in misrepresenting either the value of assets to be sold or a client's instructions concerning an acceptable settlement, is to induce another person, based on guile, to relinquish money or something else of value. The Model Rules send a message, their critics say, that lawyers can rest assured that they act ethically when they misrepresent the value of the objects of their bargaining or when they lie about their settlement instructions.[15]

These arguments have merit, but must be tempered by the reasonable expectations of those in the negotiating trenches. Many estimates of value or representations about settlement instructions, like optimistic predictions of politicians during election campaigns, are not expected to be taken as literally true, but are intended, rather, to alleviate suspicions that would be aroused by their absence. Judge Learned Hand wrote that ". . . some representations are too preposterous, jocular, suspicious, or trite to induce reasonable reliance."[16] Ultimately, the issue comes down to the subjective justifiability of reliance being placed on the representation by persons to whom it is made in all the circumstances, bearing in mind generally accepted negotiating conventions.[17]

Capturing such nuances would be no easy matter, but the Model Rules' approach is at the least an improvement on Canadian disregard of the problem. It is unrealistic to expect lawyers to aspire to high ethical standards in areas in which the rules governing their professional conduct ignore the issues.

Canadian rules of professional conduct do impose duties on lawyers in relation to three aspects of negotiation that are unrelated to issues of candour and disclosure. First, lawyers have a duty to advise and encourage clients to settle disputes whenever it is possible to do so on a reasonable basis, and should discourage clients from commencing useless legal proceedings.[18] Second, lawyers have a duty not to communicate with or attempt to negotiate with any person who is represented by a lawyer except through or with the consent of that lawyer.[19] Finally, lawyers have a duty not to advise, threaten or bring criminal or quasi-criminal prosecutions in order to secure civil advantages for clients,[20] or to advise,

---

14 See Lowenthal, *supra*, note 6, pp. 425-426.

15 Lowenthal, *supra*, note 6, pp. 438 and 441.

16 *Vulcan Metals Co. v. Simmons Manufacturing Co.*, 248 F. 2d 853 at 856 (2nd Cir., 1918).

17 See Charles Wolfram, *Modern Legal Ethics* (St Paul, Minnesota: West, 1986), pp. 720-721.

18 C.B.A. Code, chapter III, commentary 6, and chapter IX, commentary 8; Ontario rule 2.02(2). In *Jacks v. Bell* (1828), 3 C. & P. 316, Lord Tenterden said to a lawyer that he did not do his duty in neither persuading nor dissuading a client who instructed him to commence an action. "It was your duty," he said, "to tell him that he ought not to bring the action."

19 C.B.A. Code, chapter XVI, commentary 8; Ontario rule 6.03(7).

20 C.B.A. Code, chapter III, commentary 9; Ontario rule 2.02(4). The Alberta rules provide "A lawyer representing a complainant or potential complainant shall not advise, threaten or lay a criminal charge, nor advise, seek or procure its withdrawal, in consideration of a benefit to be conferred on the client." (Chapter 10, rule 4)

seek or procure the withdrawal of prosecutions in consideration of the payment of money, or transfer of property, to or for the benefit of clients.[21]

Resort to the use of the criminal justice process, and threats to do so, are condemned as a matter of policy because they are potentially oppressive uses of the criminal law to defeat just civil claims and defences. Crimes will not be reported, moreover, if threats to report are successful.[22]

---

21 C.B.A. Code, chapter III, commentary 9. The Ontario rule does not include this part of the C.B.A. commentary.

22 Wolfram, *supra*, note 17, p. 716.

16

Mediation

Heightened awareness of the drawbacks and limitations of the adversary system has resulted in recent years in more frequent resort to alternative dispute resolution alternatives. Particularly in family law, respected and experienced lawyers are often asked to serve as mediators, to assist the parties to resolve questions in dispute. The phenomenon has resulted largely from the common belief that partisan lawyers can aggravate rather than resolve problems by their adversariness.[1] Highly competitive and adversarial processes encourage parties to exaggerate their claims. Parties, and their lawyers, take extravagant positions from which it is difficult for them to resile without losing face.[1.1]

The benefits of mediation as an alternative to litigation can be significant. Mediation — if it works — is likely to exact less of an emotional toll, take less time, cost less, and provide greater opportunities for structuring solutions that are flexible and tailored to the parties' wishes. The involvement of a mediator in the early stages of a dispute can provide an excuse for negotiations that enables the parties to avoid settlement overtures from being interpreted as a sign of weakness.[1.2] In addition to family law disputes, mediation has proven successful in partnership dissolutions and even in constructing new relationships, as where firms merge, restructure, or enter into joint ventures.[2]

The role of mediator is at the same time one of the most delicate that a lawyer may assume, and this is so exactly because the role is in such dramatic contrast to the lawyer's traditional role as a single-minded and partisan champion of either one client or two or more clients with common interests. The main problem of professional responsibility presented by the lawyer's assumption of the mediator's

---

1 See Charles Wolfram, *Modern Legal Ethics* (St. Paul, Minnesota: West, 1986), p. 730.

1.1 See George W. Adams and Naomi L. Bussin, "Alternative Dispute Resolution and Canadian Courts: A Time for Change", a paper prepared for presentation at the Cornell Lectures, July 1994, pp. 10-11.

1.2 *Ibid.* p. 13.

2 *Ibid.*, pp. 727-729.

role is, of course, the conflicting interests between the clients who have engaged the lawyer.[3]

The Canadian Bar Association's Code of Professional Conduct is silent on the professional duties of the lawyer as mediator. In British Columbia and Ontario, law societies have promulgated rules that specify the lawyer's responsibilities when asked to serve as a mediator, although the British Columbia rules apply only to the mediation of family law disputes. In Ontario, the Law Society has also amended its rules of professional conduct to specify that lawyers should consider the appropriateness of alternative dispute resolution ("ADR") in every case and, if appropriate, inform their client of ADR options and, if so instructed, take steps to pursue those options.[3.1] The British Columbia rules require that written agreements be entered into between the parties and between the mediator and each party, and that the written agreements contain at least certain standard clauses.[4]

It is essential that a lawyer who is asked to serve as a mediator ensures that the parties understand fully that he or she is not acting as a lawyer for either party, but rather is acting to assist the parties jointly to resolve the matters in issue.[5] The lawyer-mediator should encourage the parties to seek the advice of separate counsel before and during the mediation process if they have not already done so.[6] The lawyer should undertake the role, in short, only with the informed consent of the parties.

But even before ensuring that the parties appreciate the nature of the mediator's role, the lawyer-mediator should be satisfied that the case is one in which there is a reasonable likelihood that mediation will be effective in resolving or at least significantly narrowing the issues. Fairly extensive consultation with the parties is likely to be necessary in most cases before the lawyer-mediator can responsibly conclude that the conditions for effective mediation are present and that each client has provided a fully informed consent.[7]

This pre-mediation consultation should cover the nature and implications of the lawyer's joint representation, and the benefits and risks of mediation. The

---

3 *Ibid.*, pp. 439, 727.

3.1 Ontario rule 2.02(3).

4 British Columbia rules, chapter 6, rule 9, and Appendix A; see also Ontario rule 4.07. The Law Society of Alberta's proposed code of professional conduct, which is expected to come into force in early 1995, provides that the conflict of interest rule prohibiting a lawyer from representing opposing parties to a dispute, does not prevent a lawyer from mediating or arbitrating a dispute between clients or former clients where the parties consent, it is in the parties' best interest that the lawyer act as mediator or arbitrator, and the parties acknowledge that the lawyer will not be representing either party and that no confidentiality will apply to material information in the lawyer's possession: chapter 6, commentary 1.2. See also Robert S. Redmount, "The Nature of Client Counselling and the Code of Professional Conduct" (1983) 47 Sask. L.R. 186; and Beverly G. Smith, *Professional Conduct for Canadian Lawyers* (Toronto: Butterworths, 1989), pp. 118-120.

5 Ontario rule 4.07.

6 Ontario rule 4.07 and accompanying commentary.

7 See Wolfram, *supra*, note 1, pp. 440, 728.

risks discussed must include the possible consequences of the parties divulging confidential information to the mediator.[8]

The fact that the parties appreciate the nature of both the mediation and the lawyer-mediator's role in it is inadequate in itself to justify proceeding. The lawyer who has been asked to mediate should be satisfied also that each party will be able to make informed decisions during the mediation, and that the risk of prejudice to either party if mediation is unsuccessful is not disproportionate to the benefits to be realized if mediation is successful. This latter factor, particularly, will require a realistic assessment of the likelihood of success, and both factors will require a consideration of the relative sophistication and bargaining power of the parties. Because the lawyer-mediator cannot assume responsibility for client decisions in the way that a lawyer representing a party to traditional negotiation or litigation does, cases in which one party dominates the other are not suitable for mediation unless the dominated party is represented by separate counsel.[9]

Before embarking upon mediation, lawyers who are asked to serve as mediators must be satisfied, finally, that they are able to do so impartially and without either being or appearing to be compromised by any other responsibilities to or relationships with any of the parties.[10]

If the lawyer undertakes to serve as a mediator, the lawyer owes duties to each party, without having a traditional solicitor-client relationship with either. Each party is entitled to rely on the mediator's legal expertise. Although both lawyer-mediators and their partners and associates must not provide legal advice to either party, they are chosen in part because of their experience as lawyers, and should provide legal information to the parties as required to promote fully informed decision-making and, ultimately, the resolution of the dispute.[11]

Each party is also entitled to rely on the lawyer-mediator's trustworthiness, impartiality, and fairness. Although confidential information divulged to the mediator will be exchanged between the parties, the mediator has a duty otherwise to maintain the information in confidence unless required by the courts to disclose it.[12] At least one commentator has recommended that parties to mediation sign a written agreement confirming that they will not subpoena the mediator to testify in any legal proceeding. The mediator should warn the parties, however, that the

---

8 Wolfram, *supra*, note 1, p. 728. See also Ontario rule 25, commentary 3.

9 Wolfram, *supra*, note 1, pp. 441, 728, 730.

10 Wolfram, *supra*, note 1, p. 728. The American Bar Association's Model Rules of Professional Conduct require as a condition of a lawyer's undertaking to act as a mediator that the lawyer "reasonably believes" that the intended mediation is compatible with the best interests of the clients and can be carried out "impartially and without improper effect on other responsibilities the lawyer has to any of the clients."

11 Ontario rule 25, commentaries 4 and 5. See also Charles Wolfram, *Modern Legal Ethics* (St. Paul, Minnesota: West, 1986), pp. 729-730.

12 See Ontario rule 4,07; C.B.A. Code, chapter IV; Ontario rule 2.03(1); and Wolfram, *ibid.*, p. 129.

court may override their agreement if, for example, it wished to hear all available evidence concerning the best interests of children involved in a custody dispute.[13]

As the mediation proceeds, the mediator must continue to bear in mind that the mediator's role is to represent all parties, and that the interests of one must not be sacrificed for the advantage of another. It is for the mediator to ensure that all parties are fully apprised of all relevant facts, legal considerations, and options, and for the parties to choose among the options. The mediator must continue to consult with the parties with a view to ensuring that their choices are voluntary and fully informed.[14]

Where the mediation is successful, resolution will normally find expression in a separation or other settlement agreement. The mediator will in most cases be in the best position to draft the agreement, as the mediator will be most familiar with the terms of the settlement, will have the necessary drafting skills, and will be impartial. It is particularly important at this stage of the process, however, that the mediator expressly advise and encourage each party to obtain independent legal advice concerning the draft contract. If possible, particularly in family law disputes, the agreement together with a certificate of independent legal advice should be signed in the offices of the parties' independent lawyers in order to obviate any suggestion of coercion on the part of the mediator.[15]

If, before a resolution of the issues is achieved, any of the preconditions to undertaking mediation ceases to obtain — if, for instance, the mediator's neutrality is called into question by one of the parties — the mediator must not thereafter represent any of the parties in relation to any matter substantially related to the issues in the mediation.[16] A similar rule obtains even if the mediation culminates in agreement, except that it is permissible for the lawyer who has served as mediator to jointly represent the parties on an uncontested divorce or other related matter in which the parties' interests are congruent.[17]

A concern that has received little attention in Canada to date is whether a lawyer serving as mediator has a duty to ensure that parties are protected by safeguards assuring procedural and substantive fairness. In disputes litigated before the courts or other public tribunals, the parties generally have a right of

---

13 Judith P. Ryan, "The Mediation Alternative", a paper presented to the Canadian Institute for the Administration of Justice, Second Judicial Conference on Family Law, August 24, 1985. See also Phillip M. Epstein and Richard W. Green, "Compellability of the Mediator as Witness", a paper presented to a Law Society of Upper Canada continuing education programme in April, 1987, in which the authors consider whether communications during mediation may be privileged either as without prejudice settlement discussions, on the basis of Wigmore's well-known test, or pursuant to such statutory provisions as s. 10(4) of the *Divorce Act*, R.S.C. 1985 (2nd Supp.), c. 3.

14 Wolfram, *supra*, note 11, pp. 440, 728-730.

15 Ryan, *supra*, note 13.

16 See American Bar Association Model Rules of Professional Conduct, Model Rule 2-2(c).

17 The Ontario Association for Family Mediation prohibits lawyer-mediators and their partners and associates from representing any party during or after the mediation process in any "contested" legal matters arising out of the issues in the mediation. See Ryan, *supra*, note 13.

access to all relevant information and documents, a right to be notified in advance of allegations made about them, and a right to be given a fair opportunity to respond to any such allegations. Although much is to be said for the informality of mediation procedures, mediators should have a duty to ensure that parties' rights are not violated by a failure to observe fundamental principles of procedural fairness.[18]

Nor should any settlements reached by the parties necessarily be deemed fair, even if procedural protections are observed. If a resolution arrived at by parties who are not represented by lawyers is conspicuously one-sided or unfair, for example because one party takes advantage of a dominant position that has not previously been evident, mediators should have a duty to refuse to act in furtherance of the agreement. In such circumstances, the mediator should inform the parties of the mediator's assessment of the fairness of the agreement, using the likely litigated outcome of the dispute as a reference point, and should urge both parties (again) to obtain independent legal representation. Should they decline to do so, the mediator should refuse to draft a settlement agreement embodying the unfair terms or otherwise to assist in completing the agreement, and he or she should withdraw. Mediators should have a duty not only to ensure procedural fairness but also to avoid unfair results.[19]

---

18 See *Nicholson v. Haldimand-Norfolk (Regional Municipality) Commissioners of Police*, [1979] 1 S.C.R. 311. See also Judith L. Monte, "Public Values and Private Justice: A case for Mediator Accountability" (1991) 4 Georgetown Journal of Legal Ethics 503 at 504-505.

19 See Monte, *ibid.*, pp. 504-508 and 531-532.

17

Real Estate

17.1 ETHICS IN REAL ESTATE PRACTICE

A disproportionately high number of disciplinary proceedings, solicitors' negligence actions, and claims to client compensation funds arise out of real estate transactions. The reasons for this are many, and include among others the inability of some lawyers to resist the temptation to attempt to realize easy profits by participating personally in speculative real estate deals, and the perniciousness of apparently innocuous conflicts of interest.

Canadian rules of professional conduct require lawyers acting on real estate transactions to discharge their duties with integrity;[1] to be competent and conscientious;[2] to decline to act or continue to act in a matter when there is or is likely to be a conflicting interest;[3] and to ensure that such outside interests as engaging in a mortgage business do not jeopardize the lawyer's professional integrity, independence or competence.[4] The Canadian Bar Association's Code of Professional Conduct makes it clear that where a lawyer is asked to act for parties whose interests are in conflict, such as a vendor and a purchaser, or a mortgagor and a mortgagee, the lawyer should recommend that each party be separately represented.[5] The C.B.A. Code also alerts lawyers to the fact that in many situations in which more than one person, for example co-purchasers of real property, may wish to retain a lawyer to handle a transaction, a potential conflict of interest may exist though their interests appear to coincide.[6]

17.2 THE ONTARIO RULES

In Ontario, the Law Society has elaborated significantly upon the general admonitions of the C.B.A. Code.

---

1 C.B.A. Code, chapter I, rule; Ontario rule 1.03(1) and 6.06(1).

2 C.B.A. Code, chapter II, rule; Ontario rule 2.02(1) and (2).

3 C.B.A. Code, chapter V, rule; Ontario rule 2.04(3).

4 C.B.A. Code, chapter VII, rule, and commentary 1 thereto; Ontario rule 6.04 and accompanying commentary.

5 C.B.A. Code, chapter V, commentary 10.

6 C.B.A. Code, chapter V, commentary 11.

The Ontario rules address the types of tasks that lawyers engaged in a real estate practice may delegate to non-lawyers. Lawyers may permit non-lawyers to attend to all matters of routine administration, and to assist in more complex transactions relating to the sale, purchase, option, lease or mortgaging of land. Non-lawyers may also draft statements of account and routine documents and correspondence, and may attend to registrations. Lawyers may not, however, delegate to non-lawyers ultimate responsibility for reviewing title search reports or documents before signing, or the review and signing of letters of requisition, title opinions, or reporting letters to clients.[10]

The Law Society of Upper Canada has also promulgated detailed rules to govern the professional conduct of lawyers in mortgage transactions. Lawyers engaged in the private practice of law in Ontario are prohibited from directly or indirectly holding a mortgage having more than one investor unless each investor client receives: (i) a complete reporting letter; (ii) a trust declaration signed by the person in whose name the mortgage is registered; and (iii) a copy of the duplicate registered mortgage.[11]

Ontario lawyers are also prohibited from directly or indirectly arranging or recommending the participation of a client as an investor in a mortgage where the lawyer is also an investor unless the lawyer can demonstrate that the client had competent independent advice in making the investment or that the client is a knowledgeable investor.[12]

Lawyers engaged in private practice in Ontario are also prohibited from directly or indirectly selling mortgages to, or arranging mortgages for, clients or other persons except in accordance with the skill, competence and integrity usually expected of a lawyer in dealing with clients.[13]

The Ontario rules require lawyers who sell or arrange mortgages for clients or other persons to disclose in writing to each client or other person the priority of the mortgage and all other information relevant to the transaction that is known to the lawyer and that would be of concern to a proposed investor.[14]

Ontario lawyers are prohibited from promoting, by advertising or otherwise, individual or joint investment by clients, or other persons who have money to lend, in any mortgage in which a financial interest is held by the lawyer, directly or indirectly.[15] The Ontario rules also forbid lawyers from guaranteeing person-

10 Ontario rule 5.01(2) and accompanying commentary. See also British Columbia rules, chapter 12, rule 8(a).

11 Ontario rule 2.06(a).

12 Ontario rule 2.06(b).

13 Ontario rule 2.06(c).

14 Ontario rule 2.06(7).

15 Ontario rule 2.06(8). The ownership of less than five percent of any class of securities of a corporation or other entity offering its securities to the public is not considered a "financial interest": rule 2.06(6).

ally any mortgage or other document securing indebtedness in which a client is involved as a borrower or lender.[16]

Finally, the Ontario rules specify mortgage transactions in which lawyers may engage in connection with the practice of law. These include the following: (a) a lawyer may act on behalf of a borrower and a lender if the lawyer makes the disclosure to and obtains the consent of both in accordance with the conflict of interest rules; (b) a lawyer may introduce a borrower to a lender, whether or not either or both are clients, and may act on behalf of either or both, again if the lawyer makes disclosure to and obtains the consent of both in accordance with the conflict of interest rules; (c) a lawyer may invest in mortgages personally or on behalf of a related person or a combination thereof; (d) a lawyer may deal in mortgages in the capacity of an executor, administrator, committee, trustee of a testamentary or *inter vivos* trust established for purposes other than mortgage investment or pursuant to a power of attorney given for purposes other than exclusively for mortgage investment; and (e) a lawyer may collect, on behalf of clients, mortgage payments that are made payable in the name of the lawyer pursuant to a written direction to that effect given by the client to the mortgagor provided that such payments are deposited into the lawyer's trust account.[17]

17.3 UNAUTHORIZED USE OF CLIENT FUNDS IN SPECULATIVE REAL ESTATE VENTURES AND THE ONTARIO SPOT AUDIT PROGRAMME

Concerns about the propriety of lawyers' conduct in speculative real estate ventures resulted in the adoption in Ontario in 1964 of its spot or blitz audit programme, which was modelled on similar programmes undertaken earlier in Saskatchewan and British Columbia. An exceptionally high number of lawyers had been disbarred in the mid to late 1950's as a result of their unauthorized use of client trust funds to finance interests in speculative land transactions. One lawyer came within a day of closing a real estate deal on which he would have made $200,000. He was disbarred and sent to jail instead. Another lawyer used client trust funds, without permission, to lend money to land speculators at two percent per month interest. When the real estate market collapsed, his borrowers defaulted, and so did he.[18]

---

16 Ontario rule 2.06(9). Personal guarantees given to financial institutions in respect of loans to lawyers or their families, and personal guarantees for the benefit of non-profit or charitable institutions, are excepted: rule 2.06(10).

17 Ontario rule 2.06(6) and accompanying commentary. In four specified exceptional circumstances a lawyer may act for both a borrower and a lender in a private mortgage or loan transaction. These include situations in which the consideration for the mortgage or loan does not exceed $50,000, and in which the loan is secured by a vendor take back mortgage: rule 2.04 (12).

18 See Murray Teigh Bloom, *The Trouble With Lawyers* (New York: Simon & Schuster, 1969), pp. 31-32.

In 1964, the Law Society conducted spot audits of 243 firms in Toronto, Windsor, and Ottawa. Disciplinary proceedings were initiated against five of the lawyers who were audited, and minor deficiencies were uncovered in a further 169 cases. The following year the programme was expanded; more than 1000 firms were audited. By 1967, spot audits had been conducted on 65 percent of the lawyers practising in the province.[19]

The programme had immediate results. In 1962 and 1963, 20 lawyers had been disbarred. In 1964, the year the spot audit programme commenced, only six lawyers were disbarred. By 1966, the number was reduced to three.[20]

17.4 CONFLICTS OF INTEREST IN REAL ESTATE PRACTICE

A lawyer's representation of a vendor and a purchaser in the same transaction is a classic example of a conflict of interest. From the outset of negotiations over such fundamental terms as price, benefits realized by one party are at the expense of concessions by the other. Almost all real estate transactions are complicated by such further interests as those of mortgage lenders, real estate agents, and tenants.[21]

Although a case could be made in support of a complete prohibition of the simultaneous representation of purchasers and vendors[22] — or mortgagors and mortgagees — Canadian rules of professional conduct recognize countervailing considerations, and permit such joint representations subject to conditions where the lawyer obtains the informed written consent of both (or all) parties. The most common, and perhaps most compelling, countervailing consideration is the impairment of the client's usual right to be represented by a lawyer of the client's choice. Although in most communities other lawyers who are competent and experienced in real estate transactions are available, other lawyers are unlikely to be familiar with the client and the client's affairs, a factor that is certain to affect client confidence. In smaller communities, moreover, another lawyer with comparable experience and experience may be unavailable; a complete prohibition might result in only the most substantial clients being represented by the most experienced lawyers. The extra cost, delay and inconvenience involved in engaging another lawyer are also valid reasons for clients who are fully apprised of the dangers of lawyer conflicts of interest to decide not to retain another lawyer. The potential for actual conflict will of course be reduced if the terms of the parties' deal are negotiated before a lawyer is retained.[23]

---

19 *Ibid.*, p. 32.

20 *Ibid.*, p. 33.

21 See Charles Wolfram, *Modern Legal Ethics* (St. Paul, Minnesota: West, 1986), p. 434.

22 *Ibid.*, pp. 434-435.

23 C.B.A. Code, chapter V, commentary 4; Ontario rule 2.04(3) and accompanying commentary. See also Wolfram, *ibid.*, pp. 318, 349-350 and 434-435.

Nevertheless, Canadian rules of professional conduct emphasize the importance of a lawyer's judgment and freedom of action on the client's behalf not being compromised by other interests or duties. The rules recognize too that where a lawyer acts for more than one party to a transaction, the client's right to insist that relevant information imparted to the lawyer in confidence not be divulged must inevitably be impaired, at least insofar as the other party to the transaction is concerned. Whenever a lawyer represents more than one party to a real estate transaction there is a risk that the lawyer may sacrifice the interests of one client in order to promote those of another, or that the lawyer may use confidential information obtained from one client to advance the interests of another.[24]

Thus the rules require adequate disclosure to enable clients to make informed decisions about whether to have a lawyer act despite the existence or possibility of a conflicting interest.[25] (British Columbia's rules require lawyers to promptly and in writing recommend that each party obtain independent legal representation).[26] A lawyer who is asked to represent more than one client must inform all potential clients that the lawyer has been asked to act for all of them, that no information received in connection with the matter from one can be treated as confidential so far as any of the others is concerned and that, if a dispute develops that cannot be resolved, the lawyer cannot continue to act for all of them and may have to withdraw completely. If one of the clients is a person with whom the lawyer has a continuing relationship and for whom the lawyer acts regularly, this fact should be revealed to the others at the outset with a recommendation that they obtain independent representation.[27]

If, following disclosure, all parties are content that the lawyer act for them, the lawyer should obtain their consent, preferably in writing, or record their consent in a separate letter to each.[28] (In British Columbia, lawyers are permitted to act for all parties even with informed client consent only if the transaction is a "simple conveyance" or if it is impracticable for the parties to be separately represented because of the remoteness of the lawyer's practice).[29]

The rules caution lawyers to guard against acting for more than one client where, despite the fact that all parties concerned consent, it is reasonably obvious

24 C.B.A. Code, chapter V, commentaries 1, 2, 3, and 4; Ontario rule 2.04(1) and (3) and accompanying commentary. See also Wolfram, *ibid.*, p. 349; and *Spector v. Ageda*, [1971] 2 All E.R. 417 at 430 (Ch. D.), *per* Megarry J.

25 C.B.A. Code, chapter V, commentary 4; Ontario rule 2.04(3) and accompanying commentary; Yukon rules, Part One, rule 8; New Brunswick rules, Part C, rule 9.

26 British Columbia rules, chapter 6, rule 10, Appendix B, paragraph 2.

27 C.B.A. Code, chapter V, commentary 5; Ontario rule 2.04(6) and (7). See also *Sinclair v. Ridout*, [1955] O.R. 167 at 182-183 (H.C.), *per* McRuer C.J.H.C.

28 C.B.A. Code, chapter V, commentary 5; Ontario rule 2.04(8).

29 British Columbia rules, chapter 6, rule 10, Appendix B, paragraph 3.

that an issue contentious between them may arise, or that their interests, rights or obligations will diverge as the matter progresses.[30]

If, after the clients involved have consented, an issue contentious between them arises, the lawyer generally must not advise any of the clients on the contentious issue, but rather must refer them to other lawyers. In such circumstances the lawyer is not necessarily precluded from continuing to advise the clients on non-contentious matters. If the contentious issue involves little or no legal advice and the clients are sophisticated, the lawyer may allow them to settle the contentious issue by direct negotiations in which the lawyer does not participate. Unless it is agreed at the outset that the lawyer will continue to advise one client and refer others to another lawyer in the event of a conflict, the lawyer must not continue to act for any of the clients between whom the contentious issue has arisen.[31]

Lawyers must avoid advising unrepresented parties to transactions, and should urge them to obtain independent legal advice. If unrepresented parties do not do so, the lawyer must take care to see that they are not proceeding on the basis of an impression that the lawyer is protecting their interests.[32]

The possible consequences to lawyers of failing to observe these precautions are exemplified by two British Columbia cases decided in the early 1980's. In the first,[33] a lawyer acted for the purchaser of a vacant lot. He prepared the statement of adjustments, prepared and registered a second mortgage that was being given back to the unrepresented vendor, and disbursed the funds due on closing to the vendor. The second mortgage went into default, and the vendor brought an action framed in negligence against the lawyer.

The trial judge found that the lawyer had a duty to the vendor and, indeed, had acted for the vendor as well as the purchaser. The lawyer's duty to the vendor was held to have arisen, despite the absence of a contractual relationship, from a fiduciary relationship created by circumstances: lawyers who place themselves in a relationship of sufficient proximity to a party incur a duty of care to that party, a duty that was both created and breached by the lawyer in this case. The decision was affirmed by the British Columbia Court of Appeal.[34]

In the second case[35] also the lawyer was retained by the transferees of real property. They were the son and daughter-in-law of the transferor, who was elderly, uneducated, and unsophisticated. Although the property was assessed to be worth $168,000, no money was to change hands. When the elderly transferor attended at the lawyer's office to sign the documents that the lawyer had prepared,

30 C.B.A. Code, chapter V, commentary 5; Ontario rule 2.04(7) and accompanying commentary.

31 C.B.A. Code, chapter V, commentary 6; Ontario rule 2.04(9) and (10) and accompanying commentary.

32 C.B.A. Code, chapter XIX, commentary 8; Ontario rule 2.04(14) and accompanying commentary.

33 *Clarence Construction Ltd. v. Lavallee* (1980), 111 D.L.R. (3d) 582 (B.C. S.C.).

34 [1982] 2 W.W.R. 760 (B.C. C.A.).

35 *Panko v. Simmonds*, [1983] 3 W.W.R. 158 (B.C. S.C.).

the lawyer asked the transferor no questions and did not explain the significance of either the documents or the transfer to her. After the transfer was completed, the transferor brought an action against the lawyer.

Again, the court held that the lawyer owed a duty of care to the unrepresented party and that he had breached that duty. The lawyer should have known, the court ruled, that the plaintiff was relying on him to protect her interest. The court observed that the lawyer had failed to recognize obvious danger signals and had failed to abide by the Law Society of British Columbia's rules of professional conduct that set forth the lawyer's responsibilities in such cases.[36]

17.5 UNDERTAKINGS

Real estate transactions are often closed on the basis of undertakings given by the parties' solicitors to complete certain aspects of the transaction at a later date. Both rules of professional conduct and the courts require lawyers to honour such undertakings personally unless they have clearly stated in the undertakings themselves that they do not intend to do so. In the absence of such a statement, the person to whom the undertaking is given is entitled to expect that the lawyer giving it will honour it personally.[37]

The rules of professional conduct of the Law Society of Upper Canada expressly provides that "the use of such words as "on behalf of my client' or "on behalf of the vendor' does not relieve the solicitor giving the undertaking of personal responsibility."[38]

Lawyers have a duty to fulfil every undertaking they give, and must give no undertaking that cannot be fulfilled. Undertakings should be reduced to writing and should be unambiguous.[39] It is professional misconduct for a lawyer, without lawful justification, not to comply with an undertaking. The fact that the client of a lawyer who is seeking to enforce an undertaking acted fraudulently will not vitiate the undertaking if the lawyer has no notice of any illegality and is not a successor in title of any person affected by the illegality.[40]

---

36 See also *Tracy v. Atkins* (1977), 83 D.L.R. (3d) 46 (B.C. S.C.), affirmed (1979), 105 D.L.R. (3d) 632 (B.C. C.A.).

37 C.B.A. Code, chapter XVI, commentary 7; Ontario rule 6.03(8) and accompanying commentary; B.C. Rules, chapter 11, rules 7-11. See also *Bank of B.C. v. M.* (1981), 120 D.L.R. (3d) 177 (B.C. C.A.); *Witten, Vogel, Binder & Lyons v. Leung* (1983), 148 D.L.R. (3d) 418 (Alta. Q.B.); *Polischuk v. Hagarty* (1983), 42 O.R. (2d) 417 (H.C.), reversed (1984), 49 O.R. (2d) 71 (C.A.); *Wong (Edward) Finance Co. v. Johnson Stokes & Master*, [1984] 2 W.L.R. 36 (P.C.); and *115 Place Cooperative Housing Association v. Burke* (1994), 116 D.L.R. (4th) 657 (B.C.C.A.).

38 Ontario rule 6.03(8) and accompanying commentary. See also British Columbia rules, chapter 11, rules 7 to 11, and Yukon rules, Part One, rule 8A, in which several undertakings are deemed to have been given in all real estate transactions unless expressly disclaimed in writing.

39 C.B.A. Code, chapter XVI, commentary 7; Ontario rule 6.03(8) and accompanying commentary.

40 *Rooks Rider v. Steel*, [1993] 4 All E.R. 716 (Ch.D.).

18

Estates

18.1 TESTAMENTARY CAPACITY AND UNDUE INFLUENCE

In taking instructions to draft a will, lawyers have a duty to satisfy themselves that the testator is not influenced by any insane delusion and that the testator understands the nature and effects of the act, the extent of the property being distributed, and the claims that ought to be fulfilled.[1]

Thus, in a 1969 Ontario case[2] a judge of the Surrogate Court, in finding against a will on the ground of lack of testamentary capacity, criticized the lawyer who prepared it. The lawyer had been asked to prepare the will not by the testator but by a person named as a major beneficiary in the will. The lawyer had never acted for the testator or indeed even met him. He knew that the testator was 82 years old and that he lived in a retirement home. The lawyer had no knowledge of the size of the estate. Although he was given a letter of instructions from the testator, the lawyer prepared a will that departed from those instructions without consulting with the testator. The lawyer arranged for the will to be executed by handing it to the beneficiary who consulted him. The lawyer kept no dockets or notes concerning his instructions.

The court identified six ways in which the lawyer's representation fell short of an acceptable professional standard: (i) he should have met with the testator to take instructions from him in person; (ii) he should have inquired into the nature and extent of the testator's property, as lawyers can advise clients on tax implications and draft wills properly only if they have such information; (iii) he should have been particularly alert to the possibility that the testator may have lacked capacity or may have been subjected to undue influence, or both, in circumstances in which the testator's instructions were being conveyed to him by a major beneficiary of the estate; (iv) he should not have drawn a will that was inconsistent with the testator's written instructions without meeting with the testator to receive

---

1 See *Banks v. Goodfellow* (1870), L.R.S. Q.B. 549; and *Murphy v. Lamphier* (1914), 31 O.L.R. 287 (H.C.), *per* Boyd C., affirmed 32 O.L.R. 19 (C.A.).

2 *Re Worrell* (1969), 8 D.L.R. (3d) 36 (Ont. Surr. Ct.).

fresh instructions; (v) he should have met with the testator personally to arrange for the will to be executed, rather than handing it to a major beneficiary for that purpose; and (vi) he should have made comprehensive docket entries reflecting his instructions and advice, and the circumstances surrounding the preparation and execution of the will.[3]

In cases in which the testator's faculties may be impaired by disease, the lawyer should obtain the opinion of the testator's doctor as to whether the testator suffers from delusions and whether the testator appreciates the nature and effect of making a will, the extent of the property being distributed, and the claims that ought to be satisfied.[4] In many cases the lawyer should also arrange for an assessment by a psychiatrist.

It is not part of the lawyer's role to suggest how the testator should dispose of the estate. The lawyer should, however, ascertain what living relatives the testator has and should explain in what ways the arrangements proposed by the testator differ significantly from those customarily made for family members.[5] The lawyer should inform the testator of the right of the testator's dependants to bring an application for relief if inadequate provision is made for them in the will. The testator's insistence on leaving the estate to others despite the lawyer's advice may raise concerns about the testator's capacity and the possibility of undue influence.[6]

The professional duties imposed on lawyers by the common law to satisfy themselves of testamentary capacity and to be on guard against undue influence are enshrined in the rules of professional conduct of the Law Society of New Brunswick. The rules require lawyers to consider obtaining an opinion where testamentary capacity is in doubt, to satisfy themselves that the testator understands the nature and consequences of the document, to obtain instructions directly from the testator to satisfy themselves that instructions conveyed by third parties reflect the testator's true wishes, and in cases in which testamentary capacity is

---

3 The New Brunswick Probate Court reached the same conclusion in *Re Carvell* (1977), 21 N.B.R. (2d) 642. There the lawyer took instructions from the testator in private but received vague answers to questions about the testator's living relatives and the nature and extent of his property. The court also invoked the doctrine of suspicious circumstances. The testator, a 78-year-old who was confined to a bed in a nursing home and whose memory was failing, left his entire estate to the owner and operator of the nursing home, though he was survived by a wife (from whom he was separated) and a daughter. The testator died about ten weeks after he executed the will.

4 *Re Johnston*, [1946] 3 W.W.R. 424 (Alta. Dist. Ct.).

5 *Wilson v. Wilson* (1875), 22 Gr. 39 (Ch. D.), *per* Blake V.C.

6 See *Re Carvell*, *supra*, note 3.

in doubt to prepare notes of their observations and the circumstances surrounding the receipt of instructions and the execution of the will.[7]

Although the rules of professional conduct of other Canadian jurisdictions do not explicitly impose these duties on lawyers who prepare wills for clients of doubtful competence, lawyers who do so without taking such precautions risk running afoul of rules regarding competence[8] and, in some cases, integrity.[9] In a 1989 Ontario case,[10] a lawyer's right to practise was terminated when he was found guilty of professional misconduct for assisting a former client to take unfair advantage of elderly clients by preparing and participating in the execution of wills in which the former client was named as a beneficiary in circumstances in which the lawyer knew that the clients did not have testamentary capacity.

18.2 WILLS BENEFITTING LAWYERS

If a testator proposes to name the lawyer as a beneficiary of the testator's estate, the lawyer must insist that the testator instruct another lawyer to draw the will, as the lawyer should not act in circumstances in which the lawyer has such a conflict of interest.[11] In such a case the lawyer should insist that the client be independently represented or at least have independent legal advice.[12]

Ontario's rules of professional conduct as framed at present may be interpreted in such a way as to permit a lawyer who is named as a beneficiary to draw the will without insisting that the client obtain independent legal advice, provided that the lawyer obtains the informed consent of the client.[13] The rules, however, require lawyers to insist ("at the very least") that clients obtain independent legal advice when investing in a corporation whose shares are not publicly traded, in which the lawyer has an interest.[14] One would expect that the lawyer's duty should be at least as exacting when the lawyer is representing a client who proposes to name the lawyer as a beneficiary. In a 1914 Ontario case,[15] in any event, the court observed that a lawyer should see that the testator obtains inde-

---

7 New Brunswick rules, Part C, rule 10. In August 1993, the C.B.A. Code of Professional Conduct was amended to include a new rule dealing with the representation of clients under a disability. The new rule is discussed in chapter 25. Commentary 1 to the new rule provides that "where a lawyer is taking instructions from a client in the preparation of a will, however, the normal standards of testamentary capacity will apply".

8 C.B.A. Code, chapter II; Ontario rule 2.01.

9 C.B.A. Code, chapter I; Ontario rules 1.03(1) and 6.01(1) and accompanying commentary.

10 *Re Dudzik*, report adopted by Convocation, October 27, 1989.

11 C.B.A. Code, chapter VI, rule, paragraph (d).

12 C.B.A. Code, chapter VI, commentary 2.

13 Ontario rule 2.04(1) and (3) and accompanying commentary.

14 Ontario rule 2.06(2) and accompanying commentary.

15 *Loftus v. Harris* (1914), 30 O.L.R. 479 (C.A.).

pendent legal advice where the testator proposes to confer a substantial benefit on the lawyer in a will.[16]

More recently, in 1990, an Ontario lawyer was disciplined for preparing a will in which he was named as a substantial beneficiary.[17] The client had previously instructed the lawyer to prepare a will in which she (the testator) made a small bequest to the lawyer, but left the bulk of her estate to others. On that occasion the lawyer had arranged for the client to obtain independent legal advice.

In time, the client became estranged from the major beneficiaries of her estate. The lawyer, in the meanwhile, assisted her increasingly as her physical health deteriorated, by performing such services as arranging for her bills to be paid. He often visited her in the nursing home where she lived.

Eventually the client instructed the lawyer to draft a new will in which the lawyer became the residuary beneficiary. The lawyer did not insist that the client obtain independent legal advice in respect of this second will, in which she conferred a much more substantial benefit on the lawyer. The will accurately expressed the client's intentions, and there was no suggestion that the client either lacked testamentary capacity or was subjected to undue influence. The lawyer, however, was found guilty of professional misconduct and publicly reprimanded.[18]

In civil proceedings concerning the validity of a bequest to a lawyer who prepared the will in issue, in order to uphold the bequest the lawyer must discharge the onus not only of satisfying the court that the will is the product of a free and competent client, but must remove any suspicion that might be raised as a result of the lawyer-client relationship.[19]

A more common benefit realized by lawyers who prepare wills, of course, is that they are often retained by the executors to act on their behalf in administering the estate. Rules of professional conduct specify that it is improper for a lawyer to insert in a client's will a clause directing the executor to retain the lawyer's services in the administration of the estate without express instructions from the client.[21] This rule enshrines a principle articulated in a 1929 judgment of the Supreme Court of Canada.[22]

---

16 The House of Lords has also held that where a solicitor receives a benefit pursuant to a settlement that the solicitor has prepared, the solicitor has a duty to see to it that the settlor has independent advice: *Willis v. Barron*, [1902] A.C. 271. See also *O'Connor v. Rentier*, [1925] 1 W.W.R. 38; and *Re Souch*, [1938] O.R. 48 at 53 (C.A.), *per* Middleton J.A.

17 *Re King*, report adopted by Convocation, November 26, 1990.

18 See also *Re McDonald*, report adopted by Convocation, November 26, 1985 (Ontario).

19 *Loftus v. Harris*, *supra*, note 15; *Farrelly v. Corrigan*, [1899] A.C. 563 at 569 (P.C.), *per* Lord Macnaghten. See also *Crompton v. Williams*, [1938] O.R. 543 (S.C.); and *Re Souch*, *supra*, note 16.

21 C.B.A. Code, chapter XIX, commentary 6.

22 *St. Denis v. Thibodeau*, [1929] S.C.R. 346 at 350, *per* Mignault J.

18.3 OTHER CONFLICTS OF INTEREST

Lawyers who are not named in the will either as beneficiaries or as solicitors for the estate must nevertheless be alert to the possibility of conflicts of interest arising in other ways. Conflicts of interest will arise, for example, where a lawyer who is named as the executor of an estate invests estate funds in a company whose shares are not publicly traded in which the lawyer, a member of the lawyer's family, or a client of the lawyer, has a substantial interest.[23] Lawyers who, in their capacity as executors, loan estate funds to themselves, members of their family, corporations whose shares are not publicly traded in which they or a member of their family has a substantial interest, or other clients, similarly, are likely to be in breach of rules of professional conduct governing conflicts of interest, and in the first three of these cases are likely also to violate rules prohibiting borrowing from clients.[24]

Thus, in a 1985 Ontario case,[25] a lawyer was disciplined where, in his capacity as executor of an estate that was independently represented, he loaned money to his wife, from whom he was separated. The loan was secured by a mortgage on the matrimonial home. Nevertheless, the discipline hearing panel held that the lawyer had contravened the Law Society's rule against borrowing from a client, and had breached his duty as executor of the estate.

In another Ontario case,[26] a lawyer who was serving as both executor and solicitor for an estate loaned $53,000 in estate funds to two other clients without obtaining security. The discipline hearing panel held that in making the loans he had acted outside the scope of his authority, and had breached his duty to protect the estate.[27]

Conflicts of interest between clients (as distinct from conflicts of interest between lawyer and client) are common in an estates practice. Lawyers are often asked by spouses, for example, to prepare wills for each of them, leaving, say, a life interest to the spouse and the remainder to the children. No potential conflicts of interest are apparent. Suppose, however, that after giving such instructions the wife calls to say that she expects to inherit her parents' cottage, that she thinks that her brother should inherit it in the event of her death, and that she does not want her husband to know; or suppose that after the wills are executed the husband

---

23 C.B.A. Code, chapters V and VI; Ontario rule 2.04(1) and 2.06(2) and accompanying commentary.

24 Ontario rule 2.06(2) and (4) and accompanying commentary.

25 *Re McDonald*, *supra*, note 18. The lawyer was suspended for one year, but the well secured loan to his wife probably played a relatively small part in that determination, as the lawyer was found guilty of much more serious misconduct which was alleged in the same complaint. In related proceedings in the Surrogate Court the lawyer's compensation was reduced.

26 *Re Cochrane*, report adopted by Convocation, November 28, 1988.

27 The lawyer, who was also found guilty of charging the estate excessive fees both in his capacity as executor and in his capacity as solicitor, was permitted to resign his membership in the Law Society.

calls to say that he would like the lawyer to prepare a codicil revoking the life interest to his wife.

Rules of professional conduct recognize that in many situations in which more than one person wishes to retain a lawyer, though their interests appear to coincide, in fact a potential conflict of interest exists.[28] In such cases, before agreeing to act, the lawyer has a duty to explain to both (or all) clients that no information received in connection with the matter from one can be treated as confidential so far as any of the others is concerned.[29]

If the lawyer were to provide such an explanation in the first situation posited above, the spouse who wants to leave her parents' cottage to her brother will be in a position to make an informed choice whether to retain a separate lawyer to prepare her will or to inform her husband of her intentions. The lawyer will be spared having to choose between concealing the wife's request from her husband and telling him that he cannot prepare his will due to a mysterious conflict of interest, on the one hand, or dishonouring the wife's request that her instructions remain confidential, on the other.

In the second situation posited above, whether or not the lawyer has provided the explanation contemplated by the rules of professional conduct, the counsel of prudence would be to decline to act on the preparation of the codicil revoking the spouse's life interest. To prepare the codicil may violate the prohibition against acting against a client in matter related to a matter on which the lawyer has previously acted for the same client.[30] Because the lawyer's initial retainer is at an end, however, the lawyer probably has no duty to divulge the husband's fresh instructions to his wife.

Conflicts of interest are also common in the administration of estates. Where a lawyer is retained by the executor of the estate, the executor is of course the lawyer's client, but the lawyer owes a duty of care in tort to beneficiaries also.[31] Executors are often beneficiaries as well. A lawyer must not act for an administrator in his or her capacity as such and in his or her capacity as a beneficiary in respect of clams by others who assert claims in the estate.[32] Conflicts of interest may also result from the lawyers' dual roles if they serve simultaneously as executors and solicitors for estates.

A few examples will serve to illustrate the type of problems that lawyers are likely to encounter as a result of the multiple relationships and dual roles involved in the administration of estates.

1. A lawyer is retained by the son of the testator, who is the sole executor of the estate. The lawyer has acted for the family for years. Contrary to the lawyer's

---

28 C.B.A. Code, chapter V, commentary 11.

29 C.B.A. Code, chapter V, commentary 5; Ontario rule 2.04(6).

30 C.B.A. Code, chapter V, commentary 8; Ontario rule 2.04(4) and accompanying commentary.

31 See *Whittingham v. Crease & Co.* (1978), 88 D.L.R. (3d) 353 (B.C. S.C.); and *Ross v. Caunters* (1979), [1980] 1 Ch. 297 (Ch. D.).

32 *Re Lloyd*, [1954] 3 D.L.R. 834 (Man. C.A.).

advice, the testator has made what may well be regarded as inadequate provision for his widow, the executor's mother, and has left the bulk of his estate to the son. The widow asks the lawyer whether there is anything she can do.

The lawyer's client in the administration of the estate is the son in his capacity as executor. The lawyer can neither advise nor represent both sides of a dispute,[33] so the lawyer should refrain from giving the widow any legal advice in relation to her rights. The provision of advice that, if accurate, may result in a financial disadvantage for the lawyer's client cannot be justified on the basis that the disadvantage is sustained by the client in his capacity as a beneficiary whereas the lawyer is acting for the client in his capacity as the executor, at least if no other lawyer is representing the client in the former capacity.

The lawyer should, however, explain to the widow the reason why the lawyer cannot advise her, and should refer her to another lawyer. Although that in itself may result indirectly in a financial disadvantage for the lawyer's client, the conflict of interest rules require lawyers to promote access to justice by referring persons in need of legal assistance to other lawyers in cases of conflict.[34]

2. The testator is survived by two grown children. The younger sibling is mentally incompetent, and is cared for by the elder. The testator names the elder sibling as executor and leaves the estate to him. The testator specifies that he expects that the elder sibling will provide financially for the younger.

The drafting of the will, however, is poor, as it is not entirely clear whether this last clause is directive or precatory. The estate's lawyer interprets it as requiring the establishment of a trust fund for the younger sibling. The executor, however, insists that the lawyer arrange for the entirety of the estate to be distributed to him. When the lawyer suggests bringing a motion for a judicial interpretation of the will, the executor says that the lawyer is making a big fuss about nothing, and refuses to instruct the lawyer to bring such a motion.

Although the lawyer's client is the elder sibling in his capacity as executor, if the lawyer were to follow the executor's instructions the lawyer would be risking breaching his or her duty to the other beneficiary. The lawyer should: (i) write to the executor to record the lawyer's advice concerning the proper interpretation of the will; (ii) urge the executor to instruct the lawyer to inform the Public Trustee without divulging confidential information, that an issue of interpretation has arisen in relation to which the elder sibling cannot serve as the younger sibling's litigation guardian because of a conflict of interest; and (iii) inform the executor that the lawyer will have no choice but to withdraw if the executor does not accept the lawyer's advice.[35]

---

33 C.B.A. Code, chapter 5, rule; Ontario rule 2.04(2).

34 See C.B.A. Code, chapter V, commentary 6, and chapter XIV, rule, and commentary 1 thereto; Ontario rule 2.04(9) and (10) and 3.01 and accompanying commentary.

35 See C.B.A. Code, chapter V, commentary 6, and chapter XII, commentaries 4 and 5; Ontario rules 2.04(9) and (10) and 2.09(2) and (7) and accompanying commentary.

3. A lawyer is retained by the executor of an estate. It quickly becomes evident that the executor expects the lawyer to perform many responsibilities that are really the executor's responsibility.

The lawyer should explain the duties of both the executor and the lawyer, and should arrange as early as possible for the compensation of each to be adjusted appropriately on consent.[36]

18.4 CONFIDENTIALITY

The confidentiality rule is dealt with in detail in chapter 3. The rule is that lawyers have a duty to hold in strict confidence all information concerning the business and affairs of clients acquired in the course of the professional relationship, and should not divulge such information unless disclosure is expressly or impliedly authorized by the client, required by law or otherwise permitted or required by rules of professional conduct.[37]

In chapter 3 it is argued that rules of professional conduct as framed at present are too inflexible, and that a preferable approach would be to weigh the competing interests of confidentiality and disclosure in each case. While it is, of course, important that clients feel free to disclose confidential information to their lawyers without fear that their lawyers will repeat it, in at least a narrow range of cases in which, for example, serious harm to innocent persons is likely to result from maintaining information in confidence while little or any harm to clients will be caused by disclosure, a balancing of the interests would achieve a more equitable and acceptable resolution.

Two illustrations from the estates field may lend support to the argument.

1. A testatrix leaves her house to her niece and divides the residue of her estate equally between the same niece and her cousin, the testatrix's nephew. She instructs the family lawyer, who drafted the will, not to disclose the terms of her will to anyone until after her death.

The testatrix's mental and physical health deteriorates, and she is hospitalized, then released to a nursing home. She is declared mentally incompetent, and the niece and nephew (her only living relatives) are appointed committees of her estate.

The niece and nephew consider whether the testatrix's house should be sold. They are inclined to think that it should, but they seek the advice of the family's lawyer, intending to retain her to act on the sale of the house if she agrees.

The lawyer recognizes that if the house is sold the testatrix's intention will be frustrated, and that the testatrix's nephew will (unbeknownst to him) realize a windfall at the expense of the niece. She is bound, however, by the testatrix's express instructions, to maintain the terms of the will in confidence. It is doubtful,

---

36 The usual duties of the executor and the lawyer are listed in Margaret Rintoul, *The Solicitor's Guide To Estate Practice in Ontario* (Toronto: Butterworths, 1986), pp. 3-6.

37 C.B.A. Code, chapter 4, rule; Ontario rule 2.03(1).

particularly in light of their conflicting interests, that the niece and nephew, in their capacity as committee, could authorize the lawyer to divulge the information to themselves in their personal capacities.

A rule that allowed for the weighing of the legitimate interests of affected persons would allow disclosure by the lawyer to the committee.

2. The testator appoints his wife as executrix of his estate. Shortly after the testator's death, the executrix retains the family's lawyer to act on the administration of the estate.

The executrix asks the lawyer to turn over to her all files on which the lawyer had acted for the testator. The lawyer is hesitant to turn over two of the files, as they contain highly sensitive information concerning allegations of sexual misconduct that were disclosed to the lawyer in confidence. Knowledge of the allegations could be devastating to the family. The lawyer nevertheless concludes that the executrix as the personal representative of the testator is as entitled to require production of the testator's files as she is entitled to require production of any other property of the estate.

It is not clear at present whether the right of a personal representative to take possession of all property of the estate extends to files in the possession of the testator's lawyer that contain confidential information. A balancing of the interests militating in favour of disclosure and confidentiality would probably result in the lawyer maintaining the potentially hurtful information in confidence.[38]

18.5 COMPETENCE AND QUALITY OF SERVICE

Rules of professional conduct require lawyers to serve clients in a conscientious, diligent and efficient manner so as to provide a quality of service at least equal to that which lawyers generally would expect of a competent lawyer in a like situation.[39]

A disproportionate number of cases in which lawyers are disciplined for breaching the duty to serve clients conscientiously arise out of retainers to administer estates. In many of these cases the lawyer serves also as executor of the estate, and the beneficiaries live far away or do not know that they have been left any interest in the testator's estate. A disproportionate number of cases in which lawyers are disciplined for misappropriating client funds also arise in similar circumstances.

Two aspects of lawyer competence and quality of service that are peculiar to an estates practice are worthy of specific mention, namely, the storing of wills and the delegation of estate administration responsibilities to non-lawyers.

---

38 In *Re Karfilis*, discipline hearing panel report adopted by Convocation, September 24, 1987 (Ontario), a lawyer was disciplined as a result of a misguided attempt to maintain confidentiality, which entailed his making false and misleading representations concerning his financial dealings with a testator.

39 C.B.A. Code, chapter II, rule; Ontario rule 2(1) and (2) and accompanying commentary.

Lawyers undertake the responsibility of storing wills that they have drafted at least largely for the purpose of increasing the likelihood that they will realize a personal financial advantage as a result of being retained to administer the estate when the testator dies. They accordingly have a higher duty of care than they would have if they were storing wills as a favour to clients, though even in circumstances in which a lawyer has no expectation of being retained to administer an estate the lawyer should not be casual in fulfilling an undertaking to keep the client's will safe and intact.

When asked to draft a will, the lawyer should of course ascertain whether the client has prepared previous wills that are still in existence. If so, the lawyer should arrange for previous wills to be destroyed. If a previous will is being stored by another lawyer, the new lawyer should ask the client to sign a direction requiring the other lawyer to send the will to the new lawyer for destruction.

Ontario's rules of professional conduct explicitly address the circumstances in which estate administration responsibilities may be delegated to law clerks or other non-lawyers. The Ontario rules allow a lawyer to permit a non-lawyer to perform tasks delegated and supervised by the lawyer so long as the lawyer maintains a direct relationship with the client and assumes full professional responsibility for the work.[40]

The Ontario rules specify that a lawyer may permit a non-lawyer to attend to all matters of routine estate administration and to assist in more complex matters, to collect information, draft routine documents and correspondence, prepare income tax returns, calculate taxes, draft executors' accounts and statements of account, and attend to filings.[41]

Under the Ontario rules a lawyer may not permit a non-lawyer (among other things) to give legal opinions, give or accept undertakings (except with the express authorization of the supervising lawyer), act finally without reference to the lawyer in matters involving professional legal judgment, be held out as a lawyer, or forward to a client any documents, other than routine documents, unless they have previously been reviewed by the lawyer.[42] Lawyers are prohibited from entering into arrangements with conveyancers to divide fees on applications for probate or administration, whether or not both participate in the work.[43]

40 Ontario rule 5.01(2) and accompanying commentary. See also British Columbia rules, chapter 12, rule 8(c).

41 Ontario rule 5.01(2) and accompanying commentary.

42 Ontario rule 5.01(3) and accompanying commentary.

43 Ontario rule 2.08(a).

19

Tax

Canadian rules of professional conduct do not address specific questions of professional responsibility encountered by lawyers engaged in tax law practices. Questions of importance, such as the extent to which lawyers are entitled to take partisan positions in advising clients who are not (at least yet) in an adversarial relationship with tax authorities, are left to be determined by general rules applicable as well to issues arising in other fields of practice.

To some extent this is true also of fields other than tax law, but in at least some other fields the ethical problems of lawyers are specifically addressed by rules of professional conduct. This is particularly true of the ethical problems of lawyers who practise in the courts.[1] Indeed, a major shortcoming of current Canadian rules of professional conduct is that they draw too slight a distinction between the professional responsibilities of lawyers acting as partisan advocates in adversarial proceedings and those of lawyers serving clients in non-adversarial work.

In the United States, the professional responsibilities of lawyers in advising on tax questions are specifically set forth in rules of professional conduct and informal opinions of the American Bar Association's Standing Committee on Ethics and Professional Responsibility.[2] In Canada, the issues must be resolved by reference to general rules concerning integrity,[3] competence and quality of service,[4] and advising clients.[5]

The ethical issues that lawyers are likely to confront in a tax practice often involve evidentiary problems, notably the state of mind of the client. In some cases, such as where the client asks the lawyer to backdate documents to change the tax consequences of a transaction, the impropriety of following the client's

---

1 See, for example, C.B.A. Code, chapter IX, and Ontario rule 10.

2 See, for example, American Bar Association Model Code of Professional Responsibility, E.C. 7-3, 7-6; American Bar Association Standing Committee on Ethics and Professional Responsibility (commonly known as the Ethics Committee), Formal Opinions 314 (1965) and 352 (1985).

3 C.B.A. Code, chapter I; Ontario rule 1.03(1) and 6.01(1) and accompanying commentary.

4 C.B.A. Code, chapter II; Ontario rule 2.01.

5 C.B.A. Code, chapter III; Ontario rule 2.02(1).

instructions will be obvious; in the example just posited, the backdating of the documents would expose the lawyer to potential allegations of professional misconduct and criminal fraud.[6]

A second problem involves the extent to which lawyers may provide advice that may tempt clients to manufacture evidence. Suppose that a client who is 50 years old tells a lawyer from whom he is seeking estate planning advice that none of his ancestors have lived to be older than 50; that he wants to put his affairs in order; and that he understands that he can avoid substantial estate taxes by setting up a trust. The lawyer explains that in the jurisdiction in which the client lives and the lawyer practises, the client could avoid paying taxes only if the authorities could be satisfied that the trust was not established in contemplation of death.

The client asks the lawyer how he could satisfy the authorities that the trust was not established in contemplation of death. The lawyer responds that the client would be well advised not to tell anyone else that he is concerned about an early death, and that he should write letters to and have conversations with friends in which he says that he is setting up the trust for reasons that have nothing to do with fears of imminent death or a desire to put his affairs in order.

On these facts, the lawyer has knowingly assisted in or encouraged dishonesty and fraud, and is in violation of lawyers' professional duties as prescribed in rules of professional conduct applicable to lawyers practising in all fields.[7] The lawyer is the active instrument in establishing a fraudulent case.[8] As discussed in chapter 4, a lawyer should not routinely assume that legal advice will be used for a fraudulent purpose, but should avoid providing legal advice in circumstances in which it is evident that that is the client's objective.[9]

A more troublesome issue is the standard that lawyers should apply in advising clients to take positions that are legally questionable. A related (but less problematic) issue is whether lawyers are entitled in advising clients to take

---

6 See Charles Wolfram, *Modern Legal Ethics* (St. Paul, Minnesota: West, 1986), p. 700.

7 C.B.A Code, chapter III, commentary 7; Ontario rule 2.02(5) and accompanying commentary. See also C.B.A. Code, chapter XIII, commentary 3 and Ontario rule 4.06(1) and accompanying commentary, both of which provide that the lawyer must not subvert the law by counselling or assisting in activities that are in defiance of it.

8 The hypothetical example is taken from Monroe H. Freedman, "Professional Responsibility of the Criminal Defense Lawyer: The Three Hardest Questions" (1966) 64 Michigan L.R. 1469. In that article, Freedman defended the lawyer's advice on the basis of his assumption that virtually every tax lawyer in the country would answer the client's question the same way, and would in due course rely in court upon the client's letters and conversations. He later wrote that he also had in mind the "I am just a law book" rationale, that is, that the lawyer would be doing no more than informing the client of what is in the applicable statute and court decisions. On reflection, Freedman changed his mind, on the ground that the lawyer was more than a law book in that the lawyer advised the client how to establish a false case. Although a probable consensus of the tax bar is relevant to making an ethical judgment, he added, it should not be conclusive in such a blatant case of manufactured evidence: Monroe H. Freedman, *Lawyers' Ethics In An Adversary System* (New York: Bobbs-Merrill, 1975), pp. 71-72.

9 See chapter 4, *supra*, part 4.12.

advantage of what is known as the tax audit lottery, that is the process whereby taxpayers and their legal advisers know that it is highly unlikely that an income tax return that is regular on its face will be audited.[10]

The first of these issues was addressed in the United States at least as early as 1965, when the American Bar Association's Standing Committee on Ethics and Professional Responsibility (commonly known as the A.B.A. Ethics Committee) issued a formal opinion that recognized the potentially adversarial relationship between the taxpayer and the government, but moderated the extravagances that sometimes characterize partisan lawyering by prohibiting lawyers from advising or furthering positions taken by clients except where there is a "reasonable basis" for such positions.[11] In time, the term "reasonable basis" came to mean something quite different from what was originally intended. One commentator wrote that by 1984, in practice, what the term meant was "anything you can articulate without laughing."[12]

As a result, the A.B.A. Ethics Committee issued a fresh formal opinion in 1985. That opinion substituted for the "reasonable basis" standard a requirement that the lawyer may advise or support positions taken by taxpayer clients only "if the lawyer has a good faith belief that those positions are warranted in existing law or can be supported by a good faith argument for an extension, modification or reversal of existing law." The opinion adds by way of elaboration that "a lawyer can have a good faith belief in this context even if the lawyer believes the client's position probably will not prevail. However, good faith requires that there be some realistic possibility of success if the matter is litigated."[13]

The A.B.A.'s section of taxation had recommended in 1984 that the Ethics Committee go much further. It recommended that the Ethics Committee recognize that "a tax return is not a submission in an adversary proceeding" and that the "reasonable basis" standard be replaced by a "meritorious position" standard, which was defined as a position "advanced in good faith, as evidenced by a practical and realistic possibility of success, if litigated . . . [or one] supported by a sound construction of the applicable statutory provision." A non-meritorious position, by way of contrast, was defined as one "advanced principally to exploit the audit selection process, [or] . . . advanced solely to obtain leverage in . . . settlement negotiations", among other things. As on all other standards, doubts based on uncertain facts rather than on a strategic desire to reach an advantageous legal position could be resolved in the client's favour. Lawyers would be forbidden, however, from advising clients to take non-meritorious positions and would

---

10 See Matthew C. Ames, "Formal Opinion 352: Professional Integrity and the Tax Audit Lottery" (1987-88) 1 Georgetown Journal of Legal Ethics 411.

11 American Bar Association Ethics Committee, Formal Opinion 314, *supra*, note 2; Ames, *ibid.*, p. 416.

12 Lee A. Sheppard, "Ethics Opinion 314 and Tax Shelters Addressed at American Bar Association Meeting"(1984), 22 Tax Notes 757, quoted by Ames, *ibid.*, p. 416.

13 American Bar Association Ethics Committee Formal Opinion 352, *supra*, note 2.

be required to withdraw from representing clients who persisted in taking such positions despite the lawyer's advice.[14]

The A.B.A. Ethics Committee has been criticized for not adopting the section of taxation's recommendation. The 1985 formal opinion does not prohibit the playing of the tax audit lottery or require lawyers to believe that positions they advise or support are meritorious; it merely requires them to believe in good faith that there is "some realistic possibility" that the position would be upheld if the issue were litigated.[15]

As discussed above, none of these issues are dealt with at all in the context of advising specifically about tax law in Canadian rules of professional conduct. The guidance that may be gleaned from rules of general application may lead one to conclude that in Canada the rejected recommendations of the A.B.A. section of taxation carry the day. The rules require lawyers to be "honest and candid when advising clients."[16] "The advice", the rules add, "must be open and undisguised, clearly disclosing what the lawyer honestly thinks about the merits and probable results."[17]

Moreover, the lawyer's duty to be "openly and necessarily partisan" in Canadian rules of professional conduct applies only when the lawyer is acting as an advocate in adversary proceedings.[18] In Ontario, the applicable rule stipulates that the principle of resolute partisanship extends to court proceedings and also to appearances and proceedings before boards, administrative tribunals and other bodies, regardless of their function or the informality of their procedures.[19] The rules provide no justification for extending the principle to legal services such as advising clients on their entitlement to claim dubious deductions on their tax returns, which may or may not create a dispute between the client and the government in the future.

Nevertheless, it would be unrealistic, based on such general formulations of lawyers' duties, to conclude that the drafters of the rules necessarily intended such a result. It would be helpful to lawyers practising in the field if the rules were amended to address the issue explicitly.

---

14 American Bar Association Section of Taxation, "Proposed Revision to Formal Opinion 314", May 21, 1984, quoted in Ames, *supra*, note 10, p. 421. See also Wolfram, *supra*, note 6, p. 701.

15 See Ames, *supra*, note 10, pp. 421-430; Wolfram, *supra*, note 6, p. 701; and American Bar Association Model Code of Professional Responsibility, E.C. 7-3.

16 C.B.A. Code, chapter III, rule; Ontario rule 2.02(1).

17 C.B.A. Code, chapter III, commentary 1; Ontario rule 2.02(1) and accompanying commentary.

18 C.B.A. Code, chapter IX, commentary 15; Ontario rule 4.01(1) and accompanying commentary.

19 Ontario rule 4.01(1) and accompanying commentary.

20

The Corporate Counsel

20.1 HOUSE COUNSEL

Most ethical issues that corporate counsel confront are common to both house counsel and outside counsel. Both must struggle with such issues as the propriety of acting for employees of their corporate employer or client, the potential conflict of interest in representing affiliated companies only partially owned by their corporate employer or client, and whether there are circumstances in which they have a duty to blow the whistle on unlawful corporate activities.

The ethical duties of house counsel and outside counsel seldom, if ever, differ.[1] When functioning as a lawyer, a house counsel can and must invoke solicitor-client privilege, and must observe all other rules of professional conduct.

A concern of particular relevance to house counsel is the possible erosion of the independence that lawyers are ethically obliged to maintain as a result of their becoming progressively more closely associated with the corporate goals of their employers. Chief executive officers want their general counsel to have the same exclusive loyalty to the company that they expect from employees who do not have professional responsibilities. Outside counsel may be similarly compromised when they become identified with the goals of an important corporate client. Nevertheless, the concern is especially acute where a lawyer's livelihood and potential for advancement are entirely dependent upon the goodwill of a single client. The concern is aggravated where a house counsel assumes executive responsibilities and becomes part of the corporation's management group.

---

1 The proposition that the professional responsibilities of house counsel are the same as those of outside counsel was expressed by Lord Denning in *Alfred Crampton Amusement Machines Ltd. v. Commissioners of Custom and Excise (No. 2)*, [1972] 2 All E.R. 353 at 376 (C.A.). See also Charles Wolfram, *Modern Legal Ethics* (St. Paul, Minnesota: West, 1986), p. 737; and Beverley G. Smith, *Professional Conduct for Canadian Lawyers* (Toronto: Butterworths, 1989), pp. 215, 219 and 225.

House counsel who also serve in executive capacities must nevertheless keep their dual roles separate if they wish to preserve solicitor-client privilege. In a 1997 decision[1.1], Justice Winkler of the Ontario Court of Justice (General Division), while affirming that solicitor-client privilege applies equally to house counsel and outside counsel, held that the privilege did not attach to a document circulated internally to all branches of a bank by the bank's Senior Vice-President, General Counsel and Secretary. Justice Winkler interpreted the document as a statement of corporate policy rather than legal advice, and inferred from that interpretation that the document was circulated by the officer in his capacity as a business executive rather than as a lawyer. Justice Winkler also inferred from the wide circulation of the document and the absence of any warning accompanying it that it was not intended to be confidential. Thus none of the three requirements of solicitor-client privilege were met: the communication was not made between a lawyer and a client; it was not made for the purpose of providing legal advice; and it was not intended to be treated as confidential.

Former United States Supreme Court Justice William O. Douglas once wrote that lawyers who are house counsel tend to become obsequious, giving the advice their "boss" wishes to hear. By way of contrast, he wrote, "Outside counsel in the Clark Clifford tradition are coldly objective and brutally frank in their advice."[2]

This assessment is at once too disparaging of house counsel and too commendatory of outside counsel. A similar dichotomy, however, was drawn by the Court of International Trade in 1983 in two cases[3] in which a company that was challenging a finding that certain competitors were not dumping steel in the United States asked the court to provide the house counsel representing it access to confidential business data that the competitors in question had submitted during the course of the investigation. The court denied the company's request, though such information was customarily released to parties' outside counsel pursuant to protective orders prohibiting counsel from sharing the information with other agents of the parties. The court held that the retention by the company of outside counsel was a reasonable way for it to satisfy its need for the information.

In justifying its distinction between employed and retained counsel, the court emphasized that the distinction was not based upon any reservation as to the integrity of house counsel, but rather was intended to avoid placing house counsel "under the unnatural and unremitting strain of having to exercise constant self-censorship in their normal working relations." The court added

---

1.1 *Toronto Dominion Bank v. Leigh Instruments Ltd. (Trustee of)* (1997), 32 O.R. (3d) 575 (Gen. Div. [Commercial List]).

2 The quotation of former Justice Douglas is from *The Court Years 1939-1975: The Autobiography of William O. Douglas* (New York: Random House, 1980), p. 187.

3 *United States Steel Corp. v. United States*, 569 F. Supp. 870 (vacated on other grounds 578 F. Supp. 415); and *Republic Steel Corp. v. United States*, 572 F. Supp. 275.

that "It is humanly impossible to control the inadvertent disclosure of some of this information in any prolonged working relationship."

The court acknowledged that these concerns would be applicable also to retained counsel in certain circumstances. It held, however, that because a closer and more sustained relationship can be presumed to be an outgrowth of the employer-employee relationship, "[a] meaningful increment of protection can be obtained by excluding in-house counsel."

On appeal, however, the United States Court of Appeals for the Federal Circuit, by a two to one margin, reversed the Court of International Trade's ruling, and held that the distinction drawn between house counsel and outside counsel was unsustainable.[4] The majority of the Circuit Court pointed out that often outside counsel have long and intimate relationships with clients, often including service on corporate boards of directors. Mobility of lawyers between companies and retained law firms is also common, the court observed. Perhaps most importantly, both employed and retained counsel must abide by the same rules of professional conduct, which of course require obedience to protective orders.

(*Continued on page 20–3*)

4 *United States Steel Corp. v. United States*, 730 F. 2d 1465 (1984). The decisions are discussed by Professor Ted Schneyer of the University of Arizona College of Law in "Professionalism

The duty of house counsel to comply with the rules of professional conduct by which all lawyers are bound was also the basis of an interesting 1991 decision of the Michigan Court of Appeals.[5] The plaintiff was a senior house counsel for an insurance company. His non-lawyer supervisors, as a cost-containment measure, ordered him to cut corners in defending policy-holders. When he refused, the plaintiff was subjected to a retaliatory demotion and, ultimately, was constructively dismissed.

The employer's attitude was exemplified by a statement made to the plaintiff by an executive of the company: "The only role a lawyer has in this company is to tell me how close to the edge I can go without falling off."

At trial, the plaintiff was awarded $1,250,000 by a jury. The jury's award was upheld on appeal. The Court of Appeals held that the plaintiff's contract of employment, which arose from the employer's policy manual and pamphlets, incorporated a term that the plaintiff was bound by the state bar's code of professional ethics. The employer thus agreed to be bound indirectly by the code. Accordingly, the house counsel's discharge for refusing to violate the code was not for good cause.

There is no difference, then, between the duties of outside counsel and house counsel in resolving ethical issues. It is doubtful that concerns about

---

and Public Policy: The Case of House Counsel" (1988-89) 2 Georgetown Journal of Legal Ethics 449 at 459-463. See also Smith, *supra*, note 1, p. 224.

5 *Mourad v. Automobile Club Insurance Association*, 465 N.W. 2d 395 (1991). This case represented a departure from earlier American authorities in which courts held that a house counsel's employment may be terminated at will just as may be an outside counsel's retainer, even if the reason for the termination is the lawyer's refusal to destroy or remove inculpatory documents requested in lawsuits (*Herbster v. North American Co.*, 501 N.E. 2d 343, appeal dismissed 508 N.E. 728, cert. denied 108 S. Ct. 150 (1987)), or the lawyer's insistence on the employer complying with environmental laws (*Willy v. Coastal Corp.*, 647 F. Supp. 116 (S.D. Tex., 1986)). See also Tom Odar, "Basic Counselling Issues" (1988-89) 2 Georgetown Journal of Legal Ethics 313 at 314-315. The result reached in *Mourad* is consistent, however, with two other recent decisions, *Balla v. Gambro Inc.*, 560 N.E. 2d 1043 (Ill. App. Ct., 1990) and *Parker v. M & T Chemicals Inc.*, 566 A. 2d 215 (N.J. Superior Ct. App. Div., 1989). These divergent lines of authority, and particularly the *Mourad* case, are discussed by Lawrence Dubin and Donald Jolliffe, "Recent Discharge Cases Focus New Attention on Counsel as Employee", National Law Journal (May 20, 1991), p. S-2. In Canada there is no doubt that in the absence of agreement to the contrary an employed solicitor may be dismissed only upon reasonable notice or payment in lieu thereof, or for cause. Although there is evidently no Canadian authority on point, it is likely that compliance by house counsel with applicable rules of professional conduct would be implied as a term of an employment contract, and that the refusal by house counsel to follow instructions that, if followed, would result in a breach of the rules, would not constitute cause for dismissal. In *Courtright v. Canadian Pacific Ltd.* (1983), 45 O.R. (2d) 52 (H.C.), affirmed (1985), 50 O.R. (2d) 560 (C.A.), a wrongful dismissal action was brought by a lawyer whose offer of employment was rescinded after his prospective employer learned that he had been charged criminally with influence peddling. Although the plaintiff was acquitted of the charges his civil action was dismissed. The court held that he had breached his duty to disclose any matter that could have a bearing on the effective performance of the lawyer's duties, and that the employer accordingly had cause for dismissal.

the greater potential for erosion of independence among house counsel are well founded. The findings of a Canadian study conducted in 1986 and 1987 included a finding that one-third of house counsel identify more with the legal profession than with their organization, one-third identify more with their organization than with the legal profession, and one-third are ambivalent.[6] One suspects that a similar survey of outside corporate counsel would yield results that are not wildly different; corporate lawyers develop fierce loyalties to their clients, and often serve on their boards of directors. The rarity of cases in which house counsel have been disciplined for professional misconduct would also suggest that the fear of compromised independence is largely illusory.[7]

20.2 MOONLIGHTING

The only professional conduct issues peculiar to house counsel arise from the question of whether they may do legal work for clients other than their employer. In Ontario, the only house counsel who have been disciplined for professional misconduct have run afoul of the Law Society not because of work undertaken for their corporate employer, but because of work undertaken for other clients.[8]

Many employers have a policy prohibiting moonlighting. In organizations that do not have such a policy, the requests that house counsel are likely to find most difficult to refuse and the most troublesome are those emanating from more senior levels of management within the same organization.

The problems that may arise as a consequence of house counsel moonlighting include the following:

1. *Competence and quality of service* — Lawyers who are full-time employees of organizations may be tempted to treat work for private clients as being of secondary importance, and may not attend to such work as diligently as they should. Concerns about quality of service are heightened if the work undertaken is outside the areas of practice in which the lawyers work as house counsel.

2. *Conflicts of Interest* — House counsel are often asked to act on transactions in which their employer and one or more of their fellow employees

---

6 The 1986-1987 study referred to was conducted by Assistant Professor Sally Gunz of the School of Accountancy at the University of Waterloo, Ontario, and is referred to in Ms. Gunz's article "Ethics and Divided Loyalties", 1 Canadian Corporate Counsel 5 (September, 1991).

7 The infrequency of disciplinary proceedings brought against house counsel is commented upon in a paper presented by Stephen E. Traviss titled "Issues of Professional Responsibility: Obligations of Counsel", which was delivered to a Law Society of Upper Canada continuing education programme on "Law for the Company Counsel" in Toronto on February 25, 1988.

8 *Ibid.*

are parties. If, for instance, a house counsel is asked to act for her employer on a mortgage loan from the employer to an employee, the house counsel must be careful to comply with rules of professional conduct governing conflicts of interest. This will entail as a minimum disabusing the employee of the notion that the house counsel is acting as his lawyer and advising the employee that he should retain a lawyer to act on his behalf. If the house counsel is asked by her employer to act for both parties, she should comply with the rules of professional conduct that govern that situation.[9]

20.3 RESPONSIBILITY TO LAW SOCIETY

Moonlighting house counsel who have been disciplined have gotten into difficulty in large part because of their failure to comply with responsibilities imposed by the law society on lawyers who are in private practice. In one Ontario case, for example, a moonlighting house counsel was reprimanded for failing to pay errors and omissions levies and for filing statutory declarations in which he swore that he was not engaged in the private practice of law. In a second case, a moonlighting house counsel was reprimanded for (among other things) failing to reply to correspondence from the Law Society concerning a complaint that the law society received from a disgruntled private client. A third house counsel was disbarred, after two prior reprimands, for breaching undertakings to the law society, failing to file required annual reports concerning his limited private practice, and misappropriating $3000.[10]

House counsel who moonlight are unlikely to encounter difficulties if they follow these guidelines:

(1) They should not act for any client other than their employer without their employer's approval.

(2) They should not allow their private practice to conflict or otherwise interfere with their duties to their employers.

(3) They should complete work for private clients conscientiously and efficiently, be accessible to clients on their own time, and keep clients fully informed.

(4) They should not undertake any legal work that they are not qualified to perform.

(5) They should not do legal work for private clients during normal business hours or at any time on the premises of their employer without their employer's approval.

(6) They must pay full errors and omissions premiums (house counsel who do

---

9 See C.B.A. Code, chapter V, commentary 5; Ontario rule 2.04(6) through (10) and accompanying commentary.

10 Traviss, *supra*, note 7, pp. 22-23.

no legal work except for their employer are exempt from paying mandatory errors and omissions premiums because errors and omissions policies do not cover legal work done by a lawyer who is an employee of the client).

(7) They must make all filings required by law societies of lawyers in private practice, and keep books, records, and accounts in connection with their private practice as required by applicable legislation.[11]

20.4 NON-LEGAL ADVICE

Whether or not they serve also as directors or officers, corporate lawyers are frequently asked for advice on such non-legal matters as the business, policy, social, or moral implications of company decisions, or which of various alternative courses the client should choose.

Rules of professional conduct[12] recognize that in many instances lawyers' experience will be such that their advice on non-legal matters will be of real benefit to the client. Although lawyers can best maintain professional detachment by not seeming to mix business and legal advice, a blending of roles may give lawyers better access to facts and give clients the benefit of detailed knowledge based upon extensive business experience.

It is important that the lawyer draw attention to any lack of experience or other qualifications to provide the advice sought, and that the lawyer clearly differentiate legal advice from non-legal advice.[13]

An important reason for distinguishing between legal and other advice is that communications between clients and lawyers that are not made for the purpose of obtaining legal advice are not privileged.[14] Some house counsel have different letterhead for legal and other advice. This practice might strengthen later claims of privilege in relation to communications recorded on legal letterhead and, at the least, will facilitate identification of written communications for which privilege is claimed.[15]

Advice about whether proposed decisions are morally right can be especially troublesome, yet can provide challenging opportunities for corporate lawyers to attempt to influence corporate behaviour for the better. Corporate lawyers are sometimes treated as the company's conscience; managers may attribute to the

---

11 *Ibid.*, pp. 20-21. At this writing, the Canadian Corporate Counsel Association is considering guidelines similar to these.

12 C.B.A. Code, chapter III, commentary 10; Ontario rule 2.01(1) and accompanying commentary. See also Charles Wolfram, *Modern Legal Ethics* (St. Paul, Minnesota: West, 1986), pp. 338-339.

13 C.B.A. Code, chapter III, commentary 10; Ontario rule 2.01(1) and accompanying commentary.

14 *Alfred Crampton Amusement Machines Ltd v. Commissioners of Custom and Excise (No. 2)*, [1972] 2 All E.R. 353 (C.A.).

15 See Beverley G. Smith, *Professional Conduct for Canadian Lawyers* (Toronto: Butterworths, 1989), p. 221.

lawyer a peculiar ability to distinguish between right and wrong. Good lawyers are sensitive to societal standards and are trained to be objective, but the legal profession enjoys no monopoly on the ability to distinguish between right and wrong. If a proposed course is legally permissible but morally questionable, the lawyer should say so. The lawyer should seek to create a consensus among other decision-makers that a morally questionable course should be resisted.[16]

By way of illustration, a government lawyer was once asked for advice concerning a contract that contained a clause requiring the parties to boycott Israeli products in purchasing supplies under the contract. The lawyer rightly advised that the clause in question may offend human rights legislation, and recommended its deletion.

The parties took the lawyer's advice, but substituted for the offensive clause a clause requiring the parties to purchase North American products when supplies were needed under the contract. The lawyer advised that on its face the clause was probably lawful. However, there could be little doubt that the purpose of the clause was to discriminate on the basis of nationality, religion, and race and, therefore, that the clause was immoral. The lawyer should have said so, advised against including such a North American content clause, and attempted to convince others involved in the negotiations to delete it.

20.5 WHO IS THE CLIENT?

Corporate activities are carried out by individuals who are directors, officers, agents, and employees. These individuals confide information to the organization's lawyers and act on the lawyers' advice. They may come to think of the organization's lawyers as their lawyers as well.

To the extent that the interests of the individual agents of the organization and the organization itself are compatible, this identification between individual agents and corporate lawyers is both natural and constructive, or at worst neutral. It is important to recognize, though, that the interests of the individual agents of the organization frequently clash with the interests of the organization itself.

In law, a lawyer retained or employed by a corporation or other organization owes allegiance to the entity and not to a shareholder, director, officer, employee, agent, or other person affiliated with the entity. The Law Society of Alberta's Code of Professional Conduct provides that a lawyer in the service of a corporation must consider the corporation to be the lawyer's client.[16.1]

It does not necessarily follow, however, that a corporate lawyer owes no duty to the individual agents who carry out the organization's activities. In a

16 See Ivan R. Feltham, "The Emerging Role of Corporate Counsel", a paper delivered to the National Conference of Corporate Counsel in Banff in 1981.

16.1 Chapter 12, rule 1.

leading American case decided in 1978,[17] the court held that a corporation's counsel owes a fiduciary duty to the corporation's shareholders, for example, to disclose material financial information to them prior to the completion of a merger. In a 1979 American decision,[18] on the other hand, the United States Court of Appeals for the Eighth Circuit held that 40 years of service by a law firm to a bank gave rise to no fiduciary duty to the bank's chairperson in the absence of evidence that the firm had performed personal legal services for the chairperson.

The triangular relationship among corporate lawyers, corporations, and corporations' individual agents accounts for most of the ethical complications in the lives of corporate lawyers. Conflicts of interest of course arise where lawyers act for two or more individual clients, but individual clients can independently give instructions if fully informed; corporate clients speak only through individual agents. The principle that corporate lawyers owe a duty to the corporation as an entity is a product of the legal fiction that the corporation is a separate person. The principle is of limited assistance in resolving the thorniest conflict of interest problems arising in corporate representations, namely those involving clashes between the interests of individual agents of the corporation and the entity itself.[19]

Additional complications arise as a result of the vast differences in the size of corporations and in the nature of the relationships between shareholders and corporations. The duty owed by a corporation's lawyer to the sole shareholder of what is in effect an incorporated proprietorship differs significantly from the duty owed by a corporation's lawyer to the holder of a few shares of a large, complex, multidivisional, multinational corporation. Both corporations are juristic entities, but they bear little resemblance to each other.

A lawyer could not ethically bring an action in a corporation's name against the corporation's only shareholder. Nor could the lawyer refuse other lawful instructions from such a corporation's only shareholder by setting up competing duties to the corporation. The sole shareholder, in effect, *is* the corporation.

By way of contrast, a lawyer for a multinational public company could quite ethically bring an action in the corporation's name against a person who owns a few shares of the company. The small shareholder could not in any sense be considered the lawyer's client. The lawyer need have no fear of conflicting interests.

---

17 *Securities and Exchange Commission v. National Student Marketing Corp.*, 457 F. Supp. 682 (U.S. District Ct., D.C., 1978). See also *Re Zimmerman*, 81 Bankr. 296 (Bankr. E.D. Pa., 1987).

18 *Lane v. Chowning*, 610 F. 2d 1385 (1979).

19 See Stephen Gillers, "Model Rule 1.13(c) Gives the Wrong Answer to the Question of Corporate Counsel Disclosure" (1987-88) 1 Georgetown Journal of Legal Ethics 289 at 294-296; Smith, *supra*, note 15, pp. 217-218 and 222-223; Wolfram, *supra*, note 12, pp. 732-736; Tom Odar, "Basic Counselling Issues" (1988-89) 2 Georgetown Journal of Legal Ethics 313 at 313 and 314; and *Re BeVill, Bresler & Schulman Asset Management Corp.*, 805 F. 2d 120 (1986), in which the United States Court of Appeals for the Third Circuit held that a corporate client may waive solicitor-client privilege in respect of communications made to the corporation's lawyer by executives acting in their capacity as officers of the corporation.

The doctrine that the corporate lawyer's client is the fictional entity and not its individual agents takes on reality and importance where the interests of the entity and the interests of its individual agents are adverse. A corporate lawyer might, for example, receive instructions to draft a pension plan from the corporation's chief executive officer who will directly benefit from the plan, or the lawyer might be asked for an opinion as to whether the company's chief executive officer has exceeded his or her authority.

Where the interests of the corporation as a whole and the interests of any of its officers or members materially diverge, the corporate lawyer has an overriding duty to serve the interests of the whole and not the divergent interests of any of its parts. It is desirable that the lawyer's contract of employment or retainer specify who within the organization has authority to call on the lawyer's professional services on the client's behalf.

The lawyer should emphasize to individual agents of the corporation whose interests clash with those of the corporation that the lawyer's allegiance lies elsewhere. Even sophisticated executives might well assume that all of their confidential communications to the corporation's lawyer are protected from disclosure by solicitor-client privilege.

In most cases, the lawyer should also advise the individual agents with interests divergent to those of the organization that they should obtain independent legal advice or representation, although in some circumstances it will be acceptable for the corporate lawyer to act for both the corporation and an officer or employee of the corporation if the lawyer informs both that no information received in connection with the matter can be treated as confidential insofar as the other party to the transaction is concerned, and that if a conflict develops that cannot be resolved the lawyer will be unable to continue to act for both and may have to withdraw completely. Should this course be adopted, the lawyer should obtain the written consent of both the corporation and the officer or employee, or record their consent in a separate letter to each.[20]

Ethical issues also arise when corporate lawyers are asked to represent companies that are affiliated with their client. Affiliated companies that the lawyer may be asked to represent range from wholly owned subsidiaries of the lawyer's client to companies in which the parent of the lawyer's client holds a minority interest.

No problems generally arise where the lawyer is instructed to represent a wholly owned subsidiary of the lawyer's client or a sister corporation that is wholly owned by the parent of the lawyer's client, as there will normally be no conflict of interest between such corporations. Even if the corporations enter into contracts with each other, in the ordinary course any differences over the terms of the contracts are likely to be negotiated and resolved at the management level.

20 C.B.A. Code, chapter V, commentaries 5 and 12; Ontario rule 2.04(8). See also Wolfram, *supra*, note 12, pp. 732-736; and *Vegetable Kingdom Inc. v. Katzen*, 653 F. Supp. 917 (N.D.N.Y., 1987).

Ordinarily no conflict will arise either where the lawyer is instructed to represent either a company that is controlled, though not wholly owned, by the lawyer's client or a sister corporation that is controlled, though not wholly owned, by the same parent as the lawyer's client. A conflict will exist, however, if the issue involves a question of the rights of the majority or minority shareholders, or both. In this situation, the lawyer may represent the lawyer's client, the majority shareholder, but should not act for the affiliated company or, of course, the minority shareholders.

Where the lawyer's client has a minority interest in an affiliated company the potential for conflicts of interest is high. In many circumstances lawyers will be unable to act for the affiliated company even if they make the disclosure and obtain the consent required by the rules of professional conduct. They may of course represent their client as a minority shareholder.[21]

20.6 WHISTLEBLOWING

The subject of whistleblowing tends to arouse strong views among lawyers and non-lawyers alike. It crystallizes a recurring tension in legal ethics. On the one hand, the lawyer has a duty to uphold the law. On the other, the lawyer has a duty not to betray the trust of a client.

Our views on whistleblowing are unavoidably influenced by the whistleblower's motivations. The self-congratulatory grandstanding that sometimes accompanies disclosures of alleged corporate wrongdoing tempts one to doubt whether the service of public morality is the whistleblower's real purpose.

The issue of whether a lawyer may or must disclose intended client wrongdoing is not peculiar to corporate representations. As in the case of various other ethical conundrums, however, the legal fiction that a corporation is a person distinct from its individual agents adds layers of complexity to an already troublesome issue.

Individual clients are autonomous in the sense that they may choose, rightly or wrongly, whether to act unlawfully contrary to their lawyer's advice. The complication that makes the issue of whistleblowing especially problematic where the client is a corporation is that the directors or shareholders or both may be ignorant of the decision of one or more individual agents of the corporation to cause the corporation to act unlawfully. Such a decision is likely to be contrary to the interests of the corporation which, as we have seen, is the client to whom the corporate lawyer owes allegiance.[22]

---

21 See Wolfram, *supra*, note 12, pp. 732-736.

22 The issue of whistleblowing is discussed by Charles Wolfram in *Modern Legal Ethics* (St. Paul, Minnesota: West, 1986), pp. 666-671 and 743-746. See also Smith, *supra*, note 15, pp. 224-225.

Two examples will serve to illustrate the difficulties.[23]

First, a lawyer learns during the course of the lawyer's work for a corporate client that two executive vice presidents of the client, from whom the lawyer takes instructions, are unlawfully furthering their own interests at the corporation's expense by causing the corporation to purchase supplies at inflated prices from a company that they secretly control.

Second, a lawyer learns during the course of the lawyer's work for the same client that the chief executive officer is causing false safety certificates to be issued.

Because the lawyer's duty is owed to the corporation, the lawyer has a duty to take measures to prevent the senior officers of the corporation from causing it harm. The lawyer also has a duty, however, to maintain in confidence all information acquired during the course of a professional relationship with a client.[24] The lawyer may not divulge any such information unless authorized by the client or required by law to do so.

Sound policy reasons underlie the confidentiality rule. Lawyers would be unable to serve clients effectively were it not for the rule, as effective lawyering requires candid and unreserved communication between clients and lawyers. Clients would refuse to confide in lawyers if they could not be assured that their communications would remain secret.[25]

There are few exceptions to the confidentiality rule. The exception most relevant to the issue of whistleblowing is that disclosure of information necessary to prevent a crime will be justified if the lawyer has reasonable grounds for believing that a crime is likely to be committed.[26] In Ontario, as a result of amendments that came into force in 2000, lawyers may breach their duty of confidentiality to prevent a crime only where they believe on reasonable grounds that there is an imminent risk to an identifiable person or group of death or serious bodily harm, including serious psychological harm that substantially interferes with health or well-being.[26.1] Even in these circumstances the lawyer has no *duty* to disclose confidential information; the exception merely *permits* disclosure. Until 1995, Canadian rules of professional conduct did not expressly address the subject of whistleblowing. That year, amendments to the Law Society of Alberta's *Code of Professional Conduct* were introduced to deal with the issue, and five years later the Law Society of Upper Canada's *Rules of Professional Conduct* were also amended to provide guidance to lawyers who encounter such issues.

---

23 The examples of unlawful conduct are adapted from Professor Stephen Gillers' article "Model Rule 1.13(c) Gives the Wrong Answer to the Question of Corporate Counsel Disclosure" (1987-88) 1 Georgetown Journal of Legal Ethics 289 at 297-298.

24 C.B.A. Code, chapter IV, rule; Ontario rule 2.03(1).

25 C.B.A. Code, chapter IV, commentary 1; Ontario rule 2.03(1) and accompanying commentary.

26 C.B.A. Code, chapter IV, commentary 11.

26.1 Ontario rule 2.03 (3)

The Law Society of Alberta's Code of Professional Conduct provides that a lawyer must not implement instructions of a corporation that would involve a breach of professional ethics or the commission of a crime or fraud.[26.2] The code also provides that if a lawyer while acting for a corporation receives information material to the interests of the corporation, the lawyer must disclose the information to an appropriate authority in the corporation.[26.3] A commentary to the latter rule provides that in some circumstances, for example where the person to whom the lawyer normally reports is guilty of misconduct, the lawyer should report material information to other, usually more senior, authorities within the corporation until satisfied that the information has been conveyed to someone who will give it appropriate consideration.[26.4] Commentary to the Law Society of Upper Canada's confidentiality rule emphasizes that the lawyer's duties are owed to the organization and not to the officers, employees, or agents of the organization; that the lawyer should therefore ask that the matter be reconsidered and, if necessary, bring the proposed misconduct to the attention of a higher (and ultimately the highest) authority in the organization despite any directions from anyone in the organization to the contrary; and that, if these measures fail, it may be appropriate for the lawyer to resign in accordance with the rules governing withdrawal from representation.[26.5]

The lawyer should take the following steps in the first example set forth above:

(1) The lawyer should confront the officers, inform them that their actions are both unlawful and contrary to the company's interest, provide reasons that this is so, and suggest that they discontinue their unlawful acts.

(2) If this is ineffective, the lawyer should provide the same advice to the officers in writing.

(3) If this is ineffective, the lawyer should inform the officers in writing that if their unlawful acts are not discontinued the lawyer will report them to their immediate superior (the lawyer should avoid jumping lines of authority).

(4) If this is ineffective, the lawyer should follow through by reporting the officers' unlawful acts to their immediate superior, the chief executive officer in this example.

(5) If the chief executive officer refuses or neglects to intervene to prevent the unlawful acts, the lawyer should inform him or her that the lawyer will report the matter to the board of directors.

26.2 Chapter 12, rule 4.

26.3 Chapter 12, rule 3.

26.4 Chapter 12, commentary 3.

26.5 Ontario rule 2.03 (3) and accompanying commentary.

(6) If this is ineffective, the lawyer should bring the matter to the attention of one or more outside members of the board of directors.

(7) If the board of directors refuses or neglects to put an end to the unlawful acts, the lawyer should resign.

The lawyer should adopt the same measures in the second case, eliminating steps four and five in view of the fact that the wrongdoer in that example is the chief executive officer.

The most difficult question is whether the lawyer, after taking the measures specified, should reveal the unlawful acts to others outside the corporate structure. The rules of professional conduct, as mentioned above, permit such a revelation of confidential information only if the lawyer has reasonable grounds for believing that a crime is likely to be committed. If the unlawful activity is continuing, and is a crime, the lawyer may divulge confidential information to the extent that it is necessary to do so to prevent the crime.

Any extra-corporate disclosure should be as restricted as possible, consistent with the goal of protecting the client. Informing a major shareholder may be adequate. If it is necessary to report the matter to the police or a regulatory authority, the lawyer may be able to negotiate confidentiality. For instance, the lawyer might instruct counsel to make the initial contact and to keep the identities of the lawyer and the client confidential until the terms of disclosure are settled.

In practice, the exception to the confidentiality rule permitting disclosure to prevent a crime is rarely invoked. Few clients confide their intention to commit a crime to their lawyer. Effective counselling may be sufficient to prevent the intended commission of crimes that are confided. The threat of disclosure outside of the corporate structure is almost certain to put an end to unlawful conduct.

Both the confidential information and the considerations that have influenced the lawyer's decision should be reduced to writing in a memorandum. Lawyers placed in the uncomfortable position of learning in their professional capacity of corporate wrongdoing would be well advised to consult such neutral sources of expert guidance as respected senior members of the profession and the professional conduct committee of the Law Society, confidentially, at an early stage.

In the United States, the Model Rules of Professional Conduct explicitly address the duty of lawyers who during the course of their professional relationship with a client learn of planned organizational illegality. In states that have adopted the Model Rules, lawyers have a duty to take reasonable steps within the corporation to protect the corporation's interests. Under the Model Rules lawyers not only have no duty to disclose illegality outside the corporation, but in fact have a duty not to disclose illegality, even to prevent a crime. The lawyer's duty is to go to the top, then stop.[27]

At least one commentator has suggested that the Model Rules should be revised to provide that a corporate lawyer should have the authority to divulge

27 Model Rule 1.13.

client confidences not only when a corporation will likely suffer substantial harm in future as a result of unlawful conduct, but also where the corporation has already suffered substantial harm.[28]

One effect of following the procedure set forth above to protect the corporation's interest may be to protect the lawyer also from being named as a party to the unlawful conduct. The lawyer's protection may well be enhanced by disclosure of information to prevent a crime or by the lawyer's resignation, or both. In a 1974 American case,[29] a lawyer who had informed the Securities and Exchange Commission of non-disclosure in a registration statement, and who had resigned his position as an associate lawyer in the law firm that prepared the statement, was held entitled to disclose the confidential information to the plaintiffs in subsequent litigation naming him as a defendant. The United States Court of Appeals for the Second Circuit held that the lawyer was entitled to disclose confidential information for the purpose of defending himself against allegations of wrongdoing, a right that lawyers also have in Canada.[30] After disclosure was made, the plaintiffs discontinued the action as against the lawyer.

---

28 Professor Stephen Gillers has suggested the revision referred to in "Model Rule 1.13(c) Gives the Wrong Answer to the Question of Corporate Counsel Disclosure" (1987-88) 1 Georgetown Journal of Legal Ethics 289 at 297-298.

29 *Meyerhofer v. Empire Fire and Marine Insurance Company*, 497 F. 2d 1190 (1974).

30 C.B.A. Code, chapter IV, commentary 12; Ontario rule 2.03(4).

21

Government Lawyers

21.1 INTRODUCTION

Government lawyers are bound to adhere to standards of conduct as high as those required by rules of professional conduct of lawyers engaged in private practice.[1] Many of the ethical problems they encounter, however, are peculiar to public service. These include such fundamental issues as, who is the client of government lawyers? Are government lawyers limited in their choice of forensic strategies in ways in which lawyers in private practice are not? May government lawyers report unlawful conduct of government officials of which they learn in the course of their employment to the Attorney General, members of Parliament or the Legislature, or the media, either to prevent the commission or continuation of the offence or to expose the perpetrators to justice? What restrictions must government lawyers observe if they leave the public service for private practice?

21.2 WHO IS THE CLIENT?

The issue of who is their client perplexes government lawyers continually.

If we take as an example a staff lawyer employed by the Ministry of the Attorney General of a province, the possible answers to the question, who is my client? include at least the lawyer's immediate superior, the Deputy Attorney General, the Attorney General, the agencies or other ministries on whose behalf the lawyer appears before courts and tribunals, the government, and the public.

The question is important, and the lack of Canadian authority is surprising. From whom does the lawyer seek instructions? What should she do if the instructions she receives from two or more of these sources conflict? Does she have a duty to keep secret from some of those possible clients communications received in confidence from others? Who, if anyone, can consent to the lawyer representing

---

1 C.B.A. Code, chapter X, rule; Ontario rule 6.05(1). Both rules are entitled "The Lawyer in Public Office", and commentary 1 to each specifies that the rule applies to lawyers who are elected or appointed to a legislative or administrative office at any level of government, regardless of whether the lawyer attained such office because of professional qualifications.

more than one client in a representation that involves a possible conflict of interest?

The answers may vary to some extent depending upon the nature of the government lawyer's duties. The Law Society of Alberta's proposed code of professional conduct, which is expected to come into force in early 1995, provides that a lawyer in government service must consider the government to be the lawyer's client.[1.1] In the United States, the Federal Bar Association has issued a formal opinion to the effect that though all government lawyers represent the public interest, the client of a lawyer who practises in a government agency is the agency itself.[2] The lawyer's responsibility to the public interest is fulfilled through the lawyer's following the "instructions" set forth in duly adopted policies and in the directions of superiors in the agency to whom the lawyer reports.[3]

The client of the most senior lawyer in the agency, on this analysis, will also be the agency itself, and that lawyer too will of course be bound to abide by duly adopted agency policies. In some agencies the submissions to be made in individual cases will be determined by the senior lawyer in the agency, subject only to general policies. In such cases, within the limitations of such policies, the client of the senior lawyer may be considered to be the public.

The considerations to be weighed in answering the questions are somewhat different in the example posited above involving the lawyer employed by the Ministry of the Attorney General of a province. That lawyer is likely to represent different ministries and agencies, while being subject to policies adopted by both her own ministry and the ministry or agency she is representing, and while receiving instructions from both her superiors in her own ministry and from the ministry or agency that she is representing.

Nonetheless, there is no reason in principle for the answer to the question to differ from the answer reached in the case of the lawyer employed full-time by a government agency. The lawyer should regard the ministry or agency that she represents to be her client, and should follow the lawful and proper instruction received by the responsible representatives of that ministry or agency. She should also abide by the policies and follow the directions of her superiors in her own ministry if they are compatible with the instructions of the ministry or agency that she represents. If the instructions or policies of that ministry or agency conflict

1.1 Chapter 12, rule 1.

2 Federal Bar Association Opinion 73-1, discussed in Daniel Schwartz, "The New Legal Ethics and the Administrative Law Bar" in David Luban (ed.), *The Good Lawyer: Lawyers' Roles and Lawyers' Ethics* (Totowa, New Jersey: Rowan & Allenhead, 1983), p. 243.

3 See District of Columbia Bar Association, "Report of Special Committee on Government Lawyers and the Model Rules of Professional Conduct" reprinted in *Washington Law* (September-October, 1988), p. 53, in which the special committee concluded that the government lawyer employed by an agency should regard the agency as her client. See also Keith W. Donahoe, "The Model Rules and the Government Lawyer, A Sword or Shield? A Response To the D.C. Bar Special Committee on Government Lawyers and the Model Rules of Professional Conduct" (1988-89) 2 Georgetown Journal of Legal Ethics 987, in which the author argues that the client of the government lawyer should be the public interest.

with the instructions of her superiors or the policies of her own ministry, and the conflict cannot be resolved, the lawyer may have no choice but to withdraw from the representation, and the ministry or agency may have no choice but to retain outside counsel.[4]

It is no doubt unnecessary to add that it would be helpful if Canadian rules of professional conduct were amended to clarify the professional duties of government lawyers in cases of conflict among the interests or instructions of the various constituencies or clients whom they may be said to serve. It is not surprising that rules of professional conduct are drafted with the paradigm of the lawyer in private practice in mind, as that is still the predominant model of the lawyer-client relationship. Recognition of other lawyer-client relationships that introduce different factors into the formation of lawyers' professional responsibilities is nevertheless overdue.

21.3 LIMITATIONS ON FORENSIC STRATEGIES

As mentioned above,[5] Canadian rules of professional conduct make it clear that government lawyers are bound to adhere to standards of conduct as high as those required of lawyers engaged in private practice. In a 1992 decision,[6] the Ontario Divisional Court held that there is no indication in the rules that government lawyers have a higher professional obligation than other lawyers.

In the United States, courts have imposed a higher duty on government lawyers than on lawyers in private practice. In a 1977 decision of the United States Court of Appeals for the Eighth Circuit,[7] for example, a member of the court wrote that it is the duty of lawyers employed by the Department of Justice not to engage in relitigation and forum shopping, strategies that are permissible for private litigants.

The rationale for imposing this higher duty on government lawyers is that all citizens are entitled to fairness in dealing with their government, and that public confidence in governmental fairness would be eroded if government lawyers were to deploy questionable negotiating strategies or tactics intended to harass, delay or obstruct.[8] Bearing in mind, however, that we are not dealing with the role of the prosecutor in criminal cases — whose professional duties differ dramatically from those of the criminal defence lawyer[9] — a preferable means of realizing the objectives of the American rule would be to proscribe strategies intended to serve such illegitimate purposes for all lawyers.

---

4 See Charles Wolfram, *Modern Legal Ethics* (St. Paul, Minnesota: West, 1986), pp. 448 and 754-755.

5 *Supra*, note 1.

6 *Everingham v. Ontario* (1992), 8 O.R. (3d) 121 (Div. Ct.).

7 *May Department Stores v. Williamson*, 549 F. 2d 1147 at 1150, *per* Lay J., concurring.

8 See Wolfram, *supra*, note 4, pp. 757-758.

9 See chapters 6 and 7.

21.4 WHISTLEBLOWING

A lawyer employed by a Canadian government department is working closely with other senior employees of the department on a sensitive contract negotiation involving a foreign government. The lawyer is told during a confidential discussion concerning the department's strategy that members of the group have been approached by a public official of the foreign government who, for a payment of $10,000, has offered to provide them with copies of documents that would embarrass and weaken the bargaining position of the foreign government. Two of the senior employees of the department who are at the meeting are among those from whom the lawyer regularly takes instructions. It is evident from the discussion that they have told the corrupt public official that they are interested in pursuing the proposal and that they intend to disguise the payment as "outside consulting fees." It is also evident from the discussion that they expect the lawyer to assist in carrying out the plan. The lawyer cannot determine whether the minister responsible for the department has been informed of the proposal.

The lawyer cannot, of course, participate in the unlawful act. But can the lawyer report the matter to the senior employees' superiors, to the minister, to other members of the Cabinet or Parliament, or to the media? Does it matter whether the lawyer's purpose in disclosing the confidential information acquired is the prevention of crime, the exposure of wrongdoing, or self-aggrandizement?

Whistleblowing is discussed in the context of corporate illegality in chapter 20. Under Canadian rules of professional conduct as framed at present the same considerations are relevant to the government lawyer: the recurring tension between the lawyer's duty to uphold the law and the lawyer's duty not to prevent senior employees of a client from causing the client harm, on the one hand, and the lawyer's duty to maintain in confidence all information acquired during the course of a professional relationship with a client, on the other.[10]

The only exception to the confidentiality rule that is relevant is the proviso that disclosure of information necessary to prevent a crime will be justified if the lawyer has reasonable grounds for believing that a crime is likely to be committed.[11] In Ontario, as a result of amendments that came into force in 2000, lawyers may breach their duty of confidentiality to prevent a crime only where they believe on reasonable grounds that there is an imminent risk to an identifiable person or group of death or serious bodily harm, including serious psychological harm that substantially interferes with health or well-being.[11.1] Even in these circumstances the lawyer has no *duty* to disclose confidential information; the exception merely makes disclosure permissible.[12]

10 C.B.A. Code, chapter IV, rule; Ontario rule 2.03(1).

11 C.B.A. Code, chapter IV, commentary 11.

11.1 Ontario rule 2.03 (3).

12 Commentary 11 to the C.B.A. rule adds that disclosure is mandatory when the anticipated crime is one involving violence. The Ontario rule does not make disclosure mandatory in any case.

The steps that lawyers should take when confronted with organizational illegality such as that described in the hypothetical example posed above are set forth in detail in chapter 20. Those steps include advising the employees in question in writing of the illegality of their proposed acts and the potential harm to the organization's interest; informing their immediate superiors and, if necessary, others more senior in the chain of command if the lawyer's advice is not heeded; and, ultimately, resigning.[13]

Although the whistleblowing problem in the government context raises issues concerning the relationships between public officials and their political superiors that are not present in the context of private corporations,[14] it is clear that the same confidentiality rules apply at present to corporate and government lawyers. There is no reason to believe that the professional duties of government lawyers are significantly different from those of corporate lawyers in situations such as the one discussed above. That leaves, however, the question of whether it is ever proper for a government lawyer, after taking the steps specified, to reveal the unlawful scheme to others outside of the government.

Most Canadian rules of professional conduct permit the revelation of confidential information if the lawyer has reasonable grounds for believing that a crime is likely to be committed. As discussed above, the Law Society of Upper Canada's *Rules of Professional Conduct* include a much more restricted exception to the confidentiality rule. In any event, where the requirements of the applicable rule are met, any disclosure must be restricted to what is necessary to prevent the anticipated crime or harm.[15] In most cases actual disclosure is unlikely to be necessary; the threat of disclosure is almost certain to put an end to an unlawful scheme.

The Law Society of Alberta's code of professional conduct provides that a lawyer must not implement instructions of a government that would involve a breach of professional ethics or the commission of a crime or fraud.[15.1] The code also provides that if a lawyer while acting for a government receives information material to the interests of the government, the lawyer must disclose the information to an appropriate authority in the government.[15.2] A commentary to the latter rule provides that in some circumstances, for example where the person to whom the lawyer normally reports is guilty of misconduct, the lawyer should report material information to other, usually more senior, authorities within the client until satisfied that the information has been conveyed to someone who will give it appropriate consideration.[15.3]

---

13 See chapter 20, part 20.6.

14 See Wolfram, *supra*, note 4, p. 758.

15 See C.B.A. Code, chapter IV, commentary 13; Ontario rule 2.03(3).

15.1 Chapter 12, rule 4.

15.2 Chapter 12, rule 3.

15.3 Chapter 12, commentary 3.

21.5 CONFLICTS OF INTEREST

Government lawyers must not allow personal or other interests to conflict with the proper discharge of their official duties. They must guard against allowing their independent judgment in the discharge of official duties to be influenced by their own interests, or by the interests of persons closely related to or associated with them, former or prospective clients, or former or prospective partners or associates.[16]

The phenomenon of lawyers entering and leaving public service and private practice raises issues of actual and apparent conflicts of interest. Rules of professional conduct provide that lawyers who have left public office[17] should not act for a client in connection with any matter for which they had substantial responsibility prior to leaving office. It is not improper, however, for a lawyer to act professionally in such a matter on behalf of the public body in question.[18]

The rules also specify that lawyers who have acquired confidential information by virtue of holding public office should keep such information confidential and not divulge or use it notwithstanding that they have ceased to hold office.[19]

16 C.B.A. Code, chapter X, commentary 2; Ontario rule 6.05(2) and accompanying commentary. The meaning of persons closely related to or associated with the lawyer is elaborated upon by commentary 3 to chapter X of the C.B.A. Code.

17 For the meaning of the term "public office" in the rules, see note 1, *supra*.

18 C.B.A. Code, chapter XIX, commentary 3; Ontario rule 6.05(5) and accompanying commentary.

19 Ontario rule 6.05(5) and accompanying commentary; C.B.A. Code, chapter X, commentary 7. See also chapter IV, commentary 14; and Daniel Schwartz, "The "New' Legal Ethics and the Administrative Law Bar" in David Luban (ed.), *The Good Lawyer: Lawyers' Role and Lawyers' Ethics* (Totowa, New Jersey: Rowan & Allenhead, 1983), p. 250.

22

Conflicts of Interest

22.1 INTRODUCTION

If lawyers are asked to identify the most common ethical problem they encounter in practice they almost invariably answer "conflicts of interest."

The prevalence of conflicts of interest in the practice of law is not new. A provision of the London Ordinance of 1280 prohibited conflicts of interest on the part of lawyers.[1] It has always been the case in a sense that every time a lawyer agrees to act for a client for a fee the representation involves a conflict of interest, in that the maximization of the fee is in the lawyer's interest, while the minimization of the fee is in the client's interest.[2]

Conflict of interest problems have nevertheless become both more common and more complex over the years. Specialized conflict of interest problems may arise today in a perplexing variety of transactions and cases, including corporate representations, shareholder derivative actions, class actions, syndicated mortgages, and indemnity insurance litigation, among many others. The problems and their solutions have been complicated also by such phenomena as the adoption of alternative means of delivering legal services, the increased mobility of lawyers, the growth of large law firms, and the increase in the cost of legal services.

The introduction of such complexities alters the analysis of conflict of interest problems that were resolved traditionally by reference to immutable principles. Even problems free of novel complexities, however, may be resolved by weighing common considerations differently depending upon the nature of the legal services performed. The representation of two parties in drafting a partnership agreement may be quite proper if the parties provide their informed consent.[3] In litigation over a partnership agreement, the representation of both parties is never proper.[4] It is for this reason that the conflict of interest problems encountered

1 Herman Cohen, *History of the English Bar* (London: Sweet & Maxwell, 1929), pp. 233-234, as cited in Charles Wolfram, *Modern Legal Ethics* (St. Paul, Minnesota: West, 1986), p. 312.

2 See Wolfram, *ibid.*, p. 313.

3 See C.B.A. Code, chapter V, rule, and commentaries 4, 5, 10 and 11; Ontario rule 2.04(3) and (6) and accompanying commentary. See also Wolfram, *ibid.*, pp. 689-690.

4 C.B.A. Code, chapter V, rule; Ontario rule 2.04(2).

by lawyers in particular fields are addressed in the chapters of this book devoted to specialized practice areas.

The most prominent of the immutable principles on the basis of which conflict of interest problems have traditionally been resolved are the two principles fundamental to the client-lawyer relationship: loyalty and confidentiality.[5] The loyalty principle finds expression in Canadian rules of professional conduct that provide that "the reason" for the conflict of interest rule is that clients may suffer serious prejudice unless their lawyers' judgment and freedom of action on the clients' behalf are as free as possible from compromising influences.[6] The principle of confidentiality is not expressed in the rules themselves to be a reason for the conflict of interest rule (though the rules emphasize the necessity of lawyers who are asked to act for more than one client in a matter or transaction advising the clients that no information received from one in connection with the matter can be treated as confidential so far as the others are concerned)[7]. The importance of the confidentiality principle to the conflict of interest rule is nevertheless apparent. Clients whose options are either to conceal relevant information from their lawyer — thereby inhibiting the lawyer's ability to provide legal services effectively[8] — or to divulge confidential information that will be disclosed to and perhaps used for the benefit of other parties, are placed in an intolerable position.

Loyalty and confidentiality are not, however, the only principles that must be considered in the analysis of conflict of interest problems. Canadian rules of professional conduct provide that lawyers may act despite actual or likely conflicts of interest if fully informed clients consent to their doing so.[9] "As important as it is to the client that the lawyer's judgment and freedom of action on the client's behalf should not be subject to other interests, duties or obligations", the rules add, "in practice this factor may not always be decisive. Instead it may be only one of several factors that the client will weigh when deciding whether to give the consent referred to in the rule. Other factors might include, for example, the availability of another lawyer of comparable expertise and experience, the extra cost, delay, and inconvenience involved in engaging another lawyer and the

5 See Wolfram, *supra*, note 1, pp. 313-314 and 316-317.

6 C.B.A. Code, chapter V, commentaries 1 and 2; Ontario rule 2.04(1) and (3) and accompanying commentary.

7 C.B.A. Code, chapter V, commentary 5; Ontario rule 2.04(6); British Columbia rules, chapter 6, rule 4.

8 See C.B.A. Code, chapter IV, commentary 1; Ontario rule 2.03(1) and accompanying commentary. See also Wolfram, *supra*, note 1, p. 317.

9 C.B.A. Code, chapter V, rule, and commentary 4 thereto; Ontario rule 2.04(3) and accompanying commentary; British Columbia rules, chapter 6, rules 3 and 4.

latter's unfamiliarity with the client and the client's affairs. In the result, the client's interests may sometimes be better served by not engaging another lawyer."[10]

The policy option of prohibiting lawyers absolutely from acting in matters when they have or may have a conflict of interest has thus been rejected in favour of a more flexible standard designed to accommodate countervailing factors. The identification of a conflict of interest is only the first step in the process of resolving the problem.

It is unfortunate that the term "conflict of interest" has acquired a pejorative connotation that implies impropriety. In fact, a conflict of interest is merely an inevitable circumstance that can be dealt with in such a way as to avoid any taint of impropriety. In the United States, the American Bar Association's 1969 Model Code of Professional Responsibility uses the term "differing interests", which perhaps better captures both the inevitability of the problem (for any lawyer except a sole practitioner with a single client) and the permissibility of lawyers acting for clients with different interests with the clients' consent. The term is nevertheless engrained in lawyers' consciousness so deeply that the use of any other term would be cumbersome and confusing.[11]

Conflict of interest problems commonly encountered by lawyers who practise in the courts are considered in chapter 5 and those commonly encountered by lawyers practising in the fields of criminal law, mediation, real estate, estates, tax, corporate law, and government practice are considered in chapters 7, 16, 17, 18, 19, 20, and 21 respectively. In this chapter we will consider at a more general level the resolution of conflict of interest problems that arise in non-litigious contexts. We will deal separately with conflicts involving lawyers' other clients and those involving lawyers' personal interests. We will also consider conflicts of interest that may arise as a result of duties owed by lawyers to non-clients. Finally, we will consider the conflict of interest that arises when lawyers learn of an error or omission that may expose them to liability for professional negligence.

22.2 OTHER CLIENT CONFLICTS OF INTEREST

As we have seen, Canadian rules of professional conduct provide that lawyers may act in matters involving conflicting interests only if they have made adequate

---

10 C.B.A. Code, chapter V, commentary 4; Ontario rule 2.04(3) and accompanying commentary. In *McCauley v. McVey*, [1980] 1 S.C.R. 165, the Supreme Court of Canada recognized that in small communities other lawyers are not always available to act on the other side of a transaction. In *Clark Boyce v. Mouat*, [1993] 4 All E.R. 268 (P.C.) the Privy Council affirmed that there is no general rule of law that the lawyer should never act for both parties in a transaction where their interests might conflict; rather, lawyers are entitled to act for both parties in transactions in such circumstances if they obtain the informed consent of both parties.

11 See Charles Wolfram, *Modern Legal Ethics* (St. Paul, Minnesota: West, 1986), p. 313; and Monroe H. Freedman, *Understanding Lawyers' Ethics* (New York: Matthew Bender & Co., 1990), pp. 173, 181.

disclosure to and have obtained the consent of the clients or prospective clients concerned.[12]

Conflicting interests are defined by the rules as interests that would be likely to affect adversely the lawyer's judgment or advice on behalf of, or loyalty to, a client or prospective client.[13] The rules specify that conflicting interests include, but are not limited to, the duties and loyalties of the lawyer or a partner or professional associate of the lawyer to any other client, whether involved in the particular transaction or not, including the obligation to communicate information.[14]

The principal issues that arise have to do with the circumstances in which the duties to make adequate disclosure and obtain consent arise, and what disclosure is adequate. The rules provide some guidance on each issue.

In many situations, the rules say, even though no actual dispute exists between the parties, their interests are in conflict. Common examples are vendor and purchaser, or mortgagor and mortgagee.[15] In other cases a potential conflict of interest exists although the clients' interests appear to coincide. Examples cited in the rules include co-purchasers of real property and persons forming a partnership or corporation.[16] The interests of multiple parties to a business transaction rarely coincide in practice. Parties with apparently common interests normally have different shares in the proceeds or subject matter of the transaction, for example.

The rules provide that before the lawyer accepts employment from more than one client in the same matter, the lawyer must inform the clients that the lawyer has been asked to act for both or all of them, that no information received in connection with the matter from one can be treated as confidential so far as any of the others is concerned and that, if a dispute develops that cannot be resolved, the lawyer cannot continue to act for both or all of them and may have

---

12 C.B.A. Code, chapter V, rule; Ontario rule 2.04(3); Quebec rules, section 3.05.04; British Columbia rules, chapter 6, rules 1 to 3, provide that lawyers must not act with divided loyalties, even with informed client consent, but that with informed client consent they may act in circumstances that might *in future* give rise to divided loyalties.

13 C.B.A. Code, chapter V, commentary 1; Ontario rule 2.04(1) expands this definition to include also interests "which the lawyer might be prompted to prefer to the interests of a client or prospective client."

14 C.B.A. Code, chapter V, commentary 3; Ontario rule 2.04(1) and accompanying commentary.

15 C.B.A. Code, chapter V, commentary 10.

16 C.B.A. Code, chapter V, commentary 11.

to withdraw completely.[17] The lawyer should also advise the clients about the desirability of obtaining independent legal advice.[17.1]

If one of the clients is a person with whom the lawyer has a continuing relationship and for whom the lawyer acts regularly, the rules add, this fact should be revealed to the other or others at the outset with a recommendation that they obtain independent representation.[18] If, following such disclosure, all parties are content that the lawyer act for them, the lawyer should obtain their consent, preferably in writing, or record their consent in a separate letter to each.[19]

Finally, the rules specify that the lawyer should "guard against" acting for more than one client where, despite the fact that all parties concerned consent, it is reasonably obvious that an issue contentious between them may arise or that their interests, rights or obligations will diverge as the matter progresses.[20]

That the interests of parties to a transaction will diverge is often not "reasonably obvious" at all. Nonetheless, a consideration of three important variables can assist greatly in formulating a prediction on the basis of which lawyers can decide whether they should represent more than one party to a transaction even with the parties' informed consent.

The first variable is the relationship between the clients. Parties to a "one-shot" transaction, for instance, are much more likely to fall into conflict than are parties with longstanding relationships, who are likely to be more disposed to iron out differences. The strength and duration of the parties' relationship is likely to be at least as important a factor in determining the likelihood of contentiousness as is their interest in the immediate transaction.[21]

The second variable is the strategic interests of the clients in the immediate transaction. If the parties stand to gain only at each other's expense, their interests conflict. Thus, a lawyer generally cannot act for both parties in negotiating the price of property that is for sale. This is known as "zero-sum" bargaining: every plus on one side is offset by a corresponding and equal minus on the other, so that the sum of the two sides is zero. If, however, the parties both stand to gain

---

17 C.B.A. Code, chapter V, commentary 5; Ontario rule 2.04(6); British Columbia rules, chapter 6, rule 4. See also *McCauley v. McVey*, [1980] S.C.R. 165; *R. v. Dunbar* (1982), 138 D.L.R. (3d) 221 (Ont. C.A.); *Davey v. Woolley, Hames, Dale & Dingwall* (1982), 35 O.R. (2d) 599 (C.A.), leave to appeal to S.C.C. refused (1982), 37 O.R. (2d) 499n (S.C.C.); *Clark Boyce v. Mouat*, [1993] 4 All E.R. 268 (P.C.); and *Skimming v. Goldberg*, [1993] 8 W.W.R. 59 (Man. Q.B.).

17.1 *Dwyer v. Spry* (1981), 27 B.C.L.R. 253 (S.C.); *Garofoli v. Kohm* (1989), 77 C.B.R. (N.S.) 84 (Man. Q.B.).

18 C.B.A. Code, chapter V, commentary 5; Ontario rule 2.04(7); British Columbia rules, chapter 6, rule 4.

19 C.B.A. Code, chapter V, commentary 5; Ontario rule 2.04(8); British Columbia rules, chapter 6, rule 4.

20 C.B.A. Code, chapter V, commentary 5; Ontario rule 2.04(7) and accompanying commentary; British Columbia rules, chapter 6, rule 4.

21 See Geoffrey C. Hazard, Jr., "A Conflict Isn't Always So Obvious", National Law Journal (February 15, 1988), pp. 13- 14.

by co-operating with each other, the potential for discord is minimized. This type of negotiation is sometimes referred to as "positive sum" bargaining: the parties both stand to realize a net gain if successful. Many transactions involve both zero-sum and positive-sum bargaining. In joint venture agreements, for example, the parties are likely to have potentially conflicting interests in the division of proceeds, but common interests in maximizing the profits to be divided. The likelihood of discord diminishes in direct proportion to the significance of common interests relative to conflicting interests.[22]

The third variable is the nature of the services that the lawyer is retained to perform. If the lawyer is asked to provide disinterested advice about legal implications of a proposed transaction the likelihood of the parties' interests diverging in a way relevant to the representation will be appreciably lower than it will be if the lawyer is asked to assist one of the parties to manoeuvre for a position of dominance over the other.[23] A lawyer should not represent both parties in the latter instance, even in the unlikely event that both provided an informed consent.

Generally, the representation of multiple parties with potentially conflicting interests is more likely to be regarded as proper (where the clients have provided informed consent) in transactional work than in litigation. This can be explained on two grounds. First, certain types of transactions, such as residential real estate deals, tend to unfold in more predictable ways than most multiple party court proceedings. This predictability enables solicitors to gauge the risks of joint representations more accurately. Second, it is as a rule less disruptive to complete a transaction with separate lawyers if a joint representation breaks down even at a late stage than it is to complete a trial if new counsel must be briefed shortly before or after the trial has begun.[24]

By prohibiting lawyers from advising or representing both sides of a dispute, and perhaps by admonishing lawyers to "guard against" acting for both sides in a transaction where it is reasonably obvious that a contentious issue may arise or that the parties' interests, rights or obligations will diverge as the matter progresses, the rules create a category of non-consentable conflicts of interest. In other words, although the right of a client to a conflict-free representation is treated by the rules as a right that a fully informed and competent client should normally be able to relinquish, in cases in which the risks of harm attributable to conflicts of interest in joint representations are particularly high, no amount of disclosure will be adequate, and even a fully informed consent will not make joint representation proper.[25]

The effectiveness of consents to lawyers acting for more than one party to a transaction will be determined by a multitude of considerations. It is clear that the burden is on the lawyer to raise the issue and that the lawyer must do so before

22 *Ibid.*

23 *Ibid.*

24 See Charles Wolfram, *Modern Legal Ethics* (St. Paul, Minnesota: West, 1986), pp. 356-357.

25 *Ibid.*, pp. 337-338.

accepting employment for more than one party.[26] Factors likely to be weighed in considering the effectiveness of client consent include the nature and strength of the interests of each affected client, the detail and intelligibility of the disclosures made by the lawyer, the capacity of the client to understand and consent, and the likelihood of conflict.[27] In disciplinary proceedings, the lawyer must bear the onus of showing good faith, that adequate disclosure was made, and that the client's consent was obtained.[28]

Canadian rules of professional conduct make it clear that if, after the clients involved have consented, an issue contentious between them or some of them arises, the lawyer must not attempt to advise them on the contentious issue.[29] The lawyer is almost certain to be in possession of confidential information whose use to the prejudice of either client is of course improper. The lawyer should generally refer the clients to other lawyers. The lawyer may continue to advise one client while referring another to a different lawyer only if it was agreed at the outset that this course would be followed in the event of a conflict arising. The lawyer is not necessarily precluded from advising both or all of the affected clients on other, non-contentious matters. If the contentious issue is one that involves little or no legal advice, and the clients are sophisticated, the lawyer may allow the clients to settle the issue by direct negotiation in which the lawyer does not participate.[30]

Disciplinary proceedings arising out of conflicts of interest in transactional work are common. In the absence of evidence that the lawyer had a personal financial interest that he or she preferred to a client's interest, the sanction imposed for a first offence is generally a reprimand.

Another consequence of a lawyer's failure to abide by the rules of professional conduct governing conflicts of interest in relation to transactions in which the lawyer represents more than one party is a greater risk of exposure to solicitor's negligence claims. In the absence of a conflict of interest, a solicitor's negligence claim is often difficult to prove. Whether the lawyer turns out to be right or wrong, decisions to include a particular clause in a contract or to require a particular form of security, for example, are likely to be regarded as non-negligent matters of professional judgment. Judges generally recognize wide ranges of acceptable choices, choices that must often be made in the heat of the moment.

A conflict of interest will often remove lawyers' choices from the realm of professional judgment by providing disgruntled clients with a plausible basis for alleging that their lawyers were at fault because the course of action that they adopted was designed to protect not the plaintiffs, but other clients with different

---

26 C.B.A. Code, chapter V, commentary 5; Ontario rule 2.04(6); British Columbia rules, chapter 6, rule 4.

27 See Wolfram, *supra*, note 24, p. 343.

28 C.B.A. Code, chapter V, commentary 13.

29 C.B.A. Code, chapter V, commentary 6; Ontario rule 2.04(9); British Columbia rules, chapter 6, rules 5 and 6.

30 C.B.A. Code, chapter V, commentary 6; Ontario rule 2.04(9) and accompanying commentary.

interests. The conflict can, in effect, reverse the presumption of which lawyers usually obtain the benefit.[31]

22.3 LAWYER-CLIENT CONFLICTS OF INTEREST

Compelling arguments could be advanced in support of a rule prohibiting lawyers from acting for other parties altogether where conflicts of interest arise not by reason of the lawyer's duties to another client, but by reason of the financial or other interest of the lawyer or an associate or family member of the lawyer. Both Canadian and American rules of professional conduct, however, assimilate the two types of conflicts of interest, and at least in some cases allow lawyers to act for other parties in both types of transaction if the lawyer obtains the informed consent of all clients involved.

Thus the Canadian Bar Association's Code of Professional Conduct provides that the principles enunciated in the rule relating to conflicts of interest between clients (as referred to above) apply *mutatis mutandis* to the Code's separate rule governing conflicts of interest between lawyer and client.[32]

The Law Society of Upper Canada's *Rules of Professional Conduct* provide that "[c]onflicting interests include, but are not limited to, the financial interest of a lawyer or an associate of a lawyer, and the duties and loyalties of a lawyer to any other client . . .."[33] The rule cites as examples cases in which the lawyer, a family member, or a law partner has a personal financial interest in the client or in the matter in which the lawyer is requested to act for the client, such as a partnership interest in a joint business venture with the client.[34]

As a result of amendments that came into force in 2000 the Ontario rules now include a separate rule titled "Doing Business with a Client".[35] The rule provides that where a client intends to enter into a transaction with his or her lawyer (or with a corporation or other entity in which the lawyer has an interest other than a corporation whose securities are publicly traded) the lawyer, before accepting any retainer must (a) disclose and explain the nature of the conflicting interest to the client or, in the case of a potential conflict, how it might develop later, (b) recommend independent legal representation and require that the client

31 See, for example, *London Loan & Savings Co. v. Brickenden*, [1933] S.C.R. 257 at 262 (affirmed [1934] 3 D.L.R. 465 (P.C.)); *McGrath v. Goldman* (1975), 64 D.L.R. (3d) 305 (B.C. S.C.); *Mastercraft Construction Corp. v. Baker* (1978), 19 O.R. (2d) 652 (H.C.), affirmed (1979), 26 O.R. (2d) 389 (C.A.); *LaPierre v. Young* (1980), 30 O.R. (2d) 319 (H.C.); *Davey v. Woolley, Hames, Dale & Dingwall* (1982), 35 O.R. (2d) 599 (C.A.), leave to appeal to S.C.C. refused (1982), 37 O.R. (2d) 499n (S.C.C.); *Ferris v. Rusnak* (1983), 50 A.R. 297 (Q.B.); and *Morris v. Jackson* (1984), 34 R.P.R. 269 (Ont. H.C.). See also Geoffrey C. Hazard, Jr., "Conflicts are Often Key in Malpractice", National Law Journal (September 10, 1990), pp. 13- 14.

32 C.B.A. Code, chapter VI, commentary 1.

33 Ontario rule 2.04(1) and accompanying commentary.

34 Ontario rule 2.04(1) and accompanying commentary.

35 Ontario rule 2.06.

obtain independent legal advice, and (c) where the client asks the lawyer to act, obtain the client's written consent.[36]

If the client elects to be represented by the lawyer who (or whose family member or associate) has an interest in the transaction, the lawyer giving independent legal advice must, prior to any advance being made on the investment, provide the client with a certificate signed by both the lawyer and the client that must include at least the following:

(1) a statement that the certifying lawyer has explained to the client the latter's right to independent legal representation and that the client has expressly waived such right and elected to rely on the representation of the original lawyer; and

(2) a statement that the certifying lawyer has explained the legal aspects of the transaction to the client, that the client appeared to understand the advice given, and further that the certifying lawyer has informed the client of the availability of qualified advisers in other fields who would be in a position to give an opinion to the client as to the desirability or otherwise of the proposed investment from a business point of view.[37]

The Ontario rules provide that if the lawyer does not wish to make disclosure of the conflicting interest or cannot do so without breaching a confidence, the lawyer must decline the retainer.[38]

Finally, the Ontario rule provides that the lawyer should not uncritically accept the client's decision to have the lawyer act in such circumstances. Lawyers must bear in mind that if they agree to act in such circumstances their first duty will be to the client. If they have any misgivings about being able to place the client's interests first, the rules say, lawyers should refuse to act.[39]

The Ontario rules specify in a separate rule the requirements that must be observed by lawyers in situations in which a client invests by way of borrowing in a corporation or other entity in which the lawyer has an interest (other than a corporation or other entity whose securities are publicly traded).[41]

Lawyers are prohibited from borrowing money from clients except:

(1) where the client is a lending institution, financial institution, insurance company, trust company or similar corporation whose business includes lending money to members of the public; or

(2) where in the case of a loan from a related person as defined by the *Income Tax Act* (Canada) the lawyer is able to discharge the onus of proving that the

---

36 Ontario rule 2.06(2) and accompanying commentary.

37 Ontario rules 1.02 (definition of "independent legal advice") and 2.06(3).

38 Ontario rule 2.06(2) and accompanying commentary.

39 Ontario rule 2.06(2) and accompanying commentary.

41 See Ontario rule 2.06(2).

client's interests were fully protected by the nature of the case and by independent legal advice.[42]

In any transaction other than one falling within the first exception ((1) above) in which money is borrowed from a client by the lawyer's spouse or by a corporation, syndicate or partnership in which either the lawyer or the lawyer's spouse has, or both of them together have, directly or indirectly, a substantial interest, the lawyer must be able to discharge the onus of proving that the client's interests were fully protected by the nature of the case and by independent legal representation.[43]

Finally, the Ontario rule governing borrowing from clients specifies that lawyers will be considered bound by the same fiduciary obligation that attaches to a lawyer in dealings with a client in every case in which the circumstances are such that the lender or investor might reasonably feel entitled to look to the lawyer for guidance and advice in respect of the loan or investment.[44]

The Canadian Bar Association's Code of Professional Conduct, while incorporating by reference *mutatis mutandis* (as noted above) the principle enunciated in relation to conflicts of interest between clients,[45] adopts a somewhat more restrictive approach to lawyer-client conflicts of interest. The Canadian Bar Association rule provides that a lawyer should not enter into a business transaction with a client, or knowingly give to or acquire from the client an ownership, security or other pecuniary interest unless:

(1) the transaction is a fair and reasonable one and its terms are fully disclosed to the client in a manner that is reasonably understood by the client;

(*Continued on page 22–11*)

42 Ontario rule 2.06(4). See also British Columbia rules, chapter 7, rule 4; and chapter 25, *infra*, part 25.4.

43 Ontario rule 2.06(5).

44 Ontario rule 2.06(4) and accompanying commentary.

45 C.B.A. Code, chapter VI, commentary 1.

(2) the client is given a reasonable opportunity to seek independent legal advice about the transaction, the onus being on the lawyer to prove that the client's interests were protected by such independent advice; and

(3) the client consents in writing to the transaction.[46]

The Canadian Bar Association rule also provides that a lawyer must not enter into or continue a business transaction with a client if:

(1) the client expects or might reasonably be assumed to expect that the lawyer is protecting the client's interests; and

(2) there is a significant risk that the interests of the lawyer and the client may differ.[47]

The Canadian Bar Association rule provides that a lawyer must not act for a client where the lawyer's duty to the client and the personal interests of the lawyer or an associate are in conflict.[48] The term "associate" is defined to include the lawyer's spouse and children, any relatives of the lawyer or the lawyer's spouse living under the same roof, any partner or associate of the lawyer in the practice of law, a trust or estate in which the lawyer has a substantial beneficial interest or for which the lawyer acts as a trustee or in a similar capacity, and a corporation of which the lawyer is a director or in which the lawyer or an associate owns or controls, directly or indirectly, a significant number of shares.[49]

The Canadian Bar Association rule provides that a lawyer who has a personal interest in a joint business venture with others may represent or advise the business venture in legal matters between it and third parties, but should not represent or advise either the joint business venture or the joint venturers in respect of legal matters as between them.[50]

The Canadian Bar Association Code also admonishes lawyers that they should avoid entering into a debtor-creditor relationship with clients; that they should not borrow money from clients who are not in the business of lending money; and that lending money to clients, except by way of advancing necessary expenses in legal matters that the lawyer is handling, is undesirable.[51]

Like its Ontario counterpart, the Canadian Bar Association rule provides an expansive definition of the term "client." Persons who are not otherwise clients may be deemed to be clients for the purpose of the rule if they might reasonably feel entitled to look to the lawyer for guidance and advice in respect

46 C.B.A. Code, chapter VI, rule, paragraph (a); see also British Columbia rules, chapter 7.

47 C.B.A. Code, chapter VI, rule, paragraph (b).

48 C.B.A. Code, chapter VI, rule, paragraph (c).

49 C.B.A. Code, chapter VI, commentary 3.

50 C.B.A. Code, chapter VI, commentary 5.

51 C.B.A. Code, chapter VI, commentary 4. See also Quebec rules, section 3.05.12 and British Columbia rules, chapter 6, rules 4 and 6.

of the transaction. The onus is imposed on the lawyer in such circumstances to establish that such persons were not in fact looking to the lawyer for guidance and advice.[52]

The Law Society of Alberta's code of professional conduct provides that "A lawyer must not act when there is a conflict or potential conflict between lawyer and client unless the client consents *and it is in the client's best interests that the lawyer so act*".[52.1] (emphasis added). The proposed code also specifies that "a lawyer must not act personally in a matter when the lawyer's objectivity is impaired to the extent that the lawyer would be unable to properly and competently carry out the representation".[52.2] Finally, the proposed code provides that "a lawyer must not engage in a business transaction with a client of the lawyer who does not have independent legal representation unless the client consents and the transaction is fair and reasonable to the client in all respects".[52.3]

Among the lessons to be learned from the many civil cases in which lawyers have been found liable to clients with whom they have entered into non-professional business transactions is the exacting nature of the lawyer's duty of disclosure. Incomplete disclosure may be taken by the courts to be a lack of candour that demonstrates bad faith on the lawyer's part. Adverse inferences to this effect may be drawn even if the lawyer-client relationship is determined before the transaction is negotiated.

Thus, in a 1987 case,[53] the Ontario Court of Appeal held that a lawyer who entered into a business transaction with former clients had a duty to disclose the fact that he was judgment proof. "As a result of the possession by the lawyer of special confidential information pertaining to clients," the court said, "he should not take advantage of that position of superiority if he enters into such a transaction with them. If he is entering into such a transaction, the lawyer is bound to make full disclosure of his position so that the client is not placed at a disadvantage. The ethics of the profession and fairness require that such a disclosure be made." The court added that "this principle must apply in many instances to former clients as well as current clients."[54]

---

52 C.B.A. Code, chapter VI, commentary 6.

52.1 Chapter 6, rule 7.

52.2 Chapter 6, rule 8.

52.3 Chapter 6, rule 9.

53 *Korz v. St. Pierre* (1987), 61 O.R. (2d) 609 (C.A.), leave to appeal to S.C.C. refused (1988), 62 O.R. (2d) ix (note) (S.C.C.).

54 *Ibid.*, p. 618. See also *Nocton v. Ashburton*, [1914] A.C. 932 (H.L.); *Demerara Bauxite Co. v. Hubbard*, [1923] A.C. 673 (P.C.); *McLellan v. Milne*, [1937] O.R. 742 (H.C.); *McMaster v. Byrne*, [1952] 3 D.L.R. 337 (P.C.), reversing [1951] O.W.N. 1, affirmed [1950] 3 D.L.R. 815; *Milligan v. Gemini Mercury Sales Ltd.* (1977), 1 B.L.R. 63 (Ont. H.C.); *Taylor v.*

The Canadian Bar Association rule stipulates that a lawyer must not prepare an instrument giving the lawyer or an associate a substantial gift from a client, whether *inter vivos* on testamentary.[55] When such a gift is contemplated, the rule adds, the prudent course for the lawyer is to insist that the client either be independently represented or have independent legal advice.[56]

The Ontario rule, oddly, contains no equivalent provisions. At common law, however, undue influence is presumed where clients make either *inter vivos* or testamentary gifts to lawyers during the currency of the client-lawyer relationship, and the Supreme Court of Canada ruled in a 1902 case[57] that it is impossible to rebut the presumption unless the donor had competent independent advice. In an English case[58] decided the following year Lord Justice Cozens-Hardy observed, moreover, that "I am inclined to think that the only competent independent advice that should be given to a man who says he has arranged to make a gift to his solicitor is to tell him not to do so."[59]

Thus, Ontario lawyers who have drafted wills in which the lawyer is named as a beneficiary, without at least insisting that the client obtain independent legal advice, have been found guilty of professional misconduct despite the absence of an explicit prohibition against doing so in that jurisdiction's rules of professional conduct.[60]

22.4 CONFLICTS OF INTEREST INVOLVING NON-CLIENTS

As mentioned above, conflict of interest problems have become both more common and more complicated over the years. Canadian rules of professional conduct, however, consider conflict of interest problems based principally upon a traditional model in which two parties to a transaction attempt to engage a lawyer to act for both.

The rules are silent on the subject of conflicts of interest created by reason of duties that may be owed by lawyers to non-clients. The issues are also undeveloped as yet by jurisprudence.

Murphy (1980), 24 B.C.L.R. 198 (S.C.); *Copperview Haven Ltd. v. Waverley Park Estates Ltd.*, [1981] 4 W.W.R. 673 (B.C. S.C.), varied [1984] 4 W.W.R. 673 (C.A.); *Davey v. Woolley, Hames, Dale & Dingwall* (1982), 35 O.R. (2d) 599 (C.A.), leave to appeal to S.C.C. refused (1982), 37 O.R. (2d) 499n (S.C.C.); *Cavallin v. King* (1984), 51 B.C.L.R. 149 (S.C.); and Charles Wolfram, *Modern Legal Ethics* (St. Paul, Minnesota: West, 1986), p. 484.

55 C.B.A. Code, chapter VI, rule, paragraph (d).

56 C.B.A. Code, chapter VI, commentary 2.

57 *Trusts & Guarantee Co. v. Hart* (1902), 32 S.C.R. 553 at 558, *per* Taschereau J.

58 *Wright v. Carter*, [1903] 1 Ch. 27 (C.A.).

59 *Ibid.*, p. 62. See also American Bar Association Model Rules of Professional Conduct, Model Rule 1.8(c); and Wolfram, *supra*, note 54, p. 487.

60 *Re McDonald*, report adopted by Convocation, November 21, 1985; and *Re King*, report adopted by Convocation, January 25, 1991.

Two examples will suffice to illustrate the types of situations in which such problems may arise.

1. A lawyer is retained by the court-appointed committee of the estate of a person who has been found mentally incompetent. The committee mismanages the estate, intermingling the estate's assets with the committee's own assets, and investing in questionable ventures in which the committee has a personal interest. The committee is replaced, and his successor brings an action against the committee's lawyer alleging that though the lawyer may have discharged her duty to her client (the committee), she had a duty of care and a fiduciary duty to the mentally incompetent person, both of which duties she breached.[61]

2. A law firm has for many years acted for a union. In most cases, the firm has taken instructions from the union's president, who tended to dominate the union. A group of dissident members of the union alleges that the union's president has made unlawful use of union dues for his personal benefit and to perpetuate himself in office. The president of the union asks the law firm to advise both the union and him, and to meet with the lawyer for the dissidents to attempt to negotiate a settlement of the dispute.[62]

Duties of care owed to non-clients have repeatedly been recognized over the last few decades.[63] Conflicts of interest may be said to arise in cases involving corporate clients and their officers and employees, and executors and beneficiaries, among many other relationships.

Canadian courts and law societies have scarcely begun the task of sorting out the conflict of interest problems that may arise as a result of the recognition of lawyers' duties to non-clients. All we can do at present is anticipate some of the issues that are likely to be raised.

The main issues are likely to turn on the nature of the duty owed to non-clients such as the mentally incompetent person in the first example above. If that duty is equated with the duty owed to clients, a potential conflict of interest will always exist. Lawyers would be required to divulge confidential information disclosed by clients to non-clients, who would be able to waive privilege and disclose the confidential information to third parties.[64]

---

61 See *Fickett v. Superior Court*, 558 P. 2d 988 (Ariz. Ct. of Appeals, 1976), in which a lawyer was found liable to the mentally incompetent person on similar facts. See also Geoffrey C. Hazard, Jr., "Triangular Lawyer Relationships: An Exploratory Analysis"(1987-88) 1 Georgetown Journal of Legal Ethics 15 at 17-18.

62 In *Yablonski v. United Mine Workers*, 448 F. 2d 1175 (D.C. Cir., 1971), the court granted a motion to disqualify a law firm from representing the union and its president in a derivative action brought on similar facts. See also Hazard, *ibid.*, pp. 19-20.

63 See, for example, *Hedley Byrne & Co. v. Heller & Partners*, [1963] 2 All E.R. 575 (H.L.); *Anns v. Merton, London Borough Council*, [1977] 2 All E.R. 492 (H.L.); *Tracy v. Atkins* (1979), 16 B.C.L.R. 223 (C.A.).

64 See Hazard, *supra*, note 61, pp. 26-28.

The duty must be defined, therefore, differently from the duty owed by a lawyer to a client. But how differently? And how will the difference affect the lawyer in analyzing and attempting to resolve conflict of interest problems?

All of the issues remain unresolved. They should be addressed in future revisions of rules of professional conduct so that courts and law societies are not compelled to resolve them in a vacuum when they arise.

22.5 ERRORS AND OMISSIONS CLAIMS

The Ontario rules of professional conduct deal explicitly with the conflict of interest that arises when lawyers learn of errors or omissions that may expose them to liability for professional negligence. The conflict of interest arises as a result of the differing interests of the client, the lawyer, and the insurer in such circumstances.

The Ontario rule[65] recognizes that the introduction of compulsory insurance imposes additional obligations upon a lawyer, but that those obligations must not impair the relationship and duties of the lawyer to the client.

The rule makes note of the lawyer's duty to preserve the insurer's rights. There may well be occasions when a lawyer believes that certain actions or failure to take action have exposed the lawyer to liability for damages when in fact no liability exists, the rule says. In every case, moreover, a careful assessment will have to be made of the damages sustained as a result of any negligence of the lawyer. Many factors must be taken into account in assessing the client's claim and damages.

The rule requires lawyers to take the following steps as soon as they become aware that an error or omission may have occurred that may involve liability to a client for professional negligence:

(1) The lawyer should immediately arrange an interview with the client and inform the client forthwith that an error or omission may have occurred that may form the basis of a claim by the client against the lawyer.

(2) The lawyer should advise the client to obtain an opinion from another independent lawyer and that in the circumstances the first lawyer might no longer be able to act for the client.

(3) Concurrently, the first lawyer should notify the insurer of the relevant facts.

(4) The lawyer must bear in mind that in order to fulfil all duties to the client, the insurer and the profession, the lawyer must co-operate to the fullest extent and as expeditiously as possible with the Society's adjusters in the investigation and eventual settlement of the claim.

(5) Upon settlement of the client's claim, the lawyer must make arrangements to pay that portion of the client's claim that is not covered by insurance, forthwith upon completion of the settlement.

---

65 Ontario rule 6.09 and accompanying commentary.

PART IV

THE REGULATION OF THE PROFESSION

23

Admission to the Bar

Our characters are the result of our conduct.[1]

23.1 INTRODUCTION

Legislation governing admission to the bar of Canadian jurisdictions generally provides that applicants are entitled to be admitted upon the successful completion of specified educational requirements, provided that the applicants are "of good character."[2] An additional requirement is imposed in Quebec, where applicants who are actively engaged in certain occupations — including police officers, bailiffs, court reporters, and employees of collection agencies — are prohibited from practising law.[3] The Supreme Court of Canada struck down a citizenship requirement in a 1989 decision.[4]

The educational requirement specified in each jurisdiction is the successful completion of the governing body's bar admission course.[5] Bar admission courses consist of a combination of formal instruction and examinations together with a period of one year's service of articled clerkship to a member of the bar in good standing. The completion of a three-year bachelor of laws degree at an accredited law school is in turn a requirement for admission to the bar admission course.

From time to time questions have been raised about such issues as whether the fact that one's membership in the bar is in good standing should be an adequate qualification for service as an articling principal. In Ontario, lawyers who wish to serve as articling principals are required to apply for the Law Society's approval,

---

1 Aristotle, *Nicomachean Ethics*, c. 335 B.C., quoted in David Shrager and Elizabeth Frost (eds.), *The Quotable Lawyer* (New York: Facts on File Publications, 1986), p. 39.

2 See *Law Society Act*, R.S.O. 1990, c. L.8, s. 27(2).

3 In *Patry c. Barreau (Québec)*, [1991] R.J.Q. 2366 (C.S.), the court upheld the constitutionality of the prohibition against persons who are actively engaged in police work becoming practising members of the bar at the same time.

4 *Andrews v. Law Society (British Columbia)*, [1989] 1 S.C.R. 143. See also *Black v. Law Society (Alberta)*, [1989] S.C.R. 591; *Casey* v. *Law Society (Newfoundland)* (1986), 58 Nfld. & P.E.I.R. 349 (Nfld. T.D.); and *Channan v. Professional Examination Board in Law* (1980), 12 Alta. L.R. (2d) 301 (Q.B.).

5 See reg. 708, R.R.O. 1990 under the *Law Society Act*, R.S.O. 1990, c. L.8, s. 2.

and that approval will be forthcoming only if the Society is satisfied of their suitability.

The most problematic issues have been raised by the requirement that applicants must be of good character. British Columbia's rules of professional conduct provide that it is the duty of every lawyer to guard the Bar against the admission to the profession of any candidate whose moral character or education renders that person unfit for admission.[6] The balance of this chapter is devoted to a consideration of the purpose, history, and application of the good character requirement, and to a consideration of whether other means of screening applicants might better accomplish the objectives of protecting the public, promoting the rehabilitation of offenders, and dealing with applicants and potential applicants in an equitable, fair, and non-discriminatory way.

23.2 PURPOSES OF THE GOOD CHARACTER REQUIREMENT

The purposes of the good character requirement are the same as the purposes of professional discipline: to protect the public, to maintain high ethical standards, to maintain public confidence in the legal profession and its ability to regulate itself, and to deal fairly with persons whose livelihood and reputation are affected.[7]

These purposes are commendable and there can be no doubt about the relevance of the good character requirement to the practice of law. The law is concerned with questions of right and wrong, and fairness and unfairness. At least one commentator has argued that as our society has become more secularized, the law has replaced religion as our primary moral touchstone.[8]

The requirement that lawyers must be of good character finds expression also in what is in most jurisdictions not coincidentally the first rule of professional conduct: lawyers must discharge with integrity all duties owed to clients, the court, the public, and other members of the profession.[9] "Integrity," the first commentary to this rule says, "is the fundamental quality of any person who seeks to practise as a member of the legal profession."[10]

---

6 British Columbia rules, chapter 1, rule 5(2).

7 The purposes of professional discipline are discussed in chapter 26, part 26.1, *infra*. See notes 1 through 3 to chapter 26 for sources. In Ontario, the Divisional Court accepted that these were also the purposes of the good character requirement in *Rajnauth v. Law Society (Upper Canada)* (1993), 13 O.R. (3d) 381 (Div. Ct.) (Montgomery, Carruthers and White JJ.).

8 Stephen M. Grant, "Sex, Lies and Legal Ethics", Law Society of Upper Canada Gazette, vol. 24, no. 2 (June, 1990), p. 103 at 108-109.

9 C.B.A. Code, chapter I, rule; Ontario rules 1.03(1) and 6.01(1) and accompanying commentary.

10 C.B.A. Code, chapter I, commentary 1; Ontario rule 6.01(1) and accompanying commentary. The rule is quoted

Lawyers who by their conduct have proven to be lacking in integrity are likely to lose their right to practise. In a 1980 case,[11] an Ontario lawyer was disbarred on the basis of a criminal conviction in the United States for an offence against the *Mann Act*, which prohibited transporting female persons across state lines for immoral purposes. Although he was not acting in his capacity as a lawyer at the time, the Divisional Court upheld the disbarment order of Convocation. Justice Craig, for a unanimous court, wrote that the appellant's conduct was not only reprehensible, but that it shattered his professional integrity to the point where the protection of the public was involved.[12]

The requirement that applicants be of good character is preventative, not punitive. It recognizes that character is the well-spring of professional conduct in lawyers. By requiring lawyers to be of good character, law societies protect the public and the reputation of the profession from potential lawyers who lack the fundamental quality of any person who seeks to practise as a member of the legal profession, namely, integrity.

This message is a frequent theme of distinguished speakers at call to the bar ceremonies. At call to the bar ceremonies in Ontario in 1981, the Honourable Sydney L. Robins of the Ontario Court of Appeal assimilated integrity and character, and quoted the following observations of Justice Benjamin Cardozo on the prosaic ways in which lawyers' characters are tested:

> The tests of character come to us silently, unaware, by slow and inaudible approaches. We hardly know that they are there, till lo! the hour has struck and the choice has been made, well or ill, but whether well or ill, a choice. The heroic hours of life do not announce their presence by drum and trumpet, challenging us to be true to ourselves by appeals to the martial spirit that keeps the blood at heat. Some unassuming, unobtrusive choice presents itself before us slyly and craftily, glib and insinuating, in the modest garb of innocence. To yield to its blandishments is so easy. The wrong, it seems, is venial. Our hyper-sensitiveness, we assure ourselves, would call it a wrong at all. These are the moments when you will need to remember the game you are playing. Then it is that you will be summoned to show the courage of adventurous youth.[13]

Two years later the Right Honourable Robert E. Megarry, also at Ontario call to the bar ceremonies, identified unbreakable confidentiality, honesty, reliability, and unimpeachable integrity as four qualities that lawyers must display. (The importance of confidentiality is discussed in chapter 3). Of honesty, Justice Megarry said that "with very few exceptions I would

---

in the context of an appeal from an order of Convocation denying admission on character grounds in *Rajnauth v. Law Society (Upper Canada)*, *supra*, note 7.

11 *Cwinn v. Law Society (Upper Canada)* (1980), 28 O.R. (2d) 61 (Div. Ct.), leave to appeal denied and appeal quashed (1980), 28 O.R. (2d) 61n (S.C.C.).

12 *Ibid.*, p. 69.

13 Sydney L. Robins, "An Address to New Lawyers", Law Society of Upper Canada Gazette, vol. 15, part 4 (December, 1981), p. 349 at 353.

accept the word of a practising barrister as readily as that of a bishop." Of reliability he said that "no longer will you easily give promises which you are not confident of being able to fulfil." Of integrity he said that the standard expected of lawyers is more comprehensive than one may expect:

> Obviously, you would never "sell out" a client in any way, and obviously you would never let him down in order to obtain some personal benefit. But the law demands more than this. You will often have to ask yourself whether you are satisfied with what you have done. Have you really done everything that is humanly possible to solve your client's problem? Did you abandon research on his behalf a little too quickly? Did you rely on your client never discovering that you had not spent enough time in preparing his case? Clients, of course, come and go; but your conscience does not, and you will have to live with it the rest of your life.[14]

The purpose of the good character requirement, considered in isolation, is commendable. We must examine the requirement's history and application to determine whether its purpose has been realized and, if so, at what cost.

23.3 HISTORY AND APPLICATION OF THE GOOD CHARACTER REQUIREMENT

The requirement that applicants for admission to the bar must be of good character reaches back to the Roman Theodesian Code, and its Anglo-American roots extend back at least 700 years, to thirteenth century England.[15]

In the nineteenth century United States, the good character requirement was invoked to exclude women from the profession. In an 1872 decision of the United States Supreme Court,[16] Justice Bradley, concurring, wrote that "the natural and proper timidity and delicacy which belongs to the female sex" disabled it from the practice of law.[17] In an 1875 decision,[18] the Supreme Court of Wisconsin wrote that the "peculiar qualities of womanhood, its gentle graces, its quick sensibility, its tender susceptibility, its purity, its delicacy, its emotional impulses, its subordination of hard reason to sympathetic feeling, are surely not qualifications for forensic strife."[19]

During the 1920's and 1930's, again in the United States, efforts were made in some jurisdictions to tighten up the enforcement of good character requirements. It is generally accepted today that at least some of these efforts

14 Robert E. Megarry, "Convocation Address", Law Society of Upper Canada Gazette, vol. 17, no. 1 (March, 1983), p. 41 at 43- 44.

15 See Deborah L. Rhode, "Moral Character as a Professional Credential", 44 Yale L.J. 491 at 493 (January, 1985).

16 *Bradwell v. Illinois*, 83 U.S. (16. Wall) 130 (1872).

17 *Ibid.*, p. 141.

18 *Re Goodell*, 39 Wis. 232 (1875).

19 *Ibid.*, p. 245.

were tainted by racial, ethnic, and class biases. In 1928, Pennsylvania implemented a registration and perceptorship system in which candidates were required to undergo character investigations both at the beginning of law school and when they applied for admission to the bar. The earlier investigation consisted of an interview that afforded the profession an opportunity to dissuade the "unworthy" from pursuing careers as lawyers. The definition of "unworthy" was flexible. Those rejected in 1929 included individuals who were regarded as "dull", "colourless", "unprepossessing", "keen", "shrewd", "arrogant", or "conceited", those who were without "well-defined ideas on religion", and those who were "not seeking admission for the best motives." Applicants who saw "no wrong" in advertising were denied admission. So too initially was an applicant who sought "fame as a woman attorney" and public official, although this rejection was later reversed. Other applicants were tainted by association, in that their family members had "poor business reputations" or "unsavoury backgrounds", or in that their sponsors were "unreliable." In all, seven percent of all candidates withdrew or were rejected. It is safe to assume others decided not to apply for fear of rejection. The proportion of Jewish lawyers dropped 16 percent, and virtually no blacks gained entry.[20]

The United States Supreme Court recognized the danger of abuse inherent in the good character requirement in a 1957 decision.[21] After observing that the term "good moral character" is "unusually ambiguous" Justice Black added that the term:

> . . . can be defined in an almost unlimited number of ways, for any definition will necessarily reflect the attitudes, experiences, and prejudices of the definer. Such a vague qualification, which is easily adapted to fit personal views and predilections, can be a dangerous instrument for arbitrary and discriminatory denial of the right to practise law.[22]

The court ruled that evidence that the applicant had attended meetings of the Communist Party at a time, many years earlier, when the party was lawful in the state in which the applicant resided, did not afford evidence that the applicant was not of good character.[23] The court reached the same conclusion in

20 See Walter C. Douglas, Jr., "The Pennsylvania System Governing Admission to the Bar" (1929) 54 Rep. A.B.A. 701 at 703-705; Jerald S. Auerbach, *Unequal Justice* (New York: Oxford University Press, 1976), pp. 127-128; and Rhode, *supra*, note 15, p. 501.

21 *Konigsberg v. State Bar of California*, 353 U.S. 252 (1957).

22 *Ibid.*, pp. 262-263.

23 The court did not consider whether the applicant's refusal to answer questions concerning his past or present membership in the Communist Party was a proper ground for refusing the applicant the right to practise law. When, at a second hearing, the same applicant refused to answer such questions, the United States Supreme Court decided by a 5-4 majority that admission was properly denied on the ground that the applicant's refusal to answer questions prevented a full investigation of his qualifications: *Konigsberg v. State Bar of California*, 366 U.S. 36 (1961).

another decision that was released the same day.[24]

In British Columbia, however, the Court of Appeal had come to the opposite conclusion several years earlier in a case[25] involving an applicant who was at the time of the application a member of the Labour-Progressive Party, which was a lawful organization. The applicant was a Canadian citizen who had successfully completed the academic requirements to be admitted to the bar. Justice O'Halloran wrote that "a Marxist Communist cannot be a loyal Canadian citizen; at best his loyalty must be divided between Canada and the Communist leadership outside Canada which is engaged ideologically through him (whether he knows it or not) and others of like indoctrination in promoting disruptively in Canada and other countries what Lenin called the 'class struggle of the proletariat' for the world revolution."[26]

Apart altogether from concerns about possible arbitrary and discriminatory denial of the right to practise law, the good character requirement raises serious concerns about unpredictability, inconsistency, and vagueness. Although the United States Supreme Court has held that any standard of qualification must be rationally connected with the applicant's fitness or capacity to practise law,[27] definitions of "good character" that have been adopted by admission committees provide little guidance to either prospective applicants or law societies. In Ontario, Convocation has adopted the following definition:

> Character is that combination of qualities or features distinguishing one person from another. Good character connotes moral or ethical strength, distinguishable as an amalgam of virtuous attributes or traits which would include, among others, integrity, candour, empathy and honesty.[28]

A review of governing bodies' dispositions of applications is even less helpful. In a Michigan case, a local committee considered an applicant's vio-

24 *Schware v. Board of Bar Examiners*, 353 U.S. 232 (1957).

25 *Martin v. Law Society (British Columbia)*, [1950] 3 D.L.R. 173 (B.C. C.A.), affirming [1949] 1 D.L.R. 105 (*sub nom. Re Martin*).

26 *Ibid.*, p. 190. See also *Re Summers*, 325 U.S. 561 (1945), in which the United States Supreme Court affirmed a decision denying admission to the Illinois bar to a conscientious objector on the ground that he was unable in good faith to take the required oath to support the constitution of the state; and *Re Pontarelli*, 393 Ill. 310 (1946), in which a conscientious objector was disbarred upon his conviction for violating the *Selective Service Act* by failing to report for induction into the armed forces.

27 *Schware v. Board of Bar Examiners*, 353 U.S. 232 (1957).

28 *Re Rizzotto*, reasons of Convocation, September 14, 1992. In *Rizzotto*, Convocation accepted this definition, which was adopted previously by an admission committee in Ontario in *Re Spicer*, in a report dated October 3, 1991. In *Spicer*, the committee modified a definition adopted by Convocation in a third Ontario case, *Re P.*, report dated September 8, 1989. In the definition adopted in *Re P.*, the adjective "socially acceptable", as well as the adjective "virtuous" modified the nouns "attributes" and "traits." The committee in the *Spicer* case was persuaded that many excellent lawyers have not exhibited "socially acceptable" qualities.

lation of a fishing licence statute ten years earlier to be sufficient cause to deny the application. The state board rejected the local committee's recommendation.[29] In a 1991 case, the Law Society of England admitted to student membership an applicant who 14 years earlier had been convicted of murder.[30] In some cases the applicant's addiction to alcohol or drugs has been considered a mitigating circumstance sufficient to justify admission.[31] In other cases the applicant's addiction to alcohol or drugs has been considered an aggravating or even independent circumstance sufficient to justify the dismissal of the application.[32]

Examples abound of applicants who have been admitted to the bar in spite of criminal records for offences involving dishonesty and other serious offences. In a 1978 Maryland case,[33] an application was granted in spite of the applicant's admission that he had been guilty of theft on two prior occasions, one of which occurred after he graduated from law school, five years prior to the hearing,

In a 1981 Florida case,[34] an application was granted in spite of the applicant's admission that he had participated in the sale of cocaine in amounts ranging from one to eight ounces on approximately 15 occasions while he was an undergraduate. The applicant had pleaded guilty to one charge of unlawfully selling cocaine, and later had pleaded *nolo contendere* to a second charge. He had been sentenced to four years in jail for the first offence and three years, concurrent, for the second.

In a 1982 Maryland case,[35] an application was granted in spite of the applicant's conviction for armed robbery, an offence for which he was sentenced to ten years in prison. The applicant had served six and one-half years in a federal penitentiary before he was released on parole. While incarcerated, the applicant had been classified as a "management problem" and was repeatedly transferred from one penitentiary to another. He had spent time in solitary confinement and, because of his conduct, was denied parole on more than five occasions.

After he was released from custody the applicant successfully completed university and law school, and applied for admission to the bar. On the state bar's character questionnaire the applicants were asked to list every place

29 See Deborah L. Rhode, "Moral Character as a Professional Credential", 44 Yale L.J. 491 at 538 (January, 1985).

30 See Evlynn Gilvarry, "Society Enrols Rehabilitated Murderer as Student", the Law Society's Gazette, no. 19 (May 22, 1991), p. 4.

31 See, for example, *Re Application of A.T.*, 408 A. 2d 1023 (1979). See also Rhode, *supra*, note 29, p. 538.

32 See, for example, *Re Monaghan*, 167 A. 2d 81 (1961); and *Re Willis*, 215 S.E. 2d 771, appeal dismissed *sub nom. Willis v. North Carolina State Board of Law Examiners*, 430 U.S. 976 (1975). See also Rhode, *supra*, note 29, p. 538.

33 *Re Application of Allan S. for Admission to the Bar of Maryland*, 387 A. 2d 271 (1978).

34 *Re Petition of Diez-Arguelles*, 401 So. 2d 1347 (1981).

35 *Re Application of G.L.S. for Admission to the Bar of Maryland*, 439 A. 2d 1107 (1982).

where they had lived during the past ten years. The applicant neglected to list any residence for the years during which he was incarcerated. Applicants were also asked to provide a complete record of all criminal proceedings to which he had been a party. The applicant wrote "11/67" and "U.S. District Court for the District of Maryland" under the headings "date" and "court" respectively, but provided no information under the headings "nature of proceedings" and "disposition." A four to three majority of the Court of Appeals of Maryland concluded that the rehabilitation that the applicant demonstrated adequately offset the evidence of imperfect character, and ordered that he be admitted to the bar.

By way of contrast, in a 1988 decision[36] the Quebec Court of Appeal held that legislation authorizing the governing body of the bar to inquire into the morals, knowledge, and qualities of candidates empowered it to delay an applicant's entry into the profession while it considered concerns that had been expressed about an applicant's mental health.

Even within the same jurisdiction it is impossible to reconcile law societies' decisions to grant or deny grounds of character applications for admission. In 1978 a bencher of the Law Society of British Columbia reviewed the 19 cases in which that Society's credentials committee had ordered full inquiries between 1971 and 1977. She reported that two of the 19 applications had been rejected, while 17 were granted. (Three of the 17 applicants were denied admission initially, but were later admitted.) One of the applicants who was admitted had been convicted five years before his application, when he was 28 years old, of four counts of obtaining money by false pretences.[37] Neither of the applicants who were denied admission had been convicted of any offence. One, while articling, had failed to commence proceedings that he was supposed to commence, and had falsely told his principal that the Registry had lost the document that he should have prepared. The other unsuccessful applicant had had a drinking problem. He had already been admitted to the bar of another province. The admission committee found that the applicant was "a decent, fairly honest person", but "weak and ineffectual", and, therefore, not "fit" to become a lawyer in the province.[38]

In Ontario, no applicants were denied admission to the bar as a result of hearings at which their good character was considered until 1989. Applicants who were admitted prior to 1989 included one who had been convicted of theft only two years prior to his admission; one who had on three separate occasions over a five-year period been convicted of possession of stolen prop-

---

36 *Lewin c. Barreau (Quebec)*, [1988] R.J.Q. 619 (Que. C.A.). See also *Hutton v. Law Society (Newfoundland)* (1992), 96 D.L.R. (4th) 670 (Nfld. T.D.).

37 Mary F. Southin, "What is 'Good Character' ", The Advocate, vol. 35 (1977), p. 129 at pp. 129, 130 and 134-135.

38 *Ibid.*, pp. 131-132.

erty twice and breaking and entering with intent to commit an indictable offence once, and who was sentenced to one year's imprisonment for his third conviction; one who had been found guilty of criminal offences including possession of LSD for the purpose of trafficking, theft, and fraud, on at least six separate occasions over a ten-year period; and several others who had been convicted of such criminal offences as theft and possession of hashish for the purpose of trafficking. In 1991 an applicant was admitted despite a lengthy criminal record that culminated in a plea of guilty to wounding, and the consequent withdrawal by the Crown of a charge of attempted murder, a charge that resulted from a shooting in a bar. (The benchers accepted evidence that the applicant had overcome a serious drinking problem that was an important factor in his criminal record).[39]

The first Ontario case in which an application for admission was denied on grounds of character was the first case that received any publicity. It involved an applicant who, shortly before he began attending law school, was arrested for sexually assaulting his daughter over a period of several years. On the day of his arrest the applicant voluntarily disclosed that he had also been involved in an unlawful sexual relationship with a second young girl. He pleaded guilty to charges of sexually assaulting his daughter and having sexual intercourse with a female person who was between the ages of 14 and 16 years.

The applicant was sentenced to eight months in prison together with three years' probation by the Chief Justice of the High Court of Justice, who was favourably impressed by the applicant's prospects for rehabilitation, which were evidenced by his lack of a prior criminal record, his good work record, his excellent academic background, his timely admission of guilt and voluntary disclosure of offences that were not known to the police, his obtaining of psychiatric assistance, and his plea of guilty, which spared the victims the trauma of being required to testify.

In imposing sentence the Chief Justice said that though a lengthier sentence would otherwise be warranted, such a sentence would destroy the applicant's opportunities of getting into law school. "I am not prepared", the Chief Justice said, "to deprive you of what may be your last opportunity to make something of yourself."

The applicant was released on probation after he served approximately three months in a reformatory between his first and second years in law school. He successfully completed his bachelor of laws degree, as well as the articling and teaching portions of the bar admission course. Contemporaneously, he complied with the terms of both his parole and probation, and continued psychiatric treatment until his treating psychiatrist considered it unnecessary for him to receive further treatment.

A hearing before a quorum of the admission committee was convened shortly after the applicant completed the bar admission course. The appli-

39 *Re C.*, report of admission committee, December 19, 1991.

cant's request for admission was supported among other evidence by letters from partners in the law firm for whom the applicant articled. One partner in the firm described the applicant as an exceptional articling student who "will no doubt be a superb lawyer and a credit to our profession." She added that the applicant was possessed of "superior intellectual skills, and was dedicated, hard working, sympathetic, insightful, and wise." She also added that the applicant showed a firm grasp of the ethics of the profession. He had disclosed his criminal record to the firm before accepting the firm's offer of employment. "I am of the opinion", she concluded, "that it would be a tragedy for him and the legal profession if such a talented person were to be shut out."

Another partner in the firm, who served as the applicant's articling principal, informed the committee that the applicant "was by far the most incisive and intelligent student that I have ever had the opportunity to work with in the ten years that I have been a member of the Bar of Ontario." He added that both during the period of his articles and during the six-month period thereafter, during which the applicant worked for the firm about 25 hours a week while he was enrolled in the teaching portion of the bar admission course, the applicant's ethical standards were never called into question.

The application was vigorously opposed by counsel retained by the Law Society, and the hearing was widely covered in the media. The Women's Legal Education and Action Fund (LEAF) was granted standing at the hearing, and joined with the Law Society's counsel in opposition to the application. Counsel for the Law Society and LEAF called several prominent psychiatrists and psychologists who had not examined the applicant, but who testified, based in part upon the applicant's demeanour in giving evidence, that they did not accept his treating psychiatrist's opinion that the likelihood of the applicant re-offending was remote.

The committee unanimously dismissed the application. The committee concluded that it was not persuaded that that applicant had been "cured" of his sexual deviation and rejected parts of his evidence. The committee defined good character by reference to moral strength, and to "virtuous or socially acceptable attributes or traits" among other things. Convocation accepted the report of the committee.[40]

A quorum of the admissions committee of the Law Society of Upper Canada held a hearing involving another applicant two years later. The applicant, before he attended law school, had served for several years as the secretary-manager of a municipality in the Northwest Territories. While serving in that capacity he attempted to alter the results of a municipal election. He did so by opening the safe (to which he had access as a result of his employment)

40 *Re P.*, report dated September 8, 1989. As noted above, the definition of "good character" that the committee adopted was modified in later Ontario decisions: see note 27, *supra*. The author acted as counsel for the applicant.

in which election documents were kept, making more than 200 photocopies of ballots, checking off the name of the mayoralty candidate of his choice on each of the photocopies that he had made, forging the initials of scrutineers and replacing genuine ballots in filled ballots boxes (to which he also had access as a result of his employment) with forged ballots. The scheme was implemented over a period of about ten hours, and was discovered when a scrutineer noticed that the initials on the back of certain ballots for his poll were not made by him. A new election had to be held as a result of the applicant's conduct.

The applicant was charged with nine counts of unlawfully forging documents in an election. Although he had previously protested his innocence, he pleaded guilty on the day set for his trial to one count of unlawfully damaging election documents contrary to subsection 335(1) of the *Criminal Code*. He was sentenced to one year in prison and fined $15,000. The applicant was 35 years old at the time he committed the offence.

A few months after he was released from prison on parole the applicant applied to law school. The application form in use at the time did not require disclosure of his criminal record, and he did not disclose it. In a personal profile that he filed in conjunction with his application the applicant wrote that between May, 1986, and September, 1987, after he ceased to be employed by the municipality, he worked in the same community as a private consultant in the fields of governmental affairs, human resources, and land use planning. In fact he was in jail several thousand miles away for much of this period.

The applicant successfully completed law school. He testified at a hearing before a quorum of the admission committee, and his counsel called character evidence on his behalf, including the evidence of the dean and the chair of admissions at the law school. The committee made unfavourable findings concerning the applicant's credibility and found that he was not of good character.[41] Convocation rejected the committee's report, however, and ordered a new hearing.

At the second hearing a differently constituted panel of the admissions committee again found that the applicant was not of good character. Again, the panel made unfavourable findings of credibility, and found that the applicant was at times evasive and combative, and did not leave the impression that he was being truthful. The panel also found that in his application to law school, the applicant had clearly attempted to mislead the reader into thinking that for a fixed period of time he had been gainfully employed in a particular community on a full-time basis, when in fact for a large part of that time he was in prison elsewhere.[42]

Again, however, Convocation declined to accept the unanimous report of the admissions committee. In written reasons in which it found that the

41 *Re Rizzotto (No. 1)*, report of admissions committee, June 14, 1991.

42 *Re Rizzotto (No. 2)*, report of admissions committee, February 3, 1992.

applicant was of good character despite the finding of the committee to the contrary, Convocation found that the committee erred in principle in undervaluing the views of the applicant's character witnesses and in holding that the applicant in effect had a duty to disclose his criminal conviction.[43]

These cases are the two leading authorities on the issue in the province of Ontario. One of them may have been correctly decided; it is difficult to accept that both were. In both cases applicants committed serious offences not long before they started law school. Both applicants were adults at the time the offences were committed; their offences could not in either case be excused as youthful indiscretions. Most people would probably consider the abhorrent and repeated sexual assaults of the first applicant to be more serious than the attempts of the second applicant to tamper with the democratic process, though the latter's sentence in the criminal courts was appreciably more severe. The second applicant's breaches of public trust were at least as relevant to the practice of law, however, as were those of the first applicant. Although most professional misconduct for which lawyers are disciplined involves white collar offences, most applicants for admission to the bar have not yet occupied positions of trust that they may be tempted to abuse.[44] The second applicant occupied such a position and yielded to that temptation.

Both applicants had favourably impressed those with whom they had had professional contact. One would expect, however, that the extraordinarily favourable reports of the partners in the firm for which the first applicant articled would have carried at least as much weight as the views of the dean and chair of admissions who knew the second applicant as a law student. The partners in the firm who supported the first applicant's candidacy worked with him intensively in a law practice for a period of 18 months.

The admission committees who heard each of the applicants testify found the evidence of each to be inadequate to convince them of the applicants' rehabilitation. Unlike that of the second applicant, however, the post-conviction conduct of the first, unsuccessful, applicant was free of any suggestion that he had attempted to mislead others concerning his personal history.

The vagueness of the good character requirement allows benchers, who determine admission application almost without objective criteria, to choose

---

43 *Re Rizzotto*, reasons of Convocation, September 14, 1992. In a third Ontario case, *Re Preyra* (April 20, 2000), a panel of benchers held that an applicant for admission who had falsified his law school marks and other academic credentials to prospective employers while seeking articles, had failed to discharge the onus of proving on a balance of probabilities that he was at the time of hearing a person of good character. The panel emphasized that the applicant had failed to be honest about his misrepresentations with people who were close to him, including his articling principal, even after his misrepresentations were discovered.

44 Deborah L. Rhode, "Moral Character as a Professional Credential", 94 Yale L.J. 491 at 516 (January, 1985).

which among aspiring lawyers who have fulfilled onerous educational requirements should be entitled to be members of the profession. The standards, values, and predispositions of the benchers vary widely. Cases are likely to be decided on the basis of wildly divergent views of human nature and individuals' capacity of reform. Many of the cases reviewed above demonstrate a sanguine view of offenders' potential for rehabilitation. A bencher in British Columbia (who later became a judge), on the other hand, has written that "I have never seen any evidence that the character of grown men and women improved with age."[45] In response to an argument that it would be harsh to refuse an applicant on the basis of, say, a student's single conviction for shoplifting, she added "I think it sad that anyone would compromise his academic career and his future career at the bar for such a trivial thing as a book or a pen. But that is the problem of the applicant, not of you, me, or the public at large."[46]

Time will tell whether an argument can successfully be marshalled that the good character requirement is unconstitutionally vague.[47] In the meantime, the mischief of the requirement's unpredictability consists less in its effect on applicants who are denied admission after a hearing than in its effect on potential lawyers who may be deterred from pursing a career in the law because of uncertainty over their prospects of admission. Even in the United States only about 50 applicants a year — .2 percent of all applicants — are denied admission.[48] There are no data on the deterrent effect of the good character requirement. It is clear, nonetheless, that subjectivity and inconsistency in the application of the requirement make predictions almost impossible. It is fair to surmise that risk-averse students and others are dissuaded from attending law school for fear of exclusion, though the likelihood of rejection is in fact slight. Others may well overestimate the likelihood of their persuading an admissions committee of their rehabilitation.[49]

Predictions are almost as impossible for law societies, who can be — and are — of little assistance to inquiring potential applicants. Both of the Ontario applicants whose cases are discussed in some detail above wrote to the Law Society before or shortly after they began law school to inquire about their prospects for admission in light of their criminal records. Both were told that

45 Southin, *supra*, note 37, p. 135.

46 *Ibid.*, p. 136.

47 See *R.* v. *Pharmaceutical Society (Nova Scotia)*, [1992] 2 S.C.R. 606; and *R. v. Wyssen* (1992), 10 O.R. (3d) 193 at 201-203 (C.A.), *per* Finlayson J.A. (concurring in the result). For a discussion of the applicability of s. 7 of the *Charter of Rights and Freedoms* in professional discipline proceedings see chapter 26, part 26.2. In the United States, the requirement has survived constitutional challenges based on vagueness on the dubious ground that long term usage has given "well-defined contours" to the term: *Law Students Civil Rights Research Council v. Wadmond*, 401 U.S. 154 at 159 (1971). See also *Konigsberg* v. *State Bar of California*, 353 U.S. 252 (1977).

48 Rhode, *supra*, note 44, p. 516.

49 Rhode, *supra*, note 44, pp. 517-518.

their records "may, *prima facie*, prevent you being called to the Bar"[50] — whatever that means. Both chose to pursue their legal education in the hope that if they were successful and conducted themselves responsibly over the next few years, they could persuade the Law Society of their rehabilitation. As we have seen, one gained admission and one did not. The unsuccessful applicant could have done nothing more than he did to prove his worthiness — no criticism was made of his post-conviction conduct. One could predict the results of the two cases as accurately by rolling dice.

The arbitrariness of the good character requirement is especially troubling in a profession devoted to the preservation of principles and the protection of the rights of the unpopular.[51] Nor is it clear that the unstated premise underlying the good character requirement — that law societies are capable of predicting future professional misconduct based on applicant's prior criminal records — is a valid one. Even highly trained psychologists and psychiatrists have poor records in predicting future deviance based on a small number of isolated prior acts, particularly if the prior acts were committed in dissimilar settings. The difficulty in formulating accurate predictions may be attributable largely to the critical importance of situational pressures in influencing conduct. Character screening has not been shown to be an effective way of identifying applicants likely to engage in professional misconduct in the future.[52]

A comparison of the procedural and substantive requirements in admission and disciplinary proceedings is instructive. In admission hearings the burden of proof is on applicants, who are required to show on a balance of probabilities that they are of good character as of the date of the hearing.[53] The meaning of "good character" has not been precisely defined, though it is now clear that it is possible for applicants to prove rehabilitation sufficient to be called to the bar regardless of the seriousness of their past offences.[54]

Although the misconduct of lawyers, who owe duties to clients, courts, and their profession, among others, is quite obviously more probative of the future risk that the same lawyers will re-offend than is the misconduct of persons in different situations who owe no such duties, both procedural and substantive requirements imposed by law societies have been consistently more solicitous of lawyers than of applicants for admission.[55] In discipline

50 See *Re Rizzotto*, reasons of Convocation, September 14, 1992, p. 5.

51 See Rhode, *supra*, note 44, pp. 512, 551-552 and 569-570.

52 Rhode, *supra*, note 44, pp. 509, 554-560.

53 *Re Rizzotto*, reasons of Convocation of the Law Society of Upper Canada, September 14, 1992, at pp. 19-20; *Re Application of Allan S.*, 387 A. 2d 271 (1978); *Re Application of G.L.S. for Admission to the Bar of Maryland*, 439 A. 2d 1107 (1982).

54 See, for example, Evlynne Gilvarry, "Society Enrols Rehabilitated Murderer as Student", Law Society of Upper Canada Gazette, no. 19 (May 22, 1991), p. 4; and *Re Rizzotto*, reasons of Convocation of the Law Society of Upper Canada, September 14, 1992, p. 20.

55 See Deborah L. Rhode, "Moral Character as a Professional Credential", Yale L.J. 491 at 546-547 (January, 1985).

proceedings the burden of proof is on the law society's counsel, who must prove specific allegations of professional misconduct based on cogent evidence of clear and convincing weight. Although the scope of the term "professional misconduct" is not exhaustively defined by legislation, the guidance provided by rules of professional conduct is virtually always sufficient to obviate debate about whether the alleged misconduct is culpable. The term has a more precise meaning than the amorphous "good character" requirement.

The legitimacy of monitoring post-admission conduct relevant to the practice of law cannot be doubted. By way of contrast, it is generally difficult to justify denying to applicants who have been guilty of offences committed at a time when they did not have the duties of lawyers, the opportunity to prove their worthiness. Contraventions of the law by persons duty-bound to uphold it assume an entirely different dimension.[56]

The primary focus of the admission and discipline functions of the governing bodies of self-governing professions should be on conduct directly relevant to the practice of law. Yet the reports are replete with instances in which lawyers who have been guilty of serious misconduct in their capacity as lawyers, and who pose a continuing danger to the public, have been permitted to continue to practise law, while others have been prevented from doing so by reason of conduct that may pose no threat to the public at all. In 1983, in Indiana, a lawyer was suspended from practising for 45 days for habitually neglecting cases, deceiving clients, and withholding clients' funds.[57] In the same year, in the same jurisdiction, a lawyer was disbarred for growing his own marijuana.[58] The state bar at the same time presided over an admission system that concerned itself among other things with "bounced cheques, political commitments, and consensual sexual activity."[59]

Law societies depend primarily on self-reporting to identify applicants who may not meet the good character standard. In some jurisdictions applicants are asked whether they have ever been found guilty of a criminal offence; in others they are asked whether other events in their past may call their character into question; in yet others they are asked more specific questions about their family, civil claims brought by or against them, voluntary and involuntary commitments to institutions, diagnoses of mental illness, and whether they have ever been dismissed from their employment for unsatisfactory work.[60] At least some such questions are objectionably intrusive, and are of doubtful value in determining an applicant's fitness to be called to the bar.

56 *Ibid.*, p. 587.
57 *Re Holloway*, 452 N.E. 2d 934 (1983).
58 *Re Moore*, 453 N.E. 2d 971 (1983).
59 Rhode, *supra*, note 55, p. 591.
60 Rhode, *supra*, note 55, pp. 573-576 and 581.

23.4 ALTERNATIVES TO THE GOOD CHARACTER REQUIREMENT

Should law societies simply abandon the requirement that applicants for admission to the bar must be of good character? An affirmative answer is tempting. It is unlikely that the composition of the bar would be altered significantly if the good character requirement were eliminated. Few applicants are excluded on character grounds now, though it is impossible to tell how many are deterred from even undertaking a legal education for fear of being excluded after years of study at considerable expense. The considerable resources now allocated to conjectural predictions of professional misconduct could be reallocated to the detection, deterrence, and redressing of actual professional misconduct.[61] The United States Supreme Court observed in a 1971 case[62] that "wise policy", if not constitutional prescription, might dictate greater reliance on post-admission sanctions rather than preliminary screening as a means of policing the bar.[63]

Nevertheless, as we have seen, the purpose of the good character requirement is commendable. In some cases, moreover, regulatory authorities *are* able to identify with reasonable certainty applicants who will likely pose a threat to the public if they are admitted to the bar. Public confidence in the profession's ability to govern itself may legitimately be called into question if, for instance, a law society were to admit an applicant who had recently been convicted of an offence involving dishonesty that was committed while the applicant was employed in a position of trust comparable to that of a lawyer.

If the screening process were abandoned by law societies altogether, clients would be required to do their own investigating.[64] The vast majority of clients would have no idea how to go about investigating whether a lawyer has a criminal record. Even if law societies made such information accessible to potential clients, it is likely that few clients would make use of the service. Only a small proportion of potential clients inquire now about lawyers' disciplinary records, though such records are public information in most jurisdictions.

A preferable alternative would be to disqualify for a specified period — say five years after the completion of service of whatever sentence is imposed — all applicants who have been convicted of one or more criminal offences involving dishonesty or violence. If applicants were convicted of no further

61 Rhode, *supra*, note 55, p. 590.

62 *Law Students Civil Rights Research Council v. Wadmond*, 401 U.S. 154 (1971).

63 *Ibid.*, p. 167; for an interesting discussion of the possibility of requiring applicants to pass an integrity test as a condition of admission, see Marvin J. Huberman, "*Integrity Testing: Is it Time?*" (1997), 76 C.B.R. 47, in which the author concludes that improved teaching of professional ethics and standards and improved enforcement of professional conduct standards would be preferable alternatives.

64 Rhode, *supra*, note 55, p. 590.

offences during the specified period, they would be entitled to be admitted.[65] By this means the unfairness and uncertainty of the good character requirement would be eliminated, without public confidence in the profession's ability to govern itself being impaired.

65 See Rhode, *supra*, note 55, pp. 586-587.

24

Regulating Lawyer Competence and Quality of Service

24.1 RULES OF PROFESSIONAL CONDUCT

Canadian rules of professional conduct impose on lawyers a duty to be competent to perform any legal services undertaken on behalf of clients,[1] and a duty to serve clients in a conscientious, diligent and efficient manner so as to provide a quality of service at least equal to that which lawyers generally would expect of a competent lawyer in a like situation.[2]

Competence in the context of these duties of course means more than formal qualification to practise law,[3] and involves more than an understanding of legal principles.[4] Clients are entitled to expect that a lawyer who undertakes a particular matter on their behalf is either competent to handle the matter or is able to become competent without undue delay, risk or expense to the client. The rules of professional conduct make it clear that lawyers who proceed on any other basis are not being honest with their clients, and that this raises ethical considerations to be distinguished from the standard of care that a court would apply for purposes of determining negligence.[5]

The rules specify that lawyers must be alert to recognize any lack of competence for a particular task and the disservice that would be done the client if they were to undertake that task. In such circumstances lawyers should either decline to act or obtain the client's instructions to retain, consult or collaborate with a lawyer who is competent in that field.[6] The rules also require lawyers to

---

1 C.B.A. Code, chapter II, rule, paragraph (a); Ontario rule 2.01(2); B.C. Rules, chapter 3, rules 1 and 2.
2 C.B.A. Code, chapter II, rule, paragraph (b); Ontario rules 2.01(1) and (2); B.C. Rules, chapter 3, rule 3.
3 C.B.A. Code, chapter II, commentary 1.
4 C.B.A. Code, chapter II, commentary 4.
5 C.B.A. Code, chapter II, commentary 3; Ontario rule 2.01(1) and accompanying commentary.
6 C.B.A. Code, chapter II, commentary 6; Ontario rule 2.01(1) and accompanying commentary; Quebec rules, section 3.01.01.

maintain competence by keeping abreast of developments in the branches of law in which they practise.[7]

The Law Society of Upper Canada's *Rules of Professional Conduct*, as a result of amendments that came into force in 2000, now contain a detailed definition of the term "competent lawyer", and require lawyers to perform any legal services undertaken on a client's behalf to the standard of a competent lawyer.[8] The definition reads as follows:

> "2.01 (1) In this rule
>
> 'competent lawyer' means a lawyer who has and applies relevant skills, attributes, and values in a manner appropriate to each matter undertaken on behalf of a client including
>
> (a) knowing general legal principles and procedures and the substantive law and procedure for the areas of law in which the lawyer practises,
>
> (b) investigating facts, identifying issues, ascertaining client objectives, considering possible options, and developing and advising the client on appropriate courses of action,
>
> (c) implementing, as each matter requires, the chosen course of action through the application of appropriate skills, including,
>
> (i) legal research,
>
> (ii) analysis,
>
> (iii) application of the law to the relevant facts,
>
> (iv) writing and drafting,
>
> (v) negotiation,
>
> (vi) alternative dispute resolution,
>
> (vii) advocacy, and
>
> (viii) problem-solving ability,
>
> (d) communicating at all stages of a matter in a timely and effective manner that is appropriate to the age and abilities of the client,
>
> (e) performing all functions conscientiously, diligently, and in a timely and cost-effective manner,
>
> (f) applying intellectual capacity, judgment, and deliberation to all functions,
>
> (g) complying in letter and in spirit with the *Rules of Professional Conduct*,
>
> (h) recognizing limitations in one's ability to handle a matter or some aspect of it, and taking steps accordingly to ensure the client is appropriately served,

---

7 C.B.A. Code, chapter II, commentary 4.

8 Ontario rules 2.01(1) and (2). See also commentary 8 to chapter II of the C.B.A. Code and Quebec rules, sections 3.02.04, 3.02.10, 3.03.02, and 4.02.01(h).

(i) managing one's practice effectively,

(j) pursuing appropriate professional development to maintain and enhance legal knowledge and skills, and

(k) adapting to changing professional requirements, standards, techniques, and practices."

Finally, the rules admonish lawyers that though a mistake, even one that may be actionable in damages for negligence, would not necessarily constitute a failure to maintain the standard set by the rules, evidence of gross neglect in a particular matter or a pattern of neglect or mistakes in different matters may be evidence of such a failure regardless of tort liability. Incompetence can give rise to disciplinary action.[9]

24.2 DISCIPLINE PROCEEDINGS

In practice, the enforcement of competency standards through disciplinary action has been limited generally to blatant cases of wilful and reckless failures to maintain even the most minimal standards of competence and quality of service. Despite the wording of the rules referred to above, incompetency and, in Ontario, unsatisfactory professional practice, are usually considered to be less culpable than professional misconduct, which traditionally has been defined as conduct that would reasonably be regarded as disgraceful or dishonourable by solicitors of good repute and competency.[10] Cases in which a lawyer's right to practise has been revoked by reason of incompetency are exceedingly rare.[11] Lesser penalties, such as suspensions and reprimands, are seldom effective in rectifying competence problems. If the legal profession's only measure of an acceptable quality of service were the standard set by the results of discipline proceedings it would never have to fear being criticized for establishing an unrealistic professional ideal. Professor Harry Arthurs has written that "law societies have exhibited an invincible repugnance to the idea that they should use their knowledge and power to discipline incompetent lawyers, the very group professional self-government

9 C.B.A. Code, chapter II, commentary 9; Ontario rule 2.01(2) and accompanying commentary.

10 *Myers v. Elman*, [1940] A.C. 282 at 288-289 (H.L.), citing with approval Justice Darling's definition in *Re Solicitor*, [1912] 1 K.B. 302. See also cases cited in note 50 to chapter 26.

11 In *Re MacDonald (No. 1)*, report of discipline hearing panel adopted by Convocation, February 20, 1981 (Ontario), a lawyer was publicly reprimanded for maintaining a standard of practice lower than that required of a competent lawyer. (The lawyer was disbarred for misappropriation on September 18, 1981.) See also Edmund B. Spaeth, "To What Extent Can a Disciplinary Code Assure the Competence of Lawyers?" (1988) 61 Temple Law Review 1211; Susan R. Martyn, "Lawyer Competence and Lawyer Discipline: Beyond the Bar?" (1981) 69 Georgetown Law Journal 705; and American Bar Association Report of the Commission on Evaluation of Disciplinary Enforcement (the McKay Commission) May, 1991, pp. 9-10.

is designed to suppress".[11.1] In discipline proceedings, the profession has regulated competence by reference to the lowest common denominator.

Fortunately, discipline proceedings are not the only possible method of regulating competence. Others include bar admission courses, continuing legal education, insurance loss prevention programmes, practice review programmes, solicitors' negligence litigation, and judicial intervention.

24.3 CONTINUING LEGAL EDUCATION

Canadian rules of professional conduct provide that lawyers should keep abreast of developments in fields in which they practise by engaging in continuing study and education.[12] In 28 American jurisdictions continuing legal education is mandatory.[13]

Mandatory continuing legal education programmes are no panacea, however. They have been criticized for requiring too few hours of continuing education, for failing to require that the programmes taken are relevant to the practitioner's field of practice, and, perhaps most importantly, for failing to address the most prevalent causes of problems. The most common competency problems are not caused by lawyers' failure to keep current in the law — the most frequent subject of continuing education programmes — but by inadequate office systems and sloppy work habits, resulting in such problems as missed limitation periods, botched title searches, and failures to communicate appropriately with clients.[14]

24.4 INSURANCE LOSS PREVENTION PROGRAMMES

Compulsory errors and omissions insurance, in those jurisdictions in which it exists, has enabled law societies to identify common problem areas and risks and to implement loss prevention programmes that have had some success.[15]

24.5 PRACTICE REVIEW PROGRAMMES

In 1986 the Law Society of Upper Canada created a standing committee of benchers with responsibility for professional standards. The impetus to form a

---

11.1 H.W. Arthurs, "The Dead Parrott: Does Professional Self-Regulation Exhibit Vital Signs?", a paper presented at a National Conference on the Legal Profession and Ethics, University of Calgary, June 10, 1994, p. 4.

12 The C.B.A. Code's requirement that lawyers maintain competence provides that lawyers should keep abreast of developments in areas in which they practise. The definition of the term "competent lawyer" in Ontario rule 2.01 (1) requires lawyers to pursue appropriate professional development to maintain and enhance legal knowledge and skills.

13 Susan R. Martyn, "Standards of Quality: Past Efforts and Future Options" in Robert M. Greene (ed.), *The Quality Pursuit* (Chicago, American Bar Association, 1989), p. 223 at 224.

14 Joel Henning, *Managing Law Firm Profitability* (New York: Hildebrandt, 1992), pp. 5-1 to 5-7.

15 Martyn, *supra*, note 13, p. 224.

professional standards committee originated in a growing consensus that concerns about professional competence were being inadequately dealt with by means of the discipline process, and that remedial means would be more effective.

At present, the Law Society's professional standards department is staffed by a lawyer who had significant experience in private practice before she joined the Law Society's staff, together with a specialist in office systems and technology, a law clerk, and a secretary.

The professional standards department also makes extensive use of experienced lawyers in private practice who conduct peer reviews of lawyers who are referred to the department. The reviewers make recommendations designed to improve the lawyer's office management procedures and the quality of legal services provided.

In late 1991, an ad hoc committee charged with the responsibility of implementing reform proposals in the discipline, complaints, and standards fields recommended that the professional standards committee be authorized to initiate random practice reviews, in addition to investigations of members' practices initiated as a result of complaints, errors and omissions claims, or audits that call the members' competence into question. This recommendation, the committee wrote in its report, calls for an important addition to the profession's ability to regulate itself. "The assumption that, once qualified for admission, a member of a profession will necessarily continue to maintain standards of competence in a rapidly changing legal environment", the committee observed, "is not, in the view of the committee, an assumption that can be justified."[16]

The recommendation requires legislative change, and has yet to be implemented. In the meantime, Convocation has addressed the persistent problem of the unco-operative lawyer who is diverted by the complaints or errors and omissions departments to the practice review programme. Experience has shown that remedial means are effective only for lawyers who recognize their shortcomings and who are willing to learn to overcome them. Lawyers who do not co-operate in the practice review programme are referred to the discipline department.[17]

24.6 SOLICITORS' NEGLIGENCE LITIGATION

The standard of care and skill enforced by courts in solicitors' negligence litigation is that of a reasonably competent and diligent lawyer practising in the

16 Law Society of Upper Canada, Report of the Reform Implementation Committee, Regulation of Professional Standards of Competence, October 8, 1991, p. 2.

17 Report of the Professional Standards Committee, approved by Convocation, October 23, 1992.

area in which the defendant practised at the time of the alleged negligence.[18] In order to succeed in establishing liability it is not enough for a plaintiff to prove that the lawyer has made an error or given advice on a view of the law that a court later holds to be untenable; the plaintiff must show that the error was such that an ordinarily competent lawyer practising in the area would not have made it.[19] A lawyer will not be found liable by reason of a violation of competency standards in a case in which there is a rift of respectable professional opinion concerning the acceptability of the measures taken by the lawyer.[20] The Supreme Court of Canada held in a 1991 case,[20.1] however, that the courts are not bound by expert evidence that the defendant's conduct conforms to the norms of practice of prudent lawyers in the same circumstances. The fact that a lawyer follows the common professional practice at the relevant time is not sufficient to avoid liability unless the common practice is demonstrably reasonable.

Lawyers may be found liable in tort as well as contract, and may be found liable not only to clients but to others who have foreseeably suffered harm as a result of their negligence.[21] The Supreme Court of Canada's decision in a 1986 case[22] that lawyers may be concurrently liable in contract and tort had the effect of extending limitation periods in some cases and broadening the categories of remedies that are available to disgruntled clients.

Frequently civil claims asserted against lawyers are framed as breaches of fiduciary duty. The courts have repeatedly affirmed, however, that not all duties of lawyers may be categorized as fiduciary duties. As Justice Southin wrote (when a member of the British Columbia Supreme Court) in a 1987 decision:[22.1]

---

18 See, for example, the judgment of Riley J. in *Millican v. Tiffin Holdings Ltd.* (1964), 50 W.W.R. 673 at 675 (Alta. T.D.) reversed (1965), 53 W.W.R. 505 (Alta. C.A.), reversed [1967] S.C.R. 183, as quoted by Haddad J.A., in *Spence v. Bell*, [1982] 6 W.W.R. 385 at 396 (Alta.C.A.), leave to appeal to S.C.C. refused (1982), 46 N.R. 179 (S.C.C.). See also *Hauck v. Dixon* (1975), 10 O.R. (2d) 605, (H.C.); and *Stronghold Investments Ltd. v. Renkema*, [1984] 3 W.W.R. 51 at 58 (B.C. S.C.).

19 See, for example, *Ormingdale Holdings Ltd. v. Ray, Wolfe, Connell, Lightbody & Reynolds* (1980), 116 D.L.R. (3d) 346 (B.C. S.C.), affirmed (1982), 135 D.L.R. (3d) 577 (B.C. C.A.); and *Stronghold Investments Ltd. v. Renkema, ibid.*

20 *Papadopoulos v. Anklewicz* (1987), 60 O.R. (2d) 198 (H.C.).

20.1 *Dorion v. Roberge* (*sub nom.* Roberge v. Bolduc) (1991), 78 D.L.R. (4th) 666 (S.C.C.); the Ontario Court of Appeal reached the same conclusion in *Glivar v. Noble* (1985), 8 O.A.C. 60 at 66: "if the risk of harm from following prevailing practice is both foreseeable and readily avoidable, a solicitor is negligent in following that practice."

21 See *Hedley Byrne & Co. v. Heller & Partners*, [1964] A.C. 465 (H.L.); *Anns v. Merton London Borough Council*, [1978] A.C. 728 (H.L.); and *Tracy v. Atkins* (1979), 16 B.C.L.R. 223 (C.A.).

22 *Central and Eastern Trust Co. v. Rafuse*, (*sub nom.* Central Trust Co. v. Rafuse), [1986] 2 S.C.R. 147, varied [1988] 1 S.C.R. 1206.

22.1 *Girardet v. Crease & Co.* (1987), 11 B.C.L.R. (2d) 361 at 362 (S.C.); see also *Fasken Campbell Godfrey v. Seven-up Canada Inc.* (1997), 142 D.L.R. (4th) 456 at 483 (Ont. Gen. Div.); and *Martin v. Goldfarb* (1997), 31 B.L.R. (2d) 265 at 279-280 (Ont. Gen. Div.), reversed in part (August 26, 1998), Doc. CA C27477 (Ont. C.A.)

"The word "fiduciary" is flung around now as if it applied to all breaches of duty by solicitors, directors of companies and so forth. But "fiduciary" comes from the Latin "fiducia" meaning "trust". Thus, the adjective, "fiduciary" means of or pertaining to a trustee or trusteeship. That a lawyer can commit a breach of the special duty of a trustee, e.g., by stealing his client's money, by entering into a contract with the client without full disclosure, by sending a client a bill claiming disbursements never made and so forth is clear. But to say that simple carelessness in giving advice is such a breach is a perversion of words. The obligation of a solicitor of care and skill is the same obligation of any person who undertakes for reward to carry out a task. One would not assert of an engineer or physician who had given bad advice and from whom common law damages were sought that he was guilty of a breach of fiduciary duty. Why should it be said of a solicitor?"

Lawyers of course have a duty to follow clients' lawful instructions, and will be responsible for any loss that may ensue as a result of their disobeying them. Lawyers have a duty to seek instructions as necessary; they must not substitute their own judgment either for actual client instructions or what they expect the client's instructions would be if the client were asked.[23]

24.7 JUDICIAL INTERVENTION

In a profession that has become increasingly specialized, it is particularly important that lawyers abide by the admonition of the rules of professional conduct that when consulted about matters in fields in which they lack expertise and experience, they have a duty either to decline to act or to retain, consult or collaborate with lawyers who are competent in those fields.[24] In a 1994 decision, the Ontario Court of Appeal allowed an appeal from conviction on the ground that the incompetence of defence counsel at trial prevented the accused from having a fair trial. Defence counsel had failed to take the rudimentary step of investigating witnesses who, he was told, would support his client's alibi. He had also failed to object to some dubious evidence of other acts of violence and had not ordered a transcript of the preliminary hearing.

In at least one American case a judge has intervened to prevent a lawyer from acting in a field in which the lawyer lacked the necessary experience.

In a 1986 Florida case,[25] a bankruptcy court judge dismissed an application because of the debtor's lawyer's failure to file a required statement and plan. The debtor's lawyer acknowledged unfamiliarity with the filing requirements and informed the court that he had relied on the advice of an assistant clerk in the bankruptcy office who had informed him that all necessary forms had been filed. The court ordered that the lawyer be discharged as the debtor's lawyer and be enjoined from further practice in the bankruptcy court until he completed a

23 See *Osler v. Ford*, [1936] O.W.N. 159 (H.C.). See also New Brunswick rules, Part C, rule 7.

24 C.B.A. Code, chapter II, commentary 6; Ontario rule 2.01(1) and accompanying commentary.

25 *Re Pearson*, 70 Bankr. 202 (Bankr. S.D. Fla., 1986).

minimum of nine hours of continuing legal education in the field of bankruptcy law. "It is outrageous", the presiding judge said by way of explanation for this order, "that an attorney who has achieved a law degree and obtained admission to the Florida bar publicly admits that he practises based on the advice of assistant court clerks and products available in a stationery store."[26]

24.8 CONCLUSION

Perhaps because of increased public scrutiny and heightened public expectations, it has become evident in recent years that incompetent legal service can be as damaging to clients and third parties as unprofessional conduct of other kinds. The legal profession has done an appreciably better job of protecting the public from lawyers who have acted dishonestly than it has of protecting the public from lawyers who have acted incompetently. Lawyers in both categories bring discredit upon the profession. Both the public interest and the self-interest of the profession demand that law societies redouble their efforts to improve the competence of their members and protect the public against lawyers who are unwilling or unable to provide legal services of an acceptable quality.[27]

---

26 *Ibid.*, p. 204.

27 See William H. Hurlburt, "Incompetent Service and Professional Responsibility" (1980) 18 Alta. L.R. 145 at 149; and Geoffrey C. Hazard, "Internal Management Controls Tend to Assure the Quality of Legal Services", National Law Journal (March 22, 1993), pp. 15-16.

25

Rules of Professional Conduct

25.1 INTRODUCTION

For the most part, the most significant and complex rules of professional conduct, together with those that are particularly relevant to specialized areas of practice, are considered in some detail in other chapters. Specifically, rules of professional conduct dealing with integrity[1] are considered in chapter 26 (Discipline Proceedings); rules dealing with competence and quality of service[2] are considered in chapter 24 (Regulating Lawyer Competence and Quality of Service); rules dealing with advising clients[3] are considered in chapter 14 (Counselling); rules dealing with confidentiality of information[4] are considered in chapters 3 (Confidentiality) and 20 (Corporate Counsel); rules dealing with conflicts of interest[5] are considered in chapters 5 (Conflicts of Interest in Litigation), 7 (Criminal Defence), 16 (Mediation), 17 (Real Estate), 18 (Estates), 20 (Corporate Counsel), 21 (Government Lawyers), and 22 (Conflicts of Interest); rules dealing with withdrawal of services[6] are considered in chapters 4 (Advocacy) and 7 (Criminal Defence); rules dealing with contingency fees[7] are considered in chapter 12 (Contingency Fees); rules dealing with the lawyer as advocate[8] are considered in chapters 4 (Advocacy), 6 (Prosecuting), and 7 (Criminal Defence); rules dealing with advertising, solicitation, and making legal services available[9] are considered in chapters 10 (Advertising) and 11 (Solicitation); rules dealing with lawyers' responsibility to other lawyers individually[10] are considered in chapter 8 (Civility); rules dealing with delegation to non-lawyers[11] are considered insofar

1 C.B.A. Code, chapter I; Ontario rule 1.03(1) and 6.01(1) and accompanying commentary.
2 C.B.A. Code, chapter II; Ontario rule 2.01.
3 C.B.A. Code, chapter III; Ontario rule 2.02.
4 C.B.A. Code, chapter IV; Ontario rule 2.03.
5 C.B.A. Code, chapters V and VI; Ontario rules 2.04 and 2.05.
6 C.B.A. Code, chapter XII; Ontario rule 2.09.
7 C.B.A. Code, chapter XI, commentary 10; Ontario rules 2.08(3) and (4).
8 C.B.A. Code, chapter IX; Ontario rules 4.01 through 4.04.
9 C.B.A. Code, chapter XIV; Ontario rules 3.01 through 3.06.
10 C.B.A. Code, chapter XVI; Ontario rule 6.03.
11 Ontario rule 5.01.

as certain specialized practice areas are concerned in chapters 4 (Advocacy), 17 (Real Estate), and 18 (Estates); rules dealing with the lawyer in public office[12] are considered in chapter 21 (Government Lawyers); rules dealing with public appearances and public statements by lawyers[13] are considered in chapter 13 (The Media); rules dealing with lawyers in mortgage transactions[14] are considered in chapter 17 (Real Estate); rules dealing with lawyers as mediators[15] are considered in chapter 16 (Mediating); and, finally, rules dealing with medical-legal reports[16] are considered in chapter 4 (Advocacy).

In this chapter we will consider the history, nature, and application of rules of professional conduct. We will also consider those rules that are not dealt with in other chapters.

25.2 HISTORY, NATURE, AND APPLICATION OF RULES OF PROFESSIONAL CONDUCT

Although the legal profession has devoted more energy and thought to formulating standards of professional responsibility than have members of other professions, it was in fact one of the last to adopt rules of professional conduct. The American Bar Association's Canons of Professional Ethics were first adopted in 1908. Over considerable opposition, the Canadian Bar Association approved a set of Canons of Legal Ethics, which were based in part on the A.B.A. model, at its fifth annual meeting, at Ottawa, in 1920. Thus, at least at a national level, rules of professional conduct are a phenomenon of the twentieth century.[17]

The 1920 C.B.A. Canons of Legal Ethics were adopted by law societies, just as the 1908 A.B.A. Canons of Professional Ethics were adopted by state bar associations.[18] Both codes have been superseded twice.

At its 1969 annual meeting, the Canadian Bar Association created a special committee to review the 1920 Canons and to recommend changes. As a result a new Code of Professional Conduct was adopted by the C.B.A. in 1974. The 1974 C.B.A. Code was in turn adopted, and in some cases adapted, by provincial and

---

12 C.B.A. Code, chapter X; Ontario rule 6.05.

13 C.B.A. Code, chapter XVIII; Ontario rule 6.06.

14 Ontario rule 2.06(6) through (11).

15 Ontario rule 4.07.

16 Ontario rule 2.02(7) through (9).

17 See Mark M. Orkin, *Legal Ethics: A Study of Professional Conduct* (Toronto: Cartwright & Sons, 1957), pp. 9-10; R.D. Gibbens, Review of *Professional Conduct for Canadian Lawyers* by Beverley G. Smith (1990) 69 Can. Bar Rev. 385 at 385- 386; Charles Wolfram, *Modern Legal Ethics* (St. Paul, Minnesota: West, 1986), p. 48; and Thomas Ehrlich, "Introduction: Common Issues of Professional Responsibility" (1987-88) 1 Georgetown Journal of Legal Ethics 3 at 5-6. The Alabama Bar Association adopted the first code of professional ethics in 1887, and the 1908 Canons were based in large part on that Code, which was in turn based on an influential set of lectures by Judge George Sharswood in 1854; see David Luban, *Lawyers and Justice: An Ethical Study* (Princeton, New Jersey: Princeton University Press, 1988), p. xxv.

18 See H.S. Drinker, *Legal Ethics* (New York: Columbia University Press, 1953), pp. 21-30.

territorial law societies. The national executive committee of the C.B.A. resolved in 1984 to appoint a committee to review and revise the 1974 Code. The committee built upon the 1974 Code rather than starting from scratch. Two new chapters, titled "conflicts of interest between lawyer and client" (chapter VI) and "public appearances and public statements by lawyers" (chapter XVIII), were added. A third chapter (chapter XIII, "making legal services available") was retitled and revised (chapter XIV, "advertising, solicitation and making legal services available"), and the other chapters were revised to varying extents.[19]

The 1974 C.B.A. Code has been used as a basis for their rules of professional conduct by all law societies in Canada and, to a lesser extent, by the Barreau du Quebec.[20] A number of law societies have adopted either the 1974 or the 1987 C.B.A. Code virtually without amendment;[21] others have added to and altered the provisions of the C.B.A. codes significantly;[22] and still others have prepared their own rules with an eye on the C.B.A. Codes, but in such a way that the final product bears almost no resemblance to either C.B.A. Code.[23]

In the United States, the 1908 A.B.A. Canons were replaced in 1969 by the A.B.A. Model Code of Professional Responsibility. The Model Code was adopted, in many cases in a revised form, by almost all state bar associations. It has been revised several times since 1969.[24]

In 1983, the A.B.A. adopted new Model Rules of Professional Conduct. A majority of state bar associations have adopted a version of the Model Rules, but a significant minority are still governed by a version of the Model Code.[25]

An important difference between the 1969 Model Code and the 1983 Model Rules exemplifies the profession's ambivalence towards the purposes of a code of professional conduct. The Model Code consists of two kinds of rules: mandatory disciplinary rules and "aspirational" ethical considerations. Thus an effort was made to separate matters of professional regulation and matters of ethics. The disciplinary rules are mandatory statements of minimally acceptable conduct,

---

19 Report of the C.B.A. Special Committee on Legal Ethics, Law Society of Upper Canada Gazette, vol. 7, no. 4 (December, 1973), p. 276; C.B.A. Code, Forward, p. v; Beverley G. Smith, *Professional Conduct for Canadian Lawyers* (Toronto: Butterworths, 1989), p. 5.

20 Quebec rule 1.

21 The Law Societies of Prince Edward Island, Newfoundland, the Northwest Territories and the Yukon have all adopted the 1987 C.B.A. Code with minor, if any, revisions.

22 The Law Societies in Saskatchewan, Manitoba, Ontario and Nova Scotia have used the 1974 and 1987 C.B.A. Codes as the basis for their rules of professional conduct, but have modified and added to the Codes significantly.

23 The Law Societies of Alberta, British Columbia and New Brunswick have adopted rules of professional conduct that bear little resemblance to the C.B.A. Codes.

24 See Luban, *supra*, note 17, pp. xxvii-xxviii.

25 Luban, *supra*, note 17, pp. xxvii-xxviii.

whereas the ethical considerations are designed to point the way to morally praiseworthy conduct.[26]

The Model Rules eliminated this dichotomy. Like the C.B.A. Code, the Model Rules consist of rules with commentaries that are intended as aids to the interpretation of the rules. For the most part, the Model Rules are confined to injunctions that are appropriate and necessary for the effective regulation of the profession in the interest of protecting clients and third parties. Little effort is expended in defining or exploring the ethical dimensions of the practice of law.[27]

The dual purposes of codes of professional conduct — though explicitly recognized for the first time in the Model Code — have been apparent from the outset. The original "canons of ethics" were soon invoked to discipline lawyers, and have since been invoked to find lawyers liable for professional negligence — peculiar uses for purely ethical prescriptions.[28] In a 1990 decision,[29] the Supreme Court of Canada held that though rules of professional conduct are not binding on courts, they should nonetheless be considered important statements of public policy that express the collective views of the profession as to the appropriate standards to which lawyers should adhere.

Canadian rules of professional conduct are patchworks that reflect both purposes. Some rules are framed in prohibitive language: "The lawyer shall not advise or represent both sides of a dispute. . . .";[30] "The lawyer shall not stipulate for, charge or accept any fee that is not fully disclosed, fair and reasonable."[31] Others exhort lawyers to strive for exemplary ethical standards of practice: "The lawyer should encourage public respect for and try to improve the administration

---

26 Luban, *supra*, note 17, pp. xxvii-xxviii; Wolfram, *supra*, note 17, p. 69; and Reed Elizabeth Loder, "Tighter Rules of Professional Conduct: Saltwater for Thirst" (1987-88) 1 Georgetown Journal of Legal Ethics 311 at 323.

27 See Wolfram, *supra*, note 17, pp. 69- 70; and Luban, *supra*, note 17, pp. xxvii-xxviii.

28 See Wolfram, *supra*, note 17, p. 69. See also *Enns v. Panju*, [1978] 5 W.W.R. 244 (B.C. S.C.); *Enerchem Shipmanagement Inc. v. "Coastal Canada" (The)* (1988), 83 N.R. 256 (Fed. C.A.); *Major v. Higgins* (1932), 53 Que. K.B. 277 at 283; and John Honsberger, "Legal Rules, Ethical Choices and Professional Conduct", Law Society of Upper Canada Gazette, vol. 21, no. 2 (June, 1987), p. 113.

29 *MacDonald Estate v. Martin*, [1990] 3 S.C.R. 1235. In *Essa (Township) v. Guergis* (1993), 15 O.R. (3d) 573, the Divisional Court held that courts should be reluctant to adopt provisions of the C.B.A. Code in preference to rules of professional conduct duly adopted by law societies in cases in which Code provisions conflict. In *Stewart v. Canadian Broadcasting Corp.* (1997), 150 D.L.R. (4th) 24 (Ont. Gen. Div.), additional reasons at (1997), 152 D.L.R. (4th) 102 (Ont. Gen. Div.), the Court emphasized that rules of professional conduct are not exhaustive of either lawyers' professional obligations or the full scope of fiduciary duties as they are defined. See text accompanying notes 15.2 and 15.3 to chapter 13, *supra*.

30 C.B.A. Code, chapter V, rule; Ontario rule 2.04(2).

31 C.B.A. Code, chapter XI, rule; see also Ontario rule 2.08(1).

of justice";[32] "The lawyer should assist in maintaining the integrity of the profession and should participate in its activities."[33]

The preface to the 1987 C.B.A. Code makes it clear that no attempt has been made in the Code to define professional misconduct or conduct unbecoming a barrister and solicitor. Although the Ontario Divisional Court held in a 1985 case[34] that in promulgating rules of professional conduct the Law Society is performing a regulatory function on behalf of the Legislature and government and is therefore vulnerable to scrutiny under the *Charter of Rights and Freedoms*, it would be a mistake to assimilate rules of professional conduct to a statute such as the *Criminal Code*. Not every breach of the rules of professional conduct necessarily amounts to professional misconduct or conduct unbecoming a barrister and solicitor.[35] Conversely, not every act that amounts to professional misconduct is explicitly proscribed by the rules. No rule specifically prohibits the misappropriation of funds held in trust for clients, for example. What constitutes professional misconduct and conduct unbecoming a barrister and solicitor is determined by discipline committees case by case.[36]

Nevertheless, codes of conduct in the United States and Canada have tended to evolve from simple statements of ideals to which members of the profession aspire to mandatory rules designed to be enforced in disciplinary proceedings. This evolutionary process is more complete in the United States. There, as mentioned above, the American Bar Association attempted to serve both ideological and regulatory functions by including in its 1969 Model Code both ethical aspirations and mandatory disciplinary rules. The American Bar Association abandoned this hybrid approach in its 1983 Model Rules, which articulate expected standards of practice in such number and detail that they are more comparable to a regulatory statute than to a traditional code of ethics. The preface to the Model

32 C.B.A. Code, chapter XIII, rule; Ontario rule 4.06(1). See also Stephen E. Sherriff, H. Reginald Watson and Shaun M. Devlin, " 'You Can Run . . . But You Can't Hide': A Guide To Understanding Lawyer Discipline In Ontario", in Franklin Moskoff (ed.), *Administrative Tribunals: A Practice Handbook for Legal Counsel* (Aurora, Ontario: Canada Law Book, 1989), pp. 117-118; and Honsberger, *supra*, note 28, p. 118.

33 C.B.A. Code, chapter XV.

34 *Klein v. Law Society (Upper Canada)* (1985), 50 O.R. (2d) 118 (Div. Ct.).

35 *Fan v. Law Society (British Columbia)* (1977), 77 D.L.R. (3d) 97 (B.C. C.A.). See also note 31, *supra*.

36 *Stevens v. Law Society (Upper Canada)* (1979), 55 O.R. (2d) 405 at 410 (Div. Ct.). See also Sherriff *et al.*, *supra*, note 32, pp. 117-118, and chapter 26, *infra*, part 26.7. The Alberta rules contain the following guide to its interpretation: "Under the *Legal Profession Act*, the Law Society has broad powers to declare conduct to be deserving of sanction and is not limited to disciplining violations that are expressly or impliedly referred to in this Code. However, the Law Society's primary concern is with conduct that reflects poorly on the profession or that calls into question the suitability of an individual to practise law. Disciplinary assessment of conduct will therefore be based on all facts and circumstances as they existed at the time of the conduct. A trivial or technical breach of this Code without significant consequences is unlikely to be sanctioned. A lawyer's intentions and the wilfulness of conduct are also relevant."

Rules describes what follows as "legal rules", while urging members of the profession to look elsewhere for ethical guidance: "The Rules do not, however, exhaust the moral and ethical considerations that should inform a lawyer, for no worthwhile human activity can be completely defined by legal rules. The Rules simply provide a framework for the ethical practice of law." At least one commentator has even suggested that the profession's traditional name for the subject-matter of codes of conduct is obsolete:

> If we are not talking about right and wrong, but simply what regulatory rules apply, for policy reasons, in particular legal situations, is there any reason to still refer to this branch of legal thought as "ethics"? Will anything be lost if we call it something else, and simply regulate without the moral overtones?[37]

The Law Society of Alberta's code of professional conduct exemplifies an approach akin to that of the Model Rules. It consists of 129 rules that are identified as such, together with many more rules that are identified as statements of principle and commentaries.

Should other Canadian jurisdictions adopt a similar approach? An affirmative answer is tempting, if only because the final step in an evolutionary process seems progressive,[38] if not inevitable. There are, moreover, several cogent reasons for elaborating upon the still quite general admonitions of most current Canadian codes of conduct.

First, some issues of professional responsibility are sufficiently complex that it is impractical to expect individual practitioners to resolve them on the basis of general principles. Guidance from specific rules of professional conduct are a practical necessity for lawyers struggling with conflict of interest problems, for example.

Second, many issues of professional responsibility — conflicts of interest again spring immediately to mind — are often addressed by the courts today, on disqualification motions and in solicitors' negligence actions in the conflict of interest example. It would be dangerously misleading to leave practitioners with the impression that such issues may be resolved on the basis of general principles when the applicable jurisprudence has developed relatively elaborate standards. The courts, moreover, will be less likely to defer to law societies if law societies have not articulated principles with sufficient clarity and detail to enable their members to resolve professional conduct problems consistently and responsibly.[39]

Third, lawyers are accustomed to applying black-letter rules, which are conducive to certainty in the law. The notion of determining a permissible course of conduct on the basis of aspirational ethical considerations seems foreign and

---

37 Mark H. Aultman, "Cracking Codes" (1994) 7 Georgetown Journal of Legal Ethics 735, 737.

38 See Nancy J. Moore, "Elaborating Standards of Professional Conduct", a paper delivered to the Law Society of Upper Canada's Strategic Planning Conference, September 25, 1992, p. 10.

39 *Ibid.*, pp. 10-13.

equivocal.[40] General ideological principles are of limited use to lawyers in answering practical questions of how they should conduct themselves in specific situations.

Finally, if the only standards articulated in a code of conduct are general, they will have to be elaborated *ex post facto* in contested disciplinary proceedings. Standards are thus developed incrementally through the adjudication process, case by case, like the common law. By inviting contested proceedings, codes of conduct that contain only general principles increase the strain on the limited resources of discipline committees, which already have ample work to do. More importantly, discipline committees are singularly ill-equipped to develop professional standards efficiently. Because the standards are not brought home to the practitioner in advance in the profession's code of conduct, discipline committees are likely to bend over backwards to avoid the unfairness to the practitioner of applying an exacting standard retrospectively. Particularly where both parties lead expert evidence, the less rigorous of two suggested standards is likely to be applied for disciplinary purposes, as a result of the heavy standard of proof that must be discharged by Law Society counsel in discipline proceedings.[40.1]

There are, nevertheless, several equally cogent reasons for codes of conduct to articulate the profession's ideals and ethical aspirations.

First, the profession over the last few years has undergone a sustained period of disillusionment both among its members and in the eyes of the public. A principal cause of disillusionment is an overemphasis by lawyers on the business dimension of the practice of law, and a corresponding belief shared by many members of the public that the profession as a whole is self-interested. Codes of ethics have traditionally served to inform the public, and remind the profession, that lawyers are quasi-public officials ("officers of the court" and "ministers of justice") who are expected to share with judges a community-minded devotion to the law.[40.2] Codes that consist of detailed, black-letter rules that are designed to serve regulatory functions cannot help but at least dilute this public service orientation.

Second, the chief objective of spelling out lawyers' professional responsibilities in a comprehensive code of black-letter rules — namely, the achievement of certainty — is exceedingly difficult to achieve in practice. Certainty is generally attainable only if rules are few, simple, relatively immutable, and clear in both statement and application. As Judge Richard Posner has pointed out, these are

40 See Reed Elizabeth Loder, "Tighter Rules of Professional Conduct: Saltwater for Thirst" (1987-88) 1 Georgetown Journal of Legal Ethics 311 at pp. 311-13.

40.1 I am indebted to Mary Eberts of the Ontario Bar, who developed this theme most effectively in an unpublished speech to a regional conference of the Council on Licensure, Enforcement, and Regulation in Toronto on April 28, 1994.

40.2 Anthony T. Kronman, *The Lost Lawyer: Failing Ideals of the Legal Profession* (Cambridge, Mass.: Harvard University Press, 1993), pp. 153, 374; W. Wesley Pue, "Becoming 'Ethical': Lawyers' Professional Ethics in Early Twentieth Century Canada", (1991) 20 Man. L.J. 227 at 227-28.

objectives that systems of legal rules rarely accomplish.[40.3] Even where these objectives seem to have been achieved, there are significant differences among judges and other adjudicators in their willingness to interpret rules flexibly and to recognize exceptions freely.[40.4]

Third, tighter and more comprehensive regulation can be achieved only at the price of diminished flexibility — flexibility that may be the greatest strength of self-government. Unanticipated situations are more likely to be accommodated by general principles than by specific rules. Moreover, the imposition of inflexible and universal solutions is generally not the optimum approach to the resolution of complex ethical issues.[40.5]

Fourth, an exhaustive code of black-letter rules is unlikely to attract the support of a professional consensus. Consensus is important in any system of self-government, partly because voluntary compliance is preferable to disciplinary sanctions. Rules of professional conduct adopted by the bars and law societies of the European Community in 1977 made the point in this way:

> Rules of professional conduct are not designed simply to define obligations the breach of which may involve a disciplinary sanction. A disciplinary sanction is imposed only as a last resort. It can indeed be regarded as an indication that the self-discipline of the profession has been unsuccessful.[40.6]

The willingness and determination of the profession to achieve widespread compliance with this Code is a more powerful and fundamental enforcement mechanism than the imposition of sanctions by the Law Society. Professor Harry Arthurs of Osgoode Hall Law School has pointed out that many, if not most, of the provisions of Canadian codes of conduct are not used as a basis for disciplining lawyers. Lawyers who are derelict in such duties as attempting to improve the administration of justice or making legal services available to the public in an efficient and convenient manner, for example, are not generally censured by law societies as a result.[40.7] Nevertheless, most lawyers subscribe to such ideals, and are likely to observe rules of conduct that capture them, whether or not they risk disciplinary proceedings if they are delinquent.

Finally, to spell out minimum prohibitions for disciplinary purposes entails regulating to the lowest common denominator. If the standards that are established

---

40.3 Richard A. Posner, *The Problems of Jurisprudence* (Cambridge, Mass. Harvard University Press, 1990), p. 48.

40.4 Ibid., pp. 48-49.

40.5 See Loder, *supra*, note 40, pp. 314, 323-24 and 327; and Reed Elizabeth Loder, "Moral Scepticism and Lawyers" (1990), 47 Utah L.R. 47 at 91-92.

40.6 Consultative Committee of the Bars and Law Societies of the European Community, "The Declaration of Perugia on the Principles of Professional Conduct of the Bars and Law Societies of the European Community 16.IX.1977", Law Society of Upper Canada Gazette, vol. 14, no. 4 (June, 1980), p. 205.

40.7 H.W. Arthurs, "The Dead Parrot: Does Professional Self-Regulation Exhibit Vital Signs?", a paper presented at a National Conference on the Legal Profession and Ethics, University of Calgary, June 10, 1994, pp. 6,8.

are calibrated too high, neither widespread compliance nor rigorous enforcement is likely. Such a code will command little respect. Rules that embody minimal standards, on the other hand, almost by definition de-emphasize ethical aspirations and are certain to discourage lawyers from reaching beyond those minimums.[40.8]

Traditional codes of ethics, with their emphasis on the collective ethical aspirations of the profession, contribute at least in some measure to this sense of pride, and to public respect for the profession. Traditional codes are at the same time insufficiently useful to practising lawyers who encounter complex professional responsibility problems with some regularity, and who require specific guidance if the profession is to resolve such problems satisfactorily and consistently.

For the reasons developed above, the tension between the ideological and regulatory functions of codes of ethics makes the accommodation of these two commendable objectives problematic. The functions are not necessarily mutually exclusive, however. Professor Nancy Moore of Rutgers Law School has suggested a hybrid approach to the drafting of codes of ethics, an approach in which certain provisions (for instance, those dealing with conflicts of interest and confidentiality) would be elaborated on in some detail, whereas other provisions would be treated at a level of generality — a more suitable approach where, for example, there is no consensus as to what the appropriate standard should be. Thus, despite the adoption of a regulatory approach to professional responsibility problems for which lawyers require specific guidance and on which there is a consensus in the profession on the appropriate standard, the promulgation of the code of ethics would not result in the abandonment of any discussions of ethical aspirations.[40.9]

Such a compromise is unlikely to satisfy the most ardent proponents of either the regulatory or the ideological approach, but it may be the strategy that is most conducive to harmonizing the conflicting objectives.

The framers of such a code of ethics might consider the adoption of a few general guidelines:

1. A primary purpose of a code of ethics should be the reinforcement of the public service orientation of the practice of law.
2. At least in areas in which there is a consensus in the profession, a code of ethics should be sufficiently specific to enable practitioners to deal effectively with the immediate professional responsibility problems that they confront regularly in practice.

40.8 See Moore, *supra*, note 38, pp. 13-14; Loder, *supra*, note 40, pp. 311-14, 319-20 and 328-32; David Luban, "Calming the Hearse Horse: A Philosophical Research Program for Legal Ethics" (1981), 40 Md. L.R. 454 at 460-61; and Stephen Toulmin, "Ethics and Equity: The Tyranny of Principles", Law Society of Upper Canada Gazette, vol. 15, no. 3 (September, 1981), p. 240, especially at p. 244.

40.9 Moore, *supra*, note 38, pp. 10, 14-15.

3. A code of ethics should nevertheless be sufficiently flexible to be responsive to unforeseen situations.

4. A code of ethics should not establish standards that are so stringent that voluntary compliance is discouraged. Rather, it should establish standards that reflect the values and practices of responsible and conscientious members of the profession.

5. At the same time, a code of ethics should not be protective of lawyers (or, particularly in the case of confidentiality rules, of clients[40.10]) at the expense of the general public. Indeed (as guideline 1 provides), fostering an ethic of public service should be one of the chief objectives of such a code.

To follow these guidelines is of course to walk a tightrope between paradoxical, though perhaps not incompatible, principles. The hard part lies in the drafting. Only when the attempt is complete can we know whether the reconciliation of the ideological and regulatory functions of codes of ethics is possible.

25.3 CLIENT PROPERTY

Canadian rules of professional conduct provide that lawyers have a duty to clients to observe all relevant rules and law regarding the preservation and safekeeping of clients' property entrusted to them.[41] Clients' property is defined to include monies; securities such as mortgages, negotiable instruments, stocks and bonds; original documents such as wills, title deeds, minute books, licences and certificates; other papers such as clients' correspondence files, reports and invoices; and chattels such as jewellery and silver.[42]

In most jurisdictions lawyers' duties with respect to safekeeping, preserving and accounting for clients' monies and other property are set out in detail in regulations separate from rules of professional conduct.[43] The C.B.A. Code of Professional Conduct specifies that in the absence of such regulations lawyers should adhere to the following minimum standards:

> (a) paying into and keeping monies received or held by the lawyer for or on behalf of clients in a trust bank account or accounts separate from the bank account of the lawyer or the lawyer's firm;
>
> (b) keeping properly written books and accounts of all monies received, held or paid by the lawyer for or on behalf of each of the lawyer's clients that clearly distinguish such monies from the monies of every other client and from the monies of the lawyer and the lawyer's firm;

40.10 *Ibid.*, p. 13.

41 C.B.A. Code, chapter VIII, rule; Ontario rule 2.07(1).

42 C.B.A. Code, chapter VIII, commentary 1.

43 See, for example, Quebec rules, sections 3.02.07, 3.02.08, 3.03.03; Manitoba rules, rule 61 ff.

(c) not retaining for an unnecessarily long period, without the express authority of the client, monies received for or on behalf of such client;

(d) subject to the rules prescribed by the governing body, no lawyer shall take fees, as opposed to disbursements, from funds held in trust for a client without the client's express authority unless the work being done by the lawyer for the client has been performed and a proper account in respect thereof has been rendered to the client. Where a client authorizes the payment of fees from trust funds before an account has been rendered, this arrangement should be recorded in writing and an interim account sent to the client forthwith;

(e) the lawyer should not estimate a lump sum that may in the aggregate be owed by a number of clients and then transfer that sum in bulk from a trust account to the lawyer's general account without allocating specific amounts to each client and rendering an account to each client.[44]

Rules of professional conduct also provide that where there are no relevant laws or rules respecting the preservation and safekeeping of clients' property, or where the lawyer is in any doubt, the lawyer should take the same care of such property as a careful and prudent owner would when dealing with property of like description.[45]

Lawyers also have a duty to promptly notify clients upon receiving any property of or relating to clients unless satisfied that the clients know that the property has come into their custody.[46] Lawyers should clearly label and identify clients' property and place it in safekeeping separate and apart from their own property.[47]

Rules of professional conduct provide that lawyers should maintain adequate records of clients' property in the lawyers' custody so that it may be promptly accounted for or delivered to or to the order of clients upon request. Lawyers should ensure that property is delivered to the right person and, in case of dispute as to the person entitled, may have recourse to the courts.[48]

The rules governing clients' property draw attention to their relationship with rules regarding confidential information. Lawyers should keep clients' papers and other property out of sight as well as out of reach of those not entitled to see them and should, subject to any right of lien, return them promptly to the clients upon request or at the conclusion of the retainer.[49]

---

44 C.B.A. Code, chapter VIII, commentary 1 and note 3.

45 C.B.A. Code, chapter VIII, rule; Ontario rule 2.07(1).

46 C.B.A. Code, chapter VIII, commentary 2; Ontario rule 2.07(2).

47 C.B.A. Code, chapter VIII, commentary 3; Ontario rule 2.07(3).

48 C.B.A. Code, chapter VIII, commentary 4; Ontario rule 2.07(4) through (6).

49 C.B.A. Code, chapter VIII, commentary 5; Ontario rule 2.07(1) and accompanying commentary. See also *Alberta Treasury Branches v. Invictus Financial Corp.* (1985), 63 A.R. 4 (Q.B.); and *Bank of Nova Scotia v. Imperial Developments (Canada) Ltd.* (1988), 49 Man. R. (2d) 53 (C.A.).

Finally, the rules provide that lawyers should be alert to claim on behalf of clients any lawful privilege respecting information about their affairs, including their files and property if seized or attempted to be seized by a third party. Lawyers should be familiar in this regard with the nature of clients' privilege, and with relevant statutory provisions such as those in the *Income Tax Act*, the *Criminal Code*, and the *Charter of Rights and Freedoms*.[50]

Until fairly recently lawyers generally considered it safe to dispose of closed files six years after a matter was completed. It is now clear that limitation periods applicable in professional negligence claims may not start to run until the client becomes aware or ought reasonably become aware of an act or omission resulting in loss or damage.[51] In combination with increased potential exposure to claims by non-clients,[52] this has necessitated the maintaining of many client files for evidentiary purposes almost indefinitely.

In most jurisdictions, interest on lawyers' mixed trust accounts is generally paid to a law foundation for such charitable purposes as legal education and research, legal aid, and law libraries.[53] Clients may, however, direct their lawyers to set up separate bank accounts into which the clients' funds are deposited so that they are not mingled with funds of other clients, and so that the clients are entitled to the interest.[54]

25.4 BORROWING FROM CLIENTS

Ontario's rules of professional conduct specifically prohibit lawyers from borrowing from clients.[55] The only exceptions to the rule are (a) where the client is a lending institution, financial institution, insurance company, trust company or similar corporation whose business includes lending money to members of the public; and (b) where in the case of a loan from a related person as defined by the *Income Tax Act* the lawyer is able to discharge the onus of proving that the client's interests were fully protected by the nature of the case and by independent legal advice.[56]

The Ontario rule does not prohibit loans by clients to lawyers' spouses or to corporations, syndicates or partnerships in which the lawyer or the lawyer's spouse has, directly or indirectly, a substantial interest. In such cases, however,

---

50 C.B.A. Code, chapter VIII, commentary 6.

51 See *Central & Eastern Trust Co. v. Rafuse* (*sub nom.* Central Trust Co. v. Rafuse), [1986] 2 S.C.R. 147, varied [1988] 1 S.C.R. 1206; and *Consumers Glass Co. v. Foundation Co. of Canada/Cie foundation du Canada* (1985), 51 O.R. (3d) 385 (C.A.).

52 *Hedley Byrne & Co. v. Heller & Partners*, [1963] 2 All E.R. 575 (H.L.); *Anns v. Merton London Borough Council*, [1977] 2 All E.R. 492 (H.L.); and *Tracy v. Atkins* (1979), 16 B.C.L.R. 223 (C.A.).

53 See, for example, *Law Society Act*, R.S.O. 1990, c. L.8, ss. 55, 57.

54 See Beverley G. Smith, *Professional Conduct for Canadian Lawyers* (Toronto: Butterworths, 1989), pp. 70-71.

55 Ontario rule 2.06(4). See also chapter 22, *supra*, part 22.3.

56 Ontario rule 2.06(4).

unless the client is a lending institution, financial institution, insurance company, trust company or similar corporation whose business includes lending money to members of the public, the lawyer must be able to discharge the onus of proving that the client's interests were fully protected by the nature of the case and by independent legal representation.[57]

The C.B.A. Code provides simply that lawyers should not borrow money from clients who are not in the business of lending money.[58] British Columbia's rules provide that lawyers must not borrow money from clients "unless the transaction is of a routine nature and in the ordinary course of business of the client."[59]

25.5 FEES[60]

(a) Fairness of Fees

Canadian rules of professional conduct stipulate that lawyers shall not undertake to act for, charge or accept any amount that is not fully disclosed, fair and reasonable.[61] The rules add that a fair and reasonable fee will depend on and reflect such factors as:

(a) the time and effort required and spent;

(b) the difficulty and importance of the matter;

(c) whether special skill or service has been required and provided;

(d) the customary charges of other lawyers of equal standing in the locality in like matters and circumstances;

(e) in civil cases, the amount involved, or the value of the subject matter;

(f) in criminal cases, the exposure and risk to the client;

(g) the results obtained;

(h) tariffs or scales authorized by local law;

(i) such special circumstances as loss of other employment, urgency and uncertainty of reward;

(j) any relevant agreement between the lawyer and the client.[62]

---

57 Ontario rule 2.06(5).

58 C.B.A. Code, chapter VI, commentary 4.

59 British Columbia rules, chapter 7, rule 4. See also Yukon rules, Part One, rule 18.

60 Contingency fees are considered in chapter 12.

61 C.B.A. Code, chapter XI, rule (a); Ontario rule 2.08(1); Quebec rules, section 3.08.01; British Columbia rules, chapter 9, rules 1 and 7; New Brunswick rules, Part E, rule 1.

62 C.B.A. Code, chapter XI, commentary 1. The Ontario rules in the commentary to rule 2.08(2), contain a similar list that does not include, however, factors (d), (f), or (j), and that does not preface factor (e) with the qualifier "in civil cases"; see also Quebec rules, section 3.08.02; and Alberta rules, chapter 13, rule 1. Rule 2 of chapter 13 of the Alberta rules requires that "A lawyer must provide to the client in writing, before or within a reasonable time after commencing a representation, as much information regarding fees and disbursements as is reasonable and practical in the circumstances, including the basis on which fees will be determined."

A fee will not be fair and reasonable and may subject the lawyer to disciplinary proceedings, the rules provide, if it is one that cannot be justified in the light of all pertinent circumstances, including the factors mentioned, or if it is so disproportionate to the services rendered as to introduce the element of fraud or dishonesty, or undue profit.[63]

The rules also recognize that it is in keeping with the best traditions of the legal profession to reduce or waive a fee in cases of hardship or poverty, or where the client or prospective client would otherwise effectively be deprived of legal advice or representation.[64]

Lawyers are prohibited from appropriating any client funds held in trust or otherwise under the lawyer's control for or on account of fees without the express authority of the client except as permitted by the rules of the governing body.[65] Law societies generally allow lawyers to draw from client trust accounts to pay their fees after a billing or other written notification is delivered, provided that the money drawn does not exceed the unexpended balance of the money held in the trust account for the client.[66]

Rules of professional conduct also specify that lawyers should give clients a fair estimate of fees and disbursements, and point out any uncertainties involved, so that the client may be able to make an informed decision.[67] This is particularly important, Ontario's rules add, in respect of fees or disbursements that the client might not reasonably be expected to anticipate.[68] When something unusual or unforeseen occurs that may substantially affect the amount of a fee or disbursement the lawyer should forestall misunderstandings or disputes by explaining this to the client. Lawyers should be ready, the rules add, to explain the basis of their charges to clients, especially if the clients are unsophisticated or uninformed as to the proper basis and measurements for fees.[69]

Ontario's rules expressly require lawyers, when asked by a client to quote a fee, to explain the nature and approximate amount of any anticipated disburse-

---

63 C.B.A. Code, chapter XI, commentary 1. The Ontario rules do not expressly mention either the possibility of disciplinary proceedings or the alternative basis for a finding that a fee is not fair and reasonable, namely, that the fee is so disproportionate to the services rendered as to introduce the element of fraud or dishonesty, or undue profit. See *Re Daley*, discipline hearing panel report adopted by Convocation, November 26, 1992 (Ontario).

64 C.B.A. Code, chapter XI, commentary 2; Ontario rule 2.08(2) and accompanying commentary. The British Columbia rules, chapter 1, rule 3(9), provide that a client's ability to pay cannot justify a charge in excess of the value of the service, though it may require a reduction or waiver of a fee.

65 C.B.A. Code, chapter XI, rule (b); Ontario rule 2.08(11).

66 See, for example, by-law 19 under the *Law Society Act*, R.S.O. 1990, c. L.8 as amended.

67 C.B.A. Code, chapter XI, commentary 3; Ontario rule 2.08(2) and accompanying commentary.

68 Ontario rule 2.08(2) and accompanying commentary.

69 C.B.A. Code, chapter XI, commentary 3; Ontario rule 2.08(2) and accompanying commentary.

ments to be incurred.[70] They also prohibit lawyers from charging any significant amount as a disbursement, such as the cost of a title search, that is not fully disclosed in a timely fashion, and is fair and reasonable.[71] The Ontario rules specify that when preparing and delivering accounts to clients, lawyers should clearly and separately identify amounts charged as fees and disbursements, and should provide a detailed statement of disbursements.[72]

In matters in which a lawyer acts for two or more clients, the lawyer has a duty to apportion the fees and disbursements equitably between them unless the clients have agreed otherwise.[73] Lawyers may charge interest on overdue accounts only as permitted by law or local practice or with the prior agreement of the client, and then only at a reasonable rate.[74]

Finally, Canadian rules of professional conduct proscribe the acceptance by lawyers of hidden fees. The fiduciary relationship between lawyer and client requires full disclosure in all financial matters, the rules provide. Thus no fee, reward, costs, commission, interest, rebate, agency or forwarding allowance or other compensation whatsoever related to the professional employment may be taken by the lawyer from anyone other than the client without full disclosure to and consent of the client or, where the lawyer's fees are being paid by someone other than the client, such as a legal aid agency, a borrower, or a personal representative, without the consent of the other person.[75] Only *bona fide* and specified payments to others may be charged as disbursements. If a lawyer has a financial interest in a person to whom disbursements are made, such as an investigating, brokerage or copying agency, the lawyer must expressly disclose that fact to the client.[76]

Lawyers are rarely disciplined for charging excessive fees. Fee disputes are generally resolved by way of assessment by a court officer.[77] Disciplinary proceedings are generally initiated only if the fee charged is so grossly excessive as to give rise to an inference that the lawyer has taken advantage of a vulnerable client, or if the lawyer has accepted a hidden fee or otherwise concealed the basis of the lawyer's charges from the client. In the United States lawyers have been disciplined for misrepresenting to clients that their cases were very difficult in

---

70 Ontario rule 2.08(1).

71 Ontario rule 2.08(1).

72 Ontario rule 2.08(5).

73 C.B.A. Code, chapter XI, commentary 5; Ontario rule 2.08(6); British Columbia rules, chapter 9, rule 5.

74 C.B.A. Code, chapter XI, commentary 4; Ontario rule 2.08(2). In Ontario, the *Solicitors Act*, R.S.O. 1990, c. S.15, s. 33, permits lawyers to charge interest on overdue accounts at the rate established for pre-judgment interest in civil litigation, beginning one month after the bill is delivered. Section 33(4) requires that the rate of interest be shown on the bill.

75 C.B.A. Code, chapter XI, commentary 7; Ontario rule 2.08(2) and accompanying commentary; British Columbia rules, chapter 9, rules 7 to 9.

76 C.B.A. Code, chapter XI, commentary 7. The Ontario rules do not include this language.

77 See Ontario rule 2.08(2) and accompanying commentary.

order to justify high fees,[78] and for failing to notify clients promptly when as a result of unexpectedly favourable developments their legal services were no longer necessary,[79] among other things.[80] In a 1994 case,[80.1] the Court of Appeals for the State of New York upheld a two-year suspension of a lawyer's right to practise where, after he was dismissed, the lawyer refused to return to clients the unearned portion of non-refundable retainers that he had received.

(b) Fee Splitting and Referral Fees

Lawyers are prohibited from sharing fees and from giving any financial or other reward to non-lawyers who bring or refer business to them.[81] This prohibition is intended to prevent unauthorized practice. Thus an arrangement between a lawyer and a conveyancer to divide fees on applications for probate or administration is improper whether both participate in the work or not. It is also improper for a lawyer, in return for a fee, to permit the lawyer's name to be placed on applications for probate or administration that have been prepared by a conveyancer.[82] Nor may a lawyer enter into a lease or arrangement whereby a landlord directly or indirectly shares in the fees or revenues generated by the law practice.[83]

Lawyers may divide fees with lawyers, however, if the other lawyer is a partner or associate, or if the client expressly or implicity consents to the employment of the other lawyer and the fee is divided in proportion to the work done and responsibility assumed.[84] Also, in Ontario, British Columbia, and Saskatchewan, and in some American jurisdictions (including California and Illinois), lawyers are now permitted to pay and accept referral fees in certain circumstances. The policy underlying the permissibility of referral fees in these jurisdictions includes encouraging lawyers to refer cases and transactions that they are poorly equipped to handle because they lack experience or expertise in a particular field or because of the volume of other work in their offices.[85] To permit referral fees also tends to treat sole practitioners and small firm lawyers equally with large firm lawyers, whose compensation policies may be structured to reward attracting work that is performed by other lawyers in the firm who have special expertise.

---

78 See *Re Rappaport*, 558 F. 2d 87 (2nd Cir., 1977); and *United States v. Blitstein*, 626 F. 2d 774 (10th Cir., 1980), cert. denied 101 S. Ct. 898 (1981).

79 See *Re Sullivan*, 494 S.W. 2d 329 (Missouri, 1973).

80 See Charles Wolfram, *Modern Legal Ethics* (St. Paul, Minnesota: West, 1986), pp. 515-522.

80.1 In *The Matter of Cooperman*, New York Court of Appeals, March 17, 1994 (unreported): see also Geoffrey C. Hazard, "New York Proposals Would Impose Substantial Safeguards for Clients", National Law Journal, August 8, 1993, p. 17.

81 C.B.A. Code, chapter XI, commentary 8; Ontario rule 2.08(9); British Columbia rules, chapter 9, rule 2.

82 These examples were cited in former Ontario rule 9, commentary 7, but were not carried forward when the rules were amended in 2000.

83 C.B.A. Code, chapter XI, commentary 9.

84 C.B.A. Code, chapter XI, commentary 6. See also Chapter 13, rule 7 of the Alberta Code of Professional Conduct.

85 See Wolfram, *supra*, note 79, pp. 510 to 513.

The Law Society of Upper Canada's *Rules of Professional Conduct* allow lawyers to charge and accept referral fees where the referral is made because of the expertise and ability of the lawyer to whom the matter is referred, unless the referral is made because of a conflict of interest. Referral fees are permitted, however, only if (a) the fee is reasonable and does not increase the total amount of the fee charged to the client, and (b) the client is informed and consents.[86]

25.6 LAWYERS AND THE ADMINISTRATION OF JUSTICE

Rules of professional conduct provide that lawyers should encourage public respect for and try to improve the administration of justice.[87] This obligation is not restricted to lawyers' professional activities but is a general responsibility resulting from their position in the community. Lawyers' responsibilities, the rules provide, are greater than those of private citizens. Lawyers must not subvert the law by counselling or assisting in activities that are in defiance of it and must do nothing to lessen the respect and confidence of the public in the legal system. Lawyers should avoid broad, irresponsible allegations of corruption or partiality that may weaken public confidence in legal institutions and authorities. Lawyers in public life must be particularly careful in this regard, the rules add, because the mere fact of being a lawyer will lend weight and credibility to public statements. For the same reason, lawyers should not hesitate to speak out against injustices.[88]

Lawyers should also lead in seeking improvements in the legal system, the rules provide, though criticisms and proposals should be *bona fide* and reasoned. By training, opportunity and experience, lawyers are positioned to observe the workings and discover the strengths and weaknesses of laws, legal institutions and public authorities.[89]

The rules recognize that because of changes in human affairs and the imperfection of human institutions, constant efforts must be made to improve the administration of justice and thereby maintain public respect for it. The admission to and continuance in the practice of law imply a basic commitment to equal justice for all in an open, ordered and impartial system. Judicial institutions will not function effectively unless they command the respect of the public.[90]

The proceedings and decisions of courts and tribunals are subject to criticism by all members of the public, including lawyers. The rules provide, however, that the fact that judges and members of tribunals are often prohibited by law or

---

86 Ontario rule 2.08 (8). See also British Columbia rules, chapter 9, rule 3, which allows referral fees only if, at the commencement of the retainer, the lawyer accepting the referral fully discloses the referral fee to the client and the client consents in writing to its payment.

87 C.B.A. Code, chapter XIII, rule; Ontario rule 4.06(1).

88 C.B.A. Code, chapter XIII, commentary 3; Ontario rule 4.06(1) and accompanying commentary.

89 C.B.A. Code, chapter XIII, commentary 2; Ontario rule 4.06(1) and accompanying commentary.

90 C.B.A. Code, chapter XIII, commentary 1; Ontario rule 4.06(1) and accompanying commentary.

custom from defending themselves places special responsibilities on lawyers. Lawyers should avoid criticism that is petty, intemperate, or unsupported by a *bona fide* belief in its real merit, bearing in mind again that in the eyes of the public professional knowledge lends weight to lawyers' judgments or criticism. If lawyers have been involved in proceedings their criticisms may be, or may appear to be, partisan rather than objective. Where courts or tribunals are the object of unjust criticism, lawyers are uniquely able to and should support them, the rules provide, both because their members cannot defend themselves and because lawyers are thereby contributing to greater public understanding of and therefore respect for the legal system.[91]

The rules provide also that lawyers who seek legislative or administrative changes should disclose whose interest is being advanced, whether it be their own interest, that of clients, or the public interest. Lawyers may advocate such changes on behalf of clients without personally agreeing with them, but lawyers who purport to act in the public interest should espouse only those changes that they conscientiously believe to be in the public interest.[92]

Ontario's rules of professional conduct specify that lawyers who have reasonable grounds for believing that a dangerous situation is likely to develop at a court facility shall inform the local police force, give particulars and, where possible, suggest such solutions to the anticipated problem as further security and that judgment ought to be reserved.[93]

25.7 RESPONSIBILITY TO THE PROFESSION

Canadian rules of professional conduct provide that lawyers should assist in maintaining the integrity of the profession and should participate in its activities.[94] The rules add that lawyers should do everything possible to assist the profession to function properly and effectively, in order that the profession may discharge its public responsibility of providing independent and competent legal services. Participation in such activities as law reform, continuing legal eduction, tutorials, legal aid programs, community legal services, professional conduct and discipline, liaison with other professions and other activities of the governing body or local, provincial or national associations, although often time-consuming and without tangible reward, is essential to the maintenance of a strong, independent and useful profession.[95]

Three commentaries to the rule have given rise to disciplinary proceedings. One of the commentaries requires lawyers to reply promptly to all communica-

91 C.B.A. Code, chapter XIII, commentary 4; Ontario rule 4.06(1) and accompanying commentary.

92 C.B.A. Code, chapter XIII, commentary 5; Ontario rule 4.06(2) and accompanying commentary.

93 Ontario rule 4.06(3) and accompanying commentary.

94 C.B.A. Code, chapter XV, rule; Ontario rule 6.01(1).

95 C.B.A. Code, chapter XV, commentary 4. The Ontario rules include no counterpart to this commentary, perhaps on the view that it is superfluous.

tions from their governing body.[96] Failures to reply to letters from the Law Society concerning complaints from clients is the single most frequent basis for disciplinary action in Ontario.

Another commentary stipulates that lawyers should not in the course of their professional practice write letters, whether to a client, another lawyer or any other person, that are abusive, offensive or otherwise totally inconsistent with the proper tone of a professional communication from a lawyer.[97]

Finally, a commentary to the rule governing lawyers' responsibility to the profession imposes on lawyers a duty to report to their governing body any occurrences involving an apparent breach of the rules of professional conduct where there is a reasonable likelihood that someone will suffer serious damage as a consequence, for example where a shortage of trust funds is involved. The only exceptions to the duty to report come into play where to report the matter would entail a breach of privilege or otherwise would be unlawful. The report to the governing body must be made *bona fide* without malice or ulterior motive.[98]

The same commentary provides that it is proper — though not obligatory — for a lawyer to report *any* occurrences involving a breach of the rules of professional conduct (unless, again, to report the matter would entail a breach of privilege or otherwise would be unlawful). Again, such a report must be made *bona fide* without malice or ulterior motive. The commentary explains that evidence of minor breaches may, on investigation, disclose a more serious situation or may indicate the beginning of a course of conduct that would lead to serious breaches in the future, and that unless lawyers who tend to depart from proper professional conduct are checked at an early stage, loss or damage to clients or others may ensue. A common observation of members of discipline hearing panels and law society counsel is that they often learn after a hearing is completed that lawyers involved in disciplinary proceedings had been regarded with suspicion or concern by colleagues and other local practitioners for some time.[99]

---

96 C.B.A. Code, chapter XV, commentary 2; Ontario rule 6.02; British Columbia rules, chapter 13, rule 3. See also *Re X*, (1920), 16 Alta. L.R. 542 at 543 (T.D.), *per* Walsh J.

97 C.B.A. Code, chapter XV, commentary 3; Ontario rule 6.03(5); Quebec rules, section 4.03.02.

98 C.B.A. Code, chapter XV, commentary 1; Ontario rule 6.01(3) and accompanying commentary; Quebec rules, section 4.04.01. The British Columbia rules, chapter 13, rules 1 and 2, provide that a lawyer must report (a) a breach of undertaking that has not been consented to or waived, (b) a shortage of trust funds, and (c) any other conduct that raises a substantial question as to a lawyer's honesty or trustworthiness. Rule 4 of chapter 3 of the Alberta rules provide that a lawyer must, subject to confidentiality, report to the Law Society any conduct of which the lawyer has personal knowledge and which in the lawyer's reasonable opinion, acting in good faith, raises a serious question about the competence, honesty or trustworthiness of another lawyer, or is likely to harm any person.

99 C.B.A. Code, chapter XV, commentary 1; Ontario rule 6.03(1) and accompanying commentary. See also Harry W. Arthurs, "Climbing Kilimanjaro: Ethics for Postmodern Professionals", an address to the Westminster Institute Conference on Legal Ethics, March 5, 1993, p. 11.

In a 1985 Ontario case,[100] two clients (who were husband and wife) learned that a lawyer had been misappropriating funds belonging to them. They retained counsel, who negotiated a settlement that called for the misappropriated funds to be repaid. The clients' counsel was instructed not to report the misappropriation to the law society. The lawyer went on to misappropriate large sums of money from other clients. Eventually his thefts were discovered. He was disbarred by the law society and was sentenced to a lengthy term of imprisonment after pleading guilty to criminal charges.

For the client's counsel to have reported the misappropriation to the law society would not have been in his client's interest, as the client in all probability would not have recovered the missing funds if the law society had learned of the misappropriation at that time. The law society concluded that it was not clear that the client's counsel had a duty to report the misappropriation under the rules of professional conduct as framed at that time.[101]

As a result of the case the Ontario rule was amended to require a lawyer in such a position to attempt to persuade the clients to report the facts to the law society before pursuing private remedies. If the client refuses to make such a report, the lawyer is required to inform the client of the policy of the law society's Lawyers' Fund for Client Compensation that claimants who have elected to take steps to recover the loss in pursuit of a private agreement with an apparently dishonest member will not be entitled to a grant unless the law society has been informed before any such steps are taken. The rules now provide that in such circumstances the lawyer should obtain instructions in writing to proceed with the client's claim without notice to the law society, and should inform the client of the provision of the *Criminal Code* dealing with the concealment of an indictable offence in exchange for an agreement to obtain valuable consideration (section 141). In the event that the client wishes to pursue a private agreement with the apparently dishonest lawyer, the rules conclude the lawyer shall not continue to act if the agreement constitutes a breach of section 141.[102]

For the same reason the 1987 revision of the Canadian Bar Association's Code of Professional Conduct includes an amendment that, subject to local rules, requires that lawyers must not act on clients' instructions to recover from another lawyer funds allegedly misappropriated by the other lawyer unless the client

100 *Re Scherer*, report adopted by Convocation, February 24, 1984.

101 See Kim Lockhart, "The Scherer Affair", *Canadian Lawyer* (April, 1985), pp. 10-14.

102 Ontario rule 6.01(4) and accompanying commentary.

authorizes disclosure to the governing body and the lawyer makes such disclosure.[103]

25.8 RETIRED JUDGES RETURNING TO PRACTICE

The C.B.A. Code provides that judges who return to practice after retiring or resigning from the bench should not (without the approval of the governing body) appear as a lawyer before the court of which the former judge was a member or before courts or tribunals of inferior jurisdiction thereto in the province where the judge exercised judicial functions. The rule in question explains that if in a given case the former judge were in a preferred position by reason of having held judicial office, the administration of justice would suffer, whereas if the reverse were true, the former judge's client might suffer. The rule also provides that there may be cases in which a governing body would consider that no preference or appearance of preference would result, for example where the judge resigned for good reason after only a very short time on the bench.[104]

Ontario's rules of professional conduct are more specific. They provide that without the express approval of Convocation, which approval may be granted only in exceptional circumstances and may be restricted as Convocation sees fit, no member who was formerly a judge of the Supreme Court of Canada, the Ontario Court of Appeal or the Federal Court of Canada, Appeal Division and who has retired, resigned or been removed from the bench and has returned to practice, may appear as counsel or advocate in any court, or in chambers, or before any administrative board or tribunal.[105]

The Ontario rule also provides that without the express approval of Convocation, which approval may be granted only in exceptional circumstances and may be restricted as Convocation sees fit, no member who was formerly a judge of the Federal Court of Canada, Trial Division, the Tax Court of Canada, the Supreme Court of Ontario, Trial Division, a County or District Court or the Ontario Court of Justice (General Division) and who has retired, resigned or been removed from the bench and has returned to practice, may appear as counsel or advocate before the court on which the judge served or any lesser court, or before any tribunal over which the court on which the judge served exercised an appellate

103 C.B.A. Code, chapter XV, commentary 1. In an American case, *Re Himmel*, 125 Ill. 2d 531 (1988), the Illinois Supreme Court suspended a lawyer for a year for failing to report a lawyer who had misappropriated client funds. The 1969 Model Code of Professional Responsibility, in DR 1-103A, requires mandatory reporting of all violations unless the information is privileged. The 1983 Model Rules of Professional Conduct, rule 8.3(a) requires only that "a violation . . . that raises a substantial question as to the other lawyer's honesty, trustworthiness, or fitness to practise" be reported. See also Geoffrey C. Hazard, Jr., "Squeal Rule' Considered for Change", National Law Journal (March 26, 1990), p. 13, in which the author suggests that mandatory reporting of all offences results in a surge of petty cases adding a burden to already overloaded disciplinary systems and corrodes already fragile relations among lawyers.

104 C.B.A. Code, chapter XIX, commentary 4.

105 Ontario rule 6.08(1) and (3).

or judicial review jurisdiction, for a period of two years from the date of retirement, resignation or removal.[106]

25.9 PRACTICE BY UNAUTHORIZED PERSONS AND DELEGATION TO NON-LAWYERS[107]

Canadian rules of professional conduct specify that lawyers should assist in preventing the unauthorized practice of law.[108]

The rules explain that statutory provisions against the practice of law by unauthorized persons are for the protection of the public: even if unauthorized persons have technical or personal ability, they are immune from control, regulation and, in the case of misconduct, from discipline by any governing body. Their competence and integrity have not been vouched for by an independent body representative of the legal profession. Moreover, the rules add, the client of a lawyer who is authorized to practise has the protection and benefit of the lawyer-client privilege, the lawyer's duty of secrecy, the professional standards of care that the law requires of lawyers, as well as the authority that the courts exercise over them. Other safeguards include group professional liability insurance, rights with respect to the assessment of lawyers' accounts, rules regarding trust funds, and requirements for the maintenance of funds financed by lawyers to compensate clients who have been victimized by dishonest lawyers.[109]

A corollary of the duty to assist in preventing the unauthorized practice of law is the lawyers' duty to assume complete professional responsibility for all business entrusted to them, and to maintain direct supervision over staff and assistants such as students, clerks, and legal assistants to whom particular tasks and functions may be delegated. Lawyers who practise alone or who operate branch or part-time offices, the rules provide, should ensure that all matters requiring a lawyer's professional skill and judgment are dealt with by a lawyer qualified to do the work and that legal advice is not given by unauthorized persons, whether in the lawyer's name or otherwise. Lawyers should approve the amount of any fee to be charged to a client.[110]

A second corollary of lawyers' duty to assist in preventing the unauthorized practice of law is the rule that lawyers should not, without the approval of the governing body, employ in any capacity having to do with the practice of law a lawyer who is under suspension as a result of disciplinary proceedings or a former

---

106 Ontario rule 6.08(2) and (4).

107 Rules of professional conduct dealing with delegation to non-lawyers are considered insofar as certain specialized practice areas are concerned in chapters 4 (Advocacy), 17 (Real Estate), 18 (Estates), and 20 (Corporate Counsel).

108 C.B.A. Code, chapter XVII, rule; Ontario rule 6.07(1).

109 C.B.A. Code, chapter XVII, commentary 1; Ontario rule 6.07(1) and accompanying commentary. See also *R. v. Lawrie & Pointts Ltd.* (1987), 59 O.R. (2d) 161 (C.A.).

110 C.B.A. Code, chapter XVII, commentary 3; Ontario rule 5.01(2) and accompanying commentary.

lawyer who has been disbarred or has been permitted to resign while facing disciplinary proceedings and who has not been reinstated.[111] Ontario's rule of professional conduct makes it clear that the prohibition extends beyond conventional employment relationships to proscribe retaining, occupying office space with, and using the services of lawyers or former lawyers who in Ontario or elsewhere have been suspended, disbarred or permitted to resign as a result of disciplinary action.[112]

The Ontario rules provide that no collection letter should be sent out over the signature of a lawyer unless the letter is on the lawyer's letterhead, prepared under the lawyer's supervision and sent from the lawyer's office.[113]

Rules of professional conduct also recognize that it is in the interests of the profession and the public for the delivery of more efficient, comprehensive and better quality legal services that the training and employment of legal assistants be encouraged, and that there are many tasks that can be performed by a legal assistant under the supervision of a lawyer.[114] The Ontario rules recognize that there exists a category of non-lawyers, generally referred to as law clerks, who have received specialized training or education and are therefore capable of doing independent work under the general supervision of a lawyer. Lawyers may in appropriate circumstances, the rules add, render services to clients with the assistance of non-lawyers of whose competence they are satisfied.[115]

The rules provide that, subject to restrictions that may be established by local rules and practice, legal assistants may perform any task delegated and supervised by a lawyer so long as the lawyer maintains a direct relationship with the client and assumes full professional responsibility for the work. Legal assistants may not perform any of the duties that lawyers only may perform or do things that lawyers themselves may not do. The rules add that, generally speaking, the question of what the lawyer may delegate to a legal assistant turns on the distinction between the special knowledge of the legal assistant and the professional legal judgment of the lawyer, which must be exercised whenever it is required.[116]

---

111 C.B.A. Code, chapter XVII, commentary 2; British Columbia rules, chapter 13, rule 5. In *Green, Carter v. Law Society (Northwest Territories)* (1980), 114 D.L.R. (3d) 762, the Northwest Territories Supreme Court held that s. 69 of the *Legal Profession Ordinance*, 1976 (N.W.T.) (2d session), c. 4, which prohibited employment by a member of a suspended or disbarred member, and which defined "member" as a member of the Law Society of the Northwest Territories, does not prevent the employment by a member of a person who has been disbarred in another jurisdiction. The C.B.A. Code's provision, however, uses the word "lawyer" rather than "member", and the Ontario rule (see note 112, *infra*) places the question beyond doubt.

112 Ontario rule 6.07(2).

113 Ontario rule 5.01(5).

114 C.B.A. Code, chapter XVII, commentary 4; British Columbia rules, chapter 12, rules 4 to 8.

115 Ontario rule 5.01(3) and accompanying commentary.

116 C.B.A. Code, chapter XVII, commentary 5; Ontario rule 5.01(2) and accompanying commentary.

The rules impose on lawyers a duty to permit legal assistants to act only under the supervision of a lawyer. The adequacy of supervision will depend on the type of legal matter, including the degree of standardization and repetitiveness of the matter as well as the experience of the legal assistant, both generally and with regard to the matter in question. The burden rests upon the lawyer who employs a legal assistant, the rules add, to educate the legal assistant about the duties to which the legal assistant may be assigned and also to supervise on a continuing basis the way in which the legal assistant carries them out.[117] The Ontario rules add that a lawyer should review the legal assistant's work at sufficiently frequent intervals to ensure its proper and timely completion.[118]

The Ontario rules also stipulate that every law office, including a branch office of a law firm, must at all times be effectively supervised by a lawyer.[119] Those rules also provide examples of tasks that may permissibly be delegated to illustrate the application to particular areas of practice of the rule governing delegation to non-lawyers.[120] They also provide the following list of tasks that a lawyer may not delegate to a non-lawyer:

The lawyer may not permit a non-lawyer to:

(a) accept cases on behalf of the lawyer, except that such persons may receive instructions from established clients if the supervising lawyer is advised before any work commences;

(b) fix fees, except where such persons use a fee schedule; provided that the lawyer has set the fee schedule and is responsible for sending the account to the client;

(c) give legal opinions;

(d) give or accept undertakings, except with the express authorization of the supervising lawyer;

(e) act finally without reference to the lawyer in matters involving professional legal judgment;

(f) be held out as a lawyer. (The lawyer should insure that the non-lawyer is identified as such when communicating orally or in writing with clients, lawyers, public officials or with the public generally whether within or outside the offices of the law firm of employment);

(g) appear in court or actively participate in formal legal proceedings on behalf of a client except as set forth above, or in a support role to the lawyer appearing in such proceedings;

---

117 C.B.A. Code, chapter XVII, commentary 6; Ontario rule 5.01(2) and accompanying commentary. See also Geoffrey C. Hazard, Jr., "Legal Staff Should Learn Principles", National Law Journal (September 9, 1991), p. 15.

118 Ontario rule 5.01(2) and accompanying commentary.

119 Ontario rule 5.01(2).

120 Ontario rule 5.01(2) and accompanying commentary. The examples are considered in chapters 4 (Advocacy), 17 (Real Estate), 18 (Estates), and 20 (Corporate Counsel).

(h) be named in association with the lawyer in any pleading, written argument or other like document submitted to a court;

(i) be remunerated on a sliding scale related to the earnings of the lawyer, except where such person is an employee of the lawyer;

(j) conduct negotiations with third parties, other than routine negotiations where the client consents and the results thereof are approved by the supervising lawyer before action is taken;

(k) take instructions from clients, unless the supervising lawyer has directed the client to the non-lawyer for that purpose;

(l) sign correspondence containing a legal opinion, but the non-lawyer who has been specifically directed to do so by a supervising lawyer may sign correspondence of a routine administrative nature, provided that the fact such person is a non-lawyer is disclosed, and the capacity in which such person signs the correspondence is indicated;

(m) forward to a client any documents, other than routine documents, unless they have previously been reviewed by the lawyer.[121]

The Ontario rules also provide that, generally speaking, a non-lawyer shall not attend on examinations or in court except in support of a lawyer also in attendance. Although exceptions are specified (including routine adjournments in provincial courts and attending on watching briefs, among others) the rules stipulate that "in no circumstances shall a non-lawyer be permitted to conduct an examination for discovery in a contested matter or a cross-examination of a witness in aid of a motion."[121.1]

In a 1996 case[121.2], Justice Maloney of the Ontario Court of Justice (General Division) held that where an examination for discovery of a defendant is conducted by a non-lawyer in breach of this rule, a transcipt of the examination may not be read into the record as part of the plaintiff's case.

25.10 OUTSIDE INTERESTS AND THE PRACTICE OF LAW

Canadian rules of professional conduct provide that lawyers who engage in another profession, business or occupation concurrently with the practice of law must not allow their outside interest to jeopardize their professional integrity, independence or competence.[122]

The rules explain that the term "outside interest" in this context covers the widest possible range and includes activities that may overlap or be connected with the practice of law, such as engaging in a mortgage business, acting as a director of a client corporation, or writing on legal subjects, as well as activities

121 Ontario rule 5.01(3) and accompanying commentary.

121.1 Ontario rule 5.01(2) and accompanying commentary.

121.2 *Dumais v. Zarnett* (1996), 30 O.R. (3d) 431, 6 O.T.C. 264 (Gen. Div.).

122 C.B.A. Code, chapter VII, rule; Ontario rule 6.04(1); Quebec rules, sections 3.05.04(b)(i) and 4.01.01. See also chapter 15 of the Alberta Rules.

not so connected such as a career in business, politics, broadcasting or the performing arts. In each case, the rules add, the questions of whether the lawyer may properly engage in the outside interest and, if so, to what extent, will be subject to any applicable law or rule of the governing body.[123]

The rules emphasize that lawyers must not allow involvement in an outside interest to impair the exercise of their independent judgment on behalf of clients.[124] The considerations declared in the rules relating to conflicts of interest should govern lawyers' conduct where social, political, economic or other considerations might influence their judgment.[125]

Where the outside interest is unrelated to the legal services being performed for clients, the rules provide, ethical considerations will usually not arise unless the lawyer's conduct brings either the lawyer or the profession into disrepute, or impairs the lawyer's competence as, for example, where the outside interest occupies so much time that clients suffer because of the lawyer's inattention or lack of preparation.[126]

The C.B.A. Code specifies that lawyers must not carry on, manage or be involved in any outside business, investment, property or occupation in such a way that makes it difficult to distinguish in which capacity the lawyer is acting in a particular transaction, or that would give rise to a conflict of interest or duty to a client. When acting or dealing in respect of a transaction involving an outside interest in a business, investment, property or occupation, the Code adds, lawyers must disclose any personal interest, must declare to all parties in the transaction or to their solicitor whether the lawyer is acting on the lawyer's own behalf or in a professional capacity or otherwise, and must adhere throughout the transaction to standards of conduct as high as those that the Code requires of a lawyer engaged in the practice of law.[127]

The C.B.A. Code also specifies that lawyers who have an outside interest in a business, investment, property or occupation must not be identified as lawyers when involved in the outside interest, and that they must ensure that monies received in respect of the day-to-day operation of the outside interest are deposited in an account other than their trust account, unless the monies are received in their professional capacities as lawyers on behalf of the outside interest.[128]

---

123 C.B.A. Code, chapter VII, commentary 1; Ontario rule 6.04(2) and accompanying commentary.

124 Ontario rule 6.04(2).

125 C.B.A. Code, chapter VII, commentary 2.

126 C.B.A. Code, chapter VII, commentary 3; Ontario rule 6.04(2) and accompanying commentary. See also *Re Weare*, [1893] 2 Q.B. 439 (C.A.); and *Cwinn v. Law Society (Upper Canada)* (1980), 28 O.R. (2d) 61 (Div. Ct.), leave to appeal denied and appeal quashed (1980), 28 O.R. (2d) 61n (S.C.C.). In 1964, Chief Justice Wylie of the Borneo High Court held that it was improper for a barrister to act also as a travelling sales representative in ladies underwear and dresses: *Re An Advocate*, [1964] M.L.J. 1.

127 C.B.A. Code, chapter VII, commentary 4; British Columbia rules, chapter 7, rule 6.

128 C.B.A. Code, chapter VII, commentary 5.

Finally, the Code provides that in order to be compatible with the practice of law, the other profession, business or occupation must be an honourable one that does not detract from the status of the lawyer or the legal profession generally, and must not be such as would likely result in a conflict of interest between the lawyer and a client.[129]

25.11 INTERPROVINCIAL LAW FIRMS[130]

Ontario's rules of professional conduct provide that lawyers may enter into agreements with lawyers in other Canadian jurisdictions to form an interprovincial law firm, that is, a firm that carries on the practice of law in more than one province or territory of Canada, provided that they comply with specified requirements.[131]

Those requirements are, first, that the members of interprovincial law firms qualified to practise in Ontario must comply with all the requirements of the Law Society;[132] second, that the members of interprovincial law firms qualified to practise in Ontario must ensure that the books, records and accounts pertaining to their practice in Ontario be available in Ontario upon demand by the Law Society's auditors or their designated agents;[133] and third, that the members of interprovincial law firms qualified to practise in Ontario must ensure that they do not permit their partners, associates, or employees who are not qualified to practise in Ontario to be held out as or to represent themselves as qualified to practise in Ontario.[134]

25.12 DUTIES OF ARTICLING PRINCIPALS AND STUDENTS

The Ontario rules of professional conduct specify that lawyers who serve as principals to articling students have a duty to provide to those students meaningful training and exposure to and involvement in work that will furnish them with knowledge and experience of the practical aspects of the law, together with an appreciation of the traditions and ethics of the profession.[135] The rules also specify that articling students have a duty to their principal and to their principal's firm

---

129 C.B.A. Code, chapter VII, commentary 6. See also New Brunswick rules, Part F, rule 3.

130 In *Black v. Law Society (Alberta)*, [1989] 1 S.C.R. 591 the Supreme Court of Canada struck down two rules of the Law Society of Alberta on the ground that they offended mobility rights guaranteed by s. 6 of the *Charter of Rights*. The first rule prohibited members of the law society from entering into a partnership with anyone who was not an active member ordinarily resident in Alberta. The second rule prohibited members from being partners in more than one firm.

131 Ontario rule 3.07(1).

132 Ontario rule 3.07(2).

133 Ontario rule 3.07(3).

134 Ontario rule 3.07(4).

135 Ontario rule 5.02(2).

to act in good faith in fulfilling all the obligations arising from the articling experience.[136]

25.13 SEXUAL HARASSMENT

The issue of whether rules of professional conduct should expressly proscribe lawyers from having sexual relations with clients while representing them and other forms of sexual harassment has been the subject of frequent debate over the last few years.[137] Lawyers have been found guilty of professional misconduct on a number of occasions even in the absence of an explicit prohibition.[138]

A particular concern has arisen in matrimonial litigation, where emotionally vulnerable clients may need protection from even consensual sexual relations initiated by lawyers on whom they are dependent.[139]

In 1992 the Law Society in Ontario adopted a new rule of professional conduct that proscribes sexual harassment of colleagues, staff, clients or other persons in a professional context.[140] The rule defines sexual harassment as one or a series of incidents involving unwelcome sexual advances, requests for sexual favours, or other verbal or physical conduct of a sexual nature:

(i) when such conduct might reasonably be expected to cause insecurity, discomfort, offence or humilation to another person or group; or

---

136 Ontario rule 5.02(3).

137 See, for example, Jody Meir, "Sexual Harassment In Law Firms: Should Attorneys Be Disciplined Under the Lawyer Codes?"(1990) 4 Georgetown Journal of Legal Ethics 169; Carrie Mennel-Meadow, "The Comparative Sociology of Women Lawyers and the "Feminization' of the Legal Profession" (1986) 24 Osgoode Hall L.J. 897; and Matthew Certosimo, "A Conflict is a Conflict is a Conflict: Fiduciary Duty and Lawyer-Client Sexual Relations" (1993), 16 Dalhousie Law Journal 446.

138 See, for example, *Re Coccimiglio*, report of discipline hearing panel adopted by Convocation, June 20, 1991, (Ontario) in which Convocation rejected a recommendation that a lawyer be suspended for three months and imposed as a penalty a one-year suspension where a lawyer in two matrimonial cases separated by a year propositioned one client to have sexual relations with him and sexually assaulted another client while propositioning her; *Re Ramsay*, report of discipline hearing panel adopted by Convocation, November 26, 1992, (Ontario) in which a lawyer was publicly reprimanded for offering to waive his fee for preparing a codicil to a client's will if she would return to his office without wearing a brassiere and give him a complete viewing of her breasts; *Re Stanton*, 708 P. 2d 325 (1985), in which a lawyer was disbarred as a result of his conviction in the criminal courts for sexually assaulting a client; *Commission on Professional Ethics and Conduct of Iowa State Bar Assn. v. Floy*, 334 N.W. 2d 739 (Iowa, 1983), in which a lawyer was suspended for 18 months as a result of his conviction in the criminal courts of the misdemeanour of making obscene telephone calls; *Cincinnati Bar Assn. v. Fettner*, 8 Ohio St. 3d 17, (1983); *Re Wood*, 265 Ind. 616, (1976); *Re Wood (No. 2)*, 489 N.E. 2d 1189 (Ind., 1986); and *Re Liebowitz*, 101 N.J. 632 (1985).

139 See Lawrence Dubin, "Sex and the Divorce Lawyer: Is the Client Off Limits?"(1987-88) 1 Georgetown Journal of Legal Ethics 585; Geoffrey C. Hazard, Jr., "Lawyer-Client Sex Relations Are Taboo", National Law Journal (April 15, 1991), p. 13; and Peter J. Riga, "Hands Off the Clients", National Law Journal (July 1, 1991), p. 13.

140 Ontario rule 5.03(2). See also chapter 1, rule 9 of the Alberta rules, which provides that "A lawyer must not sexually harass a colleague, staff member, client or other person."

(ii) when submission to such conduct is made implicitly or explicitly a condition for the provision of professional services; or

(iii) when submission to such conduct is made implicitly or explicitly a condition of employment; or

(iv) when submission to or rejection of such conduct is used as a basis for any employment decision (including, but not limited to, matters of promotion, raise in salary, job security and benefits affecting the employee); or

(v) when such conduct has the purpose or effect of interfering with a person's work performance or creating an intimidating, hostile or offensive work environment.[141]

The rule also includes the following non-exhaustive list of types of behaviour that constitute sexual harassment: sexual jokes causing embarrassment or offence, told or carried out after the joker has been advised that they are embarrassing or offensive, or that are by their nature clearly embarrassing or offensive; leering; the display of sexually offensive material; sexually degrading words used to describe a person; derogatory or degrading remarks directed towards members of one sex or one sexual orientation; sexually suggestive or obscene comments or gestures; unwelcome inquiries or comments about a person's sex life; unwelcome sexual flirtations, advances, or propositions; persistent unwanted contact or attention after the end of a consensual relationship; requests for sexual favours; unwanted touching; verbal abuse or threats; and sexual assault.[142]

Finally, the rule provides that sexual harassment can occur in the form of behaviour by men towards women, between men, between women or by women towards men.[143]

25.14 REPRESENTATION OF CLIENTS UNDER A DISABILITY

In August 1993, the Canadian Bar Association considered a proposal that its Code of Professional Conduct be amended by the addition of a new rule dealing with lawyers' professional responsibilities in circumstances in which they reasonably believe that a client's capacity to make adequately considered decisions in connection with the matter is limited, whether because of minority, mental disability or for some other reason. In such circumstances, the proposed rule would provide, lawyers are required to maintain a routine client-lawyer relationship, as far as reasonably possible.[144]

The proposed rule would provide that the lawyer must refuse to take instructions from the client, however, if the lawyer reasonably believes that the client cannot adequately instruct the lawyer to act in the client's own interests. Should

141 Ontario rule 5.03(1).

142 Ontario rule 5.03(1) and accompanying commentary.

143 Ontario rule 5.03(1) and accompanying commentary.

144 C.B.A. Code, chapter III, proposed rule, paragraph A.

the lawyer form such a belief in the course of providing legal services in which further instructions will be required, the lawyer would be required to secure the appointment of a substitute decision-maker for the client.[145]

Nothing in the proposed rule would prevent a lawyer from representing a client who is apparently incapable of instructing a lawyer if the lawyer is appointed by a court or tribunal or by operation of statute. Nor would anything in the rule prevent a lawyer from representing a client who is apparently incapable of instructing a lawyer in a proceeding in which some aspect of the client's mental capacity is in issue.[146]

The commentary to the proposed rule specifies that the lawyer should objectively consider the client's capacity (a) to understand the subject matter and the options being discussed, and (b) to appreciate the consequences of the options. The commentary would also caution that a client's capacity may change from time to time.[147]

25.15 DISCRIMINATION

In Ontario, the Law Society's rules of professional conduct prohibit lawyers from discriminating on the grounds of race, ancestry, place of origin, colour, ethnic origin, citizenship, creed, sex, sexual orientation, age, record of offences, marital status, family status or disability in the employment of other lawyers or articled students, or in dealings with other members of the profession or any other persons.[148] The Alberta rules contain a similar rule[149] as does the British Columbia Professional Conduct Handbook.[150]

145 C.B.A. Code, chapter III, proposed rule, paragraph B.

146 C.B.A. Code, chapter III, proposed rule, paragraph C.

147 C.B.A. Code, chapter III, proposed commentary, paragraph 2.

148 Ontario rule 5.04(1) and (3) and accompanying commentary. The rule also provides that lawyers have a "special responsibility" to respect human rights laws in force in Ontario. As a result of amendments that came into force in 2000, the rule now includes extensive commentary on the implications of discrimination.

149 Chapter 1, rule 8. See also "Is Bias Unethical?", National Law Journal, November 29, 1993, p. 14.

150 B.C. Rules, chapter 11, rules 1 to 4.

26

Discipline Proceedings

26.1 PURPOSES OF DISCIPLINE PROCEEDINGS

The purposes of law society discipline proceedings are not to punish offenders and exact retribution, but rather to protect the public, maintain high professional standards, and preserve public confidence in the legal profession.

In cases in which professional misconduct is either admitted or proven, the penalty should be determined by reference to these purposes. If a lawyer has committed a criminal offence it is for the criminal courts, not the legal profession, to inflict punishment. All sanctions necessarily have punitive effects, which are tolerable results of the protective and deterrent functions of the discipline process. The goals of the process are, nevertheless, nonpunitive.

The seriousness of the misconduct is the prime determinant of the penalty imposed. In the most serious cases, the lawyer's right to practise will be terminated regardless of extenuating circumstances and the probability of recurrence. If a lawyer misappropriates a substantial sum of clients' money, that lawyer's right to practise will almost certainly be determined, for the profession must protect the public against the possibility of a recurrence of the misconduct, even if that possibility is remote. Any other result would undermine public trust in the profession.[1]

---

1 The purposes of discipline proceedings are discussed in Mark M. Orkin, *Legal Ethics: A Study of Professional Conduct* (Toronto: Cartwright & Sons, 1957), p. 197, citing *Ex parte Brounsall* (1778), 2 Cowp. 829; William J. Smith, "Disciplinary Proceedings Before the Law Society", 1971 Law Society of Upper Canada Special Lectures 285 at 294; Stuart Thom, "Discipline", Law Society of Upper Canada Gazette, vol. 9, no. 2 (June, 1975), pp. 89-91; Bette Stephenson, "A Self-Governing Profession", Law Society of Upper Canada Gazette, vol. 18, no. 2 (June 1984), pp. 202-203; Charles Wolfram, *Modern Legal Ethics* (St. Paul, Minnesota: West, 1986), p. 79; Cynthia A. Kelly, "Lawyer Sanctions: Looking Back Through the Looking Glass" (1987-88) 1 Georgetown Journal of Legal Ethics 469 at 470, citing *State ex rel. Oklahoma Bar Assn. v. Raskin*, 642 P. 2d 262 at 267 (Oklahoma, 1982), and *Garlow v. State Bar of California*, 640 P. 2d 1106 (1982); American Bar Association,

Thus, in a 1985 decision[2] a discipline hearing panel in Ontario recommended that a lawyer who had been found guilty of misappropriation be disbarred notwithstanding evidence that satisfied the panel that he was "a man who for 17 years had an unblemished record, who placed service to his clients ahead of personal gain, who was a good father and respected member of his community, and who acted at a time when he was under considerable financial and emotional stress . . ." The panel's reason:

> The Society cannot countenance theft and fraud by its members, and must express its disapproval in no uncertain terms. The penalty of disbarment is not meant to be reserved only for members who are thoroughly lacking in good qualities; experience shows that the penalty attends the tragic downfall of good lawyers who succumb to pressure as frequently as it is the fitting conclusion of an evil career.

In all but the most serious cases, however, the benchers must scrutinize the offender as well as the offence to determine whether the likelihood of future misconduct justifies the revocation of the lawyer's right to practise.

Although the protection of the public is often said to be a principal objective of the discipline process, law societies also have a duty to deal fairly with members whose livelihood and reputation are affected. The Ontario Court of Appeal has emphasized that nothing is to be gained by giving one of these functions priority over the other.[3]

26.2 ARE DISCIPLINE PROCEEDINGS CIVIL OR CRIMINAL?

Many of the disciplinary issues that law societies confront today have to do with the degree to which their proceedings can fairly be analogized to the proceedings of criminal courts. The extent to which the procedural safeguards available to persons accused of criminal offences are also available to members of self-governing professions is raised at every phase of the disciplinary process. During the investigation phase, to what extent is the law society entitled to examine, copy, and seize documents, and what limitations does section 8 of the *Canadian Charter of Rights and Freedoms* impose? During the pre-hearing phase, what obligation of disclosure is placed on the law society, and what obligation of disclosure, if any, is imposed on lawyers? During the hearing phase, what is the burden of proof, and is the lawyer a compellable witness? Does the use of a transcript of evidence given by a lawyer in parallel proceedings violate the right not to have incriminating evidence used to incriminate oneself under section 13 of the *Charter*?

Standards for Lawyer Discipline , Standard 7.1; *Re McGough*, 793 P. 2d 430 at 438 (1990); and *Bolton v. Law Society*, [1993] 1 W.W.R. 512 (C.A.).

2 *Re Milrod*, report adopted by Convocation, January 30, 1986.

3 *W.D. Latimer Co. v. Bray* (1974), 6 O.R. (2d) 129 (C.A.).

In form, a discipline hearing bears a greater resemblance to a criminal proceeding than to a civil proceeding. A lawyer is accused of professional misconduct or conduct unbecoming a barrister and solicitor in a complaint that alleges that he or she is guilty of charges that often amount to criminal offences. The law society's counsel, whose role is similar in some ways to that of a crown attorney, bears the burden of proof. The standard of proof requires competent evidence of at least clear and convincing weight. Where it is alleged that the lawyer is guilty of misconduct that also amounts to a criminal offence, the standard of proof is so close to the criminal standard that there is little if any difference between them in practice.[3.1] At the conclusion of the hearing, the adjudicators must decide whether the lawyer is guilty and may impose a penalty that can be as severe as disbarment; as Laskin J.A., of the Ontario Court of Appeal observed in a dissenting opinion in a 1994 case, for some professionals a finding of professional misconduct is more serious than a criminal conviction.[3.2] Even the fact that the discipline hearing panel is likely to be dominated by members of the practitioner's profession has a parallel in the right of persons accused of serious criminal offences to be tried by a jury of their peers.[4]

Ultimately, however, the analogy breaks down. In Ontario, the rules of evidence applicable in civil proceedings apply in discipline proceedings.[5] At present, the lawyer is in theory a compellable witness;[6] the constitutionality of legislative provisions empowering disciplinary tribunals to compel members to testify at their own hearings has been upheld, since the *Charter* came into force, by the Quebec Court of Appeal.[7] Lawyers have a duty during audit investigations to provide their governing body with access to their books, records, and files, and to provide any explanations the investigators require.[8] Lawyers also have a duty

---

3.1 See part 26.17 *infra.*

3.2 *Howe v. Institute of Chartered Accountants of Ontario* (1994), 19 O.R. (3d) 483 (C.A.) at pp. 495-496.

4 See Gavin MacKenzie, "Lawyer Discipline and the Independence of the Bar: Can Lawyers Still Govern Themselves?", Law Society of Upper Canada Gazette, vol. 24, no. 4 (December 1990), p. 319 at 324-325. See also Geoffrey C. Hazard, Jr., "Grievance Machinery Grievances", National Law Journal (April 23, 1990), pp. 13-14. In *Carruthers v. College of Nurses of Ontario* (1996), 31 O.R. (3d) 377, 96 O.A.C. 41, 141 D.L.R. (4th) 325 (Div. Ct.), the Divisional Court held that the rule against multiple convictions for the same delict (the principle in *R. v. Kienapple* (1974), [1975] 1 S.C.R. 729, 26 C.R.N.S. 1, 15 C.C.C. (2d) 524, 44 D.L.R. (3d) 351, 1 N.R. 322) applies in professional discipline proceedings where there is both a sufficient factual nexus and a sufficient legal nexus between the allegations.

5 *Law Society Act*, R.S.O. 1990, c. L.8, s. 33(9).

6 *Law Society Act*, R.S.O. 1990, c. L.8, s. 33(6). In practice, the law society's counsel never calls a lawyer charged with professional misconduct as a witness, and Convocation has adopted a recommendation (which requires legislative change) that s. 33(6) be repealed.

7 In *Belhumeur c. Barreau du Québec* (*sub nom.* Belhumeur v. Discipline Committee of the Quebec Bar Association) (1983), 34 C.R. (3d) 279 (Que. S.C.), affirmed (1988), 54 D.L.R. (4th) 105 (Que. C.A.), the court held that a provision compelling a lawyer to testify at his or her own hearing offends neither s. 7 nor s. 11(c) of the *Charter of Rights.*

8 By-law 19 under the *Law Society Act*, R.S.O. 1990, c. L.8, as amended.

to reply promptly to communications from their governing body.[9] Failing to co-operate in an investigation can constitute professional misconduct.[10]

In a 1979 decision,[11] in dismissing an appeal based upon an argument that particulars in a complaint of professional misconduct were duplicitous, the Ontario Divisional Court said that charges brought against a professional person by his or her governing body should not be approached as if they were counts in an indictment alleging that the person committed offences contrary to the *Criminal Code*. The Divisional Court has also upheld orders disbarring a lawyer and cancelling the registration of a doctor for professional misconduct, notwithstanding the practitioners' acquittal of criminal charges based upon the same facts.[12]

In another 1979 decision[12.1] the same Court held that though the principles governing the procedure to be followed by a discipline committee are no different from those governing a judge on an application to sever counts in a multiple-count criminal indictment, the public interest in the former case requires an expeditious investigation into the alleged misconduct. The Court held that it should decline to interfere with a discipline committee's decision not to sever allegations of misconduct unless such a decision results in manifest prejudice or injustice.

Most importantly, for the purpose of determining whether section 11 of the *Canadian Charter of Rights and Freedoms* applies to discipline proceedings, the Supreme Court of Canada has drawn a sharp distinction between matters "of a public nature, intended to promote public order and welfare within a public sphere of activity" and "private, domestic or disciplinary matters which are regulatory, protective, or corrective and which are primarily intended to maintain discipline, professional integrity and professional standards or to regulate conduct in a limited sphere of activity." In the latter case, section 11 is applicable only if the person affected is subject to true penal consequences, such as imprisonment.[13]

---

9 C.B.A. Code, chapter XV, commentary 2; Ontario rule 6.02; British Columbia rules, chapter 13, rule 3; New Brunswick rules, Part D, rule 1.

10 *Matthews v. Board of Directors of Physiotherapy* (1986), 54 O.R. (2d) 375 (Ont. Div. Ct.), affirmed (1987), 61 O.R. (2d) 475 (C.A.).

11 *Stevens v. Law Society (Upper Canada)* (1979), 55 O.R. (2d) 405 (Div. Ct.).

12 The case in which the court upheld a disbarment order despite the lawyer's prior acquittal of criminal fraud charges is *Re Sugg and Law Society of Upper Canada*, action no. 156/86, March 30, 1988 (unreported); the case in which the court upheld an order cancelling a doctor's registration for professional misconduct despite the doctor's acquittal in parallel criminal proceedings is *Gillen v. College of Physicians & Surgeons (Ontario)* (1989), 68 O.R. (2d) 278 (Div. Ct.).

12.1 *Stone v. Law Society of Upper Canada* (1979), 26 O.R. (2d) 166, 102 D.L.R. (3d) 176 (Div. Ct.)

13 *R. v. Wigglesworth*, [1987] 2 S.C.R. 541, and three companion cases, *Burnham v. Metropolitan Toronto Chief of Police*, [1987] 2 S.C.R. 572; *Trumbley v. Metropolitan Toronto Police Force*, [1987] 2 S.C.R. 577; and *Trimm v. Durham Regional Police Force*, [1987] 2 S.C.R. 582.

(The mere fact that a tribunal is empowered to impose fines is not in itself an indicator that a practitioner is subject to true penal consequences. Justice Wilson, who delivered the majority judgment for the court, specified that "a true penal consequence which would attract the application of section 11 is imprisonment or a fine which by its magnitude would appear to be imposed for the purpose of redressing the wrong done to society at large rather than for the maintenance of internal discipline within the limited sphere of activity." She added that one indicium of the purpose of a particular fine is whether fines form part of the government's consolidated revenue fund or are used for the purpose of the governing body. In the latter case, it is more likely that fines are imposed purely to maintain discipline within the limited sphere of activity.)[14]

In the same case, the court specifically left open the question whether the procedural protections constitutionally guaranteed under section 7 of the *Charter* are available in professional discipline proceedings. Justice Wilson, however, strongly implied that they are: "It is, in my view, preferable to restrict s. 11 to the most serious offences known to our law, that is, criminal and penal matters, and to leave other 'offences' subject to the more flexible criteria of 'fundamental justice' in s. 7."[15]

The view that section 7 applies to legislation governing professions has been reinforced by later decisions of the Supreme Court of Canada.[16] Also, in

14 *R. v. Wigglesworth*, *ibid.*, p. 561. In *Spicer v. Assn. of Professional Engineers, Geologists & Geophysicists (Alberta)* (1989), 95 A.R. 132, the Alberta Court of Queen's Bench held that a maximum fine of $10,000 is not of such a magnitude that the court should conclude that it was imposed to redress a societal wrong rather than to maintain internal discipline.

15 *R. v. Wigglesworth*, *ibid.*, p. 558.

16 The later decisions of the Supreme Court of Canada that reinforce the view that s. 7 of the *Charter* applies to proceedings of professional bodies are: *Thomson Newspapers Ltd. v. Canada (Director of Investigation & Research)*, [1990] 1 S.C.R. 425; and *R. v. McKinlay Transport Ltd.*, [1990] 1 S.C.R. 627. Although it is difficult to derive any principle from a decision of a five-judge court in which one judge dissents and two others dissent in part, it does seem to be tolerably clear that subs. 11(c) and s. 13 of the *Charter* are not exhaustive of the right to remain silent and the right against self-incrimination. The British Columbia Court of Appeal, in *Wilson v. British Columbia (Medical Services Commission)* (1988), [1989] 2 W.W.R. 1 (B.C. C.A.), leave to appeal to S.C.C. refused [1989] 3 W.W.R. xxi (note) (S.C.C.) and the Nova Scotia Court of Appeal, in *Re Khaliq-Kareemi* (*sub nom.* Khaliq-Kareemi v. Nova Scotia (Health Services & Insurance Comm.) (1989), 57 D.L.R. (4th) 505 (N.S. C.A.), leave to appeal to S.C.C. refused (1989), 93 N.S.R. (2d) 269 (note) (S.C.C.) have held that the right to liberty protected by s. 7 embraces the right to practise one's profession. In *Arlington Crane Service Ltd. v. Ontario (Minister of Labour)* (1988), 67 O.R. (2d) 225 (H.C.), Justice Henry of the High Court of Justice declined to follow *Wilson*, as he felt bound by the Ontario Court of Appeal's decision in *R. v. Quesnel* (1985), 53 O.R. (2d) 338, leave to appeal to S.C.C. refused (1986), 55 O.R. (2d) 543 (S.C.C.) and by the Supreme Court of Canada's decision in *R. v. Videoflicks*, [1986] 2 S.C.R. 713 (*sub nom.* R. v. Edwards Books & Art Ltd.), to hold that the right to work is not protected by s. 7. The Ontario Divisional Court came to the same conclusion in *Feldman v. Law Society of Upper Canada* (December 3, 1987), Doc. 639/85 (Ont. Div. Ct.). The Quebec Court of Appeal came to the same conclusion in *Béliveau c. Comité de discipline (Barreau du Québec)* (1992), 101 D.L.R. (4th) 324 (C.A. Qué.). See also *Nisbett v. Manitoba (Human*

a 1992 decision of Chief Justice Hickman of the Supreme Court of Newfoundland Trial Division, section 7 of the *Charter* was invoked to set aside a suspension of a lawyer who was deprived of his right to make full answer and defence, due to the unavailability of witnesses, after his hearing was inexplicably delayed for over five years.[17] The Supreme Court of Canada has confirmed that discipline proceedings specifically involving lawyers are regulatory rather than criminal or penal in nature and that, accordingly, section 11 of the *Charter* is inapplicable to such proceedings.[18]

Thus, many of the procedural safeguards available to persons charged with criminal offences are not available to a lawyer charged with professional misconduct. The principle articulated in the American Bar Association's Model Rules of Professional Conduct applies equally in Canada: "Disciplinary proceedings are neither civil nor criminal but are *sui generis*."

26.3 IMPARTIALITY OF ADJUDICATORS AND THE INDEPENDENCE OF LAW SOCIETY'S COUNSEL

One reason for public scepticism about the disciplinary processes of self-governing professions is that representatives of the same disciplinary agency serve as investigators, prosecutors, and judges, while in the courts these functions are performed by representatives of organizations that are wholly independent of each other. It is important that the roles do not become blurred and, particularly, that the adjudicators do not become prosecutors. The law society's counsel, though their fees or salaries are paid by the organization governed by the adjudicators, must represent only the public. Adjudicators must not interfere in the conduct of cases. Counsel must be free to conduct every proceeding without taking instructions from members of the bench.

In Ontario, the *Law Society Act* states that the decision whether a lawyer should be charged with professional misconduct is to be made by one or more members of the law society's governing body. In practice, the decision is made by the chair and the vice-chairs of the discipline committee. Although the involvement of benchers in an essentially prosecutorial responsibility may appear to be inappropriate, it can be justified on the basis that the charging decision is sufficiently important for it to be made by persons in authority who are elected and, therefore, accountable. Concerns about compromising impartiality are satisfactorily answered if those responsible for authorizing a

Rights Commission), [1992] 3 W.W.R. 582 (Man. Q.B.); *Stephen v. College of Physicians & Surgeons (Saskatchewan)* (1990), 89 Sask R. 25 (Q.B.); *Kopyto v. Law Society of Upper Canada* (1993), 18 Admin. L.R. (2d) 54 (Ont. Div. Ct.); and *Markandey v. Board of Ophthalmic Dispensers (Ontario)* (March 14, 1994), Doc. Toronto RE 2661/93 (Ont. Gen. Div.). In *New Brunswick (Minister of Health) v. G.(J.)*, [1999] 3 S.C.R. 46, the Supreme Court of Canada ruled that the Charter's section 7 guarantee of security of the person extends beyond the criminal law sphere to protect against other types of civil or administrative state actions that have a "serious and profound effect on a person's psychological integrity". The case dealt with the right to legal aid in child protection proceedings.

17 *Harvey v. Law Society (Newfoundland)* (1992), 88 D.L.R. (4th) 487 (Nfld. T.D.).

18 *Pearlman v. Law Society (Manitoba)*, [1991] 2 S.C.R. 869.

complaint of professional misconduct play no further role in the prosecution of the case and are disqualified from adjudicative responsibilities.[19]

In a 1989 decision of the Alberta Court of Queen's Bench,[20] the College of Physicians and Surgeons of Alberta was prohibited from taking further disciplinary proceedings against the applicant on the ground that the college's investigating committee was empowered to make a preliminary decision, to recommend sanctions to the college's council, and to initiate new proceedings that it would also adjudicate. The Supreme Court of the Northwest Territories came to the same conclusion in a 1988 case.[20.1]

26.4 INVESTIGATION OF COMPLAINTS

Most law society investigations result from complaints received either from present or former clients or from other members of the profession. Other investigations are a result of random audits authorized by legislation, media coverage, or reports from law enforcement or other agencies.

As a result of a 1996 decision of the Saskatchewan Court of Queen's Bench[20.2] and a 1998 decision of Convocation of the Law Society of Upper Canada[20.3] it has become apparent that there are constitutional limitations on what law societies are empowered to investigate. As self-governing professional bodies whose authority is derived from provincial legislation, law societies must not encroach upon Parliament's exclusive jurisdiction over criminal law by undertaking an investigation into what is in pith and substance the commission of a specific criminal offence by a named person.

Thus, in the Saskatchewan case, the Court quashed a complaint of conduct unbecoming a lawyer in which it was alleged that a lawyer had assisted an identified person to breach section 121 of the *Criminal Code* (fraud on the government) and attempting to conceal the breach. In the Ontario case, Convocation dismissed a complaint in which it was alleged that a lawyer had failed to comply with the *Income Tax Act* by failing to report income in connection with accounts rendered to a client.

---

19 See *French v. Law Society (Upper Canada) (No. 2)* (1975), 8 O.R. (2d) 193 at 198 (C.A.), application for leave to appeal to S.C.C. dismissed without written reasons (1975), 8 O.R. (2d) 193n (S.C.); *Re French* (1982), 39 O.R. (2d) 666 at 670 (Div. Ct.); *Withrow v. Larkin*, 955 S. Ct. 1456 (1975); and Gavin MacKenzie "Lawyer Discipline and the Independence of the Bar: Can Lawyers Still Govern Themselves?" Law Society of Upper Canada Gazette, vol. 24, no. 4 (December, 1990), p. 319 at 323-324.

20 *Rosenstock v. College of Physicians and Surgeons (Alberta)*, [1989] 2 W.W.R. 611 (Alta. Q.B.).

20.1 *Barsoum v. Pape*, [1988] N.W.T.R. 368.

20.2 *Stromberg v. Law Society (Saskatchewan)*, 132 D.L.R. (4th) 470, [1996] 3 W.W.R. 389, 36 Admin. L.R. (2d) 181, 139 Sask. R. 182 (Q.B.), additional reasons at [1996] 10 W.W.R. 737, 6 C.P.C. (4th) 157, 149 Sask. R. 226, 44 Admin. L.R. (2d) 65 (Q.B.)

20.3 *Re a Solicitor*, Reasons of Convocation, July 14, 1998 (Ontario).

The fact that conduct that constitutes professional misconduct or conduct unbecoming a barrister and solicitor may also constitute a crime is not in itself a bar to disciplinary proceedings respecting that conduct.[20.4] A person may be answerable in both the criminal courts and in professional disciplinary proceedings for the same conduct.[20.5] Thus, for example, on the basis of the same incident a lawyer may be found guilty of professional misconduct for misappropriating client funds held by the lawyer in trust, and may also be found guilty of theft as defined in the *Criminal Code* by a court of criminal jurisdiction. Moreover, a lawyer who has been found guilty of a criminal offence may on the basis of such a conviction be disciplined by a law society for conduct unbecoming a barrister and solicitor. What must be determined is the dominant feature or focus of the law society investigation. The Court expressed the applicable principles as follows in the Saskatchewan case:

> The potential for a constitutional challenge increases if the description of the misconduct parallels the definition of a criminal offence, especially if the misconduct does not appear to have an "unprofessional" underpinning independent of its definition as an offence under the *Criminal Code*. In other words if the misconduct is "unbecoming" *because* it constitutes a crime, then the potential for challenge is significant. . .[20.6]
>
> . . .a disciplinary proceeding begins to go off the rails when it approaches the matter on the basis that the conduct is unprofessional because it constitutes a criminal offence not yet determined by the criminal courts. It goes completely off the rails when its net effect is to investigate and determine whether the lawyer has engaged in conduct which is directly or indirectly characterized as a specific criminal offence. It has by then unsurped the exclusive domain of the federal government and the criminal courts over criminal law and procedure, a head of power clearly assigned pursuant to the division of powers in the Constitution to the federal government.[20.7]

Lawyers are required by regulations and by rules of professional conduct to co-operate in investigations. In Ontario, they are required to produce "all evidence, vouchers, records, books, [and] papers" and to "furnish such explanations" as are required by a person designated by the chair or vice-chairs of the discipline committee to conduct an investigation for the purpose of

---

20.4 See *Imrie v. Institute of Chartered Accountants (Ontario)*, 28 D.L.R. (3d) 53 at 55, [1972] 3 O.R. 275 (H.C.); and *Rosenbaum v. Law Society (Manitoba)*, 150 D.L.R. (3d) 352, [1983] 5 W.W.R. 752, 22 Man. R. (2d) 260, 2 Admin. L.R. 210, 6 C.C.C. (3d) 472 (Q.B.), affirmed (1983), [1984] 4 W.W.R. 95, 7 Admin. L.R. 77, 8 C.C.C. (3d) 256, 3 D.L.R. (4th) 768, 25 Man. R. (2d) 154 (C.A.), leave to appeal refused (1984), 27 Man. R. (2d) 159, 55 N.R. 400 (S.C.C.).

20.5 *R. v. Wigglesworth*, [1987] 2 S.C.R. 541, [1988] 1 W.W.R. 193, 45 D.L.R. (4th) 235, 81 N.R. 161, 24 O.A.C. 321, 61 Sask. R. 105, 28 Admin. L.R. 294, 37 C.C.C. (3d) 385, 60 C.R. (3d) 193, 32 C.R.R. 219 (S.C.C.).

20.6 *Stromberg v. Law Society (Saskatchewan)*, 132 D.L.R. (4th) 470 at 488, [1996] 3 W.W.R. 389, 36 Admin. L.R. (2d) 181, 139 Sask. R. 182 (Q.B.), additional reasons at [1996] 10 W.W.R. 737, 6 C.P.C. (4th) 157, 149 Sask. R. 226, 44 Admin. L.R. (2d) 65 (Q.B.).

20.7 *Ibid.*, at 498.

determining whether regulations governing funds held in trust for clients, books and records, and the filing of annual statutory declarations and reports of public accountants have been complied with.[21] Lawyers are also required by rules of professional conduct to reply promptly to any communication from their governing body.[22] The Ontario Court of Appeal has upheld a judgment of the Divisional Court in which that court ruled that failing to co-operate in an investigation by one's governing body can constitute professional misconduct.[23]

Issues concerning the governing body's right to examine communications whose confidentiality is protected by solicitor-client privilege do not normally arise in investigations initiated as a result of a complaint from a lawyer's client because solicitor-client privilege and confidentiality are almost invariably waived by the complainant, either expressly or impliedly. Moreover, the Court of Appeal in England has held that provisions empowering investigators to require production of relevant documents override any privilege or confidence that might otherwise subsist between solicitor and client.[24] The Alberta rules expressly provide that "a lawyer must disclose confidential information to the Law Society when required to do so by the Law Society."[24.1] The governing body must itself respect the obligation of confidence and must not use privileged information for any purpose except the investigation and any consequential proceedings.[25]

In a 1995 decision, the Saskatchewan Court of Appeal upheld an order requiring a law firm that was under investigation by the Law Society to produce to the Law Society's investigating committee two legal opinions that it had obtained concerning the firm's involvement in transactions between its client and a third party. The Court of Appeal emphasized that the opinions were part of the factual nexus relating to the actual matter under investigation — the firm's decision not to report the transactions to the Law Society — and not part of the process of the members of the firm in seeking to defend themselves.[25.1]

---

21 By-law 19 under the *Law Society Act*, R.S.O. 1990, c. L.8, as amended.

22 See note 9, *supra*.

23 *Matthews v. Board of Directors of Physiotherapy* (1986), 54 O.R. (2d) 375 (Div. Ct.), affirmed (1987), 61 O.R. (2d) 475 (C.A.). In *Artinian v. College of Physicians & Surgeons (Ontario)* (1990), 73 O.R. (2d) 704, the Divisional Court held that, fundamentally, all professionals have a duty to co-operate with their governing body.

24 *Parry-Jones v. Law Society*, [1968] 1 All E.R. 177 (C.A.).

24.1 Chapter 7, rule 8(a).

25 See *Johnston v. Law Society (Prince Edward Island)* (1982), 37 Nfld. and P.E.I.R. 142 (P.E.I. S.C.), reversed (1985), 53 Nfld. & P.E.I.R. 181 (P.E.I. C.A.), in which the court observed that the privileges afforded to the legal profession and the right of self-government carry obligations to the public and require that legislation respecting the investigation of complaints be given a broad and liberal interpretation that gives the public the benefit of that interpretation.

25.1 *Law Society (Saskatchewan) v. Robertson Stromberg* (*sub nom.* Robertson Stromberg, Re) (1994), [1995] 1 W.W.R. 112, 119 D.L.R. (4th) 551, 124 Sask. R. 259 (Q.B.), affirmed, [1995] 3 W.W.R. 601, (*sub nom.* Robertson Stromberg, Re) 122 D.L.R. (4th) 433, 128 Sask. R. 107, 85 W.A.C. 107 (C.A.).

The Federal Court of Appeal has held that if signed statements given by a taxpayer to Revenue Canada under compulsion of law are communicated to the police for use in criminal proceedings, a violation of section 7 of the *Canadian Charter of Rights and Freedoms* has occurred.[26] A distinction must be drawn between documents prepared contemporaneously in relation to transactions under investigation, and statements made under compulsion of law by practitioners who have a duty to co-operate in investigations by their governing body. A profession's governing body is likely to be accused of shielding one of its number from criminal investigation if it refuses a request to provide copies of documents in the former category to the police. It should not divulge documents in the latter category.

The United States Supreme Court has held that lawyers cannot constitutionally be required to respond to a complaint of misconduct under threat of sanction for the assertion of the privilege against self-incrimination.[27] The Supreme Court of Maine has held, however, that where during the course of a disciplinary proceeding a lawyer chooses to make statements without invoking the privilege against self-incrimination, those statements may be used in a subsequent criminal proceeding.[28] The Supreme Court of Louisiana has held that the privilege against self-incrimination is applicable only if the testimony sought would subject the lawyer to criminal prosecution. The fact that compliance with a proper demand to produce documents would subject a lawyer to discipline proceedings is not a basis for invoking the privilege.[29]

The constitutionality of statutory provisions empowering the governing bodies of physicians and surgeons to inspect and copy documents in patients' files during random peer assessments has been upheld under sections 7 and 8 of the *Charter* as a reasonable means of monitoring compliance with statutory requirements.[30] It is likely that comparable provisions in legislation bestowing similar powers on law societies would be similarly upheld. In a 1992 decision,[30.1] however, the Saskatchewan Court of Queen's Bench quashed a finding that an optometrist was guilty of professional misconduct when he refused to produce to an accountant who was appointed to investigate conflict of interest allegations,

---

26 *Tyler v. Minister of National Revenue*, [1991] 2 F.C. 68 (C.A.). See also Stephen E. Sherriff, H. Reginald Watson, and Shaun M. Devlin, " 'You Can Run...But You Can't Hide': A Guide To Understanding Lawyer Discipline In Ontario" in Franklin Moskoff (ed.), *Administrative Tribunals: A Practice Handbook for Legal Counsel* (Aurora, Ontario: Canada Law Book Inc., 1989), p. 115 at 122-124.

27 *Spevack v. Klein*, 385 U.S. 511 (1967).

28 *Maine v. Horton*, 561 A. 2d 488 (Me., 1989).

29 *Louisana State Bar Assn. v. Chatelain*, 513 So. 2d 1178 (1987).

30 *Charboneau v. College of Physicians & Surgeons (Ontario)* (1985), 52 O.R. (2d) 552 (H.C.). See also *Bishop v. College of Physicians & Surgeons (British Columbia)* (1985), 22 D.L.R. (4th) 185 (S.C.), affirmed (1986), 26 D.L.R. (4th) 15 (C.A.); *Thomson Newspapers Ltd. v. Canada (Director of Investigation & Research)*, [1990] 1 S.C.R. 425; and *R. v. McKinlay Transport Ltd.*, [1990] 1 S.C.R. 627.

30.1 *Kuntz v. Assn. of Optometrists (Saskatchewan)*, [1993] 3 W.W.R. 651.

his income tax returns and financial records for the relevant years. The court held that the principles of natural justice apply at the investigative stage of proceedings, and that those principles were not complied with by the investigator. A practitioner, the court held,

> is entitled to reasonable disclosure of the purpose of the investigation before being required to produce all of his business and personal financial records. The investigator is only entitled to those documents which specifically relate to the investigation under way. The investigator is not entitled to proceed upon a 'fishing expedition' or a general audit of [the practitioner's] business without providing him with sufficient particulars of the alleged conflict such that [the practitioner] can make a reasoned decision about his position.[30.2]

Generally the law societies will maintain in confidence even the fact that they have received letters of complaint against a lawyer, at least unless and until a notice of hearing has been served. In at least three American jurisdictions (Oregon, Florida, and West Virginia), by way of contrast, clients' complaints against lawyers are completely and permanently public from the day the complaints are received. Oregon pioneered this dramatic departure from the norm in 1976. State bar officials there say that this openness has built public confidence that the state's lawyer discipline system is fair and reliable. They will release over the phone details of the number of complaints received, the number dismissed, and any penalties imposed. The state bar's files containing letters of complaint and details of investigations are available for inspection. Care is taken to ensure that inquiring members of the public understand the distinction between an allegation and a proven fact.[31]

Since law societies are empowered to require lawyers to co-operate in investigations, they almost invariably request responses from lawyers to letters of complaint and to concerns that come to light from other sources. In Ontario, the *Law Society Act* requires discipline proceedings to be initiated only upon the authorization of the discipline committee or its chair or vice-chairs. (Reform proposals approved by Convocation, but not yet enacted, call for the authorization committee to consist of an elected bencher, a lay bencher, and a non-bencher lawyer). Recommendations that proceedings be initiated are generally made by counsel on the basis of the results of investigations, including any response received from lawyers affected, who are not as a rule given a further right to be heard before the authorization committee. Complainants, similarly, do not normally appear before or make submissions to the authorization committee.

30.2 *Ibid.*, p. 661 W.W.R. See also *Broda v. Law Society (Alberta)* (1993), 7 Alta. L.R. (3d) 305 (Alta. Q.B.).

31 Oregon's open complaint process is described in the Report of the Commission on Evaluation of Disciplinary Enforcement (the McKay Commission) to the American Bar Association, May 1991, p. 23, and in Avram Goldstein, "State Bar Is Closed to Oregon's Openness", Detroit *News* (March 17, 1991).

Despite the potentially devastating effect of discipline proceedings on a lawyer's reputation — regardless of the outcome of the case — courts have held that natural justice and fairness do not require the governing body to give a lawyer an opportunity to respond before authorization.[32] This is so despite the fact that in another context the decision whether to initiate disciplinary proceedings has been said to involve the exercise of a quasi-judicial discretion,[33] which would seem to imply a right to notice and hearing on the lawyer's part.

In some American jurisdictions, letters of complaint are absolutely privileged: a lawyer who receives a letter of complaint cannot bring an action for malicious prosecution or defamation. In its May 1991 report to the American Bar Association, the Commission on Evaluation of Disciplinary Enforcement (the McKay Commission) recommended that all jurisdictions provide absolute immunity to complainants. It observed that a small minority of lawyers attempt to intimidate clients who have valid complaints against them by threatening to sue if a complaint is filed. In jurisdictions which provide immunity to complainants, courts have pointed out that the sending of a letter of complaint is almost invariably preceded by a succession of letters, phone calls, threats, and demands, so lawyers usually have many opportunities to intimidate potential complainants by threatening action. The commission concluded that the prospect of being sued as a result of writing a letter of complaint discourages the filing of valid complaints and undermines public confidence in the integrity of the process.[34]

26.5 PARALLEL CRIMINAL AND CIVIL PROCEEDINGS

Many serious discipline proceedings involve allegations of conduct that may be criminal, such as offences relating to affidavits, misappropriation,

32 *Maxwell v. Law Society (New Brunswick)* (1990), 65 D.L.R. (4th) 754 (N.B. Q.B.). In *Von Richter v. Law Society (New Brunswick)* (1991), 116 N.B.R. (2d) 325 (Q.B.), the court held that the *Law Society Act*, s. 20(8) does not require a hearing before a decision is reached that no further action is warranted.

33 *Voratovic v. Law Society (Upper Canada)* (1978), 20 O.R. (2d) 214 (H.C.), where Justice Cromarty ruled that a law society is not liable in damages for the erroneous exercise of its discretion in the absence of bad faith or malice. *Edwards v. Law Society of Upper Canada* (1998), 37 O.R. (3d) 279, 156 D.L.R. (4th) 348 (Gen. Div.) is to the same effect. See also *French v. Law Society (Upper Canada)* (1975), 9 O.R. (2d) 473 at 476 (C.A.).

34 The McKay Commission's reasons for recommending that complainants be absolutely immune from suit are set forth on pp. iv and 26-28 of its report. The New Jersey Supreme Court created the absolute immunity rule on public policy grounds in *Toft v. Ketchum*, 113 A. 2d 671, cert. denied 350 U.S. 887 (1955). The same court, in a 4-3 decision, reaffirmed the rule and commented on the opportunities for intimidation and the need for public confidence in the integrity of the process in *Re Hearing on Immunity for Ethics Complainants*, 477 A. 2d 339 at 340-342 (1984). See also James R. Zazzali, "Disciplining Attorneys: The New Jersey Experience" (1987-88) 1 Georgetown Journal of Legal Ethics 659 at 679-682; and Charles Wolfram, *Modern Legal Ethics* (St. Paul, Minnesota: West, 1986), pp. 100-101.

fraud, obstruction of justice, and sexual improprieties. As discussed above,[34.1] law societies must not encroach upon Parliament's exclusive jurisdiction over criminal law by undertaking an investigation into what is in pith and substance the commission of a specific criminal offence by a named person.

The Ontario Divisional Court has held that a discipline hearing panel of the law society may hear a complaint of professional misconduct while criminal charges are pending, as the law society's responsibility to protect the public could be compromised if it were prohibited from proceeding. Potential prejudice to the accused lawyer is minimized by such protections as the right (guaranteed by section 13 of the *Charter of Rights*) not to have evidence given in a proceeding used to incriminate him or her in subsequent criminal proceedings, the right to bring a motion for an order to change the venue of a criminal trial, and the right to challenge potential jurors peremptorily and for cause.[35] The Saskatchewan Court of Queen's Bench has reached the same conclusion in relation to proceedings before the discipline committee of the College of Physicians and Surgeons.[36]

Similarly, in a 1994 decision,[36.1] the Ontario Divisional Court dismissed an application for an order prohibiting the discipline committee of the Institute of Chartered Accountants of Ontario from proceeding with a hearing pending the final disposition of related civil actions. To permit the disciplinary proceeding to be blocked indefinitely by the existence of civil actions would be inconsistent, the Court held, with a recognition of the public interest in disciplinary proceedings.

Law societies are more likely to hold discipline hearings while criminal proceedings are pending in cases in which misconduct is alleged to have occurred in the accused lawyer's professional capacity, such as in cases involving the misappropriation of client's funds. Law societies are more likely to be willing to await the conclusion of criminal proceedings when the alleged misconduct is unrelated to the lawyer's practice.

34.1 See text accompanying notes 20.2 to 20.7.

35 *Re Cornacchia and Law Society of Upper Canada*, September 26, 1985 (unreported). See also *Stickney v. Trusz* (1974), 3 O.R. (2d) 538 (C.A.), affirmed (1974), 3 O.R. (2d) at 539 (C.A.), leave to appeal to S.C.C. refused (1974), 28 C.R.N.S. at 127 (note) (Ont. C.A.).

36 *Voutsis v. College of Physicians & Surgeons (Saskatchewan)* (1987), 34 C.C.C. (3d) 560 (Sask. Q.B.). See also *R. v. Daigle* (1982), 32 C.R. (3d) 388 at 393-394 (Que. S.C.). In *Re Whyte and Provincial Medical Board (Discipline Committee)* (1980), 113 D.L.R. (3d) 408 at 412-413, Hallett J. of the Nova Scotia Supreme Court held that discipline proceedings based upon a doctor's alleged fraud should not await the outcome of parallel criminal proceedings where the disciplinary sanction if the doctor were found guilty would likely be harsher than the sanction imposed by the criminal courts. The case involved relatively small amounts of money. The result may have been different, Justice Hallett said, if the doctor had been charged with murder.

36.1 *Howe v. Institute of Chartered Accountants (Ontario)* (1994), 21 O.R. (3d) 315, 31 Admin. L.R. (2d) 119, 121 D.L.R. (4th) 149, 77 O.A.C. 145 (Div. Ct.), affirmed (1995), 25 O.R. (3d) 96, 31 Admin. L.R. (2d) 133 (C.A.).

In either case, discipline hearing panels are much more likely to adjourn discipline hearings until criminal charges are disposed of if the lawyer has undertaken not to practise in the interim. The seriousness of the charges is also an important consideration.

From the vantage point of the law society, one attraction of awaiting the result of a lawyer's criminal trial is that proof of misconduct will be facilitated if the lawyer is convicted: proof of conviction is *prima facie* (but not conclusive) evidence of the facts on which the conviction is based.[37] Lawyers are not normally permitted to relitigate those facts in discipline proceedings. The potentially conclusive effect of the conviction is compatible with the principles of fundamental justice because the lawyer has already had an opportunity to litigate all the essential facts in the criminal prosecution. The standard of proof beyond a reasonable doubt that is applied in criminal proceedings is at least as high as the standard of proof applied in discipline proceedings.

It does not follow, however, that a lawyer *acquitted* of a criminal charge cannot be found guilty of professional misconduct. A member of a self-governing profession may be guilty of misconduct as a result of acts that are not criminal. As Justice Cardozo said in an American case, "There are . . . many forms of professional misconduct which do not amount to crimes."[38] Different evidence may be led at the lawyer's discipline hearing, and evidence may be introduced that is inadmissible at a criminal trial. In Ontario, as mentioned above, the Divisional Court has upheld an order of disbarment and an order cancelling a doctor's registration for professional misconduct despite the practitioner's acquittal on criminal charges based on the same facts.[39]

There are risks, however, in awaiting the result of criminal proceedings. In a case involving a doctor charged criminally but ultimately acquitted at a second trial after an appeal from his conviction at his first trial was allowed, the Saskatchewan Court of Appeal allowed an appeal from an order of the College of Physicians and Surgeons of Saskatchewan revoking the doctor's licence after a hearing that occurred several years after the alleged misconduct. The court ruled that a disciplinary body that awaits the outcome of a criminal charge and accepts the criminal court's finding rather than conducting its own

37 *Del Core v. Ontario College of Pharmacists* (1985), 51 O.R. (2d) 1 (C.A.), leave to appeal to S.C.C. refused (1986), 57 O.R. (2d) 296n (S.C.C.). See also *Demeter v. British Pacific Life Insurance Co.* (1983), 43 O.R. (2d) 33 (H.C.), affirmed (1985), 48 O.R. (2d) 266 (C.A.); *General Medical Council v. Spackman*, [1943] A.C. 627 (H.L.); *Rosenbaum v. Law Society (Manitoba)* (1983), 150 D.L.R. (3d) 352 (Man. Q.B.), affirmed (1984), 3 D.L.R. (4th) 768 (Man. C.A.), leave to appeal to S.C.C. refused (1984), 27 Man. R. (2d) 159n; (S.C.C.); *Taylor Estate v. Baribeau; Baribeau v. Jakob* (1985), 51 O.R. (2d) 541 (Div. Ct.); and Wolfram, *supra*, note 34, p. 90. In *Terrace Developments Limited v. Terry*, Ont. Court Doc. No. 23782/87, May 27, 1992 (unreported), Justice Mandel admitted into evidence in parallel civil proceedings (as *prima facie* evidence) the complaint, report of the discipline hearing panel, and order reprimanding the defendant lawyer in Convocation.

38 *People ex rel. Karlin v. Culkin*, 248 N.Y. 465 at 470 (1928).

39 See note 12, *supra*. See also Charles Wolfram, *supra*, note 34, p. 91.

hearing on the merits may be bound by its decision to do so if the delay caused by the wait for the criminal proceedings would result in a hearing before the disciplinary body being clearly oppressive in that the practitioner's ability to defend would be impaired.[40]

In 1996 decision[40.1], Justice Baynton of the Saskatchewan Court of Queen's Bench quashed a complaint of conduct unbecoming a lawyer on the ground that the disciplinary proceedings were *ultra vires* the Law Society of Saskatchewan in that they offended Parliament's exclusive jurisdiction over criminal law. In the complaint the Law Society alleged that one of its members had used his law firm to assist a named individual to breach section 121 of the *Criminal Code*, which includes the offence commonly known as "influence peddling." No criminal proceedings had been commenced by the time the motion was argued, though the Law Society was co-operating in a police investigation into the transactions that gave rise to the complaint.

Justice Baynton held that the complaint should be quashed on the ground that the dominant feature of the proceedings was whether the member and the other named individual (who was not a lawyer) committed acts in the nature of frauds on the government which were prohibited by section 121 of the *Criminal Code*. As such, the proceeding was in pith and substance a substitute police investigation and not a disciplinary proceeding.

Justice Baynton observed that the wording of the complaint was only one factor that influenced his decision, and that the revision of the wording of the complaint to avoid a specific allegation of criminal conduct would not salvage the constitutional validity of the proceedings. Nevertheless, he added, where a lawyer's conduct is characterized as unbecoming *because* if constitutes a specific crime not yet determined by the courts, the dominant feature and focus of the proceeding is likely to be found to be a substitute police investigation, which is a matter for the police and the criminal courts. "[A] disciplinary proceeding begins to go off the rails when it approaches the matter on the basis that the conduct is unprofessional because if constitutes a criminal offence not yet determined by the criminal courts," Justice Baynton wrote. "It goes completely off the rails when its net effect is to investigate and determine whether the lawyer has engaged in conduct which is directly or indirectly characterized as a specific criminal offence."

Convocation of the Law Society of Upper Canada, in a 1998 decision,[40.2] found a complaint of professional misconduct and conduct unbecoming a barrister and solicitor not to have been made out on the same basis. It had been alleged

40 *Misra v. College of Physicians & Surgeons (Saskatchewan)*, [1988] 5 W.W.R. 333 (Sask. C.A.), leave to appeal to S.C.C. granted (1989), 79 Sask. R. 80 (note) (S.C.C.), appeal to S.C.C. discontinued January 27, 1992.

40.1 *Stromberg v. Law Society (Saskatchewan)*, [1996] 3 W.W.R. 389, 36 Admin. L.R. (2d) 181, 132 D.L.R. (4th) 470, 139 Sask. R. 182 (Q.B.), additional reasons at [1996] 10 W.W.R. 737, 6 C.P.C. (4th) 157, 149 Sask. R. 226, 44 Admin. L.R. (2d) 65 (Q.B.).

40.2 *Re a Solicitor*, Reasons of Convocation, July 14 1998.

in the complaint that the lawyer had failed to report income from his practice, a breach of the *Income Tax Act*. No proceedings under the *Income Tax Act* had been brought against the lawyer in the criminal courts, however.

The policy of the law society in Ontario in relation to the disclosure to police and other law enforcement agencies of information and documents obtained as a result of an investigation is that no such information or documents will be released without the approval of the chair of the discipline committee or a bencher designated by the chair. In practice, if a request is received for the release of information or documents obtained as a result of a law society investigation, information and documents that may provide evidence of a criminal offence will be released except to the extent that they consist of confidential or privileged communications and statements made by lawyers whose conduct is being investigated in the discharge of their duties to co-operate in the investigation and to reply promptly to communications from the law society.

Counsel retained to act for a lawyer being investigated for alleged misconduct that may also be criminal should determine as soon as possible whether authorization has been obtained to release information to the police. If the authorization has not been obtained, the lawyer's counsel should seek a commitment from the law society's counsel that the lawyer will be notified if authorization is granted in the future. The law society's policy requires the solicitor affected to be notified immediately after the release of information or documents is approved.

Even though the law society has a policy of not releasing statements made by lawyers in the discharge of their duty to co-operate in investigations, lawyers and their counsel should insist that any demand for information be in writing, in terms that make it clear that the lawyer's response is involuntary and made with fear of prejudice or hope of advantage or both. If a subpoena is served on the law society and it is unable to avoid the production of statements made by the lawyer, this approach may at least minimize the possibility that the statements will be admitted into evidence against the lawyer in criminal proceedings.

Particularly in cases in which the outcome of an investigation by the law society is a foregone conclusion, one option the lawyer should consider is admitting misconduct that falls short of criminal wrongdoing (for instance, failing to co-operate in an investigation) and joining in a submission that the lawyer should be disbarred. That option will not always be acceptable to the law society's counsel. If the misconduct involves, for example, a large misappropriation of client funds that can easily be proven, a lawyer might wish to consider consenting to an order of disbarment, with or without an explicit admission, so that as an accused person in the criminal courts the by then disbarred lawyer can at least say to the sentencing judge that he or she co-operated fully with the law society and consented to disbarment.[41]

26.6 DISCLOSURE PENDING HEARING

It is now universally accepted that counsel for the law society have a duty of full disclosure. In Ontario, they must produce all relevant documents in the law society's possession or under its control or power, except to the extent that the documents are privileged. The term "document", for this purpose, bears the same meaning as in rule 30.01(1)(a) of the Ontario rules of civil procedure:

> "document" includes a sound recording, videotape, film, photograph, chart, graph, map, plan, survey, book of account, and information recorded or stored by means of any device.[42]

The law society's counsel must also disclose the names and addresses of all persons who might reasonably be expected to have knowledge of the matters in issue, as well as disclosing copies of any written statements. Where no written statements exist, the law society's counsel must provide a summary of the witnesses' anticipated evidence. All experts' reports must also be disclosed, whether or not the reports advance the law society's position.

These disclosure obligations were recommended by the benchers special committee on discipline reform and were approved by Convocation on September 7, 1990. The extent to which a lawyer charged with professional misconduct should have a duty of disclosure was the subject of considerable debate both among the members of the special committee and among the benchers in Convocation. The debate revolved around the perennial issue of whether discipline proceedings are more like civil or criminal proceedings. If they are more like civil proceedings, the lawyer would have a duty of full disclosure similar to the duty of the law society's counsel; if they are more like criminal proceedings, the lawyer would have a right to remain silent and to refuse to produce documents.

The issue was resolved in favour of a regime that resembles the criminal model. The only disclosure requirement on lawyers is that if they call expert evidence, a report setting out the substance of the testimony that the expert is expected to give must be provided to the law society's counsel at least ten days before the hearing. Unlike the law society's counsel, lawyers have no duty to disclose an expert's report if the expert will not be called as a witness.

---

41 Strategies for representing lawyers involved contemporaneously in professional discipline and criminal investigations and proceedings are discussed in Stephen E. Sheriff, H. Reginald Watson, and Shaun M. Devlin, " 'You Can Run...But You Can't Hide': A Guide To Understanding Lawyer Discipline In Ontario" in Franklin Moskoff (ed.), *Administrative Tribunals: A Practice Handbook for Legal Counsel* (Aurora, Ontario: Canada Law Book Inc., 1989), p. 115 at 122-124.

42 R.R.O. 1990, reg. 194.

Thus, a lawyer in Ontario has a duty to co-operate in an investigation by the law society and to produce documents required for the investigation until a decision to initiate discipline proceedings is made. At that point, subject only to the duty to provide a report setting out the substance of an expert witness's anticipated evidence, the lawyer's duty to make disclosure ceases. Similarly, the Supreme Court of California has held, in considering a physician's right to disclosure in discipline proceedings, that the criminal law analogy is appropriate.[43]

The duty of counsel to disciplinary tribunals to make full disclosure was affirmed by a judge of the Ontario Court of Justice (General Division) in a 1994 case.[43.1] Counsel is required to disclose all relevant information, whether it damages or supports the practitioner's case, the court held. At a minimum, counsel to the tribunal must produce copies of all witness statements and notes of investigators. Counsel must undertake a diligent review of the investigation before making disclosure. This duty of disclosure is operative even in the absence of a request therefor, the court added, and is a continuing obligation.

The Divisional Court in a 1993 case[43.2] drew similar conclusions on an application for judicial review of the decision of a Board of Inquiry appointed pursuant to the Ontario Human Rights Code.

In a 1995 case,[43.3] Justice Tysoe of the British Columbia Supreme Court set aside a disbarment order and remitted a complaint of professional misconduct for a new hearing on the ground that the applicant had been denied natural justice by being called as the first witness after the late disclosure of the particulars of the allegations against her and the evidence to be introduced at the hearing. The applicant, Justice Tysoe held, had not been given a proper opportunity to review her files and prepare herself after she was given disclosure.

In a 1997 decision,[43.4] the Ontario Divisional Court dismissed a motion brought by the Law Society to quash a decision of a discipline committee

---

43 *Shively v. Stewart*, 421 P. 2d 65 (1967).

43.1 *Markandey v. Board of Ophthalmic Dispensers (Ontario)*, (March 14, 1994), Doc. Toronto RE 2661/93 (Ont. Gen. Div.). For a consideration of law society counsel's duty in circumstances in which a law society investigator has received transcripts of an examination for discovery, which transcripts are generally subject to an implied undertaking that they will be used only for the purposes in which they are taken, see *Law Society (Alberta) v. Randhawa*, 39 Alta. L.R. (3d) 226, [1996] 7 W.W.R. 664, 185 A.R. 220, 48 C.P.C. (3d) 21 (Q.B.). In the *Randhawa* case the Court ordered that such transcripts may be used by the law society's counsel, without obtaining leave of the Court, for the purpose of a law society investigation of one of its members for misconduct.

43.2 *Ontario (Human Rights Commission) v. House* (1993), 67 O.A.C. 72, leave to appeal to Court of Appeal denied January 31, 1994.

43.3 A *Solicitor v. Law Society (British Columbia)* (1995), 128 D.L.R. (4th) 562, 8 B.C.L.R. (3d) 377, 40 C.P.C. (3d) 67, 33 Admin. L.R. (2d) 314 (S.C.).

43.4 *Baker v. Law Society of Upper Canada* (1997), (*sub nom. Law Society of Upper Canada v. Baker*) 143 D.L.R. (4th) 551, 97 O.A.C. 244 (Div. Ct.), leave to appeal refused (April 10, 1997), Doc. CA M19885 (Ont. C.A.).

whereby the committee ordered the Law Society to disclose two investigative reports. The committee had ordered that if portions of the reports were protected by solicitor-client privilege, edited versions of the reports were to be provided to the member. The Court held that the committee's order was not patently unreasonable and was within the committee's jurisdiction. Moreover, the Court held, the application was premature, as the order in question was made on a preliminary motion and the hearing had not commenced.

Finally, in a 1994 decision,[43.5] the Ontario Court of Appeal was asked to consider whether the Institute of Chartered Accountants of Ontario breached its duty of fairness to a practitioner against whom a complaint of professional misconduct had been lodged, by refusing to produce the report of an investigator on which the complaint was based. The majority of the court determined the appeal by holding that the judicial review application, which was brought from a prehearing decision of the chair of the Institute's discipline committee, was premature. In a strong dissent, Laskin J.A. expressed the opinion that the Institute had a duty pursuant to the requirements of natural justice and fairness to disclose the investigator's report to the practitioner. The desirability of ensuring proper disclosure is especially important, Justice Laskin observed, in proceedings before tribunals whose procedures do not provide for discovery and production of documents.[43.6]

26.7 PROFESSIONAL MISCONDUCT

Legislation governing some professions contains a code of conduct in which the term "professional misconduct" is exhaustively defined. Legislation governing the legal profession generally does not define the term but leaves it to the benchers to determine.

An example of the former type of legislation is the Ontario *Medicine Act*, whose regulations define "professional misconduct" by listing 32 offences, the commission of which may expose a doctor to discipline. Some of these offences are quite specific (for example, "offering a reduction for prompt payment of an account" and "sexual impropriety with a patient"), while others are so general that they scarcely explicate the meaning of professional misconduct (for example, "failure to maintain the standard of practice of the profession" and "conduct or an act relevant to the practice of medicine that, having regard to all the circumstances, would reasonably be regarded by members as disgraceful, dishonourable or unprofessional").[44]

In Ontario, the *Law Society Act* authorizes Convocation to make by-laws authorizing and providing for the preparation, publication, and distribution of a

---

43.5 *Howe v. Institute of Chartered Accountants of Ontario* (1994), 19 O.R. (3d) 483 (C.A.).

43.6 *Ibid.*, at page 11.

44 The illustrations of offences that define professional misconduct for doctors are from paras. 14, 29, 21, and 32 of s. 27 of reg. 448, R.R.O. 1990 under the *Health Disciplines Act*, R.S.O. 1990, c. H.4.

code of professional conduct and ethics. The Law Society of Upper Canada's *Rules of Professional Conduct*, as a result of amendments that came into force in 2000, now define "professional misconduct" for the first time:

> "professional misconduct" means conduct in a lawyer's professional capacity that tends to bring discredit upon the legal profession including
>
> (a) violating or attempting to violate one of the rules in the *Rules of Professional Conduct* or a requirement of the *Law Society Act* or its regulations or by-laws,
>
> (b) knowingly assisting or inducing another lawyer to violate or attempt to violate the rules in the *Rules of Professional Conduct* or a requirement of the *Law Society Act* or its regulations or by-laws,
>
> (c) knowingly assisting or inducing a non-lawyer partner or associate of a multi-discipline practice to violate or attempt to violate the rules in the *Rules of Professional Conduct* or a requirement of the *Law Society Act* or its regulations or by-laws,
>
> (d) misappropriating or otherwise dealing dishonestly with a client's or a third party's money or property,
>
> (e) engaging in conduct that is prejudicial to the administration of justice,
>
> (f) stating or implying an ability to influence improperly a government agency or official, or
>
> (g) knowingly assisting a judge or judicial officer in conduct that is a violation of applicable rules of judicial conduct or other law."

In jurisdictions in which professional misconduct is not defined in legislation or rules of professional conduct, not every breach of the rules of professional conduct will necessarily amount to professional misconduct.[44.1] Conversely, not every act of professional misconduct will be specifically prohibited by the rules.[45]

Misappropriation, for instance, is not specifically prohibited by many codes of professional conduct. Although some rules prohibit certain acts — such as advising or representing parties on opposite sides of a dispute, or borrowing from clients — others are designed to urge lawyers to strive for exemplary professional

---

44.1 In *Fan v. Law Society (British Columbia)* (1977), 77 D.L.R. (3d) 97, 4 B.C.L.R. 16 (C.A.), the British Columbia Court of Appeal held that a finding that a lawyer is in breach of a ruling in a Professional Conduct Handbook is not in itself a finding of professional misconduct. The Court rejected the submission that a breach of a ruling in the handbook would necessarily constitute professional misconduct.

45 See Daniel P. Iggers and John P. Twohig, "The Disciplinary Process of the Law Society of Upper Canada" (1987) 8 Advocates' Quarterly 1 at 4; and Stephen M. Grant, "Sex, Lies and Legal Ethics," Law Society of Upper Canada Gazette, vol. 24, no. 2 (June 1990), pp. 118-120. In Alberta, the *Legal Profession Act*, R.S.A. 1980, c. L-9, as amended by 1981, c. 53, proscribes "conduct incompatible with the best interests of the public or of the Society", or that "tends to harm the standing of the legal profession."

standards. For example, rule 1 of the Canadian Bar Association's *Code of Professional Conduct* specifies that "the lawyer must discharge with integrity all duties owed to clients, the courts, the public, and other members of the profession." Thus, as discussed in chapter 25, rules of professional conduct are a combination of rules and ethical admonitions.

Professor Harry Arthurs of Osgoode Hall Law School has argued that at least insofar as enforcement is concerned, Canadian codes of professional conduct are a dead letter:

> Many, if not most, of the chapters of the CBA Code are not actually used to disbar or discipline lawyers. I, personally, would be pleased to hear that someone had been suspended for not representing clients resolutely, not adhering to high standards in the discharge of public office or not trying to improve the administration of justice. I would be delighted to know that someone who was discourteous to members of the profession or derelict in his or her duty to make legal services available to the public had attracted professional censure. But alas, such professional norms are violated with virtual impunity.[45.1]

Complaints of professional misconduct, therefore, may or may not allege a violation of a rule of professional conduct. Whether conduct deserves discipline is determined case by case by the benchers, that is, by lawyers' elected peers and the public's lay representatives. Although the rules of professional conduct are generally the best evidence of whether certain conduct is unethical, they should not be read as if they were a statute such as the *Criminal Code*.[46] Justice Cory, while sitting on the Divisional Court, explained the logic of this approach:

> What constitutes professional misconduct by a lawyer can and should be determined by the discipline committee. Its function in determining what may in each particular circumstance constitute professional misconduct ought not be unduly restricted. No one but a fellow member of the profession can be more keenly aware of the problems and frustrations that confront a practitioner. The discipline committee is certainly in the best position to determine when a solicitor's conduct has crossed the permissible bounds and deteriorated into professional misconduct. Probably no one could approach a complaint against a lawyer with more understanding than a group composed primarily of members of his profession.[47]

45.1 H.W. Arthurs, "The Dead Parrott: Does Professional Self-Regulation Exhibit Vital Signs?", a paper presented to the National Conference on the Legal Profession and Ethics, University of Calgary, June 10, 1994, pages 6-7.

46 For a helpful discussion of the use that may be made of rules of professional conduct in discipline proceedings, see Sherriff *et al.*, *supra*, note 41, pp. 117-118.

47 *Stevens v. Law Society (Upper Canada)* (1979), 55 O.R. (2d) 405 at 410 (Div. Ct.). In *Klein v. Law Society (Upper Canada)* (1985), 50 O.R. (2d) 118, the Divisional Court held that a finding of professional misconduct may be based upon a contravention of a commentary to a rule of professional conduct. See also *Re French* (1982), 39 O.R. (2d) 666 (Div. Ct.); and *Emerson v. Law Society (Upper Canada)* (1984), 5 D.L.R. (4th) 294 (Ont. H.C.).

This approach has been approved by the Supreme Court of Canada,[48] which observed that benchers are in the best position to determine issues of misconduct and quoted approvingly from a decision of the Manitoba Court of Appeal:

> No one is better qualified to say what constitutes professional misconduct than a group of practising barristers who are themselves subject to the rules established by their governing body.[49]

The Ontario Court of Appeal, similarly, has held that legislation that exposes members of professions to discipline for professional misconduct is not vulnerable to attack on the ground that it contains no definition of professional misconduct, since the question of whether the conduct in question amounts to professional misconduct is for the governing body to decide.[50]

Traditionally, professional misconduct has been defined as "conduct which would reasonably be regarded as disgraceful or dishonourable by solicitors of good repute and competency."[51] Moral turpitude was an essential component. Mere negligence was not sufficient.

Today, in jurisdictions in which the law society's governing statute either defines professional misconduct or authorizes the profession to pass specific rules of professional conduct and the profession does so, this definition must be qualified in two respects. First, it is now clear that practitioners can be found guilty of professional misconduct for violating regulatory requirements and rules of professional conduct that impose specific duties, whether or not such violations could be said to be disgraceful or dishonourable. Lawyers are frequently reprimanded, for example, for failing to respond promptly to communications from

---

48 *Pearlman v. Law Society (Manitoba)*, [1991] 2 S.C.R. 869.

49 *Law Society (Manitoba) v. Savino* (1983), 1 D.L.R. (4th) 285 (Man. C.A.).

50 *Matthews v. Board of Directors of Physiotherapy* (1987), 43 D.L.R. (4th) 478 (Ont. C.A.). Other cases affirming that the courts should not readily interfere with a determination by the governing body of a profession as to what is misconduct are: *Wilson v. Law Society (British Columbia)* (1986), 33 D.L.R. (4th) 572 (B.C. C.A.); *Prescott v. Law Society (British Columbia)*, [1971] 4 W.W.R. 433 at 440 (B.C. C.A.); and *Imrie v. Institute of Chartered Accountants (Ontario)*, [1972] 3 O.R. 275 at 279 (H.C.). See also *Larson v. Land Surveyors Assn. (Saskatchewan)* (1988), 65 Sask. R. 292 (Q.B.); *Morton v. Registered Nurses Assn. (N.S.)* (1989), 92 N.S.R. (2d) 154 (T.D.); and *Laba v. Dental Assn. (Manitoba)* (1988), 54 Man. R. (2d) 17 (Q.B.). See also *Szmuilowicz v. Ontario (Minister of Health)* (1995), 24 O.R. (3d) 204, 125 D.L.R. (4th) 688, 82 O.A.C. 183 (Div. Ct.), in which the Court struck down a regulation purporting to make it professional misconduct for doctors to charge patients annual or block fees for uninsured services, on the ground that the regulation distorted the meaning of the term "professional misconduct" and pushed the term's meaning beyond permissible limits.

51 The quoted definition of professional misconduct is from the judgment of Lord Maugham in *Myers v. Elman*, [1940] A.C. 282 at 288-289, in which the House of Lords cites with approval the definition enunciated by Justice Darling in *Re Solicitor*, [1912] 1 K.B. 302. The judgment of Lord Esher in *Re Cooke* (1889), 5 T.L.R. 407 at 407-408 is to the same effect, and was adopted in *Re Solicitor* (1916), 37 O.L.R. 310 (C.A.) and *Re Solicitor*, [1935] 3 W.W.R. 428 (Sask. C.A.). See also *Re Fitzpatrick*, [1924] 1 D.L.R. 981 (Ont. S.C.), in which the court held that its disciplinary jurisdiction extends only to cases of misfeasance or dishonourable conduct and not to cases involving solicitors' negligence.

the law society and for failing to file required forms and annual reports of public accountants.[52]

Second, it is now clear that a series of acts of gross negligence may, taken together, constitute professional misconduct.[53] Since law societies have adopted codes of professional conduct, lawyers have frequently been disciplined for failing to serve clients in a conscientious, diligent, and efficient manner. Commentary 9 of chapter II of the C.B.A. Code, for example, provides that "evidence of gross neglect in a particular matter or a pattern of neglect or mistakes in different matters" may be evidence of a failure to maintain the required standard and can give rise to disciplinary action.

Nevertheless, a single mistake, even though it may be actionable in negligence, will generally not result in discipline proceedings. Negligence is not likely to be a basis for discipline unless it is gross or habitual, or both.[54]

Lawyers will generally be vulnerable to allegations of professional misconduct (rather than conduct unbecoming a barrister and solicitor) only in respect of acts performed in their professional capacity. In other words, lawyers' conduct in their private lives will not generally be considered professional misconduct unless that conduct can reasonably be regarded as an extension of their professional status or activities, as where non-clients lend money to lawyers relying on their assumed integrity and ability to repay.[55]

---

52 In *Re X.* (1920), 16 Alta. L.R. 542 (T.D.), the court held that the failure of a lawyer to reply to letters from the law society about complaints is not professional misconduct. Since 1945, however, the law society in Ontario has taken the position that a failure to reply to a letter from the law society will be treated as professional misconduct, and this duty is now enshrined as commentary 3 to rule 13 of the Ontario rules. See note 9, *supra*, for references to similar rules in other jurisdictions. In *Trace v. Institute of Chartered Accountants (Alberta)* (1988), (*sub nom. Trace v. Council of the Institute of Chartered Accountants of Alta.*) 54 D.L.R. (4th) 82, (*sub nom. Trace v. Institute of Chartered Accountants Council*) 63 Alta. L.R. (2d) 53, (*sub nom. Trace v. Institute of Chartered Accountants (Alta.)*) [1989] 2 W.W.R. 86, 91 A.R. 241 (Alta. C.A.), the Alberta Court of Appeal overruled *German v. Law Society (Alberta)*, 45 D.L.R. (3d) 535, [1974] 5 W.W.R. 217 (Alta. C.A.), and held that conduct need not be disgraceful or dishonourable to amount to professional misconduct if the governing statute either expressly defines professional misconduct or authorizes the profession to pass specific rules of professional conduct and the profession does so. The Court of Appeal relied upon *Canada (Attorney General) v. Law Society (British Columbia)*, [1982] 2 S.C.R. 307, 37 B.C.L.R. 145, [1982] 5 W.W.R. 289, 19 B.L.R. 234, 43 N.R. 451, 66 C.P.R. (2d) 1, 137 D.L.R. (3d) 1 at 27, in doing so.

53 In *Baron v. F.*, [1945] 4 D.L.R. 525 (B.C. Law Society Visitorial Trib.), Farris C.J.S.C. held that a series of acts of gross negligence may amount to a course of conduct that brings the legal profession into disrepute.

54 See Stephen M. Grant and Linda Rothstein, *Lawyers' Professional Liability* (Toronto: Butterworths, 1989), p. 6; Mark M. Orkin, *Legal Ethics: A Study of Professional Conduct* (Toronto: Cartwright & Sons, 1957), pp. 123-124; and New Brunswick rules, Part C, rule 13. The Yukon rules, Part One, rule 19, provide that "negligence in the handling of a client's transaction may be conduct unbecoming."

55 The scope of the term "professional misconduct" is discussed in Iggers and Twohig, *supra*, note 44, p. 6.

The following acts, among many others, have been found to constitute professional misconduct:

(i) misappropriation or misapplication of funds held in trust for clients or others;

(ii) failing to account for funds held in trust for clients or others;

(iii) creating false documents;

(iv) forgery;

(v) destroying or concealing documents in furtherance of an unlawful scheme;

(vi) assisting clients in an attempt to defraud creditors;

(vii) taking unfair advantage of clients, for example, by charging grossly excessive fees;

(viii) acting in circumstances in which the lawyer has a conflict of interest without adequate disclosure and consent, or to the detriment of the client, or both;

(ix) borrowing from clients, particularly when the clients do not have independent legal advice or adequate security, or both;

(x) attempting to mislead clients, other lawyers, the law society, or others;

(xi) attempting to defraud a legal aid plan;

(xii) attempting to charge clients fees in addition to amounts paid by a legal aid plan;

(xiii) attempting to obtain financial benefits to which the lawyer is not entitled by such billing practices as falsely representing that disbursements have been incurred or charging personal expenses as fees without the knowledge of clients or partners;

(xiv) suborning perjury or otherwise fabricating evidence;

(xv) making false representations to courts or tribunals;

(xvi) interfering with the orderly administration of justice, for example, by making discourteous or offensive remarks to opposing counsel;

(xvii) practising law while under suspension;

(xviii) repeatedly failing to serve clients in a conscientious, diligent, and efficient manner;

(xix) failing to honour undertakings;

(xx) failing to meet financial obligations arising out of practice, for example, failing to pay court reporters for transcripts;

(xxi) attempting to persuade complainants to withdraw complaints to the law society by offering them a benefit for doing so;

(xxii) failing to maintain books and records as required;

(xxiii) failing to file required forms or annual reports of public accountants;

(xxiv) failing to respond to communications from the law society;

(xxv) failing to co-operate in investigations by the law society; and

(xxvi) ungovernability.[56]

26.8 CONDUCT UNBECOMING A BARRISTER AND SOLICITOR

Legislation governing law societies generally empowers benchers to discipline lawyers who are found guilty of either professional misconduct or conduct unbecoming a barrister and solicitor. The distinction between professional misconduct and conduct unbecoming is that the former arises out of acts performed in lawyers' professional capacity or in connection with their professional status, while the latter arises out of acts performed in their personal or private capacity.[57]

As a result of amendments that came into force in 2000, the Law Society of Upper Canada's *Rules of Professional Conduct* now define "conduct unbecoming a barrister or solicitor" for the first time:

> "conduct unbecoming a barrister or solicitor" means conduct in a lawyer's personal or private capacity that tends to bring discredit upon the legal profession including, for example,
>
> (a) committing a criminal act that reflects adversely on the lawyer's honesty, trustworthiness, or fitness as a lawyer,
>
> (b) taking improper advantage of the youth, inexperience, lack of education, unsophistication, ill health, or unbusinesslike habits of another, or
>
> (c) engaging in conduct involving dishonesty."

---

56 The illustrations of professional misconduct are drawn in part from Stephen E. Traviss, *Synopses of Discipline Cases Considered by Convocation 1972 to 1984* (Toronto: Law Society of Upper Canada, 1987); Stephen E. Sherriff, H. Reginald Watson, and Shaun M. Devlin, " 'You Can Run...But You Can't Hide': A Guide to Understanding Lawyer Discipline In Ontario" in Franklin Moskoff (ed.), *Administrative Tribunals: A Practice Handbook for Legal Counsel* (Aurora, Ontario: Canada Law Book, Inc., 1989), p. 115 at 118-119; Iggers and Twohig, *supra*, note 45, pp. 5-6; William J. Smith, "Disciplinary Proceedings Before the Law Society," 1971 Law Society of Upper Canada Special Lectures, p. 285 at 293-294; Orkin, *supra*, note 54, pp. 207-213; Claude R. Thomson and Gavin MacKenzie, "The Defence of Disciplinary Proceedings Before the Law Society of Upper Canada's Discipline Committee", Part 2, The Advocates' Society Journal (December 1982), p. 7 at 7-8.

57 Section 34 of the *Law Society Act*, R.S.O. 1990, c. L.8, empowers the law society to impose discipline for conduct unbecoming a barrister and solicitor.

In order for lawyers' personal or private conduct to amount to conduct unbecoming a barrister and solicitor, it must tend to bring discredit upon the legal profession or the administration of justice. Since the lawyer's non-professional conduct is in issue, rules of professional conduct are generally irrelevant in conduct unbecoming cases. Two commentaries to chapter I of the C.B.A. Code, however, do provide some guidance in determining when law societies are justified in initiating discipline proceedings in relation to lawyers' personal or private activities:

> (1) Integrity is the fundamental quality of any person who seeks to practise as a member of the legal profession. If the client is in any doubt as to the lawyer's trustworthiness, the essential element in the true lawyer-client relationship will be missing. If personal integrity is lacking, the lawyer's usefulness to the client and reputation within the profession will be destroyed regardless of how competent the lawyer may be.
>
> . . .
>
> (3) Dishonourable or questionable conduct on the part of the lawyer in either private life or professional practice will reflect adversely upon the lawyer, the integrity of the legal profession and the administration of justice as a whole. If the conduct, whether within or outside the professional sphere, is such that knowledge of it would be likely to impair the client's trust in the lawyer as a professional consultant, a governing body may be justified in taking disciplinary action.[58]

Thus, lawyers may be disciplined for private conduct that calls into question their ability or willingness to practise law honestly and competently. Law societies are not otherwise justified in intruding into lawyers' non-professional lives.[59]

Deviant social or sexual behaviour that has no bearing on lawyers' trustworthiness or fitness to practise should not form the basis of a complaint of conduct unbecoming a barrister and solicitor. Nevertheless, in a 1980 Ontario case,[60] a lawyer was disbarred when he was found to have seduced teenaged girls whom he employed to work as grooms in training, riding, and showing horses. The lawyer's conduct was held, first, to seriously reflect upon his integrity to the point where the protection of the public was involved and, second, to bring discredit upon the profession as a whole.

---

58 C.B.A. Code, Chapter I, commentaries 1 and 3; Ontario rule 1.02 and accompanying commentary.

59 The circumstances in which governing bodies are justified in disciplining lawyers for non-professional activities are discussed by Charles Wolfram, *Modern Legal Ethics* (St. Paul, Minnesota: West, 1986), pp. 97-98; Iggers and Twohig, *supra*, note 45, pp. 6-7; Beverley G. Smith, *Professional Conduct for Canadian Lawyers* (Toronto: Butterworths, 1989), pp. 227-246; and Orkin, *supra*, note 54, pp. 202-209.

60 *Cwinn v. Law Society (Upper Canada)* (1980), 28 O.R. (2d) 61 (Div. Ct.), leave to appeal denied and appeal quashed (1980), 28 O.R. (2d) 61n (S.C.C.). Similarly, in *Adams v. Law Society of Alberta*, [2000] A.J. 1031, the Alberta Court of Appeal upheld a disbarment order against a lawyer who had been convicted of sexual exploitation of a 16-year old client.

In some cases it is not entirely clear whether a particular activity should be classified as professional misconduct or conduct unbecoming, or both. In an American case,[61] a lawyer gained access to a penitentiary in his professional capacity and sold heroin to inmates. In a recent Ontario case,[62] a lawyer was disbarred for conduct unbecoming as a result of his misuse of investors' funds in a mortgage brokerage business that he operated in premises that he occupied as a lawyer.

In serious cases, insofar as the discipline proceedings themselves are concerned, there is generally little if any advantage to be gained by categorizing the conduct in question as either professional misconduct or conduct unbecoming. Both may be alleged in the alternative, and complaints may be amended, so it is unlikely that a complaint will be dismissed due to the categorization of the misconduct. Nor, in a serious case, is the penalty likely to be affected by the classification of the alleged misconduct. Lawyers have often been disbarred for conduct unbecoming.[63]

The classification of a lawyer's misconduct may, however, be important in some less serious cases. If the lawyer is able to resist a suggestion that he or she was acting in a professional capacity, the lawyer may not be subject to discipline at all if the conduct in question, outside a professional sphere of activity, does not bring the legal profession or the administration of justice into disrepute.

Moreover, regardless of the seriousness of the case, a lawyer may prefer one categorization or the other as a result of parallel proceedings in the civil or criminal courts. The possible availability of insurance coverage if the lawyer was acting in a professional capacity, or the possible lack of privity of contract if the lawyer was not so acting, may give rise to a civil advantage as a result of the classification. The sentence imposed on a lawyer or former lawyer in the criminal courts might be affected by the fact that the relationship between wrongdoer and victim is also that of lawyer and client.

Most conduct unbecoming complaints involve convictions for criminal offences. Historically, only convictions for criminal offences involving moral turpitude were considered to bring discredit upon the profession. However, in a 1988 decision,[64] the Alberta Court of Appeal held that an order striking a chartered accountant from the register for conduct unbecoming was justified, even in the absence of disgraceful or dishonourable conduct, in circumstances where the penalty was the only effective one available. In the case before the court, the governing body had given the practitioner detailed advice at least three times, with no effect.

---

61 *People v. McGonigle*, 600 P. 2d 61 (1979).

62 *Re Handelman*, report adopted by Convocation, January 23, 1992.

63 See Sherriff *et al.*, *supra*, note 56, pp. 119-120.

64 *Trace v. Institute of Chartered Accountants (Alberta)*, [1989] 2 W.W.R. 86 (Alta. C.A.).

Similarly, in a 1990 case,[65] the California Supreme Court adopted a recommendation that a lawyer be publicly reproved for having been convicted of driving with an excessive blood-alcohol level, despite the fact that the offence did not involve moral turpitude. The lawyer had been convicted of the same offence two years earlier and was still on probation when the second offence was committed. The court held that her violation of a pending probation order established "a disrespect for the legal system that directly related to a lawyer's fitness to practise law." The same could be said of a conviction for most criminal offences, whether or not the offender has breached a probation order in the process. On the rationale that a lawyer has a duty to be law-abiding, the Supreme Court of Florida has upheld a public reprimand of a lawyer who had announced on a television program that he had placed football bets through a bookmaker (a misdemeanour).[66]

The breadth of the concepts of "conduct unbecoming" and "moral turpitude" clearly invite prying into private lives and the imposition of value judgments in matters unrelated to the practice of law. It is also important that law societies do not employ the discipline process to impose a supplementary punishment on people who have violated criminal laws.

The commission of some criminal offences strongly suggests deficits of character or self-control so significant that they indicate unsuitability to practise. Other offences involve neither maliciousness nor premeditation, and may, especially if unrepeated, betray uncharacteristically poor judgment rather than a settled disposition to flout the law.[67]

Proof of conviction of a criminal offence is *prima facie* proof of the facts upon which the criminal conviction was based.[68] As noted above, law societies are generally entitled to proceed with discipline hearings both while criminal charges are pending and even after such charges are dismissed.[69]

The following acts, among others, have been held to amount to conduct unbecoming a barrister and solicitor:

(1) permitting premises that a lawyer owns to be used as a brothel;[70]

(2) conspiring to distribute valium to persons in police custody;[71]

---

65 *Re Kelley*, 801 P. 2d 1126 (Cal., 1990).

66 *Florida Bar v. Levin*, 570 So. 2d 917 (Fla., 1990). See also Daniel P. Iggers and John P. Twohig, "The Disciplinary Process of the Law Society of Upper Canada" (1987) 8 Advocates' Quarterly 1 at 6-7.

67 The types of offences that should and should not give rise to disciplinary sanctions are discussed in Wolfram, *supra*, note 59, pp. 92-99.

68 *Re Ciglen*, report adopted by Convocation on October 16, 1970 (Ontario).

69 *Re Cornacchia and Law Society of Upper Canada*, Div. Ct., file no. 1943/85, September 26, 1985 (unreported). As for the risks of proceeding with a complaint of conduct unbecoming based upon a criminal conviction that is under appeal, see *Law Society (British Columbia) v. MacKrow* (1968), 68 D.L.R. (2d) 179 (B.C. C.A.).

70 *Re Weare*, [1893] 2 Q.B. 439 (C.A.).

71 *Re Caskie*, report adopted by Convocation on June 24, 1983 (Ontario).

(3) evasion of income tax;[72]

(4) conspiring to possess counterfeit money;[73]

(5) manslaughter;[74]

(6) possession of narcotics for the purpose of trafficking;[75] and

(7) conspiring to attempt to obstruct justice by interfering with the lawful disposition of informations and summonses.[76]

A conviction in the criminal courts is not the only possible basis for a finding of conduct unbecoming a barrister and solicitor. Thus, in a 1995 decision[76.1], an Ontario lawyer was found guilty of conduct unbecoming where he took steps that were calculated to ensure that a former client could not realize on a civil judgment against him. The lawyer had been criticized by a judge, on the lawyer's application to be discharged from bankruptcy, in a judgment that was made public.

26.9 PUBLIC HEARINGS

In the 1980's and 1990's, commentators and courts have repeatedly recognized the desirability of disciplinary hearings being held in public. Until the mid-1980's, most discipline hearings were held *in camera*. This fuelled public suspicion that elitist clubs were protecting their members against well-founded accusations by shrouding their proceedings in a cloak of secrecy.

The profession's resistance to holding discipline proceedings in public is understandable. The mere fact that a lawyer is before a discipline hearing panel to answer a complaint of professional misconduct will in some cases cause permanent damage to his or her reputation and livelihood. That, however, is a sacrifice that the legal profession must make to preserve its right of self-governance and the independence of the bar.

Discipline hearings involving Ontario lawyers have been held in public since 1985. The exceptional circumstances in which evidence may be received *in camera* are set forth in section 9(1) of the *Statutory Powers Procedure Act*.

---

72 *Re Ciglen*, report of discipline hearing panel adopted by Convocation on October 16, 1970, (Ontario), and numerous subsequent cases.

73 *Re Goldman*, report of discipline hearing panel adopted by Convocation on May 14, 1981 (Ontario) (the lawyer, who was disbarred, was re-admitted by Convocation in 1987).

74 *Re Shea*, report of discipline hearing panel adopted by Convocation on January 16, 1976 (Ontario); and *Re Milne*, report of discipline hearing panel adopted by Convocation on September 23, 1990 (Ontario).

75 *Re Telfer*, report of discipline hearing panel adopted by Convocation on January 16, 1981 (Ontario).

76 *Re May*, report of discipline hearing panel adopted by Convocation on January 24, 1985 (Ontario).

76.1 *Re Chodos*, report of discipline hearing panel adopted by Convocation December 8 1995 (Ontario).

9.—(1) A hearing shall be open to the public except where the tribunal is of the opinion that,

(a) matters involving public security may be disclosed; or

(b) intimate financial or personal matters or other matters may be disclosed at the hearing of such a nature, having regard to the circumstances, that the desirability of avoiding disclosure thereof in the interests of any person affected or in the public interest outweighs the desirability of adhering to the principle that hearings be open to the public,

in which case the tribunal may hold the hearing concerning any such matter in camera.

Section 32 of the *Statutory Powers Procedure Act* provides that the provisions of that statute prevail over other statutory provisions, unless other statutory provisions are expressly stated to apply notwithstanding the *Statutory Powers Procedure Act*.[77]

In considering an application to hold a hearing *in camera* under paragraph 9(1)(b) of the *Statutory Powers Procedure Act*, a discipline hearing panel may weigh the following considerations, among others:

(i) the desirability of maintaining the confidentiality of privileged communications;

(ii) the desirability of avoiding public disclosure of such intimate personal matters as psychiatric assessments; and

(iii) the effect of public disclosure on parallel criminal or civil proceedings.[78]

A hearing may be held partly in public and partly *in camera*.[79]

---

77 In *Re Pilzmaker and Law Society of Upper Canada* (1989), 70 O.R. (2d) 126, the Divisional Court dismissed an application for an order that a discipline hearing be held *in camera*. Justice Sutherland, for the court, observed that there is an important public interest in having hearings of disciplinary bodies held in public and agreed with the Law Society's conclusion that s. 9(1) of the *Statutory Powers Procedure Act* supersedes s. 33(4) of the *Law Society Act*. See also Kenneth E. Howie, "Lawyers Under Fire", Law Society of Upper Canada Gazette, vol. 25, no. 2 (June 1991), p. 164 at 167; Gavin MacKenzie, "Lawyer Discipline and the Independence of the Bar: Can Lawyers Still Govern Themselves?", Law Society of Upper Canada Gazette, vol. 24, no. 4 (December 1990), p. 319 at 322-323; Daniel P. Iggers and John P. Twohig, "The Disciplinary Process of the Law Society of Upper Canada" (1987) 8 Advocates' Quarterly 1 at 21; *Thompson v. Lambton (Board of Education)*, [1972] 3 O.R. 889 at 894-896 (H.C.); and *Y. v. Yukon Medical Council*, [1998] Y.J. 126.

78 Stephen E. Sherriff, H. Reginald Watson, and Shaun M. Devlin, " 'You Can Run...But You Can't Hide': A Guide to Understanding Lawyer Discipline in Ontario" in Franklin Moskoff (ed.), *Administrative Tribunals: A Practice Handbook for Legal Counsel* (Aurora, Ontario: Canada Law Book, Inc., 1989), p. 115 at 127-128.

79 *Canada (Solicitor General) v. Ontario (Royal Commission into Confidentiality of Health Records (sub nom. Re Inquiry into Confidentiality of Health Records in Ontario)* (1979), 24 O.R. (2d) 545 at 565 (C.A.), reversed on other grounds [1981] 2 S.C.R. 494.

The Divisional Court has held that a discipline hearing panel has no authority to order that evidence not be published.[80] (Convocation has adopted a recommendation that the *Law Society Act* should be amended to confer on discipline hearing panels the authority to make non-publication orders). In the same case, the court also held that the Law Society does not have a duty to publish a list of forthcoming hearings. Nevertheless, Convocation has adopted and is acting on a proposal that such a list be made available upon request.

The Quebec Court of Appeal has affirmed the constitutionality of a statutory provision empowering a discipline hearing panel to order that a hearing be held *in camera* in the interest of morality or public order, to preserve professional secrecy, or to protect a person's privacy or reputation. Although the provision offends subsection 2(b) of the *Charter* (which guarantees freedom of expression, including freedom of the press), the court ruled, it is justified under section 1 of the *Charter* as a reasonable limitation that is demonstrably justified in a free and democratic society.[81]

26.10 EFFECT OF DELAY

The Supreme Court of Canada has now made it clear that section 11 of the *Canadian Charter of Rights and Freedoms* is inapplicable to disciplinary matters of a regulatory nature that are designed to maintain professional integrity, discipline, and standards and that do not have true penal consequences. Thus, subsection 11(b) of the *Charter* cannot be successfully invoked to support an argument that a lawyer's right to be tried by his or her governing body within a reasonable time has been violated.[82]

The court has not decided whether the right to practise a profession is embraced by the right to life, liberty, and security of the person, as guaranteed

(*Continued on page 26–27*)

80 *Canadian Newspapers Co. v. Law Society (Upper Canada)* (1986), 10 O.A.C. 361 (Div. Ct.).

81 *Southam Inc. v. Lafrance* (1990), 71 D.L.R. (4th) 282 (C.A.).

82 Subsection 11(b) was the basis of the court's decision in *R. v. Askov*, [1990] 2 S.C.R. 1199. The court held that s. 11 of the *Charter* is inapplicable to disciplinary proceedings that do not have true penal consequences in *R. v. Wigglesworth*, [1987] 2 S.C.R. 541, and three companion cases. The court applied its holding in *Wigglesworth* to discipline proceedings involving a lawyer in *Pearlman v. Law Society (Manitoba)* (1991), 84 D.L.R. (4th) 105 (S.C.C.). See text accompanying notes 13 to 18, *supra*.

by section 7 of the *Charter*, but has strongly implied, *obiter dicta*, that it is.[83] It is doubtful, in any event, that the principles of fundamental justice in section 7 provide any greater protection than does the power to stay or dismiss proceedings as an abuse of process, for example, pursuant to section 23 of the *Statutory Powers Procedure Act* of Ontario.

The Saskatchewan Court of Queen's Bench has held that though pre-charge delay does not in and of itself involve an infringement of section 7 of the *Charter*, such a delay will infringe section 7 if it results in a denial of a practitioner's right to make full answer and defence to a complaint of professional misconduct. The court issued an order prohibiting the College of Physicians and Surgeons from proceeding in respect of four incidents of alleged sexual misconduct, each of which occurred more than 20 years earlier. It held that to allow a discipline hearing to proceed so many years after the events occurred would be oppressive and would offend the community's sense of fairness.[84]

As mentioned above, Chief Justice Hickman of the Supreme Court of Newfoundland Trial Division, in a 1992 decision, also invoked section 7 of the *Charter* in setting aside a suspension of a lawyer who was deprived of his right to make full answer and defence due to the unavailability of witnesses, after his hearing was inexplicably delayed for more than five years.[85] Chief Justice Hickman's decision was cited with approval by a discipline committee of the Law Society of Upper Canada in a 2000 decision in which allegations of professional misconduct were stayed by reason of a combination of pre- and post-charge delay. The committee based its decision on common law principles but added that in doing so it was "bolstered by the spirit of the Charter."[85.1]

In two Ontario cases,[85.2] the Divisional Court has allowed the appeals of police officers from orders whereby they were disciplined, on the ground that inexcusable delay impinged upon the officers' right to make full answer and defence. The court found it unnecessary to decide whether section 7 of the Charter was applicable.

The fact that the incidents on which allegations of professional misconduct are based occurred long before disciplinary proceedings were initiated is inadequate in itself as a ground for staying or dismissing a complaint. In two

83 In the *Wigglesworth* case, at p. 558, Justice Wilson, delivering the judgment of the court, suggested that it is preferable to leave "offences" that are neither criminal nor penal "subject to the more flexible criteria of 'fundamental justice' in section 7."

84 *Brand v. College of Physicians & Surgeons (Saskatchewan)*, [1989] 5 W.W.R. 516 (Sask. Q.B.). The Court of Appeal affirmed the court's decision "without necessarily agreeing with all of the reasoning of the chambers judge." The Court of Appeal decision is reported at [1990] 3 W.W.R. 272.

85 *Harvey v. Law Society (Newfoundland)* (1992), 88 D.L.R. (4th) 487 (Nfld. T.D.). See also text accompanying note 17, *supra*.

85.1 *Re Baker*, March 30 2000.

85.2 *Lang v. Ramsay* (1992), 11 O.R. (3d) 190 at 200-201; *Duriancik v. Ontario (Attorney General)* (1994), 114 D.L.R. (4th) 504 (Ont. Div Ct.).

1991 decisions, the Supreme Court of Canada and the Alberta Court of Appeal declined to stay or dismiss discipline proceedings that arose out of incidents that had occurred eight or more years before proceedings were initiated. The Supreme Court held that whether or not section 7 of the *Charter* applies to such proceedings (a question the court found unnecessary to decide), pre-charge delay will not violate the principles of fundamental justice when the law society acts with reasonable dispatch once it becomes aware of possible misconduct.[86] The Alberta Court of Appeal held that even if the law society has knowledge of possible misconduct for eight years before discipline proceedings are initiated, the delay in proceeding will not justify dismissal of the complaint unless the lawyer has been suspended on an interim basis or has otherwise suffered prejudice as a result of the delay.[87]

American courts have been at least equally reluctant to impose limitations on the time within which a lawyer must be notified of a complaint or the hearing process must be completed.[88]

26.11 DISQUALIFICATION FOR BIAS

The rules of natural justice require that members of tribunals exercising adjudicative functions must be both impartial and disinterested in the outcome of matters coming before them for decision. Adjudicators may be disqualified either because of actual bias or because of circumstances that give rise to a reasonable apprehension of bias.

---

86 *Pearlman v. Law Society (Manitoba)*, *supra*, note 82.

87 *Duncan v. Law Society of Alberta Investigating Committee* (1991), 80 D.L.R. (4th) 702 (Alta. C.A.), leave to appeal to S.C.C. refused (1991), 82 Alta. L.R. (2d) lxv (note) (S.C.C.). In *MacPhee v. Barristers' Society (New Brunswick)* (1983), 50 N.B.R. (2d) 61 (Q.B.), Richard C.J.Q.B., held that an inference of prejudice may be drawn from delay that is both inexcusable and unexplained. See also *Robinson v. College of Physicians & Surgeons (British Columbia)* (1986), 32 D.L.R. (4th) 589 (B.C. S.C.), in which McKenzie J. held that both the fact that a practitioner has early notice of a complaint and the fact that there are continuing proceedings are relevant in determining a motion for prohibition based upon delay; *Misra v. Council of the College of Physicians & Surgeons (Saskatchewan)*, [1988] 5 W.W.R. 333, leave to appeal to S.C.C. granted (1989), 79 Sask. R. 80 (note) (S.C.C.), appeal to S.C.C. discontinued January 27, 1992, in which the Saskatchewan Court of Appeal held that the fact that a practitioner has been suspended pending the outcome of parallel criminal proceedings may constitute prejudice sufficient to warrant the dismissal of disciplinary proceedings for delay; *Lister v. College of Physicians & Surgeons (Ontario)*, (February 12, 1987), Doc. No. 1188/85 (Ont. Div. Ct.); *Johnson v. Law Society (Alberta)* (1985), 66 A.R. 345 at 349 (Q.B.); and *Lang v. Ramsay* (1992), 11 O.R. (3d) 190, in which the Divisional Court allowed an appeal from a finding of misconduct by a police officer, without invoking the *Charter*, in part because of a delay of five and one-half years from the date of the complaint to the start of the hearing, a delay that the court considered sufficient to give rise to an inference of prejudice.

88 See Charles Wolfram, *Modern Legal Ethics* (St. Paul, Minnesota: West, 1986), pp. 101-102.

The measure of whether circumstances give rise to a reasonable apprehension of bias is whether a person, viewing all the circumstances objectively, would have a reasonable apprehension that the tribunal or a member of the tribunal would not decide the issues impartially. The circumstances giving rise to a reasonable apprehension of bias may be either personal or institutional and may include tribunal members' prior involvement in a matter before them, their relationship with parties or witnesses, or their conduct at hearings.[89]

The Supreme Court of Canada has repeatedly emphasized that fundamental justice, natural justice, and fairness are flexible standards. The content of each of these requirements varies as a result of the nature of the matter to be decided, the applicable statutory provisions, and the circumstances of the case. As a corollary, the court has expressly allowed for a flexible application of the reasonable apprehension of bias test to take into account different administrative contexts.[90] The Supreme Court of Canada held in a 1990 decision that where partiality by reason of prejudgment (as contrasted with partiality by reason of personal interest) is alleged, the party alleging disqualifying bias must establish prejudgment of the matter to the extent that any representations at variance with the view that has been adopted would be futile.[90.1]

Because tribunals' findings must be based exclusively on evidence introduced at the hearing, tribunal members who have prior knowledge of the matters in issue should generally be disqualified. This principle, however, has been applied less rigorously to disciplinary tribunals than to courts. Thus, the Supreme Court of Canada has held that the participation in a disciplinary hearing of a tribunal member who participated earlier in a decision to suspend the practitioner's licence pending the hearing does not give rise to a reasonable apprehension of bias. In the same case, the court held that a member of a

89 The leading Canadian case on disqualification on the ground of reasonable apprehension of bias is *Committee for Justice & Liberty v. Canada (National Energy Board)*, [1978] 1 S.C.R. 369. A leading American case is *Tunney v. Ohio*, 47 S. Ct. 437 (1927), in which the Supreme Court held that impartiality is a requirement of due process. The House of Lords has recently departed from the traditional test by requiring the moving party to show "a real danger of injustice having occurred as a result of the alleged bias", a test that both de-emphasizes the importance of appearances and dispenses with the need to look at the alleged bias through the eyes of a reasonable person: *R. v. Gough*, [1993] A.C. 646, [1993] 2 W.L.R. 883 (H.L.). It remains to be seen whether Canadian courts will follow the House of Lords' lead. See also J. M. Evans, *de Smith's Judicial Review of Administrative Action*, 4th ed. (London: Stevens & Sons Ltd., 1980), p. 156; and Richard Steinecke and Donald Posluns, "Professional Misconduct Proceedings" (1988) 9 Advocates' Quarterly 160 at 176-183.

90 See *R. v. L. (T.P.)*, [1987] 2 S.C.R. 309 at 361; *Knight v. Indian Head School Division No. 19*, [1990] 1 S.C.R. 653 at 682; *Syndicat des employés de production du Québec & de l'Acadie v. Canada (Canadian Human Rights Commission)*, [1989] 2 S.C.R. 879 at 895-896; and *Committee for Justice & Liberty v. Canada (National Energy Board)*, *ibid.*

90.1 *Old St. Boniface Residents Assn. v. Winnipeg (City)*, [1990] 3 S.C.R. 1170, 46 Admin. L.R. 161, 2 M.P.L.R. (2d) 217, [1991] 2 W.W.R. 145, 116 N.R. 46, 69 Man. R. (2d) 134, 75 D.L.R. (4th) 385 at 408-409.

committee that referred the matter in issue to a hearing, but who did not personally participate in the referral decision, is not disqualified.[91] Foreknowledge of the allegations against a practitioner and of some of the evidence expected to be called at the hearing, and even the formation of tentative views on the matters in issue, have not always resulted in disqualification.[92]

A tribunal member will not be disqualified by reason of having sat as a member of the tribunal at a previous hearing involving the same practitioner, as long as the allegations in the two hearings are distinct and no serious adverse findings of credibility were made at the first hearing.[93] On the other hand, a tribunal member who has attempted to negotiate with the practitioner a resolution of the complaint that is the subject of the hearing will be disqualified.[94]

The prior involvement of tribunal members in a matter that would otherwise give rise to a reasonable apprehension of bias is unobjectionable in cases in which the tribunal's constituent statute specifically authorizes procedures

---

91 *Ringrose v. College of Physicians & Surgeons (Alberta)*, [1977] 1 S.C.R. 814 at 823-824.

92 Cases in which foreknowledge and the formation of tentative views have not resulted in disqualification include: *Allen v. Manitoba (Judicial Council)*, [1990] 5 W.W.R. 236 (Man. Q.B.), reversed (1990), 78 D.L.R. (4th) 576 (Man. C.A.); *French v. Law Society (Upper Canada) (No. 2)* (1975), 8 O.R. (2d) 193 at 198 (C.A.), application for leave to appeal to S.C.C. dismissed without written reasons (1975), 8 O.R. 193n (S.C.C.); *Mady v. Royal College of Dental Surgeons (Ontario)* (1974), 5 O.R. (2d) 414 at 421-422 (Div. Ct.); *Sutherland v. Pembroke Hospital* (1973), 1 O.R. (2d) 438 at 441 (Div. Ct.); *W.D. Latimer Co. v. Bray* (1974), 6 O.R. (2d) 129 at 140 (C.A.); and *Brett v. Board of Directors of Physiotherapy (Ontario)* (1992), 9 O.R. (3d) 613 (Div. Ct.). See, however, *Barsoum v. Pape*, [1988] N.W.T.R. 368 (S.C.) in which the court granted an order in the nature of prohibition requiring a board of inquiry constituted under the *Pharmacy Act* to desist from holding a hearing into allegations of professional misconduct where the board, which had reached certain conclusions about the practitioner's conduct based on an investigation that it had directed, had allowed its investigative and adjudicative functions to overlap; and *Leshner v. Ontario (Deputy Attorney General)* (1992), 10 O.R. (3d) 732 (Div. Ct.) in which the court found that certain proceedings were vitiated by a reasonable apprehension of bias where an official who had conducted an investigation into allegations of misconduct was also appointed to adjudicate on those allegations. See also *Assoc. des officiers de direction du service de police de Québec (Ville) v. Québec (Commission de police)* (1995), 119 D.L.R. (4th) 484, [1994] R.J.Q. 1505 (C.A.), in which a second inquiry was established to investigate the conduct of senior police officers whose conduct had been the subject of adverse criticism by an earlier inquiry into the conduct of other officers.

93 Cases involving tribunal members who have sat on previous hearings include: *French v. Law Society (Upper Canada) (No. 2)*, *ibid.*, pp. 198-199; *Re French* (1982), 39 O.R. (2d) 666 at 670-671 (Div. Ct.); *Batorski v. Moody* (1983), 42 O.R. (2d) 647 at 649-650 (Div. Ct.); *Vespra (Township) v. Ontario (Municipal Board)* (1983), 43 O.R. (2d) 680 at 684 (Div. Ct.); and *Huerto v. College of Physicians & Surgeons (Saskatchewan)*, [1994] 9 W.W.R. 457, 117 D.L.R. (4th) 129, 26 Admin. L.R. (2d) 169, 124 Sask. R. 33 (Q.B.).

94 *McGavin Toastmaster Ltd. v. Powlowski* (1973), 37 D.L.R. (3d) 100 at 118-119 (*sub nom.* B.C.T.W. v. Manitoba (Man. Human Rights Comm.)) (Man. C.A.).

involving overlapping functions. Thus, in a 1991 decision,[95] the Alberta Court of Appeal, by a two-to-one majority, held that no reasonable apprehension of bias arose where the Convocation of the Law Society of Alberta had approved a grant out of the law society's compensation fund — a grant based on a lawyer's dishonesty — before discipline proceedings were initiated.

Similarly, if a statute authorizes a tribunal to receive and investigate complaints in order to decide whether they should be referred for hearing, and then to hold a hearing to decide the matter, the members of the tribunal are not disqualified by reason of reasonable apprehension of bias because the statute authorizes their participation at each stage and because the questions to be determined (whether a hearing is warranted and whether the practitioner is guilty of misconduct) are different at each stage.[96] Even a preliminary determination may be authorized by statute.[97] The doctrine that prior involvement of tribunal members may be authorized by statute has survived *Charter* scrutiny.[98]

In two cases involving law society discipline proceedings, lawyers have argued unsuccessfully that provisions of the law society's constituent statute have created a financial interest in the adjudicators that has given rise to a reasonable apprehension of bias. In a 1987 Ontario case, the Divisional Court rejected an argument based on the law society's operation of its compulsory liability insurance program. The lawyer argued that the law society has an interest in disbarring members and thereby reducing insurance claims and that this interest gave rise to a reasonable apprehension of bias on the part of lawyers charged with professional misconduct. The court held that the very fact that both the insurance and the discipline functions were provided for by the *Law Society Act* was fatal to the lawyer's argument.[99]

---

95 *Duncan v. Law Society of Alberta Investigating Committee* (1991), 80 D.L.R. (4th) 702 (Alta. C.A.), leave to appeal to S.C.C. refused (1991), 85 D.L.R. (4th) viii (note) (S.C.C.). The New Brunswick Court of Appeal reached the same conclusion in *Russell v. Law Society (New Brunswick)* (1991), 117 N.B.R. (2d) 32, in which the appellant's objection was based on the participation of 11 of the 21 members of Council who imposed penalty after having been present when Council had made an interim suspension order.

96 *W.D. Latimer Co. v. Bray*, *supra*, note 92, pp. 140-141. See also *Ringrose v. College of Physicians & Surgeons (Alberta)*, *supra*, note 91, pp. 824-825; *Prescott v. Law Society (British Columbia)* (1971), 19 D.L.R. (3d) 446 at 454-455 (B.C. C.A.); and *Schabas v. University of Toronto* (1974), 6 O.R. (2d) 271 at 281-282 (Div. Ct.).

97 *Stone v. Public Accountants Council (Ontario)*, [1972] 3 O.R. 801 at 804-805 (H.C.); *R. v. Public Accountants Council (Ontario)*, [1960] O.R. 631 at 641-642 (*sub nom.* Public Accountancy Act v. Stoller) (C.A.).

98 See *Duncan v. Law Society of Alberta Investigating Committee*, *supra*, note 95; *Barry v. Alberta (Securities Commission)* (1986), 25 D.L.R. (4th) 730 at 735-736 (Alta. C.A.), affirmed [1989] 1 S.C.R. 301; and *Malartic Hygrade Gold Mines (Canada) Ltd. v. Ontario (Securities Commission)* (1986), 54 O.R. (2d) 544 at 549-550 (Div. Ct.), leave to appeal to Ont. C.A. refused (1986), 19 Admin. L.R. xliv (note) (Ont. C.A.).

99 *Feldman v. Law Society (Upper Canada)* (November 1, 1988), Doc. No. 639/85 (Ont. Div. Ct.).

The second case is a 1991 decision of the Supreme Court of Canada in which a lawyer contended that a provision in the Manitoba *Law Society Act* that empowers the law society to order lawyers found guilty of professional misconduct or conduct unbecoming a barrister and solicitor to pay costs gave rise to a reasonable apprehension of bias. The court held that the provision did not create a perception of pecuniary interest that was sufficient to put into doubt the impartiality of the governing body.[100]

In a 1989 decision, however, the Alberta Court of Queen's Bench made an order prohibiting the College of Physicians and Surgeons of Alberta from pursuing disciplinary action against a doctor on the ground that the college's investigating committee was empowered to make a preliminary determination of the case, recommend sanctions to the council of the college, and initiate new proceedings that it would also adjudicate. The investigating committee, the court held, acted as both accuser and judge.[101]

Similar considerations apply when the basis of a reasonable apprehension of bias argument is either improper conduct or a relationship between an adjudicator and either a party or a witness. Again, discipline panels are not held to the same standard as are courts. In a 1988 decision, the Ontario Divisional Court held that though the questioning of an unrepresented lawyer by members of a discipline hearing panel of the law society was frequent and sometimes significant and excessive, it did not indicate a reasonable apprehension of bias, since such tribunals are not held to the same standard as are courts.[102] In a 1998 decision of the Nova Scotia Court of Appeal,[102.1] however, the Court applied a higher standard to a discipline committee of the Nova Scotia Barristers' Society: administrative tribunals that are primarily adjudicative in their functions will be expected to comply with the standard applicable to courts. The Court of Appeal allowed the lawyer's appeal and set aside the discipline committee's finding that he was guilty of professional misconduct on the ground that the committee members' questioning of the lawyer left them "cast with the demeanour of prosecutors" as they examined on matters not relevant to the complaint and made suggestions of bad faith and unfair conduct in doing so.

A reasonable apprehension of bias may be created by questions asked by members of the tribunal that appear to prejudge the merits of the case or the character of a party. An attitude of hostility toward a party or the adoption of

---

100 *Pearlman v. Law Society (Manitoba)* (1991), 84 D.L.R. (4th) 105 (S.C.C.).

101 *Rosenstock v. College of Physicians & Surgeons (Alberta)*, [1989] 2 W.W.R. 611 (Alta. Q.B.).

102 *Rusonik v. Law Society (Upper Canada)* (1988), 28 O.A.C. 57 (Div. Ct.).

102.1 *Solicitor "X" v. Nova Scotia Barristers' Society* (1998), 171 D.L.R. (4th) 310 (N.S. C.A.). The Court applied, in the context of Law Society discipline proceedings, the Supreme Court of Canada's decision in *Newfoundland Telephone Co. v. Newfoundland (Board of Commissioners of Public Utilities)*, [1992] 1 S.C.R. 623 at 636, 638-39, 134 N.R. 241, 89 D.L.R. (4th) 289, 4 Admin. L.R. (2d) 121, 95 Nfld. & P.E.I.R. 271, 301 A.P.R. 271.

a prosecutorial role may also infect proceedings with a reasonable apprehension of bias. Again, whether a reasonable apprehension of bias is created in law depends on the context of the adjudicator's comments and questions and the circumstances as a whole.[103]

In a 1993 decision,[103.1] the Quebec Court of Appeal held, by a two-to-one majority, that the fact that a party has filed a complaint with the Canadian Judicial Council concerning the judge's rulings and attitudes during the course of the hearings in question is an insufficient reason in itself to order the disqualification of the judge on the basis of a reasonable apprehension of bias. It if were otherwise, the majority observed, it would not be hard "to imagine the dishonest manoeuvres of a party wishing to paralyze the proceedings or trying to avoid a decision that he anticipates will be unfavourable to him".[103.2]

A member of a tribunal must not have a pecuniary or other relationship with a party or witness that would reasonably compromise confidence in the tribunal member's impartiality.[104] A 1999 decision of the Ontario Divisional Court[104.1] provides an example of a case in which a discipline hearing panel member's relationship with a witness was held to give rise to a reasonable apprehension of bias. In that case one of the members of a discipline hearing panel of the College of Nurses of Ontario regularly attended meetings of a hospital committee with the immediate superior of the nurse who was alleged to be guilty of professional misconduct. The immediate superior was one of the main witnesses called on behalf of the College, as she had conducted the investigation that led to the allegations of misconduct. Although the panel ruled

---

103 See *Deep v. College of Physicians & Surgeons (Ontario)* (1974), 5 O.R. (2d) 435 (Div. Ct.); *Golomb v. College of Physicians & Surgeons (Ontario)* (1976), 12 O.R. (2d) 73 at 88 and 92 (Div. Ct.); *Bernstein v. College of Physicians & Surgeons (Ontario)* (1977), 15 O.R. (2d) 447 at 472 and 479 (Div. Ct.); *Milstein v. College of Pharmacy (Ontario) (No. 2)* (1978), 20 O.R. (2d) 283 at 295-296 (C.A.); *College of Physicians & Surgeons (Ontario) v. Casullo*, [1977] 2 S.C.R. 2; *Connor v. Law Society (British Columbia)*, [1980] 4 W.W.R. 638 at 643 (B.C. S.C.); *Re Rodrigues* (1987), (*sub nom.* Rodrigues v. Newfoundland Dental Board) 44 D.L.R. (4th) 689 (Nfld. T.D.); and *Misra v. College of Physicians & Surgeons (Saskatchewan)*, [1988] 5 W.W.R. 333 (Sask. C.A.), leave to appeal to S.C.C. granted (1989), 79 Sask. R. 80 (note) (S.C.C.), appeal to S.C.C. discontinued January 27, 1992.

103.1 *S. (P.) v. C.(A.J.)* (1993), 101 D.L.R. (4th) 345 (Que. C.A.).

103.2 *Ibid.*, p. 360.

104 *Moskalyk-Walker v. College of Pharmacy (Ontario)* (1975), 8 O.R. (2d) 609 at 611-612 (Div. Ct.); *Hirt v. College of Physicians & Surgeons (British Columbia)* (1986), 63 B.C.L.R. 185 at 205 (S.C.), affirmed (1986), 10 B.C.L.R. (2d) 314 (C.A.); and *Wasylyshen v. Law Society (Saskatchewan)* (1987), 36 D.L.R. (4th) 214 at 223 (Sask. C.A.), leave to appeal to S.C.C. refused [1987] 5 W.W.R. lxiii (note) (S.C.C.). In *Dulmage v. Ontario (Police Complaints Commissioner)* (1994), 21 O.R. (3d) 356, 75 O.A.C. 305, 120 D.L.R. (4th) 590, 30 Admin. L.R. (2d) 203 (Div. Ct.), the Ontario Divisional Court granted a judicial review application and prohibited a board of inquiry from proceeding with an inquiry into the conduct of police officers, in part on the basis that a member of the panel was the president of a chapter of a group of which an officer from another chapter had made a statement at a press conference that reflected apparent prejudgment of the issue at the hearing.

104.1 *Roberts v. College of Nurses of Ontario*, [1999] O.J. 2281 (Div. Ct.).

that the panel member should be disqualified on the ground that there could well be a reasonable apprehension of bias, the panel member continued to attend the hearing after her disqualification, was present in the public gallery on the day on which the panel heard evidence and submissions on penalty, and spoke to other members of the panel in a coffee room at the beginning and end of the day. The Divisional Court held that the reasonable apprehension of bias in the one member of the tribunal was sufficient to disqualify the whole tribunal, and ordered a stay of the proceedings.

Potential objections based on a reasonable apprehension of bias may be waived either explicitly or by conduct. A party must be aware of the existence of the adjudicator's potentially disqualifying interest for the waiver to be effective.[105]

Tribunal members who would otherwise be disqualified because of a reasonable apprehension of bias will nonetheless be required to decide a matter if, without their participation, there would not be a tribunal competent to decide the case.[106]

26.12 DUTY TO ACT JUDICIALLY

In the words of former Chief Justice McRuer of the Ontario High Court of Justice, tribunals empowered to impose discipline sanctions "must act judicially as distinct from merely acting judiciously."[107] This means that the tribunal must give all parties whose rights may be affected by its order both notice of the nature of the proceedings to be taken and a full opportunity to be heard and to meet any case put against them. The tribunal also has a duty to approach the issues without bias and to listen fairly to both sides.[108]

105 Courts have considered the elements of an effective waiver of a potentially disqualifying reasonable apprehension of bias in *Wasylyshen v. Law Society (Saskatchewan)* (1985), 39 Sask. R. 187 at 192 (C.A.); and *R. v. Broker-Dealers' Assn. of Ontario*, [1971] 1 O.R. 355 at 365-366 (H.C.).

106 The doctrine of necessity, requiring tribunal members to decide a case if there would not otherwise be a competent tribunal, was applied to a Canadian discipline proceeding in *Johnston v. Law Society (Prince Edward Island)* (1991), 91 Nfld. & P.E.I.R. 126 (P.E.I. C.A.), leave to appeal to S.C.C. refused (1991), 93 Nfld. & P.E.I.R. 270 (note) (S.C.C.). The doctrine was applied many years earlier to an American discipline proceeding in *Brinkley v. Hassig*, 83 F. 2d 351 (1936). See also *Re Ashby*, [1934] O.R. 421 at 431 (C.A.); *Kalina v. Directors of Chiropractic (Ontario)* (1981), 35 O.R. (2d) 626 at 628 (Div. Ct.), leave to appeal to Ont. C.A. refused (1982), 35 O.R. (2d) 626 (C.A.); *Milne v. Joint Chiropractic Professional Review Committee (Saskatchewan)*, [1992] 3 W.W.R. 354 (Sask. C.A.); *Bennett v. British Columbia (Securities Commission)* (1992), 94 D.L.R. (4th) 339 (C.A.), leave to appeal to Supreme Court of Canada dismissed [1992] 6 W.W.R. lvii (note); and *E.A. Manning Ltd. v. Ontario (Securities Commission)* (1994), 18 O.R. (3d) 97 (Div. Ct.).

107 *Mehr v. Law Society (Upper Canada)*, [1954] O.R. 337 at 343 (H.C.), affirmed [1954] O.R. 692 (C.A.), reversed on other grounds [1955] S.C.R. 344.

108 In *Re F. (sub nom. Re Legal Professions Act & Benchers Society of British Columbia)*, [1945] 4 D.L.R. 702 at 703-704 (B.C. Law Visitorial Trib.), Farris C.J.S.C. held that a discipline committee empowered to hear a complaint of professional misconduct has a duty

The rights created by the duty to act judicially for lawyers alleged to be guilty of professional misconduct or conduct unbecoming include the right to notice of the allegations, the right to a hearing, the right to cross-examine the complainant and all other witnesses, the right to examine all the evidence that will be tendered, the right to testify, the right to lead evidence, the right to present argument, and the right to be represented by counsel of choice.[109]

Two of these rights, the right to cross-examine witnesses and the right to notice of the allegations, require comment. In Ontario, section 15 of the *Statutory Powers Procedure Act* provides that a tribunal may admit as evidence and act upon any oral testimony, document or other thing that is relevant, whether or not it would be admissible in evidence in a court, unless the testimony, document, or thing would be inadmissible in a court by reason of any privilege under the law of evidence or is inadmissible under any statute. That section permits the admission of hearsay evidence.[110]

Nevertheless, Canadian courts have uniformly held that the right of cross-examination is so highly valued in our legal system that it cannot be denied to a party on a vital fact in issue and that a refusal of the right of cross-examination will be fatal to the proceedings.[111] Subsection 33(9) of the Ontario *Law Society Act*, which provides that the rules of evidence applicable in civil proceedings are also applicable in discipline proceedings before the law society, probably has the effect independently of making hearsay evidence on vital facts in issue inadmissible.

As for the right to notice of the allegations, courts have distinguished between the degree of precision required in criminal prosecutions and that required in discipline proceedings. Justice Cory, while sitting on the Divisional Court, made this distinction in the following way:

> The charges brought against a professional person by his governing body should not, in most cases, be approached as though they were counts in an indictment alleging that he committed an offence or offences contrary to the Criminal Code . . . Charges . . . should . . . specify that there has been

to act judicially, citing *O'Connor v. Waldron*, [1935] A.C. 76 at 82 (P.C.), and *St. John v. Fraser*, [1935] S.C.R. 441.

109 The procedural rights created by the duty to act judicially are commented upon generally in *Banks v. Hall*, [1941] 2 W.W.R. 534 at 542 (Sask. C.A.), and in numerous American cases including *Re Ruffalo*, 88 S. Ct. 1222 (1968); *Withrow v. Larkin*, 95 S. Ct. 1456 (1975); *Re Jones*, 506 F. 2d 527 (8th Cir., 1974); and *Giddens v. State Bar*, 621 P. 2d 851 (Cal., 1981).

110 See *Lischka v. Ontario (Criminal Injuries Compensation Board)* (1982), 37 O.R. (2d) 134 (Div. Ct.).

111 In *Brethour v. Law Society (British Columbia)*, [1951] 2 D.L.R. 138 at 140 (B.C. C.A.), O'Halloran J. held that refusal of the right to cross-examine the complainant is fatal to the proceedings. *Mehr v. Law Society (Upper Canada)*, [1955] S.C.R. 344 at 349, and *Golomb v. College of Physicians & Surgeons (Ontario)* (1976), 12 O.R. (2d) 73 (Div. Ct.), are to the same effect. See also Richard Steinecke and Donald Posluns, "Professional Misconduct Proceedings" (1988) 9 Advocates' Quarterly 160 at 196.

> professional misconduct and set out the particulars relied upon to demonstrate such conduct. Those particulars should not be given the designation of "count" which may imply that the procedure to be followed is that provided by the Criminal Code.[112]

Nevertheless, governing bodies must not admit evidence or find lawyers guilty of professional misconduct that is not alleged in the complaint. The complaint limits the scope of the proceeding.

It does not follow that all evidence supporting the allegation must be set forth in the complaint. In proceedings governed by the Ontario *Statutory Powers Procedure Act,* the parties must be given reasonable notice of the hearing, and the notice of hearing must include information about the time, place, and purpose of the hearing, a reference to the statutory authority under which the hearing will be held, and a statement that if the notified party does not attend, the tribunal may proceed in the party's absence and the party will not be entitled to any further notice in the proceedings. The Act also specifies, in a separate section, that where the good character, propriety of conduct, or competence of a party is an issue, the party is entitled to be furnished prior to the hearing with reasonable information of any allegations with respect thereto.[113]

The Act does not require the reasonable information of allegations to be set out in the complaint itself, and the Divisional Court has held that no denial of natural justice will result if evidence not referred to in the complaint is disclosed prior to the hearing.[114] The ultimate test is whether lawyers know the case they have to meet so that they are not taken by surprise.[115] The complaint need not refer to either the precise rule of professional conduct allegedly violated or the precise sanction that will be sought if the allegations are established.

Where more than one incident of misconduct is alleged in a complaint, evidence in relation to each incident may be introduced at the same hearing. The hearing panel should, however, be careful to consider each allegation separately in making its findings. Except in the unusual situation in which evidence introduced to prove one allegation is admissible in relation to another

---

112 *Stevens v. Law Society (Upper Canada)* (1979), 55 O.R. (2d) 405 (Div. Ct.). The Divisional Court had made the same point in *Golomb v. College of Physicians & Surgeons (Ontario), ibid.*, p. 82, in which the court emphasized the prejudicial effect of evidence of misconduct not alleged in the notice of hearing. See also *Percheson v. College of Physicians & Surgeons (Ontario)* (1985), 51 O.R. (2d) 91 at 95-96 (Div. Ct.).

113 Sections 6 and 8.

114 *Cwinn v. Law Society (Upper Canada)* (1980), 28 O.R. (2d) 61 at 70 (Div. Ct.), leave to appeal denied and appeal quashed (1980), 28 O.R. (2d) 61n (S.C.C.).

115 The notice of hearing must make it clear to practitioners that it is a hearing, and not just a preliminary investigative meeting, that they are being given a right to attend: *R. v. Ontario (Racing Commission)*, [1970] 1 O.R. 458 at 462-463 (H.C.). See also Charles Wolfram, *Modern Legal Ethics* (St. Paul, Minnesota: West, 1986), pp. 102-103.

allegation because of the striking similarity of the lawyer's conduct, each allegation must be proven separately.[116]

Discipline hearing panels should exercise similar care where allegations against two or more lawyers are made in the same complaint. The hearing panel must consider separately the evidence in relation to each lawyer. Despite the need for such care, a common proceeding involving more than one lawyer is generally preferable to separate proceedings against each, both in the interest of efficiency and, more importantly, in the interest of avoiding inconsistent decisions.[117]

The Ontario Divisional Court has held that the *audi alteram partem* rule requires a tribunal that is considering imposing a penalty harsher than the one recommended by the parties in a joint submission to inform the parties that it is considering imposing such a penalty and to request submissions on that issue.[118]

26.13 ADJOURNMENTS AND INTERIM SUSPENSIONS

Most law societies are now authorized by statute to order the interim suspension of members pending a hearing.[119] The Ontario Divisional Court has held, moreover, that both a discipline committee and Convocation may require a member who has admitted serious misconduct to undertake not to practise as a condition of granting a request for an adjournment.[120]

The courts have held that where statutes expressly empower governing bodies to issue interim suspension orders, such orders should be used sparingly. An interim suspension order may be made when it is necessary to protect the public or when a practitioner has flouted the authority of the governing body.[121]

---

116 *College of Physicians & Surgeons (Ontario) v. K.* (1985), 59 O.R. (2d) 1 (C.A.); see also *R. v. Litchfield*, [1993] 4 S.C.R. 333.

117 See *Law Society (Manitoba) v. Crump* (1982), 14 Man. R. (2d) 405 at 410-411 (C.A.); *Threader v. Canada (Treasury Board)*, [1987] 1 F.C. 41 (C.A.); and *Ontario (Ministry of Transportation & Communications) v. Eat 'N Putt Ltd.* (1985), 50 O.R. (2d) 503 at 505-506 (Div. Ct.).

118 *College of Physicians & Surgeons (Ontario) v. Petrie* (1989), 68 O.R. (2d) 100 (Div. Ct.).

119 See, for example, section 16.1 of *Statutory Powers Procedure Act*, R.S.O. 1990, c. S. 22, as amended.

120 *Amourgis v. Law Society of Upper Canada* (1984), 48 O.R. (2d) 91, 12 D.L.R. (4th) 759, 5 O.A.C. 286 (Div. Ct.).

121 The rare circumstances in which interim suspension orders may be justified are discussed in *Wilson v. Law Society (British Columbia) (No. 2)* (1975), 64 D.L.R. (3d) 512 at 516-517 (B.C. S.C.); *James v. Law Society (British Columbia)*, [1982] 2 W.W.R. 647 at 651-654 (B.C. S.C.); and *College of Physicians & Surgeons (Manitoba) v. Morgentaler* (1986), 28 D.L.R. (4th) 283 at 286 (Man. C.A.).

Where governing bodies are authorized to order interim suspensions, certain natural justice requirements will be read into the statute if no proce-

(*Continued on page 26–37*)

dural protections are specified, though the notice and evidentiary rules that govern the conduct of the ultimate hearing are likely to be relaxed at the hearing of a motion for an interim suspension.[122]

Common law rules governing motions for adjournment apply in disciplinary proceedings. The decision whether to grant an adjournment is a discretionary matter that must must be determined by balancing the right to a fair hearing against the desirability of an expeditious process. The wrongful refusal of a request for an adjournment may result in a denial of natural justice in exceptional cases.[123]

26.14 HEARING PANEL'S USE OF OWN EXPERTISE

Because the *audi alteram partem* rule applies to discipline proceedings, the decisions of hearing panels must be based upon the evidence introduced at hearings, including any facts agreed upon by the parties.[124] Hearing panels may take notice of any generally recognized scientific or technical facts within their specialized knowledge, in addition to taking notice of any facts that may be judicially noticed. Indeed, the specialized knowledge of members of professional regulatory bodies is one of the most important justifications for self-governance.[125]

Members of discipline tribunals may thus use their expertise in making findings of fact. However, they must have an evidentiary basis for those findings. They cannot decide disputed issues purely on the basis of their own beliefs, though they may act upon evidence by supplementing it with their own expertise, particularly when dealing with issues of prevailing professional standards. As former Associate Chief Justice MacKinnon of the Ontario

---

(B.C. S.C.); and *College of Physicians & Surgeons (Manitoba) v. Morgentaler* (1986), 28 D.L.R. (4th) 283 at 286 (Man. C.A.).

122 *Taylor v. Law Society (British Columbia)* (1980), 116 D.L.R. (3d) 41 (B.C. S.C.); and *College of Physicians & Surgeons (Manitoba) v. Morgentaler*, *ibid.*, p. 286.

123 *Morgan v. Land Surveyors Assn. (Ontario)* (1980), 28 O.R. (2d) 19 at 22-23 (Div. Ct.); *Mulvihill v. R.* (1914), 22 C.C.C. 354 (B.C. C.A.), extension of time for appeal refused (1914), 49 S.C.R. 587; *Mady v. Royal College of Dental Surgeons (Ontario)* (1974), 5 O.R. (2d) 414 at 423 (Div. Ct.); and *Jain v. College of Physicians & Surgeons (British Columbia)* (1974), 52 D.L.R. (3d) 616 at 622 (B.C. S.C.).

124 *Prescott v. Law Society (British Columbia)*, [1971] 4 W.W.R. 433 at 444 (B.C. C.A.). That the parties may agree upon some or all of the facts was affirmed by Justice Henry in *Emerson v. Law Society (Upper Canada)* (1983), 44 O.R. (2d) 729 at 755 (H.C.). Section 4 of the Ontario *Statutory Powers Procedure Act*, R.S.O. 1990, c. S.22, also makes it clear that proceedings to which the Act applies may be disposed of by agreement.

125 Section 16 of the Ontario *Statutory Powers Procedure Act* provides that a tribunal may take notice of any generally recognized scientific or technical facts within its specialized knowledge. The use by disciplinary tribunals of the specialized knowledge of their members has been judicially sanctioned in *Stout v. College of Pharmacy (Ontario)* (1977), 15 O.R. (2d) 650 at 655-657 (C.A.); and *Ringrose v. College of Physicians & Surgeons (Alberta) (No. 2)*, [1978] 2 W.W.R. 534 at 553-556 (Alta. C.A.), leave to appeal to S.C.C. refused May 16, 1978.

Court of Appeal said in a 1983 decision, members of discipline tribunals may use their own expertise in assessing evidence before them, but the evidence must be before them before they can assess it. The expertise used by members of tribunals must not be at variance with the evidence.[126]

26.15 USE OF TRANSCRIPTS OF PREVIOUS TESTIMONY — SECTION 13 OF THE CHARTER

Section 13 of the *Canadian Charter of Rights and Freedoms* provides that a witness in any proceedings has the right not to have any incriminating evidence given there used to incriminate him or her in any other proceedings, except in a prosecution for perjury or for giving contradictory evidence.

The Ontario Divisional Court has held that the admission into evidence in a discipline hearing of statements made by a lawyer to the police pursuant to a promise of immunity does not offend section 13 because the lawyer could not be considered a witness at the time the statements were made.[127] The Saskatchewan Court of Queen's Bench, similarly, has held that the admission into evidence of a doctor's response to correspondence from his governing body, in circumstances in which he had a statutory duty to provide the information requested, does not violate section 13 because the doctor could not be considered a "witness."[128]

In a 1984 decision,[129] the British Columbia Court of Appeal held that a transcript of a lawyer's evidence in a civil proceeding is not admissible in a later discipline hearing as evidence that the lawyer had acted in an unbecoming manner because section 13 protects a witness from the use of incriminating evidence in any other proceedings, including proceedings in which the witness may be subjected to penalties.

Three years later the same court held that counsel for the law society may cross-examine a lawyer on evidence given in a previous proceeding for

126 Cases in which decisions of tribunals have been reversed for lack of an evidentiary basis for findings of fact informed by the specialized knowledge of tribunal members include: *Hosein v. College of Physicians & Surgeons (Ontario)* (1974), 5 O.R. (2d) 204 at 206 and 210 (H.C.); *Burns v. Chiropractic Assn. (Alberta)* (1981), 125 D.L.R. (3d) 475 (Alta. C.A.); *Reddall v. College of Nurses (Ontario)* (1983), 42 O.R. (2d) 412 at 416-417 (C.A.) (from which the quotation of Associate Chief Justice MacKinnon is taken); *Del Core v. Ontario College of Pharmacists* (1985), 51 O.R. (2d) 1 (C.A.), leave to appeal to S.C.C. refused (1986), 57 O.R. (2d) 296n (S.C.C.); and *Knippel v. Institute of Chartered Accountants of Saskatchewan (Discipline Committee)*, 1991 S.J. No. 184 (Sask. Q.B.), April 10, 1991 (unreported). See also Richard Steinecke and Donald Posluns, "Professional Misconduct Proceedings" (1988) 9 Advocates' Quarterly 160 at 191-193.

127 *Prousky v. Law Society of Upper Canada and Attorney General of Ontario* (1987), 61 O.R. (2d) 37 (H.C.), affirmed (1987), 62 O.R. (2d) 224 (C.A.).

128 *Bassett v. College of Physicians & Surgeons (Saskatchewan)* (1987), 63 Sask. R. 45 (Appeal Trib. under the Medical Professions Act), affirmed (1988), 70 Sask. R. 283 (C.A.).

129 *Donald v. Law Society (British Columbia)*, [1984] 2 W.W.R. 46 (B.C. C.A.), additional reasons at [1985] 2 W.W.R. 671 (B.C. C.A.), leave to appeal to S.C.C. refused (1984), 55 N.R. 237 (S.C.C.).

the purpose of impeaching credibility, but that if the main purpose of using a transcript of previous evidence in cross-examination is to incriminate, the use of the transcript would contravene section 13.[130]

In 1988 the Ontario Divisional Court considered an appeal from a finding that a lawyer was guilty of professional misconduct because he gave misleading evidence under oath in an affidavit and on a cross-examination in previous proceedings. The court held that section 13 did not prevent the law society's counsel from introducing the affidavit and a transcript of the cross-examination into evidence in discipline proceedings if the giving of false or misleading evidence is the *actus reus* of the offence.[131] The court adopted a distinction drawn by the Saskatchewan Court of Appeal and approved by the Supreme Court of Canada in a criminal case in which the same issue was raised, between occasions on which persons testifying under oath are required when answering truthfully to disclose the commission by them of an offence — on which occasions the testimony generally cannot be used against them — and occasions on which persons testifying under oath are alleged to have made false statements — on which occasions the statements are admissible in a subsequent proceeding in which the allegedly false evidence forms the very substance of the offence with which the persons are charged.[132]

All these cases either predate or were decided without reference to the Supreme Court of Canada's decision that section 11 of the *Charter* does not apply to disciplinary proceedings that do not subject practitioners to true penal consequences.[133] Since the Supreme Court of Canada's ruling, the Saskatchewan Court of Appeal has assimilated the right protected by section 13 to the rights protected by subsections 11(c) and (d) of the *Charter* — the rights of non-compellability and the presumption of innocence — and has held that the scope of sections 11 and 13 should generally be the same. Thus, the court held, one may incriminate oneself pursuant to section 13 only in respect of criminal or quasi-criminal charges or other proceedings with penal consequences. The court pointed out that the 1984 decision of the British Columbia Court of Appeal, referred to above, antedated the Supreme Court of Canada's ruling on the applicability of section 11 of the *Charter* to disciplinary proceedings that do not involve true penal consequences, and it distinguished that case on the basis that the British Columbia statute empowered the law society to impose a fine of up to $10,000, a sanction that "would, in all likelihood, have been found to be a true penal consequence."[134]

---

130 *Johnstone v. Law Society (British Columbia)*, [1987] 5 W.W.R. 637 (B.C. C.A.). The Supreme Court of Canada came to a similar conclusion in *R. v. Kuldip*, [1990] 3 S.C.R. 618.

131 *Spring v. Law Society (Upper Canada)* (1988), 64 O.R. (2d) 719 (Div. Ct.).

132 *R. v. Staranchuk* (1983), 3 D.L.R. (4th) 574 at 576 (Sask. C.A.), affirmed [1985] 1 S.C.R. 439.

133 *R. v. Wigglesworth*, [1987] 2 S.C.R. 541. See also text accompanying notes 13 to 18, *supra*.

134 *Knutson v. Registered Nurses' Assn. (Saskatchewan)* (1990), 75 D.L.R. (4th) 723 (Sask. C.A.). The test for determining whether a fine is a true penal consequence is articulated by

Although this last proposition, particularly, is highly questionable, there is nevertheless little room in the present state of the law to successfully invoke section 13 in disciplinary proceedings. To summarize: section 13 is not violated by the introduction of statements made by a lawyer to the police or to the lawyer's governing body, nor is it violated by the use of a transcript of a lawyer's evidence in previous proceedings if the main purpose of referring to the transcript is to impeach credibility. Evidence in previous proceedings may be relied upon to prove an allegation that the same evidence was false or misleading. Even in cases involving complaints of misconduct unrelated to the giving of false or misleading evidence and in which the transcript is used to prove the governing body's case rather than to impeach credibility, section 13 will not be violated unless the proceedings can be said to expose the lawyer to true penal consequences, a possibility only if a fine is so large that it appears to be imposed to redress the wrong done to society at large rather than to maintain internal discipline.

It is unlikely that section 7 of the *Charter* will be interpreted to prohibit the use of a transcript of a lawyer's evidence in prior proceedings. Although section 7 may provide some residual protection when section 13 is inapplicable, the Supreme Court of Canada has held that it was not intended to provide a generalized right against self-incrimination based on the United States model.[135]

26.16 STANDARD OF PROOF

The standard of proof required to establish a complaint of professional misconduct or conduct unbecoming a barrister and solicitor has been defined differently over the years. It is now established that:

(a) The standard is a civil standard rather than the criminal standard of proof beyond a reasonable doubt, even if the misconduct alleged is also

---

Justice Wilson in *R. v. Wigglesworth, ibid.*, p. 561. As for the use of a transcript of disciplinary proceedings in a related civil action, see *Baumann v. Bonderove* (1986), 45 Alta. L.R. (2d) 168 (C.A.); *Duarte v. Perreault* (1991), 83 Alta. L.R. (2d) 92 (Master); *Hamulka v. Golfman*, [1985] 5 W.W.R. 597 (Man. C.A.); and *Merrill Lynch, Royal Securities Ltd./Ltée. v. Granove*, [1985] 5 W.W.R. 589 (Man. C.A.). See also *R. v. Dubois*, [1985] 2 S.C.R. 350; and *McDonald v. Law Society (Alberta)*, [1994] 3 W.W.R. 697 (Alta. Q.B.).

135 *Thomson Newspapers Ltd. v. Canada (Director of Investigation & Research)*, [1990] 1 S.C.R. 425. See also *British Columbia (Securities Commission) v. Branch* (1992), 88 D.L.R. (4th) 381 (B.C. C.A.), leave to appeal to S.C.C. granted [1992] 6 W.W.R. lvii (note) (S.C.C.). Where the previous evidence is given on examination for discovery, its use may violate the implied undertaking that it will not be used for any purpose other than the litigation: see *Reichmann v. Toronto Life Publishing Co.* (1988), 28 C.P.C. (2d) 11 (Ont. H.C.), leave to appeal to Ont. Div. Ct. refused (1988), 29 C.P.C. (2d) 66 (Ont. H.C.); *755568 Ontario Ltd. v. Linchris Homes Ltd.* (1990), 1 O.R. (3d) 649 (Ont. Gen. Div.); but see also *Kyuquot Logging Ltd. v. B.C. Forest Products Ltd.* (1986), 5 B.C.L.R. (2d) 1 (C.A.).

a criminal offence;[136]

(b) The standard nevertheless rises in direct proportion to the gravity of the allegation and the seriousness of the consequences, and accordingly, if the allegations are serious, the trier of fact must scrutinize the cogency of the evidence with greater care than would be required, for example, in an ordinary negligence case; and

(c) In order to find an allegation of professional misconduct or conduct unbecoming a barrister and solicitor made out, clear and convincing proof based on cogent evidence is required.[137]

In some cases, courts have held that in the assessment of the evidence the lawyer's explanation should be accepted if there is a reasonable probability of it being true.[138] In others, courts have expressly stated that where the allegation is one of criminal misconduct, it must be proven beyond a reason-

---

136 In *Camgoz v. College of Physicians & Surgeons (Saskatchewan)* (1989), (*sub nom re Camgoz*) 74 Sask. R. 73 (C.A.), the Saskatchewan Court of Appeal held that in a case in which the allegation is that the practitioner is guilty of a criminal offence the standard of proof is the highest possible standard applicable in a civil case, which, however, is not proof beyond a reasonable doubt. In *Miller v. Saskatchewan Psychiatric Nurses' Association* (1992), 103 Sask. R. 61 (Q.B.) the court referred to *R. v. Oakes*, [1986] 1 S.C.R. 103, in which Dickson C.J.C. quoted Lord Denning's statement in *Bater v. Bater*, [1950] 2 All E.R. 458 (C.A.) that "A civil court, when considering a charge of fraud, will naturally require a higher degree of probability than that which it would require if considering whether negligence were established. It does not establish so high a standard as a criminal court, even when considering a charge of a criminal nature, but still it does require a degree of probability which is commensurate with the occasion" (at p. 77). See also *Hryciuk v. Ontario (Lieutenant Governor)* (1994), 18 O.R. (3d) 695 (Div. Ct.); *Re Khaliq-Kareemi (sub nom. Khaliq-Kareemi v. Nova Scotia (Health Services & Insurance Commission)* (1988), 84 N.S.R. (2d) 425 (T.D.), reversed on other grounds (1989), 89 N.S.R. (2d) 388 (C.A.), leave to appeal to S.C.C. refused (1989), 93 N.S.R. (2d) 269 (note) (S.C.C.); and *Glassman v. College of Physicians & Surgeons (Ontario)*, [1966] 2 O.R. 81 (C.A.).

137 In *Coates v. Ontario (Registrar of Motor Vehicle Dealers & Salesmen)* (1988), 52 D.L.R. (4th) 272, the Ontario Divisional Court articulated the "clear and convincing proof based on cogent evidence" test and cited *R. v. Oakes*, [1986] 1 S.C.R. 103 at 137, *per* Dickson C.J.C. for the proposition that the standard of proof rises with the gravity of the allegations and the seriousness of the consequences. See also *Hryciuk v. Ontario (Lieutenant Governor)* (1994), 18 O.R. (3d) 645 (Div. Ct.); *Beckon v. Ontario (Deputy Chief Coroner)* (1992), (*sub nom. Re Beckon*) 9 O.R. (3d) 256 (C.A.); *Lanford v. General Medical Council* (1989), [1990] 1 A.C. 13 (P.C.); and *Gillen v. College of Physicians & Surgeons (Ontario)* (1989), 68 O.R. (2d) 278 (Div. Ct.). Earlier civil cases to the same effect include *Briginshaw v. Briginshaw* (1938), 60 C.L.R. 336, *per* Sir Owen Dixon J.; *Bater v. Bater*, [1950] 2 All E.R. 458 at 459 (C.A.), *per* Lord Denning; *Smith v. Smith*, [1952] 2 S.C.R. 312 at 331-33, *per* Cartwright J.; *Hanes v. Wawenesa Mutual Insurance Co.*, [1963] S.C.R. 154 at 161; *Bernstein v. College of Physicians & Surgeons (Ontario)* (1977), 15 O.R. (2d) 447 at 470 and 485-86 (Div. Ct.) *per* O'Leary J. and Garrett J., respectively; and *Continental Insurance Co. v. Dalton College Co.* (1982), 131 D.L.R. (3d) 559 at 563-64 (S.C.C.) *per* Laskin C.J.C.

138 *Brethour v. Law Society (British Columbia)* (1950), 1 W.W.R. 34 at 38 (B.C. C.A.), *per* O'Halloran J.A.; *Shumiatcher v. Law Society (Saskatchewan), ibid.*, p. 328.

able doubt.[139] None of these authorities have been explicitly overruled, but the propositions for which they stand should now be considered to be qualified, at least in Canada, by the principles that clear and convincing proof based upon cogent evidence is required and that the standard of proof rises with the gravity of the allegation and the seriousness of the consequences. One is tempted to surmise that in a case in which it is alleged that a lawyer is guilty of misconduct that is also a criminal offence, there is little if any difference in practice between this sliding civil standard and the criminal standard of proof beyond a reasonable doubt.

In considering whether a discipline committee has applied the correct test, a court on appeal will examine not only the test the committee has articulated, but also whether, on a review of all the evidence, the proper test has in fact been applied.[140] A tribunal is not required in law to express the degree of proof it has required.[141]

The failure of a lawyer to testify may be weighed by the tribunal once counsel for the law society has established a *prima facie* case. Thus the lawyer's failure to testify may materially bolster a *prima facie* case.[142] However, a finding that a lawyer is guilty of professional misconduct cannot rest entirely on an obverse inference, that is, a conclusion drawn by the discipline hearing panel that the lawyer's denials of wrongdoing are false.[143]

26.17 PENALTY

Centuries ago, in England, disbarment was common and painful. In public ceremonies, barristers who misconducted themselves were physically

---

139 Cases in which it has been held that where the allegation is one of criminal misconduct, it must be proven beyond a reasonable doubt include: *Baron v. F.*, [1945] 4 D.L.R. 525 at 527 (B.C. Law Society Visitorial Trib.), *per* Farris C.J.S.C.; *Re Barrister* (1953), [1954] 1 D.L.R. 814 (N.B. C.A.); and *Shumiatcher v. Law Society (Saskatchewan)* (1966), 60 D.L.R. (2d) 318 at 328 (Sask. C.A.), *per* Culliton C.J.S., leave to appeal refused (1967), 61 D.L.R. (2d) 520 (Sask. C.A.). in *Bhandari v. Advocates Committee*, [1956] 3 All E.R. 742 at 744, the Judicial Committee of the Privy Council approved the statement that a professional person should not be condemned on a mere balance of probabilities.

140 *Ringrose v. College of Physicians & Surgeons (Alberta) (No. 2)*, [1978] 2 W.W.R. 534 (Alta. C.A.), leave to appeal to Supreme Court of Canada refused May 16, 1978.

141 *Rak v. British Columbia (Superintendent of Brokers)* (1990), 51 B.C.L.R. (2d) 27 (C.A.).

142 *Sen v. College of Physicians & Surgeons (Saskatchewan)* (1969), 6 D.L.R. (3d) 520 at 525 *(sub nom. R. v. Sask. College of Physicians & Surgeons; Ex parte Sen)* (Sask. C.A.); *Patterson v. College of Physicians & Surgeons (British Columbia)* (1974), 49 D.L.R. (3d) 219 at 231 (B.C. S.C.); and *Golomb v. College of Physicians & Surgeons (Ontario)* (1976), 12 O.R. (2d) 73 at 99-100 (Div. Ct.). See also Richard Steinecke and Donald Posluns, "Professional Misconduct Proceedings" (1988) 9 Advocates' Quarterly 160 at 200.

143 *Edmondson v. State Bar*, 625 P. 2d 812 (Cal., 1981). See also Charles Wolfram, *Modern Legal Ethics* (St. Paul, Minnesota: West, 1986), p. 110.

thrown over the wooden railing — the "bar" (thus the term "disbarment") — that separated the judges' and lawyers' half of the courtroom from the spectators' gallery.[144]

The penalties imposed today range from a reprimand or admonition that is not announced publicly by the law society, to disbarment. Between these extremes, in order of severity, the most frequently imposed penalties are reprimands that are announced publicly, suspensions, and the granting of permission to resign.

The consequences of the penalties enable cases to be classified into three categories of seriousness: those in which the main objective of the lawyer's counsel is to avoid publication of a reprimand so as to protect the lawyer's reputation; those in which the main objective of the lawyer's counsel is to avoid a suspension and thus protect the lawyer's ability to earn a livelihood as a lawyer; and those in which disbarment is inevitable and the main objective is to protect or improve the lawyer's position in the criminal courts.[145]

Although most participants in the discipline process might agree that similar penalties should be imposed for similar cases of misconduct, the penalties imposed for similar misconduct differ widely, both within and among jurisdictions. This is largely due to the fact that one of the main purposes of the process is to protect the public. It may be entirely appropriate that a lawyer who has proven to be incorrigible be disbarred for the same conduct for which a different lawyer is reprimanded if the discipline hearing panel and Convocation are reasonably satisfied that the likelihood of recurrence is minimal in the latter case.[146]

Factors frequently weighed in assessing the seriousness of a lawyer's misconduct include the extent of injury, the lawyer's blameworthiness, and the penalties that have been imposed previously for similar misconduct. In assessing each of these factors, the discipline hearing panel focuses on the offence rather than on the offender and considers the desirability of parity

---

144 Martin Garbus and Joel Seligman, "Sanctions and Disbarment: They Sit in Judgement" in Ralph Nader and Mark Green (eds.), *Verdicts on Lawyers* (New York: Thomas Y. Crowell Co., 1976), p. 49.

145 See Claude R. Thomson and Gavin MacKenzie, "The Defence of Disciplinary Proceedings Before the Law Society of Upper Canada's Discipline Committee", Part 1, Advocates' Society Journal (October, 1982), p. 9.

146 The desirability of imposing similar sanctions for similar misconduct is argued by Cynthia A. Kelly in "Lawyers' Sanctions: Looking Back Through the Looking Glass" (1987-88) 1 Georgetown Journal of Legal Ethics 469. American cases in which the courts have said that sanctions should be applied consistently include *Re Fogel*, 422 A. 2d 966 (D.C., 1980), and *Re McLennan*, 443 N.E. 2d 553 at 556 (1982). In *Stevens v. Law Society of Upper Canada* (1979), 55 O.R. (2d) 405 at 411, Cory J. (as he then was), for the Divisional Court, wrote that "a conscious comparison should be made between the case under consideration and similar cases wherein sentences were imposed. If the comparison with other cases is not undertaken, there may well be such a wide variation in the result as to constitute not simply unfairness but injustice."

and proportionality in sanctions and the need for deterrence. The panel also considers an array of aggravating and mitigating factors, many of which are relevant to the likelihood of recurrence. These aggravating and mitigating factors include the lawyer's prior discipline record, the lawyer's reaction to the discipline process, the restitution (if any) made by the lawyer, the length of time the lawyer has been in practice, the lawyer's general character, and the lawyer's mental state. Alcoholism, drug addiction, stress caused by financial and matrimonial difficulties, and mental illness are common factors in discipline cases and are material to the assessment of penalty in cases where a causal relationship exists between the lawyer's condition and the misconduct being considered. These conditions have not generally been regarded as sufficient to excuse misconduct altogether; it is sufficient for the law society's counsel to show that the lawyer knowingly and without coercion committed the misconduct alleged in the complaint.[147] The lawyer's motives are not relevant to the finding, as opposed to the penalty.[148]

Both the British Columbia Court of Appeal in a 1994 case[148.1] and Convocation of the Law Society of Upper Canada in a 1995 case[148.2] have held that principles of sentencing developed in criminal cases should not be imported into the process of imposing penalty by disciplinary tribunals. In the latter case Convocation rejected an approach recommended by a discipline committee that involved allocating a portion of a lawyer's suspension to general and specific deterrence. "Two significant objectives of the discipline process are the protection of the public and the protection of the reputation of the profession," Convocation observed. "To allocate specified portions of a suspension to general and specific deterrence may suggest that those significant objectives are being subordinated, if not disregarded."[148.3]

In a 1989 Ontario decision,[149] Convocation adopted a report of a discipline hearing panel in which the panel held that a lawyer charged with professional misconduct should have available the defence of insanity if it can be established that by reason of a disease of the mind the lawyer was incapable of appreciating

---

147 Mitigating and aggravating factors in assessing penalty are listed in section 11 of the American Bar Association's *Standards for Imposing Lawyer Sanctions* (Washington: A.B.A. Centre for Professional Responsibility, 1986), and are discussed in Wolfram, *supra*, note 143, pp. 122-126. Wolfram discusses the differing weight that should be accorded different factors. See also Stuart Thom, "Discipline", Law Society of Upper Canada Gazette, vol. 9, part 2 (June 1975), p. 89 at 90-91.

148 *Re Friedman*, 392 N.E. 2d 1333 (Ill. S.C., 1979).

148.1 *McKee v. College of Psychologists (British Columbia)*, 116 D.L.R. (4th) 555, 95 B.C.L.R. (2d) 66, [1994] 9 W.W.R. 374, (*sub nom. McKee v. College of Psychologists (British Columbia) (No. 2)*) 47 B.C.A.C. 189, 76 W.A.C. 189 (C.A.).

148.2 *Re O'Donnell*, Reasons of Convocation dated September 28 1995.

148.3 At page 2.

149 *Re Perreault*, report adopted by Convocation on May 28, 1989. The possible availability of the defence of insanity was also recognized but rejected on the evidence in *Re Stewart*, report of discipline hearing panel adopted by Convocation on June 25, 1988 (Ontario).

the nature of his or her act or the fact that it was wrong. On the evidence in that case, the discipline hearing panel found that the defence was not established.

In a 1993 English decision,[149.1] the Court of Appeal held that because the main purpose of imposing penalty in discipline cases is not punishment, but rather the maintenance of public confidence in the profession, mitigating circumstances are entitled to less weight than they would be in a criminal case.

Some types of evidence in mitigation of penalty are more reliable indicators of the likelihood of recurrence than are others. Character evidence is common and can be persuasive, but it is much less valuable if the witnesses are not fully informed of the facts. Even then, it is difficult to gauge the extent to which the evidence is affected by factors such as friendship. Virtually all lawyers are responsible for some good deeds, and virtually all are held in high esteem by some other lawyers and clients. The discipline hearing panel must ensure that the process is not transformed from a deliberative process into a referendum among members of the profession.[149.2]

Evidence that a lawyer's misconduct occurred during a period of stress caused by financial or matrimonial pressures may also be of doubtful value in mitigation of the penalty. The fact that lawyers yield to temptation while under stress may, indeed, be regarded as a sign that they lack the moral strength necessary to be lawyers. As an Ontario discipline committee stated in a 1995 case,[149.3] "[i]t is exactly when the stresses are greatest, when compliance with our profession's rules of conduct are most difficult, that members must faithfully hew to the line. Those are the times when lawyers must be worthy of being 'trusted to the ends of the earth', no matter what difficulties they face."

Neither the fact that a lawyer has a heavy workload nor the fact that a lawyer relied on employees should be compelling mitigating factors, because both are within the lawyer's control.[150]

Other factors may, nevertheless, suggest strength of character in ways germane to a lawyer's ability to function responsibly in practice. The fact that a lawyer has made restitution is always relevant (except perhaps in cases in which it has been effected by the exercise by the victim of a right of set-off or

---

149.1 *Bolton v. Law Society*, [1993] 1 W.L.R. 512 (C.A.). Similarly, in *McKee v. College of Psychologists (British Columbia)* (1994), 95 B.C.L.R. (2d) 66, [1994] 9 W.W.R. 374, 116 D.L.R. (4th) 555, (*sub nom.* McKee v. College of Psychologists (British Columbia) (No. 2)) 47 B.C.C.A. 189, 76 W.A.C. 189 (C.A.) the British Columbia Court of Appeal observed that principles of criminal sentencing are inappropriate in cases of professional discipline.

149.2 Apart altogether from mitigation of penalty, character evidence is admissible in support of the credibility of the lawyer, and as the basis of an inference that the lawyer is unlikely to have committed the act of professional misconduct alleged: *Re Curtis*, report of discipline hearing panel of Law Society of Upper Canada, September 29, 1993, p. 8, citing *R. v. Profit* (1992), 11 O.R. (3d) 98 (C.A.) at p. 105.

149.3 *Re Reilly*, Report adopted by Convocation June 22 1995.

150 See *Disciplinary Board v. Amundson*, 297 N.W. 2d 433 (N.D., 1980); and *Attorney Grievance Commission of Maryland v. Goldberg*, 441 A. 2d 338 (Md., 1982).

other legal process), but it is much more likely to be indicative of a genuinely altered attitude if made prior to discovery by the law society of the lawyer's misconduct. Similarly, a lawyer who voluntarily discloses wrongdoing to the law society before it learns of the lawyer's misconduct — and before it has become inevitable that the misconduct will come to light — may properly be regarded as a more suitable person to continue in practice than one who merely co-operates with the law society after it uncovers misconduct as a result of the initiatives of others.

Despite the current absence of medieval physical consequences, disbarment is a sanction that, in addition to the loss of one's licence to practise, still carries a significant stigma. The Ontario Divisional Court has described disbarment as the professional equivalent of capital punishment.[151] The impact of disbarment on particular lawyers varies: for some, it means only the cancellation of a licence to practise law; for others, it means the loss of identity. One former lawyer said that, for him, being disbarred was far worse than going to jail: "The law was really a jealous mistress for me."[152]

It would be a mistake, however, to assume that disbarment is a penalty reserved for cases that combine the worst imaginable offence with the worst imaginable offender. In cases involving fraud or theft, in spite of evidence of prior good character and financial or other pressures, lawyers are almost certain to be disbarred.[153] In one such case, a discipline hearing panel held that "disbarment is as much required for the lawyer who throws away a hard-earned reputation for integrity as it is for the scoundrel who caps a disreputable career with more of the same."[154] Thus the profession sends an unequivocal message in the interest of maintaining public trust and the reputation of the profession.

An informal survey of 83 misappropriation cases in Ontario between 1980 and 1988 disclosed that 67 (81 percent) resulted in disbarment, 12 (14 percent) resulted in the lawyer being granted permission to resign, three (four percent) resulted in suspension, and one (one percent) resulted in a reprimand in Convocation.[155] Discipline hearing panels have frequently held that acts of misappropriation should result in disbarment unless exceptional extenuating circumstances exist. An order of disbarment in such cases is made to preserve

151 *Stoangi v. Law Society (Upper Canada) (No. 2)* (1979), 25 O.R. (2d) 257 (Div. Ct.). In light of the fact that disbarred lawyers are entitled to apply for readmission (see part 26.22 *infra*) the analogy breaks down.

152 The disbarred criminal lawyer, Edmond Rosner, is quoted by Alan M. Dershowitz in *The Best Defence* (New York: First Vintage Books, 1983), p. 379.

153 See *Re Milrod*, report of discipline hearing panel adopted by Convocation, January 30, 1986 (Ontario). See also *R. v. Logiacco* (1984), 2 O.A.C. 177, 111 C.C.C. (3d) 374 (C.A.)

154 *Re Cooper*, discipline hearing panel report adopted by Convocation, May 23, 1991. See also Thom, *supra*, note 147, pp. 90-91.

155 Stephen E. Sherriff, H. Reginald Watson, and Shaun M. Devlin, " 'You Can Run...But You Can't Hide': A Guide to Understanding Lawyer Discipline in Ontario" in Franklin Moskoff (ed.), *Administrative Tribunals: A Practice Handbook for Legal Counsel* (Aurora, Ontario: Canada Law Book Inc., 1989), p. 115 at 135-139.

public confidence, to protect the public, and to deter other lawyers from breaching the trust of their clients.[156]

In some American jurisdictions, notably New Jersey, courts have held that disbarment is the only appropriate discipline for misappropriation, that in such cases it should be permanent, that there should be no significant exceptions to the rule, and that the result should be almost invariable. Since 1979, when the Supreme Court of New Jersey articulated these general principles, disbarment has been the result in every misappropriation case in the state, including cases involving the unauthorized temporary use of client funds for lawyers' own purposes, whether or not the lawyers derive any personal benefit. Mitigating factors, including restitution before or after discovery, are considered irrelevant.[157]

---

156 Examples of cases in which discipline committees have held that acts of misappropriation will result in disbarment in the absence of most exceptional extenuating circumstances include *Re Robb* and *Re Coffee*, both of which are decisions of discipline hearing panels that were adopted by Convocation on September 23, 1982. The purposes served by a disbarment order are discussed in *Re Bradbury*, report adopted by Convocation on May 27, 1983 (Ontario). For a discussion of the point at which prohibited borrowing from an estate by a lawyer serving as executor becomes misappropriation, see *Re Black*, report of discipline committee dated August 16 1993 at pages 11 to 12, report adopted by Convocation November 25 1993.

157 The principle that misappropriation should almost invariably result in disbarment was established in *Re Wilson*, 409 A. 2d 1153 (1979), and has been applied in *Re Noonan*, 506 A. 2d 722 (1986); *Re Fleischer*, 508 A. 2d 1115 (1986); *Re Lennan*, 509 A. 2d 179 (1986); *Re Romano*, 516 A. 2d 1109 (1986); *Re Hein*, 516 A. 2d 1105 (1986); *Re Warhaftig*, 524 A. 2d 398 (1987); and in other jurisdictions in *Re Marks*, 424 N.Y.S. 2d 229 (1980); *Re Okerman*, 310 N.W. 2d 569 (Minn., 1981); and *Oklahoma ex rel. Oklahoma Bar Assn. v. Raskin*, 642 P. 2d 262 (1982). See also James R. Zazzali, "Disciplining Attorneys: The New Jersey Experience" (1987-88) 1 Georgetown Journal of Legal Ethics 659 at 663-668. By way of contrast, in Ontario, a lawyer was suspended for three months after a $2,500 misappropriation that occurred in 1978 was discovered eight years later: *Re Milloy*, report adopted by Convocation on February 19, 1989. In that case the lawyer's conduct was influenced by alcohol abuse and personal problems and was uncharacteristic. In another Ontario case, *Re Biderman*, report adopted by Convocation on March 28, 1991, a lawyer was suspended for 18 months, prohibited from operating a trust account and required to practise under supervision for three and a half years thereafter. The lawyer had borrowed from his trust account to cover short-term bills in anticipation of transactions closing within days or weeks thereafter. For several months he replaced the missing funds as transactions closed, but then he fell behind. His total misappropriation reached a maximum of $6,000 but was reduced to $400 when a spot audit was performed by the law society. No client suffered any loss, and the misappropriation would not have been detected were it not for the spot audit. A total of $32,150 had been misappropriated over an 18-month period. The lawyer co-operated with the law society, was candid with the discipline hearing panel, and accepted responsibility for his actions. Similarly, in *Re Horman*, report adopted by Convocation on February 24, 1994, a lawyer was suspended for six months, prohibited from operating a trust account for three years, and required to be subject to co-signing controls for a further two years if he operates a trust account thereafter. The amounts misappropriated were relatively small and were repaid after only a short interval, before the Law Society's investigation. The clients suffered no loss. Examples of cases in which lawyers have been disbarred for misappropriating small amounts include *Re Cannon*, no.

Most non-misappropriation cases in which lawyers have been disbarred involve convictions for serious criminal offences. Lawyers have been disbarred as a result of criminal convictions for fraud, tax evasion, conspiring to possess counterfeit money, manslaughter, bribery of public officials, and sexual offences involving children (all involving a breach of trust).[158] Disbarment is not reserved exclusively, however, for cases involving fraud or convictions for serious criminal offences. In a 1997 Ontario case[158.1], for example, a lawyer was disbarred on the basis of his admission that he was guilty of a great many allegations of professional misconduct, including failing to serve at least nine clients competently and diligently, failing to honour financial obligations incurred in connection with his practice on at least four occasions, failing to respond to the Law Society regarding complaints on at least 90 occasions, breaching an undertaking to the Law Society, breaching an order of Convocation that he suspend his practice for failing to pay his annual fees, and using his

---

92-1, March 26, 1992 (Saskatchewan); and *Re Shuckett, No. 2*, January 7, 1992 (Manitoba). In the latter case the lawyer misappropriated $755.32. In *Re Baum*, Reasons of Convocation dated September 28 1995, Convocation of the Law Society of Upper Canada rejected the suggestion that there is a threshold level at which disbarment automatically becomes the appropriate penalty by reason of the amount misappropriated. "One can readily imagine cases involving the misappropriation of relatively small amounts in which disbarment would be the most appropriate penalty," Convocation stated. "One can similarly imagine cases involving the misappropriation of larger amounts in which, because of compelling extenuating circumstances, a penalty other than disbarment is the most appropriate penalty." For cases in which lawyers have been permitted to resign or suspended for misappropriation, see notes 158.2 and 159.1.

158 Stephen Traviss has collected and summarized all cases during a 12-year period in which Convocation of the Law Society in Ontario has imposed a reprimand in Convocation or a more severe penalty in *Synopses of Discipline Cases Considered by Convocation, 1972-1984* (Toronto: Law Society of Upper Canada, 1987). Ontario cases in which lawyers have been disbarred as a result of criminal convictions include: *Re Hargrave*, report adopted by Convocation on March 21, 1980 (conspiracy to defraud public); *Re Cross*, report adopted by Convocation on April 23, 1982 (conspiracy to defraud client's creditors, defrauding client and bank); *Re Ciglen*, report adopted by Convocation on October 16, 1970 (conspiring to evade taxes); *Re Goldman*, report adopted by Convocation on May 14, 1981 (conspiring to possess counterfeit money); *Re Shea*, report adopted by Convocation on January 16, 1976 (manslaughter); *Re Morgan*, report adopted by Convocation (which delivered separate reasons) on September 24, 1998 (assault, contempt of court, and repeatedly disobeying court orders without lawful excuse); and *Re Cwinn*, report adopted by Convocation on September 12, 1979 (conviction in United States under the *Mann Act* for transporting young girls over state lines for immoral purposes), upheld on appeal (1980), 28 O.R. (2d) 61 (Div. Ct.). In *Adams v. Law Society of Alberta*, [2000] A.J. 1031 (C.A.) the Alberta Court of Appeal upheld a disbarment order against a lawyer who was convicted in the criminal courts of sexual exploitation of his 16-year old client. See also *Prescott v. Law Society (British Columbia)*, [1971] 4 W.W.R. 433 (B.C. C.A.) (conviction under *Income Tax Act* based on gross negligence in keeping personal accounts). In *Re Kopyto*, report adopted by Convocation on November 8, 1989 (Ontario), a lawyer was disbarred for defrauding the legal aid plan.

158.1 *Re Kinnaird*, Reasons of Convocation dated April 9 1997.

trust account for personal transactions, among other things. In the absence of compelling evidence of mitigating circumstances, Convocation held, the Law Society's duty to protect the public requires disbarment in such a case by reason of the harm caused to the public and the need to ensure the misconduct is not repeated.

Cases in which lawyers have been permitted to resign are usually those in which the misconduct is sufficiently serious to justify disbarment but in which mitigating circumstances persuade the benchers that the stigma of disbarment in addition to the withdrawal of the lawyer's right to practise law would be unfair. The practical result of the penalty is the same, except to the extent that an admission committee may give more favourable consideration to an application for readmission brought by a former lawyer who has been given permission to resign.[158.2]

Suspensions have been imposed in cases involving lawyers who have taken unfair advantage of elderly clients; who have sexually harassed a client by making unwelcome comments and sexual overtures; who have participated in attempts to fabricate transactions and destroy documents; who have made false submissions to courts and tribunals; who have advised and assisted clients who were involved in matrimonial disputes to conceal assets; who have obtained funds from clients for investment without advising them to obtain independent legal advice or representation; who have falsified documents and lied to clients in attempts to cover up their inaction; who have failed to attend in court because of intoxication and have attended in court in an intoxicated condition; who have cheated their partners and clients by representing that they have made disbursements that have not been made, taking retainers for themselves rather than depositing them in their firm's trust account, and charging personal expenses as fees; who have cheated on bar admission course

---

158.2 See, for example, *Re Korman* and *Re Boughner*, both of which are reports adopted by Convocation on April 21, 1994. Ontario cases in which lawyers found guilty of misappropriating client funds have been given permission to resign by reason of extenuating circumstances include *Re Lapedus*, order of Convocation dated February 26 1987; *Re Gray*, order of Convocation dated October 22 1992; *Re Fraser*, order of Convocation dated November 26 1992; *Re Mallal*, order of Convocation dated March 25 1993; *Re Jarson*, order of Convocation dated September 23 1993; *Re Steponaitus*, order of Convocation dated November 25 1993; *Re Box*, order of Convocation dated November 24 1994; *Re McDonald*, order of Convocation dated January 26 1995; *Re Flak*, order of Convocation dated September 28 1995; *Re Trapp*, order of Convocation dated May 23 1996; *Re Heslin*, order of Convocation dated September 26 1996; and *Re Parsons*, order of Convocation dated September 26 1996. In *Re Parker*, order of Convocation dated September 29 1995, a lawyer was given permission to resign where he failed to provide to clients investing in mortgages a level of skill and competence that the clients were entitled to expect, thereby endangering $2.5 million in client mortgage investments. For a thorough discussion of the circumstances in which permission to resign may be justified in a case in which the misconduct established would otherwise require disbarment, see *Nova Scotia Barristers Society v. Steele*, [1995] L.S.D.D. No. 261 (Discipline Subcommittee "A").

examinations; who have caused real estate agents to receive gift certificates as a reward for referring business; who have practised law while suspended for non-payment of annual fees or other levies; who have taken steps calculated to ensure that a former client could not realize on a civil judgment against the lawyer; and who have been convicted in the criminal courts of conspiring to distribute valium, possessing narcotics for the purpose of trafficking, making false or deceptive statements on income tax returns, uttering forged documents, conspiring to obstruct justice by "fixing" traffic tickets, and sexually assaulting clients.[159] In several cases involving exceptional mitigating circumstances,[159.1]

159 Ontario cases in which lawyers have been suspended include: *Re Burk*, report adopted by Convocation on May 24, 1984 (one-year suspension for deliberately taking advantage of an elderly and incompetent client); *Re Zuker*, reasons of Convocation June 24, 1999 (six-month suspension for a second offence of sexual harassment of a client; dissenting members of Convocation issued reasons for their conclusion that the solicitor should be disbarred); *Re McDonald*, report adopted by Convocation on November 21, 1985 (one-year suspension for preparing a will for an elderly and infirm client without being instructed to do so, whereby the solicitor was named executor and beneficiary); *Re Ciglen*, report adopted by Convocation on September 18, 1980 (three-month suspension for participating in the formulation of a plan to fabricate a transaction and participating in the destruction and concealment of documents to assist in the evasion of income taxes); *Re Dubinsky*, report adopted by Convocation on September 21, 1984 (one-month suspension for making false submissions as to sentence in a criminal court); *Re Rovet*, report adopted by Convocation on January 23, 1992 (one-year suspension for making false submission to labour board and charging $35,000 of personal expenses as fees without knowledge of partners or clients); *Re Brooks*, Reasons of Convocation dated November 14, 1996 (three-month suspension for advising and assisting client involved in matrimonial dispute to conceal assets); *Re Faraci*, report adopted by Convocation on May 24, 1984 (eight-month suspension for obtaining $157,500 from eight clients for investment without advising them to obtain independent legal representation among other things); *Re Vanular*, report adopted by Convocation on January 28, 1993 (nine-month suspension for guaranteeing client's indebtedness and dishonouring guarantee); *Re Farkas*, report adopted by Convocation on March 24, 1983 (two-year suspension for forging court documents to mislead clients as to lawyer's inaction); *Re Gower*, reported adopted by Convocation on April 23, 1992 (one-year suspension for forging court documents and misleading client as to lawyer's inaction, among other things); *Re Iannetta*, Reasons of Convocation dated September 28, 1995 (three-month suspension for failing to serve clients conscientiously, misleading clients as to lawyer's inaction, and falsifying abstract page from land registry office to corroborate misleading of clients); *Re McKeown*, report adopted by Convocation on March 25, 1983 (18-month suspension for having been convicted of contempt of court for having appeared in court in an intoxicated condition, having failed to attend in court because of intoxication, and having been found in an intoxicated condition in a barrister's gown in a public place); *Re Posen*, report adopted by Convocation on January 21, 1972 (two-year suspension for falsely representing that disbursements were made and taking retainers personally rather than depositing them in firm's trust account); *Re Squires*, report adopted by Convocation on March 21, 1985 (one-year suspension for wrongfully depriving solicitor's firm of money to which it was entitled); *Re Donaldson*, report adopted by Convocation on June 26, 1992 (two-year suspension for using foreign exchange credits to which clients were entitled for business development purposes, among other things); *Re Ramati*, report adopted by Convocation on July 15, 1982 (two-year delay in call to the bar for cheating on a bar admission course examination); *Re Shub*, report adopted by Convocation on February 25, 1983 (three-year suspension for causing real estate agents to receive gift certificates as a

lawyers found guilty of misappropriating client funds have been suspended, though (as discussed above) in the vast majority of misappropriation cases the offending lawyer has been disbarred.

In Ontario, Convocation has established as a general rule that lawyers who practise while under suspension should be penalized by being suspended for a period equal to the period during which they have practised while under suspension, plus one month.[159.2] The rationale for this rule, of course, is that lawyers who practise while under suspension should not be put in a better position as a result of being disciplined than they would have been in if they had complied with their obligations not to practise. Convocation has made it clear in cases that have been determined since the general rule was established, however, that the specific penalty in each case should reflect a multitude of considerations, many of which are not susceptible to the application of a mathematical formula.[159.3] "The principle should not become an inflexible, irreducible tariff," a discipline committee stated in recommending a nine-month suspension in a case in which a lawyer had practised under suspension for a period of almost 18

---

reward for referring business to the lawyer's firm); *Re MacGregor*, report adopted by Convocation on April 22, 1993 (five-month suspension for practising for four months while suspended for non-payment of fees); *Re Chodos*, report adopted by Convocation on December 8 1995 (six-month suspension for taking steps that were calculated to ensure that a former client could not realize on a civil judgment against the lawyer); *Re Caskie*, report adopted by Convocation on June 24, 1983 (six-month suspension for conviction under *Criminal Code* of conspiring to distribute valium to persons in police custody); *Re Telfer*, report adopted by Convocation on January 16, 1981 (one-year suspension for conviction for possession of a narcotic for the purpose of trafficking); *Re Greening*, report adopted by Convocation on May 17, 1974 (one-year suspension for conviction under *Income Tax Act* of making false or deceptive statements on tax returns); *Re Maloney*, report adopted by Convocation on March 28, 1991 (six-month suspension for conviction under *Income Tax Act* of making false or deceptive statements on tax returns); *Re Radigan*, report adopted by Convocation on April 23, 1982 (two-year suspension for conviction for witnessing a forged document, namely an affidavit of value of the consideration respecting a conveyance to be filed in land registry offices); *Re May*, report adopted by Convocation on January 24, 1985 (one-year suspension for conviction for conspiring to obstruct justice by fixing traffic tickets); and *Re Coccimiglio*, report adopted by Convocation on September 26, 1991 (one-year suspension for conviction for sexually assaulting a client and making an indecent proposition to another client, both of whom the lawyer was representing in matrimonial litigation).

159.1 Ontario cases in which lawyers found guilty of misappropriating client funds have been suspended include *Re Benaiah*, order of Convocation dated September 22, 1993; *Re Davies*, order of Convocation dated June 23, 1994; *Re Reilly*, order of Convocation dated June 22, 1995; *Re Baum*, order of Convocation dated September 28, 1995; *Re McKay*, order of Convocation dated September 28, 1995; *Re Stewart*, order of Convocation dated June 27, 1996; and *Re Kramer*, order of Convocation dated September 25, 1997. See also cases cited in note 157.

159.2 *Re MacGregor*, Reasons of Convocation dated April 23, 1993; *Re Laan*, Reasons of Convocation dated March 24, 1994.

159.3 See for example, *Re O'Donnell*, Reasons of Convocation dated September 28, 1995.

months. "Otherwise, the imposition of penalty is reduced to slavery to a mathematical formula without consideration of individual circumstances or the principle of totality of the penalty".[159.4]

Lawyers have been reprimanded in Convocation (that is, publicly) for submitting false accounts to the Ontario Legal Aid Plan; attempting to persuade a complainant to withdraw a complaint to the law society by offering a benefit for doing so; practising law while under suspension for non-payment of annual fees or other levies; failing to serve clients conscientiously; failing to honour an undertaking; taking advantage of a client by making grossly excessive charges; charging clients an amount for disbursements in excess of the amount actually incurred; destroying correspondence evidencing neglect of a client's litigation for the purpose of interfering with a law society investigation; misleading staff in a correctional facility to enable an unauthorized person (i.e., a client's girlfriend) to have access to the facility; interfering with the orderly administration of justice by repeatedly making unwarranted, personal, and offensive remarks to opposing counsel during a cross-examination in an official examiner's office; being found guilty in the criminal courts of attempting to obstruct justice by allowing a client to testify using an alias; repeatedly failing to respond to communications from the law society; repeatedly failing to keep required books and records or file required forms including public accountants' reports; being found liable in civil proceedings for breaching a lawyer's fiduciary duty to a client by using confidential information for the lawyer's benefit; and being found guilty in the criminal courts of possessing narcotics.[160]

159.4 *Re Fejes*, Report of Discipline Committee dated May 9, 1994, at page 14; adopted by Convocation June 23, 1994.

160 Ontario cases in which lawyers have been publicly reprimanded include: *Re Girones*, report adopted by Convocation on January 19, 1973 (submitting false accounts to legal aid plan); *Re Hendin (No. 1)*, report adopted by Convocation on July 15, 1982 (attempting to persuade complainant to withdraw complaint to law society by offering a benefit); *Re Sankey*, report adopted by Convocation on January 26, 1984 (continuing to practise while under suspension for non-payment of annual fees); *Re Dingle*, report adopted by Convocation on September 21, 1984 (failing to serve client conscientiously in three litigation matters, among other things); *Re Shane*, report adopted by Convocation on October 29, 1982 (failing to honour an undertaking given to another lawyer); *Re Stanbrook*, report adopted by Convocation on January 21, 1977 (taking advantage of client by making grossly excessive charges, among other things); *Re Tencer (No. 1)*, report adopted by Convocation September 18, 1981 (charging clients an amount for disbursements exceeding the amount actually incurred); *Re Chodos (No. 2)*, report adopted by Convocation on April 16, 1989 (destroying correspondence evidencing neglect of client's litigation for the purpose of interfering with a law society investigation); *Re Breault*, report adopted by Convocation on September 21, 1984 (misleading staff at correctional facility to enable unauthorized person access to facility); *Re Balaban*, report adopted by Convocation on May 24, 1984 (interfering with the orderly administration of justice by repeatedly making unwarranted, personal, and offensive remarks to opposing counsel during cross-examination in official examiner's office); *Re Brown*, report adopted by Convocation March 27, 1997 (conviction in criminal courts of wilfully attempting to obstruct the course of justice by allowing client to testify using an alias); *Re Freedman*, report adopted by Convocation on September 22, 1983 (repeatedly

Private reprimands or admonitions (formerly known in Ontario as reprimands in committee) are generally reserved for first offenders who are guilty of relatively minor misconduct in cases in which no significant injury has resulted. Examples of cases in which private reprimands have been imposed include cases involving isolated failures to reply to correspondence from the law society; failures to file necessary forms; books and records offences; minor conflicts of interest; and signing affidavits in one's role as a commissioner for the taking of oaths where the deponent is not present to accommodate clients in cases in which the lawyer believes that no harm can result.[161]

In some jurisdictions, fines have been imposed for professional misconduct and conduct unbecoming a barrister and solicitor. Partly because of concerns that a substantial fine may be regarded as a penal consequence attracting the applicability of section 11 of the *Charter of Rights*, fines are seldom imposed in Ontario. When fines have been imposed, they have been modest. Lawyers have more often been required to pay or contribute toward the costs of investigations and hearings.[162]

The Ontario *Law Society Act* provides for the possibility of lawyers being invited to attend before the discipline committee in cases of minor breaches of discipline. Where these invitations are extended, the committee generally advises lawyers with respect to their conduct. Lawyers do not acquire discipline records when matters are dealt with by way of invitations to attend; the procedure is considered therapeutic rather than disciplinary. Examples of cases dealt with by way of invitations to attend include cases in which lawyers have been guilty of discourtesy, have resorted to intemperate language, or have threatened for tactical

---

failing to answer letters from law society); *Re Applebaum*, report adopted by Convocation on July 15, 1982 (failure to keep books and records current, failure to file required forms including public accountants' report, conviction for possession of heroin and hashish); and *Re Chodos (No. 1)*, report adopted by Convocation on November 22, 1986 (being found liable in civil action for breaching fiduciary duty to client by using confidential information for lawyer's benefit).

161 The types of cases in which private reprimands may be imposed are discussed by Claude R. Thomson and Gavin MacKenzie in "The Defence of Disciplinary Proceedings Before the Law Society of Upper Canada's Discipline Committee" (Part 2), The Advocates' Society Journal (December 1982), p. 7 at 7-8. In British Columbia, offences involving the signing of affidavits by commissioners when the deponent is not present are generally visited with a penalty of a one-month suspension.

162 Section 34 of the *Law Society Act*, R.S.O. 1990, c. L. 8, as amended, lists a fine not exceeding $10,000 as one of the orders that may be made as a result of a finding of professional misconduct or conduct unbecoming a barrister or solicitor. Section 40 of the Act provides that a person found guilty of professional misconduct or conduct unbecoming a barrister and solicitor may be ordered to pay all or part of the expense incurred by the law society in the investigation or hearing of any complaint in respect of which he or she has been found guilty. Stephen G. Bene urges more widespread use of fines in discipline proceedings in "Why Not Fine Attorneys?: An Economic Approach to Lawyer Disciplinary Sanctions" (1991) 43 Stanford Law Review 907.

reasons to report the supposedly unprofessional conduct of opposing lawyers to the law society.[163]

The State Bars of California, Virginia, and Florida have established a different system for dealing with minor breaches of ethical rules — they have established ethics schools. Lawyers guilty of minor lapses may trade a few hours of their time and pay a modest fee (75 dollars in California) for a clean discipline record. The students include lawyers who have habitually neglected to return clients' phone calls and who have let clients' cases slide. One student explained that he had to attend because he had "one client too many." When a corporate client sued its president for embezzlement, the lawyer decided to represent both.

The students write an examination at the end of the course, and if they pass they receive in the mail an Ethics School Certificate of Completion. Many of the students specifically request that the envelope be marked "personal and confidential."[164]

26.18 DECISION AND REASONS

Discipline hearings are multiple-stage proceedings. A discipline hearing panel must first determine whether the alleged facts have been made out. If all or some have been made out, the panel must then decide whether the proven facts constitute professional misconduct or conduct unbecoming a barrister and solicitor. If the panel decides that they do, it must impose or recommend a penalty.[165] The panel's decision may be set aside if it can be shown that the committee failed to direct its mind to one of these steps.[166]

The decision of a discipline hearing panel must be in writing, and the panel must provide reasons for its decision if requested to do so by a party.[167] On appeal

163 Invitations to attend before the discipline committee are authorized by section 36 of the *Law Society Act*, R.S.O. 1990, c. L.8, as amended.

164 The Ethics School of the State Bar of California is described in Amy Stevens, "What Can a Lawyer Learn in One Day in Downtown L.A.?", *The National* (July-August 1991), pp. 19 and 24. See also Rosalind Resnick, "Lawyer "Ethics School' Created", National Law Journal (June 29, 1992), pp. 1 and 34.

165 Formerly, in Ontario, a discipline hearing panel was authorized to impose penalty only in cases in which it concluded that a private reprimand was appropriate. In cases in which the panel concluded that a harsher penalty was warranted, it recommended that that penalty be imposed by Convocation. Since the *Law Society Act* was amended in 1999, discipline hearing panels have been authorized to impose all penalties including disbarment. Members have a right of appeal to an appeal panel, and a further right of appeal to the Divisional Court: see sections 35, and 49.29 to 49.41, of the *Law Society Act*, R.S.O. 1990, c. L. 8, as amended.

166 See *Golomb v. College of Physicians & Surgeons* (1976), 12 O.R. (2d) 73 at 92-94 (Div. Ct.); *Fan v. Law Society (British Columbia)* (1977), 77 D.L.R. (3d) 97 at 102-103 (B.C. C.A.); *Milstein v. College of Pharmacy (Ontario)*(1978), 20 O.R. (2d) 283 at 292-293 (C.A.); and *Fenton v. College of Physicians & Surgeons (Ontario)* (1974), 6 O.R. (2d) 193 at 197-199 (Div. Ct.). See also Richard Steinecke and Donald Posluns, "Professional Misconduct Proceedings" (1988) 9 Advocates' Quarterly 160 at 200-201.

167 *Statutory Powers Procedure Act*, R.S.O. 1990, c. S.22, as amended, s. 17.

or judicial review, the reviewing court may draw adverse inferences concerning the panel's findings where reasons have not been provided.[168]

The decision and reasons must be those of the discipline committee. A clerk who is responsible to the committee, who does not participate in the committee's deliberations, and who is not in any way involved in the prosecution of the complaint may provide journalistic and administrative assistance by preparing a draft report for the committee if the report is reviewed and, if necessary, revised by the committee to ensure that the report accurately and completely reflects the reasoning of the committee.[169] In practice, discipline hearing panels in Ontario prepare their own reasons.

---

168 *Stoangi v. Law Society (Upper Canada)* (1978), 22 O.R. (2d) 274 at 277 (H.C.); and *Stoangi v. Law Society (Upper Canada) (No. 2)* (1979), 25 O.R. (2d) 257 at 265-266 (Div. Ct.).

169 The permissibility of a clerk to the discipline hearing panel preparing draft reasons in the circumstances stated was decided by the Ontario Court of Appeal in *Khan v. College of Physicians & Surgeons (Ontario)* (1992), 9 O.R. (3d) 641, and by the Ontario Divisional Court (by a 2-to-1 majority) in *Spring v. Law Society (Upper Canada)* (1988), 64 O.R. (2d) 719 (Div. Ct.). Earlier, in *Emerson v. Law Society (Upper Canada)* (1983), 44 O.R. (2d) 729 at 760-762 (H.C.), Justice Henry held that reasons may not be drafted by the Secretary of the Society who is, in effect, the prosecutor. See also *Bernstein v. College of Physicians & Surgeons (Ontario)* (1977), 15 O.R. (2d) 447 (Div. Ct.); *Sawyer v. Ontario (Racing Commission)* (1979), 24 O.R. (2d) 673 (C.A.); *Del Core v. Ontario College of Pharmacists* (1985), 51 O.R. (2d) 1 at 8 (C.A.); 2747-3174 *Québec Inc. c. Québec (Régie des permis d'alcool)*, [1994] R.J.Q. 2440, 65 Q.A.C. 245, 122 D.L.R. (4th) 553 (C.A.), leave to appeal allowed (1995), (*sub nom. 2747-3174 Québec Inc. v. Régie des permis d'alcool du Québec*) 189 N.R. 160n (S.C.C.), reversed [1996] 3 S.C.R. 919, (*sub nom. 2747-3174 Québec Inc. v. Québec (Régie des permis d'alcool du Québec*) 205 N.R. 1, 42 Admin. L.R. (2d) 1, 140 D.L.R. (4th) 577; and the comments of Martin Teplitsky and Gavin MacKenzie on the *Khan* decision in (1992) 2 Reid's Administrative Law at 72 and 75, respectively. The role of independent counsel to disciplinary tribunals (who are considered unnecessary in the case of tribunals that consist in whole or in part of lawyers) is also considered in *Matthews v. Board of Directors of Physiotherapy (Ontario)* (1990), 44 Admin. L.R. 147 (Ont. Div. Ct.); *Venczel v. Assn. of Architects (Ontario)* (1990), 45 Admin. L.R. 288 (Ont. Div. Ct.); *Brett v. Board of Directors of Physiotherapy (Ontario)* (1991), 77 D.L.R. (4th) 144 (Ont. Div. Ct.); *Omenica Enterprises Ltd. v. British Columbia Minister of Forests* (1992), 7 Admin. L.R. (2d) 95 (S.C.); *Després v. Assn. des Arpenteurs — Géomètres du Nouveau Brunswick* (1992), 8 Admin. L.R. (2d) 136 (N.B. C.A.); *Adair v. Health Disciplines Board (Ontario)* (1993), 15 O.R. (3d) 705 (Div. Ct.); *Bovbel v. Canada (Minister of Employment & Immigration)* (1994), 18 Admin. L.R. (2d) 169 (Fed. C.A.); *Mitchell v. Institute of Chartered Accountants (Manitoba)*, [1994] 10 W.W.R. 768, 97 Man. R. (2d) 66, 79 W.A.C. 66; R.W. Macaulay, *Practice and Procedure Before Administrative Tribunals* (Toronto: Carswell, 1988) at 22-10 to 22-10.21; and David J. Mullan, "The Role of Lawyers to Professional Disciplinary Bodies", 13 Advocates' Society Journal 10 (1994). For a discussion of the obligations of the separate, prosecutorial branch of professional disciplinary tribunals, see Gavin MacKenzie, "Procedural Fairness and the Role of Tribunal Counsel in Professional Discipline Proceedings", 1992 Law Society of Upper Canada Special Lectures, *Administrative Law — Principle, Practice and Pluralism* (Toronto: Carswell, 1993), p. 391.

26.18.1 COSTS

In some Canadian jurisdictions, legislation governing law society discipline proceedings provides that a lawyer who has been disciplined may be ordered to pay all or part of the expense incurred by the Law Society in the investigation or hearing of any complaint in respect of which the lawyer has been found guilty.[169.1] In Ontario, Convocation has held that the expense that a disciplined lawyer may be required to pay may include an amount, calculated on the basis of an hourly rate, in respect of the time devoted to the case by salaried staff counsel.[169.2] This interpretation of the legislation was the subject of a vigorous dissent, and has not yet been tested in the courts.

In most Canadian jurisdictions, the governing legislation also provides that where discipline proceedings were unwarranted the law society may be ordered to pay costs to the lawyer whose conduct has been the subject of the proceedings. In a 1994 decision,[169.3] a special committee of Convocation held that the lawyer must discharge the onus of establishing, on a balance of probabilities, that the discipline proceedings were unwarranted.[169.4] The lawyer in that case was awarded 75 per cent of his costs on a party-and-party scale, as the special committee concluded that three of the four particulars on which the Law Society proceeded were unwarranted.[169.5]

26.19 JUDICIAL REVIEW AND APPEAL

In Ontario, lawyers who have been the subject of a conduct order issued by a hearing panel have a right of appeal to an appeal panel,[170] and a further right of appeal to the Divisional Court.[171] On both appeals, the appeal may be based on any grounds.[172] The Law Society also has a right of appeal to the appeal panel[173] and a further right of appeal to the Divisional Court,[174] but the grounds of appeal are limited to grounds that do not involve a question of fact alone

---

169.1 See, for example, *Law Society Act*, R.S.O. 1990, c. L.8, s. 49.28; *Law Society Act*, R.S.M. 1987, c. L.100, s. 52(4); *Legal Profession Act*, S.A. 1990, c. L.9-1, s. 69(2)(b).

169.2 *Re Clark*, report adopted by Convocation January 22, 1993. In *Re Bagambiire*, June 1 1997, an admission committee of the Law Society of Upper Canada held by a two-to-one majority that Convocation has no authority under the *Law Society Act* to award costs of a hearing convened to determine whether an applicant for admission is of "good character" for the purpose of section 27 of the *Act*.

169.3 *Re Speciale*, February 25, 1994; see also *Grochowski v. Assn. of Architects (Alberta)* (1996), 184 A.R. 233, 38 Admin. L.R. (2d) 132, 122 W.A.C. 233 (Alta. C.A.).

169.4 At p. 25.

169.5 At pp. 37-40.

170 The legislative provisions governing the two-stage procedure prescribed for serious cases are ss. 33, 34, and 37 of the *Law Society Act*, R.S.O. 1990, c. L.8, as amended, s. 49.32(1).

171 *Ibid.*, s. 49.38.

172 *Ibid.*, ss. 49.33(1) and 49.39(1).

173 *Ibid*, s. 49.32(1).

174 *Ibid*, s. 49.38.

(except, in the case of appeals to the Divisional Court, where the appeal is from an order for costs, in which case the Society's appeal may be on any grounds).[175]

At least in Ontario, the standard of review is correctness,[175.1] rather than mere reasonableness, though in a 1997 case the Manitoba Court of Appeal took a different view.[175.2]

An order disciplining a lawyer is not automatically stayed pending appeal. In Ontario, the appellant may bring a motion to a judge of the Divisional Court for a stay of the order appealed from, but on the present state of the law it is difficult to obtain a stay. The onus is on the applicant, who must show that the appeal is brought in good faith and that special circumstances justify a stay. The applicant's financial difficulty alone is not a ground upon which a stay should be granted, although hardship or prejudice resulting from the refusal of the stay is a factor to be weighed. The protection of the public and the interests of justice are the paramount considerations.[176]

The jurisdiction of the Divisional Court on appeal is not limited to questions of law or jurisdiction, but in most cases in which reasons for judgment have been delivered the issues dealt with have been natural justice or *Charter of Rights* issues that could be raised on an application for judicial review.[177] Most appeals based upon arguments that findings are not supported by the evidence have been dismissed.[178] In a 1985 Ontario case,[179] however, an appeal was allowed and the matter was remitted for further consideration on the basis of the court's conclusion that the discipline hearing panel's recommendation as to penalty might have been different if additional evidence had been put before it.

---

175 *Ibid*, s. 49.39(2).

175.1 See *Richmond v. College of Optometrists (Ontario)* (1995), 25 O.R. (3d) 448, 85 O.A.C. 379 (Div. Ct.); and *Cox v. College of Optometrists (Ontario)* (1988), 65 O.R. (2d) 461, 28 O.A.C. 337, 33 Admin. L.R. 287, 52 D.L.R. (4th) 298 (Div. Ct.), leave to appeal to C.A. refused (1988), 33 Admin. L.R. xliv (Ont. C.A.).

175.2 *Law Society (Manitoba) v. Frohlinger*, 148 D.L.R. (4th) 710, [1997] 7 W.W.R. 747, 47 Admin. L.R. (2d) 1, 118 Man. R. (2d) 89, 149 W.A.C. 89 (C.A.). In Nova Scotia, where section 32(13) of the *Barristers and Solicitors Act*, R.S.N.S. 1989, c. 30, confers a power of "intervention" on the Court of Appeal, the Court of Appeal will exercise its power of intervention only if it can be shown that the discipline committee made an error of law on the face of the record or breached the rules of natural justice: *Markus v. Barristers' Society (Nova Scotia)* (1989), 90 N.S.R. (2d) 156, 230 A.P.R. 156 (C.A.); *Ayre v. Barristers' Society (Nova Scotia)* (June 8, 1998), Doc. C.A. 139683 (N.S. C.A.).

176 Factors to be considered on a motion for a stay are discussed in *Tan v. College of Physicians & Surgeons (Saskatchewan)* (1985), 39 Sask. L.R. 152 (Q.B.); and *Dudzic v. Law Society (Upper Canada)* (1989), 36 O.A.C. 314 (Div. Ct.).

177 The powers of the Divisional Court on appeal are specified in s. 44(5) of the *Law Society Act*, R.S.O. 1990, c. L.8.

178 *Rusonik v. Law Society (Upper Canada)* (1988), 28 O.A.C. 57 (Div. Ct.), is an example of a case in which an appeal based in part upon an argument that a finding of fact was not supported by the evidence was dismissed. See also *Valente v. General Dental Council* (1990), 123 N.R. 311 (P.C.); and *Brown v. General Dental Council* (1990), 123 N.R. 315 (P.C.).

179 *Tencer v. Law Society (Upper Canada)*, Ont. Div. Ct., July 29, 1985 (unreported).

Appeal courts have frequently stated that they will not intervene in the exercise by law societies of their statutory powers except in cases involving a breach of the rules of natural justice or other jurisdictional error, a manifest wrong, an error in principle, or a substantial miscarriage of justice.[180] Nonetheless, in some cases less rigorous tests have been applied, and appeals have been allowed on the grounds that the discipline committee has not critically examined the evidence or that the penalty appealed from is not justified on the evidence.[181]

Thus in a 1991 decision the Saskatchewan Court of Appeal,[182] by a two-to-one majority, reduced the penalty imposed on a lawyer from a two-year suspension to a one-year suspension in a case involving serious misconduct in which alcohol abuse and the use of cocaine were major contributing factors. The majority held that the facts that the lawyer had voluntarily sought treatment and that his medical prognosis was favourable warranted a variation of the length of his suspension. The dissenting member of the court was of the view that the decision of the discipline hearing panel reflected no error in principle and, accordingly, should not be disturbed.

26.20 SPECIAL CASES: CROWN ATTORNEYS, JUDGES, LEGISLATORS

Determining the circumstances in which law societies may initiate and maintain discipline proceedings against crown attorneys involves a consideration of the scope of the independence of the office of attorney general. In 1985, the British Columbia Court of Appeal held that a law society does not have jurisdiction to inquire into the conduct of crown attorneys in exercising their discretion as to whether criminal proceedings should be initiated or proceeded with because

---

180 Cases in which appeal courts have expressed unwillingness to intervene in the exercise by law societies of their statutory powers except in unusual circumstances include: *Hall v. Ball* (1923), 54 O.L.R. 147 at 153-154 (H.C.) ("manifest wrong"); *Harris v. Law Society (Alberta)*, [1936] S.C.R. 88; *McCafferty v. Law Society (Alberta)*, [1941] S.C.R. 430; *Sandberg v. F.*, [1945] 4 D.L.R. 446 at 447-448 (Law Society of B.C. (Visitorial Trib.)) ("matters of principle" or "substantial miscarriage of justice"); *Re Solicitor*, [1956] 3 All E.R. 516 (Q.B.); *McCoan v. General Medical Council*, [1964] 3 All E.R. 143 (P.C.); *Stoangi v. Law Society (Upper Canada) (No. 2)* (1979), 100 D.L.R. (3d) 639 (Ont. S.C.) at 650; *Haunholter v. Law Society (Alberta)* (1988), 88 A.R. 313 (C.A.); and *Bolton v. Law Society*, [1994] 1 W.L.R. 512 at 516 (C.A.). These standards, and the expertise of the tribunal, are irrelevant, however, in cases of jurisdictional error: *National Corn Growers Assn. v. Canada (Canadian Import Tribunal)*, [1990] 2 S.C.R. 1324; and *Canada (Attorney General) v. P.S.A.C.*, [1991] S.C.R. 614.

181 In *Brethour v. Law Society (British Columbia)* (1950), 1 W.W.R. 34 (B.C. C.A.), the court held that it was entitled to go into the evidence taken by the benchers when the lawyer was denied the right of cross-examination; when the discipline hearing panel has not critically examined the evidence; and when, in the opinion of the court, the penalty appealed from was not justified on the evidence. See also *College of Nurses (Ontario) v. Quiogue* (1993), 13 O.R. (3d) 325 (Div. Ct.).

182 *Lamontagne v. Law Society (Saskatchewan)*, [1991] 4 W.W.R. 481 (Sask. C.A.), leave to appeal to S.C.C. refused (1991), 137 N.R. 384 (note) (S.C.C.).

attorneys general and their agents are accountable only to parliament or the legislature in the exercise of prosecutorial discretion.[183]

The court based its holding, however, largely upon the policy considerations that at that time precluded civil actions for malicious prosecution against attorneys general and their agents. Four years later the Supreme Court of Canada ruled that though the crown itself is immune from suit for malicious prosecution even when malice is shown, attorneys general and crown prosecutors are not.[184] If crown attorneys may now be vulnerable to civil actions for malicious prosecution in relation to the exercise of prosecutorial discretion in cases in which malice is shown, there may be no sound reasons in such cases for continuing their immunity to discipline proceedings brought at the instance of their governing body. The issue has not, however, been addressed by the courts.

Crown attorneys may be disciplined for professional misconduct or conduct unbecoming a barrister and solicitor in cases that do not involve the exercise of prosecutorial discretion as to whether criminal proceedings should be initiated or continued. Thus, for example, crown attorneys who breach their professional duty to make timely disclosure of evidence may be disciplined for the breach[185] at least where the failure is alleged to have been attributable to dishonesty or bad faith.[185.1]

In a 1987 decision,[186] the Yukon Supreme Court dismissed a motion brought by the territorial Minister of Justice for an order prohibiting the law society from proceeding with a complaint alleging professional misconduct in relation to public statements made during a dispute concerning a court crest. The court was not persuaded that the member's statements were made solely in the proper discharge

---

183 *Hoem v. Law Society (British Columbia)* (1985), 63 B.C.L.R. 36 (C.A.).

184 *Nelles v. Ontario*, [1989] 2 S.C.R. 170.

185 See *Re Cunliffe v. Law Society (British Columbia)*, [1984] 4 W.W.R. 451 (B.C. C.A.).

185.1 See *Krieger v. Law Society (Alberta)*, [2000] A.J. 1129 (C.A.). In the *Krieger* case the Court of Appeal did not decide the issue of whether the Alberta rule (chapter 10 rule 28(d)) requiring a prosecutor to make timely disclosure of all known relevant facts and witnesses whether tending toward guilt or innocence, is *intra vires* the Law Society. Rather, the Court chose to characterize the Law Society's consideration of the complaint of a defence counsel who had complained also to the Attorney General, as a review of the decision of the Attorney General. Although the Attorney General had reprimanded Crown Attorney Krieger for an error in judgment in delaying disclosure of preliminary results of blood tests, the senior Crown Attorney who conducted the investigation into the complaint had concluded that Krieger had not acted dishonestly or in bad faith. Because a commentary to rule 28(d) specifies that the Law Society's scrutiny would be limited to circumstances in which the Crown Attorney's discretion is exercised dishonestly or in bad faith, the Court held that rule 28 (d) did not apply "because there has been a finding of no bad faith or dishonesty." The Court added that "[f]or the Law Society to continue to pursue this matter, it is necessarily reviewing whether the Attorney General erred in its (*sic*) conclusions regarding Krieger's action. We are of the opinion that the Law Society has no authority to conduct a review of a decision of the Attorney General because it has no jurisdiction over the Crown as an entity or over the office of Attorney General."

186 *Kimmerly v. Law Society of Yukon* (1987), 3 Y.R. 54 (S.C.).

of ministerial responsibilities, that they were entirely divorced from the minister's status as a member of the law society, or that the principle of ministerial responsibility was established.

The Supreme Court of Canada held in a 1989 case that under the *Law Society Act* of Saskatchewan, which provides that discipline proceedings may be brought only against members of the law society, the law society lacked jurisdiction to discipline former members who have since been appointed to the bench, even in respect of their conduct while they were members.[187] The same result would obtain in Ontario.

26.21 INCAPACITY PROCEEDINGS

In Ontario, if the law society has reason to believe that one of its members may be incapable of practising law because of physical or mental illness, including addiction to alcohol or drugs, or any other cause, a committee of benchers may be appointed to conduct a capacity hearing.[188] Such hearings are not discipline proceedings, though on some occasions Convocation has authorized a discipline hearing panel to concurrently conduct a capacity hearing and hear a complaint of professional misconduct or conduct unbecoming a barrister and solicitor.

Whether or not a capacity hearing is held concurrently with a discipline hearing, it must be conducted in accordance with the principles of natural justice. A member is entitled to notice of the evidence to be introduced, to be represented by counsel, to cross-examine witnesses, and to be heard by an impartial panel.

If the committee finds that a lawyer is incapable of practising, Convocation will usually suspend the lawyer's rights and privileges for as long as the incapacity exists. In some cases the lawyer's rights may be limited rather than suspended; for example, the lawyer may be restricted to practising under the supervision of another lawyer.[189]

26.22 READMISSION

A former lawyer who has been disbarred or given permission to resign may apply to be readmitted.[191] As the Alberta Court of Appeal pointed out in a 1988 case, "[t]he removal of a lawyer from the rolls of the Society is not "a life sentence'."[191.1] Applications for readmission in Ontario are heard by a panel of

---

187 *Maurice v. Priel*, [1989] 1 S.C.R. 1023.

188 *Law Society Act*, R.S.O. 1990, c. L.8, ss. 37 and 38.

189 See Daniel P. Iggers and John P. Twohig, "The Disciplinary Process of the Law Society of Upper Canada" (1987) 8 Advocates' Quarterly 1 at 8-9; and Stephen E. Sherriff, H. Reginald Watson, and Shaun M. Devlin, " 'You Can Run...But You Can't Hide': A Guide to Understanding Lawyer Discipline in Ontario" in Franklin Moskoff (ed.), *Administrative Tribunals: A Practice Handbook for Legal Counsel* (Aurora, Ontario: Canada Law Book Inc., 1989), p. 115 at 139.

191 *Law Society Act*, R.S.O. 1990, c. L.8, as amended, s. 49.42.

191.1 *Haunholter v. Law Society (Alberta)* (1988), 88 A.R. 313 at 316 (Alta. C.A.).

three benchers sitting as a quorum of the admission committee, which makes a recommendation to Convocation.

In Ontario, the standard that an applicant for readmission must meet has been articulated as follows:

1. As a general rule, an order of disbarment for serious professional misconduct is intended to be permanent. Readmission should be the exception rather than the rule.
2. Applicants must show by a long course of conduct that they are persons to be trusted, who are in every way fit to be lawyers.
3. Applicants must show that their conduct is unimpeached and unimpeachable, and this can only be established by evidence of trustworthy persons, especially members of the profession and persons with whom applicants have been associated since disbarment.
4. A sufficient period of time must have elapsed before an application for readmission will be granted.
5. Applicants must show by substantial and satisfactory evidence that it is extremely unlikely that they will misconduct themselves in future if permitted to resume practice.
6. Applicants must show that they have entirely purged their guilt.
7. Applicants must show that they have remained current in the law through participating in continuing legal education since the termination of their membership in the Law Society, or at least that they have a plan acceptable to the Law Society that will enable them prior to readmission to become sufficiently current in the law to fulfil their responsibilities as lawyers.[191.2]

(*Continued on page 26–63*)

191.2 *Re Weisman*, report to Convocation dated January 27, 1997, at pages 20-21.

This seven-part test was a restatement of a standard articulated in previous Ontario decisions. The committee that devised the restatement of the test also emphasized the importance of the legal profession recognizing rehabilitation by allowing readmission, but only in cases in which there is independent evidence that claimed rehabilitation is genuine:

> In our view, the legal profession of all professions has a special responsibility to recognize cases of true rehabilitation. At the same time, however, we must bear in mind that rehabilitation will be claimed by virtually all applicants for readmission, and we must look to independent corroborating evidence before being satisfied that professed rehabilitation is genuine.[191.3]

An earlier version of these onerous stipulations were found to have been met in a 1987 case. In that case,[192] the applicant had been disbarred in 1981 after he was convicted in the criminal courts and imprisoned for conspiring to possess counterfeit money. At the time of the offence and for a number of years before that, the applicant had been addicted to gambling.

A psychiatrist retained by the law society to assess the applicant testified that at the time of his offence the applicant had suffered from a recognized psychiatric disorder involving impulse control which, however, had been arrested for a number of years by the time his readmission application was heard. The psychiatrist's evidence supported impressive character evidence that the applicant was a different person from the addict who had committed a criminal offence for which he was disbarred several years earlier and that the applicant's case was one of true rehabilitation.

The applicant had also participated willingly as a panellist at programs sponsored by the Canadian Bar Association and the law society at which he shared his mistakes with younger members of the bar and tried to impress upon them the dangers of becoming too closely associated with their clients. He had also kept current in the law by reading of recent developments in his field in law libraries.

Convocation has also held that "as a rule, those who are disbarred are meant to be permanently disbarred".[192.1] In a 1993 case,[192.2] an admissions committee of the Law Society in Ontario applied the same presumption in considering an application for admission to the Ontario Bar brought by a former lawyer who had been disbarred in British Columbia. "We are of the view," the committee observed, "that it would be inappropriate to review the disposition of another regulatory body unless in the rarest of cases, it had been demonstrated that the proceedings, including disposition, were seriously defective . . . Further,

---

191.3 *Ibid.*, at page 21.

192 *Re Goldman*, report of Convocation, May 5, 1987.

192.1 *Re Cirillo*, report of admissions committee of Law Society of Upper Canada, adopted by Convocation, October 22, 1992.

192.2 *Re Jones*, report of admissions committee of Law Society of Upper Canada, August 31, 1993.

we believe that this principle of reciprocal discipline or deference to the decisions of other professional bodies is in accord with the orderly administration of regulatory affairs."[192.3]

In a 1999 decision[192.4] a committee of inquiry of the Law Society of Alberta was called upon to consider an application for readmission brought by a former lawyer who, approximately 11 years earlier, had been convicted of second degree murder of his wife, sentenced to life imprisonment, and disbarred.

The applicant had been released on full parole after serving approximately ten years of his sentence. About ten months later he applied for readmission.

The committee of inquiry received uncontradicted evidence of rehabilitation that was both extensive and compelling. The applicant had not had a drink since the fateful evening. The applicant received psychiatric and psychological treatment and counselling. He developed coping mechanisms that enabled him to manage his anger and remain sober. He participated in programs in prison, and eventually led programs dealing with rehabilitation from addictions. Indeed one of his primary motivations for seeking readmission was to enhance his ability to help others suffering from addictions. He acknowledged the enormity of his crimes. He developed a new relationship with a supportive companion. The committee found that his progress was "remarkable and admirable", and added that "we very much admire the inner strength he has demonstrated on his continuing journey to personal redemption and rehabilitation."

In dismissing the application the committee accepted the submission of the Law Society's counsel that the paramount factor in its deliberations should not be rehabilitation, but rather the committee's view of what effect readmission "would have on the standing of the legal profession in the eyes of a reasonable person." Rehabilitation and other factors "pale in significance", the committee wrote, beside the standing of the legal profession. "As a self-governing profession," the committee added, "we are all too aware that the public sometimes sees us as self-serving rather than fulfilling our mandate which is to govern in the public interest and to protect the public interest."

The committee accordingly recommended rejection of the application. It also recommended that a period of ten years should elapse before another application may be entertained. The committee emphasized that in making such a recommendation (which had the effect of extending the two-year period prescribed by Law Society rules) it did not mean to imply that an application at that time would be *favourably* entertained.

The benchers of the Law Society of Alberta accepted the committee of inquiry's recommendation, which was not contested at that level by the applicant.

192.3 *Ibid.*, at p. 16.

192.4 *Re Sychuk and Law Society of Alberta*, [1999] L.S.D.D. No. 15 (Quicklaw).

In a 1989 American case,[193] the Supreme Court of Washington applied an eight-factor test in granting an application for readmission. The court considered, first, the applicant's pre-disbarment character, standing, and professional reputation in the community; second, the applicant's ethical standards in law practice; third, the type of misconduct that had led to disbarment; fourth, the sufficiency of discipline and restitution; fifth, the applicant's post-disbarment attitude, conduct, and reformation; sixth, the elapsed time since disbarment; seventh, the applicant's current proficiency in law; and eighth, the applicant's sincerity, truthfulness, and frankness in presenting and discussing issues surrounding his or her disbarment and readmission.

Although in a 1924 Alberta case[194] the Court of Appeal held that an applicant who had been disbarred for failing to account for funds entrusted to him by clients should not be readmitted unless all the claims of former clients were completely satisfied, the weight of authority is to the effect that restitution is only one factor among many to be considered in evaluating the applicant's professed rehabilitation. Restitution may be made merely for the purpose of contributing useful evidence at applicants' readmission hearings. It may measure applicants' wealth, borrowing ability, or good fortune rather than any personal qualities that suggest either that their original misconduct was out of character or that they have reformed and are unlikely to cause harm in the future.[195]

In two recent California cases, courts have held that an applicant's failure to make restitution may be considered on a readmission application even though the applicant's debt to clients has been discharged in bankruptcy.[196]

In readmission applications, the sufficiency of the punishment imposed upon the applicant is of secondary importance at most. The chief concern is whether the benchers are sufficiently confident that the applicant will not re-offend in the future.[197]

An order readmitting an applicant may be made conditional, for example, upon the applicant fulfilling certain educational requirements or practising

193 *Re Moynihan*, 778 P. 2d 521 (Wash., 1989).

194 *Re Eaton*, [1924] 3 W.W.R. 562 (Alta. C.A.). See also *Re V.*, [1924] 3 W.W.R. 552 (Alta. C.A.).

195 In *Re Solicitor* (1914), 7 W.W.R. 87 (Sask. S.C.), the court held that the mere fact that restitution has been made will not in itself entitle an applicant to readmission. In *Re Solicitor* (1915), 9 W.W.R. 480 (Alta. C.A.), a readmission application was granted upon the payment of 25 percent of the money misappropriated. See also *Re Wilson*, 409 A. 2d 1153 at 1156 (1979); Mark M. Orkin, *Legal Ethics: A Study of Professional Responsibility* (Toronto: Cartwright & Sons, 1957), pp. 224-225; and Charles Wolfram, *Modern Legal Ethics* (St. Paul, Minnesota: West, 1986), p. 136.

196 *Brookman v. State Bar*, 46 Cal. 3d 1004 (1988); *Re Hippard*, 782 P. 2d 440 (Cal., 1989).

197 *Re Harris* (1914), 6 W.W.R. 628 (Alta. C.A.). In *Bakht v. College of Physicians & Surgeons (New Brunswick)* (1989), 95 N.B.R. (2d) 81, the New Brunswick Court of Appeal upheld an order that an applicant for readmission undergo a five-month evaluation and clinical training period. See also *Laba v. Dental Assn. (Manitoba)* (1989), 61 Man. R. (2d) 24 (Q.B.), reversed in part (1990), 70 D.L.R. (4th) 154 (Man. C.A.)

under supervision. No specific time before which an application for readmission may be brought is specified in the Ontario *Law Society Act* or in the cases, although in a 1924 Nova Scotia decision the court held that a period of one year was too short.[198] It would be unusual for an application to be granted until at least three to five years had elapsed from the date on which the applicant's membership was cancelled. In a 1984 case,[199] however, the Saskatchewan Court of Appeal held that the benchers must not fetter their discretion by establishing a minimum time requirement. In cases in which the original misconduct continued for a period of years, it is likely that a lengthier waiting period would be required. A relatively substantial period of time must generally elapse before a readmission application will be considered favourably both for deterrent and, perhaps more important, evaluative purposes.

In 1975, the Massachusetts Supreme Court allowed the readmission application of Alger Hiss, who had been convicted of perjury 25 years earlier in a notorious case that still generated controversy. The court ordered readmission despite the fact that Hiss was utterly unrepentant; he had consistently protested his innocence. The case is considered to stand for the proposition that no inference of unfitness to practise may be drawn from the applicant's refusal to admit that he or she was correctly convicted. Applicants may be readmitted also if they hold the sincere belief that they were victims of a miscarriage of justice. One hopes that Canadian law societies will adopt the same approach.[200]

In a 1994 decision,[201] the Iowa Supreme Court denied a petition to posthumously reinstate the law licence of Charles Howard Sr., who was a co-founder of the National Bar Association in the 1920s, at a time when African-American lawyers were refused admission to the American Bar Association. Mr. Howard had voluntarily surrendered his law licence in the early 1950s during a disciplinary investigation that had been initiated against him. He died in 1969.

The court acknowledged Mr. Howard's outstanding contributions, but held that the governing legislation did not authorize the posthumous re-admission of a former lawyer. Even if such relief could be granted, the court added, it would decline to do so because of the numerous disciplinary problems that Mr. Howard had encountered during his career.

---

198 *Re Moseley* (1924), 57 N.S.R. 209 (T.D.).

199 *Deptuck v. Law Society (Saskatchewan)* (1984), [1985] 2 W.W.R 433 (Sask. C.A.). See also Wolfram, *supra*, note 195, p. 133. In *Re Cappe*, report of admission committee adopted by Convocation on June 20, 1991 (Ontario) a lawyer who had been given permission to resign after admitting misappropriating client funds was readmitted to the bar three years after his membership was terminated.

200 *Re Hiss*, 368 Mass. 447 (1975). See also David Pannick, *Advocates* (Oxford: Oxford University Press, 1992), pp. 124-125.

201 *In Re Howard*, 512 N.W. 2d 300 (Iowa 1994); see also Lawrence A. Dubin, "When Should a State Posthumously Readmit a Former Attorney to the Bar?", National Law Journal, January 31, 1994, p. A-15; and Lawrence A. Dubin, "The Court Had the Opportunity to Honor a Lawyer Who Fought for Justice", National Law Journal, March 28, 1994, p. A-21.

Thus, at least in the view of the Iowa Supreme Court, the re-admission process cannot be used to publicly honour a former lawyer who is deceased; the contribution of the former lawyer and the fact that the re-admission would in no way pose a danger to the public are insufficient reasons to grant such relief.

The Florida Supreme Court, however, came to the opposite conclusion in 1988, when it ordered the posthumous re-admission of Virgil Darnell Hawkins to the Florida Bar.[202] Mr. Hawkins too was a civil rights hero, whose litigation during the 1950s was responsible for desegregating the public universities in Florida.

202 *In Re Hawkins*, 532 So. 2d 669 (Fla. 1988); see also Dubin, *ibid.*, at p. A-15.

27

The Independence of the Bar

27.1 INTRODUCTION

In the late 1980s, after almost two centuries,[1] the right of the legal profession in Ontario to govern its members came under attack as a result of what became known as the Lang Michener case,[2] a case that raised the eternal Platonic question of who will guard the guardians.

Five partners in Lang Michener, who were the members of the firm's executive committee at the material time, were charged with professional misconduct. The law society alleged that the five lawyers had failed to make timely disclosure, to either the law society or the firm's clients, of information that had come to their attention that had led them to conclude that another partner in the firm, Martin Pilzmaker, had engaged in unethical conduct in his immigration practice. Pilzmaker was disbarred.[3] The five members of the firm's executive committee were reprimanded,[4] as were two other lawyers in the firm who had worked closely with Pilzmaker and who had failed to disclose his wrongful conduct in a timely way.

The public controversy surrounding the case was aroused by allegations of favouritism in the decision as to which partners in the firm should be charged with professional misconduct. One of the firm's partners who was not charged had been the chair of the law society's discipline committee and was at the time the complaint was authorized the chair of the law society's professional conduct committee.

---

1 In *Hands v. Law Society (Upper Canada)* (1888), 16 O.R. 625 (Q.B.), Chancellor Boyd, after reviewing the responsibilities of the law society as derived from the Statutes of Upper Canada for 1797 and later amendments, concluded that "the result of all this progressive legislation now is, that the profession represented by the Benchers is clothed with plenary powers of self-government and self-discipline." This decision was reversed by the Divisional Court on a separate point (17 O.R. 300) but was restored by the Court of Appeal (17 O.A.R. 41).

2 *Re Gnat et al.*, report of discipline hearing panel, January 9, 1990 (Ontario).

3 *Re Pilzmaker*, report adopted by Convocation, January 25, 1990.

4 *Supra*, note 2.

Due to these allegations of favouritism, the law society retained a respected retired judge from Manitoba, the Honourable Archibald S. Dewar, to investigate the law society's handling of the case. He concluded that the law society "was not influenced or affected by bias, partiality or oblique motive. There was no favouritism."[5]

Nevertheless, the Lang Michener case focused public attention on the question of whether lawyers should be responsible for disciplining lawyers. Even though the process was found to have been uncontaminated by bias in the Lang Michener case, shouldn't the potential for this type of abuse be removed? Should the government step in to regulate the legal profession?

27.2 THE INDEPENDENCE OF THE BAR FROM THE STATE

For lawyers, self-governance means something qualitatively different from what it means for members of other professions. In the legal profession the right of self-governance is at the heart of the independence of the bar. The importance of the legal profession remaining independent from government control was emphasized by Justice Estey in a unanimous 1982 judgment of the Supreme Court of Canada:[6]

> The independence of the bar from the State in all its pervasive manifestations is one of the hallmarks of a free society. Consequently, regulation of these members of the law profession by the State must, so far as by human ingenuity it can be so designed, be free from state interference, in the political sense, with the delivery of services to the individual citizens in the State, particularly in fields of public and criminal law. The public interest in a free society knows no area more sensitive than the independence, impartiality and availability to the general public of the members of the bar and through those members, legal advice and services generally.[7]

In an article published in 1985,[8] a former Treasurer of the Law Society of Upper Canada, George D. Finlayson Q.C. (now the Honourable Justice Finlayson of the Ontario Court of Appeal), while acknowledging that the legal profession is not free from regulation by the Legislature, articulated at least some of the reasons why the legal profession cannot be equated with other

---

5 A.S. Dewar, *"The Lang Michener Matter" Report* (Toronto: Law Society of Upper Canada, April, 1990), p. 38.

6 *Canada (Attorney General) v. Law Society (British Columbia) (sub nom. Jabour v. Law Society (British Columbia))*, [1982] 2 S.C.R. 307. This passage was quoted with approval and applied by the Supreme Court of Canada in *Pearlman v. Law Society (Manitoba)* (1991), 84 D.L.R. (4th) 105 at 119. See also *Beltz v. Law Society (British Columbia)* (1986), 31 D.L.R. (4th) 685 (B.C. S.C.).

7 *Ibid.*, p. 335.

8 George D. Finlayson, "Self-Government and the Legal Profession — Can it Continue?" (1985) 4 Advocates' Society Journal 11.

self-governing professions, and wrote eloquently of the importance of an independent bar in a modern democracy:

> The legal profession has a unique position in the community. Its distinguishing feature is that it alone among the professions is concerned with protecting the person and property of citizens from whatever quarter they may be threatened and pre-eminently against the threat of encroachment by the State. The protection of rights has been a historic function of the law, and it is the responsibility of lawyers to carry out that function. In order that they may continue to do so there can be no compromise in the principle of freedom of the profession from interference, let alone control, by government.
>
> A vital role of the lawyer is to stand between the citizen and the state, and this role is more important now than ever before. . . . Lawyers could not advise citizens as to their responsibilities with respect to particular legislation or governmental action if they cannot maintain their independence as individuals. It is almost impossible to do this if the Society that governs them is under the day-to-day control of government. It is imperative that the public have a perception of the legal profession as entirely separate from and independent of government, otherwise it will not have confidence that lawyers can truly represent its members in their dealings with government. . . .
>
> I am not talking only about a high profile case where counsel appear in court to defend accused persons against charges that directly reflect government policy, even though many examples come readily to mind. I am talking about every situation in which a client walks into your office and asks you what his rights are in a traffic case, a real estate transaction, or the filing of an income tax form. That client must know that we represent him and him alone. When you tell him what the law is and what his remedies are, he must be confident that you are not influenced by any government ties.[9]

In 1961 Lord Birkett made a similar point:

> When men and women are brought into the civil and criminal courts, for whatever reason, they should be able to turn for assistance at what may be the critical moments of their lives to a trained body of advocates, independent and fearless, who are pledged to see that they are protected against injustice and that their rights are not wrongly invaded from any quarter.[10]

We can appreciate the fundamental importance of an independent bar only by contrasting the treatment of lawyers in Western democracies in repressive

---

9 *Ibid.*, pp. 11 and 15. See also George D. Finlayson, "The Lawyer as a Professional", Law Society of Upper Canada Gazette, vol. XIV, no. 3 (September, 1980), p. 229 at 234; and B. Clive Bynoe, "Unprofessional Conduct: The Role of the Discipline Committee", Law Society of Upper Canada Gazette, vol. 10, no. 3 (September, 1976), p. 256 at 256-257.

10 Norman Birkett, *Six Great Advocates* (London: Penguin Books, 1961), p. 110, quoted by Arthur Maloney in "The Role of the Independent Bar", 1979 Law Society of Upper Canada Special Lectures 49 at 64. A thorough and thoughtful discussion of the meaning of the term "independence" in this context may be found in a paper written by Simon H. Hodgett of the Ontario bar for the LL.M. program at the London School of Economics.

regimes. In the regimes of Stalin, Hitler, the Greek Colonels, and the Chinese Cultural Revolutionaries, among others, vigorous and independent lawyers who have acted for clients whose views or conduct the government has deplored or feared have been harassed, ill-treated, prevented from practising their profession and in some instances even murdered, either by or with the complicity of the government. The cunning revolutionary in Shakespeare's *King Henry VI* who said "First, let us kill all the lawyers" knew that totalitarianism could not survive a strong and independent bar.[11]

The importance of the regulation of the profession being free of direct government control was recognized in England early on. Barristers have always been subject to discipline only by the Inns of Court to which they were admitted, whereas solicitors were subject to discipline first by the courts and, later, by the law society.[12]

When the Law Society of Upper Canada came into being in 1797, it was modelled on the Inns of Court. Its constituent statute conferred rule-making authority on it under inspection of the judges as visitors of the law society. The power of visitation was never a significant factor in the operation of the law society, and in modern times it has been removed from the statute. The importance of the power of visitation is that it provides a clear indication that the Legislature did not intend the law society to be its creature.[13]

Succeeding legislation, however, is framed progressively in the language of delegated authority.[14] In a 1985 case,[15] the Divisional Court held that the *Law Society Act* is today "part of a regulatory scheme established by the Ontario Legislature to govern the affairs and activities of the various professions."[16] It is not, the court added, "a private body whose powers derive from some vague form of contract or articles of association found in the mists of antiquity."[17] In promulgating rules of professional conduct, the court concluded, "the Law Society is performing a regulatory function on behalf of the "Legislature and government' of Ontario."[18] The rules are accordingly vulnerable to *Charter* scrutiny.

Despite its ringing endorsement of the principle of the independence of the bar in the 1982 case referred to above,[19] the Supreme Court of Canada in

11 William Shakespeare, *King Henry VI*. See also David Pannick, *Advocates* (Oxford: Oxford University Press, 1992), p. 147; and Alan M. Dershowitz, *The Best Defence* (New York: First Vintage Books, 1983), p. 415.

12 See part 27.5, "Independence From the Courts", *infra*.

13 See James J. Carthy, "The Law Society of Upper Canada" in *Professional Responsibility Reference Material* (Toronto: Law Society of Upper Canada, 1990-91), pp. 1-2.

14 See Carthy, *ibid.*, pp. 1-2.

15 *Klein v. Law Society (Upper Canada)* (1985), 16 D.L.R. (4th) 489 (Ont. Div. Ct.).

16 *Ibid.*, p. 528.

17 *Ibid.*

18 *Ibid.*

19 *Canada (Attorney General) v. Law Society (British Columbia) (sub nom. Jabour v. Law Society (British Columbia)*, [1982] 2 S.C.R. 307.

the same case wrote about the right of provincial governments to regulate legal services and to select for that purpose as its administrative technique an agency such as the law society.[20]

Perhaps the most startling development for those who regard the independence of the bar as one of our society's main means of ensuring individual rights and freedoms is a 1970 amendment to the Ontario *Law Society Act* that designates the Attorney General of the province as "the guardian of the public interest in all matters within the scope of this Act or having to do with the legal profession in any way."[21] That provision, which fortunately for other jurisdictions is peculiar to Ontario, is alarming to anyone concerned about the attenuation of the independence of the bar from government intervention. How would we react to a provision designating the Attorney General as the guardian of the public interest in all matters having to do with the judiciary?[22]

The 1970 amendment has never been invoked by the Attorney-General of Ontario. Since its enactment, the profession has continued to assert its independence, perhaps most notably in its commitment to maintaining control over legal aid plans and to ensuring that even government funded legal services are free of government control.[23]

The issue of whether legislation that purported to place the admission and discipline of lawyers directly under governmental control would be constitutional — in other words, whether the independence of the bar is a constitutional imperative — has not, of course, been decided.[24]

In a decision released in 2000,[24.1] however, the Ontario Divisional Court held that a provision of the *Securities Act* (R.S.O. 1990, c. S.5) which a lawyer was alleged to have contravened (exposing him to a reprimand by the Securities Commission) did not encroach upon the independence of the bar and should not be declared unconstitutional and read down so as not to apply to lawyers. The allegation against the lawyer was that he had made misleading statements to the Commission while he was representing a public company in the course of a prospectus review. The Court held that nothing in the *Law Society Act* (R.S.O. 1990, c. L.8) suggests that a lawyer should be immune from proceedings under the *Securities Act* solely because the lawyer is acting in a professional capacity. The Commission's purpose in proceedings under the *Securities Act*, the Court held, is not to discipline a lawyer for professional misconduct but to remedy a breach of its own statute that violates the public interest in fair and efficient

20 *Ibid.*, p. 336.

21 R.S.O. 1990, c. L.8, s. 13(1).

22 See S. Ronald Ellis, "The Independent Bar" in *Professional Responsibility Reference Materials* (Toronto: Law Society of Upper Canada, 1990-91) (originally published 1983), p. 2-6.

23 *Ibid.*, pp. 2-5 and 2-7.

24 *Ibid.*, p. 2-4.

24.1 *Wilder v. Ontario Securities Commission* (2000), 47 O.R. (3d) 361 (Div. Ct.).

capital markets. As such, the Court held, the Commission was not usurping the quite different public interest role of the Law Society.

27.3 RULES OF PROFESSIONAL CONDUCT

The preservation of their independence is a professional duty imposed on lawyers by some codes of professional conduct. Under the heading "Independence of the Bar," New Brunswick's rules of professional conduct provide that "[i]t is the duty of a lawyer to resist any attempt to coerce or influence him in the execution of his duties to his client. Historically the independence of the Bar has proven to be a bulwark against improper social or judicial interference with his duty to his client."[25] The same duty is found in the Code of Ethics of the International Bar Association.[26]

A similar duty was also adopted as a principle of professional conduct in 1977 by the bars and law societies of the European Community.[27] Three features of this particular principle of professional conduct are worthy of note. First, rules against conflicting interests and rules prohibiting certain outside interests are both treated as aspects of the independence of the bar. "The multiplicity of duties to which a lawyer is subject require his absolute independence, free from all other influences," the principle provides, "especially such as may arise from his personal interests."[28] Second, the principle provides that "[t]his independence is necessary in non-contentious matters as well as in litigation . . ."[29] Finally, the principle makes it clear that though the public is the beneficiary of an independent bar, and though it is primarily the government from which the bar must maintain independence, lawyers must maintain their independence as well both from the courts and, paradoxically, from their clients. "The disinterestedness of the lawyer is as necessary to trust in the process of justice as the impartiality of the judge. A lawyer must therefore show himself to be as independent of his client as of the court and be careful not to curry favour with the one or the other."[30]

27.4 INDEPENDENCE FROM CLIENTS

To say that lawyers must be independent of their clients means a number of different things. It means that lawyers have a right to represent any client

---

25 New Brunswick rules, Part B, rule 5.

26 International Code of Ethics of the International Bar Association, section 3, reproduced in Law Society of Upper Canada Gazette, vol. 15, no. 4 (December, 1981), pp. 443 and 444.

27 Consultative Committee of Bars and Law Societies of the European Community, "The Declaration of Perugia on the Principles of Professional Conduct of the Bars and Law Societies of the European Community 16. IX. 1977", reproduced in Law Society of Upper Canada Gazette, vol. 14, no. 2 (June 1980), p. 205.

28 *Ibid.*, p. 207.

29 *Ibid.*

30 *Ibid.*

— a right that they have a duty to assert at all costs and in the face of any opposition.[31] Although, as we have seen, Canadian lawyers do not in most circumstances have a duty to act for any client who wishes to retain them (as do English barristers) they have a right and in some cases a duty to act for clients whose views they find distasteful, and to advance positions with which they personally disagree.[32] Lawyers are better able to argue cases against governmental impropriety or oppression if they can maintain a spirit of independence from their clients.[33]

To say that lawyers must be independent of their clients also means that lawyers must not blindly do as their clients wish. Justice Sydney Robins of the Ontario Court of Appeal advised the graduating class at the Law Society of Upper Canada's call to the bar ceremonies in 1981 that "you . . . should regard yourselves as having clients rather than being someone's lawyer. A lawyer too personally associated in his client's affairs, one who lacks objectivity, the capacity to exercise the power of disinterested analysis, is seldom the best advocate or adviser."[34]

Lawyers' independence from their clients gives them considerable latitude — and great responsibility — in the conduct of clients' cases in court. In a 1979 lecture on the role of an independent bar,[35] the late Arthur Maloney quoted approvingly from an 1876 Scottish judgment:[36]

> . . . the nature of the advocate's office makes it clear that in the performance of his duty he must be entirely independent, and act according to his own discretion and judgment in the conduct of the case for his client. His legal right is to conduct the case without any regard to the wishes of his client, so long as his mandate is unrecalled, and what he does *bona fide* according to his own judgment will bind his client, and will not expose him to any action for what he has done, even if the client's interests are thereby prejudiced.[37]

---

31 See Mark M. Orkin, *Legal Ethics: A Study of Professional Conduct* (Toronto: Cartwright & Sons, 1957), p. 39.

32 See chapter 4, *supra*, part 4.2.

33 The independence of the bar has been invoked to explain the English cab rank rule, pursuant to which barristers have a duty to represent any client willing and able to pay them a proper fee who wishes to retain them to act in a field in which they practise: lawyers are better able to argue a case against government oppression if they can justify having done so not because they associate themselves with their client's views but because they have a duty to act for a client with whom they disagree. See David Pannick, *Advocates* (Oxford: Oxford University Press, 1992), pp. 47- 48.

34 Sydney L. Robins, "An Address to New Lawyers", Law Society of Upper Canada Gazette, vol. 15, part 4 (December, 1981), p. 349 at 353. See also Stuart Thom, "The Independence of the Legal Profession", Law Society of Upper Canada Gazette, vol. 13, no. 3 (September, 1979), p. 173 at 180.

35 Arthur Maloney, "The Role of the Independent Bar", 1979 Law Society of Upper Canada Special Lectures 49 at 62.

36 *Batchelor v. Pattison and Mackersy* (1876), 3 R. 914 (Scot. Ct. of Sess.).

37 *Ibid.*, p. 918.

Thus in a 1978 case,[38] the Ontario Court of Appeal held that a trial judge erred in allowing a party to share control of a trial with the party's counsel, as such an arrangement is "inconsistent with the complete control which counsel must have over the conduct of the case."[39]

27.5 INDEPENDENCE FROM THE COURTS

The independence of lawyers from the courts is of greater importance to the regulation of the profession than is their independence from their clients. This is because the principal practical issue that arises is whether the independence of the bar protects lawyers who are not in contempt of court from being subject to judicial discipline. The issue is most likely to arise today in the context of proposed orders that lawyers pay costs personally.

Historically, solicitors in England were subject to discipline by the courts, whereas barristers could be disciplined only by their Inns, as they were considered a self-governing profession. The distinction is generally explained on the basis that solicitors are officers of the court, whereas barristers are not. In 1888, the Council of the Law Society was empowered to investigate complaints against solicitors, and in 1919 the discipline committee of the law society was given by statute the authority to strike off the roll, to suspend, or to order payment of costs. However, the disciplinary jurisdiction of the courts was continued. The courts maintain disciplinary authority over solicitors concurrently with the law society to this day.[40] The authority to strike solicitors off the roll or to suspend solicitors, however, is never exercised by the courts today.[41]

English courts have nevertheless continued to exercise disciplinary jurisdiction over solicitors by ordering them to pay costs personally, either to their own clients or to parties adverse in interest, or both. The basis of such orders is that the solicitors have been guilty of professional misconduct that is not, however, sufficiently serious as to justify striking them off the roll or suspending them.[42]

In such proceedings the court exercises a summary jurisdiction. The judge is required to see that the solicitor is given adequate notice of the complaint and a full opportunity to answer it. The complaint need not involve dishonesty. Gross neglect or inaccuracy in a matter that it is the solicitor's duty to ascertain with accuracy may suffice as a basis for awarding costs against a solicitor

38 *Sherman v. Manley* (1978), 19 O.R. (2d) 531 (C.A.).
39 *Ibid.*, p. 534.
40 *Solicitors Act* (U.K.), 1974, c. 47, s. 50(2).
41 See *Myers v. Elman*, [1940] A.C. 282 at 318 (H.L.), *per* Lord Wright.
42 *Ibid.*, pp. 317-319.

personally,[43] but costs will not be awarded against solicitors personally unless they are guilty of "a serious dereliction of duty"[44] or "serious misconduct."[45]

Costs have been awarded against solicitors in England in cases in which they have been found guilty of abusing the process of the court or of oppressive conduct. Solicitors have been ordered to pay costs where they have unreasonably commenced or continued actions that have had no or substantially no chance of success[46] or that are impossible to prove.[47]

In a 1987 decision,[48] the Master of the Rolls, Sir John Donaldson, observed that the court's jurisdiction to award costs personally "falls to be exercised with care and discretion and only in clear cases."[49] In cases in which the complaint is that litigation was initiated or continued in circumstances in which to do so constituted serious misconduct, he added, "it must never be forgotten that it is not for solicitors or counsel to impose a pre-trial screen through which a litigant must pass before he can put his complaint or defence before the court."[50] On the other hand, he wrote, solicitors should not lend their assistance to actions brought *mala fide* or for an ulterior purpose.[51] The Master of the Rolls also observed that in cases in which solicitors' ability to answer complaints is hampered by their duty of confidentiality, justice requires that they be given the benefit of any doubt.[52]

One of the members of the House of Lords observed in 1940, in one of the leading cases, that the court's jurisdiction is not merely punitive but compensatory in that the order is for the payment of costs thrown away or lost by a litigant due to a solicitor's misconduct.[53] In a 1990 decision of the Court of Appeal,[54] however, the Chief Justice, Lord Lane, observed that there is nevertheless a punitive element to such an order in that the solicitor must pay a bill that would otherwise have to be paid by one of the parties to the litigation,

---

43 *Ibid.*, p. 319.

44 *Edwards v. Edwards*, [1958] P. 235, *per* Sachs J., quoting Viscount Maugham in *Myers v. Elman, ibid.*

45 *Orchard v. South Eastern Electricity Board*, [1987] 1 All E.R. 95 at 100 (C.A.), *per* Donaldson M.R.

46 *Edwards v. Edwards, supra*, note 44, pp. 248 and 254; *Davy-Chiesman v. Davy-Chiesman*, [1984] 1 All E.R. 321 at 334 (C.A.), *per* Dillon L.J.; and *Orchard v. South Eastern Electricity Board, ibid.*, p. 100. See also *Holmes v. National Benzole Co.* (1965), 109 S.J. 971 (Q.B.), where Lyell J., held that the court's jurisdiction may be exercised if the case is "hopeless."

47 *Wilkinson v. Wilkinson*, [1963] P. 1 at 10 (C.A.), *per* Ormerod L.J.

48 *Orchard v. South Eastern Electricity Board*, [1987] 1 All E.R. 95 (C.A.).

49 *Ibid.*, p. 100.

50 *Ibid.*

51 *Ibid.*

52 *Ibid.*

53 *Myers v. Elman*, [1940] A.C. 282 at 302-304 (H.L.), *per* Lord Atkin. See also *Weston v. Central Criminal Court's Administrator*, [1976] 2 All E.R. 875 at 883 (C.A.), *per* Stephenson L.J.

54 *Holden & Co. v. Crown Prosecution Service*, [1990] 1 All E.R. 368 (C.A.).

and in that the solicitor must incur the additional expense and adverse publicity that the exercise of the court's jurisdiction entails.[55]

The history of Canadian courts' exercise of disciplinary jurisdiction over lawyers bears some resemblance, as one would expect, to the English experience. In 1780, the Court of Common Pleas of the Province of Quebec purported to suspend two lawyers, but later vacated the suspensions as a result of opposition from La Communauté des Avocats.[56] When the Law Society of Upper Canada came into being in 1797, no disciplinary powers were conferred on it by its constituent statute. The law society was granted the right to admit persons "to practise in the law" and "to the Bar of any of His Majesty's courts of this province."[57]

The scheme of the legislation suggested the creation of an Inn of Court. The law society was granted rule making authority under inspection of the judges as visitors of the law society. The law society soon usurped the disciplinary jurisdiction of the superior courts of the province, with the courts' acquiescence. One may venture to surmise that like the English courts before them, the superior courts of Upper Canada were happy to be relieved of "the unpleasant duty of disbarring barristers."[58]

As early as 1823, the law society justified its exercise of disciplinary authority by reference to its intended similarity, as contemplated by the 1797 statute, to the Inns of Court. "The power of degradation and expulsion as well as other powers belonging to the Inns of Court in England," the law society contended, "are also by law vested in this Society."[59]

In 1876, the law society was by statute empowered to "make all necessary rules, regulations, and by-laws . . . respecting all . . . matters relating to the interior discipline and honour of members of the bar."[60] An 1881 statute clarified the powers conferred.[61] Any powers of the visitors respecting discipline were vested in the benchers.[62] By then, the law society had been exercising disciplinary authority for more than half a century. The Legislature was merely formalizing the status quo.[63]

---

55 *Ibid.*, p. 372. See also *Currie & Co. v. Law Society*, [1976] 3 All E.R. 832 at 839, *per* May J.

56 See Mark M. Orkin, *Professional Autonomy and the Public Interest: A Study of the Law Society of Upper Canada* (Osgoode Hall Law School of York University, Doctor of Jurisprudence Thesis, 1971), p. 46.

57 *Ibid.*

58 *Re Justices of Antigua* (1830), 1 Knapp 267, *per* Lord Wynford. See also Orkin, *supra*, note 56, p. 46.

59 Law Society of Upper Canada Minute Book, vol. 1, p. 487, cited by Orkin, *supra*, note 56, p. 44.

60 S.O. 1876, c. 31, ss. 1 and 2; R.S.O. 1877, c. 138, ss. 38 and 46.

61 S.O. 1881, c. 17. See also *Mehr v. Law Society (Upper Canada)*, [1954] O.R. 692 at 669 (C.A.), *per* Laidlaw J.A., reversed [1955] S.C.R. 344.

62 S.O. 1881, c. 17, s. 4. See also Orkin, *supra*, note 56, pp. 46-47.

63 See Orkin, *supra*, note 56, pp. 46-47.

Canadian statutes governing law societies, unlike their English counterparts, do not expressly retain the original disciplinary jurisdiction of the courts, although parties affected by disciplinary orders made by law societies generally have a right to appeal those orders to the courts.[64] On appeal, courts have been reluctant to interfere with orders made by law societies within jurisdiction, particularly on issues of what constitutes professional misconduct, as that determination is based on a professional standard that only members of the profession can properly apply.[65]

Canadian rules of civil procedure, however, empower courts to order lawyers to pay costs personally,[66] and Canadian courts have made such orders. Canadian courts have repeatedly emphasized, however, that orders requiring lawyers to pay costs personally should be sparingly made, that such orders should be made only in clear cases,[67] and that such orders should be made only in cases involving gross negligence or a failure to carry out one's professional duty.[68] Where the complaint against the lawyer is that the litigation should not have been brought, an order of costs against the lawyer personally will be made only where the case is "so hopelessly deficient that the defendant should not have been brought into court to answer for it."[69]

In a 1990 case,[70] the British Columbia Court of Appeal allowed an appeal from an order that the entire costs of an unsuccessful civil action be paid on a solicitor-client basis by the plaintiff's lawyer. The Law Society of British Columbia intervened on the appeal to support the position that the order of costs against the plaintiff's lawyer personally be set aside. The following were among the reasons of the court for setting aside the costs order:

(1) The lawyer's conduct, though less than impeccable, was not such as to engage the contempt power of the court, and was if anything a matter for the disciplinary process of the law society. Although it was not necessary to decide whether the court's power to visit costs on counsel on the basis of their

---

64 See, for example, *Law Society Act*, R.S.O. 1990, c. L.8, s. 49.38. See also *Young v. Young* (1990), 50 B.C.L.R. (2d) 1 at 68 (C.A.), *per* Cumming J.A., leave to appeal to S.C.C. granted (1991), 54 B.C.L.R. (2d) xxxiv (note) (S.C.C.).

65 *Young v. Young, ibid.*, pp. 68-69; *Wilson v. Law Society (British Columbia)* (1986), 9 B.C.L.R. (2d) 260 at 264 (C.A.), *per* MacFarlane J.A.; *Prescott v. Law Society (British Columbia)*, [1971] 4 W.W.R. 433 at 440-441 (B.C. C.A.), *per* Branca J.A. See also *Imrie v. Institute of Chartered Accountants (Ontario)*, [1972] 3 O.R. 275 at 279 (H.C.); and cases cited at notes 180 through 182 to chapter 26, *supra*.

66 See, for example, rule 57(3) of the British Columbia Rules of Court (1976), and rule 57.07 of the *Ontario Rules of Civil Procedure*, R.R.O. 1990, reg. 194.

67 See *Young v. Young, supra*, note 64, p. 6; and *Pacific Mobile Corp. v. Hunter Douglas Canada Ltd.*, [1979] 1 S.C.R. 842 at 845.

68 *Cini v. Micallef* (1987), 60 O.R. (2d) 584 (H.C.). See also cases cited at notes 192 through 197 to chapter 4, *supra*.

69 *WorldWide Treasure Adventures Inc. v. Trivia Games Inc.* (1987), 16 B.C.L.R. (2d) 135 at 138 (S.C.), *per* Gibbs J.

70 *Young v. Young, supra*, note 64.

conduct of trials can properly be applied only in cases of contempt, the court expressed the tentative view that its power should be limited to such cases.[71]

(2) Courts should exercise their powers to award costs against lawyers personally with care and discretion and only in clear cases because lawyers should not be dissuaded from advancing points that they honestly believe to be fairly arguable, by fear of being mulcted in costs. To hold a lawyer to be guilty of misconduct because he or she takes a point that the court holds to be bad would have a chilling effect and provide an unwelcome disincentive against acting fearlessly and in the best interests of the profession.[72]

(3) An award of costs should not be made against a lawyer personally in respect of his role in the management and conduct of a case in court or in the preliminary work that is related to the conduct of the case in court in light of the traditional immunity of barristers from suit.[73]

(4) An award of costs should not be made against a lawyer personally on the ground that proceedings brought on behalf of a client lack merit unless it is beyond doubt, not only that the proceedings are devoid of merit and the lawyer knew or ought to have known them to be so, but also that the responsibility for continuing with the proceedings despite their lack of merit lies with the lawyer rather than the client. Lawyers should not prejudge clients' cases, for to do so is to usurp the function of the court. Moreover, unless clients waive privilege, lawyers are helpless to defend

---

71 *Young v. Young, supra*, note 64, pp. 73-75. See also Mary F. Southin, "An Independent Bar: Sham or Reality" (1967) 25 The Advocate 227 at 228- 229.

72 *Young v. Young, supra*, note 64, pp. 62-64, citing *Abraham v. Jutson*, [1963] 2 All E.R. 402 at 404 (C.A.), *per* Lord Denning M.R.; and *Geller v. Brisseau*, [1979] 6 W.W.R. 416 at 424-425 (B.C. C.A.), *per* Taggart J.A.

73 *Young v. Young, supra*, note 64, pp. 66-67, and 70, citing *Rondel v. Worsley*, [1969] 1 A.C. 191 (H.L.) and *Rees v. Sinclair*, [1974] 1 N.Z.L.R. 180 at 186-187 (C.A.), *per* McCarthy P. This basis for the decision is highly doubtful, at least in the unequivocal language in which it is framed. As pointed out in chapter 4, *supra*, at part 4.18 it is generally accepted today that Canadian lawyers are not immune from suit for negligently performed barristers' work: *Demarco v. Ungaro* (1979), 21 O.R. (2d) 673 (H.C.). Cumming J.A., in the *Young* case, moreover, writes at p. 37 of his reasons "I leave for another day the question as to whether a lawyer in British Columbia may be held liable for negligence in his capacity as a barrister. . . ." It is difficult to understand how one can conclude without qualification that an award of costs should not be made against a lawyer in respect of barristers' work without answering that question in the negative. A conclusion that courts should be loath to award costs on the basis of a lawyer's conduct of a trial in light of the nature and number of judgments that counsel must make, however, would be defensible. In any event, as discussed in part 4.18, *supra*, in *Arthur J.S. Hall & Co. v. Simons*, [2000] H.L. J. 43, the House of Lords in effect overruled *Rondel v. Worsley* and abolished the immunity of advocates from claims cast in negligence for the conduct of cases in court.

such complaints by showing that they have advised clients of the unlikelihood of success but that their clients have nevertheless insisted on proceeding.[74]

In addition to its jurisdiction to award costs against lawyers personally in cases of misconduct, the courts have jurisdiction also over fee disputes between lawyers and clients. Assessment officers, who are judicial officers under the control of the judiciary, rather than law societies, are empowered to adjudicate such disputes.[75]

In summary, it is apparent that though in both England and Canada the courts initially had disciplinary authority over lawyers, they have entirely and willingly ceded that authority to law societies insofar as the powers to disbar, strike from the rolls, and suspend lawyers are concerned; and that even insofar as the power to penalize lawyers for less serious misconduct occurring during litigation before the courts is concerned, the courts have been loath to award costs against lawyers personally except in clear cases, despite clear rules of civil procedure empowering them to do so. The courts' reluctance to exercise disciplinary authority is a direct result of their solicitude for the principle of the independence of the bar, a principle that they have invoked frequently and forcefully.

27.6 THE AMERICAN EXPERIENCE: DISCIPLINE BY THE COURTS

In 1970, a special committee of the American Bar Association chaired by a retired judge of the United States Supreme Court, Tom Clark, published a report in which it warned that the inadequacy of the disciplinary processes of state bar associations made for a "scandalous situation" that called out for "the immediate attention of the profession." Discipline was administered at that time on a part-time basis by elected bar officials in private. Disciplinary functions were insufficiently funded, and examples abounded of cases in which miscreants escaped detection and disbarment for years while continuing to misappropriate clients' funds or otherwise misconduct themselves. The committee found that a substantial number of malefactors continued to practise law.[76]

In 1989, the A.B.A. struck another special committee (known as the McKay Commission) to assess the progress made in the field in the interim. The McKay Commission found that revolutionary changes had occurred:

74 *Young v. Young, supra*, note 64, pp. 71-72.

75 See S. Ronald Ellis, "The Independent Bar" in *Professional Responsibility Reference Materials* (Toronto: Law Society of Upper Canada, 1990-91) (originally published 1983), p. 7.

76 American Bar Association Special Committee on Disciplinary Enforcement, *Problems and Recommendations in Disciplinary Enforcement* (1970), pp. 1 and 3.

today almost all states have full-time professional disciplinary staff, and funding has increased dramatically. In 1988, almost 75 million dollars was spent on lawyer discipline across the country. In a majority of states, discipline hearings are public.[77] A separate study concluded that when disciplinary matters were transferred by the Illinois courts from the Chicago Bar Association to an independent Attorney Regulation and Disciplinary Commission, the proportion of complaints about lawyers that were investigated rose from 17 to 43 per cent, and the proportion carried through to hearings rose from 3.5 per cent to 13.5 per cent.[77.1]

In the intervening two decades, authority over discipline was transferred in many cases from state bar associations to state supreme courts, which typically delegated their authority to independent disciplinary agencies responsible to the court. In some jurisdictions this transfer of authority took place over the objection of state bar associations; in others it took place at their request.[78]

In some quarters this system has continued to be regarded as inadequate to answer concerns about accountability. A non-profit activist organization known as HALT, for example, whose aim is to improve the quality and integrity of the legal profession, has lobbied for the removal of the disciplinary system outside the bar to a public agency.[79]

The McKay Commission report focused not on whether the transfer of disciplinary authority from the bar to the courts compromised the independence of the bar, but on whether that authority should be transferred to a legislatively created regulatory agency responsible not to courts but to legislatures. The commission concluded that self-policing by the organized bar is, in the words of one commentator, "not only a lost cause but a bad one."[80] It recommended that authority over lawyer discipline should be retained or assumed by the court system of each state.[81]

"Elected bar officials, their appointees and employees should have no investigative, prosecutorial, or adjudicative functions in the disciplinary process,"[82] the commission concluded. "Despite the many reforms made in the

---

77 Report of American Bar Association Commission on Evaluation of Disciplinary Enforcement (the McKay Commission), May 1991, pp. xix-xx and 49. See also Mary M. Devlin, "The Development of Lawyer Disciplinary Procedures in the United States" (1994) 4 Georgetown Journal of Legal Ethics 911.

77.1 Richard L. Abel, *American Lawyers* (New York: Oxford University Press, 1989), p. 147.

78 See David A.A. Stager and Harry Arthurs, *Lawyers In Canada* (Toronto: University of Toronto Press, 1990), pp. 49-51; and *R. v. Kopyto* (1987), 62 O.R. (2d) 449 (C.A.), *per* Dubin J.A.

79 See Geoffrey C. Hazard, Jr., "Disciplinary Process Needs Major Reform", National Law Journal (August 1, 1988), p. 13.

80 Fred Strasser, "Call for Disciplinary Reform", National Law Journal (June 3, 1991), p. 1.

81 *Supra*, note 77, recommendations 1, 5 and 6.

82 *Supra*, note 77, recommendation 5.2, p. xi.

disciplinary process in the last twenty years," the committee reasoned, "there is significant distrust of the fairness and impartiality of self-regulation."[83]

The commission justified its recommendation that the regulation of the legal profession should remain under the authority of the judicial branch of government on both ideological and practical grounds. Apart altogether from the principle that the bar should be independent from the state, the commission "found no persuasive evidence that legislative regulation of other professions has resulted in better protection of the public."[84]

These recommendations of the McKay Commission were adopted by the American Bar Association's House of Delegates in February, 1992.

27.7 CONCLUSION

We shall end where we began. In spite of such salutary reforms as open discipline hearings many members of the public will continue to consider self-government by lawyers to be regulation by and for a self-interested, unaccountable elite. Pressure will be renewed to entrust the regulation of the legal profession, and particularly its disciplinary function, to a public agency responsible directly to the government.

This would be a fundamental mistake. The main threat to the independence of the bar comes from government, and independence from government is crucial in a democracy. The independence of the bar from the courts is also important, but the courts have always been involved to a degree in the regulation of the profession, and generally have proven sensitive to the indispensability of an independent bar. One hopes that the legal profession will maintain high ethical standards; that it will administer discipline firmly, fairly and visibly; and that it will command public respect for, and instill public confidence in, its ability to govern itself. To cede regulatory control to the courts would be by far the lesser of two evils — at least as long as the courts retain *their* independence — but would be nonetheless a retrogressive step.

---

83 *Supra*, note 77, p. 19.

84 *Supra*, note 77, recommendation 1, pp. 1, 3 and 4.

Appendix

CODE OF PROFESSIONAL CONDUCT

Reproduced with the permission of the Canadian Bar Association

Contents

	Foreword	A-v
	Preface	A-vii
	Interpretation	A-xi
Chapter I	Integrity	A-1
Chapter II	Competence and Quality of Service	A-5
Chapter III	Advising Clients	A-9
Chapter IV	Confidential Information	A-13
Chapter V	Impartiality and Conflict of Interest Between Clients	A-17
Chapter VI	Conflict of Interest Between Lawyer and Client	A-23
Chapter VII	Outside Interests and the Practice of Law	A-27
Chapter VIII	Preservation of Clients' Property	A-31
Chapter IX	The Lawyer as Advocate	A-35
Chapter X	The Lawyer in Public Office	A-45
Chapter XI	Fees	A-49
Chapter XII	Withdrawal	A-53
Chapter XIII	The Lawyer and the Administration of Justice	A-59
Chapter XIV	Advertising, Solicitation and Making Legal Services Available	A-63
Chapter XV	Responsibility to the Profession	A-67
Chapter XVI	Responsibility to Lawyers Individually	A-69
Chapter XVII	Practice by Unauthorized Persons	A-73
Chapter XVIII	Public Appearances and Public Statements by Lawyers	A-77
Chapter XIX	Avoiding Questionable Conduct	A-81
	Abbreviations	A-85
	Bibliography	A-87

FOREWORD

At the meeting of the National Executive Committee of The Canadian Bar Association in January of 1984, a resolution was adoted unanimously to review the 1974 Code of Professional Conduct. The then President Robert McKercher, Q.C. appointed Robert P. Fraser, Q.C. to chair the Committee to Revise The Code of Professional Conduct.

The National Council of the Canadian Bar Association in August of 1987 adopted without a dissenting vote the Revised Code of Professional Conduct (1987).

In his report to Council, Robert P. Fraser, Q.C. stated:

> "You will recall that this Association approved a Code in 1974. Since that time, that Code has been used by and large, as the authority in terms of ethics and discipline matters by all Law Societies in Canada, and to a lesser extent, by the Barreau du Québec. It has been adopted by some provinces in its entirety, others have used it as the basis of their own provincial publication."

In drafting the new Code, the Committee began its work with the conscious decision to build upon the 1974 document, (delivered to The Canadian Bar Association by the then Committee Chairman S.E. Fennell, Q.C., Past President of the CBA), and to bring forward only those changes that reflect the realities of practising law in today's society.

In adopting the 1987 Code of Professional Conduct, The Canadian Bar Association recognized the extraordinary effort on the part of the Committee in bringing to realization the revised document after numerous consultations with Council, CBA Branches, and the Law Societies. The Association is grateful to the Committee for its professional contribution to the practice of law in Canada.

The Honourable Jean Bazin, Q.C.
President
Ottawa, June 1988

PREFACE[1]

The legal profession has developed over the centuries to meet a public need for legal services on a professional basis. Traditionally, this has involved the provision of advice and representation to protect or advance the rights, liberties and property of a client by a trusted adviser with whom the client has a personal relationship and whose integrity, competence and loyalty are assured.[2]

In order to satisfy this need for legal services adequately, lawyers and the quality of service they provide must command the confidence and respect of the public. This can only be achieved if lawyers establish and maintain a reputation for both integrity and high standards of legal skill and care. The lawyers of many countries in the world, despite differences in their legal systems, practices, procedures and customs, have all imposed upon themselves substantially the same basic standards. Those standards invariably place their main emphasis on integrity and competence.

In Canada, the provincial legislatures have entrusted to the legal profession through its governing bodies responsibility for maintaining standards of professional conduct and for disciplining lawyers who fail to meet them. Generally, the preparation and publication of codes of ethics and professional conduct have been left to the profession. It is a responsibility that must be accepted and carried out by the profession as a whole.

The pertinent laws in Canada use various terms to describe conduct that subjects the lawyer to discipline, for example, "professional misconduct", "conduct unbecoming" and "acts derogatory to the honour or dignity of the Bar". Some statutes also provide that disciplinary action may be taken if a lawyer is convicted of an indictable offence, or for "misappropriation or wrongful conversion", or "gross negligence" or for conduct "incompatible with the best interests of the public or the members of the [Law] Society", or for breach of the applicable statute itself or the rules made under it.[3]

With few exceptions the statutes do not specify the kinds of conduct that will subject a lawyer to discipline. For its part, the Code does not attempt to define professional misconduct or conduct unbecoming, nor does it try to evaluate the relative importance of the various rules or the gravity of a breach of any of them. Those functions are the responsibility of the various governing bodies. The rules that follow are therefore intended to serve as a guide, and the commentaries and notes appended to them are illustrative only. By enunciating principles of what is and is not acceptable professional conduct, the Code is designed to assist governing bodies and practitioners alike in determining whether in a given case the conduct is acceptable, thus furthering the process of self-government.

The essence of professional responsibility is that the lawyer must act at all times *uberrimae fidei*, with utmost good faith to the court, to the client, to other lawyers, and to members of the public. Given the many and varied demands to which the lawyer is subject, it is inevitable that problems will arise. No set of rules can foresee every possible situation, but the ethical principles set out in the Code are intended to provide a framework within which the lawyer may, with courage and dignity, provide the high quality of legal services that a complex and ever-changing society demands.[4]

The extent to which each lawyer's conduct should rise above the minimum standards set by the Code is a matter of personal decision. The lawyer who would enjoy the respect and confidence of the community as well as of other members of the legal profession must strive to maintain the highest possible degree of ethical conduct. The greatness and strength of the legal profession depend on high standards of professional conduct that permit no compromise.

The Code of Professional Conduct that follows is to be understood and applied in the light of its primary concern for the protection of the public interest. This principle is implicit in the legislative grants of self-government referred to above. Inevitably, the practical application of the Code to the diverse situations that confront an active profession in a changing society will reveal gaps, ambiguities and apparent inconsistencies.[5] In such cases, the principle of protection of the public interest will serve to guide the practitioner to the applicable principles of ethical conduct and the true intent of the Code.

NOTES

1. The footnotes relate the provisions of the Code to pertinent earlier Codes, rulings, by-laws, statutes, judicial dicta, text books and articles, as well as to certain other materials. They are selective, not exhaustive, and merely supplement the text. For abbreviations and bibliography, see pages 85 and 87.

2. "The core of the proposition is that problems of . . . rights or property call for a personal relationship with a trusted adviser, whose discretion is absolute, who serves no master but his client, and whose competence is assured. The codes and traditions of the professions who supply these services support the basic proposition. They also display the uniformity that its truth would lead one to expect." *Bennion*, p. 16.

3. Abstract of disciplinary provisions:

   Alberta: *Legal Profession Act*, R.S.A. 1980, c. L-9
   s. 47 "conduct incompatible with the best interests of the public or the members of the Society"
   "tends to harm the standing of the legal profession generally"

   British Columbia: *Barristers and Solicitors Act*, R.S.B.C. 1979, c. 26
   s. 50 "misappropriation or wrongful conversion"
   "professional misconduct"
   "conduct unbecoming a member"
   "breach of this Act or the rules made under it"
   s. 55 "convicted of an indictable offence"

   Manitoba: *Law Society Act*, R.S.M. 1970, c. L-100
   s. 45 "professional misconduct"

"conduct unbecoming a barrister, solicitor, or student"

New Brunswick: *Barristers Society Act*, 1931, S.N.B., c. 50 as am. by S.N.B. 1954, c. 99

s. 19 "professional misconduct"
default *re* clients' moneys
breach of Act or regulation

Newfoundland: *Law Society Act*, R.S.N. 1970, c. 201

s. 37 "conduct unbecoming a barrister, solicitor, student-at-law or articled clerk"

Nova Scotia: *Barristers and Solicitors Act*, R.S.N.S. c. B-2

s. 29 "professional misconduct"
"conduct unbecoming a barrister or articled clerk"
s. 31 "absconding, insane or insolvent"

Ontario: *Law Society Act*, R.S.O. 1980, c. 233

s. 34 "professional misconduct"
"conduct unbecoming a barrister and solicitor"
s. 38 "conduct unbecoming a student member"

Prince Edward Island: *Law Society and Legal Profession Act*, R.S.P.E.I. 1974, c. L-9

s. 27 "professional misconduct"
"conduct unbecoming a member"

Quebec: *Bar Act*, R.S.Q. 1977, c. B-1

s. 107 "derogatory to the honour or dignity of the Bar or prejudicial to the discipline of its members"
"position or office . . . incompatible with the practice of the profession of advocate"
"occupation, industry or trade carried on or the position held is incompatible with the honour or dignity of the Bar"
s. 111 "conviction of an indictable offence"

Saskatchewan: *Legal Profession Act*, R.S.S. c. L-10

s. 59 "conduct unbecoming a barrister and solicitor"
s. 70 "convicted of an indictable offence"

England: *Cordery on Solicitors* (7th ed., 1981), p. 333

". . . because he has been guilty of an act or omission for which the Act or some other statute prescribes that penalty, or because he has committed an act of misconduct which renders him unfit to be permitted to continue in practice."

(at p. 335): "Misconduct which makes a solicitor unfit to continue in practice may be divided into three kinds: criminal conduct, professional misconduct and unprofessional conduct."

(at p. 336): "The jurisdiction is not limited to cases where the misconduct charged amounts to an indictable offence, or is professional in character, but extends to all cases where the solicitor's conduct is 'unprofessional', i.e., such as renders him unfit to be an officer of the court."

"Is it a personally disgraceful offence or is it not? Ought any respectable solicitor to be called upon to enter into that intimate discourse with (the offender) which is necessary between two solicitors even though they are acting for opposite parties?" per Lord Esher M.R., in *Re Weare* (1893), 2 Q.B. 439 at 446 (C.A.).

"Counsel . . . takes the position that the expressions (unprofessional conduct and professional misconduct) are synonymous . . . I agree . . . that the phrases are often used interchangeably but cannot agree that this is always so . . . . Accepting as I do that the terms are not synonymous . . .", per McKay J. in *Re Novak and Law Society* (1973) 31 D.L.R. (3d) 89 at 102 (B.C.S.C.).

4. "The law and its institutions change as social conditions change. They must

change if they are to preserve, much less advance, the political and social values from which they derive their purposes and their life. This is true of the most important of legal institutions, the profession of law. The profession, too, must change when conditions change in order to preserve and advance the social values that are its reason for being." Cheatham, *Availability of Legal Services: The Responsibility of the Individual Lawyer and the Organized Bar* (1965) 12 U.C.L.A.L. Rev. 438, 440.

5. "It is not possible to frame a set of rules which will particularize all the duties of the lawyer in all the varied relations of his professional life . . .". Sask. *Preamble.*

INTERPRETATION

In this Code the field of professional conduct and ethics is divided into nineteen chapters, each of which contains a short statement of a rule or principle followed by commentary and notes. Although this division gives rise to some overlapping of subjects, the principle of integrity enunciated in Chapter I underlies the entire Code so that some of the rules in subsequent chapters represent particular applications of the basic rule set out in Chapter I. Again there are instances where substantially the same comment appears more then once. Such duplication is considered desirable in order to provide clarity and emphasis and to reduce cross-references.

The commentary and notes to each rule contain a discussion of the ethical considerations involved, explanations, examples and other material designed to assist in the interpretation and understanding of the rule itself. Each rule should therefore be read with and interpreted in the light of the related commentary and notes.

Certain terms used in the Code require definition as follows:

"client"	means a person on whose behalf a lawyer renders or undertakes to render professional services;
"court"	includes conventional law courts and generally all judicial and quasi-judicial tribunals;
"Governing Body"	means the body charged under the laws of a particular jurisdiction with the duty of governing the legal profession (e.g., the Benchers, General Council, Convocation or Council);
"lawyer"	means an individual who is duly authorized to practise law;
"legal profession"	refers to lawyers collectively;
"person"	includes a corporation or other legal entity, an association, partnership or other organization, the Crown in right of Canada or a province and the government of a state or any political subdivision thereof.

It will be noted that the term "lawyer" as defined above extends not only to those engaged in private practice but also to those who are employed on a full-time basis by governments, agencies, corporations and other organizations. An employer-employee relationship of this kind may give rise to special problems in the area of conflict of interest,[1] but in all matters involving integrity[2] and generally in all professional matters, if the requirements or demands of the employer conflict with the standards declared by the Code, the latter must govern.

NOTES

1. See Chap. V.
2. See Chap. I. The involvement of various lawyers in The Watergate Affair most graphically illustrates some of the hazards.

CHAPTER I

INTEGRITY

RULE

The lawyer must discharge with integrity all duties owed to clients, the court, other members of the profession and the public.[1]

Commentary

Guiding Principles

1. Integrity is the fundamental quality of any person who seeks to practise as a member of the legal profession. If the client is in any doubt about the lawyer's trustworthiness the essential element in the lawyer-client relationship will be missing. If personal integrity is lacking the lawyer's usefulness to the client and reputation within the profession will be destroyed regardless of how competent the lawyer may be.[2]

2. The principle of integrity is a key element of each rule of the Code.

Disciplinary Action

3. Dishonourable or questionable conduct on the part of the lawyer in either private life or professional practice will reflect adversely upon the lawyer, the integrity of the legal profession and the administration of justice as a whole.[3] If the conduct, whether within or outside the professional sphere, is such that knowledge of it would be likely to impair the client's trust in the lawyer as a professional consultant, a governing body may be justified in taking disciplinary action.[4]

Non-professional Activities

4. Generally speaking, however, a governing body will not be concerned with the purely private or extra-professional activities of a lawyer that do not bring into question the integrity of the legal profession or the lawyer's professional integrity or competence.

NOTES

1. Cf. CBA-COD 1. *O.E.D.*: "Integrity . . . soundness of moral principle, esp. in relation to truth and fair dealing; uprightness, honesty, sincerity, candour."
   Cf. IBA. "Introductory". "The rules of professional conduct enforced in various countries . . . uniformly place the main emphasis upon the essential need for integrity and, thereafter, upon the duties owed by a lawyer to his client, to the Court, to other members of the legal profession and to the public at large."
2. "Integrity, probity or uprightness is a prized quality in almost every sphere of life . . . . The best assurance the client can have . . . is the basic integrity of the professional consultant . . . . Sir Thomas Lund says that . . . his reputation is the greatest asset a solicitor can have . . . . A reputation for integrity is an indivisible whole; it can therefore be lost by actions having little or nothing to do with the profession . . . . Integrity has many aspects and may be displayed (or not) in a wide variety of situations . . . the preservation of confidences, the display of impartiality, the taking of full responsibility are all aspects of integrity. So is the question of competence . . . . *Integrity is the fundamental quality, whose absence vitiates all others." Bennion, passim,* pp. 108-12 (emphasis added).
3. Illustrations of conduct that may infringe the Rule (and often other provisions of this Code) include:
   (a) committing any personally disgraceful or morally reprehensible offence that reflects upon the lawyer's integrity (whereof a conviction by a competent court would be *prima facie* evidence);
   (b) committing, whether professionally or in the lawyer's personal capacity, any act of fraud or dishonesty, e.g., by knowingly making a false tax return or falsifying a document, even without fraudulent intent, and whether or not prosecuted therefor;
   (c) making untrue representations or concealing material facts from a client with dishonest or improper motives;
   (d) taking improper advantage of the youth, inexperience, lack of education or sophistication, ill health, or unbusinesslike habits of a client;
   (e) misappropriating or dealing dishonestly with the client's monies;
   (f) receiving monies from or on behalf of a client expressly for a specific purpose and failing, without the client's consent, to pay them over for that purpose;
   (g) knowingly assisting, enabling or permitting any person to act fraudulently, dishonestly or illegally toward the lawyer's client;
   (h) failing to be absolutely frank and candid in all dealings with the Court, fellow lawyers and other parties to proceedings, subject always to not betraying the client's cause, abandoning the client's legal rights or disclosing the client's confidences;
   (i) failing, when dealing with a person not legally represented, to disclose material facts, e.g., the existence of a mortgage on a property being sold, or supplying false information, whether the lawyer is professionally representing a client or is concerned personally;
   (j) failure to honour the lawyer's word when pledged even though, under technical rules, the absence of writing might afford a legal defence.

   Other examples are specifically dealt with in subsequent chapters.
   (The foregoing are drawn largely from IBA A-1 to A-24 and from disciplinary records. For illustrative cases in the same area see, e.g., 36 *Halsbury* (3d) pp. 222-26 and *Orkin*, pp. 204-14. In *Re Weare* (1893), 2 Q.B. 439 (C.A.) the striking off of a solicitor who had knowingly rented his premises for use as a brothel was upheld by the Court.)
   As to the distinction between "professional misconduct" and "unprofessional conduct" in disciplinary proceedings, see note 3 to the *Preface, supra.*

4. Cf. IBA, Chapter 2.
"The public looks for a hallmark bestowed by a trusted professional body, and evidenced by entry on a register or members' list." (p. 36). "Membership of a . . . professional body is generally treated as an indication of good character in itself . . .", *Bennion,* p. 111.

CHAPTER II

COMPETENCE AND QUALITY OF SERVICE

RULE

(a) The lawyer owes the client a duty to be competent to perform any legal services undertaken on the client's behalf.[1]

(b) The lawyer should serve the client in a conscientious, diligent and efficient manner so as to provide a quality of service at least equal to that which lawyers generally would expect of a competent lawyer in a like situation.[2]

Commentary

Knowledge and Skill

1. Competence in the context of the first branch of this Rule goes beyond formal qualification to practise law. It has to do with the sufficiency of the lawyer's qualifications to deal with the matter in question. It includes knowledge, skill, and the ability to use them effectively in the interests of the client.[3]

2. As members of the legal profession, lawyers hold themselves out as being knowledgeable, skilled and capable in the practice of law. The client is entitled to assume that the lawyer has the ability and capacity to deal adequately with any legal matters undertaken on the client's behalf.[4]

3. The lawyer should not undertake a matter without honestly feeling either competent to handle it, or able to become competent without undue delay, risk or expense to the client. The lawyer who proceeds on any other basis is not being honest with the client. This is an ethical consideration and is to be distinguished from the standard of care that a court would apply for purposes of determining negligence.

4. Competence involves more than an understanding of legal principles: it involves an adequate knowledge of the practice and procedures by which such principles can be effectively applied. To accomplish this the lawyer should keep abreast of developments in all branches of law wherein the

lawyer's practice lies.

5. In deciding whether the lawyer has employed the requisite degree of knowledge and skill in a particular matter, relevant factors will include the complexity and specialized nature of the matter, the lawyer's general experience, the lawyer's training and experience in the field in question, the preparation and study the lawyer is able to give the matter and whether it is appropriate or feasible to refer the matter to, or associate or consult with, a lawyer of established competence in the field in question. In some circumstances expertise in a particular field of law may be required; often the necessary degree of proficiency will be that of the general practitioner.

Seeking Assistance

6. The lawyer must be alert to recognize any lack of competence for a particular task and the disservice that would be done the client by undertaking that task. If consulted in such circumstances, the lawyer should either decline to act or obtain the client's instructions to retain, consult or collaborate with a lawyer who is competent in that field. The lawyer should also recognize that competence for a particular task may sometimes require seeking advice from or collaborating with experts in scientific, accounting or other non-legal fields. In such a situation the lawyer should not hesitate to seek the client's instructions to consult experts.

Quality of Service

7. Numerous examples could be given of conduct that does not meet the quality of service required by the second branch of the Rule. The list that follows is illustrative, but not by any means exhaustive:

(a) failure to keep the client reasonably informed;
(b) failure to answer reasonable requests from the client for information;
(c) unexplained failure to respond to the client's telephone calls;
(d) failure to keep appointments with clients without explanation or apology;
(e) informing the client that something will happen or that some step will be taken by a certain date, then letting the date pass without follow-up information or explanation;
(f) failure to answer within a reasonable time a communication that requires a reply;
(g) doing the work in hand but doing it so belatedly that its value to the client is diminished or lost;
(h) slipshod work, such as mistakes or omissions in statements or documents prepared on behalf of the client;
(i) failure to maintain office staff and facilities adequate to the lawyer's practice;
(j) failure to inform the client of proposals of settlement, or to explain them properly;

(k) withholding information from the client or misleading the client about the position of a matter in order to cover up the fact of neglect or mistakes;
(l) failure to make a prompt and complete report when the work is finished or, if a final report cannot be made, failure to make an interim report where one might reasonably be expected;
(m) self-induced disability, for example from the use of intoxicants or drugs, which interferes with or prejudices the lawyer's services to the client.[5]

Promptness

8. The requirement of conscientious, diligent and efficient service means that the lawyer must make every effort to provide prompt service to the client. If the lawyer can reasonably foresee undue delay in providing advice or services, the client should be so informed.[6]

Consequences of Incompetence

9. It will be observed that the Rule does not prescribe a standard of perfection. A mistake, even though it might be actionable for damages in negligence, would not necessarily constitute a failure to maintain the standard set by the Rule, but evidence of gross neglect in a particular matter or a pattern of neglect or mistakes in different matters may be evidence of such a failure regardless of tort liability. Where both negligence and incompetence are established, while damages may be awarded for the former, the latter can give rise to the additional sanction of disciplinary action.[7]

10. The lawyer who is incompetent does the client a disservice, brings discredit to the profession, and may bring the administration of justice into disrepute.[8] As well as damaging the lawyer's own reputation and practice, incompetence may also injure the lawyer's associates or dependants.

NOTES

1. Cf. CBA-COD 2; IBA B-1; ABA-MR 1.1; ABA Canon 6, ECs 6-1 to 6-5, DR 6-101 (A).
"The public looks for a hallmark bestowed by a trusted professional body, and evidenced by entry on a register or members' list (p. 36) . . . Having bestowed a hallmark of competence, a professional institute has some responsibility for ensuring that it remains valid.", *Bennion*, p. 48.
See also Bastedo, *A Note on Lawyers' Malpractice*, (1970) 7 Osg. Hall L.J. 311.

2. As a matter of law, the English and Canadian courts have consistently held that actions by clients against their lawyers for breach of duty stem from the contract of employment made or implied from the retainer, or from the fiduciary relationship that exists between lawyer and client and not on any general tort basis. A contractual or fiduciary relationship must be established: see, e.g., *Groom* v. *Crocker et al.* (1938), 2 All E.R. 394 (C.A.); *Rowswell* v. *Pettit et al.* (1968), 68 D.L.R. (2d) 202 (Ont. H.C.J.) at pp. 209-12 (affd. with variations as to damages, *sub nom. Wilson et al.* v. *Rowswell* (1970)

S.C.R. 865).

3. "Incompetence goes wider than lack of professional skill, and covers delay, neglect and even sheer disobedience to the client's instructions.", *Bennion,* p. 53.

4. "This solicitor's very presence as a lawyer . . . is an assurance to the public that he has the training, the talent and the diligence to advise them about their legal rights and competently to aid in their enforcement. Having regard to the faith which a citizen ought to be able to place in a member of the Law Society . . .", per Porter, J.A. in *Cook v. Szott et al.* (1968), 68 D.L.R. (2d) 723 at 726 (Alta. App. Div.).

5. Cf. *Orkin,* pp. 123-25, and para. 9, *post.*
"A client has a right to honest explanations for delay on the part of his solicitor, and it is clear that the Benchers . . . concluded that the solicitor had not given an honest explanation for the delay, but on the contrary had deceived his client as to the reason for such delay . . .", per Farris, C.J.S.C. in *Re Legal Professions Act; Sandberg* v. *"F"* (1945), 4 D.L.R. 446 at 447 (B.C. Visitorial Tribunal).
Cf. IBA D-1. In some jurisdictions (e.g., Ontario, *Law Society Act,* R.S.O. 1980, c. 233, s. 35) provision is made for inquiry and suspension of members incapacitated by reason of age, physical or mental illness including addiction to alcohol or drugs, or other cause.

6. For a denunciation of dilatory practices of solicitors, see *Allen* v. *McAlpine et al.* (1968), 2 W.L.R. 366 (C.A.).

7. "I take the law as to the standard of care of a solicitor to be accurately stated in Charlesworth on Negligence . . . it must be shown that the error or ignorance was such that an ordinary competent solicitor would not have made or shown it", per Lebel, J. in *Aaroe & Aaroe* v. *Seymour* (1957), 6 D.L.R. (2d) 100 at 101 (Ont. H.C.J.).
"As a future guide to Benchers [this Visitorial Tribunal] expresses the opinion that the words 'good cause' in the *Legal Professions Act* are broad enough . . . to justify the Benchers in suspending a member . . . who has been guilty of a series of acts of gross negligence which, taken together, would amount to a course of conduct sufficient to bring the legal profession into disrepute", per Farris, C.J.S.C. in *Re Legal Professions Act; Baron* v. *"F"* (1945), 4 D.L.R. 525 at 528 (B.C. Visitorial Tribunal).

8. For an instance of "inordinate and inexcusable delay" see *Tiesmaki* v. *Wilson* (1972), 23 D.L.R. (3d) 179 per Johnson, J.A. at 182 (Alta. App. Div.).

CHAPTER III

ADVISING CLIENTS

RULE

The lawyer must be both honest and candid when advising clients.[1]

Commentary

Scope of Advice

1. The lawyer's duty to the client who seeks legal advice is to give the client a competent opinion based on sufficient knowledge of the relevant facts, an adequate consideration of the applicable law and the lawyer's own experience and expertise. The advice must be open and undisguised, clearly disclosing what the lawyer honestly thinks about the merits and probable results.[2]

2. Whenever it becomes apparent that the client has misunderstood or misconceived what is really involved, the lawyer should explain as well as advise, so that the client is informed of the true position and fairly advised about the real issues or questions involved.[3]

3. The lawyer should clearly indicate the facts, circumstances and assumptions upon which the lawyer's opinion is based, particularly where the circumstances do not justify an exhaustive investigation with resultant expense to the client. However, unless the client instructs otherwise, the lawyer should investigate the matter in sufficient detail to be able to express an opinion rather than merely make comments with many qualifications.

4. The lawyer should be wary of bold and confident assurances to the client, especially when the lawyer's employment may depend upon advising in a particular way.[4]

Second Opinion

5. If the client so desires, the lawyer should assist in obtaining a second opinion.

Compromise or Settlement

6. The lawyer should advise and encourage the client to compromise or settle a dispute whenever possible on a reasonable basis and should discourage the client from commencing or continuing useless legal proceedings.[5]

Dishonesty or Fraud by Client

7. When advising the client the lawyer must never knowingly assist in or encourage any dishonesty, fraud, crime or illegal conduct, or instruct the client on how to violate the law and avoid punishment. The lawyer should be on guard against becoming the tool or dupe of an unscrupulous client or of persons associated with such a client.[6]

Test Cases

8. A *bona fide* test case is not necessarily precluded by the preceding paragraph and, so long as no injury to the person or violence is involved, the lawyer may properly advise and represent a client who, in good faith and on reasonable grounds, desires to challenge or test a law and this can most effectively be done by means of a technical breach giving rise to a test case.[7] In all such situations the lawyer should ensure that the client appreciates the consequences of bringing a test case.

Threatening Criminal Proceedings

9. Apart altogether from the substantive law on the subject, it is improper for the lawyer to advise, threaten or bring a criminal or quasi-criminal prosecution in order to secure some civil advantage for the client, or to advise, seek or procure the withdrawal of a prosecution in consideration of the payment of money, or transfer of property to, or for the benefit of the client.[8]

Advice on Non-legal matters

10. In addition to opinions on legal questions, the lawyer may be asked for or expected to give advice on non-legal matters such as the business, policy or social implications involved in a question, or the course the client should choose. In many instances the lawyer's experience will be such that the lawyer's views on non-legal matters will be of real benefit to the client. The lawyer who advises on such matters should, where and to the extent necessary, point out the lawyer's lack of experience or other qualification in the particular field and should clearly distinguish legal advice from such other advice.[9]

Errors and Omissions

11. The duty to give honest and candid advice requires the lawyer to inform the client promptly of the facts, but without admitting liability, upon discovering that an error or omission has occurred in a matter for

which the lawyer was engaged and that is or may be damaging to the client and cannot readily be rectified. When so informing the client the lawyer should be careful not to prejudice any rights of indemnity that either of them may have under any insurance, client's protection or indemnity plan, or otherwise. At the same time the lawyer should recommend that the client obtain legal advice elsewhere about any rights the client may have arising from such error or omission and whether it is appropriate for the lawyer to continue to act in the matter. The lawyer should also give prompt notice of any potential claim to the lawyer's insurer and any other indemnitor so that any protection from that source will not be prejudiced and, unless the client objects, should assist and co-operate with the insurer or other indemnitor to the extent necessary to enable any claim that is made to be dealt with promptly. If the lawyer is not so indemnified, or to the extent that the indemnity may not fully cover the claim, the lawyer should expeditiously deal with any claim that may be made and must not, under any circumstances, take unfair advantage that might defeat or impair the client's claim. In cases where liability is clear and the insurer or other indemnitor is prepared to pay its portion of the claim, the lawyer is under a duty to arrange for payment of the balance.[10]

Giving Independent Advice

12. Where the lawyer is asked to provide independent advice or independent representation to another lawyer's client in a situation where a conflict exists, the provision of such advice or representation is an undertaking to be taken seriously and not lightly assumed or perfunctorily discharged. It involves a duty to the client for whom the independent advice or representation is provided that is the same as in any other lawyer and client relationship and ordinarily extends to the nature and result of the transaction.

NOTES

1. Cf. CBA-COD 3; CBA 3(1); Que. 3.01.01; IBA A-10; *Orkin* at pp. 78-79.
2. The lawyer should not remain silent when it is plain that the client is rushing into an "unwise, not to say disastrous adventure", per Lord Danckwerts in *Neushal* v. *Mellish & Harkavy* (1967), 111 Sol. Jo. 399 (C.A.).
3. For cases illustrating the extent to which a lawyer should investigate and verify facts and premises before advising see, e.g., those collected in 43 E. & E.D. (Repl.) at pp. 97-115.
4. Cf. CBA 3(1) and Eaton, "Practising Ethics" (1966) 9 Can. B.J. 349.
5. Cf. CBA 3(3) and *Orkin* at pp. 95-97. N.B. C-3: "The lawyer has a duty to discourage a client from commencing useless litigation; but the lawyer is not the judge of his client's case and if there is a reasonable prospect of success the lawyer is justified in proceeding to trial. To avoid needless expense it is the lawyer's duty to investigate and evaluate the proofs or evidence upon which the client relies *before* the institution of proceedings. Similarly, when possible the lawyer must encourage the client to compromise or settle the dispute."

"[The litigation process] operates to bring about a voluntary settlement of a large proportion of disputes . . . . This fact of voluntary settlement is an essential feature of the judicial system", Jackett, C.J.F.C.C., *The Federal Court of Canada, A Manual of Practice* (1971) at pp. 41-42.

6. Cf. CBA 3(5): ". . . the great trust of the lawyer is to be performed within and not without the bounds of the law." See also ABA DR 7-102(A).
Any complicity such as abetting, counselling or being an accessory to a crime or fraud is obviously precluded.
Cf. ABA ECs 7-3 and 7-5: "Where the bounds of law are uncertain . . . the two roles [of advocate and adviser] are essentially different. In asserting a position on behalf of his client, an *advocate* for the most part *deals with past conduct* and must take the facts as he finds them. By contrast, a lawyer serving as *adviser* primarily *assists* his client *in determining* the course of *future conduct* and relationships . . . . A lawyer should never encourage or aid his client to commit criminal acts or counsel his client on how to violate the law and avoid punishment . . ." (emphasis added).
"The arms which [the lawyer] wields are to be the arms of the warrior and not of the assassin. It is his duty to accomplish the interest of his clients *per fas*, but not *per nefas*.", per Cockburn, L.C.J. in a speech in 1864 quoted as being derived from Quintilian in Rogers, "The Ethics of Advocacy" (1899) 15 L.Q.R. 259 at 270-71.
Applied to a solicitor in a "very clear case where the solicitor has been guilty of misconduct" and is "floundering in a quagmire of ignorance and moral obliquity" (he having, pending trial of an action and in anticipation of an adverse outcome, advised his client to dispose of its property and, after verdict, taking an assignment of part of that property). *Centre Star* v. *Rossland Miners Union* (1904-05) 11 B.C.R. 194 at 202-03 (B.C. Full Ct.).

7. For example, to challenge the jurisdiction for or the applicability of a shop-closing by-law or a licensing measure, or to determine the rights of a class or group having some common interest.

8. See article, "Criminal Law May Not be Used to Collect Civil Debts" (1968) Vol. 2, No. 4 Law Soc. U.C. Gaz. 36; and cf. B.C. E-5; Alta. 41; ABA DR 7-105(A).

9. Summarized from Johnstone and Hopkins, *Lawyers and Their Work* (1967), Bobbs-Merrill, Indianapolis, pp. 78-81. The lawyer's advice is usually largely based on the lawyer's conception of relevant legal doctrine and its bearing on the particular factual situation at hand. Anticipated reactions of courts, probative value of evidence, the desires and resources of clients, and alternative courses of action are likely to have been considered and referred to. The lawyer may indicate a preference and argue persuasively, or pose available alternatives in neutral terms. The lawyer makes the law and legal processes meaningful to clients; the lawyer explains legal doctrines and practices and their implications; the lawyer interprets both doctrines and impact. Often legal and non-legal issues are intertwined. Much turns on whether the client wants a servant, a critic, a sounding board, a neutral evaluator of ideas, reassurance, authority to strengthen his hand . . . . The real problem may be one, not of role conflict, but of role definition. The lawyer may spot problems of which the client is unaware and call them to his attention.

10. See Bastedo, "A Note on Lawyers' Malpractice" (1970) 7 Osg. Hall L.J. 311.

CHAPTER IV

CONFIDENTIAL INFORMATION

RULE

The lawyer has a duty to hold in strict confidence all information concerning the business and affairs of the client acquired in the course of the professional relationship, and should not divulge such information unless disclosure is expressly or impliedly authorized by the client, required by law[1] or otherwise permitted or required by this Code.

Commentary

Guiding Principles

1. The lawyer cannot render effective professional service to the client unless there is full and unreserved communication between them. At the same time the client must feel completely secure and entitled to proceed on the basis that without any express request or stipulation on the client's part, matters disclosed to or discussed with the lawyer will be held secret and confidential.[2]

2. This ethical rule must be distinguished from the evidentiary rule of lawyer and client privilege with respect to oral or written communications passing between the client and the lawyer. The ethical rule is wider and applies without regard to the nature or source of the information or to the fact that others may share the knowledge.[3]

3. As a general rule, the lawyer should not disclose having been consulted or retained by a person unless the nature of the matter requires such disclosure.

4. The lawyer owes a duty of secrecy to every client without exception, regardless of whether it be a continuing or casual client. The duty survives the professional relationship and continues indefinitely after the lawyer has ceased to act for the client, whether or not differences have arisen between them.[4]

Confidential Information Not to be Used

5. The fiduciary relationship between lawyer and client forbids the lawyer to use any confidential information covered by the ethical rule for the benefit of the lawyer or a third person, or to the disadvantage of the client. The lawyer who engages in literary works, such as an autobiography, memoirs and the like, should avoid disclosure of confidential information.[5]

6. The lawyer should take care to avoid disclosure to one client of confidential information concerning or received from another client and should decline employment that might require such disclosure.[6]

7. The lawyer should avoid indiscreet conversations, even with the lawyer's spouse or family, about a client's affairs and should shun any gossip about such things even though the client is not named or otherwise identified. Likewise the lawyer should not repeat any gossip or information about the client's business or affairs that may be overheard by or recounted to the lawyer. Apart altogether from ethical considerations or questions of good taste, indiscreet shop-talk between lawyers, if overheard by third parties able to identify the matter being discussed, could result in prejudice to the client. Moreover, the respect of the listener for the lawyers concerned and the legal profession generally will probably be lessened.[7]

8. Although the Rule may not apply to facts that are public knowledge, the lawyer should guard against participating in or commenting upon speculation concerning the client's affairs or business.

Disclosure Authorized by Client

9. Confidential information may be divulged with the express authority of the client concerned and, in some situations, the authority of the client to divulge may be implied. For example, some disclosure may be necessary in a pleading or other document delivered in litigation being conducted for the client. Again, the lawyer may (unless the client directs otherwise) disclose the client's affairs to partners and associates in the firm and, to the extent necessary, to non-legal staff such as secretaries and filing clerks. This implied authority to disclose places the lawyer under a duty to impress upon associates, students and employees the importance of non-disclosure (both during their employment and afterwards) and requires the lawyer to take reasonable care to prevent their disclosing or using any information that the lawyer is bound to keep in confidence.[8]

Disclosure Where Lawyer's Conduct in Issue

10. Disclosure may also be justified in order to establish or collect a fee, or to defend the lawyer or the lawyer's associates or employees against any allegation of malpractice or misconduct, but only to the extent necessary for such purposes. (As to potential claims for negligence, see Commentary 10 of the Rule relating to Advising Clients.)[9]

Disclosure to Prevent a Crime

11. Disclosure of information necessary to prevent a crime will be justified if the lawyer has reasonable grounds for believing that a crime is likely to be committed and will be mandatory when the anticipated crime is one involving violence.[10]

12. The lawyer who has reasonable grounds for believing that a dangerous situation is likely to develop at a court facility shall inform the person having responsibility for security at the facility and give particulars. Where possible the lawyer should suggest solutions to the anticipated problem such as:

(a) the need for further security;
(b) that judgement be reserved;
(c) such other measures as may seem advisable.

Disclosure Required by Law

13. When disclosure is required by law or by order of a court of competent jurisdiction, the lawyer should always be careful not to divulge more information than is required.[11]

14. The lawyer who has information known to be confidential government information about a person, acquired when the lawyer was a public officer or employee, shall not represent a client (other than the agency of which the lawyer was a public officer or employee) whose interests are adverse to that person in a matter in which the information could be used to the material disadvantage of that person.

NOTES

1. Cf. CBA-COD 4; CBA 3(7); Que. 3.05.01, .02, .03; Ont. 4; Alta. 15; N.B. C-3; IBA B-8; ABA-MR 1.6; ABA Canon 4, DRs 4-101(A), (B), (C).

2. ". . . [I]t is absolutely necessary that a man, in order to prosecute his rights or defend himself . . . should have recourse to lawyers, and . . . equally necessary . . . that he should be able to place unrestricted and unbounded confidence in the professional agent, and that the communications he so makes to him should be kept secret, unless with his consent (for it is his privilege and not the privilege of the confidential agent) . . .", per Jessell, M.R. in *Anderson* v. *Bank of British Columbia* (1876), L.R. 2 Ch.D. 644 at 649 (C.A.).

3. Cf. *Orkin*, pp. 83-86, and Tollefson, "Privileged Communications in Canada" in Proceedings of 4th Int. Comp. Law Symp. (1967) (Univ. of Ottawa Press) 32 at 36-41.

4. ". . . [A] fundamental rule, namely the duty of a solicitor to refrain from disclosing confidential information unless his client waives the privilege . . . . Because the solicitor owes to his former client a duty to claim the privilege when applicable, it is improper for him not to claim it without showing that it has been properly waived.", per Spence, J. in *Bell et al.* v. *Smith et al.* (1968), S.C.R. 644 at 671. To waive, the client must know of his rights and show a clear intention to forgo them: *Kulchar* v. *March & Benkert* (1950), 1 W.W.R. 272 (Sask. K.B.).

5. Misuse by a lawyer for his own benefit of his client's confidential information may

render the lawyer liable to account: *McMaster* v. *Byrne* (1952), 3 D.L.R. 337 (P.C.); *Bailey* v. *Ornheim* (1962), 40 W.W.R. (N.S.) 129 (B.C.S.C.).

6. "*Joint Retainer.* When two parties employ the *same solicitor,* the rule is that communications passing between either of them and the solicitor, in his *joint capacity,* must be disclosed in favour of the other — e.g., a proposition made by one, to be communicated to the other; or instructions given to the solicitor in the presence of the other; though it is otherwise as to communications made to the solicitor in his *exclusive* capacity." (quotation from *Phipson on Evidence* cited and approved by Atkins, J. in *Chersinoff* v. *Allstate Insurance* (1968), 69 D.L.R. (2d) 653 at 661 (B.C.S.C.).
   As to the duties of lawyers instructed by insurers in the defence of the insured in motor accident cases, see *Groom* v. *Crocker et al.* (1938), 2 All E.R. 394 (C.A.).
7. See Eaton, "Practising Ethics" (1967), 10 Can. B.J. 528.
8. "When a solicitor files an affidavit on behalf of his client . . . it should be assumed, until the contrary is proved, or at least until the solicitor's authority to do so is disputed by the client, that the solicitor has the authority to make the disclosure.", per Lebel, J. in *Kennedy* v. *Diversified* (1949), 1 D.L.R. 59 at 61 (Ont. H.C.).
9. There is no duty or privilege where a client conspires with or deceives his lawyer: *The Queen* v. *Cox* (1885), L.R. 14 Q.B.D. 153 (C.C.R.). Cf. *Orkin* at p. 86 as to the exceptions of crime, fraud and national emergency.
10. To oust privilege the communication must have been made to execute or further a crime or fraud — it must be prospective as distinguished from retrospective: *R.* v. *Bennett* (1964), 41 C.R. 227 (B.C.S.C.) and cases there cited.
11. Cf. Freedman, "Solicitor-Client Privilege Under the Income Tax Act" (1969), 12 Can. B.J. 93.

CHAPTER V

IMPARTIALITY AND CONFLICT OF INTEREST BETWEEN CLIENTS

RULE

The lawyer shall not advise or represent both sides of a dispute and, save after adequate disclosure to and with the consent of the clients or prospective clients concerned, shall not act or continue to act in a matter when there is or is likely to be a conflicting interest.

Commentary

Guiding Principles

1. A conflicting interest is one that would be likely to affect adversely the lawyer's judgement or advice on behalf of, or loyalty to a client or prospective client.[1]

2. The reason for the Rule is self-evident. The client or the client's affairs may be seriously prejudiced unless the lawyer's judgement and freedom of action on the client's behalf are as free as possible from compromising influences.[2]

3. Conflicting interests include, but are not limited to the duties and loyalties of the lawyer or a partner or professional associate of the lawyer to any other client, whether involved in the particular transaction or not, including the obligation to communicate information.[3]

Disclosure of Conflicting Interest

4. The Rule requires adequate disclosure to enable the client to make an informed decision about whether to have the lawyer act despite the existence or possibility of a conflicting interest. As important as it is to the client that the lawyer's judgement and freedom of action on the client's behalf should not be subject to other interests, duties or obligations, in practice this factor may not always be decisive. Instead it may be only one of several factors that the client will weigh when deciding whether to give the consent referred to in the Rule. Other factors might include, for

example, the availability of another lawyer of comparable expertise and experience, the extra cost, delay and inconvenience involved in engaging another lawyer and the latter's unfamiliarity with the client and the client's affairs. In the result, the client's interests may sometimes be better served by not engaging another lawyer. An example of this sort of situation is when the client and another party to a commercial transaction are continuing clients of the same law firm but are regularly represented by different lawyers in that firm.

5. Before the lawyer accepts employment from more than one client in the same matter, the lawyer must advise the clients that the lawyer has been asked to act for both or all of them, that no information received in connection with the matter from one can be treated as confidential so far as any of the others is concerned and that, if a dispute develops that cannot be resolved, the lawyer cannot continue to act for both or all of them and may have to withdraw completely. If one of the clients is a person with whom the lawyer has a continuing relationship and for whom the lawyer acts regularly, this fact should be revealed to the other or others at the outset with a recommendation that they obtain independent representation.[4] If, following such disclosure, all parties are content that the lawyer act for them, the lawyer should obtain their consent, preferably in writing, or record their consent in a separate letter to each. The lawyer should, however, guard against acting for more than one client where, despite the fact that all parties concerned consent, it is reasonably obvious that an issue contentious between them may arise or their interests, rights or obligations will diverge as the matter progresses.[5]

6. If, after the clients involved have consented, an issue contentious between them or some of them arises, the lawyer, although not necessarily precluded from advising them on other non-contentious matters, would be in breach of the Rule if the lawyer attempted to advise them on the contentious issue. In such circumstances the lawyer should ordinarily refer the clients to other lawyers. However, if the issue is one that involves little or no legal advice, for example a business rather than a legal question in a proposed business transaction, and the clients are sophisticated, they may be permitted to settle the issue by direct negotiation in which the lawyer does not participate. Alternatively, the lawyer may refer one client to another lawyer and continue to advise the other if it was agreed at the outset that this course would be followed in the event of a conflict arising.

Lawyer as Arbitrator

7. The Rule will not prevent a lawyer from arbitrating or settling, or attempting to arbitrate or settle, a dispute between two or more clients or former clients who are *sui juris* and who wish to submit the dispute to the lawyer.[6]

Acting Against Former Client

8. A lawyer who has acted for a client in a matter should not thereafter act against the client (or against persons who were involved in or associated with the client in that matter) in the same or any related matter, or take a position where the lawyer might be tempted or appear to be tempted to breach the Rule relating to confidential information. It is not, however, improper for the lawyer to act against a former client in a fresh and independent matter wholly unrelated to any work the lawyer has previously done for that person.[7]

9. For the sake of clarity the foregoing paragraphs are expressed in terms of the individual lawyer and client. However, the term "client" includes a client of the law firm of which the lawyer is a partner or associate, whether or not the lawyer handles the client's work. It also includes the client of a lawyer who is associated with the lawyer in such a manner as to be perceived as practising in partnership or association with the first lawyer, even though in fact no such partnership or association exists.

Acting For More Than One Client

10. In practice, there are many situations where even though no actual dispute exists between the parties their interests are in conflict. Common examples in a conveyancing practice are vendor and purchaser, or mortgagor and mortgagee. In cases where the lawyer is asked to act for more than one client in such a transaction, the lawyer should recommend that each party be separately represented. In all such transactions the lawyer must observe the rules prescribed by the governing body.

11. There are also many situations where more than one person may wish to retain the lawyer to handle a transaction and, although their interests appear to coincide, in fact a potential conflict of interest exists. Examples are co-purchasers of real property and persons forming a partnership or corporation. Such cases will be governed by Commentaries 4 and 5 of this Rule.

12. A lawyer who is employed or retained by an organization represents that organization acting through its duly authorized constituents. In dealing with the organization's directors, officers, employees, members, shareholders or other constituents, the lawyer shall make clear that it is the organization that is the client when it becomes apparent that the organization's interests are adverse to those of the constituents with whom the lawyer is dealing. The lawyer representing an organization may also represent any of the directors, officers, employees, members, shareholders or other constituents, subject to the provisions of this Rule dealing with conflicts of interest.

Burden of Proof

13. Generally speaking, in disciplinary proceedings arising from a breach

of this Rule the lawyer has the burden of showing good faith and that adequate disclosure was made in the matter and the client's consent was obtained.

NOTES

1. Cf. CBA-COD 5; CBA 3(2), 3(7); Que. 3.05.04; Ont. 5; B.C. B-1, B-2, B-9(b); N.B. C-9; IBA B-7; ABA-MR 1.7, 1.8, 1.9; ABA DRs 5-101(A), 5-105; *Orkin* at pp. 98-101.
2. Cf. ABA EC 5-1.
3. "A solicitor must put at his client's disposal not only his skill but also his knowledge, so far as it is relevant .... What he cannot do is to act for the client and at the same time withhold from him any relevant knowledge that he has . . .", per Megarry, J. in *Spector* v. *Ageda* (1971), 3 All E.R. 417 at 430 (Ch. D.).
"Applying this [*dictum* of Cozens-Hardy, M.R. in *Moody* v. *Cox et al.* (1917), 2 Ch. D. 71] to a simple circumstance which arises in every conveyancing transaction, does a solicitor acting for both parties disclose the previous purchase price to the purchaser . . .? If he does there may be a breach of duty .... This example alone faces a solicitor with an unanswerable dilemma, which may only be resolved by his refusing to act for one . . . or . . . possibly stepping back from a situation in which both clients really need positive advice.", article in (1970) Law Soc. Gazette 332; and see thirteen examples of difficulties there listed. In *Cornell* v. *Jaeger* (1968), 63 W.W.R. 747 (Man.) the non-disclosure by a solicitor of his personal interest in a property to the clear detriment of his client was held to amount to fraud.
4. "Notwithstanding that [the solicitor] had acted for the plaintiff and had been introduced to the defendants by the plaintiff and acted for both the plaintiff and R while they were negotiating the purchase . . . he divorced himself from his responsibilities . . . and acted for the defendants while they acquired the property . . . and, after the writ was issued . . . acted for both defendants .... I refer to *Bowstead on Agency*: 'It is the duty of a solicitor . . . (8) not to act for the opponent of his client, of or a former client, in any case in which his knowledge of the affairs of such client or former client will give him an undue advantage . . .' *This is a principle of ethical standards which admits to no fine distinctions but should be applied in its broadest sense,* and it makes no difference whether the solicitor was first acting for two parties jointly who subsequently disagreed and became involved over the subject-matter of his joint retainer, or acted for one party with respect to a matter and took up a case for another party against his former client about the same matter.", per McRuer, C.J.H.C. in *Sinclair* v. *Ridout & Moran* (1955), 1 O.R. 167 at 182-83 (Ont. H.C.) (emphasis added). See Knepper, "Conflicts of Interest in Defending Insurance Cases" (1970), Defence L.J. 515, and "Guiding Principles", *ibid.*, pp. 540-44.
5. Cf. Ont. 5(5). Common "multiple client" situations where there is real danger of divergence of interest arising between clients include the defending of co-accused, the representation of co-plaintiffs in tort cases or of insureds and their insurers, the representation of classes or groups such as beneficiaries under a will or trust and construction lien and bankruptcy claimants.
See for examples *Orkin* at p. 100.
[Leave to appeal granted] ". . . by reason of the same solicitor appearing for R and D, and it being apparent that there was a conflict of interest between R and D, each one blaming the other for the injuries of the children, he should not have acted for D after having acted for R.", *Regina* v. *DePatie* (1971), 1 O.R. 698 at 699

(Ont. C.A.).

6. Cf. Que. 55; ABA 5-20.

7. "The appellant had for many years been the respondent's solicitor, and a quarrel . . . brought about a rupture . . . . It was then . . . that the appellant by his letters to the wife incited her and improperly encouraged her to prosecute an action . . . thus stirring up a litigation against the respondent.", per Taschereau, J. in *Sheppard* v. *Frind* (1941), S.C.R. 531 at 535 (S.C.C.).
"The solicitor acting for the defendant . . . drew the mortgage and advised the said defendant on the effect thereof. Later the same solicitor acting for the mortgagee bank brought action against his former client based on a claim arising out of and related to that mortgage. Solicitors should not so conduct themselves even with the knowledge and consent of all parties . . .", *La Banque Provinciale* v. *Adjutor Levesque Roofing* (1968), 68 D.L.R. (2d) 340 at 345 (N.B.C.A.).

CHAPTER VI

CONFLICT OF INTEREST BETWEEN LAWYER AND CLIENT

RULE

(a) The lawyer should not enter into a business transaction with the client or knowingly give to or acquire from the client an ownership, security or other pecuniary interest unless:

- (i) the transaction is a fair and reasonable one and its terms are fully disclosed to the client in writing in a manner that is reasonably understood by the client;
- (ii) the client is given a reasonable opportunity to seek independent legal advice about the transaction, the onus being on the lawyer to prove that the client's interests were protected by such independent advice; and
- (iii) the client consents in writing to the transaction.

(b) The lawyer shall not enter into or continue a business transaction with the client if:

- (i) the client expects or might reasonably be assumed to expect that the lawyer is protecting the client's interests;
- (ii) there is a significant risk that the interests of the lawyer and the client may differ.

(c) The lawyer shall not act for the client where the lawyer's duty to the client and the personal interests of the lawyer or an associate are in conflict.

(d) The lawyer shall not prepare an instrument giving the lawyer or an associate a substantial gift from the client, including a testamentary gift.

Commentary

Guiding Principles

1. The principles enunciated in the Rule relating to impartiality and conflict of interest between clients apply *mutatis mutandis* to this Rule.

2. A conflict of interest between lawyer and client exists in all cases where the lawyer gives property to or acquires it from the client by way of

purchase, gift, testamentary disposition or otherwise. Such transactions are to be avoided. When they are contemplated, the prudent course is to insist that the client either be independently represented or have independent legal advice.

3. This Rule applies also to situations involving associates of the lawyer. Associates of the lawyer within the meaning of the Rule include the lawyer's spouse, children, any relative of the lawyer (or of the lawyer's spouse) living under the same roof, any partner or associate of the lawyer in the practice of law, a trust or estate in which the lawyer has a substantial beneficial interest or for which the lawyer acts as a trustee or in a similar capacity, and a corporation of which the lawyer is a director or in which the lawyer or an associate owns or controls, directly or indirectly, a significant number of shares.[1]

Debtor-Creditor Relationship to be Avoided

4. The lawyer should avoid entering into a debtor-creditor relationship with the client. The lawyer should not borrow money from a client who is not in the business of lending money.[2] It is undesirable that the lawyer lend money to the client except by way of advancing necessary expenses in a legal matter that the lawyer is handling for the client.

Joint Ventures

5. The lawyer who has a personal interest in a joint business venture with others may represent or advise the business venture in legal matters between it and third parties, but should not represent or advise either the joint business venture or the joint venturers in respect of legal matters as between them.

When Person to be Considered a Client

6. The question of whether a person is to be considered a client of the lawyer when such person is lending money to the lawyer, or buying, selling, making a loan to or investment in, or assuming an obligation in respect of a business, security or property in which the lawyer or an associate of the lawyer has an interest, or in respect of any other transaction, is to be determined having regard to all the circumstances. A person who is not otherwise a client may be deemed to be a client for purposes of this Rule if such person might reasonably feel entitled to look to the lawyer for guidance and advice in respect of the transaction. In those circumstances the lawyer must consider such person to be a client and will be bound by the same fiduciary obligations that attach to a lawyer in dealings with a client. The onus shall be on the lawyer to establish that such a person was not in fact looking to the lawyer for guidance and advice.

NOTES

1. Cf. ABA-COD 5. As to corporations, cf. ABA-MR 1.13; ABA EC 5-18: "A lawyer employed or retained by a corporation or similar entity owes his allegiance to the entity and not to a stockholder, director, officer, employee, representative, or other person connected with the entity. In advising the entity, a lawyer should keep paramount its interests . . .".

2. Cf. Ont. 5; Alta. 34; and B.C. B-13: ". . . in a number of instances of professional misconduct . . . the borrowing of money by [the lawyers] in question has been a factor leading to the . . . misconduct. [A lawyer] should not borrow money from his clients save in exceptional circumstances, and in that case the onus of proving that the client's interests were fully protected by the nature of the case or by independent legal advice will rest upon [the lawyer] . . . . [Attention is called to] the various transactions and dealings that the courts have held to be improper or reprehensible conduct in violation of these principles, and which, in addition to their consequences at law, constitute professional misconduct."
Cf. ABA EC 5-8.

CHAPTER VII

OUTSIDE INTERESTS AND THE PRACTICE OF LAW

RULE

The lawyer who engages in another profession, business or occupation concurrently with the practice of law must not allow such outside interest to jeopardize the lawyer's professional integrity, independence or competence.[1]

Commentary

Guiding Principles

1. The term "outside interest" covers the widest possible range and includes activities that may overlap or be connected with the practice of law, such as engaging in the mortgage business, acting as a director of a client corporation, or writing on legal subjects, as well as activities not so connected such as a career in business, politics, broadcasting or the performing arts. In each case the question of whether the lawyer may properly engage in the outside interest and to what extent the lawyer will be subject to any applicable law or rule of the governing body.[2]

2. Whenever an overriding social, political, economic or other consideration arising from the outside interest might influence the lawyer's judgement, the lawyer should be governed by the considerations declared in the Rule relating to conflict of interest between lawyer and client.[3]

3. Where the outside interest is in no way related to the legal services being performed for clients, ethical considerations will usually not arise unless the lawyer's conduct brings either the lawyer or the profession into disrepute,[4] or impairs the lawyer's competence as, for example, where the outside interest occupies so much time that clients suffer because of the lawyer's lack of attention or preparation.

4. The lawyer must not carry on, manage or be involved in any outside business, investment, property or occupation in such a way that makes it difficult to distinguish in which capacity the lawyer is acting in a particular

transaction, or that would give rise to a conflict of interest or duty to a client.[5] When acting or dealing in respect of a transaction involving an outside interest in a business, investment, property or occupation, the lawyer must disclose any personal interest, must declare to all parties in the transaction or to their solicitors whether the lawyer is acting on the lawyer's own behalf or in a professional capacity or otherwise, and must adhere throughout the transaction to standards of conduct as high as those that this Code requires of a lawyer engaged in the practice of law.

5. The lawyer who has an outside interest in a business, investment, property or occupation:

(a) must not be identified as a lawyer when carrying on, managing or being involved in such outside interest; and

(b) must ensure that monies received in respect of the day-to-day carrying on, operation and management of such outside interest are deposited in an account other than the lawyer's trust account, unless such monies are received by the lawyer when acting in a professional capacity as a lawyer on behalf of the outside interest.

6. In order to be compatible with the practice of law the other profession, business or occupation:

(a) must be an honourable one that does not detract from the status of the lawyer or the legal profession generally; and

(b) must not be such as would likely result in a conflict of interest between the lawyer and a client.

NOTES

1. Cf. CBA-COD 6; B.C. B-8; N.B. F-3; IBA D-1. This Rule is closely connected with the Rule relating to conflict of interest between lawyer and client.

2. In Quebec, s. 122(1)(b) of the *Bar Act* provides that a person shall become disqualified from practising as an advocate when "he holds a position or an office incompatible with the practice or dignity of the profession of advocate."
Sask. 7 and Que. 4.01.01(c) prohibit lawyers from having an interest in collection agencies. Cf. *Orkin* at pp. 188-90.

3. B.C. B-8 identifies the dangers ". . . that make it difficult for a client to distinguish in which capacity [the lawyer] is acting in a particular instance or which could give rise to a conflict of interest or duty to a client."
For a discussion of "independent judgment" as it may be impaired by outside interests, see Weddington, "A Fresh Approach to Independent Judgment" (1969) 11 Ariz. L.R. 31.

4. In *Re Weare* (1893), 2 Q.B. 439 (C.A.) the striking off of a solicitor who had knowingly rented his premises for use as a brothel was sustained by the court.

5. Further examples of outside interests that could, unless clearly disclosed and defined, confuse or mislead persons dealing with a lawyer engaging in them include:
- professions such as accountancy and engineering;
- occupations such as those of merchant, land developer or speculator, building

contractor, real estate, insurance or financial agent, broker, financier, property manager, or public relations adviser.

CHAPTER VIII

PRESERVATION OF CLIENTS' PROPERTY

RULE

The lawyer owes a duty to the client to observe all relevant laws and rules respecting the preservation and safekeeping of the client's property entrusted to the lawyer. Where there are no such laws or rules, or the lawyer is in any doubt, the lawyer should take the same care of such property as a careful and prudent owner would when dealing with property of like description.[1]

Commentary

Guiding Principles

1. The lawyer's duties with respect to safekeeping, preserving and accounting for the clients' monies and other property are generally the subject of special rules.[2] In the absence of such rules the lawyer should adhere to the minimum standards set out in the note.[3] "Property", apart from clients' monies, includes securities such as mortgages, negotiable instruments, stocks, bonds, etc., original documents such as wills, title deeds, minute books, licences, certificates, etc., other papers such as clients' correspondence files, reports, invoices, etc., as well as chattels such as jewelry, silver, etc.[4]

2. The lawyer should promptly notify the client upon receiving any property of or relating to the client unless satisfied that the client knows that it has come into the lawyer's custody.[5]

3. The lawyer should clearly label and identify the client's property and place it in safekeeping separate and apart from the lawyer's own property.

4. The lawyer should maintain adequate records of clients' property in the lawyer's custody so that it may be promptly accounted for, or delivered to, or to the order of, the client upon request. The lawyer should ensure that such property is delivered to the right person and, in case of dispute as to the person entitled, may have recourse to the courts.[6]

5. The duties here expressed are closely related to those concerning confidential information.[7] The lawyer should keep clients' papers and

other property out of sight as well as out of reach of those not entitled to see them and should, subject to any right of lien,[8] return them promptly to the clients upon request or at the conclusion of the lawyer's retainer.

Privilege

6. The lawyer should be alert to claim on behalf of clients any lawful privilege respecting information about their affairs, including their files and property if seized or attempted to be seized by a third party. In this regard the lawyer should be familiar with the nature of clients' privilege, and with relevant statutory provisions such as those in the *Income Tax Act*,[9] the *Criminal Code*, the *Canadian Charter of Rights and Freedoms* and other statutes.

NOTES

1. Cf. CBA-COD 7; CBA 3 (8); Que. 3.02.06; ABA-MR 1.15; ABA DR 9-102(B). Although the basic duty here declared may parallel the legal duty under the law of bailment, it is reiterated as being a matter of professional responsibility quite apart from the position in law.
2. For example, in Ontario, secs. 13 to 18 captioned "Books, Records and Accounts" of O.Reg. 573 enacted pursuant to the *Law Society Act*, R.S.O. 1980, c. 233. Similar provisions exist in the other provinces and territories.
3. The minimum standards are:
   (a) paying into and keeping monies received or held by the lawyer for or on behalf of clients in a trust bank account or accounts separate from the bank account of the lawyer or the lawyer's firm;
   (b) keeping properly written books and accounts of all monies received, held or paid by the lawyer for or on behalf of each of the lawyer's clients which clearly distinguish such monies from the monies of every other client and from the monies of the lawyer and the lawyer's firm;
   (c) not retaining for an unnecessarily long period, without the express authority of the client, monies received for or on behalf of such client;
   (d) subject to rules prescribed by the governing body of the province, no lawyer shall take fees, as opposed to disbursements, from funds held in trust for a client without the client's express authority unless the work being done by the lawyer for the client has been performed and a proper account in respect thereof has been rendered to the client. Where a client authorizes the payment of fees from trust funds before an account has been rendered, this arrangement should be recorded in writing and an interim account sent to the client forthwith;
   (e) the lawyer should not estimate a lump sum that may in the aggregate be owed by a number of clients and then transfer that sum in bulk from a trust account to the lawyer's general account without allocating specific amounts to each client and rendering an account to each client.
4. In some provinces statutes authorize the depositing of valuable documents with public officials for safekeeping. As to wills, see *Comment* in (1970) 4 Law Soc. U.C. Gaz. 117.
5. Cf. ABA DR 9-102 (B)(1).
6. For example, by seeking leave to interplead.
7. Cf. the Rule relating to confidential information.

8. Cf. para. 10 of the Rule relating to withdrawal. As to the proper disposition of papers, which is frequently a perplexing problem, see *Cordery on Solicitors* (6th ed. 1968) at pp. 118-20 for a discussion of law and principles and a table of categories with supporting authorities.
The lawyer's arrangements and procedures for the storage and eventual destruction of completed files should reflect the foregoing considerations and particularly the continuing obligation as to confidentiality.
Further, statutes such as the *Income Tax Act* and the operation of limitations statutes pertinent to the client's position may preclude the destruction of files or particular papers. In several provinces statutes provide for the appointment of a custodian or trustee or the intervention of the syndic to conserve clients' property where a lawyer has died, absconded or become incapable. See, e.g., *Barristers and Solicitors Act*, R.S.B.C. 1979, c. 26, s. 69; *Bar Act*, R.S.Q. 1977, c. B-1, s. 76(2); *Law Society Act*, R.S.O. 1980, c. 233, s. 43.

9. See Freedman, "Solicitor-Client Privilege under the Income Tax Act" (1969) 12 Can. B.J. 93.

CHAPTER IX

THE LAWYER AS ADVOCATE

RULE

When acting as an advocate, the lawyer must treat the tribunal with courtesy and respect and must represent the client resolutely, honourably and within the limits of the law.[1]

Commentary

Guiding Principles

1. The advocate's duty to the client "fearlessly to raise every issue, advance every argument, and ask every question, however distasteful, which he thinks will help his client's case" and to endeavour "to obtain for his client the benefit of any and every remedy and defence which is authorized by law"[2] must always be discharged by fair and honourable means, without illegality and in a manner consistent with the lawyer's duty to treat the court with candour, fairness, courtesy and respect.[3]

Prohibited Conduct

2. The lawyer must not, for example:
   (a) abuse the process of the tribunal by instituting or prosecuting proceedings that, although legal in themselves, are clearly motivated by malice on the part of the client and are brought solely for the purpose of injuring another party;[4]
   (b) knowingly assist or permit the client to do anything that the lawyer considers to be dishonest or dishonourable;[5]
   (c) appear before a judicial officer when the lawyer, the lawyer's associates or the client have business or personal relationships with such officer that give rise to real or apparent pressure, influence or inducement affecting the impartiality of such officer;[6]
   (d) attempt or allow anyone else to attempt, directly or indirectly, to influence the decision or actions of a tribunal or any of its officials by any means except open persuasion as an advocate;[7]
   (e) knowingly attempt to deceive or participate in the deception of

a tribunal or influence the course of justice by offering false evidence, misstating facts or law, presenting or relying upon a false or deceptive affidavit, suppressing what ought to be disclosed or otherwise assisting in any fraud, crime or illegal conduct;[8]

(f) knowingly misstate the contents of a document, the testimony of a witness, the substance of an argument or the provisions of a statute or like authority;[9]

(g) knowingly assert something for which there is no reasonable basis in evidence, or the admissibility of which must first be established;[10]

(h) deliberately refrain from informing the tribunal of any pertinent adverse authority that the lawyer considers to be directly in point and that has not been mentioned by an opponent;[11]

(i) dissuade a material witness from giving evidence, or advise such a witness to be absent;[12]

(j) knowingly permit a witness to be presented in a false or misleading way or to impersonate another;

(k) needlessly abuse, hector or harass a witness;

(l) needlessly inconvenience a witness.

Errors and Omissions

3. The lawyer who has unknowingly done or failed to do something that, if done or omitted knowingly, would have been in breach of this Rule and discovers it, has a duty to the court, subject to the Rule relating to confidential information, to disclose the error or omission and do all that can reasonably be done in the circumstances to rectify it.[13]

Duty to Withdraw

4. If the client wishes to adopt a course that would involve a breach of this Rule, the lawyer must refuse and do everything reasonably possible to prevent it. If the client persists in such a course the lawyer should, subject to the Rule relating to withdrawal, withdraw or seek leave of the court to do so.[14]

The Lawyer as Witness

5. The lawyer who appears as an advocate should not submit the lawyer's own affidavit to or testify before a tribunal save as permitted by local rule or practice, or as to purely formal or uncontroverted matters. This also applies to the lawyer's partners and associates; generally speaking, they should not testify in such proceedings except as to merely formal matters. The lawyer should not express personal opinions or beliefs, or assert as fact anything that is properly subject to legal proof, cross-examination or challenge. The lawyer must not in effect become an unsworn witness or put the lawyer's own credibility in issue. The lawyer who is a necessary witness should testify and entrust the conduct of the

case to someone else. Similarly, the lawyer who was a witness in the proceedings should not appear as advocate in any appeal from the decision in those proceedings.[15] There are no restrictions upon the advocate's right to cross-examine another lawyer, and the lawyer who does appear as a witness should not expect to receive special treatment by reason of professional status.

Interviewing Witnesses

6. The lawyer may properly seek information from any potential witness (whether under subpoena or not) but should disclose the lawyer's interest and take care not to subvert or suppress any evidence or procure the witness to stay out of the way.[16] The lawyer shall not approach or deal with an opposite party who is professionally represented save through or with the consent of that party's lawyer.[17]

Unmeritorious Proceedings

7. The lawyer should never waive or abandon the client's legal rights (for example an available defence under a statute of limitations) without the client's informed consent. In civil matters it is desirable that the lawyer should avoid and discourage the client from resorting to frivolous or vexatious objections or attempts to gain advantage from slips or oversights not going to the real merits, or tactics that will merely delay or harass the other side. Such practices can readily bring the administration of justice and the legal profession into disrepute.[18]

Encouraging Settlements

8. Whenever the case can be settled fairly, the lawyer should advise and encourage the client to do so rather than commence or continue legal proceedings.[19]

Duties of Prosecutor

9. When engaged as a prosecutor, the lawyer's prime duty is not to seek a conviction, but to present before the trial court all available credible evidence relevant to the alleged crime in order that justice may be done through a fair trial upon the merits.[20] The prosecutor exercises a public function involving much discretion and power and must act fairly and dispassionately. The prosecutor should not do anything that might prevent the accused from being represented by counsel or communicating with counsel and, to the extent required by law and accepted practice, should make timely disclosure to the accused or defence counsel (or to the court if the accused is not represented) of all relevant facts and known witnesses, whether tending to show guilt or innocence, or that would affect the punishment of the accused.[21]

Duties of Defence Counsel

10. When defending an accused person, the lawyer's duty is to protect the

client as far as possible from being convicted except by a court of competent jurisdiction and upon legal evidence sufficient to support a conviction for the offence charged. Accordingly, and notwithstanding the lawyer's private opinion as to credibility or merits, the lawyer may properly rely upon all available evidence or defences including so-called technicalities not known to be false or fraudulent.[22]

11. Admissions made by the accused to the lawyer may impose strict limitations on the conduct of the defence and the accused should be made aware of this. For example, if the accused clearly admits to the lawyer the factual and mental elements necessary to constitute the offence, the lawyer, if convinced that the admissions are true and voluntary, may properly take objection to the jurisdiction of the court, or to the form of the indictment, or to the admissibility or sufficiency of the evidence, but must not suggest that some other person committed the offence, or call any evidence that, by reason of the admissions, the lawyer believes to be false. Nor may the lawyer set up an affirmative case inconsistent with such admissions, for example, by calling evidence in support of an alibi intended to show that the accused could not have done, or in fact had not done, the act. Such admissions will also impose a limit upon the extent to which the lawyer may attack the evidence for the prosecution. The lawyer is entitled to test the evidence given by each individual witness for the prosecution and argue that the evidence taken as a whole is insufficient to amount to proof that the accused is guilty of the offence charged, but the lawyer should go no further than that.[23]

Agreement on Guilty Plea

12. Where, following investigation,
   (a) the defence lawyer *bona fide* concludes and advises the accused client that an acquittal of the offence charged is uncertain or unlikely,
   (b) the client is prepared to admit the necessary factual and mental elements,
   (c) the lawyer fully advises the client of the implications and possible consequences of a guilty plea and that the matter of sentence is solely in the discretion of the trial judge, and
   (d) the client so instructs the lawyer, preferably in writing,

it is proper for the lawyer to discuss and agree tentatively with the prosecutor to enter a plea of guilty on behalf of the client to the offence charged or to a lesser or included offence or to another offence appropriate to the admissions, and also on a disposition or sentence to be proposed to the court. The public interest and the client's interests must not, however, be compromised by agreeing to a guilty plea.[24]

Undertakings

13. An undertaking given by the lawyer to the court or to another lawyer in the course of litigation or other adversary proceedings must be strictly

and scrupulously carried out. Unless clearly qualified in writing, the lawyer's undertaking is a personal promise and responsibility.[25]

Courtesy

14. The lawyer should at all times be courteous and civil to the court and to those engaged on the other side. Legal contempt of court and the professional obligation outlined here are not identical, and a consistent pattern of rude, provocative or disruptive conduct by the lawyer, even though unpunished as contempt, might well merit disciplinary action.[26]

Role in Adversary Proceedings

15. In adversary proceedings, the lawyer's function as advocate is openly and necessarily partisan. Accordingly, the lawyer is not obliged (save as required by law or under paragraphs 2(h) or 7 above) to assist an adversary or advance matters derogatory to the client's case. When opposing interests are not represented, for example in *ex parte* or uncontested matters, or in other situations where the full proof and argument inherent in the adversary system cannot be obtained, the lawyer must take particular care to be accurate, candid and comprehensive in presenting the client's case so as to ensure that the court is not misled.[27]

Communicating with Witnesses

16. When in court the lawyer should observe local rules and practices concerning communication with a witness about the witness's evidence or any issue in the proceeding. Generally, it is considered improper for counsel who called a witness to communicate with that witness without leave of the court while such witness is under cross-examination.[28]

Agreements Guaranteeing Recovery

17. In civil proceedings the lawyer has a duty not to mislead the court about the position of the client in the adversary process. Thus, where a lawyer representing a client in litigation has made or is party to an agreement made before or during the trial whereby a plaintiff is guaranteed recovery by one or more parties notwithstanding the judgement of the court, the lawyer shall disclose full particulars of the agreement to the court and all other parties.[29]

Scope of the Rule

18. The principles of this Rule apply generally to the lawyer as advocate and therefore extend not only to court proceedings but also to appearances and proceedings before boards, administrative tribunals and other bodies, regardless of their function or the informality of their procedures.[30]

NOTES

1. Cf. CBA-COD 8; CBA 2(1), 3(5); ABA-MR 3; ABA Canon 7.
   "The concept that counsel is the mouth-piece of his client and that his speech is the speech of the client is as unfortunate as it is inaccurate. He is not the agent or delegate of his client. Within proper bounds, however, counsel must be fearless and independent in the defence of his client's rights .... He must be completely selfless in standing up courageously for his client's rights, and he should never expose himself to the reproach that he has sacrificed his client's interests on the altar of expediency...", per Schroeder, J.A., "Some Ethical Problems in Criminal Law" in Law Soc. U.C. Special Lectures (1963) 87 at 102.

2. The sources of the quotations are (a) per Lord Reid in *Rondel* v. *Worsley* (1969), 1 A.C. 191 at 227 and (b) CBA 3(5).

3. Cf. CBA 3(5). "... [H]e must be a man of character. The Court must be able to rely on the advocate's word; his word must indeed be his bond .... The advocate has a duty to his client, a duty to the Court, and a duty to the State; but he has above all a duty to himself that he shall be, as far as it lies in his power, a man of integrity. No profession calls for higher standards of honour and uprightness, and no profession, perhaps offers greater temptations to forsake them...", from Hyde, *Lord Birkett* (1964, Hamish Hamilton, London) at p. 551. Courtesy and respect, as used herein, include the duty to be prompt and punctual.

4. Cf. IBA A-19; ABA DR 7-102 (A)(1).

5. Cf. IBA A-15.

6. Cf. ABA Canon 9, DR 9-101; IBA E-3.

7. Cf. CBA 2(4), 5(5); Que. 2.03, 3.05; N.B. B-6; ABA 9 ECs 7-34 and 7-35, DR 7-110; IBA A-16.
   In *Toronto Transit* v. *Aqua Taxi* (1955) O.W.N. 857 (Ont. H.C.), where a sealed letter improperly attempting to influence a decision had been delivered to a judge, the Court, while exonerating the lawyers concerned, made it clear that any involvement in such conduct would be most improper.

8. Where a lawyer joined in a scheme to mislead the Court by arranging proceedings to result in an apparent acquittal which could then be used to answer prior pending proceedings for the same offence (a justice, a constable and another lawyer being misled in the process), the Court said: "These facts establish a stupid, but nevertheless unworthy, attempt to pervert the course of justice, and most certainly constitute conduct unbecoming a barrister and solicitor in the pursuit of his profession.", *Banks* v. *Hall* (1941), 2 W.W.R. 534 (Sask. C.A.).
   A lawyer counselling false evidence would be guilty of perjury if it were given (*Criminal Code*, ss. 22, 120), and of counselling if it were not (*ibid.*, s. 422).
   It is an offence to fabricate anything with intent that it be used as evidence by any means other than perjury or incitement to perjury (*ibid.*, s. 125).
   Similarly, it is an offence wilfully to attempt in any manner to obstruct, pervert or defeat the course of justice (*ibid.*, s. 127).
   "The swearing of an untrue affidavit ... is perhaps the most obvious example of conduct which a solicitor cannot knowingly permit .... He cannot properly, still less can he consistently with his duty to the Court, prepare and place a perjured affidavit upon file .... A solicitor who has innocently put on the file an affidavit by his client which he has subsequently discovered to be certainly false owes it to the Court to put the matter right at the earliest date if he continues to act ...". per Viscount Maugham in *Myers* v. *Elman* (1940), A.C. 282 at 293-94 (H.L.).
   "[Counsel] had full knowledge of the impropriety of the paragraphs in the affidavit ... [and] is bound to accept responsibility for [them] .... If he knows that his client is making false statements under oath and does nothing to correct it,

his silence indicates, at the very least, a gross neglect of duty.", per McLennan, J.A. in *Re Ontario Crime Commission* (1962), 37 D.L.R. (2d) 382 at 391 (Ont. C.A.).

9. Cf. N.B. B-1; IBA A-14; ABA DR 7-102 (A) (5).

10. Cf. N.B. B-7; ABA EC 7-25; DR 7-106 (C) (1).

11. Cf. CBA 1(1); N.B. B-3; IBA A-14; ABA EC 7-23, DR 7-106 (B) (1).
See *Glebe Sugar* v. *Greenock Trustees* (1921), W.N. 85 (H.L.) for a strong statement by Lord Birkenhead on the duty of counsel to disclose to the court authorities bearing one way or the other: "The extreme impropriety of such a course [withholding a known pertinent authority] could not be made too plain." See also *Plant* v. *Urquhart* (1922), 1 W.W.R. 632 (B.C.C.A.) per McPhillips, J. at 638-39.

12. Cf. IBA A-18; ABA DR 7-109(B).

13. Cf. N.B. B-8; ABA DRs 7-102(B) and 4-101(C) (2).

14. Cf. ABA DR 2-110(B) (2); N.B. B-8: "Upon learning of fraudulent testimony participated in by his client, counsel has a duty to withdraw from the case and to advise the court and the adverse party of the fraud." See also *Orkin* at p. 127.

15. Cf. CBA 2(3); N.B. C-11; ABA EC 7-24, DR 7-106 (C) (3), (4).
"It is to be borne in mind that the function of counsel in any Court is that of an advocate; he is there to plead his client's cause upon the record before the Court and he does not in any sense occupy the dual position of advocate and witness.", per McGillivray, J.A. in *Cairns* v. *Cairns* (1931), 3 W.W.R. 335 at 345 (Alta. App. Div.).
"It is improper, in my opinion, for Counsel for the Crown to express his opinion as to the guilt or innocence of the accused. In the article to which I have referred it is said that it is because the character or eminence of a counsel is to be wholly disregarded in determining the justice or otherwise of his client's cause that it is an inflexible rule of forensic pleading that an advocate shall not, as such, express his personal opinion of or his belief in his client's cause.", per Locke, J. in *Boucher* v. *The Queen* (1955), S.C.R. 16 at 26.
As to the impropriety of a lawyer witness later appearing as counsel, see *Imperial Oil* v. *Grabarchuk* (1974), 3 O.R. (3d) 783 (Ont. C.A.); *Phoenix* v. *Metcalfe* (1974), 5 W.W.R. 661 (B.C.C.A.).

16. Cf. B.C. D-1 (b); N.B. B-8; IBA A-18; ABA DR 7-109(A), (B), (C). "I do not know of any rule that a defence counsel cannot interview a witness that may be called for the Crown . . . . The Crown, by issuing a lot of subpoenas, cannot throw a cloud over a lot of witnesses, excluding the defence from the preparation of their case.", per Roach, J.A. in *R.* v. *Gibbons* (1946), 86 C.C.C. 20 at 28-29 (Ont. C.A.).

17. Cf. B.C. D-1(b); N.B. D-7, D-8; ABA EC 7-19, DR 7-104(A)(1).
B.C. D-1(b) discusses situations where it is difficult to tell whether one is dealing with a witness (which is proper) or communicating with an opposite party who is legally represented (which is improper). The problem may arise where the opposite party is a corporation or government agency. The test suggested is: "Is he likely to be involved in the decision-making process of the party, or does he merely carry out the directions of others?"
"The principle was laid down long ago . . . that once it appears a person has an attorney there can be no effective dealing except through him." ". . . [A] lawyer 'should never in any way . . . attempt to negotiate or compromise the matter directly with any party represented by a lawyer, except *through* such lawyer' . . . . To notify the lawyer that the matter is settled is not to negotiate through him". per J.A. in *Nelson* v. *Murphy* (1957), 22 W.W.R. 137 at 142 (Man. C.A.).

18. Cf. CBA 4(4); N.B. D-4; ABA ECs 7-38, 7-39, DR 7-106(C)(5). See *Orkin* at pp.

60-63 for instances of dilatory tactics held to be improper.

19. Cf. CBA 3(3); *Orkin* at pp. 95-97; and see paragraph 5 of the Rule relating to advising clients.

20. But see para. 10, *post.*

21. Cf. CBA 1(2); N.B. C-12; ABA ECs 7-13, 7-14, DR 7-103; *Orkin* at pp. 116-20. "It cannot be overemphasized that the purpose of a criminal prosecution is not to obtain a conviction, it is to lay before the jury what the Crown considers to be credible evidence relevant to what is alleged to be a crime. Counsel have a duty to see that all available legal proof of the facts is presented; it should be done firmly and pressed to its legitimate strength but it must also be done fairly. The role of prosecutor excludes any notion of winning or losing; his function is a matter of public duty than which in civil life there can be none charged with greater personal responsibility. It is to be performed with an ingrained sense of the dignity, the seriousness and the justness of judicial proceedings.", per Rand, J. in *Boucher* v. *The Queen* (1955), S.C.R. 16 at 23-24.
See also *Richard* v. *The Queen* (1960), 126 C.C.C. 255 per Bridges, J.A. at p. 280; *Regina* v. *Lalonde* (1972), 5 C.C.C. (2d) 168; and Martin, "Preparation for Trial", Law Soc. U.C. Special Lectures (1969) p. 221 at 235 *et seq.*

22. Cf. CBA 2(6); N.B. C-6; IBA B-5; ABA EC 7-24, DR 7-106(C)(4).

23. See *Orkin*, p. 115, and Boulton, *Conduct and Etiquette at the Bar*, pp. 71-73, reproducing the substance of 1912 Annual Statement of the General Council of the Bar; also quoted and commented on by Schroeder, J.A., *supra*, note 1, at pp. 94-97.
See also Martin, "The Role and Responsibility of the Defence Advocate" (1969-70) 12 Crim. L.Q. 376 at 386-87.

24. See guidelines laid down in *R.* v. *Turner* (1970), 2 All E.R. 281 at 285 (C.A.); panel discussion in Law Soc. U.C. Special Lectures (1969) at pp. 299-311; Ratushny, "Plea Bargaining and the Public" (1972) 20 Chitty's L.J. 238.

25. Cf. CBA 4(3); IBA A-21, A-23; ABA EC 7-38, DR 7-106(C)(5);
N.B. D-5: "Undertakings should be written and the terms should be unambiguous. Counsel when giving an undertaking accepts personal responsibility unless expressly excepted."
"It has more than once been determined by the Court that if attorneys choose to practice upon loose understandings . . . they cannot expect aid from the Court if difficulties arise in carrying them out . . . .", per Barry, J. in *Ferguson* v. *Swedish-Canadian* (1912), 41 N.B.R. 217 at 220 (N.B.C.A.).
Where solicitors wrote: "on behalf of our client . . . we undertake . . ." it was held that, in the circumstances, the solicitors were personally responsible: *Re Solicitors* (1971), 1 W.W.R. 529 (B.C.C.A.).
". . . [O]ne's word should be one's bond . . . .", Lund, 1950 Lecture to the Law Society (Law Society of Upper Canada, 1956, pp. 33-34).

26. Cf. CBA 2(1); N.B. B-3, D-4; IBA C-1; ABA EC 7-36, DR 7-106(C)(6).

27. Cf. N.B. C-8; IBA A-20; ABA EC 7-19.

28. Commentary 15 to Rule 10 of the Rules of Professional Conduct of the Law Society of Upper Canada provides as follows:
"15. The lawyer should observe the following guidelines respecting communication with witnesses giving evidence:
(a) During examination-in-chief: it is not improper for the examining lawyer to discuss with the witness any matter that has not been covered in the examination up to that point;

(b) during examination-in-chief by another lawyer of a witness who is unsympathetic to the lawyer's cause: the lawyer not conducting the examination-in-chief may properly discuss the evidence with the witness;
(c) between completion of examination-in-chief and commencement of cross-examination of the lawyer's own witness: there ought to be no discussion of the evidence given in chief or relating to any matter introduced or touched upon during the examination-in-chief;
(d) during cross-examination by an opposing lawyer: while the witness is under cross-examination the lawyer ought not to have any conversation with the witness respecting the witness's evidence or relative to any issue in the proceeding;
(e) between completion of cross-examination and commencement of re-examination: the lawyer who is going to re-examine the witness ought not to have any discussion respecting evidence that will be dealt with on re-examination;
(f) during cross-examination by the lawyer of a witness unsympathetic to the cross-examiner's cause: the lawyer may properly discuss the witness's evidence with the witness;
(g) during cross-examination by the lawyer of a witness who is sympathetic to that lawyer's cause: any conversations ought to be restricted in the same way as communications during examination-in-chief of one's own witness;
(h) during re-examination of a witness called by an opposing lawyer: if the witness is sympathetic to the lawyer's cause there ought to be no communication relating to the evidence to be given by that witness during re-examination. The lawyer may, however, properly discuss the evidence with a witness who is adverse in interest.

If there is any question whether the lawyer's behaviour may be in violation of a rule of conduct or professional etiquette, it will often be appropriate to obtain the consent of the opposing lawyer and leave of the court before engaging in conversations that may be considered improper or a breach of etiquette."

However, "It is submitted with respect that in some respects [this commentary] may inhibit the discovery of truth and go beyond what was the practice in High Court.", per Sopinka and Polin, *The Trial of an Action*, p. 106.

In Nova Scotia the rule has long existed that it is improper for counsel to communicate with a witness called in chief during a break or adjournment until the witness's cross-examination has concluded.

29. See *J. & M. Chartrand Realty Ltd.* v. *Martin* (1981), 22 C.P.C. 186 (Ont. H.C.J.).

30. Cf. ABA EC 7-15.

CHAPTER X

THE LAWYER IN PUBLIC OFFICE

RULE

The lawyer who holds public office should, in the discharge of official duties, adhere to standards of conduct as high as those that these rules require of a lawyer engaged in the practice of law.[1]

Commentary

Guiding Principles

1. The Rule applies to the lawyer who is elected or appointed to legislative or administrative office at any level of government, regardless of whether the lawyer attained such office because of professional qualifications.[2] Because such a lawyer is in the public eye, the legal profession can more readily be brought into disrepute by failure on the lawyer's part to observe its professional standards of conduct.

Conflicts of Interest

2. The lawyer who holds public office must not allow personal or other interests to conflict with the proper discharge of official duties. The lawyer holding part-time public office must not accept any private legal business where duty to the client will or may conflict with official duties. If some unforeseen conflict arises, the lawyer should terminate the professional relationship, explaining to the client that official duties must prevail. The lawyer who holds a full-time public office will not be faced with this sort of conflict, but must nevertheless guard against allowing the lawyer's independent judgement in the discharge of official duties to be influenced by the lawyer's own interest, or by the interests of persons closely related to or associated with the lawyer, or of former or prospective clients, or of former or prospective partners or associates.[3]

3. In the context of the preceding paragraph, persons closely related to or associated with the lawyer include a spouse, child, or any relative of the lawyer (or of the lawyer's spouse) living under the same roof, a trust or estate in which the lawyer has a substantial beneficial interest or for which the lawyer acts as a trustee or in a similar capacity, and a corporation of which the lawyer is a director or in which the lawyer or some closely related

or associated person holds or controls, directly or indirectly, a significant number of shares.[4]

4. Subject to any special rules applicable to a particular public office, the lawyer holding such office who sees the possibility of a conflict of interest should declare such interest at the earliest opportunity and take no part in any consideration, discussion or vote with respect to the matter in question.[5]

Appearances before Official Bodies

5. When the lawyer or any of the lawyer's partners or associates is a member of an official body such as, for example, a school board, municipal council or governing body, the lawyer should not appear professionally before that body. However, subject to the rules of the official body it would not be improper for the lawyer to appear professionally before a committee of such body if such partner or associate is not a member of that committee.[6]

6. The lawyer should not represent in the same or any related matter any persons or interests that the lawyer has been concerned with in an official capacity. Similarly, the lawyer should avoid advising upon a ruling of an official body of which the lawyer either is a member or was a member at the time the ruling was made.[7]

Disclosure of Confidential Information

7. By way of corollary to the Rule relating to confidential information, the lawyer who has acquired confidential information by virtue of holding public office should keep such information confidential and not divulge or use it even though the lawyer has ceased to hold such office.[8] (As to the taking of employment in connection with any matter in respect of which the lawyer had substantial responsibility or confidential information, see Commentary 3 of the Rule relating to avoiding questionable conduct.)

Disciplinary Action

8. Generally speaking, a governing body will not be concerned with the way in which a lawyer holding public office carries out official responsibilities, but conduct in office that reflects adversely upon the lawyer's integrity or professional competence may subject the lawyer to disciplinary action.[9]

NOTES

1. Cf. CBA-COD 9; IBA E-3; ABA-MR 1.11; ABA EC 8-8, DR 8-101(A).
2. Common examples include Senators, Members of the House of Commons, members of provincial legislatures, cabinet ministers, municipal councillors, school trustees, members and officials of boards, commissions, tribunals and departments, commissioners of inquiry, arbitrators and mediators, Crown pro-

secutors and many others. For a general discussion, see Woodman, "The Lawyer in Public Life", Pitblado Lectures (Manitoba, 1971) p. 129.

3. Cf. generally the Rule relating to conflict of interest between lawyer and client. "When a lawyer is elected to . . . (a) public office of any kind, or holds any public employment . . . his duty as the holder of such office requires him to represent the public with undivided fidelity. His obligation as a lawyer . . . continues; . . . it is improper for him to act professionally for any person . . . [who] is actively or specially interested in the promotion or defeat of legislative or other matters proposed or pending before the public body of which he is a member or by which he is employed, or before him as the holder of a public office or employment." from Brand, *Bar Associations, Attorneys and Judges* (Chicago, 1956) p. 179.

4. Both human and financial relationships are envisaged.

5. For example, Premier Davis of Ontario issued "Conflict of Interest Guidelines" to provincial ministers in September 1972, requiring them "while holding office . . . [to] abstain from day-to-day participation in any . . . professional activity." Specific "conflict of interest" laws have been introduced in several Canadian jurisdictions.

6. Cf. Ont. 13; B.C. B-9(a). The Ontario ruling related specifically to municipal councillors. Local authorities have increasingly been concerned with zoning, planning and development matters in which lawyers frequently act professionally.

7. Cf. ABA DR 9-101(A), (B): ". . . not accept private employment in matters in which the lawyer has acted in a judicial capacity or had substantial responsibility while he was a public employee."

8. Statutory oaths of office commonly impose obligations of "official secrecy".

9. In *Barreau de Montreal* v. *Claude Wagner* (1968), Q.B. 235 (Que. Q.B.) it was held that the respondent, then provincial Minister of Justice, was not subject to the disciplinary jurisdiction of the Bar in respect of a public speech in which he had criticized the conduct of a judge, because he was then exercising his official or "Crown" functions. In *Gagnon* v. *Bar of Montreal* (1959), B.R. 92 (Que.) it was held that on the application for readmission to practice by a former judge his conduct while in office might properly be considered by the admissions authorities.

CHAPTER XI

FEES

RULE

The lawyer shall not

(a) stipulate for, charge or accept any fee that is not fully disclosed, fair and reasonable;

(b) appropriate any funds of the client held in trust or otherwise under the lawyer's control for or on account of fees without the express authority of the client, save as permitted by the rules of the governing body.[1]

Commentary

Factors to be Considered

1. A fair and reasonable fee will depend on and reflect such factors as:

   (a) the time and effort required and spent;
   (b) the difficulty and importance of the matter;
   (c) whether special skill or service has been required and provided;
   (d) the customary charges of other lawyers of equal standing in the locality in like matters and circumstances;
   (e) in civil cases the amount involved, or the value of the subject matter;
   (f) in criminal cases the exposure and risk to the client;
   (g) the results obtained;
   (h) tariffs or scales authorized by local law;
   (i) such special circumstances as loss of other employment, urgency and uncertainty of reward;
   (j) any relevant agreement between the lawyer and the client.

A fee will not be fair and reasonable and may subject the lawyer to disciplinary proceedings if it is one that cannot be justified in the light of all pertinent circumstances, including the factors mentioned, or is so disproportionate to the services rendered as to introduce the element of fraud or dishonesty, or undue profit.[2]

2. It is in keeping with the best traditions of the legal profession to reduce or waive a fee in cases of hardship or poverty, or where the client or

prospective client would otherwise effectively be deprived of legal advice or representation.[3]

Avoidance of Controversy

3. Breaches of this Rule and misunderstandings about fees and financial matters bring the legal profession into disrepute and reflect adversely upon the administration of justice. The lawyer should try to avoid controversy with the client over fees and should be ready to explain the basis for charges, especially if the client is unsophisticated or uninformed about the proper basis and measurements for fees. The lawyer should give the client an early and fair estimate of fees and disbursements, pointing out any uncertainties involved, so that the client may be able to make an informed decision. When something unusual or unforeseen occurs that may substantially affect the amount of the fee, the lawyer should forestall misunderstandings or disputes by explaining this to the client.[4]

Interest on Overdue Accounts

4. Save where permitted by law or local practice, the lawyer should not charge interest on an overdue account except by prior agreement with the client and then only at a reasonable rate.[5]

Apportionment and Division of Fees

5. The lawyer who acts for two or more clients in the same matter is under a duty to apportion the fees and disbursements equitably among them in the absence of agreement otherwise.

6. A fee will not be a fair one within the meaning of the Rule if it is divided with another lawyer who is not a partner or associate unless (a) the client consents, either expressly or impliedly, to the employment of the other lawyer and (b) the fee is divided in proportion to the work done and responsibility assumed.[6]

Hidden Fees

7. The fiduciary relationship that exists between lawyer and client requires full disclosure in all financial matters between them and prohibits the lawyer from accepting any hidden fees. No fee, reward, costs, commission, interest, rebate, agency or forwarding allowance or other compensation whatsoever related to the professional employment may be taken by the lawyer from anyone other than the client without full disclosure to and consent of the client. Where the lawyer's fees are being paid by someone other than the client, such as a legal aid agency, a borrower, or a personal representative, the consent of such other person will be required. So far as disbursements are concerned, only *bona fide* and specified payments to others may be included. If the lawyer is financially interested in the person to whom the disbursements are made, such as an investigating, brokerage or copying agency, the lawyer shall expressly disclose this fact to the client.[7]

Sharing Fees with Non-lawyers

8. Any arrangement whereby the lawyer directly or indirectly shares, splits or divides fees with notaries public, law students, clerks or other non-lawyers who bring or refer business to the lawyer's office is improper and constitutes professional misconduct. It is also improper for the lawyer to give any financial or other reward to such persons for referring business.[8]

9. The lawyer shall not enter into a lease or other arrangement whereby a landlord or other person directly or indirectly shares in the fees or revenues generated by the law practice.[9]

Contingent Fees

10. Except where prohibited by the laws of the jurisdiction in which the lawyer practises, it is not improper for the lawyer to enter into an arrangement with the client for a contingent fee, provided such fee is fair and reasonable and the lawyer adheres to any rules of court or local practice relating to such an arrangement.[10]

NOTES

1. Cf. CBA-COD 10; CBA 3(8), (9); Que. 3.08.01, .02; 81; B.C. B-5; Alta. 32; N.B. E-1; IBA A-8; ABA DR 2-106.

2. The proper "factors of fairness" have been many times declared by the courts. For a compilation and discussion see, e.g., *Re Solicitors* (1972), 3 O.R. 433 (Ont. H.C.) per McBride, M. at 436-37: " . . . I have not set down these factors in any sense in order of importance. In my view most of these eight factors should be considered in every case . . . time expended is not, in most cases, the overriding factor, nor even the most important. On the other hand, there are comparatively few cases where the time factor can be completely ignored."
As to the utility of consensual local "minimum fees tariffs", see *Re Solicitors* (1970), 1 O.R. 407 (Ont. H.C.).
"Certainty is a desirable feature of any system of law. But there are certain types of conduct . . . which cannot be satisfactorily regulated by specific statutory enactment, but are better left to the practice of juries and other tribunals of fact. They depend finally . . . on proof of the attainment of some degree [followed by a page of illustrations, most related to 'reasonableness'].", per Lord Simon, L.C. in *Knuller Ltd.* v. *D.P.P.* (1972), 2 All E.R. 898 at 929-30 (H.L.).

3. See *TWA* v. *The King* (1948), 4 D.L.R. 833 at 837 (Ont. H.C.); and cf. CBA 3(9).

4. Cf. CBA 3(10). "The question of compensation for solicitors has long been the anxious concern of the Court, both in the interests of clients and their solicitors . . . . [M]uch legislative and judicial activity was directed to the reform and settlement of procedures for fair and reasonable fees. . . . [In Ontario] there is a procedure for determining in every case where it is invoked, that a solicitor's charges are fair and reasonable.", per Wright, J. in *Re Solicitor* (1972), 1 O.R. 694 at 697 (Ont. H.C.).
"The object of a bill of costs is to 'secure a mode by which the items of which the total bill is made up should be clearly and distinctly shown, so as to give the client an opportunity of exercising his judgment as to whether the bill was reasonable or not'.", per Riddell, J.A. in *Millar* v. *The King* (1922), 67 D.L.R. 119 at 120 (Ont.

App. Div.).
In certain provinces local law requires that clients be expressly advised of their right to have any agreement agreeing to fees in advance judicially reviewed: see N.B. E-2; *Law Society Act* R.S.M. 1970, c. L-100, s. 49; Alberta Supreme Court Rule 616(1)(f).

5. Cf. *Solicitors Act*, R.S.O. 1980, c. 478, s.35, re-enacted by 1983, c. 21, s. 1, amended 1984, c. 11, s. 214(5), permitting interest at the rate established for pre-judgement interest from the expiration of one month after delivery of the bill. The rate of interest "shall be shown on the bill delivered", *ibid.*, s.35(4).

6. Cf. B.C. B-5(b) and Alta. 35 (proscribing "agency fees" in consideration of the "mere introduction" of business). Cf. also ABA DR 2-107(a). The intention is not to interfere with routine agency arrangements for such services as searches or document registration in county towns or provincial capitals, etc.

7. See particularly the Rule and Commentary respecting conflict of interest between lawyer and client for the reasons underlying these proscriptions, and *Orkin* at pp. 154-55.
The lawyer may not profit from interest on clients' trust monies in the lawyer's hands. In some provinces payment of such interest to Law Foundations and legal aid plans is now authorized.
The general principles and fiduciary duties of the law of agency apply to the lawyer-client relationship, particularly with respect to fidelity, the obligation to account, and against "secret profits". See Fridman, *The Law of Agency* (3rd ed. 1971) at pp. 30-31, 132-39, and other standard authorities on agency. It would, for example, be improper for a lawyer without express disclosure and consent to take any commission, procuration or other fee or reward from a lender, a stockbroker, a real estate or insurance agent, a trust company, a bailiff or a collection agent in consideration of the introduction by the lawyer of business from which professional work resulted to the lawyer in which the lawyer acted for or the lawyer's fees were paid by the person whose business was so introduced.
As to disbursements: "In any case where there is liability upon the part of the solicitor and there is no dishonesty, the mere fact that the amount has not been paid ought not to prevent recovery. If there should be shown any dishonesty the case would be very different . . .". per Middleton, J. in *Re Solicitor* (1920), 47 O.L.R. 522 at 525 (Ont. H.C.).

8. Cf. Ont. 9(7).

9. *Ibid.*

10. See Williston, "The Contingent Fee in Canada" (1968) 6 Alta. L.R. 184; Arlidge, "Contingent Fees" (1974) Ottawa L.R. 374; *Thomson* v. *Wishart* (1910), 19 Man. R. 340 (Man. C.A.); *Monteith* v. *Caladine* (1965), 47 D.L.R. (2d) 322 (B.C.C.A.); *Hogan* v. *Hello* (1969), 1 N.B.R. (2d) 306. Alberta, British Columbia, Manitoba, New Brunswick, the Northwest Territories, Nova Scotia and Quebec permit regulated "contingent fees"; the remaining Canadian jurisdictions do not.

CHAPTER XII

WITHDRAWAL

RULE

The lawyer owes a duty to the client not to withdraw services except for good cause and upon notice appropriate in the circumstances.[1]

Commentary

Guiding Principles

1. Although the client has a right to terminate the lawyer-client relationship at will, the lawyer does not enjoy the same freedom of action. Having once accepted professional employment, the lawyer should complete the task as ably as possible unless there is justifiable cause for terminating the relationship.[2]

2. The lawyer who withdraws from employment should act so as to minimize expense and avoid prejudice to the client, doing everything reasonably possible to facilitate the expeditious and orderly transfer of the matter to the successor lawyer.[3]

3. Where withdrawal is required or permitted by this Rule, the lawyer must comply with all applicable rules of court as well as local rules and practice.

Obligatory Withdrawal

4. In some circumstances, the lawyer will be under a duty to withdraw. The obvious example is following discharge by the client. Other examples are (a) if the lawyer is instructed by the client to do something inconsistent with the lawyer's duty to the court and, following explanation, the client persists in such instructions; (b) if the client is guilty of dishonourable conduct in the proceedings or is taking a position solely to harass or maliciously injure another; (c) if it becomes clear that the lawyer's continued employment will lead to a breach of these Rules such as, for example, a breach of the Rules relating to conflict of interest; or (d) if it develops that the lawyer is not competent to handle the matter. In all these situations there is a duty to inform the client that the lawyer must

withdraw.[4]

Optional Withdrawal

5. Situations where a lawyer would be entitled to withdraw, although not under a positive duty to do so, will as a rule arise only where there has been a serious loss of confidence between lawyer and client. Such a loss of confidence goes to the very basis of the relationship. Thus, the lawyer who is deceived by the client will have justifiable cause for withdrawal. Again, the refusal of the client to accept and act upon the lawyer's advice on a significant point might indicate such a loss of confidence. At the same time, the lawyer should not use the threat of withdrawal as a device to force the client into making a hasty decision on a difficult question.[5] The lawyer may withdraw if unable to obtain instructions from the client.[6]

Non-payment of Fees

6. Failure on the part of the client after reasonable notice to provide funds on account of disbursements or fees will justify withdrawal by the lawyer unless serious prejudice to the client would result.[7]

Notice to Client

7. No hard and fast rules can be laid down as to what will constitute reasonable notice prior to withdrawal. Where the matter is covered by statutory provisions or rules of court, these will govern. In other situations the governing principle is that the lawyer should protect the client's interests so far as possible and should not desert the client at a critical stage of a matter or at a time when withdrawal would put the client in a position of disadvantage or peril.[8]

Duty Following Withdrawal

8. Upon discharge or withdrawal the lawyer should:
   (a) deliver in an orderly and expeditious manner to or to the order of the client all papers and property to which the client is entitled;
   (b) give the client all information that may be required about the case or matter;
   (c) account for all funds of the client on hand or previously dealt with and refund any remuneration not earned during the employment;
   (d) promptly render an account for outstanding fees and disbursements;
   (e) co-operate with the successor lawyer for the purposes outlined in paragraph 2.

The obligation in clause (a) to deliver papers and property is subject to the lawyer's right of lien referred to in paragraph 11. In the event of conflicting claims to such papers and property, the lawyer should make every effort to have the claimants settle the dispute.[9]

9. Co-operation with the successor lawyer will normally include providing any memoranda of fact and law that have been prepared by the lawyer in connection with the matter, but confidential information not clearly related to the matter should not be divulged without the express consent of the client.

10. The lawyer acting for several clients in a case or matter who ceases to act for one or more of them should co-operate with the successor lawyer or lawyers to the extent permitted by this Code, and should seek to avoid any unseemly rivalry, whether real or apparent.[10]

Lien for Unpaid Fees

11. Where upon the discharge or withdrawal of the lawyer the question of a right of lien for unpaid fees and disbursements arises, the lawyer should have due regard to the effect of its enforcement upon the client's position. Generally speaking, the lawyer should not enforce such a lien if the result would be to prejudice materially the client's position in any uncompleted matter.[11]

Duty of Successor Lawyer

12. Before accepting employment, the successor lawyer should be satisfied that the former lawyer approves, or has withdrawn or been discharged by the client. It is quite proper for the successor lawyer to urge the client to settle or take reasonable steps toward settling or securing any account owed to the former lawyer, especially if the latter withdrew for good cause or was capriciously discharged. But if a trial or hearing is in progress or imminent, or if the client would otherwise be prejudiced, the existence of an outstanding account should not be allowed to interfere with the successor lawyer acting for the client.[12]

Dissolution of Law Firm

13. When a law firm is dissolved, this will usually result in the termination of the lawyer-client relationship as between a particular client and one or more of the lawyers involved. In such cases, most clients will prefer to retain the services of the lawyer whom they regarded as being in charge of their business prior to the dissolution. However, the final decision rests in each case with the client, and the lawyers who are no longer retained by the client should act in accordance with the principles here set out, and in particular commentary 2.[13]

NOTES

1. Cf. CBA-COD 11; Que. 3.03.04, .05; B.C. G-5; IBA B-4; ABA-MR 1.16; ABA EC 2-32, DR 2-110(A), (C). For cases, see 4 Can. Abr. (2d) under "Barristers and Solicitors: Termination of Relationship", paras. 101-02 and supplements. See also *Orkin*, pp. 90-95.

2. In appeals to the Supreme Court of Canada see Rule 14(1) of that Court, whereunder the lawyer of record in the court below may be deemed to represent the client for purposes of the appeal.

3. Cf. ABA DR 2-110(A).
Provincial Rules of Court provide for the giving of notice of change of solicitors and for the making of applications for leave to withdraw.
For cases see 4 Can. Abr. (2d) under "Barristers and Solicitors: Change of Solicitors", paras. 342-58 and supplements.
In legal aid cases provincial regulations may also require notice to the plan administrators; see, e.g., in Ontario O. Reg. 59/86 as amended, s. 62(1)(a).
On an application under the Ontario rules for an order that the lawyer has ceased to act, the supporting material must show the particular facts warranting the lawyer's ceasing to act: *Ely* v. *Rosen* (1963), 1 O.R. 47 (Ont. H.C.).
"I have no doubt that the learned trial Judge seriously erred in law when he purported to direct counsel for the accused that he could not withdraw from the case, notwithstanding the fact that the accused, his client, apparently wished to discharge him.", per Jessup, J.A. in *Regina* v. *Spataro* (1971), 3 O.R. 419 at 422 (Ont. C.A.).

4. Cf. CBA 3(2) and 5(5); IBA B-7; ABA DR 2-110(B).
". . . this case where [N.R.] is held to have sworn affidavits of discovery which were false and where the solicitor . . . should not have allowed them to be sworn if he had done his duty which he owed to the Court . . . . The solicitor cannot simply allow the client to make whatever affidavit of documents he thinks fit nor can he escape the responsibility of careful investigation or supervision. If the client will not give him the information he is entitled to require or if he insists on swearing an affidavit which the solicitor knows to be imperfect or which he has every reason to think is imperfect, then the solicitor's proper course is to withdraw from the case.", per Lord Wright in *Myers* v. *Elman* (1940), A.C. 282 at 322 (H.L.).
For a panel discussion chaired by Gale, C.J.O. on the rights and obligations of lawyers with respect to withdrawal in criminal cases, see Law Society of Upper Canada, *Special Lectures* (1969) at pp. 295-99.

5. Cf. ABA DR 2-119(C).
"No solicitor . . . need put up with abuse and accusations such as were alleged to have been made here and would be fully entitled, after them, to withdraw from the case. An accusation of fraud, in fact, would make it improper for the solicitor to continue to act for the client, since it showed that the client had lost confidence in him.", per Urquhart, J. in *Re Solicitors Act*; *Collison* v. *Hurst* (1946), O.W.N. 668 at 671 (Ont. H.C.).

6. Failure to instruct counsel constitutes repudiation which counsel could accept and terminate the employment.

7. "An attorney is ordinarily justified in withdrawing if the client fails or refuses to pay or secure the proper fees or expenses of the attorney after being reasonably requested to do so.", proposition in *Corpus Juris Secundum* approved and applied in *Johnson* v. *Toronto* (1963), 1 O.R. 626 (Ont. H.C.).

8. "If the case is scheduled to be tried on a date which will afford the accused ample time to retain another counsel, a lawyer who has not been paid the fee agreed upon may withdraw . . . . But if he waits until the eve of the trial so that there is no time for another counsel to prepare adequately . . . it becomes too late for him to withdraw. He must continue on . . . .", from panel discussion, note 4, *supra*, at pp. 295-96; and cf. Alta. 8: "If a member accepts a retainer to represent an accused at a preliminary hearing and not at the trial . . . [he] should have a clear and unambiguous understanding with his client to that effect and . . . should advise the Court at the beginning of the inquiry . . .".

9. "... [C] ounsel should be generous in accounting for any moneys which have been received but not yet earned, bearing in mind that a great deal of the time he has spent ... may be of little value to the other counsel who is required to take over.", *ibid.*, at p. 296.
As to the proper disposition of papers, which is frequently a perplexing problem, see *Cordery on Solicitors* (6th ed.) at pp. 118-20 for a discussion of law and principles and a table of categories with supporting authorities.

10. "It is quite apparent ... that the applicant dismissed the ... solicitor without just cause.... The common law right of a solicitor to exercise a lien on documents in his possession where he has been discharged without cause by his client is well recognized, subject, however, to certain exceptions ... where third parties are involved, the Court may interfere ... always upon the basis that whereas a solicitor may assert a lien ... he should not be entitled to embarrass other parties interested.", per McGillivray, J.A. in *Re Gladstone* (1972), 2 O.R. 127 at 128 (Ont. C.A.).

11. See Morden, "A Succeeding Solicitor's Duty to Protect the Accounts of the Former Solicitor" (1971) 5 Law Soc. U.C. Gaz. 257.

12. Cf. CBA 4(1).

13. "Subject to any question of lien, the client's papers in possession of the firm belong to the client and cannot be the subject of agreement as against him, but as *between themselves* solicitors can agree that on dissolution the clients of the old firm and their papers shall either be divided between the dissolving partners, or belong to those continuing the business of the firm ....", *Cordery on Solicitors* (6th ed.) at pp. 463-64 (emphasis added).

CHAPTER XIII

THE LAWYER AND THE ADMINISTRATION OF JUSTICE

RULE

The lawyer should encourage public respect for and try to improve the administration of justice.[1]

Commentary

Guiding Principles

1. The admission to and continuance in the practice of law imply a basic commitment by the lawyer to the concept of equal justice for all within an open, ordered and impartial system. However, judicial institutions will not function effectively unless they command the respect of the public. Because of changes in human affairs and the imperfection of human institutions, constant efforts must be made to improve the administration of justice and thereby maintain public respect for it.[2]

2. The lawyer, by training, opportunity and experience, is in a position to observe the workings and discover the strengths and weaknesses of laws, legal institutions and public authorities. The lawyer should, therefore, lead in seeking improvements in the legal system, but any criticisms and proposals should be *bona fide* and reasoned.[3]

Scope of the Rule

3. The obligation outlined in the Rule is not restricted to the lawyer's professional activities but is a general responsibility resulting from the lawyer's position in the community. The lawyer's responsibilities are greater than those of a private citizen. The lawyer must not subvert the law by counselling or assisting in activities that are in defiance of it and must do nothing to lessen the respect and confidence of the public in the legal system of which the lawyer is a part. The lawyer should take care not to weaken or destroy public confidence in legal institutions or authorities by broad irresponsible allegations of corruption or partiality. The lawyer in public life must be particularly careful in this regard because the mere fact of being a lawyer will lend weight and credibility to any public statements.[4]

For the same reason, the lawyer should not hesitate to speak out against an injustice. (As to test cases, see commentary 8 of the Rule relating to advising clients.)

Criticism of the Tribunal

4. Although proceedings and decisions of tribunals are properly subject to scrutiny and criticism by all members of the public, including lawyers, members of tribunals are often prohibited by law or custom from defending themselves. Their inability to do so imposes special responsibilities upon lawyers. Firstly, the lawyer should avoid criticism that is petty, intemperate or unsupported by a *bona fide* belief in its real merit, bearing in mind that in the eyes of the public, professional knowledge lends weight to the lawyer's judgements or criticism. Secondly, if the lawyer has been involved in the proceedings, there is the risk that any criticism may be, or may appear to be, partisan rather than objective. Thirdly, where a tribunal is the object of unjust criticism, the lawyer, as a participant in the administration of justice, is uniquely able to and should support the tribunal, both because its members cannot defend themselves and because the lawyer is thereby contributing to greater public understanding of and therefore respect for the legal system.[5]

Improving the Administration of Justice

5. The lawyer who seeks legislative or administrative changes should disclose whose interest is being advanced, whether it be the lawyer's interest, that of a client, or the public interest. The lawyer may advocate such changes on behalf of a client without personally agreeing with them, but the lawyer who purports to act in the public interest should espouse only those changes that the lawyer conscientiously believes to be in the public interest.[6]

NOTES

1. Cf. CBA-COD 12. IBA, "Duty to the Court": "In view of the vital part played by lawyers in the administration of justice, they are under an obligation to strive to maintain respect for that administration . . .".
2. Cf. the traditional barristers' oath: ". . . to protect and defend the right and interest of such of your fellow-citizens as may employ you . . . . You shall not pervert the law to favour or prejudice any man . . .".
   ABA ECs 8-1, 8-2 and 8-9: "Changes in human affairs and imperfections in human institutions make necessary constant efforts to maintain and improve our legal system. This system should function in a manner that commands public respect and fosters the use of legal remedies to achieve redress of grievances . . . . Rules of law are deficient if they are not just, understandable and responsive to the needs of society . . . . The advancement of our legal system is of vital importance in maintaining the rule of law and in facilitating orderly changes . . .".
3. ABA ECs 8-1, 8-2: "By reason of education and experience, lawyers are especially qualified to recognize deficiencies in the legal system and to initiate corrective

measures therein . . . . [The lawyer] should encourage the simplification of laws and the repeal or amendment of laws that are outmoded. Likewise, legal procedures should be improved whenever experience indicates a change is needed."

4. Cf. CBA Preamble: "The lawyer is more than a mere citizen . . .". "[L]awyers, because of *what* they are as opposed to *who* they are . . . are required to assume responsibilities of citizenship well beyond [the basic requirements of good citizenship] . . . This . . . is necessary because we are the profession to which society has entrusted the administration of law and the dispensing of justice.", MacKimmie, "Presidential Address" (1963) 6 Can. B.J. 347 at 348. For lucid and divergent views as to the limits to which lawyers may properly go in "defying the law" see editorial "Civil Disobedience and the Lawyer" (1967) 1(3) Law Soc. U.C. Gaz. 5 and response thereto in (1968) 2 Law Soc. U.C. Gaz. 44.

5. Cf. CBA 2(2) and ABA EC 8-6. Tribunals generally possess summary "contempt" powers, but these are circumscribed and are not lightly resorted to. Means exist through Attorneys-General and Judicial Councils for the investigation and remedying of specific complaints of official misbehaviour and neglect; in particular cases these should be resorted to in preference to public forums and the media.

6. Cf. ABA EC 8-4.

CHAPTER XIV

ADVERTISING, SOLICITATION AND MAKING LEGAL SERVICES AVAILABLE

RULE

Lawyers should make legal services available to the public in an efficient and convenient manner that will command respect and confidence, and by means that are compatible with the integrity, independence and effectiveness of the profession.[1]

Commentary

Guiding Principles

1. It is essential that a person requiring legal services be able to find a qualified lawyer with a minimum of difficulty or delay. In a relatively small community where lawyers are well known, the person will usually be able to make an informed choice and select a qualified lawyer in whom to have confidence. However, in larger centres these conditions will often not obtain. As the practice of law becomes increasingly complex and many individual lawyers restrict their activities to particular fields of law, the reputations of lawyers and their competence or qualification in particular fields may not be sufficiently well known to enable a person to make an informed choice. Thus one who has had little or no contact with lawyers or who is a stranger in the community may have difficulty finding a lawyer with the special skill required for a particular task. Telephone directories, legal directories and referral services may help find a lawyer, but not necessarily the right one for the work involved.[2] Advertising of legal services by the lawyer may assist members of the public and thereby result in increased access to the legal system. Where local rules permit, the lawyer may, therefore, advertise legal services to the general public.

2. When considering whether advertising in a particular area meets the public need, consideration must be given to the clientele to be served. For example, in a small community with a stable population a person requiring a lawyer for a particular purpose will not have the same difficulty in selecting one as someone in a newly-established community or a large city. Thus the governing body must have freedom of action in determining the

nature and content of advertising that will best meet the community need.[3]

3. Despite the lawyer's economic interest in earning a living, advertising, direct solicitation or any other means by which the lawyer seeks to make legal services more readily available to the public must comply with any rules prescribed by the governing body, must be consistent with the public interest and must not detract from the integrity, independence or effectiveness of the legal profession. They must not mislead the uninformed or arouse unattainable hopes and expectations, because this could result in distrust of legal institutions and lawyers. They must not adversely affect the quality of legal services, nor must they be so undignified, in bad taste or otherwise offensive as to be prejudicial to the interests of the public or the legal profession.

Finding a Lawyer

4. The lawyer who is consulted by a prospective client should be ready to assist in finding the right lawyer to deal with the problem. If unable to act, for example because of lack of qualification in the particular field, the lawyer should assist in finding a practitioner who is qualified and able to act. Such assistance should be given willingly and, except in very special circumstances, without charge.[4]

5. The lawyer may also assist in making legal services available by participating in legal aid plans and referral services, by engaging in programs of public information, education or advice concerning legal matters, and by being considerate of those who seek advice but are inexperienced in legal matters or cannot readily explain their problems.

6. The lawyer has a general right to decline particular employment (except when assigned as counsel by a court) but it is a right the lawyer should be slow to exercise if the probable result would be to make it very difficult for a person to obtain legal advice or representation. Generally speaking, the lawyer should not exercise the right merely because the person seeking legal services or that person's cause is unpopular or notorious, or because powerful interests or allegations of misconduct or malfeasance are involved, or because of the lawyer's private opinion about the guilt of the accused. As stated in commentary 4, the lawyer who declines employment should assist the person to obtain the services of another lawyer competent in the particular field and able to act.[5]

Enforcement of Restrictive Rules

7. The lawyer should adhere to rules made by the governing body with respect to making legal services available and respecting advertising, but rigid adherence to restrictive rules should be enforced with discretion where the lawyer who may have infringed such rules acted in good faith in trying to make legal services available more efficiently, economically and conveniently than they would otherwise have been.

NOTES

1. Cf. CBA-COD 13; ABA-MR 7; ABA Canon 2, EC 2-1; IBA at p. 30.
2. Cf. ABA ECs 2-6, 2-7.
3. At present the governing bodies and professional conduct committees, through rulings, by-laws, rules and opinions, regulate the details of permissible and impermissible advertising within their jurisdictions. Such matters as signs, name-plates, professional cards, announcements, letterheads, listings, firm names and "specialist" representations are dealt with. The regulations vary considerably from place to place and change from time to time. No attempt is here made to collect or epitomize them. For summaries of rulings and of illustrative decisions in these areas see *Orkin* at pp. 177-88, *Cordery on Solicitors* (6th ed.) at pp. 486-87.
4. Cf. ABA EC 2-8.
5. Cf. N.B. C-4; ABA ECs 2-26 to 2-29; *Orkin* at pp. 87-88.

CHAPTER XV

RESPONSIBILITY TO THE PROFESSION GENERALLY

RULE

The lawyer should assist in maintaining the integrity of the profession and should participate in its activities.[1]

Commentary

Guiding Principles

1. Unless the lawyer who tends to depart from proper professional conduct is checked at an early stage, loss or damage to clients or others may ensue. Evidence of minor breaches may, on investigation, disclose a more serious situation or may indicate the beginning of a course of conduct that would lead to serious breaches in the future. It is, therefore, proper (unless it be privileged or otherwise unlawful) for a lawyer to report to a governing body any occurrences involving a breach of this Code. Where, however, there is a reasonable likelihood that someone will suffer serious damage as a consequence of an apparent breach, for example where a shortage of trust funds is involved, the lawyer has an obligation to the profession to report the matter unless it is privileged or otherwise unlawful to do so. In all cases, the report must be made *bona fide* without malice or ulterior motive.[2] Further, subject to local rules, the lawyer must not act on a client's instructions to recover from another lawyer funds allegedly misappropriated by that other lawyer unless the client authorizes disclosure to the governing body and the lawyer makes such disclosure.

2. The lawyer has a duty to reply promptly to any communication from the governing body.[3]

3. The lawyer should not in the course of a professional practice write letters, whether to a client, another lawyer or any other person, that are abusive, offensive or otherwise totally inconsistent with the proper tone of a professional communication from a lawyer.[4]

Participation in Professional Activities

4. In order that the profession may discharge its public responsibility of

providing independent and competent legal services, the individual lawyer should do everything possible to assist the profession to function properly and effectively. In this regard, participation in such activities as law reform, continuing legal education, tutorials, legal aid programs, community legal services, professional conduct and discipline, liaison with other professions and other activities of the governing body or local, provincial or national associations, although often time-consuming and without tangible reward, is essential to the maintenance of a strong, independent and useful profession.[5]

NOTES

1. Cf. CBA-COD 14; CBA 5(1); ABA-MR 8; ABA Canon 1.
   "The legal profession . . . has emerged over the centuries in order to fill a pressing public need for protection . . . under the law of the rights and liberties of the individual, however humble, if necessary against the state itself.", IBA introductory.
   "Public confidence in the profession would be shaken if such conduct were tolerated . . . no solicitor could escape [striking off] simply by showing that there had been no dishonesty and no concealment, and that no client had suffered . . .", per Parker, L.C.J. in *re a Solicitor* (1959), 193 Sol. Jour. 875 (Q.B.D.).
2. Cf. CBA 5(1); Ont. 13; B.C. F-3; ABA DR 1-103, EC 1-4. Alta. 22: "It is conduct unbecoming . . . not to [report instances] when they clearly involve a shortage of trust funds or a breach of an undertaking."
3. Cf. Ont. 13(3); Alta. 18; N.B. D-1; Sask. 12. "The reprehensible thing about the solicitor's conduct is his indefensible ignoring of the communications of the Law Society . . .", per Walsh, J. in *In re X., a Solicitor* (1920), 16 Alta. L.R. 542 at 543.
4. Cf. IBA D-6.
5. Cf. ABA ECs 1-4, 2-25, 6-2, 8-1, 8-2, 8-3, 8-9, 9-6.

CHAPTER XVI

RESPONSIBILITY TO LAWYERS INDIVIDUALLY

RULE

The lawyer's conduct toward other lawyers should be characterized by courtesy and good faith.[1]

Commentary

Guiding Principles

1. Public interest demands that matters entrusted to the lawyer be dealt with effectively and expeditiously. Fair and courteous dealing on the part of each lawyer engaged in a matter will contribute materially to this end. The lawyer who behaves otherwise does a disservice to the client, and neglect of the Rule will impair the ability of lawyers to perform their function properly.[2]

2. Any ill feeling that may exist or be engendered between clients, particularly during litigation, should never be allowed to influence lawyers in their conduct and demeanour toward each other or the parties. The presence of personal animosity between lawyers involved in a matter may cause their judgement to be clouded by emotional factors and hinder the proper resolution of the matter. Personal remarks or references between them should be avoided. Haranguing or offensive tactics interfere with the orderly administration of justice and have no place in our legal system.[3]

3. The lawyer should accede to reasonable requests for trial dates, adjournments, waivers of procedural formalities and similar matters that do not prejudice the rights of the client. The lawyer who knows that another lawyer has been consulted in a matter should not proceed by default in the matter without enquiry and warning.[4]

Avoidance of Sharp Practices

4. The lawyer should avoid sharp practice and not take advantage of or act without fair warning upon slips, irregularities or mistakes on the part of other lawyers not going to the merits or involving any sacrifice of the

client's rights. The lawyer should not, unless required by the transaction, impose on other lawyers impossible, impractical or manifestly unfair conditions of trust, including those with respect to time restraints and the payment of penalty interest.

5. The lawyer should not use a tape-recorder or other device to record a conversation, whether with a client, another lawyer or anyone else, even if lawful, without first informing the other person of the intention to do so.[5]

6. The lawyer should answer with reasonable promptness all professional letters and communications from other lawyers that require an answer and should be punctual in fulfilling all commitments.[6]

Undertakings

7. The lawyer should give no undertaking that cannot be fulfilled, should fulfill every undertaking given, and should scrupulously honour any trust condition once accepted. Undertakings and trust conditions should be written or confirmed in writing and should be absolutely unambiguous in their terms. If the lawyer giving an undertaking does not intend to accept personal responsibility, this should be stated clearly in the undertaking itself. In the absence of such a statement, the person to whom the undertaking is given is entitled to expect that the lawyer giving it will honour it personally.[7] If the lawyer is unable or unwilling to honour a trust condition imposed by someone else, the subject of the trust condition should be immediately returned to the person imposing the trust condition unless its terms can be forthwith amended in writing on a mutually agreeable basis.

8. The lawyer should not communicate upon or attempt to negotiate or compromise a matter directly with any party who is represented by a lawyer except through or with the consent of that lawyer.[8]

Acting Against Another Lawyer

9. The lawyer should avoid ill-considered or uninformed criticism of the competence, conduct, advice or charges of other lawyers, but should be prepared, when requested, to advise and represent a client in a complaint involving another lawyer.[9]

10. The same courtesy and good faith should characterize the lawyer's conduct toward lay persons lawfully representing others or themselves.

11. The lawyer who is retained by another lawyer as counsel or adviser in a particular matter should act only as counsel or adviser and respect the relationship between the other lawyer and the client.

NOTES

1. Cf. CBA-COD 167; CBA 4(1), (2), (4); Ont. 14; ABA ECs 7-37 and 7-38, DR 7-101(A)(1).

2. "...besides the duty which an attorney owes to the court and his client, he is bound as regards the opposite party and his professional brethren, to conduct his business with fairness and propriety.", *Dobie* v. *McFarlane* (1832), 2 U.C.Q.B. (O.S.) 285 at 323. See also N.B. D-4.

3. Cf. CBA 4(2); *Orkin* at pp. 131-32. N.B. D-4: "... it is the duty of counsel to 'try the merits of the cause and not to try each other'."

4. Cf. CBA 4(2); ABA ECs 7-38 and 7-39. "... the attorney, I think, is not bound to lay before his client every opportunity he may have of shutting out the other party from a hearing, nor bound to take or follow the direction of his client as to the degree of liberality which he shall observe in his practice.", per Robinson, C.J. in *Shaw et al.* v. *Nickerson* (1850), 7 U.C.Q.B. 541 at 544.

5. Cf. CBA 4(4), "Truth and not trickery, simplicity and not duplicity, candour and not craftiness in the conduct of legal affairs ...", per Chancellor Boyd in "Address on Legal Ethics" (1905) 4 Can. L. Rev. 85. ABA EC 7-38: "He should follow local customs of courtesy or practice, unless he gives timely notice to opposing counsel of his intention not to do so." The lawyer who intends to insist on "Peremptory Rules" should make this clear.

   "... [T]o build up a client's case on the slips of an opponent is not the duty of a professional man ... Solicitors do not do their duty to their clients by insisting upon the strict letter of their rights. That is the sort of thing which, if permitted, brings the administration of justice into odium.", per Middleton, J. in *Re Arthur and Town of Meaford* (1915), 34 O.L.R. 231 at 233-34 (Ont. H.C.).

   "... [W]e do not think that [the defendant's attorney's] conduct was marked with candor in not drawing the plaintiff's attorneys' notice to such objections in the procedure as he had or intended to insist upon until the day before the opening of the court at which the trial was to be had ...", per Gwynne, J. in *Cushman et al.* v. *Reid* (1869), 20 U.C.C.P. 147 at 153-54.

   As to tape recordings, see (1972) 6 Law Soc. U.C. Gaz. 15.

6. Alta. 20: "Failure to reply to letters or other communications from another member is at the very least discourteous ... this practice frequently places the other member in an awkward and embarrassing position ... and tends to lower the reputation of the whole profession."

7. Cf. paragraph 11 of the Rule relating to the lawyer as advocate; Ont. 14(6); Alta. 17: "... [T]he use of such words as 'on behalf of my client' or 'on behalf of the vendor' does not relieve the solicitor giving the undertaking of personal responsibility." B.C. D-2: "... [D]ifficulties may arise if [members] give undertakings on behalf of clients since clients may change instructions or solicitors. An undertaking given by one solicitor to another can be released or altered only by the latter and not by his client. The giving of an uncertified cheque is an undertaking, except in the most unusual and unforeseen circumstances the justification for which rests upon the member, that such cheque will be paid ...".

8. Cf. CBA 4(3); B.C. D-1(a); Alta. 16; N.B. D-3; ABA EC 7-18; *Nelson* v. *Murphy et al.* (1957), 9 D.L.R. (2d) 195 (Man. C.A.) per Tritschler, J.A. at p. 213: "The principle was laid down long ago ... that once it appears a person has an attorney there can be no effective dealing except through him ... a lawyer 'should never in any way ... attempt to negotiate or compromise the matter directly with any party represented by a lawyer except *through* such lawyer'."

   "... [The lawyer should] not hold any communication of the kind that passed here, except with the solicitor of the opposite party, and even had the defendants come to the office of then plaintiff's solicitor, as the latter alleges, of his own accord, he should have refused to negotiate with him personally", per Van Koughnet, C. in *Bank of Montreal* v. *Wilson* (1867), 2 Chy. Chs. 117 and 119 (U.C. Chy. Chs. 117 and 119 (U.C. Chy.).

9. Cf. CBA 5(1); IBA C-4; ABA EC 2-28; *Orkin* at pp. 97-98. See also paragraph 9 of the Rule relating to making legal services available.

CHAPTER XVII

PRACTICE BY UNAUTHORIZED PERSONS

RULE

The lawyer should assist in preventing the unauthorized practice of law.[1]

Commentary

Guiding Principles

1. Statutory provisions against the practice of law by unauthorized persons are for the protection of the public. Unauthorized persons may have technical or personal ability, but they are immune from control, regulation and, in the case of misconduct, from discipline by any governing body. Their competence and integrity have not been vouched for by an independent body representative of the legal profession. Morever, the client of a lawyer who is authorized to practise has the protection and benefit of the lawyer-client privilege, the lawyer's duty of secrecy, the professional standards of care that the law requires of lawyers, as well as the authority that the courts exercise over them. Other safeguards include group professional liability insurance, rights with respect to the taxation of bills, rules respecting trust monies, and requirements for the maintenance of compensation funds.[2]

Suspended or Disbarred Persons

2. The lawyer should not, without the approval of the governing body, employ in any capacity having to do with the practice of law (a) a lawyer who is under suspension as a result of disciplinary proceedings, or (b) a person who has been disbarred as a lawyer or has been permitted to resign while facing disciplinary proceedings and has not been reinstated.[3]

Supervision of Employees

3. The lawyer must assume complete professional responsibility for all business entrusted to the lawyer, maintaining direct supervision over staff and assistants such as students, clerks and legal assistants to whom particular tasks and functions may be delegated. The lawyer who practises

alone or operates a branch or part-time office should ensure that all matters requiring a lawyer's professional skill and judgement are dealt with by a lawyer qualified to do the work and that legal advice is not given by unauthorized persons, whether in the lawyer's name or otherwise. Furthermore, the lawyer should approve the amount of any fee to be charged to a client.[4]

Legal Assistants

4. There are many tasks that can be performed by a legal assistant working under the supervision of a lawyer. It is in the interests of the profession and the public for the delivery of more efficient, comprehensive and better quality legal services that the training and employment of legal assistants be encouraged.

5. Subject to general and specific restrictions that may be established by local rules and practice, a legal assistant may perform any task delegated and supervised by a lawyer so long as the lawyer maintains a direct relationship with the client and assumes full professional responsibility for the work. Legal assistants shall not perform any of the duties that lawyers only may perform or do things that lawyers themselves may not do. Generally speaking, the question of what the lawyer may delegate to a legal assistant turns on the distinction between the special knowledge of the legal assistant and the professional legal judgement of the lawyer, which must be exercised whenever it is required.

6. A legal assistant should be permitted to act only under the supervision of a lawyer. Adequacy of supervision will depend on the type of legal matter, including the degree of standardization and repetitiveness of the matter as well as the experience of the legal assistant, both generally and with regard to the particular matter. The burden rests on the lawyer who employs a legal assistant to educate the latter about the duties to which the legal assistant may be assigned and also to supervise on a continuing basis the way in which the legal assistant carries them out so that the work of the legal assistant will be shaped by the lawyer's judgement.

NOTES

1. Cf. CBA-COD 15; CBA 5(1), (2); IBA E-5 and E-6; ABA-MR 5.5; ABA Canon 3, DRs 3-101 (A), (B) and 3-103(2).
2. Cases and statutes provide that certain acts amount to "the practice of law"; see, for example:
   B.C.: *Barristers and Solicitors Act*, R.S.B.C. 1979, c. 26, ss. 1, 80.
   Man.: *Law Society Act*, R.S.M. 1970, c. L-100, s. 48(1), (2).
   N.B.: *Barristers Society Act*, S.N.B. 1931, c. 50, s. 14A as amended by S.N.B. 1937, c. 30.
   Nfld.: *Law Society Act*, R.S.N. 1970, c. 201, s. 76(2).
   N.S.: *Barristers and Solicitors Act*, R.S.N.S. c. B-2, s. 4(2).
   P.E.I.: *Law Society and Legal Profession Act*, R.S.P.E.I. 1974, c. L-9, s. 21.

Que.: *Bar Act*, R.S.Q. 1977, c. B-1, s. 128.
The statutes of all provinces prohibit the practice of law by unauthorized persons:
Alta.: *Legal Profession Act*, R.S.A. c. L-9, s. 93.
B.C.: *supra*, s. 77.
Man.: *supra*, s. 48(1).
N.B.: *supra*, s. 14(3).
Nfld.: *supra*, s. 76(1).
N.S.: *supra*, s. 4(1).
Ont.: *Law Society Act*, R.S.O. 1980, c. 233, s. 50(1), (2).
P.E.I.: *supra*, s. 19.
Que.: *supra*, ss. 132 et seq.
Sask.: *Legal Profession Act*, R.S.S. c. L-10, s. 5.
"To protect the public against persons who . . . set themselves up as competent to perform services that imperatively require the training and learning of a solicitor, although such persons are without either learning or experience to qualify them, is an urgent public service.", per Robertson, C.J.O. in *Rex ex rel. Smith* v. *Ott* (1950) O.R. 493 at 496 (Ont. C.A.)
"When a man says in effect, I am not a lawyer but I will do the work of a lawyer for you he is offering his services as a lawyer. In offering his services as a lawyer he is holding himself out as a lawyer even though he makes it clear he is not a properly qualified lawyer.", per Miller, C.C.J. in *Regina* v. *Woods* (1962), O.W.N. 27 at 30.
See, generally, *Orkin* at pp. 350-53, *Bennion* at p. 54.

3. Cf. Ont. 19, 20; B.C. F-4. In cases of hardship or illness and for other good cause governing bodies may well permit regulated and limited employment, for example to help rehabilitate an offender or one recovering from a disability. Their concern is to protect the public, not necessarily to inhibit individuals.

4. Cf. B.C. G-2; Alta. 40; IBA E-4 and E-6; ABA ECs 3-5 and 3-6. See also "Delegation of Authority by Solicitors" (1968) 3 Law Soc. U.C. Gaz. 23.

CHAPTER XVIII

PUBLIC APPEARANCES AND PUBLIC STATEMENTS BY LAWYERS

RULE

The lawyer who engages in public appearances and public statements should do so in conformity with the principles of the Code.

Commentary

Guiding Principles

1. The lawyer who makes public appearances and public statements should behave in the same way as when dealing with clients, fellow practitioners and the courts. Dealings with the media are simply an extension of the lawyer's conduct in a professional capacity. The fact that an appearance is outside a courtroom or law office does not excuse conduct that would be considered improper in those contexts.

Public Statements Concerning Clients

2. The lawyer's duty to the client demands that before making a public statement concerning the client's affairs, the lawyer must first be satisfied that any communication is in the best interests of the client and within the scope of the retainer. The lawyer owes a duty to the client to be qualified to represent the client effectively before the public and not to permit any personal interest or other cause to conflict with the client's interests.

3. When acting as an advocate, the lawyer should refrain from expressing personal opinions about the merits of the client's case.

Standard of Conduct

4. The lawyer should, where possible, encourage public respect for and try to improve the administration of justice. In particular, the lawyer should treat fellow practitioners, the courts and tribunals with respect, integrity and courtesy. Lawyers are subject to a separate and higher standard of conduct than that which might incur the sanction of the court.

5. The lawyer who makes public appearances and public statements

must comply with the requirements of commentary 3 of the Rule relating to advertising, solicitation and making legal services available.

Contacts with the Media

6. The media have recently shown greater interest in legal matters than they did formerly. This is reflected in more coverage of the passage of legislation at national and provincial levels, as well as of cases before the courts that may have social, economic or political significance. This interest has been heightened by the enactment of the *Canadian Charter of Rights and Freedoms*. As a result, media reporters regularly seek out the views not only of lawyers directly involved in particular court proceedings but also of lawyers who represent special interest groups or have recognized expertise in a given field in order to obtain information or provide commentary.

7. Where the lawyer, by reason of professional involvement or otherwise, is able to assist the media in conveying accurate information to the public, it is proper for the lawyer to do so, provided that there is no infringement of the lawyer's obligations to the client, the profession, the courts or the administration of justice, and provided also that the lawyer's comments are made *bona fide* and without malice or ulterior motive.

8. The lawyer may make contact with the media in a non-legal setting to publicize such things as fund-raising, expansion of hospitals or universities, promoting public instiitutions or political organizations, or speaking on behalf of organizations that represent various racial, religious or other special interest groups. This is a well-established and completely proper role for the lawyer to play in view of the obvious contribution it makes to the community.

9. The lawyer is often called upon to comment publicly on the effectiveness of existing statutory or legal remedies, on the effect of particular legislation or decided cases, or to offer an opinion on causes that have been or are about to be instituted. It is permissible to do this in order to assist the public to understand the legal issues involved.

10. The lawyer may also be involved as an advocate for special interest groups whose objective is to bring about changes in legislation, government policy or even a heightened public awareness about certain issues, and the lawyer may properly comment publicly about such changes.

11. Given the variety of cases that can arise in the legal system, whether in civil, criminal or administrative matters, it is not feasible to set down guidelines that would anticipate every possible situation. In some circumstances, the lawyer should have no contact at all with the media; in others, there may be a positive duty to contact the media in order to serve the client properly. The latter situation will arise more often when dealing with administrative boards and tribunals that are instruments of government policy and hence susceptible to public opinion.

12. The lawyer should bear in mind when making a public appearance or giving a statement that ordinarily the lawyer will have no control over any editing that may follow, or the context in which the appearance or statement may be used.

13. This Rule should not be construed in such a way as to discourage constructive comment or criticism.

CHAPTER XIX

AVOIDING QUESTIONABLE CONDUCT

RULE

The lawyer should observe the rules of professional conduct set out in the Code in the spirit as well as in the letter.[1]

Commentary

Guiding Principles

1. Public confidence in the administration of justice and the legal profession may be eroded by irresponsible conduct on the part of the individual lawyer. For that reason, even the appearance of impropriety should be avoided.[2]

2. Our justice system is designed to try issues in an impartial manner and decide them upon the merits. Statements or suggestions that the lawyer could or would try to circumvent the system should be avoided because they might bring the lawyer, the legal profession and the administration of justice into disrepute.[3]

Duty after Leaving Public Employment

3. After leaving public employment, the lawyer should not accept employment in connection with any matter in which the lawyer had substantial responsibility or confidential information prior to leaving, because to do so would give the appearance of impropriety even if none existed. However, it would not be improper for the lawyer to act professionally in such a matter on behalf of the particular public body or authority by which the lawyer had formerly been employed.[4] As to confidential government information acquired when the lawyer was a public officer or employee, see commentary 14 of the Rule relating to confidential information.

Retired Judges

4. A judge who returns to practice after retiring or resigning from the bench should not (without the approval of the governing body) appear as a lawyer before the court of which the former judge was a member or before

courts of inferior jurisdiction thereto in the province where the judge exercised judicial functions. If in a given case the former judge should be in a preferred position by reason of having held judicial office, the administration of justice would suffer; if the reverse were true, the client might suffer. There may, however, be cases where a governing body would consider that no preference or appearance of preference would result, for example, where the judge resigned for good reason after only a very short time on the bench. In this paragraph "judge" refers to one who was apppointed as such under provincial legislation or section 96 of the *Constitution Act, 1982* and "courts" include chambers and administrative boards and tribunals.[5]

5. Conversely, although it may be unavoidable in some circumstances or areas, generally speaking the lawyer should not appear before a judge if by reason of relationship or past association, the lawyer would appear to be in a preferred position.[6]

Inserting Retainer in Client's Will

6. Without express instructions from the client, it is improper for the lawyer to insert in the client's will a clause directing the executor to retain the lawyer's services in the administration of the estate.[7]

Duty to Meet Financial Obligations

7. The lawyer has a professional duty, quite apart from any legal liability, to meet financial obligations incurred or assumed in the course of practice when called upon to do so. Examples are agency accounts, obligations to members of the profession, fees or charges of witnesses, sheriffs, special examiners, registrars, reporters and public officials as well as the deductible under a governing body's errors and omissions insurance policy.[8]

Dealings with Unrepresented Persons

8. The lawyer should not undertake to advise an unrepresented person, but should urge such a person to obtain independent legal advice and, if the unrepresented person does not do so, the lawyer must take care to see that such person is not proceeding under the impression that the lawyer is protecting such person's interests. If the unrepresented person requests the lawyer to advise or act in the matter, the lawyer should be governed by the considerations outlined in the Rule relating to impartiality and conflict of interest between clients.[9] The lawyer may have an obligation to a person whom the lawyer does not represent, whether or not such person is represented by a lawyer.

Bail

9. The lawyer shall not stand bail for an accused person for whom the lawyer or a partner or associate is acting, except where there is a family

relationship with the accused in which case the person should not be represented by the lawyer but may be represented by a partner or associate.

Standard of Conduct

10. The lawyer should try at all times to observe a standard of conduct that reflects credit on the legal profession and the administration of justice generally and inspires the confidence, respect and trust of both clients and the community.

NOTES

1. Cf. CBA-COD 17; CBA 5(6): ". . . [T]he oath of office . . . is not a mere form, but is a solemn undertaking." ABA Canon 9: "A lawyer should avoid even the appearance of professional impropriety."
   Cf. dictum of Hewart, L.C.J. in *The King* v. *Sussex Justices* (1924), 1 K.B. 256 at 259 (K.B.D.): ". . . [It] is of fundamental importance that justice should not only be done, but should manifestly and undoubtedly be seen to be done."
2. Cf. ABA EC 9-1. In *Re Novak and Law Society* (1973) 31 D.L.R. (3d) 89 (B.C.S.C.) (sustaining the disbarment of a lawyer who had negotiated a reward through the police for the return of stolen securities) the Discipline Committee said (at p. 95): "In exposing himself to these situations the Respondent divested himself of the dignity and forthright dealing that one may expect of a lawyer, gave rise to the reasonable conclusion that he was associated with the possessors of the goods, and that he was participating in some way in the reward . . . . Whether in fact he was doing so is perhaps not important."
3. Cf. ABA EC 9-4: "There should be the very contrary to the secrecy and subterfuge which marks every step of this transaction, dishonourable alike to counsel and the magistrate.", per Baxter, C.J. in *The King* v. *LeBlanc and Long* (1938-39) 13 M.P.R. 343 at 357 (N.B. App. Div.).
4. Cf. ABA DR 9-101(B).
5. Cf. Ont. 15: ". . . [I]f a man should step down [from the Bench] and . . . perhaps challenge the decisions which he pronounced, or even fail to support them in argument, he will shake the authority of the judicial limb of government, and mar the prestige and dignity of the Courts of Justice . . .", per Kennedy, C.J. in *Re Solicitors Act and O'Connor* (1930) I.R. 623 at 631 (Irish H.C.).
6. Cf. paragraph 1(c) of the Rule relating to the lawyer as advocate; *Orkin* at p. 43.
7. Cf. Alta. 28. Such a direction does not bind the executor: *Re Croft* (1960) O.W.N. 171 (Ont. H.C.).
8. Art. 19 of the International Code of Ethics provides: "A lawyer who engages a foreign colleague to advise on a case or to cooperate in handling it, is responsible for the payment of the latter's charges except express agreement to the contrary. When a lawyer directs a client to a foreign colleague he is not responsible . . .". Cf. also IBA D-10.
9. Cf. *Orkin* at pp. 127-28.
   "In every case where there is the least doubt . . . as to whether the other party is capable of protecting himself, it is the duty of [the] solicitor . . . to see, if possible, that the other party is adequately represented; and, in the absence of such independent representation, it is the duty of the Court to scrutinize . . . to see whether . . . there has been any overreaching or unconscionable dealing.", per

Orde, J. in *Chait & Leon* v. *Harding* (1920-21) 19 O.W.N. 20 at 21 (Ont. H.C.). "It was [the solicitor's] duty to see that the infirm person was adequately protected or had independent advice. If [he] regarded himself as the adviser of the aged plaintiff, he should have insisted that proper arrangements protecting [him] were entered into . . .", per Middleton, J. in *Finney* v. *Tripp* (1922) 22 O.W.N. 429 at 430 (Ont. H.C.).

CHAPTER XX

NON-DISCRIMINATION

RULE

The lawyer shall respect the requirements of human rights and constitutional laws in force in Canada, and in the respective provinces and territories thereof, and shall not discriminate on grounds, including, but not limited to, of race, language, national or ethnic origin, colour, religion, age, sex, sexual orientation, marital status, family status, or disability.

Commentary

Duty of Non-Discrimination

1. The lawyer has a duty to respect the dignity and worth of all persons and to treat persons equally, without discrimination. Discrimination is defined as any distinction that disproportionately and negatively impacts on an individual or group identifiable by the grounds listed in the Rule, in a way that it does not impact on others. This duty includes, but is not limited to:

(a) the requirement that the lawyer does not deny services or provide inferior services on the basis of the grounds noted in the rule;
(b) the requirement that the lawyer not discriminate against another lawyer in any professional dealings;
(c) the requirement that the lawyer act in accordance with the legal duty to accommodate and not engage in discriminatory emloyment practices; and
(d) the requirement that the lawyer prohibit partners, co-workers and employees and agents subject to the lawyer's direction and control from engaging in discriminatory practices.

Extent of Duty of Non-Discrimination

2. As a member of the legal profession, the lawyer must ensure that he or she is at all times acting in compliance with the law. The law applicable in this context is human rights legislation. According to the law, discrimination can be constituted by the effect of action or omission.

Intent to discriminate is not a prerequisite to a finding of discrimination. Discrimination can also arise though the adverse impact of neutral practices on the basis of the grounds noted in the Rule. Failure by the lawyer to take reasonable steps to prevent or stop discrimination by the lawyer's partner, co-worker or by any employee or agent also violates the duty of non-discrimination.

Special Programs

3. Discrimination does not include special programs designed to relieve disadvantage for individuals or groups on the grounds noted in the Rule.

Responsibility

4. Discriminatory attitudes on the part of partners, employees, agents or clients do not diminish the responsibility of the lawyer to refrain from discrimination in the provision of service or employment.

Discrimination in Employment

5. The Rule applies to discrimination by the lawyers in any aspect of employment and working conditions, including recruitment, promotion, training, allocation of work, compensation, receipt of benefits, dismissal, lay-offs, discipline, performance appraisal and hours of work.

It applies to all discrimination with repercussions for employment and workplace conditions including physical work sites, washrooms, conferences, business travel and social events. Examples of discrimination in employment include:

a) setting unnecessary or unfair hiring criteria that tend to exclude applicants on prohibited grounds;
b) asking questions during an employment or promotion interview that are not logically related to the essential requirements of the job;
c) assigning work on the basis of factors or assumptions other than individual ability or denying work to lawyers on the basis of prohibited grounds;
d) failing to provide appropriate maternity and parental leave thereby discriminating on the basis of sex or family status;
e) failing to accommodate religious holidays or religious practices thereby discriminating on the basis of religion;
f) requiring billable hour targets or workload expectations which effectively exclude those who have child care responsibilities and adversely affect such persons on the basis of family status or sex.

ABBREVIATIONS

Short-form references to Canons, Codes, Rulings and particular writings are as follows:

Alta	Rulings of the Benchers of the Law Society of Alberta, contained in the *Professional Conduct Handbook* published by that Society at Calgary in 1968, as amended.
ABA	*Code of Professional Responsibility* of the American Bar Association (Chicago), adopted with effect from January 1, 1970. The ABA is divided into Canons, Ethical Considerations (ECs) and Disciplinary Rules (DRs).
ABA-MR	*Model Rules of Professional Conduct* of the American Bar Association, adopted August 2, 1983.
Bennion	F.A.R., *Professional Ethics, The Consultation Professions and Their Code* (London: Charles Knight, 1969).
B.C.	Rulings of the Benchers of the Law Society of British Columbia contained in the *Professional Conduct Handbook* published by that Society at Vancouver in 1970, as amended.
CBA	*Canons of Legal Ethics* of the Canadian Bar Association adopted in 1920.
CBA-COD	*Code of Professional Conduct* of the Canadian Bar Association adopted in 1974.
IBA	*Professional Ethics*, by Sir Thomas Lund, being Book II of the International Bar Association published in 1970 by that Association (London: Sweet & Maxwell). IBA includes as an Appendix the "International Code of Ethics" of the International Bar Association adopted in 1956, as amended.
N.B.	Rules of the Barristers' Society of New Brunswick contained in the *Professional Conduct Handbook* published by that Society at Fredericton in 1971, as amended.
Ont.	Rules of Professional Conduct of the Law Society of Upper Canada contained in the *Professional Conduct Handbook* published by that Society at Toronto in 1987, as amended.
Orkin	M.M., *Legal Ethics: A Study of Professional Conduct* (Toronto: Cartwright & Jane, 1957).
Que.	*Code of Advocates*, An Act respecting the Barreau du Québec, R.S.Q. c. B-1, s. 15.
Sask.	*Canons of Legal Ethics and Etiquette* of the Law Society of Saskatchewan, published by the Benchers of that Society at Regina in 1962, as amended.

BIBLIOGRAPHY

The following is a selected bibliography of texts and other sources helpful to those concerned with matters within the general ambit of this Code:

Arthurs, H.W. and Bucknall, B.D.: *Bibliographies on the Legal Profession & Legal Education in Canada.* (1968, York University, Toronto).

Bennion, F.A.R., *supra.* For further bibliographies see at p. 238-40.

Boulton, W.W.: *Conduct and Etiquette at the Bar.* (1971 (5th ed.), Butterworths, London).

Cordery on Solicitors (6th ed. 1968; 7th ed. 1981, Butterworths, London).

Drinker, H.: *Legal Ethics.* (1965) Columbia U.P., New York).

Johnston, Q., and Hopson, D.: *Lawyers and Their Work* (1967, Bobbs-Merrill, Indianapolis).

Lund, Sir T.: *A Guide to the Professional Conduct and Etiquette of Solicitors.* (1960, The Law Society, London).

Maru, O., and Clough, R. L.: *Digest of Bar Association Ethics Opinions.* (1970, American Bar Foundation, Chicago).

Mathews, R. E.: *Problems Illustrative of the Responsibilities of Members of the Legal Profession* (2nd ed., Council on Legal Education for Professional Responsibility, New York). For further bibliographies see at pp. xii-xiv.

Orkin, M.M., *supra.* For further bibliographies see at pp. 295-96.

Pirsig, M.: *Professional Responsibility* (1970, West, St. Paul, Minn.).

Trumball, W.M.: *Materials on the Lawyer's Professional Responsibility.* (1957, Little, Brown, Boston).

Index

[All references are to part numbers]

Access to justice
generally 9
legal aid 9
legal benefits plans 9
pro bono work 9

Adjournments
discipline proceedings 26.13

Admission to the bar
generally 23.1
good character requirement
alternatives 23.3
application 23.3
definition 23.3
examples 23.3
history 23.3
purposes 23.3
readmission to the bar 26.22
substantive and procedural requirements 23.3
compared to discipline proceedings 23.3
vagueness 23.3

Adversary system
confidentiality 2.3
duty of professional detachment 2.3, 4.2
duty to court 2.1
excesses of 2.1, 4.1
on discovery 4.6
justifications 2.3
protection of individual rights 2.3
search for truth 2.3
partisanship 2.3
prisoner's dilemma 2.3
public perception 2.2
reforms in civil procedure 2.4
sporting theory of justice 2.1

Advertising
freedom of expression 10
generally 10

Advising clients. *See also* **Counselling** 14
allegations of fraud 4.4
concerning possible litigation 4.4
generally 14
non-legal advice 20.4
moral advice 20.4
tax 19

Advocacy
control of 4.22
contempt citations 4.22
cost awards 4.22
disciplinary sanctions 4.22
evidentiary and procedural rulings 4.22
ethics of 4.1

Agreements guaranteeing recovery (Mary Carter agreements)
duty of lawyer to disclose 4.21

Alternative dispute resolution 2.1, 2.4, 4.8, 16

See also **Mediation**

American Bar Association Model Code of Professional Responsibility 25.2

American Bar Association Model Rules of Professional Conduct 25.2

Appeals
discipline proceedings 26.19
stay pending appeal 26.19

Argument
forensic excesses 4.16
personal opinions 4.2, 4.16, 4.19
lawyers' duties 4.16
adverse authorities 4.16

Articling
duties of principals 25.12
duties of students 25.12

Barrister's oath 4.2

Bias
discipline proceedings 26.11
See also **Discipline proceedings,** bias

Borrowing from clients 22.3, 25.4

Branch offices
supervision by lawyer 25.9

Burden of proof. *See* **Discipline proceedings**

Canadian Bar Association Code of Professional Conduct 25.2
adoption by Law Societies 25.2

Character. *See* **Admission to the bar**

Character evidence 26.17

Charter of Rights and Freedoms
discipline proceedings 26.2
  section 2(b) 26.9
  section 7, 26.2, 26.4, 26.10, 26.15
  section 8, 26.4
  section 11 26.2, 26.10, 26.15
  section 13 26.15

Civility
duty of courtesy and good faith 4.7, 8
generally 8
regulating through rules of professional conduct 8

Class actions
conflicts of interest 5.12
permissibility of contingency fees in Ontario 12

Client property
preservation and safekeeping 25.3

Clients under disability 25.14

Code of Conduct for Lawyers in European Community 3.1, 3.6

Commercialism 1.3, 1.5

Competence and quality of service
continuing legal education 24.3
disciplinary action 24.1, 24.2
estates administration 18.5
generally 24.1, 24.8
house counsel 20.2
insurance loss prevention programmes 24.4
judicial intervention 24.7
practice review programmes 24.5
rules of professional conduct 24.1
  maintaining competence 24.1
  unsatisfactory professional practice 24.1
solicitors' negligence litigation 24.6

Competency hearings 26.21

Complaints to law societies. *See* **Discipline proceedings,** investigations

Conduct unbecoming a barrister and solicitor
criminal convictions 26.8
definition 26.8
effect of categorization 26.8
insurance 26.8

Confidentiality
adversary system 2.3
balancing other interests 3.6
communications with professionals other than lawyers 3.2
  psychotherapists 3.2, 3.5
  religious advisors 3.2
corporate clients 3.3
  whistleblowing 20.6
duration of duty 3.2
  death of client 3.2
  termination of retainer 3.2
estates 18.4
ethical duty 3.2
  compared to evidentiary
  rule of solicitor-client privilege 3.2
  indiscreet conversations 3.2
exceptions to rule
  future crime 3.4
  malpractice and misconduct proceedings 3.5
  proceedings to collect legal fees 3.5

explanation of principle to clients 4.4
generally 3.1, 3.2
identity of client 3.2

Confidentiality—*Continued*
lawyers' duties 3.2
  not to divulge information 3.2
  not to use information
  for own benefit or benefit of other clients 3.2
medical-legal reports 4.5
rule 3.2
solicitor-client privilege 3.2
  requirements 3.2
waiver 3.2
  by mistake 3.2
when may be raised 3.2
  execution of search warrant 3.2
Wigmore test 3.2

Conflicts of interest. *See also* **Conflicts of interest in litigation, Corporate counsel, Criminal defence, Estates, Government lawyers, Mediation** and **Real estate**

acting for multiple parties 22.2
  non-consentable conflicts of interest 22.2
  variables 22.2
between clients 22.2
  consent 22.2
  disclosure 22.2
between lawyer and client 22.3
  borrowing from clients 22.3
  business transactions 22.3
  gifts from clients 22.3
  independent legal advice or representation 22.3
  investments in which lawyer interested 22.3
disciplinary proceedings 22.2
errors and omissions 22.5
  duty to client 22.5
  duty to insurer 22.5
generally 22.1
independence of the bar 27.4
negligence claims
  from clients 22.2
  from non-clients 22.4

Conflicts of interest in litigation 5.1
acting against current clients in unrelated litigation 5.4
acting against former clients 5.6
  delay in bringing disqualification motion 5.6
acting against former co-clients and co-parties 5.7
acting for adverse parties in same litigation 5.3
  uncontested divorce actions 5.3
acting for co-parties in same litigation 5.5
  employers and employees 5.5
appearance of impropriety standard 5.2
class actions 5.12
derivative proceedings 5.3
imputed disqualification 5.10
  C.B.A. and Law Society recommendations on
screening devices 5.10
  conflict information systems 5.10
indemnity insurance litigation 5.14
issue conflicts between clients 5.8
lawyer-client conflicts of interest 5.9
  contingency fees 12
  married, engaged, co- habiting, dating lawyers 5.9
motions for disqualification 5.2
orders
  effect of delay 5.6
  tactical motivations 5.2, 5.6, 5.10
payment of fees by non-clients 5.11
procedural conflicts between clients 5.8
unions 5.13

Contempt of court
affronts to judicial authority 4.22(b)
criticizing decisions of courts 4.22(b)
defiance of judicial authority 4.22(b)
disruption of judicial proceedings 4.22(b)
double booking 4.22(b)
failure to attend in court 4.22(b)
inflammatory language 4.22(b)
interference with pending judicial proceedings 4.22(b)

Contingency fees
agreements 12
  termination 12
    right of lawyer to compensation 12
arguments for and against 12
Canadian fee-shifting cost system 12
class actions in Ontario 12
criminal proceedings 12
definition 12
generally 12
lawyer-client conflicts of interest 12
matrimonial proceedings 12
permissibility in Canadian, British, and American jurisdictions 12
review by court 12

Continuing legal education 24.3

Corporate counsel
conflicts of interest
  between affiliated companies 20.5
  between corporation and agents 20.5
  minority interests 20.5
  parent and subsidiary 20.5
  sister companies 20.5
generally 20.1
house counsel 20.1
  independence 20.1
  moonlighting 20.2
    competence and quality of service 20.2
    conflicts of interest 20.2
    responsibility to Law Society 20.3
  non-legal advice 20.4
    moral advice 20.4
  professional duties 20.1
    outside counsel compared 20.1
  whistleblowing 20.6
  who is the client? 20.5
    duty owed to shareholders 20.5

Cost awards against lawyers personally 4.17, 4.22(a), 27.5

Costs (discipline proceedings) 26.18.1

Counsel's liability in negligence
arguments favouring liability 4.18
conduct of case in court 4.18
justification for English immunity rule 4.18
pre-trial work 4.18

Counselling
duty of objectivity 14
duty to inform client upon discovering error 14
duty to inform insurer upon discovering error 14
generally 14
independent legal advice or representation 14
  lawyer's duty 14
lawyer's duties in advising clients 14
  advising on limits of law 14
  encouraging fraud or illegality 14
  non-legal questions 14
legal opinions for third parties 14

Criminal defence
confidentiality duties 7.2
conflicts of interest 7.6
  effective assistance of counsel 7.6
  representation of co-accused 7.6
criminal record 7.1
  duty to disclose 7.1
cross-examining the truthful witness 7.4
duty not to destroy or conceal physical evidence 7.3
general 7.1
perjury of client 7.5
plea bargaining 7.7
withdrawal as counsel 7.8

Criminal proceedings. *See* **Discipline proceedings,** parallel criminal proceedings

Criminal record
duty to disclose 7.1

Cross-examination
credibility 4.14
duty to give witness opportunity to explain conflicting evidence 4.14
duty not to abuse or harass witnesses 4.14
duty not to attack witnesses' character 4.14

Cross-examination—*Continued*
truthful witnesses
civil cases 4.14
criminal cases
defence 7.1, 7.2, 7.4
prosecution 4.14, 6.6

Crown Attorneys. *See* **Prosecuting, Discipline proceedings, Delay**
as tactic in litigation 4.9
duty of lawyer to avoid 4.9
estates administration 18.5
generally 25.9
real estate 17.2
reasons for 4.9

Derivative proceedings
conflicts of interest 5.13

Disability, Client Under 25.14

Disbarment 26.17
See also **Discipline proceedings,** penalty

Discipline proceedings
adjournments 26.13
American experience 27.6
appeals 26.19
stay pending appeal 26.19
bias 26.11
disqualification for
reasonable apprehension of bias 26.11
test 26.11
waiver 26.11
burden and standard of proof 26.2, 26.16
effect of solicitor's failure to testify 26.16
review on appeal 26.16
Charter of Rights and Freedoms 26.2
See also **Charter of Rights and Freedoms**
civil or criminal? 26.2
disclosure pending hearing 26.6
conduct unbecoming a barrister and solicitor. *See* **Conduct unbecoming a barrister and solicitor**
conflicts of interest 22.2
costs 26.18.1
criminal convictions 26.17
Crown Attorneys 26.20
independence of attorney-general 26.20
decision 26.18
defences
insanity 26.17
delay 26.10
discourtesy in litigation 4.22(c)
disclosure pending hearing 26.6
duty to act judicially 26.12
right to cross-examine 26.12
right to notice of hearing 26.12
ethics schools 26.17
evidence 26.2
character evidence 26.17
compellability of solicitor 26.2
hearsay 26.12
rules in civil proceedings 26.2
transcripts of previous testimony 26.15
examples 26.17
fines 26.17
hearing in Convocation 26.19
hearings 26.9
in camera or in public 26.9
non-publication orders 26.9
impartiality of adjudicators 26.3
independence of Law Society's counsel 26.3
investigations 26.2, 26.4
confidentiality of complaints 26.4
disclosure to police
and other law enforcement agencies 26.4, 26.5
duty to co-operate 26.2
self-incrimination 26.2
privilege claims 26.4
judges 26.20
jurisdiction of law societies 26.20
judicial review 26.19
legislators 26.20
jurisdiction of law societies 26.20
misleading court 4.22(c)
parallel criminal proceedings 26.5
admissibility and effect of
conviction in discipline proceedings 26.5
disclosure to police and
other law enforcement agencies
stay pending determination of criminal proceedings 26.5

Discipline proceedings—*Continued*
penalty 26.17
  disbarment 26.17
  factors 26.17
  misappropriation 26.17
  mitigating circumstances 26.17
    character evidence 26.17
    disclosure of misconduct 26.17
    financial or matrimonial pressures 26.17
    remorse 26.17
    restitution 26.17
    substance abuse 26.17
  permission to resign 26.17
  reprimand 26.17
  suspension 26.17
procedural and substantive requirements
  contrasted with admission hearings 23.3
professional misconduct. *See* **Professional misconduct**
purposes 26.1
readmission 26.22
reasons 26.18
  participation of clerks in drafting reasons 26.18
suspensions
  interim 26.13
transcripts of previous testimony 26.15
tribunal's use of own expertise 26.14

Disclosure
by Crown 6.4

Disclosure pending hearing. *See* **Discipline proceedings,** disclosure pending hearing

Discovery
abuses 4.6, 8
  rules of civil procedure 4.6
production of documents 4.6
rules of civil procedure 4.6

Discrimination 25.15

Dismissal by client 4.10

Dissolution of law firms
duties to clients 4.10

Duty to client
resolute partisanship 2.1, 4.12

Duty to court 2.1, 4.12, 4.23

Duty to report misconduct 25.7

Effective assistance of counsel
effect of conflict of
interest 7.6

Employment of disbarred or suspended members 25.9

Errors and omissions
conflicts of interest 22.2, 22.5
duty to inform client 14
duty to inform insurer 14
insurance loss prevention programmes 24.4
solicitor's negligence litigation 24.6
  effect of categorizing
  misconduct as conduct unbecoming 26.8

Estates
competence and quality of service 18.5
  storing wills 18.5
confidentiality 18.4
conflicts of interest 18.3
  acting for multiple parties in
    administration of estates 18.3
    between executors and
      beneficiaries 18.3
    qua executor and
      qua lawyer 18.3
  loans and investments in which lawyer or other clients have interest 18.3
delegation to non-lawyers 18.5
testamentary capacity 18.1
undue influence 18.1
wills benefitting lawyers 18.2
  clauses directing executor to retain lawyer 18.2
  independent legal advice 18.2

Ethics schools 26.17

Evidence
discipline proceedings. *See* **Discipline proceedings**
physical
duty not to destroy or conceal 7.3

***Ex parte* proceedings**
lawyers' duty 4.20

Family law
mediation 16

Fees 25.5
contingency fees 12
See also **Contingency fees**
fairness of fees 25.5(a)
fee splitting 25.5(b)
with non-lawyers 25.5(b)
with lawyers 25.5(b)
hidden fees 25.5(a)
referral fees 25.5(b)
trust transfers 25.3, 25.5(a)

Fines 26.17
See also **Discipline proceedings,** penalty

Good character requirement. *See* **Admission to the bar**

Government lawyers
conflicts of interest 21.5
entering and leaving public service 21.5
imputed disqualification 5.10
generally 21.1
limitations on forensic strategies 21.3
whistleblowing 21.4
who is the client? 21.2

Gross negligence

discipline for 26.7

House counsel. *See* **Corporate counsel**

Incapacity proceedings 26.21

Incompetent clients
duty of lawyer for child 4.3
duty to litigation guardians 4.3
representation of children 4.3

Independence of the bar
American experience 27.6
from clients 27.3, 27.4
from the courts 27.3, 27.5
judicial discipline 27.5
orders requiring
lawyers to pay costs personally 27.5
from the state 27.2
self-governance 27.2
generally 27.1, 27.7
non-contentious matters 27.1, 27.3
rules of professional conduct 27.3

Independent legal advice or representation
lawyer's duty 14, 22.3

Instructions of clients
authority of lawyer to make tactical decisions 4.11
concerning settlement 4.8
duty to follow 4.11
inability to obtain 4.10

Insurance. *See also* **Errors and omissions**
indemnity insurance litigation
conflicts of interest 5.14
insurance loss prevention programmes 24.4

Integrity 26.7, 26.8

Interprovincial law firms 25.11

Investigations. *See* **Discipline proceedings**

Judges
controlling discovery abuse 4.6
criticism by lawyers 4.23, 25.6
neutrality
ex parte communications 4.23
lawyers' personal or business relationships 4.23
retired judges returning to practice 25.8
selection 2.1
See also **Discipline proceedings,** judges

Judicial review
discipline proceedings 26.19

Jurors
communication with 4.23

Lang Michener case 27.1

Law clerks. *See* **Delegation to non-lawyers**

Law societies
replies to communications 25.7

Lawyers
as witnesses 4.19
  evidence of counsel's partners and associates 4.19
  submitting own affidavit 4.19
  testifying at trial 4.19
duty to other lawyers individually 4.7
  adjournment requests 4.7
  courtesy and good faith 4.7
  slips and errors 4.7
education and training 1.2, 1.5
public perception 1.1, 2.2
qualities 1.1, 1.2, 1.5, 2.1
  competitiveness 1.2, 1.5, 2.1
  industry 1.1

Lawyers' ethics
commercialism 1.3
importance 1.4
improvement 1.5
legal education and training 1.2
public perception 1.1
public's ethics 2.2

Legal aid 9

Legal benefits plans 9

Legal education and training
articling students and principals 25.12
continuing legal education 24.3
professional responsibility 1.2, 1.5

Legislators. *See* **Discipline proceedings,** legislators

Letters
abusive, offensive, or unprofessional 25.7
replies to communications from governing body 25.7

Mary Carter Agreements. *See* **Agreements guaranteeing recovery**

Media
generally 13
lawyer communications with media 13
  attempts to influence courts and tribunals 13
  confidentiality duties 13
  freedom of expression 13
  improving public awareness 13
  lawyer's duty to be qualified to represent client in media 13
  obtaining client consent 13
prosecution press conferences 6.3

Mediation
advantages over litigation 16
conflicts of interest 16
family law 16
generally 16
preparation of settlement agreements 16
  independent legal advice 16
procedural and substantive fairness safeguards 16
when appropriate 16

Medical-legal reports 4.5

Misappropriation 26.17
penalty 26.17

Model Code of Professional Responsibility (A.B.A.) 25.2

Model Rules of Professional Conduct (A.B.A.) 25.2

Mortgage transactions
recommending investments 17.2
selling or arranging mortgages 17.2
syndicated mortgages 17.2

Negligence. *See* **Counsel's liability in negligence, errors and omissions**

Negotiation
disclosure obligations 15
generally 15
permissible representations 15
reasons for lack of regulation 15

Non-publication orders 26.9

Outside interests and the practice of law 25.10

penalty 26.17
See also **Discipline proceedings,** penalty

Perjury. *See* **Witnesses, Criminal defence**

Personal opinions. *See* **Argument, Prosecuting**

Physical evidence
duty not to destroy or conceal 7.3

Plea bargaining 6.5, 7.7

Practice review programmes 24.5

Prisoner's dilemma 2.3

***Pro bono* work** 9

Professional detachment 2.3, 4.2

Professional misconduct 26.7
definition 26.7
examples 26.7
failing to reply to Law Society 26.7
gross negligence 26.7
pattern of negligence 26.7

Professional responsibility
teaching 1.2, 1.5

Property
client property 25.3
  preservation and safekeeping 25.3

Prosecuting
adversarial and magisterial styles 6.7
charging decisions 6.3
disclosure 6.4
duty to do justice 6.1
impermissible tactics 6.6
  personal opinions 6.6
  prejudicial remarks 6.6
plea bargaining 6.5
  duty to fulfil bargain 6.5
  propriety of threat of further charges if plea bargain not accepted 6.5
press conferences 6.3
substantial likelihood of conviction test 6.3
who is the client? 6.2

Psychotherapists
confidentiality of patient communications 3.2, 3.5

Public appearances. *See* **Media**

Public hearings 26.9

Public office. *See* **Government lawyers**

Public statements. *See* **Media**

Readmission to the bar 26.22

Real estate
conflicts of interest 17.4
  simultaneous representation of multiple parties 17.4
    disclosure and consent 17.4
delegation to non-lawyers 17.2
generally 17.1
Mortgages. *See* **Mortgage transactions**
reporting letters 17.2
speculative real estate transactions 17.3
  spot audit programmes 17.3
  title searches 17.2
undertakings 17.5
  personal responsibility 17.5
unrepresented parties 17.4

Regulating lawyer competence. *See* **Competence and quality of service**

Reinstatement 26.22
See also **Readmission to the bar**

Religious advisors
confidentiality of communications 3.2

Reporting misconduct 25.7

Represented parties
duty of lawyers not to communicate directly 4.7, 4.12

Reprimand 26.17

See also **Discipline proceedings,** penalty

Resignation
permission to resign 26.17
See also **Discipline proceedings,** penalty

Retainer 4.2
right to decline employment 4.2
as justification for immunity in negligence 4.18
termination by client 4.10
termination by lawyer 4.10
See **Withdrawal as counsel**

Retired judges returning to practice 25.8

Right to decline employment 4.2
as justification for immunity in negligence 4.18

Rules of professional conduct
advertising. *See* **Advertising**
advising clients. *See* **Advising clients, Counselling**
application 25.2
articling students and principals 25.12
borrowing from clients 25.4
client property 25.3
preservation and safekeeping 25.3
clients under disability 25.14
competence and quality of service 24.1
maintaining competence 24.1
unsatisfactory professional practice 24.1
confidentiality. *See* **Confidentiality**
conflicts of interest. *See* **Conflicts of interest**
delegation to non-lawyers 25.9
discrimination 25.15
fees. *See* **Fees**
generally 25.1, 25.2
history 25.2
independence of the bar 27.3
integrity 26.7, 26.8
interprovincial law firms 25.11
lawyers and the administration of justice 25.6
allegations of corruption, partiality 25.6
criticism of courts, judgments 25.6
lawyers as mediators. *See* **Mediation**
lawyers in public office. *See* **Government lawyers**
medical-legal reports. *See* **Medical-legal reports**
mortgage transactions. *See* **Mortgage transactions**
nature 25.2
outside interests and the practice of law 25.10
practice by unauthorized persons 25.9
See **Unauthorized practice of law**
public appearances and statements. *See* **Media**
purposes 25.2
responsibility to other lawyers individually. *See* **Civility**
responsibility to the profession 25.7
duty to report apparent misconduct 25.7
replies to communications from governing body 25.7
unprofessional, abusive, or offensive letters 25.7
retired judges returning to practice 25.8
sexual harassment 25.13
solicitation. *See* **Solicitation**
withdrawal of services. *See* **Withdrawal of services**

Security of court facilities 25.6

Settlement
apparent authority of counsel to settle 4.8
effect of misapprehension of counsel 4.8
duty to inform clients of settlement offers 4.8
duty to settle litigation 4.8

Sexual harassment 25.13

Solicitation
generally 11

Solicitors' negligence claims. *See* **Errors and omissions**

Sporting theory of justice 2.1, 4.1

Spot audit programmes 17.3

Suspensions 26.17

See also **Discipline proceedings,** penalty
interim suspensions
pending discipline hearings 26.13

Tactics
impermissible tactics in prosecuting 6.6

Tax
advising clients 19
  manufacturing evidence 19
  meritorious position standard 19
  reasonable basis standard 19
evidentiary issues 19
state of mind 19
generally 19

Testamentary capacity 18.1

Unauthorized practice of law
duty to prevent 25.9
  employing disbarred or suspended members 25.9
fee splitting with non-lawyers 25.5(b)
generally 25.9

Undertakings 17.5
real estate transactions 17.5
  personal responsibility 17.5

Undue influence 18.1

Unions
conflicts of interest 5.13

Unrepresented parties
duty of lawyers 4.7
real estate 17.4

Watergate
introduction, 2.1

Whistleblowing
corporate counsel 20.6
government lawyers 21.4

Wills. *See* **Estates**

Withdrawal as counsel
appropriate notice 4.10
consequences to client 4.10
criminal cases 7.8
duties of successor lawyers 4.10
failure of client to provide funds 4.10
improper instructions 4.10
inability to obtain instructions 4.10
justification for 4.10
  duty to withdraw 4.10
  right to withdraw 4.10
lawyer's duties upon withdrawal 4.10
  effect on right to claim lien 4.10
loss of confidence 4.10

Witnesses
communication with, while testifying 4.15
  cross-examination 4.15
  examination in chief 4.15
  re-examination 4.15
compensation 4.12
  expert witnesses 4.12
cross-examination 4.14
See also **Cross-examination**
interviewing 4.12
  disclosure of lawyer's interest 4.12
  use of tape recorder 4.12
lawyers as. *See* **Lawyers**
orders excluding 4.15
  lawyer's duty 4.15
perjury 4.13
  duty of criminal defence lawyer 7.2, 7.5
  duty of lawyer if witness unexpectedly testifies falsely 4.13
preparing 4.12
  influencing testimony 4.12
  modifying demeanour or use of speech 4.12
presenting in false or misleading way 4.12, 4.13
providing legal advice 4.12
  use of leading questions 4.12
provoking misidentification 4.14